MARKETING RESEARCH

Measurement & Method

FIFTH EDITION

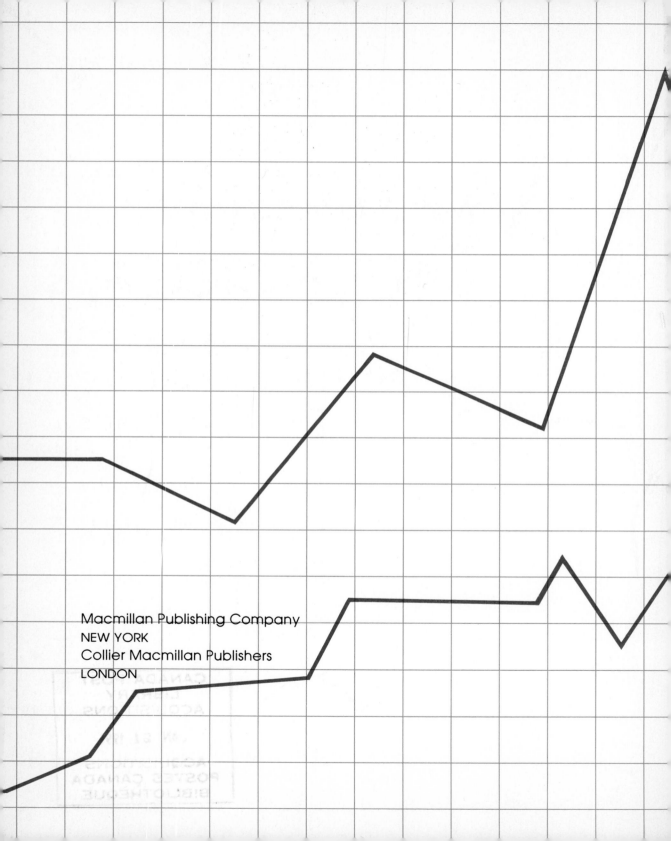

Macmillan Publishing Company
NEW YORK
Collier Macmillan Publishers
LONDON

FIFTH EDITION

MARKETING RESEARCH.

Measurement & Method

Donald S. Tull
Del I. Hawkins

Department of
Marketing and Business Environment
University of Oregon, Eugene

A TEXT WITH CASES

Editor: Michele Rhoades
Production Supervisor: J. Edward Neve
Production Manager: Richard C. Fischer
Text Designer: Patrice Fodero
Cover Design and Illustration: Patrice Fodero

This book was set in Caledonia by Progressive Typographers, Inc., printed and bound by R. R. Donnelley & Sons. The cover was printed by Phoenix Color Corp.

Macmillan Publishing Company
866 Third Avenue, New York, New York 10022

Collier Macmillan Canada, Inc.

LIBRARY OF CONGRESS CATALOGING IN PUBLICATION DATA

Tull, Donald S.
  Marketing research : measurement and method : a text with cases /
Donald S. Tull and Del I. Hawkins.—5th ed.
      p.   cm.
    Includes indexes.
    ISBN 0-02-421821-9
    1. Marketing research.   2. Marketing research—Case studies.
  I. Hawkins, Del I.   II. Title.
  HF5415.2.T83   1990
  658.8′3—dc20   89-34951
                                                                                      CIP

Printing: 1 2 3 4 5 6 7 8   Year: 0 1 2 3 4 5 6 7 8 9

The Macmillan Series in Marketing

Preface to the Fifth Edition

This is an introductory text in marketing research. As such, it is primarily concerned with *decisional* research rather than *basic* research. Decisional research is done to provide information for a pending decision. Basic research is done primarily to advance the level of scientific knowledge.

A "good" decisional research project results in helping to make the best decision that can be made at the least cost of making it. A good basic research project results in the best estimate that can be made or the best hypothesis test that can be run. These differing objectives result in differing ways of deriving *meaning*, applying *methods*, and making *measurements* in the two types of research.

This book is concerned with the doing of good decisional research, specifically good marketing research. The competently conducted marketing research project provides information to help identify, structure, and solve a marketing problem. The information it provides will have *meaning* to the manager who is to use it so that it will be relevant to his perception of the problem and will have the required level of accuracy. It will have been obtained by using the *methods* and making the *measurements* appropriate for the problem. The project will have been designed in such a way that the information will be *worth more than it costs* to obtain and will be provided at the *time* it is needed.

As those who have some acquaintance with decisional research projects are aware, meeting these requirements is not easy. The problems of proper design and sound implementation in basic research are serious ones; they are compounded in decisional research by the insistent constraints of time and of the economics of information acquisition.

In this text we have attempted to deal with these problems as clearly and directly as possible. Our continuing concern has been the illustration of the concepts and techniques discussed by the use of actual examples. Students, whether they are users or doers of research, are better motivated and taught when they can see how a concept is applied or learn how a technique is used in actual situations.

This edition is a comprehensive revision that both updates and extends the topics covered in the fourth edition. In it, we have made a conscious effort to include even more examples of marketing problems whose solution was aided, or could have been aided, by applying one or more of the techniques that we discuss. Also *new to this edition* are several other changes which bear mentioning, as they make the text easier for instructors and students to use:

- A more open, attractive design, including the functional use of color to highlight important material.
- More, but shorter and more focused, chapters.
- Up-to-date coverage of the electronics and computer revolution sweeping the marketing research field.
- A continuing real-world case that runs throughout the text, allowing students to apply new material to a familar context.

We share the difficulty of most authors of giving adequate recognition to those who have contributed to their work. Our students have been a continuing source of helpful comments and suggestions. Our colleagues, both here at Oregon and at other universities, have also provided many useful suggestions. The reviewers for this edition each provided unusually perceptive comments, and so deserve individual recognition. They are:

Panos Apostolidis	University of Scranton
Joseph Bellizzi	Arizona State University
Ray DeCormier	Central Connecticut State University
Lawrence Feick	University of Pittsburgh
Donald Fuller	University of Central Florida
Roger Gates	University of Texas — Arlington
Pat Kennedy	University of Oregon
Peter LaPlaca	University of Connecticut
D. B. Lund	University of Nevada — Reno
Suzanne McCall	East Texas State University
Steve Perkins	Pennsylvania State University
Paul Prabhaker	DePaul University
Arno Rethans	California State University — Chico
David Santee	Hallmark Cards

Ken Schneider	St. Cloud University
Bruce Smackey	Lehigh University
Richard Skinner	Kent State University
Hale Tongren	George Mason University
Tom Yokum	DePaul University

We are also indebted to the many practicing marketing researchers and research organizations that supplied examples, illustrations, and material for cases.

They each have contributed to this being a much better book than it could possibly have been without their help. All have our sincere thanks. None are in any way responsible for any shortcomings that may remain.

Particular thanks must go to Michael Capizzi of Burgoyne, Inc. His comments, criticisms, and suggestions were invaluable in anchoring this text solidly in reality. He is a practicing marketing researcher who is not only concerned about the education of future marketing managers but is willing to invest considerable time and effort to improve the educational process.

Finally, we thank Jan Clayton, who not only deciphered our frequently illegible notes, but typed with speed, accuracy, and a constant sense of humor.

Eugene, Oregon

D. S. T.
D. I. H.

Supplementary Material for the Text

Markstat Statistical Package   We have responded to the increased attention given to microcomputers and their applicability in solving marketing problems with an integrated version of **MARKSTAT**, a microcomputer package developed for the marketing research course by Peter LaPlaca at the University of Connecticut. This software is packaged with a student exercise manual which has been integrated with the data and underlying research concepts found in the Tull/Hawkins text.

Data Disks   For those who wish only to have the data from several cases and applications found in the text, these data are also available separately on computer disk to adopters.

Instructor's Manual   This comprehensive resource contains teaching objectives, quiz and demonstration questions and problems, review questions, and transparencies.

Test Bank   This edition of Tull/Hawkins provides a separate test bank that contains a large selection of over 2700 multiple choice and true/false questions, many of which have been class tested.

Microtest   A microcomputer testing system is available to adopters that provides the test bank on computer disk for the **IBM**, **Apple**, and **TRS-80** microcomputers.

Contents

SECTION 2 CASES   247

3 Measurement Techniques in Marketing Research   255

SECTION 4 CASES   676

5 Marketing Research Reports and Ethical Issues   691

22 Marketing Research Reports   693

23 Ethical Issues in Marketing Research   719

SECTION 5 CASES   743

APPENDIXES   746

GLOSSARY   793

INDEXES   815

To the Student

What you will want to learn from the course in which this text is being used will depend in part on whether you plan to be in a management position in which you will *use* marketing research, or whether you intend to be a marketing researcher and *do* research.

Those who are going to be users of research need to learn to judge how useful research information would be to help solve specific marketing problems, and how to evaluate the quality of the information promised by a research proposal. Those who are going to be marketing researchers need to learn how to design and conduct sound research projects at the least possible cost.

We have kept both of these objectives in mind in writing this text. We have attempted to give a thorough description of the underlying principles in each of the topic areas to enable a researcher to design and conduct a sound research project. In addition most of the topic areas have suggested step-by-step procedures for applying these principles in practice (how to design a research project, how to set up a sampling plan, how to prepare a questionnaire, and how to select the methods of analysis to use are examples.

Wherever possible we have used actual examples to illustrate the application of these principles and procedures. We have provided the opportunity to evaluate the quality of research proposals or information in each of the topic areas through an extensive use of examples, illustrations, discussion questions, problems, and cases.

In studying this material, we recommend that you read the review questions at the end of the chapter *before* you read the chapter. They will prepare you for the key terms and ideas in the chapter. After you read the chapter, try to answer each review question. This will serve as a review and a measure of your surface knowledge of the key terms and concepts. Once you are comfortable with these questions, examine the discussion questions/problems. They are designed to enhance your *understanding* and *ability to use* the material in the chapter. Answering these questions requires only the textbook and, for some, a calculator. The project questions require you to "leave the room" to interview people, use library or computer resources, or otherwise actually *do* marketing research.

Whether you intend to be a user or a doer of research, this is a textbook that you may want to keep. It has been said that knowledge is of two kinds: to know a subject ourselves, or to know where we can find information about it. We have attempted to make this book useful for both purposes.

Donald S. Tull
Del I. Hawkins

The Nature of Marketing Research

Marketing research serves a single purpose—*that of providing information to assist marketing managers to make better decisions.*

Each year more than two billion dollars is spent in the United States for marketing research. This money is spent on research projects that help to *identify* marketing problems and opportunities, to *select* the problems to solve and the opportunities to consider, and then to obtain information to help *solve* the problems and take advantage of the opportunities that are selected. A discussion of these functions of marketing research, along with the way in which it is organized, the nature of the research industry, and career opportunities in marketing research comprises the first chapter.

A marketing information system is a system designed to generate, store, and disseminate an orderly flow of pertinent information to marketing managers. Marketing decision support systems are data bases with associated models and software that allow managers to interact directly with the data base. They are designed to assist with specific types of marketing decisions. Chapter 2 covers both marketing information systems and marketing decision support systems.

The design of a research project is clearly critical to its success or failure. The steps involved in designing the project, how they are carried out, and estimating the value of the information that the proposed design will provide are the concern of the third chapter.

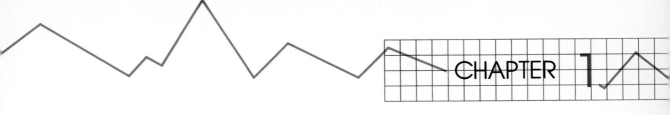

CHAPTER 1

The Nature of Marketing Research

One of the most successful new consumer package products of the 1980s was Taylor California Cellars wine. Marketing research played a vital role in this success:

> The entrepreneurial efforts that resulted in this new business were guided and, to a great degree, stimulated by research. The commitment to act on the research, to integrate it not only into decision making, but also into the creative process, was what made the $100 million difference.

> Marketing research was, and is, involved in all stages of the brand's development and marketing. The opportunity for the new product was discovered as a result of a thorough analysis of existing industry, demographic, and consumption data.

> The initial efforts involved an analysis of the projected growth rates of various types of wine. This analysis showed that one of the fastest growing segments was premium California jug wine. It was projected to grow at a rate of 21 per cent annually.

> The next step was an analysis of the competition in this market segment. At the time, Almaden, Inglenook, Paul Masson, and Sebastiani dominated this market. They had combined sales of $500 million but jointly spent only $11 million on advertising. This advertising-to-sales ratio of 2 per cent was taken as a sign of competitive vulnerability. (The advertising-to-sales ratios for spirits and beer are, in contrast, 6% and 5%, respectively.)

3

Through these and similar analyses, a large, growing market segment with relatively passive competitors was identified. The next step was to see if a product position could be developed that would appeal to a significant portion of this segment.

At the time of the initial investigation, about one-third of all American adults drank wine. Numerous focus group interviews and large-scale national surveys were available that showed that most wine drinkers (1) knew very little about wine, (2) were afraid of it, and (3) drank it mainly on social, romantic, or celebratory occasions.

Based on this research, moderately priced wines were advertised as fun to drink; easy to drink; appropriate for all occasions; good for sentimental, celebratory, or romantic occasions; or some combination of these. The focus was strictly on the usage situation and the user, not the product.

However, as management analyzed the consumption data in depth, it found that only 4 per cent of the population (10 per cent of all wine drinkers) were frequent consumers (4 times a week or more) of table wine. Furthermore, this 4 per cent was found to consume 53 per cent of the premium California jug wine! Because of the small numbers of individuals involved, it appeared that the other firms had ignored this heavy user segment.

A special study revealed that about one half of these consumers lived in California. Taylor wines, which had always been New York wines, had a distinct flavor and had only limited distribution west of the Rockies. Management initially planned to abandon the well-established Taylor name and introduce a completely new brand name. However, a series of controlled experiments on both the East and West coasts found Taylor to have a stronger association with the terms *quality* and *premium* than it did with *New York*. The Taylor label outperformed other options in generating interest in the new product. Thus, the experiments revealed that management's initial inclination to abandon the Taylor name was incorrect.

The frequent user study revealed that these individuals differed dramatically from the average wine consumer in both knowledge and values. Frequent users were reasonably well informed about wines. Their purchase criteria were taste, dryness, crispness, and other *product* features. No competitor was stressing the product in its advertising.

The study also revealed that about 60 per cent of the frequent users had recently attended a wine tasting. This led to a creative strategy of showing taste superiority by advertising the results of taste tests against Inglenook, Almaden, and Sebastiani brands. A follow-up campaign featured recognized wine authorities commenting on the taste characteristics of Taylor California Cellars.

The result of combining skillful marketing research, with a superior new product and sound management judgment, is one of the leading wine brands.[1]

The Function of Marketing Research

The Taylor California Cellars example illustrates the function of marketing research. The *function of marketing research is to provide information that will assist marketing managers in recognizing and reacting to marketing opportunities and problems.* In essence, marketing research exists to help marketing managers make better decisions. These decisions range from such global ones as "Is there a marketing opportunity or problem that I am not aware of?" to very specific decisions such as "Should we set the price at $1.79 or $1.69?" An appropriate definition of *marketing research,* therefore, is that it is *a formalized means of obtaining information to be used in making marketing decisions.* The official American Marketing Association definition of marketing research reflects this theme, but in greater detail:

> Marketing Research is the function which links the consumer, customer, and public to the marketer through information — information used to identify and define marketing opportunities and problems; generate, refine, and evaluate marketing actions; monitor marketing performance; and improve understanding of marketing as a process.
>
> Marketing Research specifies the information required to address these issues; designs the method for collecting information; manages and implements the data collection process; analyzes the results; and communicates the findings and their implications.

These definitions are not theoretical abstractions; rather, they reflect the practice of marketing research. Consider the match between these definitions and the "mission statement" of the Market Research Department at Thomas J. Lipton, Inc.:

> The mission of the Market Research Department is to gather, analyze, and interpret marketing and other relevant information needed for decision making at all levels of management. These activities are to be carried out in a cost-effective manner consistent with high professional standards.[2]

Think for a minute about the marketing manager's job. He or she must make decisions concerning which consumers to serve (market segmentation), and what product features, price levels, promotional strategies, and distribution channels to use. The example that opened this chapter described how information generated by the research process helped Taylor's management

Exhibit 1-1 *Marketing Research Applications*

- "It is our attention to basic research that has made Soft Care Apparel the largest manufacturer of infant apparel in the United States." Soft Care conducts a quarterly telephone survey that "gives us a snapshot of the marketplace, tracks trends, and offers us a picture of how attitudes change over time." Focus groups (moderated discussions involving 8–12 customers) are used to evaluate new product ideas. Test marketing (selling the product in a few cities) is used to determine demand for new products. Mall intercept interviews (questioning people in shopping malls) are also used to test new product ideas and new products. Research is also used to develop and test premiums and advertising appeals.[3]

- General Motors conducted a major research program to guide overall corporate strategy and particularly its communications strategy in the United Kingdom. It first conducted 14 focus groups with the general public and 6 with local audiences living near GM plants. It simultaneously conducted depth interviews with dealers, fleet operators, garage operators, insurance agents, pro- and anti-automobile pressure group members, governmental officials, members of the automobile press, the general editorial press and television, trade union leaders, and suppliers. Following this, 10 special surveys were developed, tested, and administered to approximately 4,000 respondents. The results produced major changes in GM's operations in the UK.[4]

- Spectra is Polaroid's most successful new product. "The market research effort was placed on a level of formal equality with every other link in the system." Positioning testing, targeting studies, and Polaroid's first use of name-generation research were used. Mall intercept interviews were conducted throughout Spectra's development. Consumers were given prototypes of the camera to use, then participated in extensive interviews concerning the camera and their attitudes towards it. These findings were used to revise the design of the camera.[5]

- US WEST was formed as one of seven regional telecommunications firms as a result of the AT&T divestiture. Shortly after divestiture, US WEST decided to reorganize around markets rather than products or functions. This resulted in a major research effort involving secondary research, depth interviews, focus groups, and thousands of questionnaires (mail, telephone, and personal) to industries and households that had needs relating to the transmission of

> information (voice or data). The result was a revised understanding of the market, a complete restructuring of the organization, and the initiation of hundreds of follow-up studies focused on specific customer needs.

select a market segment, design a product, and develop an advertising campaign. The research projects described in Exhibit 1 – 1 illustrate other applications of marketing research.

Note that it is the output of the research process, *information*, that is useful to the manager. In today's highly competitive environment, the effective use of information is a critical managerial skill. Taylor California Cellars was able to take $100 million of business away from entrenched competitors because the management group was more skilled at requesting and using information than were its competitors!

As information technology continues to improve, the ability to use information will become even more critical. The effective use of information requires a thorough understanding of the types of information available and how this information is created. In this text, we are concerned with the general questions of *when, how* and *how much* marketing research should be conducted. If you understand these issues, you will be a much better *consumer* of marketing research. That is, not only will you be able to evaluate the worth of a particular research project or proposal, but you will also know when and how to use the resultant information.

Information and Decision Making

The decision-making process in marketing is essentially the same as it is in any other area of human affairs. The management of Taylor California Cellars had to go through the same general steps in deciding to develop and introduce the wines as did Congress in voting the latest defense budget or the Metropolitan Museum of Art in deciding to hold an exhibition of the paintings of Vincent van Gogh. In each case it was necessary for those involved in making the decision to (1) establish objectives, (2) measure performance/potential, (3) select the problem/opportunity to pursue, (4) develop alternatives, (5) choose the best alternative, and (6) implement the alternative. These steps, which are illustrated in Figure 1 – 1, can be summarized under the headings of problem/opportunity identification, problem/opportunity selection, and problem/opportunity resolution.

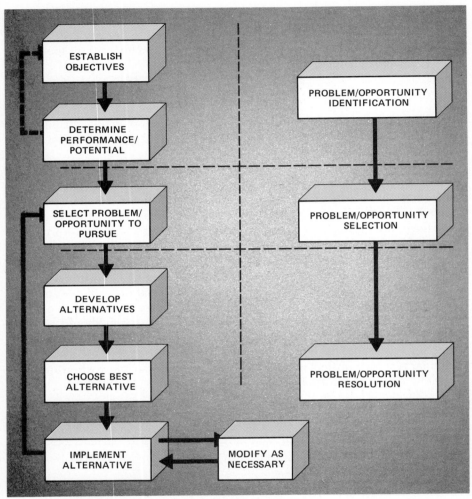

Figure 1–1 *Steps in the Decision-Making Process*

Problem/Opportunity Identification

The Taylor research described earlier is an example of research designed to identify opportunities. As Table 1 – 1 indicates, both opportunity and problem identification studies are common. For example, research for a major Canadian vacation package wholesaler, Suntours, revealed that despite two consecutive years of record sales and profits, its market share had declined by almost a third. Once the problem was recognized, Suntours was able to take steps to recapture its lost market share.[6]

Problems are identified when (1) objectives are established and (2) a mea-

Table 1 – 1 Problem/Opportunity Identification Research Conducted by Companies

Type of Research	Companies Doing (in %)	Done by Marketing Research Department (in %)	Done by Other Departments (in %)	Done by Outside Firms (in %)
Market potential	97	88	04	05
Market share	97	85	06	06
Market characteristics	97	88	03	06
Sales analysis	92	67	23	02
Short-range forecasting	89	51	36	02
Long-range forecasting	87	49	34	04
Studies of business trends	91	68	20	03

Source: D. W. Twedt, *1983 Survey of Marketing Research* (Chicago: American Marketing Association, 1983), 41.

surement of performance indicates that the objectives are not being met. Opportunities occur when the potential to exceed objectives using a new approach is discovered. Marketing research can assist in setting objectives, measuring performance, and identifying opportunities.

Think for a minute about setting or evaluating a market share or sales objective for a particular brand. What information would you like to have? Such data as number of customers, average purchase amount by customers, percentage of customers who are "heavy users," consumer purchase criteria, the nature of market segments, the number of competitors, marketing expenditures per competitor, relative product/service quality, and so forth would be useful. Marketing research can provide these types of data.

Marketing research can also be used to gather performance data such as sales by the firm and each competitor by customer type. And, as the Taylor example illustrated, it can provide information on untapped marketing opportunities.

Opportunities, and problems, often arise quickly for firms. During the third week of January 1988, the National Institute of Health announced that regular use of aspirin might lower the incidence of some heart attacks. How much, and what type of action, should aspirin marketers and competing pain remedy marketers take? The answer depends, in part, on the impact the announcement has had on the public. On February 1st, an R.H. Bruskin Associates syndicated marketing research report revealed that 90 per cent of America's adults were aware of the announcement and one third of these said they would be likely to take an aspirin every other day because of it.[7] Clearly,

---

Exhibit 1–2 *The Federal Trade Commission's Mandatory Research Requirement for* Encyclopedia Britannica

Until recently, *Encyclopedia Britannica* was required by the FTC to state "persons who reply as requested may be contacted by a salesperson" in all ads which were used to generate sales leads (i.e., "For a free brochure write . . ."). Now, it may use its own judgment in wording ads as long as three out of four consumers understand that responding to the ad will result in a contact by a salesperson.

Under the agreement, anytime the FTC requests proof, *Encyclopedia Britannica* must conduct a series of shopping mall intercept interviews using a methodology and questionnaire specified by the FTC. Seventy-five percent of the individuals interviewed must answer "yes" to: "Based on your reading of the coupon (which the consumer is viewing), would you expect a sales representative from *Encyclopedia Britannica* to contact you if you send in the coupon?" If less than 75 percent state "yes," the firm is in violation of the FTC ruling and is subject to sanctions.

Source: "FTC Test Agreement Frees Ad Format for Encyclopedia," *Advertising Age,* November 8, 1982, 88.

---

the research quickly revealed a major opportunity and problem for various firms.

Nonprofit organizations and regulatory agencies also conduct problem-identification research. For example, a problem-identification program that has been initiated by the Federal Trade Commission is described in Exhibit 1–2 as it applies to the *Encyclopedia Britannica.*

Problem/Opportunity Selection

Organizations often identify more problems and opportunities than they can work on at once. Research can often help prioritize identified problems and opportunities. Two dimensions determine the priorities—time and impact. The larger the impact and the less time until the problem occurs (or until the opportunity is lost), the higher is the priority.

Consider the following research program and its outcome:

Two million dollars was spent on research for the Ronald Reagan presidential campaign. Sixteen national surveys, eighty-two statewide studies, and more than fifty focus groups were conducted early in the campaign. During twenty days in October, an average of more than 2,400 persons were interviewed each night to provide information on voter awareness and attitudes.

This information went into a computerized simulation model known as the Political Information System (PINS). It was used to simulate the election to determine which were the major issues and what were the key coalitions of voters. Almost three hundred simulations were conducted.[8]

The PINS simulations, by allowing the major issues and key coalitions to be identified, permitted priorities to be set for both the content and the primary target audiences of Reagan campaign advertising and personal appearances.

Marketing research is commonly used to determine which new competitive activities—new products, advertising strategies, channels, and so forth—are most threatening. Those that pose serious threats in the near future are countered first.

Problem/Opportunity Resolution

Problem/opportunity resolution consists of two separate steps: (1) developing alternatives to meet objectives and (2) evaluating these alternatives in terms of the objectives.

Exhibit 1–3 describes one of the earliest formal marketing research studies. In this case, information was provided through research that helped a potential customer evaluate an alternative (the alternative of advertising in the *Saturday Evening Post*). In the Taylor example that we have been discussing, information was used to select the target market, design the product, and develop the advertising campaign.

In general, problems in marketing are related to choosing the right products and the appropriate levels of price and promotion, and selecting and maintaining the right distribution channels to reach the appropriate market segments. Table 1–2 provides an indication of the extent to which problem-solving research is conducted by companies, marketing research departments, other departments, and outside firms.

More firms are spending more on marketing research of this nature than ever before. For example, Lotus now spends about one million dollars a year on pricing studies for its software.[9] Taco Bell used marketing research to help redesign the exterior and interior of its outlets.[10] The *Seattle Post-Intelligencer* newspaper used extensive research before redesigning its editorial and feature content. Changes resulting from consumer research included the hiring of a science writer, an increased emphasis on stories by its medical reporter, and the addition of science and technology as a theme for its Tuesday "Living Section."

We do not want to leave the impression that marketing research projects

Exhibit 1–3 *The Beginning of Marketing Research*

The Curtis Publishing Company is the company generally acknowledged to have the first marketing research department in the United States, and a man named Charles Coolidge Parlin was the first head of it. In the early days of this century, a Curtis sales representative was attempting to sell the Campbell Soup Co. space in The *Saturday Evening Post.* He was told that the *Post* was the wrong medium for prepared soup advertising—that it was a magazine read mainly by working people, whereas prepared soups were bought primarily by families with higher incomes. The wife in a working class family prepared soup from scratch to save money, the argument went, while only the rich would pay 10¢ for a soup already prepared.

Parlin was asked to get data that would indicate whether or not the Campbell advertising department's view of the market for canned soups was correct. To do so, he drew a sample of garbage routes in Philadelphia and arranged to have the collected garbage from each dumped in a specified area of a National Guard Armory he had rented for that purpose. He then had the number of Campbell soup cans counted in each of the piles. He found that the piles from the garbage collection routes that served the wealthier parts of the city had few Campbell cans. Rather than buy canned soups, the wealthier families had their servants make it from scratch.

Most of the cans came from the blue-collar areas. Parlin theorized that it was probably more economic for the blue-collar wife to take the time saved in making soup and devote it to making clothes for herself and her family, an activity that really would save money.

When presented with these findings, Campbell soon became an advertiser in the *Post,* an association that lasted until that magazine was no longer published.

Source: "Garbage Dump Marks Long Ago Beginnings of Market Research," *Advertising Age,* April 30, 1970, 70.

either are, or should be, conducted to help with all marketing decisions. For example, California Cooler (and the entire "cooler" wine drink industry) was launched with absolutely no marketing research.[12] Moreover, "cooler" wine drinks are at least as large a success story as Taylor California Cellars. (The issue of when research should be conducted is discussed in Chapter 3.) However, failure to conduct research greatly increases risks. TreeSweet Products spent $12 million to develop TreeSweet Lite, a line of six reduced-calorie

Table 1–2 Research for the Resolution of Marketing Problems/ Opportunities

	Companies Doing (in %)	Done by Marketing Research Department (in %)	Done by Other Departments (in %)	Done by Outside Firms (in %)
Product research				
Competitive product studies	87	71	10	06
New product acceptance and potential	76	59	11	06
Testing of existing products	80	55	19	06
Packaging research	65	44	12	09
Test markets, store audits	59	43	07	09
Pricing research				
Promotion research				
Studies of ad effectiveness	76	42	05	29
Media research	68	22	14	32
Promotional studies of premiums, coupons, sampling, deals, etc.	58	38	14	06
Copy research	61	30	06	25
Distribution research				
Distribution channel studies	71	32	38	01
Plant and warehouse location	68	29	35	04

Source: D. W. Twedt, *1983 Survey of Marketing Research* (Chicago: American Marketing Association, 1983), 41.

juices. To beat competition, the product was launched nationally without test marketing. It failed completely and virtually forced the company into bankruptcy.[13]

The Marketing Decision

It is important to recognize that managers use information as they make decisions. The information may come from marketing research, as in the Taylor

California Cellars case, or it may come from intuition and experience, as in the California Cooler case. No matter the source, the *manager* needs to determine the information required and to decide how he or she will use it to reach a decision. If research is used, the researcher should work with the manager to ensure that the proper information is sought and that it is interpreted correctly.

Suppose you as a manager needed to estimate the maximum market potential for a new video game. You might request the research department to estimate how many households own the appropriate hardware to play the game. And, you might request them to measure consumers' reactions to a proposed price. Here is what happened when management at Atari did this:

> When research estimated the computer-hardware population in the U.S. at 19–20 million households, we used this as a base for calculating software sales — ignoring the fact that millions of units are stuck on the top shelves of closets (i.e., not used). And when focus groups of a handful of consumers said they would spend $40 for an E.T. videogame, we produced more than 20 million, many of which can be found in a landfill in New Mexico.[14]

Both management and research failed in this situation. Management needed information on computers *being used*, not computers *owned*. Both the manager and the researcher should have recognized this. The researcher should have warned management that individuals who agree to participate in long discussions (focus groups) on video games are likely to be enthusiasts who will pay more for a game than the general population.

It is our hope that this text will enhance your appreciation of both the power and the pitfalls of market research.[15] As one executive states:

> Research can be a very useful guide, but it has its limits. We need both the experienced management decision-maker and the best of what the research community can offer, integrated in a productive way and with a healthy respect for the benefits and limitations of each.[16]

The Marketing Research Department

The location of the marketing research function in the organization and the extent to which it is staffed vary from firm to firm.[17] Some firms do most of their own research, whereas others depend heavily on their advertising agency, marketing research firms, and independent consultants. Some companies have only a single marketing research department that is responsible for all research projects conducted, whereas others have decentralized the research responsibilities by functional departments. Where decentralized, sales and distribution cost analyses are conducted by the accounting department, advertising research by the advertising department, and forecasting by the staff of the chief executive. The remaining areas requiring research (studies of market potential, market share, market characteristics, sales call effectiveness, sales quotas, distribution channel effectiveness, location of plants and distribution facilities, price policies and their effects on sales, and so on) are the responsibility of the marketing research department. Still others decentralize by operating or sales divisions. Various combinations of these approaches are also utilized. There is no one optimum method of organization; the best organization for a particular company depends on its needs and the way it has organized the marketing and other functions of the firm.

As indicated by Tables 1–1 and 1–2, it is not unusual for companies to have marketing research studies, or portions of studies such as the interviewing, conducted by outside firms. Many firms do research on a contract or fee basis, including all major advertising agencies, marketing research firms, and management consulting firms, as well as independent consultants, university bureaus of business and economic research, and some trade associations. Seven factors are involved in the "make or buy" decision.[18]

1. *Economic factors:* Can an outside agency provide the information more economically? In the aspirin example described earlier, the cost of the consumer survey was shared by all the firms subscribing to the service. Thus, using an outside agency was substantially more economical than conducting a special survey in-house.

2. *Expertise:* Is the necessary expertise available internally? Carnation did not have the expertise to conduct a laboratory test market for a prospective new product and so the company contracted with an outside agency to do it.

3. *Special equipment:* Does the study require special equipment not currently available in the firm? The acquisition of special rooms for focus group interviews, sophisticated devices for measuring physiological responses to commercials, and so forth are seldom justified for one-time studies.

4. *Political considerations:* Does the study involve deeply controversial issues within the organization? Studies designed to help resolve bitter internal disputes or that may reflect unfavorably on some segment of the organization should generally be conducted by an outside organization.

5. *Legal and/or promotional considerations:* Will the results of the study be used in a legal proceeding or as part of a promotional campaign? In

either case, the presumption (not necessarily correct) that an outside agency is more objective suggests that one be used.

6. *Administrative facets:* Are current work loads and time pressures preventing the completion of needed research? If so, outside agencies can be used to handle temporary overloads.

7. *Confidentiality requirements:* Is it absolutely essential that the research be kept secret? As the need for confidentiality increases, the desirability of using an outside agency decreases.

It is not unusual for a research department to contract out parts of a study. In fact, most studies involving direct contact with consumers, such as surveys and taste tests, involve outside suppliers of research services. Thus, the pertinent question is often "What parts of this research project do we conduct ourselves and what parts do we contract out?" The seven factors we have just listed form the basis for answering this question, as well.

The Research Industry

Well over $2 billion was spent on commercial research in the United States in 1988. This figure does not include in-house work by governments, business firms, or advertising agencies. Thus, there is a large industry whose function is to supply research services to other organizations.[19]

The firms that comprise this industry range in size from one person working part time to the A. C. Nielsen Co., which generated about $765 million in worldwide research revenues in 1987.[20] The services offered range from conducting depth interviews or the analysis of questionnaire data to the installation and management of a complete marketing information system and decision support system. The most complete listing and description of the individual firms in the industry is the *Green Book*.[21] A brief overview of the industry follows.

Custom Research. Firms that supply custom research will work with the client to develop and implement a complete research project. They help management specify the information needed and they collect the information. Some of these firms specialize in particular industries or types of problems, others are generalists.

Custom research firms are particularly useful for firms with small or nonexistent research departments. They are also frequently used by larger firms when their own research department is overloaded, when a new type of problem or environment is encountered, when a "fresh" approach is desired, when specialized equipment such as an eye-tracking machine is required (Chapter 14), and so forth.

Field Services. Most interviewing is conducted by firms that specialize in this activity. This is particularly common in consumer interviews. The term *field* is generally used in the research industry to refer to that part of the research process in which data are actually collected from respondents. The asking of questions of respondents, whether done in person, over the phone, or by mail, and the recording of their answers is referred to as *fieldwork.* Companies that specialize in interviewing are called *field organizations* or *field service organizations.*

Field organizations range from small offices with a few telephones to large multinational WATS-line interviewing services to extensive facilities for personal interviews in shopping malls (see Chapters 5 and 6 for detailed descriptions). Many field organizations specialize in *qualitative research.* Most such organizations offer *focus group* interviews, which involve eight to fifteen individuals and a moderator discussing a particular topic in depth. The interviews are generally videotaped (see Chapter 13).

Data Analysis. Firms that specialize in data analysis are sometimes referred to as *tab houses.* This term arose because such firms initially supplied simple tabulations (counts) and cross tabulations for surveys. Even though the spread of computers and related software has given many firms the ability to conduct their own statistical analyses, substantial demand still exists for outside analyses. This is particularly true for sophisticated multivariate analyses (Chapter 19 and 20), trade-off analyses, and perceptual mapping (Chapter 12).

Syndicated Services. A number of research organizations, known as syndicated services, routinely collect information that they provide to firms subscribing to their services. A. C. Nielsen's television viewing panel is the most widely known service of this type. Reports on wholesale and retail sales, radio listening, household purchasing patterns, food preparation and consumption, and other behaviors are available on a subscription basis from syndicated services (Chapter 5).

Branded Research Products. Many research firms have developed specialized techniques for the collection of information relevant to specific types of marketing problems. These techniques are given brand names and are marketed like branded products. Examples include:

NameLab: A specialized approach to developing brand names.

BehaviorScan: A test marketing service of Information Resources Inc.

BASES: Burke Marketing Services, Inc.'s program for incorporating consumer attitude measures into sales estimates throughout the new product development process.

PRIZM: **A Claritas Corporation technique for identifying potential market segments based on lifestyle classifications of residential neighborhoods.**

Marketing Research Careers

Relatively few students in marketing research classes go on to careers in marketing research. However, marketing research has become a major staff function in many organizations. And, as the previous section indicates, there is a large marketing research industry consisting of a wide array of research suppliers. Thus, a variety of career paths are available in marketing research.

Marketing research organizations typically look for strong basic skills in analysis and communication, rather than expertise in a particular industry or methodology. As indicated by Table 1 – 3, strong writing, analytic, and verbal

Table 1 – 3 Qualities Sought in Researchers

Qualities	Entry Level — %*	Junior Staff — %*	Senior Staff — %*
Strong writing skills	57	71	90
Strong analytic skills	50	67	90
Strong verbal skills	49	57	82
A professional appearance	19	28	59
Good grades	15	4	7
Strong quantitative (statistical) skills	13	19	41
Potential new business development skills	10	23	54
A graduate degree/some graduate training	6	11	16
Good schools	3	—	1
Managerial skills	°°	°°	49
Client-handling skills	°°	°°	83
A national reputation	°°	°°	1
Expertise in a specific industry/–industries	°°	°°	1
Expertise in a specific methodology/–methodologies	°°	°°	4

° Indicating "very important" on four-point scale (very important, important, less important, not important at all)
°° Not asked for this level
Source: Survey conducted by the Council of American Research Organizations of 74 (responding) large marketing research companies and reported in "Talking and Writing and Analysis," *Advertising Age*, October 26, 1981, S-28.

Exhibit 1–4   *Jobs in Marketing Research*

skills are the qualities that are most highly sought by research organizations. Exhibit 1–4 contains several advertisements that indicate the nature of the researcher's job as well as the skills required to perform the job.[22]

If interest and abilities qualify one, an entry level position in marketing research offers a number of advantages. It is interesting work that provides wide exposure to marketing problems at an early stage of one's career. It brings one in contact with the top management of the company for which the research is being conducted sooner and more often than almost any other position.

There are disadvantages, however. It is a *staff position,* and staff people always *recommend* rather than decide. And the line of promotion for top corporate positions typically does not pass through the marketing research director's office.

If one is to consider taking a job in marketing research upon graduation, therefore, it is probably wise to decide in advance to reevaluate it after several years. If you decide you want to stay in research, it can be an interesting and personally rewarding career. If you decide you would like to move into a line position, that is usually a good time to do it.

Review Questions

1.1.   What is the primary function of marketing research?

1.2.   What is the definition of marketing research used in this text?

1.3.   Describe the decision process.

1.4.   How is research used in problem/opportunity identification?

1.5.   How is research used in problem/opportunity selection?

1.6.   How is research used in problem/opportunity resolution?

1.7.   Is research always needed to assist with marketing decisions?

1.8.   What are the considerations involved in deciding whether to do a research project "in-house" versus having it done by an outside agency?

1.9.   Is most research done "in-house"? Why?

1.10.   What is meant by *custom research?*

1.11.   What is meant by *field services?*

1.12.   What is meant by *fieldwork?*

1.13.   What is meant by *data analysis?*

1.14.   What is meant by *syndicated services?*

1.15.   What is meant by *branded research projects?*

1.16.   What are the three most important characteristics that marketing research organizations look for in entry-level job applicants.

Discussion Questions/Problems

1.17. Does the role of marketing research include a responsibility for providing information on ethical questions? Explain.

1.18. Should the marketing research department only provide information to help in decision making or should it also recommend courses of action? What are the advantages and disadvantages of each approach?

1.19. Can a parallel be drawn between an accounting system in providing information on costs of products and a marketing information system on providing information on demand for products? Explain.

1.20. Approximately fifty times as much is spent in the United States each year on informing and persuading consumers to buy (advertising) as it is on determining what they would like to buy and how it should be priced, distributed, and promoted (marketing research). Does this seem to be the (approximate) appropriate ratio for these two types of expenditures for a free-enterprise economy? Explain.

1.21. How can universities use "marketing" research?

1.22. Should more or less marketing research be necessary in a planned economy (e.g., Russia) than in a free-enterprise economy (e.g., the United States)? Explain.

1.23. Should companies generally reduce, maintain at the same level, or increase their research expenditures during a recession? Explain.

1.24. The following statement appeared in an advertisement run by Xerox a few years ago:
"If you pick up a newspaper these days, it's easy to walk away with the impression that there's a worldwide shortage of everything.
"There is an energy crisis and a food crisis and any number of other crises, all caused by vanishing resources.
"But there is one that involves not a shortage, but an excess. A crisis where the resource isn't dwindling, but growing almost uncontrollably.
"That resource is information.
"Consider: Seventy-five per cent of all the information available to mankind has been developed within the last two decades. Millions of pieces of information are created daily. And the total amount is doubling every ten years. . . .
"With 72 billion new pieces of information arriving yearly, how do you cope with it all?"
Is the information "explosion" a problem or an opportunity for marketing research? Explain.

1.25. As you seek employment after graduation, you will, in a sense, be a "product" that you are trying to "sell" to potential employers. What types of research should you be doing now to help design and position yourself as an "attractive" product?

1.26. Would you enjoy a career in marketing research? Why?

Projects

1.27. Examine a recent copy of *Business Week* to determine what information it contains, if any, that would be of value to the chief marketing officer of
   a. a West Coast fast food chain
   b. a wholesaler of plumbing supplies in New England
   c. Sears
   d. an exporter of wines to Europe
   e. a life insurance company

1.28. Interview someone who has worked in marketing research for five years or more. Report on their perceptions of this type of career.

1.29. Interview someone in sales or marketing management. Determine their use of and attitudes toward marketing research.

1.30. Review publications such as the *Wall Street Journal, Advertising Age,* and *Business Week.* Find and report on five applications of marketing research.

1.31. Review the help wanted sections of the *Wall Street Journal, Advertising Age,* and/or *Marketing News.* Find 10 advertisements for marketing research analysts or other entry- or near-entry level research positions. List the attributes required and desired. What do you conclude?

References

[1] Based on C. E. Overholser, "Digging Beyond Research," *Marketing News,* April 26, 1985, 6; and C. E. Overholser, "Using Research to Create a $100 Million Brand," *ARF 31st Annual Conference* (New York: Advertising Research Foundation, 1985).

[2] D. W. von Arx, "The Many Faces of Market Research," *Journal of Consumer Marketing* (Spring 1986), 88.

[3] E. E. Hinds, "Research Basic to Baby-Wear Business," *Marketing News,* February 13, 1987, 26.

[4] E. Fountain, I. Parker, J. Samuels, "The Contributions of Research to General Motors' Corporate Communications Strategy in the UK," *Journal of the Market Research Society,* January 1986, 25–42.

[5] K. T. Higgins, "Polaroid Stages Marketing Blitz," *Marketing News,* June 6, 1986, 4.

[6] J. A. Schauer, "Use Research to Analyze Marketing Success," *Marketing News,* January 4, 1985, 53. Share had declined because market demand was shifting to areas not served by Suntours.

[7] "New Aspirin Claim," *Bruskin Report* 149, March 1988, 1.

[8] "Reagan's $2 Million Marketing Research Budget Paid Off," *Marketing News,* March 5, 1982, 12.

[9] R. Brandt, "For Buyers of Business Programs, Money Is No Object," *Business Week*, August 10, 1987, 70.

[10] T. Carsen, "Taco Bell Wants to Take a Bite Out of Burgers," *Business Week*, August 4, 1986, 63.

[11] R. Edel, "Research Serves Editorial, Advertising Interests," *Advertising Age*, January 23, 1986, 24.

[12] The Concoction That's Raising Spirits in the Wine Industry," *Business Week*, October 8, 1984, 182.

[13] J. E. Davis, "A Juice Maker Squeezes Itself Dry," *Business Week*, August 10, 1987, 42.

[14] R. D. Arroyo, "Rapid Success Begat Atari Failure," *Marketing News*, May 10, 1985, 11.

[15] See A. Dunkin, "Pepsi's Marketing Magic," *Business Week*, February 10, 1986, 52–57; and J. K. Johansson and I. Nonaka, "Market Research the Japanese Way," *Harvard Business Review* (May 1987), 16–22.

[16] J. E. Duffy, "TV, Researchers Must Blaze New Trails—Together," *Marketing News*, May 10, 1985, 8.

[17] For a detailed treatment see L. Adler and C. S. Mayer, *Managing the Marketing Research Function* (Chicago: American Marketing Association, 1977), 89–110.

[18] Based on ibid., 56–70.

[19] An excellent overview of this industry is P. Barnard, "Research in the USA," *Journal of the Market Research Society* (October 1984), 273–293.

[20] J. Honomichl, "Top 50 U.S. Research Organizations," *Advertising Age*, May 23, 1988, S–4.

[21] P. Ryan, *Green Book: International Directory of Marketing Research Houses and Services* (New York Chapter, American Marketing Association, annually).

[22] See B. Hulin-Salken, "Shortage Yields Hot Market for Job Candidates," *Advertising Age*, May 23, 1985, 42–43.

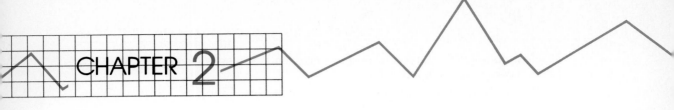

Marketing Information and
Decision Support Systems

Motorola Inc. has developed a computer-based strategic information system
that "collects and distributes information on the general business environment, domestic and international events, companies, and related areas that are
critical to market awareness and competitive success." Motorola personnel
describe the development of the system as follows:

> Motorola believes that information as a competitive resource is becom-
> ing a major goal at many top companies. We began to organize and
> focus resources in this area in 1984. At that time, the company saw a
> need for more informed strategic planning. We began by looking for a
> software package that would support the information needs of the strat-
> egy office and the operational planning and marketing staffs.
>   The demands of the users and the range of sources used to support
> the system required software with special capabilities. The system has
> to handle large volumes of text with a significant amount of flexibility.
> We have large quantities of random-sized abstracts. We need the ability
> to handle anything from a paragraph to a complete paper. When we do a
> search, we need the ability to look at the data from different analytical
> points of view. INQUIRE/Text software was selected for its ability to
> provide the needed flexibility.
>   A wide variety of data sources, including newspapers, books, in-
> dustry studies, government documents, on-line data services, market-
> ing reports, consulting reports, technical analyses, and competitor
> reports are used in the system. However, we deal only with publicly
> available information. When we are searching for information, we
> always identify ourselves as representatives of Motorola. The key to

building the system is knowing where the information exists and systematically collecting it.

There is a distinction between simply collecting information and applying that knowledge strategically. Our department's primary objective is to develop actionable information. Information is analyzed and delivered to the individual in the company who can act on it.[1]

Marketing Information Systems (MIS)

Marketing research was defined earlier as a formalized means of obtaining information to be used in making marketing decisions. A marketing information system (MIS) can be defined as a system designed to generate, store, and disseminate an orderly flow of pertinent information to marketing managers. Thus, marketing research is concerned with the act of generating information, whereas the marketing information system is focused on managing the flow of information to marketing decision makers. Motorola's system is an example of a marketing information system that focuses on strategic issues.

The Nature of the Marketing Information System

The information provided by an MIS is used to assist in each of the three major tasks of marketing decision making; that is, the system helps to identify, select, and resolve marketing problems or opportunities. For example, the J. C. Penney Co. has an MIS that provides data for all of these purposes.[2] A variety of sources of information is used to keep abreast of changes in consumer attitudes and purchasing behavior. The marketing research department monitors government and trade association data along with subscribing to consumer spending forecasts from outside agencies (identification, selection). The company participates in a consumer purchase panel that provides detailed data on the purchases made by 7,000 U.S. households each month (identification, selection, resolution).

The marketing research department also conducts periodic surveys to track consumer awareness and attitudes on each major merchandise category (identification, selection, resolution). Each of the 1,700 Penney stores has electronic point-of-sale terminals (EPOS terminals) tied to a central computer that records the item number, size, style or model, and price of each unit sold. This information permits the early identification of changes in spending patterns, as well as the efficient management of inventories (identification, selection, resolution). In addition, tailored consumer research studies are conducted to help develop merchandising and marketing plans (resolution).

Figure 2–1 illustrates an MIS. The key task of an MIS is to provide needed information to the appropriate managers in a usable format in a timely fashion.

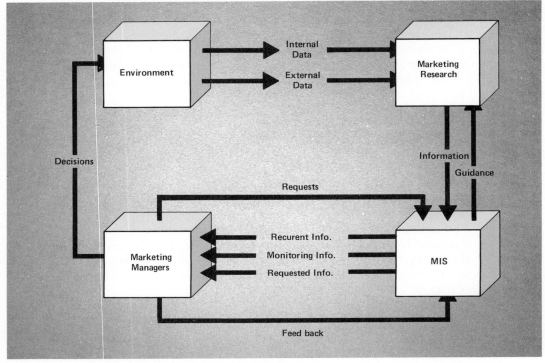

Figure 2–1 *The Nature of a Marketing Information System*

Obviously, this is a complicated task. Different managers require different types of information. Further, their information needs change, often in an unpredictable manner, over time. Flooding managers with more information than they need is generally counterproductive, as managers soon begin to ignore the relevant as well as the irrelevant information.

Thus, the most difficult task is to specify who receives what information when and in what format.[3] This task requires considerable managerial effort. Once initiated, successful MISs continue to evolve and change over time.

Types of Information in an MIS

Three distinct types of information are generally supplied to marketing managers through the MIS—recurrent, monitoring, and requested.

Recurrent Information. Recurrent information is information that is provided on a periodic basis. Market share by region, customer awareness of the firm's advertising, prices of the three leading competitors, customer satisfaction with the firm's products, and customer purchase intentions are examples of information that managers frequently receive on a weekly, monthly, quarterly, or annual basis. Recurrent information is particularly useful for indicating problems and opportunities. It can also be used to determine the effects of solutions to potential problems. For example, regular market share reports can be used to analyze the impact of price changes.

Recurrent information is based on both internal and external data sources. Accounting records and sales call reports are major internal sources. Consumer surveys, consumer panels, and store audits are important external sources.

Monitoring Information. Monitoring information is information derived from the regular scanning of certain sources. For example, a marketing manager may desire a summary of any articles on the competition or the industry. All relevant journals including trade association publications, government reports, and the general business press are examined as they are issued. Article summaries are prepared and distributed any time a relevant article appears.

Monitoring information comes primarily from external sources. Government reports, patents, articles, annual reports of competitors, and public activities of competitors are common sources that are monitored. Internal sales call reports and accounting records are also subject to monitoring. For example, sales call reports may be monitored for any mention of new product development activity by key competitors. If such activity is mentioned, the relevant marketing managers are notified.

Monitoring information is particularly useful for alerting firms to potential problems such as new competitors or new marketing activities by existing competitors. It can also help identify opportunities such as new product uses, new market segments, and improved product features.

Requested Information. Requested information is developed in response to a specific request by a marketing manager. Without such a request the information would not flow to the manager and might not exist in the system.

For example, a manager might request information on the size of a market not currently served by the firm along with an assessment of the intensity of competitive rivalry in the market and the level of customer satisfaction with the current brands in the market. Much of this information would not be available in the system and would have to be generated.

Another request might involve the response of one or more specific competitors to price changes initiated by other competitors. This information may well be in the system but may be difficult to access. Recall that the ability to access data from a variety of perspectives was a major concern of Motorola in our opening example.

Figure 2–2 provides examples of the types of information an MIS system may provide to various marketing personnel. This figure, which lists only a small portion of the types of information available, provides an indication of the tremendous difficulty of designing an MIS that will meet Motorola's ob-

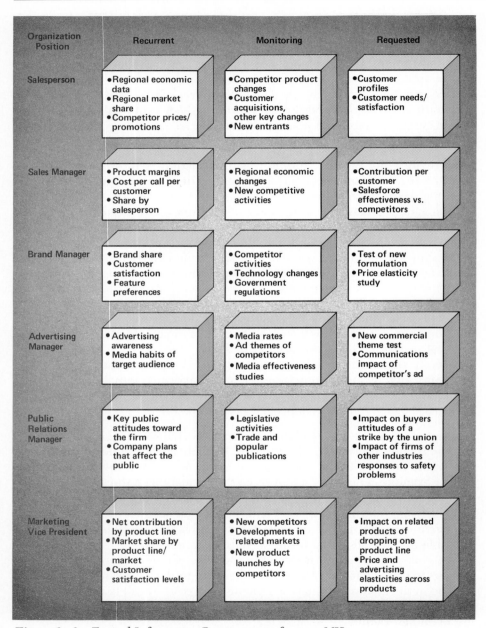

Organization Position	Recurrent	Monitoring	Requested
Salesperson	• Regional economic data • Regional market share • Competitor prices/promotions	• Competitor product changes • Customer acquisitions, other key changes • New entrants	• Customer profiles • Customer needs/satisfaction
Sales Manager	• Product margins • Cost per call per customer • Share by salesperson	• Regional economic changes • New competitive activities	• Contribution per customer • Salesforce effectiveness vs. competitors
Brand Manager	• Brand share • Customer satisfaction • Feature preferences	• Competitor activities • Technology changes • Government regulations	• Test of new formulation • Price elasticity study
Advertising Manager	• Advertising awareness • Media habits of target audience	• Media rates • Ad themes of competitors • Media effectiveness studies	• New commercial theme test • Communications impact of competitor's ad
Public Relations Manager	• Key public attitudes toward the firm • Company plans that affect the public	• Legislative activities • Trade and popular publications	• Impact on buyers attitudes of a strike by the union • Impact of firms of other industries responses to safety problems
Marketing Vice President	• Net contribution by product line • Market share by product line/market • Customer satisfaction levels	• New competitors • Developments in related markets • New product launches by competitors	• Impact on related products of dropping one product line • Price and advertising elasticities across products

Figure 2–2 *Typical Information Requirements from an MIS*

jective of analyzing data and providing it to the person in the organization who can act on it. However, the very difficulty of doing this means that those firms that succeed will have a sustainable competitive advantage over their competitors.

Exhibit 2–1   *An MIS for Competitor Intelligence*

Situation

This competitor MIS would work for virtually any product category. This system is particularly relevant for frequently purchased consumer goods such as soft drinks, beer, detergents, and personal care items. The data are collected, analyzed, and summarized by a central staff. Periodic and "as needed" reports are sent to the relevant managers. In addition, the data summaries are stored on a computer system which all the managers can access from their offices.

Recurrent Information

Recurrent information in this system generally measures competitor actions and consumer responses to those actions after they have occurred.

Type, Frequency	Source	Recipient
Sales, market share trends by model and region, weekly	Nielsen Audits NDP Consumer Panel	Brand and sales manager, regional sales managers
Customer satisfaction and perceptions, monthly	Special survey	Summary to all marketing personnel, details to brand, sales, and advertising managers.
Advertising levels and themes, monthly	Advertising tracking service	Brand and advertising manager
Price levels, monthly	Nielsen Audits	Brand and sales managers
Promotional activities (coupons, price reductions), monthly	Nielsen Audits	Brand, advertising, and sales managers
Customer mix by model by region, monthly	NDP Consumer Panel	Brand manager
General strategies, strengths, and problems, annually	Arthur D. Little annual industry report	All marketing managers

---

Monitoring Information

Although the monitoring of information indicates prior competitor activities and consumer responses, its primary objective is to alert management to *future* actions by competitors.

Type	Source	Recipient
New product plans	Trade press, competitor's local newpaper, salesforce reports (including a "hot line")	Brand manager
New product tests	Sales force reports, Nielsen audits, trade press	Brand manager
New research and development efforts	Trade press, annual and quarterly reports, want ad analysis	Brand manager
Production expansion, change	Local newpapers, building permit offices	Brand manager, production manager
New advertising themes	Trade press, sales force reports, ad agency personnel	Brand manager advertising manager
New promotions	Sales force reports, ad agency personnel	Brand manager advertising manager

Requested Information

These could involve a wide range of activities including quality testing of competitive products, cost analyses of competitor products or distribution systems, cash flow position of competitors, profiles of key competitor managers, and so forth. A sound system will build a base of this type of information over time and then update it periodically.

Specialized MISs

Thus far, we have discussed the MIS as though each firm had a single, integrated system designed to meet all the information needs of all the marketing managers. However, such systems are very rare. Instead, firms typically evolve smaller, specialized systems designed to meet the needs of a subset of managers such as sales managers or brand managers. Or, systems are developed for specific types of information such as data on competitors.

Specialized MISs frequently involve some duplication of effort and may not provide available information to all managers who could benefit from it. However, these systems have the tremendous advantage of being doable within the resources of most organizations. Furthermore, their benefits accrue to a few managers who are aware of the need for the data and who will therefore "champion" the system. Exhibit 2–1 provides a description of a specialized MIS focused on competitor activities.

Marketing Decision Support Systems (MDSS)

The term *decision support system* (DSS) is often used synonymously with *information system,* or, in a marketing context, with *marketing information system.*[4] However, it is preferable to distinguish between the two concepts. MISs are centralized suppliers of information, as is shown in Figure 2–1. Although the managers can sometimes access information directly, it is generally supplied to them by staff personnel on a periodic, as-it-is-available, or requested basis as described in Exhibit 2–1.

DSSs are decentralized and allow the managers to interact directly with the data base. The systems are generally computerized and have one or more models (formulas) built in. These models are developed to assist with specific decisions faced by marketing personnel. Therefore, DDSs typically provide the results of analyses of decision situations rather than the more "factual" information generally supplied by an MIS.[5] Figure 2–3 illustrates a typical

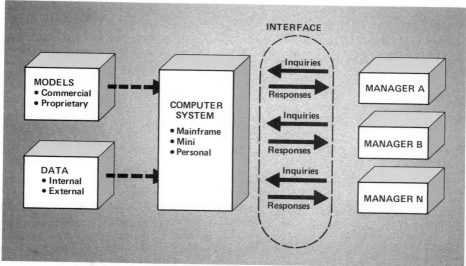

Figure 2–3   *A Typical Marketing Decision Support System*

DSS. A marketing decision support system (MDSS) is one that is designed specifically for marketing decisions.

Consider a simple MDSS. An industrial salesperson handles a product that allows substantial customization. At a customer's site 1,500 miles from the home office, she is asked if she can match the price and delivery time of a competitor for a unique product configuration. A sound MDSS would allow the salesperson to plug a portable computer directly into a phone jack. The portable computer could then communicate with a mini- or mainframe computer in the home office. The salesperson types in the product configuration and desired delivery time. The data base contains costs, inventory availability, assembly time needed, and margin requirements as well as a model to relate these variables. In a matter of minutes, the salesperson can respond with a price and delivery date. Even this very simple system involves all five of the components illustrated in Figure 2–3.

While the MDSS we have described is very valuable for the salesperson, it would have little value to the brand manager, strategic planner, advertising manager, or even the sales manager. Thus, rather than *a* MDSS, most firms have a series of MDSSs, some with shared components and some completely independent.

Components of a MDSS

As Figure 2–3 illustrates, MDSSs require five components: models, data, computers, an interface system, and managers.

Models

Models, as used in the context of a MDSS, are *mathematical statements of the presumed relationship between two or more variables.* A very simple model is

$$\text{Sales revenue} = \text{units sold} \times \text{average price per unit}$$

Although extremely simple, this model allows the manager to conduct *what-if* analyses. What-if analyses involve determining *what* the impact on a decision outcome (sales revenue in our example) would be *if* one or more of the unknown or predicted variables (units sold and average price in our example) were different from its assumed value.

Suppose a manager believes that about 1,000 units of a new product will be sold at an average price of $100:

$$\text{Sales revenue} = 1,000 \times \$100$$
$$= \$100,000$$

However, the manager is uncertain about the exact number that will be sold and about the average price level that will be obtained. Therefore, a series of what-if analyses are appropriate:

What if we only sell 900 units at $100 each?

What if we could sell 1,200 units at $90 each?

What if we could sell 800 units at $110 each?

Obviously, a model this simple requires no more than a pencil and paper to manipulate. Let's expand the model slightly to see how useful formal models can be.

Suppose management is considering introducing a new product. The firm uses a three-year planning horizon. Initial marketing research indicates that (1) the market demand is between 800,000 and 1,200,000 units a year, (2) the demand will grow between 10 and 14 per cent a year, (3) the firm's market share will be between 20 and 30 per cent, and (4) the average price will decline by $0.50 per year from the current $10.00 level.

If the manager has a reasonable understanding of the product's cost structure and the firm's marketing plans, a three-year projected income statement based on the initial marketing research estimates can be prepared. The first projection would be the "most likely" estimates produced by the researchers: perhaps 1,000,000 units current demand, a 12 per cent growth rate, a 25 per cent market share, and a $0.50 price decline each year.

A MDSS system for this situation might involve putting the projected income statements in formula form on a spreadsheet program such as *Lotus 1-2-3* or *Excel.* The manager can then conduct what-if analyses.

For example, the manager might ask, "What would our projected profits be if the initial market size were 900,000 units rather than 1,000,000?" Exhibit 2–2 illustrates a very simple version of this type of analysis.

In addition to what-if analyses, models such as this allow managers to conduct sensitivity analyses. *Sensitivity analysis* is determining at what level or value, if any, each of the unknown variables has a meaningful impact on the decision to be made. Assume our manager needs to break even the first year and show a 20 per cent return on sales for each of the next two years to justify launching the product. A simple sensitivity analysis could be done by conducting a what-if analysis with each unknown set at its highest and lowest likely value. If the decision would remain the same whether the variable was at its highest or lowest likely value, that variable could be ignored as far as the decision is concerned. If the decision would change, a critical variable has been identified. Additional research to specify its precise value may be justified.

A more thorough sensitivity analysis would involve varying the values of combinations of variables. Thus, it might be that the decision in our example would not change if the initial market size was 800,000 *given that all other unknowns were at their most likely values.* Likewise, the decision might not change if our market share was as low as 20 per cent, *again given that all other*

Exhibit 2-2 "What-If" Analysis

Assumptions

	Most Likely	Most Favorable	Least Favorable
Market Size	1,000,000	1,200,000	800,000
Market Growth	12%	14%	10%
Market Share	25%	30%	20%
Price	$10.00 first year		
Price Decline/Year	$0.50	$0.20	$1.00
Cost of Goods Sold (COGS)	$5.00 first year		
Annual Decline in COGS	5%		
Marketing Expenses	$750,000 first year plus $0.50 per unit, $0.50 unit years 2-3		

Results

Most Likely	Year 1	Year 2	Year 3
Sales	$2,800,000	$2,979,200	$3,161,088
Cost of Goods	1,400,000	1,489,600	1,668,352
Gross Profits	1,400,000	1,489,600	1,492,736
Marketing Expense	890,000	156,800	175,616
Contribution	$ 510,000	$1,332,800	$1,317,120

Most Favorable			
Sales	$4,104,000	$4,584,989	$5,120,216
Cost of Goods	2,052,000	2,222,316	2,533,440
Gross Profits	2,052,000	2,362,637	2,586,776
Marketing Expense	955,200	233,928	266,678
Contribution	$1,096,800	$2,128,745	$2,320,098

Least Favorable			
Sales	$1,760,000	$1,742,400	$1,703,680
Cost of Goods	880,000	919,600	1,011,560
Gross Profits	880,000	822,800	692,120
Marketing Expense	838,000	96,000	106,480
Contribution	$ 42,000	$ 726,000	$ 585,640

unknowns are at their most likely levels. However, if *both* initial market size *and* market share were low (800,000 and 20 per cent), the decision might differ. Thus, a complete sensitivity analysis must cover all relevant combinations of unknown or assumed variables.

Models are frequently developed for a specific decision such as the one just described. In addition, there are commercially available models for categories of problems that can be used "as is" or modified slightly to fit the situation at hand.[6] We describe several of these models in the final section of this chapter.

Data

MDSSs require varying amounts and types of data. In our first example of a price/delivery MDSS, only internal, "factual" data were involved. The new product launch MDSS that we just described required internal cost data as well as research data and assumptions about external factors such as market size, market share, and price level over time.

Suppose a brand manager for Procter & Gamble learns from the MIS that Colgate is test marketing a new competitive product in Denver and Buffalo. The manager would want answers to several questions, including, "How much share will my brand lose if Colgate goes national and I don't change my marketing mix?" Responding would require data on Procter & Gamble's brand's share trend nationally and in Denver and Buffalo, a measure of whether it or Colgate is unusually strong or weak in Denver or Buffalo, a reading of how its share is being affected in the two test cities, and estimates of how other competitors will respond if Colgate goes national.

As we will see in Chapters 4 and 5, such data is available from a variety of sources. However, for the data to prove useful, Procter & Gamble will have to have anticipated the need for it, arranged to acquire it, entered it into the system, and developed a model that will allow the data to be analyzed.

Computer System

Theoretically, the data in a MDSS could be analyzed using the relevant models and manual calculations. However, this is impractical for all but the very simplest systems. Increasingly, MDSSs are being developed for mini-computers and personnel computers rather than mainframes. Given the fairly limited data storage requirements of most MDSSs and the rapidly increasing power and speed of personal computers, this trend toward personal computer systems will undoubtedly continue.

Interface

More critical than the computer system is the software that allows the manager to interact with the data and the model. Most managers have limited computer programming skills and lack both the time and inclination to acquire these skills. Therefore, successful MDSSs are exceedingly user friendly.

A MDSS has value only to the extent that *managers* will use it to test hypotheses and assumptions, change parameters, and clarify options. Thus, the interface must be more than "doable"; it must also be fun or at least easy.

A successful system was adopted by Kraft, Inc. Kraft has a five-member MDSS staff. They acquired a general system called ACCESS Marketing Analysis System from Dialogue, Inc.; to this, they added a series of sophisticated analysis functions addressing issues specific to Kraft. Today, over 200 managers in brand marketing, marketing services, sales, and advertising are active users of the system. With a staff of only five supporting over two hundred users, it is clear that the managers are very comfortable interfacing with the system on their own.[7]

Managers

As stated earlier, managers are the most important aspect of a MDSS. If they fail to use the system or use it improperly, the system has no (or negative) value. Thus, not only must the interface system be user friendly, but managers also must understand how to do *what if* and other relevant analyses. They must also understand and accept the models involved. Hence, managers should be actively involved in developing the models. In fact, active involvement in all aspects of the design of the system by all potential users is the key to a successful system.

Examples of MDSSs

A wide array of MDSSs are used by firms, ranging from Coca-Cola to General Electric, to J. C. Penney, to Esco (a specialty steel producer).[8] In this section, we describe two applications of publicly or commercially available systems.

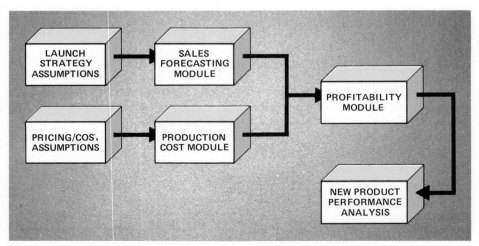

Figure 2–4 *B.E.I.I. Decision Support System*

New Industrial Product Sales Forecast and Launch Strategy MDSS

A MDSS for evaluating various launch strategies and forecasting sales (and profits) for each strategy has been developed and used successfully by a number of European firms.[9] This MDSS, called Banque d'Experiences d'Innovations Industrielles (B.E.I.I.), has three modules or models, shown in Figure 2–4 and described below.

> The *Salesforecasting Model* takes assumptions about market structure, entry strategy, and the development process. It then computes a four-year sales projection. The variables used and the formula relating these variables to sales and market penetration were derived from a five-year analysis of 112 new industrial products.

> The *Production Cost Model* uses relevant experience curves, economy of scale figures, and marketing plans to project annual production, marketing, and distribution costs for the product.

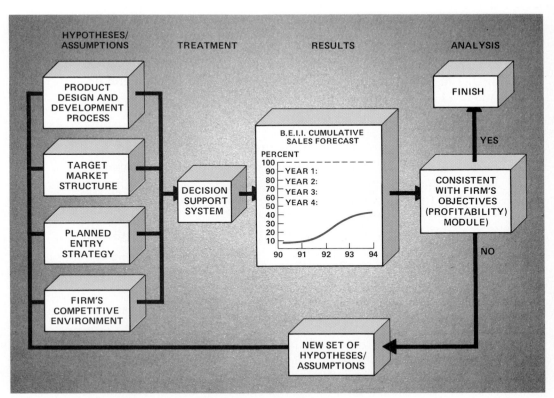

Figure 2–5   *The B.E.I.I. New Product Sales Forecast Module*

The *Profitability Model* takes cost, volume, and relevant expense projections and produces appropriate financial projections.

Figure 2–5 illustrates how this model might be used to forecast sales and profits, given a set of assumptions and a planned marketing strategy. More significantly, it allows the manager to run sensitivity analyses on the various assumptions and to easily evaluate the profit impact of differing marketing strategies.

Marketing Budget

ADVISOR is a MDSS that is used to help set and allocate marketing budgets for industrial products.[10] It focuses primarily on the communications element of industrial marketing budgets. ADVISOR is based on an analysis of over 300 products marketed by over 100 different companies.

Based on both theory and experience, 19 factors that might influence the appropriate level and mix of marketing communications expenditure for an industrial product were identified. Data on these 19 factors were collected for each of the 300 products in the database as was marketing mix expenditure data. Using sophisticated regression analysis techniques, these data were analyzed to determine how marketing communications expenditures tend to vary as the 19 factors change. This analysis identified the following nine general characteristics of industrial marketing situations that have a meaningful impact on the level and type of communications mix.

1. Current sales level
2. Number of users (customers) for the product
3. Degree of customer concentration (share of purchases accounted for by the largest customers)
4. Fraction of the sales made directly by the manufacturer to the customers rather than through intermediaries
5. Difference between the attitudes of customers and prospects toward the product
6. Fraction of sales made to fulfill orders
7. Life cycle stage of the product
8. Marketing plans for the product (aggressive, hold share, harvest, etc.)
9. Product complexity

A firm using the ADVISOR MDSS provides data on each of the nine key factors. The regression models (mathematical formulas) derived from the 300 products in the database are then used to calculate the amount and mix of marketing communications expenditures an "average" firm in the database would spend on a product with similar levels of the nine factors. (A norm or most likely amount is reported as are high and low boundary levels.)

The ADVISOR norms have been used by companies in a number of different ways: (1) as a screening device to identify communication plans that are unusual and should be subjected to a second evaluation; (2) as a standard of comparison and as guidelines in budget preparation; (3) to provide insight into the appropriate changes that might be indicated by different marketing scenarios; (4) to estimate the communication budgets of competitors; and (5) to provide justification for communication plans.

Review Questions

2.1. What is a *marketing information system* (MIS)? How does it relate to marketing research?

2.2. What is *recurrent information?* Provide an example.

2.3. What is *monitoring information?* Provide an example.

2.4. What is *requested information?* Provide an example.

2.5. What is a *specialized MIS?*

2.6. Describe a *competitor intelligence MIS.*

2.7. What is a *decision support system?* How does it differ from a *marketing decision support system?*

2.8. How does a MDSS differ from a MIS?

2.9. What are the components of a MDSS? Describe each.

2.10. What is a *model?*

2.11. What is a *what-if analysis?*

2.12. What is a *sensitivity analysis?*

2.13. Describe the B.E.I.I. MDSS.

2.14. Describe the ADVISOR MDSS.

Discussion Questions/Problems

2.15. The developer of the Motorola DSS that we described at the beginning of the chapter stated: "There is a distinction between simply collecting information and applying that information strategically." What does this mean?

2.16. How would you determine what types of information an MIS should provide to different members of an organization?

2.17. How would you improve the system shown in Exhibit 2–1?

2.18. How would you determine which types of MDSSs are required by different members of an organization?

2.19. Run a five-year what-if analysis using Exhibit 2–2 as the base.[11] Use the most likely values and the following changes:
 a. market share = 21%
 b. market share = 24%
 c. market share = 29%
 d. market growth = 10%
 e. market growth = 13%
 f. market size = 800,000
 g. market size = 1,100,000
 h. price decline = $.60 per year
 i. price decline = $.20 per year
 j. a and d
 k. c and g

2.20. How do you insure that managers will make effective use of a MDSS?

Projects

2.21. Interview the managers of _____. Describe in detail a sound MIS for that organization.
 a. your student union
 b. the university bookstore
 c. a campus restaurant
 d. a local shopping center

2.22. Interview the managers of _____. Describe in detail a sound MDSS for that organization.
 a. your student union
 b. the university bookstore
 c. a campus restaurant
 d. a local shopping center

2.23. Read the article by Choffray and Lilien, listed in reference 9. Could this same method be used for retail stores? Financial services?

References

[1] "Company Sees Benefits in Centralizing Its System of Competitor Intelligence," *Marketing News*, September 12, 1986, 4. See also J. P. Herring, "Building a Business Intelligence System," *Journal of Business Strategy* (May 1988), 4–9.

[2] Based on private correspondence and "Penney Sees 'Fairly Good' Retail Gains," *Advertising Age*, November 2, 1982, 20. See also H. G. M. Brinkhoff,

"How Does Unilever Work with Its MIS?" *European Research* (April 1984), 88–95.

[3] See C. W. Stryker, "The Power of the Sales Information System," "Putting the System to Use," and "How to Keep Your Sales Information System Up to Date," *Business Marketing* (June 1985), 120–128; (July 1985), 80–84; and (August 1985), 104–110.

[4] M. C. A. van Nievell, "Decision Support Systems Contribute to Better Marketing," *European Research* (April 1984), 74–83.

[5] M. D. Goslar and S. W. Brown, "Decision Support Systems," *Journal of Consumer Marketing* (Summer 1986), 43–50.

[6] See M. L. Laric and R. Stiff, *Lotus 1-2-3^R For Marketing and Sales* (Prentice-Hall Inc.), 1984; G. L. Lilien, *Marketing Mix Analysis with Lotus 1-2-3^R,* (The Scientific Press), 1986; and G. L. Lilien, *Marketing Management: Analytic Exercises with Lotus 1-2-3^R,* (The Scientific Press), 1988.

[7] J. E. Ohlon, "Modified Computer System Helps Kraft Make Plans," *Marketing News*, May 23, 1986, 31.

[8] See M. L. Laric and R. Stiff, op. cit.

[9] J. M. Choffray and G. L. Lilien, "A Decision-Support System for Evaluating Sales Prospects and Launch Strategies for New Products," *Industrial Marketing Management* (1986), 75–85.

[10] See Lilien, *Marketing Mix;* and Lilien, *Marketing Management.*

[11] A Lotus 1-2-3 program is available in the software package available through Macmillan.

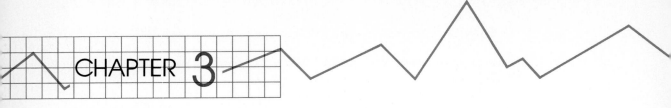

CHAPTER 3

The Research Process and Research Design

While doing research on the formula for what would become diet *Coke*, Coca-Cola USA chemists came up with a syrup that tasted "smoother" than regular *Coke*. Over the next three years the company conducted a series of taste tests comparing this and other formulations of *Coke* with the various cola brands on the market. During that time, the taste preferences of more than 190,000 persons were measured in the United States and selected foreign countries. The results of these taste tests ultimately convinced Coca-Cola USA management that "new" *Coke* should be introduced.

Although the overall design differed in some of the tests, the central design elements were as follows:

1. the tests were held in shopping malls;
2. quota samples of 200 to 400 persons representing demographic groups of interest were selected;
3. all taste tests were conducted on a *double-blind* basis. That is, neither the person administering the test nor the person taking the test knew what actual brands and/or formulations were used in the tests in which they were involved;
4. the tests were conducted using two different designs, *double triangle discrimination* and *sequential monadic preference tests*.
    For the double triangle discrimination tests each sample member was asked to taste, in random order, two samples of *Coke* and one sample of *Pepsi-Cola*, and was then asked to tell the interviewer the one that was different from the other two. In a second triangle test, the sample

member was asked to taste, in random order, two samples of *Pepsi* and one sample of *Coke,* and again was asked to identify which sample was different from the other two.

After the second triangle discrimination test, the sequential monadic preference test was conducted. The procedure for this test was to give each sample member, in random order, samples of *Pepsi* and *Coke* and ask them to state a taste preference between the two.

Analysis of the results of the tests was performed on the total sample (including discriminators and nondiscriminators);

5. the taste preference tests were conducted on a paired comparison basis involving more than one formulation of *Coke.* For example, for the preference tests between regular Coke (now *Coca-Cola Classic*), regular *Pepsi,* and a new formulation of regular *Coke,* the sample member was asked to make the following comparisons:

(i) regular *Coke* — regular *Pepsi;*
(ii) new formulation of regular *Coke* — regular *Pepsi;*
(iii) new formulation of regular *Coke* — regular *Coke.*

These pairs were administered in random order. The sample member was asked to rinse out her or his mouth with water and eat some unsalted crackers between tastes.

[See Case IV-4, 'Classic Coke, New Coke, Pepsi-Cola Taste Test,' with its accompanying data bank for an example of an actual taste test.]

In this chapter we provide an overview of *research design* within the framework of the general research process. To do this, we first discuss the research process. We then consider the nature of research design, provide a description of the steps that it involves, and conclude with an analysis of the potential errors that a good research design attempts to minimize.

The Research Process

The *research process* involves *identifying a management problem or opportunity; translating that problem/opportunity into a research problem; and collecting, analyzing, and reporting the information specified in the research problem.*

A *management problem* deals with decisions managers must make. A *research problem* deals with providing information that will help management make better decisions. The management problem that had been faced by Coca-Cola USA for a number of years was a continuing loss in the market share to Pepsi-Cola. The research problem was to discover the reasons for that loss, and how it could be reversed.

The Nature of Research Design

Research design is the specification of procedures for collecting and analyzing the data necessary to help identify or react to a problem or opportunity, such that the difference between the cost of obtaining various levels of accuracy and the expected value of the information associated with each level of accuracy is maximized.

Several aspects of this definition deserve emphasis. First, research design requires the *specification of procedures*. These procedures involve decisions on what information to generate, the data collection method, the measurement approach, the object to be measured, and the way in which the data are to be analyzed. Second, the data *are to be collected to help identify or react to a problem or opportunity*.

All data collected should eventually relate to decisions faced by management. Obviously, the efficient collection of data relevant to a decision requires a clear definition of the problem/opportunity.

A third implication of the preceding definition is that *information has value*. Information acquires value as it helps improve decisions. The fourth major implication is that *varying levels of accuracy of information can be generated in response to the same problem*. Information accuracy is affected by the occurrence of a number of potential errors. Finally, the goal of applied research design is not to generate the most accurate information possible. Rather, the objective is to *generate the most valuable information in relation to the cost of generating the information*.

Thus, a primary goal of research design is to maximize the accuracy of the information generated for a given expenditure. Stated another way, research design attempts to minimize the occurrence of potential errors at any specified budget level.

Steps in the Research Design Process

Describing the research design process as a sequential series of distinct or separate steps is inherently misleading. The steps in the design process interact and often occur simultaneously. For example, the design of a measurement instrument is influenced by the type of analysis that will be conducted. However, the type of analysis is also influenced by the specific characteristics of the measurement instrument.

Because written communications must be presented sequentially, we present the research design process as a distinct series of steps. These steps are shown in Table 3–1 and represent the general order in which decisions are made in designing a research project. However, we must emphasize the fact

Table 3 – 1 Steps in the Research Design Process

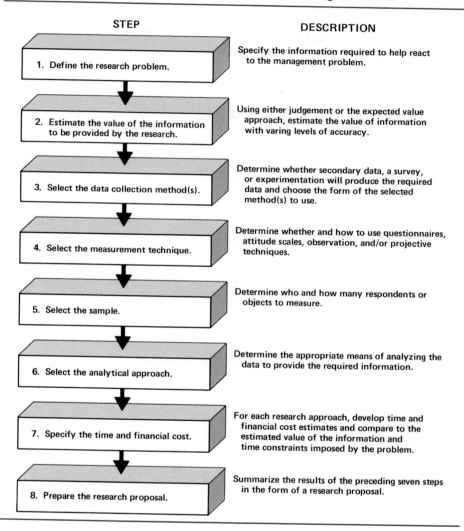

STEP	DESCRIPTION
1. Define the research problem.	Specify the information required to help react to the management problem.
2. Estimate the value of the information to be provided by the research.	Using either judgement or the expected value approach, estimate the value of information with varing levels of accuracy.
3. Select the data collection method(s).	Determine whether secondary data, a survey, or experimentation will produce the required data and choose the form of the selected method(s) to use.
4. Select the measurement technique.	Determine whether and how to use questionnaires, attitude scales, observation, and/or projective techniques.
5. Select the sample.	Determine who and how many respondents or objects to measure.
6. Select the analytical approach.	Determine the appropriate means of analyzing the data to provide the required information.
7. Specify the time and financial cost.	For each research approach, develop time and financial cost estimates and compare to the estimated value of the information and time constraints imposed by the problem.
8. Prepare the research proposal.	Summarize the results of the preceding seven steps in the form of a research proposal.

that the "early" decisions are made with a simultaneous consideration of the "later" decisions. Furthermore, there is a constant reconsideration of earlier decisions in light of the later decisions.

Step 1: Define the Research Problem

Problem definition is the most critical part of the research process. Unless the problem is properly defined, the information produced by the research process is unlikely to have any value.[2] *Research problem definition involves specifying the types of information that are needed by management.*

Research problem definition involves four interrelated steps: (1) management problem/opportunity clarification, (2) situation analyses, (3) model development, and (4) specification of information requirements.

Management Problem/Opportunity Clarification.   In a meeting with a marketing research consultant, the president of a chamber of commerce discussed a research project that would help merchants reduce the amount of shopping residents of their community do in two larger communities nearby. The management problem was apparently clear: how to reduce "outshopping" and so increase the amount of shopping done locally. Stated in this way, the task of the researcher was to help identify and evaluate various ways for increasing the local merchants' share of the shopping done by residents.

Although this seemed like a clear and straightforward statement of the problem, probing revealed that his underlying problem was to convince a majority of the local retailers that there was a sufficient outflow of local trade to warrant joint action to reverse the flow. Only after the retailers were convinced of this would it be possible to utilize information on why local residents were shopping in surrounding communities. The more precise statement of the management problem implied a very different research problem than did the initial statement. Now the researcher would become concerned with measuring the level of the retail trade outflow, in addition to the reasons for the outflow.

The basic goal of problem clarification is to ensure that the decision maker's initial description of the management decision is accurate and reflects the appropriate area of concern for research. If the wrong management problem is translated into a research problem, the probability of providing management with useful information is low.[3]

Situation Analysis.   The management problem can only be understood within the context of the decision situation. The situation analysis focuses on the variables that have produced the stated management problem or opportunity. The factors that have led to the problem/opportunity manifestations and the factors that have led to management's concern with the problem/opportunity should be isolated. The situation analysis is seldom limited to an armchair exercise in logic, although this may be a valuable part of it. It also involves giving careful attention to company records; appropriate secondary sources such as census data, industry sales figures, economic indicators, and so on; and interviews with knowledgeable individuals both internal and external to the firm. The persons interviewed will include the manager(s) involved and may include salespersons, other researchers, trade association officials, professionals, and consumers.

46

A situation analysis of the retail trade outflow problem revealed, among other things, that (1) the local population had grown 25 per cent over the previous five years, (2) buying power per capita appeared to be growing at the national rate of three per cent a year, and (3) local retail sales of nongrocery items had increased approximately 20 per cent over the past five years. Thus, the local retailers' sales are clearly not keeping pace with the potential in the area.

Model Development. Once the researcher has a sound understanding of the decision situation, it is necessary to get as clear an understanding as possible of the *situation model* of the manager. A situation model is a *description of the outcomes that are desired, the relevant variables, and the relationships of the variables to the outcomes.* The researcher is therefore interested in having the manager answer the following questions:

1. What objective(s) is desired in solving the problem or taking advantage of the opportunity?
2. What variables determine whether the objective(s) will be met?
3. How do they relate to the objective(s)?

For example, the chamber president gave the following explanation about why local consumers shop in the larger communities nearby:

It could be any of several things. Our prices are about the same as theirs but I'm not sure our local people recognize this. They advertise a lot more than we do and they have larger stores. Maybe it's just the excitement or fun of getting out-of-town. I think if more people recognized the impact on our local economy, they would spend more money in town. We really need to capture at least a third of the trade we are now losing.

Note that the president has suggested several causes for outshopping. He also has suggested a potential solution. In addition, he has stated his objective with respect to the problem. However, the researcher should not be satisfied to operate with only the manager's model of the problem. Instead, there should be an attempt to develop the best possible model of the decision at hand. Although there will usually be little latitude with respect to the objectives of the firm, the researcher should examine carefully the list of variables developed thus far that are believed to be the determining ones. Are all of these variables relevant? Are these the only relevant variables? How does each variable affect the outcome of the decision?

At least two sources of information may be helpful in this phase of research design. First, *secondary data* sources beyond those concerned directly with the situation analysis should be reviewed. These sources range from trade journal articles and special reports concerning the variable in a specific situation to more abstract theoretical treatments of the variable.

A second approach for getting information to help the researcher to develop a problem situation model involves using selected *case analyses*. Assume that a firm is concerned with the sales performance of its various branch offices. The case approach would involve an in-depth comparison of a "successful" branch and an "unsuccessful" branch. Those variables that differed the most between the two branches would then be considered relevant for additional study.

At the end of the model development stage, the researcher will have developed a list of variables relevant to the management problem *and* some known or tentative sets of relationships between the variables.

Specification of Information Requirements. Research cannot provide solutions. Solutions require executive judgment. Research provides information relevant to the decisions faced by the executive. The output of the problem-definition process is a clear statement of the information required to assist the decision maker. Thus, part of the information to be generated for the chamber president might include a price comparison of selected nongrocery items in the three towns and a measure of local residents' beliefs concerning the relative prices for the same items in the three towns.

A common temptation is to try to collect data on all possible variables. Unfortunately, this is generally impractical and always costly. The best approach for ensuring that any data collected is indeed relevant is to ask questions concerning the ultimate use of the data. Specifically, the researcher should list the research findings that seem possible and, in conjunction with the manager, trace the implications of each with respect to the decision. That is, the researcher must ask the question, "Given this finding, what would the firm do?"

The emphasis is on *what it will do,* or at least, *is likely to do, given certain findings.* In some companies such as Carnation it is the practice to have final research proposals signed by both the research director and the manager involved, and to include a statement to the effect that if X_1 results are obtained, Y_1 action will be taken; if X_2 is the finding, Y_2 action will be taken, and so on.

Categories of Research. A number of researchers have found it useful to consider three general categories of research based on the type of information required. These three categories are *exploratory, descriptive,* and *causal.*

Exploratory research is concerned with *discovering the general nature of the problem and the variables that relate to it.* Exploratory research is characterized by a high degree of flexibility, and it tends to rely on secondary data, convenience or judgment samples, small-scale surveys or simple experiments, case analyses, and subjective evaluation of the results.

Descriptive research is focused on *the accurate description of the variables in the problem model.* Consumer profile studies, market-potential studies, product-usage studies, attitude surveys, sales analyses, media research, and price surveys are examples of descriptive research. Any source of information can be used in a descriptive study, although most studies of this nature rely heavily on secondary data sources and survey research.

Causal research attempts *to specify the nature of the functional relationship between two or more variables in the problem model.* For example, studies on the effectiveness of advertising generally attempt to discover the extent to which advertising causes sales or attitude change. We can use three types of evidence to make inferences about causation: (1) *concomitant variation,* (2) *sequence of occurrence,* and (3) *absence of other potential causal factors.*

Concomitant variation, or invariant association, is a common basis for ascribing cause. Suppose we note that our advertising expenditures vary across a number of geographic areas and measure sales in each area. To the extent that high sales occur in areas with large advertising expenditures and low sales occur in areas with limited advertising expenditures, we may infer that advertising is a cause of sales. It must be stressed that we have only *inferred* this; we have not proven that increased advertising causes increased sales.

Sequence of occurrence can also provide evidence of causation. For one event to cause another, it must always precede it. An event that occurs after another event cannot be said to cause the first event. The importance of sequence can be demonstrated in our last example of advertising causing sales. Suppose that further investigation showed that the advertising allocation to the geographic regions had been based on the last period's sales such that the level of advertising was directly related to past sales. Suddenly, the nature of our causal relationship is reversed. Now, because of the sequence of events, we can infer that changes in sales levels cause changes in advertising levels.

A final type of evidence that we can use to infer causality is the *absence of other potential causal factors.* That is, if we could logically or through our research design eliminate all possible causative factors except the one we are interested in, we would have established that the variable we are concerned with was the causative factor. Unfortunately, it is never possible to control completely or to eliminate all possible causes for any particular event. Always we have the possibility that some factor of which we are not aware has influenced the results. However, if all reasonable alternatives are eliminated except one, we can have a high degree of confidence in the remaining variable.

Step 2: Estimate the Value of the Information

A decision maker normally approaches a problem with some information. If the problem is, say, whether a new product should be introduced, enough information will normally have been accumulated through past experience with other decisions concerning the introduction of new products and from various other sources to allow some preliminary judgments to be formed about the desirability of introducing the product in question. There will rarely be sufficient confidence in these judgments that additional information relevant to the decision would not be accepted if it were available without cost or delay. There might be enough confidence, however, that there would be an unwillingness to pay very much or wait very long for the added information.

Willingness to buy additional information depends on the quality of the information as well as the price. If perfect information — that is, information that would remove all uncertainty from the decision — were available, our decision maker would no doubt be willing to pay more for it than for information that would still leave some uncertainty about the proper decision.

The principle involved in deciding whether to do more research is that *research should be conducted only when it is expected that the value of the information to be obtained will be greater than the cost of obtaining it.*

Two approaches can be taken to arrive at an assessment of whether the expected value of the information in a proposed research project is greater than its estimated cost: the *intuitive* and the *expected value* approaches to the problem.

The Intuitive Approach to Making the *Do Research — Decide Without Research* Decision. The intuitive approach relies entirely on the private judgment of the person making the assessment. Because it is a private process, it is not possible to specify exactly what kinds of considerations the person(s) involved took into account. We can, however, specify what minimum considerations *ought* to be weighed in making the decision. For example, if the decision by the Coca-Cola USA management concerning whether or not to conduct taste tests had been made using the intuitive approach, the following considerations would have been relevant:

1. *The alternative actions that could be taken.* Coca-Cola management believed that a majority of the cola drinkers in the United States might prefer a cola that tasted sweeter than *Coke.* Given this belief, and an observed slow, but continuing loss of market share, the alternatives management had were (1) to decide without research to change to a sweeter formula, (2) to do research before deciding whether or not to make the formula sweeter, and (3) to decide without research to leave the formula unchanged.

The alternatives available in any marketing problem are always these same three: (1) to decide without doing research to take the action being considered, (2) to do research before deciding whether to take the action being considered, and (3) to decide without doing research not to take the action being considered.

2. *The possible states of the market and their payoffs (possible outcomes resulting from uncontrollable factors affecting the market).* Coca-Cola management must have had sales, market share, and profit forecasts made, conditional on whether or not there actually was a majority of cola drinkers who preferred a sweeter taste, assuming that (1) management changed the formula to make it sweeter, or (2) it left the formula unchanged. If the consequences of changing the formula were slight, there would have been little incentive to do the taste tests. On the other hand, if the forecast effects on sales and market share of changing the formula were substantial, there was potentially much more to be gained by conducting the taste tests.

If Coca-Cola decided to change to a sweeter formula, a market situation in which a majority of the cola drinkers preferred a sweeter formula would constitute a "favorable" market state. One ought always to define, and consider the consequences of, "favorable" and "unfavorable" states of the market on each action being considered.

3. *The degree of uncertainty concerning which state of the market is the actual state.* If Coca-Cola management had been very sure what the taste preferences were concerning the degree of sweetness, it would have had substantially less interest in conducting taste tests than if it had been uncertain about those preferences.

Research is conducted to reduce uncertainty. If the persons involved already feel reasonably sure that they know what the state of the market is, the incentive to do research is reduced.

4. *The ability to forecast the actual state of the market given the research findings.* If Coca-Cola management had expected that the taste tests would be unreliable predictors of the preferences (and purchases) of the cola-drinking population, there would obviously have been little incentive to conduct them.

The predictive accuracy of the research information must always be considered in assessing the expected value of research information. Other things being equal, the higher the predictive accuracy the more the information will be worth.

5. *The risk preferences of the decision maker(s).* A principal element in the corporate culture of every company is its attitude toward risk. Some companies have fast-moving, risk-taking managements whereas others are more cautious and conservative. For similar situations, the information from a research project will be valued more highly by risk-averting managers than it will be by those who are risk-takers.

In addition to the considerations just outlined, decisions to *do research — decide without research* using the intuitive approach are routinely influenced by such considerations as company policy, available funding, intrafirm politics, and other factors.

The persons using the intuitive approach weigh the considerations outlined, plus any others they think are relevant to the situation at hand, and estimate the value of information given varying degrees of accuracy. The intuitive approach is the most commonly used procedure. This wide usage reflects its principal advantage of requiring *the same general type of decision that marketing executives are accustomed to making.* It has some distinct disadvantages, however. Since a private, informal judgmental process is involved, (1) *the method is subject to unknown biases,* (2) *it is difficult to resolve differences between two reasonable people who reach opposite conclusions about the same research situation,* and (3) *it is difficult to improve in any systematic way the quality of the decisions made over time.*

The Expected Value Approach to Making the *Do Research — Decide Without Research* Decision. The expected value approach uses the same five items of information just described for the intuitive approach, but it uses them within an explicit *quantitative* model. This model involves the application of *Bayesian* statistics, a branch of statistics that allows personal (judgmental) probabilities to be used. The model is explained in some detail in Appendix A, where it is applied to an actual decision by the General Mills Company.

The essential differences between the expected value and the intuitive approaches are that for the expected value model (1) *all judgments about the likelihood of outcomes and the accuracies of the research project(s) being considered have to be expressed as numerical probabilities* (called personal probabilities); (2) *the expected value of the information from each prospective project is calculated and compared to its estimated cost;* and (3) *explicit consideration is given to the risk preferences (the utility function) of the person making the decision.*

Go back and reread this listing of differences. They are required for the expected value approach because, as the name implies, the approach assumes an *expected value decision maker.* Such a decision maker is one who chooses between alternative actions on the basis of possible payoffs (expressed either in amount of *money* or in *amounts of utility*), each weighted by the probability of its occurring.

The expected value approach has some very real advantages when compared to the intuitive approach. Since it is an explicit decision model, the expected value approach (1) *allows persons who reach opposite conclusions about whether a particular research project should be carried out to determine on what specific judgments they disagree* (what the states of the market are, what the payoff associated with each state is, what the predictive accuracy of the project will be, and so forth), and it (2) *allows* (in fact, requires) *explicit recognition of the risk preferences of the decision maker(s).*

The expected value approach has the disadvantages, as compared to the intuitive approach, that (1) *many people do not like to have to quantify judgments of probabilities* (most of us prefer to express judgments of probabilities by the use of verbal descriptors [there is a 'good chance' that . . .] rather than quantitatively [there is a 60 per cent chance that . . .]) and (2) *obtaining stable and accurate measurements of the risk preferences of the executive(s) involved in the decision is difficult.*

Step 3: Select the Data Collection Approach

There are three basic data collection approaches in marketing research: (1) *secondary data,* (2) *survey data,* and (3) *experimental data. Secondary data* were collected for some purpose other than helping to solve the current problem, whereas *primary data* are collected expressly to help solve the problem at hand. Survey and experimental data are therefore secondary data if

Table 3−2   Major Data Collection Methods

I. *Secondary Research* — Utilization of data that were developed for some purposes other than helping solve the problem at hand.
   A. *Internal secondary data* — data generated within the organization itself, such as salesperson call reports, sales invoices, and accounting records.
   B. *External secondary data* — data generated by sources outside the organization, such as government reports, trade association data, and data collected by syndicated services.

II. *Survey Research* — Systematic collection of information directly from respondents.
   A. *Telephone interviews* — collection of information from respondents via telephone.
   B. *Mail interviews* — collection of information from respondents via mail or similar technique.
   C. *Personal interviews* — collection of information in a face-to-face situation.
      1. *Home interviews* — personal interviews in the respondent's home or office.
      2. *Intercept interviews* — personal interviews in a central location, generally a shopping mall.
   D. *Computer interviews* — respondents enter data directly into a computer in response to questions presented on the monitor.

III. *Experimental Research* — The researcher manipulates one or more variables in such a way that its effect on one or more other variables can be measured.
   A. *Laboratory experiments* — manipulation of the independent variable(s) in an artificial situation.
      1. *Basic designs* — consider the impact of only one independent variable.
      2. *Statistical designs* — consider the impact of more than one independent variable.
   B. *Field experiments* — manipulation of the independent variable(s) in a natural situation.
      1. *Basic designs* — consider the impact of only one independent variable.
      2. *Statistical design* — consider the impact of more than one independent variable.

they were collected earlier for another study; they are primary data if they were collected for the present one. These data-collection approaches and their major subareas are described in Table 3–2.

Secondary data are virtually always collected first because of their time and cost advantages. However, a researcher does not necessarily choose one of these approaches over the others. For example, in collecting data for a decision about introducing a new product, a researcher may (1) examine company records for information relating to past introductions of similar products (secondary data); (2) conduct a series of mall interviews to determine current consumer attitudes about the product category (survey data); and (3) conduct a controlled store test in which the impact of different package designs is measured (experimental data).

The selection of the data-collection method(s) is one of the key aspects of the research design. Although creativity and judgment play a major role in this stage of the design process, the decision is constrained by the type of information required and its cost.

Table 3–3 Primary Measurement Techniques

I. *Questionnaire* — a formalized instrument for asking information directly from a respondent concerning behavior, demographic characteristics, level of knowledge, and/or attitudes, beliefs, and feelings.

II. *Attitude Scales* — a formalized instrument for eliciting self-reports of beliefs and feelings concerning an object(s).
   A. *Rating scales* — require the respondent to place the object being rated at some point along a numerically valued continuum or in one of a numerically ordered series of categories.
   B. *Composite scales* — require the respondent to express a degree of belief concerning various attributes of the object such that the attitude can be inferred from the pattern of responses.
   C. *Perceptual maps* — derive the components or characteristics an individual uses in comparing similar objects and provide a score for each object on each characteristic.
   D. *Conjoint analysis* — derive the value an individual assigns to various attributes of a product.

III. *Observation* — the direct examination of behavior, the results of behavior, or physiological changes.

IV. *Projective Techniques and Depth Interviews* — designed to gather information that respondents are either unable or unwilling to provide in response to direct questioning.
   A. *Projective techniques* — allow respondents to project or express their own feelings as a characteristic of someone or something else.
   B. *Depth interviews* — allow individuals to express themselves without any fear of disapproval, dispute, or advice from the interviewer.

Step 4: Select the Measurement Technique

There are four basic measurement techniques used in marketing research: (1) *questionnaires*, (2) *attitude scales*, (3) *observation*, and (4) *depth interviews* and *projective techniques*. Each of these approaches is briefly described in Table 3–3. (Chapter 9 provides a discussion of the theory of measurement on which all four techniques are based. Chapters 10–14 provide discussions of each technique.)

As was the case with selecting the data-collection method, selection of a measurement technique is influenced primarily by the nature of the information required and secondarily by the value of the information. Selection of the measurement technique interacts with both the preceding and following steps in the design process. For example, it is difficult or impossible to use many projective techniques in telephone interviews. Similarly, it is impossible to use complex questionnaires or scales with young children. Selection of the appropriate measurement technique requires the simultaneous consideration of other characteristics of the research design.

Step 5: Select the Sample

Most marketing studies involve a *sample* or subgroup of the total population relevant to the problem, rather than a *census* of the entire group. The population is generally specified as a part of the problem-definition process. As was indicated in the previous section, the sampling process interacts with the other stages of the research design. For example, in most statistical techniques, probability sampling techniques are assumed. Therefore, the use of nonprobability samples restricts the types of analyses that can be performed. (The major considerations in sampling are described in Table 3–4 and discussed more fully in Chapters 15 and 16.)

Step 6: Select the Method(s) of Analysis

Data are useful only after analysis. Data analysis involves converting a series of recorded observations into descriptive statements and/or inferences about relationships. The types of analyses that can be conducted depend on the nature of the sampling process, the measurement instrument, and the data collection method.

It is imperative that the researcher select the analytic techniques *prior* to collecting the data. Once the analytic techniques are selected, the researcher should generate fictional responses (dummy data) to the measurement instrument. These dummy data are then analyzed by the analytic techniques selected to ensure that the results of this analysis will provide the information required by the problem at hand. Failure to carry out this step in advance can result in a completed research project that fails to provide some or all of the information required by the problem.[4] Further, it sometimes reveals that unneeded data are about to be collected.

Table 3–4 Primary Considerations in Sampling

   I. *Population*—determine who (or what objects) can provide the required information.
  II. *Sample Frame*—develop a list of population members.
 III. *Sampling Unit*—determine the basis for drawing the sample (individuals, households, city blocks, etc.).
  IV. *Sampling Method*—determine how the sample will be selected.
    A. *Probability*—members are selected by chance and there is a known chance of each unit being selected.
    B. *Nonprobability*—members are selected on the basis of convenience or judgment or by some other means rather than chance.
   V. *Sample Size*—determine how many population members are to be included in the sample.
  VI. *Sample Plan*—develop a method for selecting and contacting the sample members.
 VII. *Execution*—carry out the sampling plan.

Step 7: Estimate Time and Financial Requirements

Once the research design(s) has been devised, the researcher must estimate the resource requirements. These requirements can be broken down into two broad categories: *time* and *financial*. Time refers to the time period needed to complete the project. The financial requirement is the monetary representation of personnel time, computer time, and materials requirements. The time and finance requirements are not independent. As we shall see, on occasion, time and money are interchangeable.

Time Requirements and PERT. The *program evaluation review technique* (**PERT**) coupled with the *critical path method* (**CPM**) offers a useful aid for estimating the resources needed for a project and clarifying the planning and control process. PERT involves dividing the total research project into its smallest component activities, determining the sequence in which these activities must be performed, and attaching a time estimate for each activity. These activities and time estimates are presented in the form of a flow chart that allows a visual inspection of the overall process. The time estimates allow one to determine the *critical path* through the chart—that series of activities whose delay will hold up the completion of the project.

Financial Requirements. Estimates of financial requirements must include the direct and indirect manpower costs, materials, transportation, overhead, and other costs. Commercial research organizations, particularly those that specialize in specific types of research, are often able to derive accurate rules of thumb. A common approach to estimating the cost of a survey is to use a variable cost of Y dollars per completed interview, plus a fixed cost of X dollars. Once the sample size is determined, the cost estimate can be quickly calculated.

Time-Cost Analysis. It is frequently possible to substitute financial resources for time. For example, it may be possible to gather information by personal interview or by mail. Although a number of variables may affect this decision, cost and time frequently play a major role. Personal interviews are generally faster and more expensive than mail questionnaires. But, if time is more critical in a given research project than the additional cost, personal interviews can be substituted. However, if a PERT analysis has been made, the chart may indicate that this is worthwhile only if this part of the data-collection procedure falls on the critical path. In other words, the completion of a project can be advanced only by shortening the time requirement of the critical path.

Step 8: Prepare the Research Proposal

The research design process provides the researcher with a blueprint, or guide, for conducting and controlling the research project. This blueprint is written in the form of a *research* proposal. A written research proposal should precede any research project. The word *precede* here may be somewhat misleading. Obviously, a substantial amount of research effort is involved in the research planning process that must precede the research proposal. The research proposal helps ensure that the decision maker and the researcher are

Table 3–5 Elements of the Research Proposal

1. *Executive Summary* — a brief statement of the major points from each of the other sections. The objective is to allow an executive to develop a basic understanding of the proposal *without* reading the entire proposal.
2. *Background* — a statement of the management problem and the factors that influence it.
3. *Objectives* — a description of the types of data the research project will generate and how these data are relevant to the management problem. A statement of the value of the information should generally be included in this section.
4. *Research Approach* — a nontechnical description of the data-collection method, measurement instrument, sample, and analytical techniques.
5. *Time and Cost Requirements* — an explanation of the time and costs required by the planned methodology accompanied by a PERT chart.
6. *Technical Appendixes* — any statistical or detailed information in which only one or a few of the potential readers may be interested.

still in agreement on the basic management problem, the information required, and the research approach.

The basic elements of the research proposal are described in Table 3–5.

As is emphasized in the definition given earlier in the chapter, one of the primary goals of research design is to minimize the extent of the errors at any given budget level. It is therefore appropriate to consider the types of errors that can reduce the accuracy of research data.

Potential Errors Affecting Research Designs

Most readers of this text will have already completed one or more statistics courses. In these courses, you most likely covered sampling error and confidence intervals. In studying confidence intervals, you learned the meaning of such statements as "based on a random sample of households, we have a penetration percentage of 20 per cent with a 99 per cent confidence interval of plus or minus 2 per cent." Seeing this statement, you might interpret it to mean, "I can be almost certain that our actual household penetration percentage is between 18 and 22 per cent." However, if you were to interpret the statement in this way, you would have made a common mistake. The mistake is confusing estimates of potential *sampling* error with estimates of *total error.* Unfortunately, sampling error is only one of eight types of potential errors that can influence research results. Research design must attempt to reduce this total error, *not* just one or two aspects of total error. Table 3–6 provides brief descriptions of each type of error. These are expanded in the following sections.

Table 3–6   Potential Sources of Error in Research Information

1. *Surrogate information error*—Variation between the information required to solve the problem and information sought by the researcher.
2. *Measurement error*—Variation between the information sought by the researcher and the information produced by the measurement process.
3. *Experimental error*—Variation between the actual impact of the independent variable(s) and the impact attributed to the independent variable(s).
4. *Population specification error*—Variation between the population required to provide the needed information and the population selected by the researcher.
5. *Frame error*—Variation between the population as defined by the researcher and the list of population members used by the researcher.
6. *Sampling error*—Variation between a representative sample and the sample obtained by using a probability sampling method.
7. *Selection error*—Variation between a representative sample and the sample obtained by using a nonprobability sampling method.
8. *Nonresponse error*—Variation between the selected sample and the sample that actually participates in the study.

Types of Errors

Surrogate Information Error

Surrogate information error is caused by *a variation between the information required to solve the problem and the information sought by the researcher.* The so-called price–quality relationship, where a consumer uses the price of a brand to represent its quality level, is a common example of a measure that is subject to surrogate information error (because price level does not always reflect quality level).

It has been argued that, in part, the taste test research done by Coca-Cola USA resulted in surrogate information. It is reported that "there was—as nearly as I can tell—no research to get at consumer attitudes about the pending change before the new formula introduction." [5] The company based its decision on taste preferences. The resultant consumer backlash was caused by surrogate information error, as consumers purchase *Coke* for reasons other than taste alone.

Measurement Error

Measurement error is caused by *a difference between the information desired by the researcher and the information provided by the measurement process.* In other words, not only is it possible to seek the wrong type of information (surrogate information error) but it also is possible to gather information that is different from what is being sought. This is one of the most common and serious errors. For example, respondents may exaggerate their income in order to impress an interviewer. The reported income will then reflect an unknown amount of measurement error. Measurement error is particularly difficult to control because it can arise from many different sources. (The various sources of measurement are described in some detail in Chapter 9 and means of reducing measurement error are described in Chapters 10–14.)

Experimental Error

Experiments are designed to measure the impact of one or more independent variables on a dependent variable. *Experimental error* occurs when *the effect of the experimental situation itself is measured rather than the effect of the independent variable.* For example, a retail chain may increase the price of selected items in four outlets and leave the price of the same items constant in four similar outlets, in an attempt to discover the best pricing strategy. However, unique weather patterns, traffic conditions, or competitors' activities may affect the sales at one set of stores and not the other. Thus, the experimental results will reflect the impact of variables other than price.

Like measurement error, experimental error can arise from a number of sources. (The various sources of experimental error and the methods by which they can be controlled are described in Chapters 7 and 8.)

Population Specification Error

Population specification error is caused by *selecting an inappropriate universe or population from which to collect data.* This is a potentially serious problem in both industrial and consumer research. A firm wishing to learn the criteria that are considered most important in the purchase of certain machine tools might conduct a survey among purchasing agents. Yet, in many firms, the purchasing agents do not determine or necessarily even know the criteria behind brand selections. These decisions may be made by the machine operators, by committee, or by higher-level executives. A study that focuses on the purchasing agent as the person who decides which brands to order may be subject to population specification error. (Population specification is described in more detail in Chapter 15.)

Frame Error

The *sampling frame* is the list of population members from which the sample units are selected. An ideal frame identifies each member of the population once and only once. *Frame error* is caused by *using an inaccurate or incomplete sampling frame.* For example, using the telephone directory as a sampling frame for the population of a community contains a potential for frame error. Those families who do not have listed numbers, both voluntarily and nonvoluntarily, are likely to differ from those with listed numbers in such respects as income, gender, and mobility. (Frame error is discussed in more detail in Chapters 6 and 15.)

Sampling Error

Sampling error is caused by the *generation of a nonrepresentative sample by means of a probability sampling method.* For example, a random sample of one hundred university students *could* produce a sample composed of all females (or all seniors or all business majors). Such a sample would not be representative of the overall student body. Yet it could occur using probability sampling techniques. Sampling error is the focal point of concern in classical statistics. (It is discussed in more detail in Chapters 17–19.)

Selection Error

Selection error occurs when a *nonrepresentative sample is obtained by nonprobability sampling methods.* For example, one of the authors talked with an interviewer who was afraid of dogs. In surveys that allowed any freedom of choice, this interviewer avoided homes with dogs present. Obviously, such a practice may introduce error into the survey results. Selection error is a major problem in nonprobability samples. (It is discussed in more detail in Chapters 6, 7, and 15.)

Nonresponse Error

Nonresponse error is caused by (1) *a failure to contact all members of a sample, and/or* (2) *the failure of some contacted members of the sample to respond to all or specific parts of the measurement instrument.* Individuals who are difficult to contact or who are reluctant to cooperate will differ, on at least some characteristics, from those who are relatively easy to contact or who readily cooperate. If these differences include the variable of interest, nonresponse error has occurred. For example, people are more likely to respond to a survey on a topic that interests them. If a firm were to conduct a mail survey to estimate the incidence of athlete's foot among adults, nonresponse error would be of major concern. Why? Those most likely to be interested in athlete's foot, and thus most likely to respond to the survey, are current or recent sufferers of the problem. If the firm were to use the percentage of those responding who report having athlete's foot as an estimate of the total population having athlete's foot, the company would probably greatly overestimate the extent of the problem. (Methods for dealing with nonresponse error are described in Chapter 6.)

Strategies for Handling Potential Research Errors

As stated earlier, the purpose of research design is, in part, to maximize the accuracy of the information that can be obtained for a given expense. Maximizing the accuracy of information requires minimizing errors in the information. There are three basic strategies for dealing with potential errors: (1) minimize individual errors through effective research design, (2) minimize total error through error trade-offs, and (3) measure or estimate the amount and/or impact of any residual error.

Strategy 1: Minimize Individual Error

The bulk of this book is devoted to describing techniques for reducing individual errors. Consider sampling error as an example. The probability and magnitude of sampling error can be reduced by increasing sample size; but, increasing sample size also increases costs. However, it may be possible to reduce sampling error (and possibly sample size, as well) by moving from a simple random sample to a stratified sample (see Chapter 15).

The first stage of research design is generally devoted to selecting those research methods that will minimize each individual source of error, given budget (or value of information) constraints.

Strategy 2: Trade-off Individual Errors to Reduce Total Error

Assume that a researcher has initially selected a large sample for a mail survey. The sample is large enough to provide a low level of sampling error, but it has taken such a large proportion of the research budget that there are sufficient funds remaining for only one follow-up mailing. Past experience with surveys of this type indicates that, with one follow-up mailing, the total response rate will reach 40 per cent; with four follow-ups, it will climb to 55 per cent. Given the nature of the survey, the researcher thinks that the nonrespondents may differ significantly from the respondents.

One solution would be to ask for an increase in the budget. However, such funds may not be available or the resultant data may not justify additional expenditures. A second solution is to "trade" sampling error for nonresponse error. Sample size could be reduced, which would increase the probable amount of sampling error. However, the funds thus freed could provide additional mailed follow-up questionnaires and telephone calls to the final group of nonrespondents. These efforts may reduce nonresponse error more than enough to offset the increase in sampling error. Thus, the result is a reduction in total error and an increase in total accuracy.

Strategy 3: Measure or Estimate Residual Error

It is seldom possible to eliminate all possible errors. Statisticians and others have recognized this with respect to sampling error. Virtually all studies dealing with random samples report confidence intervals and/or confidence levels. This is explicit recognition that sampling error may have occurred. Unfortunately, many researchers have tended to ignore the presence of other types of errors.

Measuring and/or estimating errors is preferred to ignoring them. Potential errors should never be completely ignored. It is possible and fairly common to estimate that the net effect of these errors is so small as to warrant no specific action. However, this is *not* the same as ignoring the potential errors. At a minimum, the researcher should *explicitly*, if subjectively, estimate the extent of each type of potential error. If individual errors or the combined effects of the errors are large, they should be reduced by means of the research design or their effects taken into account in the analysis of the data. Although a complete discussion of estimating and measuring individual and total error is beyond the scope of this text,[6] both approaches are described in detail with respect to nonresponse error in Chapter 6.

Review Questions

3.1. What are the steps in the *research process?*

3.2. What is the difference between the *management problem* and the *research problem?*

3.3. What is the definition of *research design?*

3.4. What are the steps involved in the *research design process?*

3.5. What are the three *basic data-collection approaches* in marketing research?

3.6. How do the three categories of *exploratory, descriptive,* and *causal* research differ from each other?

3.7. What are the *four basic measurement techniques* used in marketing research?

3.8. For what purposes are PERT charts used?

3.9. What are the five considerations that, as a minimum, ought to be involved in an intuitive approach to the assessment of the value of the information that would be provided by a proposed research project?

3.10. What are the five considerations involved in an expected value approach to the assessment of the value of the information that would be provided by a proposed research project?

3.11. What are the essential differences between the *intuitive* and the *expected value* approaches to assessing the value of the information that would be provided by a proposed research project?

3.12. What are the *potential errors* affecting research designs?

3.13. What are the *strategies for dealing with potential research errors?*

Discussion Questions/Problems

3.14. Do you agree with the assertion "Research cannot provide solutions"? Explain.

3.15. It has been stated that "Marketing research need not be used only to predict future behavior; it can be used to predict present or past behavior as well." Is it ever useful to a company to predict present or past behavior? Explain.

3.16. Review the list of potential errors in Table 3–6. Provide four examples of error trade-offs whereby the potential impact of one error might be increased to achieve a greater reduction in another error.

3.17. An underlying assumption of the Coca-Cola taste tests is that *taste preferences* lead to *purchase preferences.* Is this necessarily true? Explain.

3.18. As a newly hired researcher for Ford you have been asked to investigate the "probable family structure of the 25–30-year-old population in 2005."

    a. How will you obtain a more precise statement of the management problem?

    b. Develop two distinct management problems that could have produced this request.

    c. To what extent do the two problems developed in (b) require different information?

3.19. Most new products are not commercial successes despite the presence of a large research industry. Why is the case?

3.20. How would you go about determining why market share for a particular brand has declined for three straight quarters?

3.21. In a research project for a chain of shoe stores, mothers of young children were asked about the importance of various features of childrens' shoes and shoe outlets. Which types of error do you think would be most critical for this study?

3.22. As a one-person research staff for a manufacturer of men's shirts, you are asked to do a study to recommend in what market segments the marketing program of the firm should be concentrated.
a. How would you obtain a more precise problem statement? and
b. Give a plausible statement of the management's problem and translate it into a statement of the research problem to be conducted to help solve it.

Projects

3.23. a. With two other members of your class, prepare a research design for problem 3.22.
b. Prepare a PERT chart of your design with the same two other class members who helped develop the research design.

3.24. Conduct a taste test of 7-Up, Sprite, and Ginger Ale on five friends or acquaintances. Before telling them which soft drink they preferred, ask them which brand they would buy if they were going to stop by a store to buy a six-pack of soft drink. Compare their taste preference with their (stated) purchase preference. What do you conclude?

3.25. Interview a marketing manager and identify a marketing problem or opportunity with which the manager is concerned. Translate this into a research problem.

3.26. Prepare a research design for the research problem in 3.25 and prepare a proposal. What types of errors would be likely to affect the findings if the project were actually carried out?

3.27. Determine the value of the information associated with the research project proposed in 3.26.

References

[1] This description of the taste tests has been reviewed and approved by the corporate staff of the Coca-Cola Company.

[2] S. Jones, "Problem-Definition in Marketing Research," *Psychology & Marketing* (Summer 1985), 83–92.

[3] For an elaboration of this point, see P. W. Conner, "Research Request Step Can Enhance Use of Results," *Marketing News,* January 4, 1985, 41.

[4] A. R. Andreason, " 'Backward' Market Research," *Harvard Business Review* (May–June 1985), 176–182.

[5] J. Honomichl, "Missing Ingredient in 'New' Coke's Research," *Advertising Age,* July 22, 1985, 1, 58.

[6] See D. S. Tull and G. S. Albaum, *Survey Research: A Decisional Approach* (Intext Educational Publishers, 1973), 67–77; and L. Bailey, "Toward a More Complete Anlaysis of the Total Mean Square Error of Census and Sample Survey Statistics," Bureau of the Census, undated.

CASE I-1 WEYERHAEUSER COMPANY I: THE ROLE OF MARKETING RESEARCH

Weyerhaeuser Company was founded in 1900 in Tacoma, Washington. Starting from a forest base in the Pacific Northwest, Weyerhaeuser has become the largest private owner of timber in the world and the leader in productive management of commercial forests. At the same time, Weyerhaeuser has grown from a domestic wood products company into an international marketing organization and has expanded its product line to include nursery plants and supplies, real estate development, home mortgages, insurance and investment products, pulp, paper, packaging, engineered building systems, a variety of composite and structural panels, and an array of nonwood building products.

Today, Weyerhaeuser Company is composed of three principal business groupings: (1) forest products, (2) pulp, paper, and packaging, and (3) real estate, financial services, and diversified businesses.

Forest Products

The forest products business applies the technology and marketing skills to one of the world's oldest building materials — wood. Weyerhaeuser has long been the largest softwood lumber manufacturer in the world as well as a leader in lumber marketing. The company supplies customers with lumber in a wide variety of dimensions and grades for the full range of building needs.

Weyerhaeuser also produces and markets hardwood, reconstituted wood panels, doors, engineered strand products, fiber and molded products, gypsum, laminated products, wall paneling, plywood and veneers, and raw materials in the form of timber, logs, and wood chips.

In addition to traditional wood products, the company markets fencing, windows, nails, fasteners, roofing, and insulation.

For the commercial and industrial builder, Weyerhaeuser offers an automated design service. By using Weyerhaeuser Building Systems, a building owner, architect, or engineer can plan and see the final structure on a computer screen before the building goes up. Weyerhaeuser offers a 25-year limited warranty with this service.

Pulp, Paper, and Packaging

The pulp, paper, and paperboard packaging operations are conducted as the Weyerhaeuser Paper Company. Weyerhaeuser is the world's largest marketer of wood pulp and containerboard, and one of the three largest producers of basic pulp and paper commodities.

The pulp division produces a full line of high-quality pulps including papergrade kraft for fine papers; fluff for towels and disposable diapers; and specialty grades for molding compounds, explosives, lacquers, artificial silk, photographic papers, and other specialty products. In addition, the company produces and markets printing and writing papers, newsprint, and bleached paperboard.

Real Estate, Financial Services, and Diversified Businesses

Real estate, financial services, and diversified businesses form a multifaceted business grouping. Weyerhaeuser Real Estate Company (WRECO), a wholly owned subsidiary, serves as holding company for 10 regional real estate development and building companies and for a real estate joint-venture operation. It also is the parent for Weyerhaeuser Mortgage Company (one of the nation's largest mortgage bankers) and for Republic Federal Savings and Loan. WRECO also has a land development department and insurance subsidiaries.

The diversified business organization produces personal care products (it is the world's largest private-label producer of disposable diapers), markets nursery and garden supplies nationwide and in Europe, produces and markets a line of chemicals, and markets vegetables that it grows hydroponically.

Other subsidiaries include the GNA annuity and insurance business and several transportation businesses, including Westwood Shipping Lines, which offers service to both Transatlantic and Transpacific markets.

Corporate Decisions

Weyerhaeuser's product offerings have become increasingly diverse over the years. This has prompted Weyerhaeuser's executives to examine the role of the Weyerhaeuser name, in terms of product-branding strategies. Should the Weyerhaeuser name be associated with all Weyerhaeuser products, including disposable diapers, hydroponically grown vegetables, and turpentine, or should the Weyerhaeuser name be reserved for building products? Weyerhauser's executives want to understand the benefits, costs, and risks associated with corporate branding, product-line branding, specific-product branding, private branding, and no branding in order to develop and implement appropriate branding strategies for the company's products.

Operating Unit Decisions

In addition to corporate level marketing decisions, such as the use of the Weyerhaeuser name, a multitude of other marketing decisions are made daily in the decentralized operating units. Decisions about pricing, promotion, product modification, addition, deletion, and distribution are made for each product area in a largely decentralized manner.

Support Staff

Supporting the operations of the three principal business groupings is a group of professional staff members. Departments that provide expertise and services include Corporate Planning, Organization and Employee Relations, Tax, Energy/Environmental Regulatory Affairs, Research and Engineering, Law, Corporate Services, Information Systems, Government Relations, Financial Services, a Treasurer's Department, and Corporate Communications.

Discussion Questions

1. What role should marketing research play in the daily operations of Weyerhaeuser?
2. How should a research department fit into a multibusiness firm such as Weyerhaeuser?
3. How would you develop a MIS for Weyerhaeuser? How would it be structured?
4. What types of MDSSs would be appropriate for Weyerhaeuser?
5. How could marketing research help Weyerhaeuser develop a corporate brand strategy?
6. If Weyerhaeuser decides to use research to help develop a brand strategy, should it "make or buy"?

CASE I–2 WEYERHAEUSER II: PROBLEM DEFINITION AND RESEARCH DESIGN

The U.S. forest products industry is composed of numerous small producers, substantial competition from Canada, and two major U.S. firms — Weyerhaeuser (see Case I–1) and Georgia-Pacific. It is characterized by largely homogeneous, unbranded products, periods of substantial industry oversupply, and high fixed costs.

Weyerhaeuser's Building Products Group had been focusing considerable attention on the do-it-yourself (DIY) portion of the residential repair and remodel market for lumber. The repair and remodel market consumes between 25–30 per cent of the lumber used in the United States with rapid growth projected for the next 10 years. DIYers purchase about half this total, with contractors buying the balance. The repair and remodel lumber market is also less subject to fluctuations in the overall economy and interest rates than either the home or industrial construction markets.

As this market has grown, the distribution channel has changed radically. Distribution of lumber materials to DIYers is now dominated by large "home center" and similar chains. Since most lumber products, particularly dimensional lumber (2×4's and similar items), are sold by grade rather than brand name, producers compete primarily on price and secondarily on delivery and service to the retailer. This allows large buyers to exert strong price pressures on producers. To counter these price pressures, provide greater value to customers, and take advantage of superior product quality, Weyerhaeuser was considering expanding its use of branding beyond the few specialty items currently branded.

In the past, Weyerhaeuser Corporation had run a series of successful general corporate image campaigns aimed at the general public, stockholders, and public opinion leaders. A very high-impact aspect of these campaigns focused on Weyerhaeuser's reforestation and other environmental activities. Its slogan at that time — "The tree growing company" — emphasized the company's strong traditional link to forestry. Broad based corporate advertising was continuing.

While the general corporate campaigns had been quite successful in reaching their objective, they did little to increase product awareness among potential buyers, including DIYers. For Weyerhaeuser to succeed in marketing premium quality products to DIYers, it was felt that both its general image and its product specific image among this segment would have to improve. Image was conceptualized to include knowledge about the firm's offerings as well as beliefs about quality, value, trustworthiness, and so forth.

In addition, management was very interested in determining the relationship between a firm's image and the willingness of its customers to pay a premium for its products. Finally, management felt it needed more knowledge about the characteristics of DIYers, their homes, and their projects.

A series of 9 focus groups (a 1.5–3-hour open discussion on a topic, by 6–12 individuals led by a researcher) conducted among DIYers over the previous two years had provided some tentative insights into consumers' patterns:

- Most do not understand the lumber grading system and buy based on appearance
- Price is important only for large jobs

- Quality is important but most judge this based on appearance (they look for straightness, straight grain, few knots, sharp corners, dryness)
- Most desire helpful, skilled retailers but do not believe that many exist
- Most believe you get what you pay for
- Most are not satisfied with the quality of available lumber and do not believe that grade standards are enforced
- They neither know nor care whose (which producer) wood they are buying. They do not look for brand names
- Most are familiar with Weyerhaeuser and Georgia-Pacific but lack specific knowledge about either (though they remember Weyerhaeuser's reforestation ads)

Secondary data suggested that DIYers (1) are primarily married males, although females are increasingly active, (2) range in age from 25 to 44, (3) are both blue-collar and white-collar workers, (4) are home-owners, (5) earn middle-income salaries, and (6) are geographically disperse.

As management was discussing options relating to the DIY market, the sponsorship of "This Old House" became available. "This Old House" is a very popular program on PBS (Public Broadcasting Service), providing advice and instruction on home repair and remodeling. While a firm sponsoring a PBS program is severely restricted in terms of the type of "commercials" it can show, it is possible to highlight the sponsor's name and products related to the DIY market. Owens-Corning had sponsored the show for several years.

Weyerhaeuser opted to sponsor the show with the objective of improving the company's image among viewers. Before its first season as sponsor, the company decided to develop a means of determining the effectiveness of the sponsorship. It also desired to determine (1) the impact the show had had on Owens-Corning's image, (2) the relationship between corporate image and price sensitivity, and (3) the characteristics of DIYers.

Discussion Questions

1. What are the management problems confronting Weyerhaeuser? How would you clarify these problems?
2. What is the research problem facing Weyerhaeuser's researchers?
3. Design a research project to provide Weyerhaeuser with the required information. What errors would be of most concern to you?
4. Describe how you would develop a MIS system for Weyerhaeuser focused on the DIY market.

CASE I–3 LEMONADE PRICE LEVEL PROPOSAL*

PRODUCT ACCEPTANCE & RESEARCH
AN ORGANIZATION ENGAGED IN TOTAL RESEARCH SERVICES

SEAMAN & ASSOCIATES, INCORPORATED
POST OFFICE BOX 3126 • EVANSVILLE, INDIANA 47731
• AREA CODE 812, TELEPHONE 425-3533

Dear Steve:

Subject: Preliminary Research Proposal #2895
Lemonade Pricing Study

Herein, we will confirm our recent phone conversations on the subject study.

Purpose:	To determine which of three specific retail prices maximizes unit sales and share and profits, as measured by consumer sales using controlled store methods.
Location:	Evansville, Indiana, and Atlanta, Georgia.
Number of Stores:	Totally there would be thirty-two (32) supermarkets used in the study, equally divided between the two cities.
Tentative Starting Date:	To be determined.
Length of Study:	Twelve (12) weeks, divided into a four (4) week base period and an eight (8) week test period.
Test Brand:	Chilled Lemonade.
Audit Brands:	Audits would be made of the chilled lemonades and chilled punches. It is estimated that the category would not exceed 25 item/sizes.
Product Handling:	PAR would not assume distribution of any item. PAR would request that all stores carry extra product in the backroom to guard against out-of-stock conditions during the test period.
Number of Facings:	The number of facings has been established. PAR's function would be report accurately to same.
Retail Pricing:	Retail prices in the base period would be "normal." Retail prices of the test product during the test period would be set in accordance with our sample design.

* Used with permission.

Test Procedure: On the initial call to each store, an audit would be made of the audit items. A second audit would be taken two (2) weeks later. The final base period audit would be taken two (2) weeks later. Using the data developed during the first two (2) weeks of the base period, the stores would be divided into four (4) panels of four (4) stores each in each city. Criteria for panelization would be sales and share of the test product and total category sales. Panelization would be:

Panel	# of Stores°	Variable
A	4	Normal pricing — control
B	4	Normal pricing — plus 10¢
C	4	Normal pricing — plus 20¢
D	4	Normal pricing — minus 10¢

° per city. In the final analysis, eight (8) stores per variable would be examined.

On the initial call of the test period, an audit would be conducted, and price changes made to meet our panelization.

Audits would continue on a four (4) week sales period basis throughout the test period.

In addition to the audit calls, policing calls would be made to each store once a week during audit weeks and twice a week on non-audit weeks.

A 35mm. picture would be taken in each store each week to show the test product in its in-store surroundings.

If more frequent than twice a week calls are necessary to control properly the study, the client would be immediately notified for a decision.

A research design is attached which shows store activity by week of the study.

Reporting: Flash sales of the test product would be made available every week during the test period. This information would be made available within one week following the service call.

An interim report would be submitted within three (3) weeks following the close of each four (4) week audit period. These reports would include:

1. Unit sales by brand, by size, by store, and by panel.
2. Unit shares by brand, by size, by store, and by panel.
3. Dollar sales by brand, by size, by store, and by panel.
4. Dollar shares by brand, by size, by store, and by panel.
5. Number of shelf facings.
6. Retail price.
7. Competitive activity found on each scheduled store call.
8. Newspaper advertising report.

There would be a final report submitted to the client within four (4) weeks after the conclusion of the study.

Budget: To execute the study as outlined in this proposal would require a research budget of $XXXX.° In addition to the research budget, store cooperation payments (currently estimated at $XXX) would be billed at actual cost.

If chilled grapefruit were to be added to the study, and the same design used, an additional $XXXX should be added to the research fee and $XXX to the store payments.

All budgets are plus or minus the usual 10%.

These quotations will remain in effect for thirty (30) days. At the end of this period, they will be subject to review and possible revision by **PAR**.

Should **PAR**, as a result of a request of the client, or their agency, incur any special costs in connection with this project, and the project not be subsequently initiated, all such expenses will be billed to the client.

° Cost figures are not available due to the competitive nature of bids such as this.

Steve, I believe this covers our discussion. Your questions are welcome and invited. Thank you for the opportunity to submit this preliminary proposal. We will look forward to working with you on this project.

Best regards,

E. Harvey Seaman

EHS/zc

Discussion Questions

1. Evaluate the adequacy of this proposal as a *research proposal*.
2. Evaluate the proposed research design.

The Sources of Research Data

The design of the research project specifies both the data that are needed and how they are to be obtained. The first step in the data-collection process is to look for *secondary data*. These are data that were developed for some purpose other than for helping to solve the problem at hand. The data that are still needed after that search is completed will have to be developed specifically for the research project, and are known as *primary data*.

The secondary data that are available are relatively quick and inexpensive to obtain, especially now that computerized bibliographic search services and data bases are available. Chapter 4 is concerned with describing the various sources of the secondary data and how they can be obtained and used.

Most secondary data are generated by specialized firms and are sold to marketers to help them deal with a category of problems. Nielsen's television ratings, which marketers use in making advertising decisions, is the best-known example. Many of these services, broadly categorized as audits, commercial surveys, and panels, allow some degree of customization and thus fall between secondary and primary data. These sources are treated in detail in Chapter 5.

An important source of primary data is *survey research*. The various types of surveys (personal, mail, computer, and telephone), are described in Chapter 6.

Experiments are another important source of data for marketing research projects. The nature of experimentation, the types of experimental designs, and the uses and limitations of this method of obtaining data are the subjects of Chapter 7.

Experiments are conducted in either a laboratory setting (most advertising copy pretests) or in a field setting (test marketing). Electronic and computer technologies have revolutionized both these environments which are described in Chapter 8.

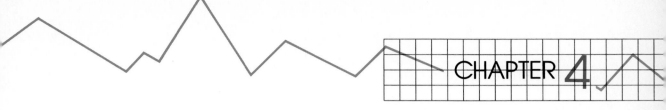

CHAPTER 4

Secondary Data

A site selection analyst for the Safeway supermarket chain (headquartered in Oakland, California) is evaluating two potential sites for a new market in Binghampton, New York. Using the modem for the minicomputer on her desk, she gets access to the *Marketing Statistics* database (produced by the Marketing Statistics Co. of New York City) and enters the zip code for the first site. Shortly, data on population, number of households, family income distribution, family size distribution, age distribution, median income, total income, population growth, ethnic composition, number of retail stores, retail trade statistics, and the Buying Power Index for the area covered by the zip code appear on the screen. The analyst prints the data and enters the second zip code. A printed copy of the same data for the neighborhood for the second site is obtained. These data, along with traffic flow information obtained from the Binghampton city manager's office, and competitive store locations determined from the Yellow Pages of the Binghampton telephone directory (accessed online through Instant Yellow Page Service), permit a comparative evaluation of the two sites before a confirming visit is made and purchase negotiations begun.

In a few short years the increase in the number of commercially available databases and of computers on which to access them have brought about dramatic changes in the utilization of secondary data. In this chapter we describe this development and discuss the traditional sources of secondary data.

The Nature of Secondary Data

Primary data are data that are collected to help solve a problem or take advantage of an opportunity on which a decision is pending. The approach used in making the evaluation of the two sites was to use *secondary data,* which are *data that were developed for some purpose other than helping to solve the problem at hand.* In this case the data provided by the database came from the *Census of Population,* the *Census of Business,* and Bureau of the Census reports, along with information from the U.S. Postal Service. The data from each of these sources, along with those from the city manager's office (traffic flow information) and the local telephone company (Yellow Pages information on the location of existing supermarkets in Binghampton) were all obviously developed for purposes other than the determination of which was the better site for a Safeway supermarket.

Advantages of Secondary Data

Why did the Safeway company use secondary data in the situation described here? Secondary data can be gathered *quickly* and *inexpensively,* compared to primary data (data gathered specifically for the problem at hand). For the site evaluation problem, it clearly would be foolish for the Safeway management to collect information directly on the population, income, ethnic origins, and other demographic characteristics of the residents of the neighborhoods of the two prospective sites. Such data are already available and can be obtained much faster and at a fraction of the cost of collecting them again. Similarly, there is no reason to measure traffic flows in the neighborhood if they are readily available from the city, or to search out the location of competing supermarkets if they can be found by simply referring to the Yellow Pages of the telephone directory.

Problems Encountered with Secondary Data

Secondary data tend to cost substantially less than primary data and can be collected in less time. Why, then, do we ever bother with primary data?

Before secondary data can be used as the only source of information to help solve a marketing problem, they must be *available, relevant, accurate,* and *sufficient.* If one or more of these criteria are not met, primary data may have to be used.

Availability

For some marketing problems, no secondary data are *available*. For example, suppose J. C. Penney's management was interested in obtaining consumer evaluations of the physical layout of the company's current catalog as a guide for developing next year's catalog. It is unlikely that such information is available from secondary sources. It is probable that no other organization that had collected such data would be willing to make it available. Sears or Spiegels may have performed such a study to guide in the development of their catalogs; it is, however, unlikely that a competitor would supply it to Penney's. In this case, the company would have to conduct interviews of consumers to obtain the desired information.

Relevance

Relevance refers to the extent to which the data fit the information needs of the research problem. Even when data are available that cover the same general topic as that required by the research problem, they may not fit the requirements of the particular problem.

Four general problems reduce the relevance of data that would otherwise be useful. First, there is often a *difference in the units of measurement*. For example, many retail decisions require detailed information on the characteristics of the population within the "trade area." However, available demographic statistics may be for counties, cities, census tracts, or zip code areas that do not match the trade area of the retail outlet. (This was true to some extent in the Safeway site evaluations.)

A second factor that can reduce the relevance of secondary data is the necessity in some applications to use *surrogate data*. Surrogate data are a *substitute for more desirable data*. This was discussed in Chapter 3 as surrogate information error. For example, if in the Safeway site evaluation the traffic flow information were for peak periods only, it would be of less value than if it were for, say, each hour from 7AM to 11PM.

A third general problem that can reduce the relevance of secondary data is the *definition of classes*. If the data on retail sales appearing in the database used by the Safeway analyst are for all retail stores in the zip code area, when the desired data are for grocery stores only, the data would obviously be less relevant than desired. Social class, age, income, firm size, and similar category-type breakdowns found in secondary data frequently do not coincide with the exact requirements of the research problem.

The final major factor affecting relevancy is *time*. Generally, research problems require current data. Most secondary data, on the other hand, have been in existence for some time. For example, the *Census of Retail Trade* is conducted only every five years, and two years are required to process and publish the results. The researcher working on the site location evaluation therefore conceivably could have been forced to use data that were over six years old.

Accuracy

Accuracy is the third major concern of the user of secondary data. The real problem is not so much obvious inaccuracy as it is *the difficulty of determining how inaccurate the data are likely to be.*

When using secondary data, the original source should be consulted if possible. This is important for two reasons. First, the original report is generally more complete than a second or third report. It often contains warnings, shortcomings, and methodological details not reported by the second or third source. For example, most studies reported by the federal government, such as the *Annual Survey of Housing,* report the magnitude of potential sampling errors and some give indications of the possible extent of nonsampling errors.

Second, using the original source allows the data to be examined in context and may provide a better basis for assessing the *competence* and *motivation* of the collector.

Examine Exhibit 4–1 before reading further:

Exhibit 4–1 *Reported Annual Expenditures of a Sample of Consumers on Selected Products*

Total Annual Expenditures	Sample (in %)	Estimated No.	Projected Expenditures
$199 or less	6.4	1,000	$ 200,000
$200 to $399	15.3	2,300	920,000
$400 to $599	13.2	2,000	1,200,000
$600 to $799	9.1	1,350	1,080,000
$800 to $999	8.7	1,325	1,325,000
$1,000 to $1,199	11.1	1,675	2,010,000
$1,200 to $1,399	4.9	750	1,050,000
$1,400 to $1,599	6.6	1,100	1,980,000
$1,600 to $1,799	5.9	950	1,710,000
$1,800 or more	19.0	2,900	5,800,000
Total	100.0	15,350	$17,275,000

The table in Exhibit 4–1 is in error, in that the total expenditure category should not be determined by multiplying the number of individuals in the category by the minimum expenditure in the next highest category. This procedure grossly overstates the total expenditures. The appropriate multiplier is the midpoint of each category. This table was taken from a report of a research project designed to persuade advertisers to purchase space in the newspaper that commissioned the project.

Few sources "cheat" in the sense of supplying outright false data. However, writers with a strong point of view often report only those aspects of a study that support their position. In addition, some sources are more competent than others, both from a technical point of view and from the standpoint of having sufficient resources to perform adequately the task at hand. Thus, the reputation of the source is an important criterion for deciding whether to use a particular piece of secondary data.

Sufficiency

Secondary data may be *available, relevant* and *accurate* but still may not be *sufficient* to meet all the data requirements for the problem being researched. For example, had traffic flow information not been available, the secondary data for the Safeway site decision would have been insufficient. In such cases, primary data must be obtained (or the decision made without complete information).

Internal Sources of Secondary Data

Internal sources can be classified into four broad categories: *accounting records, sales force reports, miscellaneous records,* and *internal experts.*

Accounting Records

The basis for the accounting records concerned with *sales* is the *sales invoice.* The usual sales invoice has a sizeable amount of information on it, which generally includes *name of customer, location of customer, items ordered, quantities ordered, quantities shipped, dollar extensions, back orders, discounts allowed, date of shipment,* and *method of shipment.* In addition, the invoice often contains information on sales territory, sales representative, and warehouse of shipment.

This information, when supplemented by data on costs and industry and product classification, as well as from sales calls, provides the basis for a comprehensive analysis of sales by product, customer, industry, geographic area, sales territory, and sales representative, as well as the profitability of each sales category.

Unfortunately, most firms' accounting systems are designed primarily for tax reasons rather than for decision support. Currently, only a few organizations can readily retrieve the data required for the types of analyses just described. Competitive pressures, increasingly sophisticated managers, and enhanced computer systems are beginning to improve this situation.

Advertising expenditures, sales force expenditures, and *data on inventories* are other types of data available from accounting records that are useful for research purposes. For example, a management trainee was asked to estimate the "best" price reduction for a store that frequently sold paint at a reduced price. An examination of the firm's advertising records allowed her to identify the timing of numerous sales at different discounts over the past several years. The firm's inventory records allowed a close estimate of the units sold during each sale. By combining these two data sources, the trainee was able to develop a useful estimate of the price elasticity of demand for the firm's paint. In addition, she was able to isolate one season of the year when the elasticity of demand was unusually high and one season when it was relatively low.

Sales Force Reports

Sales force reports represent a rich and largely untapped *potential* source of marketing information. The word *potential* is used because evidence indicates that valuable marketing information is generally *not* reported by sales personnel. An unfortunately typical example is reported in Exhibit 4 – 2.

As Exhibit 4 – 2 suggests, sales personnel often lack the motivation and/or the means to communicate key information to marketing managers. To obtain the valuable data available from most sales forces, several elements are necessary: (1) a clear, concise statement, repeated frequently, of the types of information desired; (2) a systematic, *simple* process for reporting the information; (3) financial and other rewards for reporting information; and (4) concrete examples of the actual use of the data.

Miscellaneous Reports

Miscellaneous reports represent the third internal data source. Previous marketing research studies, special audits, and reports purchased from outside for prior problems may have relevance for current problems. As a firm becomes more diversified, the more likely it is to conduct studies that may have relevance to problems in other areas of the firm. For example, Procter and Gamble sells a variety of distinct products to identical or similar target markets. An analysis of the media habits conducted for one product could be very useful for a different product that appeals to the same target market. Again, this requires an efficient marketing information system to ensure that the relevant reports can be found by those who need them.

Exhibit 4–2   *A Failure to Communicate*

A manufacturer of specialized moldings had a serious sales decline in one of its major lines for almost a year. The marketing manager could not explain the decline and was considering either revising the firm's sales incentive plan to increase the rewards for selling this line or reducing the price of the line. At the annual industry trade show, the manager noticed that a major competitor had developed a clearly superior competitive product. Inquiry revealed that the launch of the competitive product coincided with the beginning of his line's sales decline. None of the 73 sales people had reported the new product to management.

Why did these individuals fail to report such a significant piece of information? A variety of reasons emerged as illustrated by the following statements:

"I figure management *knows* what's going on in the market. They don't need me to tell them."

"I used to tell them everything and they just ignored me. Not so much as a Thank You. So I figure the hell with it."

"I'm putting 60–70 hours a week trying to make a living *selling* this stuff. I don't have time to pass on every bit of gossip in the industry."

"I felt I should tell someone when I first saw it but Bob (the sales manager) is always on the road and I didn't know who to call at corporate."

"They knew about it. I told Bob's secretary right after it came out. We were talking about the new bonus plan and I said 'XYZ's new molding is going to give us fits.' She should have told Bob."

Exhibit 4–3 describes how one consumer goods firm ensures that prior studies are consulted before primary data is collected.

Internal Experts

One of the most overlooked sources of internal secondary data is internal experts. An internal expert is anyone employed by the firm who has special knowledge related to the question at hand. While this knowledge is stored in individuals' minds rather than on paper or computer disk, it can be as valid and valuable as more formal sources.

Reconsider Exhibit 4–2. Had the marketing manager quickly asked the most obvious internal experts—members of the sales force—to explain the

---

Exhibit 4-3 *An Effective Research Reports Library*

The following statement by a senior research manager at a major consumer goods firm describes why his organization developed a research reports library and how they ensure its use.

On the average, each brand is assigned a new brand manager every two years. These brand managers are young, aspiring, talented MBA-types and they believe in the value of marketing research. They also know that their own upward mobility is pegged to the mark they leave on the brand. So, the first thing they require is marketing research: segmentation studies or attitude/usage surveys, typically followed by lots of qualitative studies in the copy concept or positioning/ad strategy areas. Hell, for most brands you don't need new segmentation or positioning studies every two years! Go to the file and find the last one done, learn from it before you decide a new study is required. The same is true for copy concept issues. If the concept is worth a damn, it has been researched before.

Reuse data, stretch it out to the max and reserve your budget for truly new, necessary primary studies. That's why we developed our "research library." Every thing we've ever done is in there, *including subsequent actions and results*. And, it is organized for easy access. Now it is company policy that any research request has to include *proof* that the library has already been searched and found lacking—*before any new research can be conducted!*

---

sales decline, work on a competitive new product could have begun almost a year earlier. In addition to the sales force, companies have discovered that marketing research personnel, technical representatives, advertising agency personnel, product managers, and public relations personnel often have expert knowledge of relevance to marketing problems.

External Sources of Secondary Data

Numerous sources external to the firm may have data relevant to the firm's requirements. Seven general categories of external secondary information are described in the sections that follow: (1) computerized databases, (2) associations, (3) government agencies, (4) syndicated services, (5) directories, (6) other published sources, and (7) external experts.

The best way to begin a search for external secondary data is to consult a general guide to secondary data sources. For example, suppose you are asked to develop background information on the brewing industry to help evaluate a loan request by a group starting a micro brewery. Where would you begin? Exhibit 4–4 shows the information sources that are referenced by one general guide, the *Encyclopedia of Business Information Sources.* This information would provide direction for beginning the search for secondary data. Note that this source provides references to computerized bibliographic databases as well as to printed reference works. Table 4–1 lists several general and specific guides to secondary data.

Rather than conduct an external search "in house," it is sometimes more efficient to hire an *information broker.*[1] These firms specialize in searching for external data using both computerized and manual techniques. Large firms such as IBM and General Electric use information brokers to supplement their

---

Exhibit 4–4   *Data Sources on the Brewing Industry from the Encyclopedia of Business Information Sources*

BREWING INDUSTRY
See also: BEVERAGE INDUSTRY; DISTILLING INDUSTRY

General Works

Malting and Brewing Science, 2nd edition. J.S. Hough and others. Halsted Press, 605 Third Ave., New York, NY 10158. (212) 850-6418. 1983. $95.00. Two volumes.

A Strategic Model of the U.S. Brewing Industry, 1952–1971. Kenneth J. Hatten, Dan E. Schendel and Arnold C. Cooper Institute for Research in the Behavioral, Economic and Management Sciences, Krannert Graduate School of Management, Purdue University, Lafayette, IN 47907. 1976.

Almanacs and Yearbooks

Brewers Almanac. United States Brewers Association, 1750 K Street, N.W., Washington, DC 20006. (212) 466-2400. Annual.

Brewing Industry Survey. Research Co. of America, 654 Madison Ave., New York, NY 10021. Annual.

Bibliographies

Information Sources on the Beer and Wine Industry. United Nations Industrial Development Organization, Lerchenfelderstrasse 1, P.O. Box 707, Vienna, Austria A-1011. 1977. $4.00.

Directories

Beer Wholesaler-Directory and Buyers Guide. 75 S.E. Fourth Ave., Delray Beach, FL 33444. (305) 272-1223. Annual. $25.00

Brewers Digest-Buyers Guide and Brewery Directory. Siebel Publishing Co., 4049 W. Peterson Ave., Chicago, IL 60646. (312) 463-3400. Annual. $8.00.

Modern Brewery Age Blue Book. Business Journals, Inc., 22 S. Smith St., Norwalk, CT 06855. (203) 853-6015. Annual. $50.00.

National Licensed Beverage Association — Industry Directory. National Licensed Beverage Association, 309 N. Washington St., Alexandria, VA 22314. (703) 683-6633. Annual.

Encyclopedias and Dictionaries

Dictionary of the History of the American Brewing and Distilling Industries. William L. Downard. Greenwood Press, 88 Post Rd. W., Westport, CT 06881. (203) 226-3571. 1980. $55.00.

Financial Ratios

Cost of Doing Business — Corporations. Dun and Bradstreet Inc., 99 Church St., New York, NY 10007. (212) 285-7000. Irregular. Single copies free.

Handbooks and Manuals

Grossman's Guide to Wines, Spirits, and Beers. Harold J. Grossman and Harriet Lembeck. Charles Scribner's Sons, 115 Fifth Ave., New York, NY 10003. (212) 614-1300. Seventh revised edition. $29.95.

The World Guide to Beer. Michael Jackson. Running Press, 125 S. 22nd St., Philadelphia, PA 19103. (215) 567-5080. Reprint 1982. $28.40.

On-Line Data Bases

Foods Adlibra. Foods Adlibra Publications, 9000 Plymouth Ave., N., Minneapolis, MN 55427. (612) 540-2720. Semimonthly. $125.00 per year. Food industry literature, 1974 to present. Inquire as to online cost and availability.

Periodicals and Newsletters

American Society of Brewing Chemists Journal. American Society of Brewing Chemists Journal, 3340 Pilot Knob Rd., Saint Paul, MN 55121. (612) 454-7250. Quarterly. $75.00 per year.

ASBC Newsletter. ASBC Newsletter, 3340 Pilot Knob Rd., Saint Paul, MN 55121. (612) 454-7250. Quarterly. $16.00 per year.

Brewers Digest. 4049 W. Peterson Ave., Chicago, IL 60646. (313) 463-3400. Monthly. $14.00 per year.

Brewing and Distilling International. William Reed, Limited, 5 Southwark St., London, England SE1 1RQ. Monthly. Thirty pounds per year.

MBAA Technical Quarterly. Master Brewers Association of America. 4513 Vernon Blvd., Madison, WI 53705. (608) 231-3446. Quarterly.

Modern Brewery Age. Business Journals., Inc., 22 S. Smith St., Norwalk, CT 06855. (203) 853-6015. Monthly. $40.00 per year.

Price Sources

Beverage Media Limited. 161 Sixth Ave., New York, NY 10013. (212) 620-0100. Monthly. $15.00 per year.

Feedstuffs. Miller Publishing Co., 2501 Wayzata Blvd., Minneapolis, MN 55405. Weekly. $18.50 per year.

Journal of Commerce. Twin Coast Newspapers, Inc., 110 Wall St., New York, NY 10005. (212) 425-1616. Daily, except Saturday and Sunday. $145.00 per year.

Research Centers and Institutes

Cereal Crops Research Unit. 501 N. Walnut St., Madison, WI 53705. (608) 262-3355.

Statistics Sources

Agricultural Prices. Economics, Statistics, and Cooperatives Service, U.S. Dept. of Agriculture, Available from U.S. Government Printing Office, Washington, DC 20402. Monthly. $27.00 per year.

Liquor Handbook. Gavin-Jobson Associates, 488 Madison Ave., New York, NY 10022. Annual.

Study of American Markets: Liquor. Marketing Concepts, Incorporated. U.S. News and World Report, 2400 N Street, N.W., Washington, DC 20037. (202) 955-2000. 1975.

Trade Yearbook. Food and Agricultural Organization of the United Nations. Unipub, 205 E. 42nd St., New York, NY 10017. (212) 916-1659. Annual.

United States Census of Business. Bureau of the Census, Washington, DC 20233. (301) 763-1584. Quinquennial. Most recent: 1982. Results presented in reports and tape files.

Trade Associations and Professional Societies

American Society of Brewing Chemists (ASBC). 3340 Pilot Knob Rd., Saint Paul, MN 55121. (612) 454-7250.

Brewers Association of America. 541 W. Randolph St., Chicago, IL 60606. (312) 782-2305.

Brewery and Soft Drink Workers Conference: U.S.A. and Canada. 1400 Renaissance Dr., Suite 406, Park Ridge, IL 60068. (312) 299-3406.

Master Brewers Association of the Americas. 4513 Vernon Blvd., Madison, WI 53705. (608) 231-3446.

National Beer Wholesalers' Association of America (NBWA). 5205 Leesburg Pike, Suite 505, Falls Church, VA 22041. (703) 578-4300.

National Women's Association of Allied Beverage Industries. 1250 Eye St., N.W., Suite 900, Washington, DC 20005. (202) 628-3544.

United States Brewers Association. 1750 K St., N.W., Washington, DC 20006. (202) 466-2400.

Other Sources

Beer Market. Business Trend Analysts, 2171 Jericho Turnpike, Commack, NY 11725. (516) 462-5454. 1984. $595.00. Market data and forecasts.

Imported Beer Market. Find/SVP, 500 Fifth Ave., New York, NY 10110. (800) 346-3787 or (212) 354-2424. 1985. $1,250.00. Market data.

Liquor Control Law Reports. Commerce Clearing House, Inc., 4025 W. Peterson Ave., Chicago, IL 60646. (312) 583-8500. Nine looseleaf volumes. $1,480.00 per year. Periodic supplementation. Federal and state regulation and taxation of alcoholic beverages.

U. S. Beer Market. Packaged Facts. Available from Find/SVP, 500 Fifth Ave., New York, NY 10110. (800) 346-3787 or (212) 354-2424. 1985. $995.00. Market data.

Value Line Investment Survey. Arnold Bernhard and Co., 711 Third Ave., New York, NY 10017. (212) 687-3965. Weekly. Looseleaf. $365.00 per year.

Source: P. Wasserman et al., *Encyclopedia of Business Information Sources,* 6th Ed. (Gale Research, Inc. 1986), 166–167.

in-house expertise. Smaller firms use them in lieu of developing in-house expertise.

Computerized Databases

A *computerized database* is defined as *a collection of numeric data and/or textual information that is made available in computer-readable form for electronic distribution.*[2] In the spring of 1987, more than 3,600 databases were available from over 550 on-line service enterprises. Databases are available that are useful in bibliographic search, site location, media planning, market planning, forecasting, and for many other purposes of interest to marketing researchers.

Table 4 – 1 Guides to Secondary Data

American Statistics Index Microfiche, (Washington, D.C.: Congressional Information Service, Annual, monthly updates): an index of statistical data available to the public from any agency of the federal government.

Directory of Directories, 6th ed. (Detroit: Gale Research, 1988): lists commercial and manufacturing directories, directories of individual industries, trades, and professions, rosters of professional and scientific societies, and others.

Directory of Online Databases (Santa Monica, Calif.: Cuadra Associates, Inc., Quarterly): describes more than 275 bibliographic and nonbibliographic databases.

Encyclopedia of Associations (Detroit: Gale Research, Annual): lists trade, business, and professional associations and describes their activities and publications.

Encyclopedia of Business Information Sources, 5th ed. (Detroit: Gale Research, 1986): a guide to the information available on various subjects, including basic statistical sources, associations, periodicals, directories, handbooks, and general literature.

Fuld, Leonard, M., *Competitor Intelligence* (New York: John Wiley & Sons, 1985): focus on sources relating to market and competitor characteristics.

Kruzas, Anthony T., and Linda Varekamp Sullivan, eds., *Encyclopedia of Information Systems and Services,* 6th ed. (Detroit: Gale Research, 1985): describes over 3,000 organizations involved in data storage and retrieval including data base producers and publishers, on-line vendors, information centers, research centers, banks, and data base producers and publishers.

Nelson, Theodore A., *Measuring Markets: A Guide to the Use of Federal and State Statistical Data* (Washington, D.C.: Department of Commerce, 1979): a guide to both federal and state statistical data.

Social Sciences Citation Index (Philadelphia: Institute for Scientific Information, three times annually): indexes all articles in about 1,400 social science periodicals and selected articles in approximately 1,200 periodicals in other disciplines.

Wasserman, Paul et al., *Statistics Sources,* 11th ed. (Detroit: Gale Research, 1989): a guide to federal, state, and private sources of statistics on a wide variety of subjects.

To use an on-line computerized database, the user links the receiving computer to the sending computer by telephone, using a coupler called a *modem*. The user dials a local telephone number, enters a special password to gain access to the sending computer, and then uses the interaction language of the system to retrieve and display the information of interest.

There is, of course, a charge for using a commercial database. The way charges are assessed and the amounts charged for using different databases both vary substantially. One is well advised to investigate not only the content but also the price of potential databases before making a selection. A number of directories provide information on databases (see Table 4–1).

Exhibit 4–5 *Examples of Specialized Bibliographic Databases*

The Information Bank Advertising & Marketing Intelligence Service

Advertising and marketing articles from over 60 trade and professional journals are summarized on topics such as new products, consumer trends, and sales promotions.

Bank Marketing Association: Financial Industry Information Service

Contains about 50,000 citations on the marketing of financial services by banks, credit companies, insurance firms, investment and real estate firms, thrift operations, and governmental agencies. Topics include advertising, pricing, sales, marketing, and new technologies.

FINDEX Reports and Studies

Indexes and describes all industry and market research reports, studies, and surveys (more than 12,000 citations) from more than 450 worldwide publishers.

Frost & Sullivan Research Reports Abstracts

Contains citations and abstracts from approximately 1,500 market research reports providing analyses and forecasts of market size and share by product and company. Industries represented include chemicals, communications, consumer products, data processing, electronics, food, health, instrumentation, machinery, and transportation.

Bibliographic Databases

A number of bibliographic databases are available for a wide variety of marketing research applications.

Two databases that are broadly applicable to marketing research problems are *ABI/Inform* (an acronym from *Abstract Business Inform*ation) and the *PREDICAST Terminal System.* ABI/Inform contains 200-word abstracts of articles published in more than 680 journals. More than 350,000 citations are included. (Among the users of the service are sales representatives who are preparing proposals for potential customers. They use it to access available articles concerning the company so that a more customized presentation can be made.)[3]

The **PREDICAST** Terminal System (PTS) has data files that provide domestic and international time series and forecasts, as well as bibliographic searches. The two bibliographic databases that are most widely used by marketing researchers are *PTS F&S Indexes* and *PTS Prompt*. *PTS F&S Indexes* contains about 3 million citations on companies, products, and industries. Its coverage includes information from more than 2,500 business, financial, and trade magazines and newspapers with weekly updating. *PTS Prompt* contains over 1.3 million citations and abstracts from more than 1,200 business and technical publications that relate to new products, markets, end uses, technology, foreign trade, and allied topics. It too is updated weekly.

Descriptions of several specialized bibliographic databases are given in Exhibit 4–5.

Numeric Databases

A large number of Census-based numeric databases are useful for *market potential studies, segmentation studies,* and *site location evaluations.* These databases use the 1980 Census of Population and Housing (with proprietary and government updating) and provide data to the census tract and zip code levels. Included among the databases for the United States are those provided by the Bureau of the Census, Donnelly Marketing Information Services, CACI, Inc., National Decision Systems, and the National Planning Data Corporation. Compusearch Market and Social Research, Ltd. produces a similar database for Canada.

Many on-line databases that provide time-series data for the economy and for specific industries are useful for *tracking* and *forecasting.* Included are those produced by the Boeing Computer Services Co., Data Resources, Evans Economics, Chase Econometrics, and the Office of Economic Coordination and Development (foreign as well as U.S.).

Still another type of numeric database is that produced by *syndicated services.* Syndicated services collect data by conducting periodic surveys and sell them on a subscription basis. Included in these services are surveys of

---

Exhibit 4–6   *Profit Impact of Market Strategies (PIMS) Database*

Profit Impact of Market Strategies (PIMS) program is an ongoing program of research and analysis on business strategy conducted by the Strategic Planning Institute (SPI) in Cambridge, Mass. More than 250 companies provide data on over 2,000 separate businesses. For each business there are at least 4 years of data. The data involve over 200 variables relating to the business's operating environment, operating decisions, and financial and market performance.

Participating firms must provide data from their own operations and pay a share of the costs of maintaining the database. For this, they receive (1) the results of studies done by the SPI staff, (2) reports that compare the performance of their business with businesses operating in similar environments, and (3) the ability to conduct special studies using the database. The database is designed so that it is impossible to isolate the input of any particular firm.

---

attitudes and lifestyles (Monitor, Claritas), surveys of purchases by panels of households (NPD Research, BehaviorScan, Market Research Corporation of America), information about movement of products at the retail level (Nielsen), movement of products at the wholesale level (SAMI), television viewing and radio listening (Nielsen, Arbitron), and magazine and newspaper readership (Simmons, Mediamark). We discuss these databases in the next chapter.

Finally, there are special-purpose numeric databases that do not fit into any of these categories. For example, the PIMS database described in Exhibit 4–6 is a widely used nonstandard data base.[4]

Database Systems

Finding the appropriate database, arranging to use it, and learning the access system is time-consuming. For firms needing to use a variety of specific databases, this time loss quickly cancels any advantage of using a computerized database. A number of firms have responded by acquiring the right to distribute numerous specific databases through their computer system. Other firms then subscribe to this system and can access any database contained on it using the same interaction language. Users are typically billed a subscription fee and a usage fee.

The largest of these systems is called DIALOG. It contains over 200 specific databases. NEXIS is another large system. Its bibliographic data contain entire articles rather than abstracts and a large selection of newspaper databases. SDC/Orbit contains over 80 databases focused on scientific and technical data. It contains the most complete collection of patent information available.

Most of these database systems offer Selective Dissemination of Information (SDI). SDI allows a researcher to specify a company name or any specific subject and to receive all new information on that company or subject each time the database is updated.

Associations

Associations frequently publish or maintain detailed information on industry sales, operating characteristics, growth patterns, and the like. Furthermore, they may conduct special studies of factors relevant to their industry.

These materials may be published in the form of annual reports, as part of a regular trade journal, or as special reports. In some cases, they are available only on request from the association. Most libraries maintain reference works, such as the *Encyclopedia of Associations*, that list the various associations and provide a statement of the scope of their activities.

Suppose you were assigned the responsibility of researching the travel industry in the United States. The keyword index of the *Encyclopedia of Associations* lists fifty associations dealing with this area. One of these associations, The *Travel and Tourism Research Association*, provides the following services and publications:

- Sponsors Travel Research Student Contest and dissertation competition
- Provides reference service to assist the travel industry in finding information sources and solving business problems
- Maintains a library of 10,000 volumes
- Publishes (1) *The Journal of Travel Research,* quarterly; (2) Member's Newsletter, 5/year; (3) *Directory of Members*, annual; (4) *Proceedings of the Annual Conference*; (5) *Travel Research Suppliers Directory*, semiannual.[5]

Clearly, one of your first steps would be to contact this association.

Many other associations provide useful research and statistics for their areas of interest. For example, in 1984 the Food Marketing Institute conducted retailer surveys concerning a large number of operating characteristics and results. Included were items that are standard for these surveys such as sales, profit as a per cent of sales, floor space, and average number of items carried, as well as more unusual items such as sales per customer transaction, sales per labor hour, per cent of stores with checkout scanning, and per cent of stores with automatic teller machines.[6]

Government Agencies

Federal, state, and local government agencies produce a massive amount of data that are of relevance to marketers. In this section, the nature of the data produced by the federal government is briefly described. However, state and local government data should not be overlooked by the researcher.

The federal government maintains five major agencies whose primary function is to collect and disseminate statistical data. They are the Bureau of the Census, Bureau of Labor Statistics, National Center for Educational Statistics, National Center for Health Statistics, and the Statistical Reporting Service, Department of Agriculture. There are also a number of specialized analytic and research agencies, numerous administrative and regulatory agencies, and special committees and reports of the judicial and legislative branches of the government.

These sources produce five broad types of data of interest to marketers. There are data on (1) *population, housing, and income;* (2) *agricultural, industrial, and commercial product sales of manufacturers, wholesalers, retailers, and service organizations;* (3) *financial and other characteristics of firms;* (4) *employment;* and (5) *miscellaneous reports.*

Data on Population, Income, and Housing

Data of these types are of interest primarily for *estimating market potential* and for *segmenting markets* for consumer products. The number of persons/households in a given area, along with the distribution of income and such demographic variables as age, marital status, education, income and occupations are associated with the market potential for many consumer products. These same variables, along with data on ethnic origin, durable goods, home ownership, and home characteristics, are useful for market segmentation. A recent development by the Census Bureau called the Tiger system allows access to this data by such geographic regions as telephone area code and zip code as well as the traditional census tracts and political boundaries.

The principal federal sources for these data are the *Census of Population and Housing* (taken each ten years) updated annually by the *Current Population Reports — Population Characteristics* and — *Consumer Income.*

Data on Industrial and Commercial Product Sales of Manufacturers, Agricultural Producers, Wholesalers, Retailers, and Service Organizations

Sales data for product categories can be used for such purposes as locating a plant, warehouse, retail store, or sales office, for setting sales quotas, or allocating advertising budgets by areas. The statistics published by the federal government on domestic sales are the most extensive available.

Sales statistics are available for each of the levels of distribution — manufacturers, agricultural producers, wholesalers, retailers for products, and suppliers for services. The principal sources of sales data for each of these levels are the censuses conducted for each. The *Census of Manufacturers, Census of Agriculture, Census of Wholesale Trade, Census of Retail Trade* and *Census of Selected Services* are each conducted every five years (during years ending in "2" and "7"). The *Current Industrial Reports, Agricultural Statistics, Current Wholesale Trade, Current Retail Trade*, and *Monthly Selected Services* series update these censuses at least annually.

Reference to the *Standard Industrial Classification (SIC)* system definition is necessary for a full understanding of what products are included in the sales statistics. For example, SIC Code 521 is for "lumber and other building materials dealers." If one were considering using the sales for SIC Code 521 by area as a correlate of market potential for the do-it-yourself homeowner market, certain questions about the type of establishments and type of sales by those establishments must be answered. For example, what happens to the sales of those establishments selling both to contractors and to the do-it-yourselfers — are they included in SIC 521, excluded from SIC 521 and assigned to a wholesale trade code number, or are they somehow split, with part assigned to SIC 521 and part to a wholesale trade number? "Sales of hardware stores" is the definition given SIC Code 525. What happens to the hardware sales of SIC

Exhibit 4–7 *Description of SIC Major Group 52 and Industry 5211*

Standard Industrial Classification
Major Group 52. — Building Materials, Hardware, Garden Supply, and Mobile Home Dealers

The Major Group as a Whole

This major group includes retail establishments primarily engaged in selling lumber and other building materials; paint; glass and wallpaper; hardware; nursery stock; lawn and garden supplies; and mobile homes.

It includes lumber and other building materials dealers and paint, glass and wallpaper stores selling to the general public, even if sales to contractors account for a larger proportion of total sales. These establishments are known as "retail" in the trade. Establishments primarily selling these products but not selling to the general public are classified in Wholesale Trade.

Establishments primarily selling plumbing, heating and air conditioning equipment and electrical supplies are classified in Wholesale Trade.

LUMBER AND OTHER BUILDING MATERIALS DEALERS

Group No.	Industry No.	
521	5211	**Lumber and Other Building Materials Dealers**

Establishments engaged in selling primarily lumber, or lumber and a general line of building materials, to the general public. While these establishments may also sell to contractors, they are known as "retail" in the trade. The lumber which they sell may include rough and dressed lumber, flooring, molding, doors, sashes, frames and other millwork. The building materials may include roofing, siding, shingles, wallboard, paint, brick, tile, cement, sand, gravel and other building materials and supplies. Hardware is often an important line of retail lumber and building materials dealers. Establishments which do no selling to the general public or those which are known in the trade as "wholesale" are classified in Group 503.

Brick and tile dealers — retail
Building materials dealers — retail
Building prefabricated — retail
Cabinets, kitchen: to be installed — retail
Cement dealers — retail
Concrete and cinder block dealers — retail
Fallout shelters — retail
Fencing dealers — retail
Flooring, wood — retail
Garage doors, sale and installation — retail
Insulation material, building — retail
Jalousies — retail
Lime and plaster dealers — retail
Lumber and building material dealers — retail
Lumber and planing mill product dealers — retail
Millwork and lumber dealers — retail
Roofing material dealers — retail
Sand and gravel dealers — retail
Storm windows and sash, wood or metal — retail
Structural clay products — retail
Wallboard (composition) dealers — retail

Source: Standard Industrial Classification Manual (Washington, D.C.: U.S. Government Printing Office, 1972).

Code 521 establishments? Are structured steel dealer sales included in SIC 521 sales? What about cement dealers? Floor covering dealers?

The answers to these and other questions can be found by looking up the definition of SIC group 521 and industry 5211 in the *Standard Industrial Classification Manual*.[7] These definitions are given in Exhibit 4–7. Given these definitions, what are the answers to the questions just raised?

It is often possible to obtain special computer runs from the issuing agency on finer breakdowns of data than those published. In some industries, products are assigned five- and even six-digit codes. If, after inspecting the appropriate definitions and code assignments in the *SIC Manual*, it appears that such is the case for products or services of interest to you, contact the issuing federal agency.

Data on Financial and Other Characteristics of Firms

Data on the financial characteristics, product line sales, joint ventures, staffing, and company history are valuable for market potential and segmentation studies, acquisition analyses, and competitor analyses. All publicly traded firms in the United States must provide detailed reports to the Securities and Exchange Commission (SEC). These SEC filings are available to the public.

The 10-K report is the most widely used. It must be filed annually and contains such data as the income statement, balance sheet, sales by product line, debt structure, earnings per share, plants and property, subsidiaries, industry description, and so forth. This form is updated quarterly, though in less detail, by the 10-Q report.

Obtaining SEC data is simple. Disclosure, Inc. is the SEC's sole vendor for the private distribution of its data.[8] A call to Disclosure (800-638-8241) will produce any desired SEC material quickly and inexpensively.

Data on Employment

Employment data are used as an indicator of market potential for industrial products. They can be found in each of the economic censuses (Manufacturers, Wholesale, Trade, Retail Trade, Services, and Agriculture), in the *Annual Survey of Manufacturers*, and in *Employment and Earning Statistics, States and Areas* published by the U.S. Department of Labor.

Miscellaneous Reports

The federal government issues a staggering number of special reports each year covering a wide diversity of topics. Many of these are of interest to market researchers working on particular projects. Examples range from the *Construction Review*, a bimonthly report on residential and other construction published by the Department of Commerce, to *China: International Trade Annual Statistical Supplement*, published by the CIA.

The *National Technical Information Service* (NTIS) of the U.S. Department of Commerce provides many useful services to the marketing researcher. One of the most valuable services is its NTI Search. This is an on-line computer search of over 1,000,000 unrestricted technical publications. It is updated every two weeks. For less than $50, an on-line search of the entire database can be made for an hour. (An average search requires considerably less time than that.) NTIS also has reports from more than 3,000 searches that have been made that can be purchased as documents through a catalog the service provides.

Syndicated Services

A wide array of data on both consumer and industrial markets is collected and sold by commercial organizations. This source of data is so important and complex that the next chapter is devoted to it.

Directories

Any sound marketing strategy requires an understanding of existing and potential competitors and customers. Suppose you were asked to prepare a report on the forest products industry, to aid your organization in developing a sales and marketing approach to lumber manufacturers. How would you identify the potential customers and competitors by location and characteristics? A number of services and directories would prove useful.

A general industry directory such as *Thomas Register of American Manufacturers* (Thomas Publishing Company) is a good starting place. This sixteen-volume set lists manufacturers' products and services by product category. It provides the company name, address, telephone number, and an estimate of its asset size. It also contains an extensive trademark listing and samples of company catalogs.

Most industries have specific directories and buyers' guides published by a trade journal or the industry trade association. For the lumber industry, *Crow's Buyers and Sellers Guide of the Forest Products Industries* (C. C. Crow Publications) lists over 5,000 lumber products manufacturers indexed geographically, by product, and by firm name. In addition, *Forest Industries — Annual Equipment Catalog & Buyers' Guide Issue* lists numerous suppliers of equipment to the lumber industry by product.

Another type of directory is provided by the Instant Yellow Page Service (Omaha, Nebraska), a computer directory containing the listings of all firms advertising in the Yellow Pages in the United States. Firms can be accessed by SIC code and geographic region (zip code, county, state, or nation).

Finally, there are a number of trade show directories (see Table 4–1). A trade show directory allows one to identify the trade shows associated with an industry. The trade show organizer or sponsor can then be contacted and a list of exhibitors can usually be obtained, often with details about their products.

Other Published Sources

There is a virtually endless array of periodicals, books, dissertations, special reports, newspapers, and the like that contain information relevant to marketing decisions. Any attempt to list or describe the more important of these sources is beyond the scope of this book.

A starting point in a *manual* search for published sources on any particular topic is the subject heading in the local library's card catalog. This should be followed by consulting the relevant abstracts or literature guides, such as *Dissertation Abstracts, Psychological Abstracts, Sociological Abstracts, Business Periodicals Index*, the *Social Science Citation Index*, and the *Reader's Guide to Periodical Literature*. After consulting these sources, the reader should ask the librarian to provide additional suggestions. The librarian can frequently produce references that even a thorough search by a person without specialized training would not reveal. Finally, a telephone call to one of the associations involved in the area will often produce useful references.

One should consider starting with a *computerized* search rather than a manual one, however. The use of a computerized bibliographic service and the resulting printout of the references relating to the topic of interest may provide a more comprehensive search in the time available and, in many cases, is less costly. As an alternative, an information broker can be hired to conduct the search.

External Experts

External experts are individuals outside your organization whose job provides them with expertise on your industry or activity. State and government officials associated with the industry, trade association officials, editors and writers for trade and business publications, financial analysts focusing on the industry, government and university researchers, and distributors often have expert knowledge relevant to marketing problems. Referring to Exhibit 4–2, a phone call to a few key retail department managers as soon as sales turned down would have most likely provided management with the required information.

While not traditionally viewed as a source of secondary data, knowledgeable outsiders are frequently the fastest and most up-to-date sources available.

An Application of Secondary Data

The following example of the use of secondary data illustrates their value. The situation involves the use of federal government data in developing the *Buying Power Index*, a widely used measure of relative market potential among areas for consumer products.

The "Buying Power Index" — An Indicator of Relative Market Potential

Each year *Sales and Marketing Management* magazine publishes a "Survey of Buying Power" issue that contains data for the United States on population, income, retail sales, and a "buying power index" (**BPI**) down to the metropolitan area, county, and city levels. Similar data are also provided for Canada at the provincial and metropolitan area levels.

This issue is widely used as a source of data for planning marketing programs for consumer products. The same magazine also publishes an annual "Survey of Industrial Purchasing Power."

The buying power index is basically a multiple factor index of *relative* market potential between geographic territories.

Multiple factor indexes usually take the form

$$RMP_i = \frac{f_{1,i}W_1}{f_{1,t}} + \frac{f_{2,i}W_2}{f_{2,t}} + \cdots + \frac{f_{n,i}W_n}{f_{n,t}}$$

where

RMP_i is the market potential in area i relative to that for the total marketing area of the company,

$f_{1,i}$ is a measure of factor 1 in area i,
$f_{1,t}$ is a measure of factor 1 for the total marketing area of the company, and
W_1 is the weight assigned factor 1.

Note that if $f_{1,i}$ is, say, the population of the Davenport-Rock Island-Moline (D-RI-M), metropolitan area, and $f_{1,t}$ is the population of the United States, $f_{1,i}/f_{1,t}$ is the *proportion* of the population that lives in the D-RI-M metropolitan area. If $f_{1,i}/f_{1,t}$ is multiplied by 100, it becomes the *percentage* of the population that lives in the D-RI-M metropolitan area.

The "Buying Power Index" is a three-factor index of this form. The factors and the factor weights are

$$\frac{f_{1,i}}{f_{1,t}} \times 100 = \text{percentage of population in area } i, \ W_1 = .2,$$

$\dfrac{f_{2,i}}{f_{2,t}} \times 100$ = percentage of retail sales in area i, $W_2 = .3$, and

$\dfrac{f_{3,i}}{f_{3,t}} \times 100$ = percentage of effective buying income (disposable personal income) in area i, $W_3 = .5$.

In 1987 the buying power index for the D-RI-M metropolitan area was 0.1628 and for the Waterloo-Cedar Falls (W-CF) metropolitan area it was 0.0621. On a *relative* basis, therefore, the two index numbers indicate that the D-RI-M area had slightly more than two and one half times (0.1628/.0621 = 2.62) the potential for sales of an average consumer good in 1987 than the W-CF area. The calculation of the D-RI-M index number is given in Exhibit 4–8.

In addition to the general buying power index, three specific indexes are also provided: one each for economy-, moderate-, and premium-priced products. The BPI is widely used to set relative advertising budgets, to allocate sales force efforts, to select areas for new product introductions or market tests, and to estimate market potential.

The BPI is concerned solely with the buying power of an area, *not* with product need. Therefore, the BPI should *not* be used to compare locations for products subject to strong geographic variations in demand unless the geo-

---

Exhibit 4–8   *Calculation of Buying Power Index (BPI) for the Davenport-Rock Island-Moline Metropolitan Statistical Area (Davenport-Rock Island-Moline MSA)*

Data on factors°	$\dfrac{f_{j,i}}{f_{j,t}} \times 100$	$\times W_j =$	Weighted Factor Value
Population			
D-RI-M MSA = 386,000	0.1587	$\times$ .2 =	0.0317
United States = 243,211,700			
Retail sales			
D-RI-M MSA = $2,251 mil.	0.1525	$\times$ .3 =	0.0458
United States = $1,476,173 mil.			
Effective Buying Income			
D-RI-M MSA = $5,086 mil.	0.1706	$\times$ .5 =	0.0853
United States = $2,981,721 mil.			
Total — Buying Power Index Value =			0.1628

° Given in the "1987 Survey of Buying Power," *Sales and Marketing Management,* July 27, 1987, B9, B23, B31.

graphic influences are similar. Thus, comparisons for snow shovels between Houston and Denver would not make much sense, whereas they would be more reasonable for Denver and Salt Lake City.

Review Questions

4.1. What are *secondary data?*

4.2. What are the *major problems* encountered with secondary data?

4.3. What are the major sources of *internal* secondary data?

4.4. What are the major sources of *external* secondary data?

4.5. What is an SIC code?

4.6. What are the *five broad types of data* published by the federal government that are of interest to marketers?

4.7. What is a *computerized* database?

4.8. Describe a specialized on-line database of use to marketing managers.

4.9. What are *two on-line bibliographic databases* that are broadly applicable to marketing research problems?

4.10. What is the *PIMS database?*

4.11. What is an *information broker?*

4.12. What is a numeric database?

4.13. What is a database system? What advantages does one offer?

4.14. What types of data are available from trade associations?

4.15. What is the *Buying Power Index?* What cautions should be observed in using the BPI?

4.16. Does the *Buying Power Index* provide a measure of *absolute* or *relative* market potential? Why?

Discussion Questions/Problems

4.17. Describe a system that would enable a company to avoid the problems encountered in Exhibit 4–2.

4.18. Most firms do not make effective use of internal secondary data. Why? How could this be altered?

4.19. Rank order the first 10 sources you would use from Exhibit 4–4.

4.20. Why are bibliographic databases useful?

4.21. Describe the steps you would go through to develop an estimate of market size for bathtubs. Use only secondary data.

4.22. Describe the steps you would go through to develop a competitor profile on IBM, Xerox, or Hewlett-Packard.

4.23. Describe the steps you would go through to develop a list of users of sheet metal.

Projects

4.24. Give at least five *specific* potential sources of secondary data that you would consult to estimate market potential for a new product (choose a product of interest to you).

4.25. Select a specialty retail store type — health foods and indoor plants are examples — that interests you. Assume that you are interested in opening such a store in the general area of the campus. Precisely what is your management problem? What is the research problem? What secondary sources are available that would provide data to help you decide whether to open such a store? Identify the specific individuals you would want to consult with to help in this decision. Gather and summarize the available secondary data that would bear on your decision of whether or not to open such a store.

4.26. Obtain data on cigarette sales in your state for the latest available year. Calculate the per-capita sales for your state and compare it to that for the country as a whole. Which is higher? What factors do you think explain the difference?

4.27. Select a company of interest to you and develop a competitive profile of that firm, indicating the source for each bit of data used.

4.28. Select a product category of interest and develop an estimate of market size, number of customers, number of competitors, geographic concentrations of customers and competitors, and a forecast of sales growth.

4.29. What database(s) would you use to develop sales leads, overseas representation opportunities, and the identity of competitors for a commercial saw manufacturer that sells directly to residential and commercial construction firms?

4.30. What database(s) would you use to help determine market size and future growth, industry capacity, average selling price, and imports and exports for laser scanners?

4.31. For each of these products, which associations would you contact?
a. saddles
b. tropical fish supplies
c. paper cups
d. industrial solvents
e. fertilizer

References

[1] C. T. Johnson, "Information Brokers," *Marketing News*, February 27, 1987, 14.

[2] Adapted from a definition given in R. N. Cuadra, *Directory of Online Databases* (Santa Monica, Calif.: Cuadra/Elsevier, Jan. 1988), 9(1), vii.

[3] For a discussion of this in practice see C. R. Milsap, "On-Line and On Target," *Business Marketing* (October 1985), 52–63.

[4] See R. O. Buzzell and B. T. Gale, *The PIMS Principles* (New York: The Free Press, 1987).

[5] *Encyclopedia of Associations*, Vol. 1 (Gale Research Inc., 1989), 353.

[6] *The Food Marketing Industry Speaks* (Washington, D.C.: Food Marketing Institute, 1984).

[7] *Standard Industrial Classification Manual* (Washington, D.C.: U.S. Government Printing Office, 1972). There is also a 1977 supplement to the Manual that should be consulted to see if any changes have been made in definitions. For a description of SIC codes and their application to marketing see R. W. Haas, "Sources of SIC Related Data for More Effective Marketing," *Industrial Marketing* (May 1977), 32–42. For a discussion of some of the SIC system shortcomings see I. Belth, "The SIC Code Needs Therapy," *Business Marketing* (August 1984), 50, 52.

[8] Disclosure, Inc., 5161 River Road, Bethesda, MD 20816.

CHAPTER 5

Commercial Surveys, Audits, and Panels

Brand managers at Procter & Gamble have substantial sales evidence that cents-off coupons produce significant sales increases. However, the coupons also lower margins and increase costs.

There are a variety of ways by which coupons can be distributed. Each method has a distinct cost and redemption rate. One approach to deciding whether to use coupons and how to distribute them is to calculate the gross contribution change during and immediately after the coupon period minus the cost of distributing the coupons. This is generally done by distributing coupons into selected regions and withholding them from a "matched" set of regions.

The brand manager can determine the coupon redemption rate through accounting records. However, accounting records would not reveal actual brand sales during the period. Why? Shipments into the channel of distribution precede retail sales by varying lengths of time. Therefore, to conduct this type of analysis, the brand manager at Procter & Gamble must obtain a measure of brand sales at retail.

Several sources are available. Nielsen Marketing Research provides weekly universal product code (UPC) scanner-based product-movement data from more than 3,000 stores. In addition, it audits brand sales in an additional 2,500 nonscanner-equipped stores every two months.

SAMSCAN®, operated by SAMI/Burke, provides weekly brand-sales data based on computerized UPC scanner reports from approximately 2,500 retail outlets. Information Resources, Inc., (IRI) provides a similar service called INFOSCAN.®

In this situation, the Procter & Gamble brand manager felt that *who* redeemed the coupons was more critical than the absolute number redeemed. The specific objective of couponing for this brand was to capture new users, not to encourage current users to stock up on the brand. How could this data be obtained?

NPD/Nielsen and IRI, among others, operate panels in which individual household purchases over time are recorded. By monitoring coupon redemption by specific households, the brand manager can determine the effect of various types of coupons on specific types of users. One such study revealed the following redemption patterns:[1]

	Redemption Rate	
Customer Type	FSI Coupons	Target Direct Mail Coupons
New Users	13%	48%
Non-loyal Buyers	16%	27%
Loyal Buyers	71%	25%
Total	100%	100%

The data we have just described were not generated solely to solve Procter & Gamble's marketing problem. Therefore, they could be considered secondary data. However, these data are collected specifically to address this category of problem for firms like Procter & Gamble. Thus, they have much in common with primary data. Commercial surveys, audits, and panels occasionally generate primary data, sometimes secondary data, and, most often, data with characteristics of each. In this chapter we will describe the characteristics of each of these three important data sources and then describe the major ways these data are used by marketing managers.

Commercial Surveys

Commercial surveys are conducted by research organizations and fall into three categories: periodic, panel, and shared. *Periodic surveys* measure the same attitudes, knowledge, and/or behaviors using different samples at regular points in time. *Panel surveys* generally measure differing attitudes, knowledge, and/or behaviors using the same basic set of respondents at either regular or unique time intervals. Finally, *shared surveys* are surveys that are administered by a research firm and are composed of questions submitted by multiple clients.

Periodic Surveys

Periodic surveys are conducted at regular intervals, ranging from weekly to annually. They use a new sample of respondents (individuals, households, or stores) for each survey, focusing on the same topic and allowing the analysis of trends over time, though changes in individual respondents cannot be traced. These surveys cover topics ranging from values to media usage and food preparation. Standard reports and special analyses are available to firms that subscribe to the service. Exhibit 5–1 describes an annual periodic survey that Audits & Surveys has offered since 1964.

Periodic surveys are conducted by mail, personal interview, and telephone. They are subject to all of the problems of questionnaire design, sampling, and survey method that affect custom surveys (these issues are discussed in the next chapter). In addition, when periodic surveys are conducted at known intervals, they may affect the behavior being measured. For example, periodic surveys are used to measure television viewing. Telecasters

---

Exhibit 5–1 *Audits & Surveys National Restaurant Market Index*

- *Timing* — Annually in May.
- *Sample* — National probability sample of approximately 6,000 restaurants projectable to all commercial restaurants in the U.S.
- *Procedure* — Personal interviews with the chef, manager, or owner and an inspection of equipment and inventories.
- *Classification Data* — U.S. Census definitions as to type, service offered (counter, table, drive-in, etc.), and whether it is free standing or part of another establishment such as a hotel or retail store. Annual sales volume and the number of full and part-time employees are also recorded.
- *Variables Measured* — The usage of specific categories of food and supplies (cleaning products, paper and plastic goods, dishes, and so forth), and the presence of specified equipment. Brand names of products actually found in the kitchen are recorded.
- *Reports* — Brands and sizes, equipment, product category usage and so forth reported by total U.S., type of restaurant, U.S. census, geographic region, and client sales regions.

have responded by scheduling specials and particularly popular shows to coincide with these surveys.

Panel Surveys

Panel surveys, sometimes called *interval panels,* are conducted among a group of respondents who have agreed to respond to a number of mail, telephone, or, occasionally, personal interviews over time. The interviews may cover virtually any topic and need not occur on a regular basis. In contrast, a *panel,* a *continuous panel,* or *panel data* refers to a group of individuals who agree to report specified behaviors over time. This type of panel is discussed in the next section of this chapter.

In an interval panel, the research firm initially gathers detailed data on each respondent, including demographics and attitudinal and product-ownership items. Because the researchers need not collect this basic demographic data again, they can now obtain more relevant information from each respondent. These basic data also allow researchers to select very specific samples. For example, a researcher can select only those families within a panel that have one or more daughters between the ages of 12 and 16, or that own a dog, or that wear contact lens. This ability to select allows a tremendous savings over a random survey procedure if a study is to be made for a product for teenage girls, dog owners, or contact lens wearers, and so on.

It is possible to survey the same interval panel members several times to monitor changes in their attitudes and purchase behavior in response to changes in the firm's or a competitor's marketing mix. However, interval panels are used more often for cross-section (one-time) surveys. A major advantage is the high response rate obtained by most interval panels. Return rates in the range of 70 to 90 percent are often obtained. In addition, the firm does not have to generate a sampling frame, a process that is both time consuming and costly. Finally, since panel members are convinced of the legitimacy of the firm maintaining the panel, they may supply more detailed and accurate data to both neutral and sensitive questions.

Interval panels exist for the general U.S. and Canadian populations, for specific geographic regions within either country, and for specialized populations such as farmers or consumers age 50 or over. For example, the Doane Countrywide Farm Panel is composed of approximately 25,000 farmers and ranchers. Data are normally collected by mail, but telephone, personal, and even focus groups can be used. Clients can survey the entire panel, a stratified random sample of the larger panel, or a specific type, size, or location category. Exhibit 5–2 describes two major consumer panels.

Panel surveys obtain very high response rates. However, the response rate when individuals are initially asked to join a panel may be quite low. Thus, panels do not eliminate nonresponse error. This issue is discussed in depth in the section on continuous panels.

Exhibit 5–2 *Two Major Interval Panels*

NFO

Size: Over 400,000 households (nearly 1 million people) with 40 continuously maintained subpanels of 5,000 households, each of which matches the demographics from the latest Census Bureau statistics.

Access: Mail-out/mail-back, mail-out/telephone collection, telephone, in-home videotape demonstrations, ability to recontact individual respondents, product placement for use testing.

Pre-identified Characteristics: Geographic region; ADI (area of dominant influence); city size; stage of household life cycle; age; education; occupation (over 50 categories); employment status of household members; size and income of household; geodemographic and value segments (ACORN, ClusterPlus, PRIZM, VISION, and VALS); dwelling type and ownership; ownership of various products (6); travel patterns; and dog or cat ownership.

CMP (Market Facts, Inc.)

Size: 270,000 households with nationally balanced subsamples available within geographic regions. An additional 30,000 households are available in Canada.

Access: Primarily mail-out/mail-back with phone interviewing also available. Products can be distributed for use testing and daily, or weekly diary reports from panel members can be obtained.

Pre-identified Characteristics: Geographic region, ADI (area of dominant influence); city size; stage of household life cycle; age; education; occupation; employment status of household head; age of children, size and income of household, employment status of adult female household members; type and ownership of dwelling unit; and presence of dogs and/or cats.

Shared Surveys

Shared surveys, sometimes referred to as *omnibus surveys,* are administered by a research firm and consist of questions supplied by multiple clients. Such surveys can involve mail, telephone, or personal interviews. The respondents may be drawn from either an interval panel or randomly from the larger population. Exhibit 5–3 briefly describes several major shared surveys. Exhibit 5–4 is a shared survey from Data Gage (Market Facts Inc).

Exhibit 5–3 *Shared Surveys*

Service	Method	Frequency	Sample
AIM (R. H. Bruskin Associates)	In-home personal	Bi-monthly	2,000 homes, national probability, adults, half male
OmniTel (R. H. Bruskin Associates)	Telephone (CATI)	Weekly (Fri.–Sun.)	1,000 adults, half male, random digit dialing
TeleNation (Market Facts, Inc.)	Telephone (CATI)	Weekly (Fri.–Sun.)	1,000 adults, half male, random digit dialing
TeleNation Canada (Market Facts of Canada Limited)	Telephone (CATI)	Weekly (Thurs.–Sun.)	1,000 adults, half male, random digit dialing
Data Gage (Market Facts, Inc.)	Mail	Monthly	1,000 to 150,000 randomly selected from CMP's interval panel (see Exhibit 5–2)
CMP National Omnibus (Market Facts of Canada, Limited)	Mail	Quarterly	3,000, 6,000, 10,000, or 14,000 randomly selected from CMP's Canadian mail panel (Exhibit 5–2)
Multicard Survey (NFO)	Mail	Twice Monthly	5,000 increments to 150,000 quota samples from NFO's interval panel (Exhibit 5–2)
Insta-Vue (Home Testing Institute)	Mail	Monthly	5,000 increments to 150,000 quota samples from HTI's interval panel

Exhibit 5–4   *A Shared Survey from Data Gage (Market Facts Inc.)*

(Please Read and Answer <u>these</u> questions)

1a. Are you currently married or are you planning to be married within the next 12 months?

Yes . . . . . □ 1   No . . . . . □ 2 (**SKIP TO QU. 2**)   (9)

1b. "X" one box below to indicate the date of your wedding.

Before <u>1985</u> . . . . □ 1   (10)
Between January and June, <u>1985</u> . . . . □ 2
Between July and December, <u>1985</u>. . . . . □ 3
Between January and June, <u>1986</u> . . . . □ 4
Between July and December, <u>1986</u>. . . . . □ 5
During <u>1987</u>. . . . . □ 6

2. What kind of video cassette recorder (VCR) do you own? (A video cassette recorder records and plays back TV shows, movies, etc.)

No VCR owned . . . . □ 1   VHS . . . . □ 2   (11)
                                        Beta . . . . □ 3

3. What kind of cameras are currently used by people in your household? ("X" **ALL THAT APPLY**.)

35 mm camera . . . . □ 1   (12)
110 cartridge camera. . . . . □ 2
126 cartridge camera. . . . . □ 3
Disc camera . . . . □ 4
Instant print camera. . . . . □ 5
Video camera/camcorder . . . . □ 6
No cameras used . . . . □ X

4. Does any member of your household currently <u>smoke</u> <u>cigars</u> at least two times a week?

Yes . . . . □ 1   No . . . . □ 2   (13)

5. Which, if any, of the following <u>credit cards</u> are currently owned by any member of your household? ("X" **ALL THAT APPLY**)

Choice . . . . □ 1   (14)
Diner's Club. . . . . □ 2
Discover . . . . □ 3
NONE OF THESE . . . . □ 4

111

6. Which, if any, of the following types of "specially-flavored" block or sliced cheese — <u>not</u> spreads — (that is cheeses that have been flavored with added bits and pieces of pepper, meats, onions, herbs/spices/seeds or have been smoked or are wine-flavored) have you or other members of your household purchased and eaten <u>in the past year</u>? ("X" ALL THAT APPLY)

Block or Sliced . . .   (15)

Pepper cheese (jalapeno, red, black pepper, etc.) . . . ☐ 1
Cheeses with bits of meat (pepperoni, bacon, ham, salami, etc.) . . . . ☐ 2
Mexican or Cajun cheese . . . . ☐ 3
Cheese with herbs/spices/seeds (onion, garlic, dill, chives, etc.) . . . . ☐ 4
Smoked cheese (hickory smoked cheddar, etc.) . . . . . ☐ 5
Wine-flavored cheese . . . . ☐ 6
NONE OF THESE . . . . ☐ X

7. "X" one box below to indicate how often you, or others in your household, <u>buy</u> . . .

	Once/ Week Or More Often	1–3 Times Per Month	1–2 Times Every Three Mos.	Less Than Every Three Mos.	Never
					(16)
Chocolate chip cookies	☐ 1	☐ 2	☐ 3	☐ 4	☐ 5
Sandwich cookies	☐ 1	☐ 2	☐ 3	☐ 4	☐ 5
Iced cookies.	☐ 1	☐ 2	☐ 3	☐ 4	☐ 5
Other types of cookies	☐ 1	☐ 2	☐ 3	☐ 4	☐ 5
Frozen cakes	☐ 1	☐ 2	☐ 3	☐ 4	☐ 5
Frozen sweet rolls/coffee cake	☐ 1	☐ 2	☐ 3	☐ 4	☐ 5
Potato/corn chips	☐ 1	☐ 2	☐ 3	☐ 4	☐ 5
Saltines	☐ 1	☐ 2	☐ 3	☐ 4	☐ 5
Snack crackers.	☐ 1	☐ 2	☐ 3	☐ 4	☐ 5
					(24)

Source: Reprinted with permission from Market Facts Inc.

Exhibit 5–5   *R. H. Bruskin Associates' OmniTel*

This weekly omnibus survey is conducted with 2 freshly drawn samples of 1,000 adults, 18 years of age and older . . . half of the interviews are with men and half with women.

Each study is based on a comparably selected sample of homes utilizing our own random digit dialing computer generated national probability sample. This RDD design thus takes into account unlisted, as well as listed telephone households.

Our on-premise computer assisted telephone interviewing (CATI) speeds up both the data collection and data processing of **OmniTel.** The Central Telephone Research Division (CTR) maintains continuous monitoring and supervision, thus providing both quality interviewing and a well-controlled field operation for this 105-line facility.

OmniTel has had many types of client studies including: point-in-time and multi-wave awareness, attitude and usage surveys; concept testing; impact of ad campaigns; advertising claim substantiation; screening for qualified respondents for follow-up marketing and product placement studies; determination of incidence levels; media audience studies; and many others.

Regularly Scheduled:

- **OmniTel** is conducted **WEEKLY.**
- Questionnaire deadline noon each Thursday.
- Top-line results on following Monday and complete tabs on Tuesday.

National Probability Sample:

- 1,000 telephone interviews each week; 52,000 per year.
- Male and female adults, 18 and over.
- Conducted on CATI on-premises by Bruskin's 10 line Central Telephone Research (CTR) division.
- Random digit dialing sample based on latest updated telephone data.

Cost:

- Full sample $750 for first question.
- Special low incidence rates.
- Quantity and special question discounts.
- Discounts for multi-wave studies.

Extra:

- All questions tabbed by sex, age, income and geographic region.
- Other demos available for cross-tab at low cost.
- Teenage and children augmentation available as needed.
- Respondents qualified through **OmniTel** can be recontacted for follow-up special studies.

OMNITEL PRICES: *Effective June 1988*

Number of Questions	Full Sample (1000)	Male/Female Sample (500)
1st – 2nd(per)	$ 750	$550
3rd – 4th(per)	$ 700	$500
5th or more	$ 550	$400
Open End	$1,200	$900

NOTE:

(1) Prices based on "yes-no" or "multiple choice" type questions.

(2) Special low prices available for participations based on low incidence qualifications and multiple waves.

(3) Cost includes tabulation by sex, age, income and area. Other variables available at a small additional cost.

Employment Status	Race
Heads of Household	ADI's
Nine Census Regions	MSA's
Family Size/Composition	Education
Metro Area Vs. Non-Metro	Marital Status
Nielsen County Classifications	Home Ownership

Source: Used with permission from R. H. Bruskin Associates.

Shared surveys offer the client several advantages. First, since the fixed cost of sample design and most of the variable surveying costs are shared by several clients, the cost per question is generally quite low. For example, a multiple-choice question asked of 1,000 respondents with the results cross tabulated by four demographic variables costs only $750 in a shared telephone survey. The cost per question declines as the number of questions increases.

Since these data are collected frequently — weekly for telephone surveys — responses can be obtained *very* quickly. This feature is useful for measuring consumers' responses to competitive moves, adverse publicity, and environmental changes.

The frequent administration of the questionnaires also allows tracking of advertising awareness, product use, attitudes, and so forth. Note that such tracking or monitoring involves aggregate measures and does not measure *individual* changes over time since different respondents are involved in each wave.

Shared surveys conducted among interval panel members have the additional advantage of allowing the extensive demographic data associated with each panel member to be used in an analysis of the responses. They also represent an economical way to develop a larger sample of individuals with unique characteristics such as allergies. These individuals can then be sent a custom survey on the topic of interest.

Exhibit 5–5 contains part of an advertisement and rate sheet for the Omnitel (R. H. Bruskin) shared telephone survey.

Audits

Audits involve the physical inspection of inventories, sales receipts, shelf facings, prices, and other aspects of the marketing mix to determine sales, market share, relative price, distribution, or other relevant information. There are two major types of audits — store audits and product audits.

Store Audits

The simple accounting arithmetic of

$$
\begin{aligned}
&\text{opening inventory} \\
+\ &\text{net purchases (receipts — transfers out — returned} \\
&\text{inventory + transfers in)} \\
-\ &\underline{\text{closing inventory}} \\
=\ &\text{sales}
\end{aligned}
$$

is the basis for the audit of retail store sales.

Exhibit 5–6 *Burgoyne Observation Systems (BOS)*

BOS can be applied within any defined set of retail outlet types or across outlet types for any given product category. Field work is normally completed in 72–96 hours minimizing any time related or competitor distortions. For the client's brand and its competitors, BOS measures on a one-time or ongoing basis:

- Distribution and Out-of-Stock
- Retail Price Levels and Feature Price Activity
- Shelf Space Allocation and Positioning
- In-Store Stocking Locations
- Display Activity
- Point-of-Purchase Material Presence
- Age-of-Stock/Type of Package/Damaged Product
- Depth-of-Line

BOS samples cover 200 major markets. Clients can share costs when using standard outlet samples. Standard sample panels correspond to other leading data sources such as **SAMI** so that sales results can be related to distribution intensity. Custom outlet samples can be created to cover any product category.

Common applications include:

- Evaluate sales force/broker distribution efforts
- Track retail build for new/competitive products
- Guarantee sufficient penetration levels *prior* to advertising
- Gauge the quality of distribution at retail
- Determine channel strengths and weaknesses
- Investigate new items/categories/outlet types
- Integrate distribution data with sales/consumer information for an actionable **MIS**

The most widely used true store audit service is the Nielsen Retail Index. It is based on audits every 30 or 60 days of a large national sample of food, drug, and mass merchandise stores. The index provides sales data on all the major packaged-goods product lines carried by these stores—foods, pharmaceuticals, drug sundries, tobacco, beverages, and the like (but not soft goods or durables). Nielsen contracts with the stores to allow their auditors to conduct the audits and pays for that right by providing them with their own data plus cash.

The clients receive reports on the sales of their own brand and of competitors' brands, the resulting market shares, prices, shelf facings, in-store promotional activity, stockouts, retailer inventory and stock turn, and local advertising. These data are provided for the entire United States and by region, by size classes of stores, and by chains versus independents. The data are available to subscribers on-line via computer as well as in printed reports.

Product Audits

Product audits, such as Audits and Surveys' National Total Market Index, are similar to store audits but focus on products rather than store samples. Whereas product audits provide information similar to that provided by store audits, product audits attempt to cover all the types of retail outlets that handle a product category. Thus, a product audit for automotive wax would include grocery stores, mass merchandisers, and drugstores (in this way it is similar to the Nielsen store audits). In addition, it would include automotive supply houses, filling stations, hardware stores, and other potential outlets for automotive wax.

Retail Distribution Audits

Similar to true store audits are retail distribution audits or surveys. These surveys do not measure inventory or sales; instead, they are observational studies at the retail level. Field agents enter stores unannounced and without permission. They observe and record the brands present, price, shelf facings and other relevant data for selected product categories. NRTI (Erhardt-Babic) and BOS (Burgoyne, Inc.) are the major suppliers of this type of data. Exhibit 5–6 provides additional information on the Burgoyne system.

Panels

A panel is a group of individuals or organizations that have agreed to provide information to a researcher over a period of time. A *continuous panel*, the focus of this section, has agreed to report specified behaviors on a regular basis. Such panels exist at the wholesale, retail, and consumer levels.

Wholesale Panels

SAMI offers a service called *Census of Warehouse Shipments*. It contracts with every food chain and major wholesaler in the United States to provide shipment data every four weeks. In return, it agrees to pay them a percentage of the revenue it receives from selling the data. It also agrees to provide these organizations with the data on all shipments for their specific market areas.

SAMI warehouse withdrawal data report the movement of brands in 476 product categories in 54 television market areas. These market areas account for approximately 89 per cent of the food sales in the United States.

Purchasers of the SAMI reports receive data for the most recent 4-week period, with 12 and 52 week summaries. They have the option of buying the report for any product category for any of the 54 SAMI market areas. The reports are available within 3 weeks after the close of the 4-week reporting period. The data are also available on tape and disk. Other firms maintain wholesale panels covering other product categories.

Retail Panels

A number of organizations offer services based on sales data from the checkout scanner tapes of a sample of supermarkets that use electronic scanning systems. An estimated 99 per cent of all packaged products in supermarkets carry the universal product code (UPC), often referred to as a bar code, and so are amenable to scanning. UPC codes are rapidly being expanded to soft goods and hardware; stores such as K mart, Wal-Mart and Toys "R" Us have or are installing scanners in all their outlets.[2]

Closely related to UPC scanner methods are Electronic Point-of-Sale (EPOS) systems. EPOS systems are generally unique to a particular retail chain. They are common in catalog showrooms, home-improvement centers, hardware stores, many speciality chains, and fast-food outlets. The item code is either read electronically or is entered into the system manually. Research organizations arrange to buy UPC scanners or EPOS data from the retailers.

A. C. Nielsen's *SCANTRACK*, Information Resources' *Infoscan*, and SAMI/Burke's *SAMSCAN* are three of the larger scanning services. Scanning data are collected from a national sample of supermarkets (each system has over 2,000 supermarkets in over 40 cities). Data on displays, advertising, couponing, and so forth are also collected. These data are analyzed to provide information on purchases by brand, size, price, flavor or formulation, and market share by user-specified definitions of time, area, and store classification. The results are available on-line and in hard copy.

Custom retail scanners and EPOS services are also offered by firms such as Burgoyne. These panels focus on unique markets or account types, geographic regions, and time periods. Such custom approaches greatly extend the range of applications for scanner panel data.

Scanning data have many applications in marketing research. Safeway Stores, for example, has a manager of scanner marketing research whose department conducts studies on such topics as price elasticities, placement of products in the stores, and the effects of in-store advertising. For example, one scanner test showed that the sales of candy bars increased 80 per cent when they were put on front-end racks near the checkout stands. Another study indicated that foil-packaged sauce mixes sold better when they were placed near companion products—spaghetti sauce near the spaghetti, meat sauce in the refrigerated meat cases, and so on—rather than when they were displayed with other sauces.[3]

Scanner data, as compared to store audit data, have the advantages of (1) *greater frequency*—weekly instead of bimonthly collection, (2) *elimination of breakage and pilferage losses being counted as sales,* and (3) *more accurate price information.* They have certain problems, however, including (1) *only the larger supermarkets have scanners,* and (2) *the quality of the scanner data is heavily dependent upon the checkout clerk.* Clerks sometimes do not lift heavy items (e.g., dog food and flour) for scanning, but ring them up instead. Rather than scan each individually packaged different flavor (of say, yogurt) in a multipackage purchase of the same product, the clerk will often put only one package through the scanner and ring in the number of packages. The purchase is then incorrectly recorded as consisting of only one flavor instead of the several different flavors actually purchased.

Consumer Panels

Continuous consumer panels allow firms to monitor shifts in individual or specific household behaviors or attitudes over time. This allows the firm to determine how its own or competitors' marketing mix changes affect specific consumers or market segments. Consumer panel data are collected either electronically by UPC scanners or by diaries.

Diary Panels

A diary panel, as the name implies, *is a panel of households who continuously record in a diary their purchases of selected products.* It is used for those product categories for which purchase is frequent—primarily food, household, and personal-care products.

The largest suppliers of diary panel data are NPD/Nielsen and MRCA. NPD/Nielsen maintains two national panels of 6,500 families and a panel of

1,500 nonfamily households (primarily singles), plus a number of regional and other panels that are subsamples of the national ones. The client thus has the option of receiving purchase data from a sample of as many as 14,500 households.

Each panel household provides information on its purchases of products in each of approximately 50 product categories each month. For each product category, the respondent records the date of the purchase, the number and size(s) of the packages, the total cash paid, whether coupons were used or if there was a special price promotion, and the store at which the purchase was made. Special questions are asked for each product category; for example, for ready-to-eat breakfast cereals, *"Does the cereal have a special flavor or fruit or nuts added?--If yes, write in . . . ,"* and *"Is this cereal purchased specifically for one family member? If yes, write in age and sex."* The reporting forms for three products are shown in Exhibit 5–7.

The panelists are classified by three geodemographic systems (**PRIZM**, ClusterPlus, **VISION**)[4] and SRI's **VALS** attitude and lifestyle classification typology.[5] The data are available to subscribers on-line.

NPD/Nielsen provides the following information in its reports based on consumer panel data:

1. brand share (including brand and private label detail) by type of outlet.
2. industry and brand volume (lbs., units, equivalent cases) by type of outlet.
3. number of households buying (projected to U.S. total).
4. penetration (per cent of area households buying).
5. buying rate (units per buying occasion).
6. purchase frequency (number of purchases within a period).
7. per cent of volume bought with a cents-off deal.
8. type of deal.
9. dollars and dollar share.
10. average price paid (by deal versus nondeal sales).

MRCA maintains a panel of 7,500 nationally and regionally representative households that report purchases weekly (as opposed to NPD's monthly diaries). MRCA provides information similar to that provided by NPD/Nielsen.

While the members of the NPD/Nielsen and MRCA panels report a wide range of purchase behaviors over a period of several years, other diary panels are established to collect relatively specific data over shorter intervals. For example, both A. C. Nielsen and Arbitron establish panels four times per year.

BRAND NAME
as shown on label

USE OFFER CODES ON PAGE 4 ▶

COFFEE

Ground, Instant, Freeze Dried, Other Types

STORE TRIP #

PANCAKE MIXES

Include: ALL PURPOSE BAKING MIXES that can be used to make Pancakes, Crepes and Waffles

STORE TRIP #

OTHER BAKING MIXES

Include: Baking Mixes for Bread, Cornbread, Muffins, Biscuits, Dinner Rolls, Cookies, Coffee Cake, Sweet Rolls, Doughnuts, and other similar baking mixes

STORE TRIP #

Coffee section column headers:

- NUMBER OF PACKAGES
- TOTAL CASH PAID (not including taxes) $ ¢
- SPECIAL PRICE OFFER — SEE CODE LIST — ENTER CODE(S) BELOW — CENTS OFF
- NUMBER OF POUNDS AND OUNCES PER CON-TAINER
- TYPE OF COFFEE (✓ One): GROUND, INSTANT, FREEZE DRIED
- IF GROUND COFFEE TYPE OF GRIND (✓ One): REGULAR OR ALL PURPOSE, WHOLE BEAN, DRIP, FINE, ELECTRIC PERCOLATOR, AUTOMATIC DRIP
- TYPE OF CONTAINER (✓ All That Apply): GLASS JAR, TIN, BAG, SPECIAL REUSABLE CONTAINER, OTHER
- KIND OF COFFEE (✓ One): PURE COFFEE, COFFEE MIXED WITH OTHER PRODUCTS (CHICORY, etc.), DECAFFEINATED COFFEE
- MANUFACTURER'S CODE — WRITE IN ALL NUMBERS OF THIS 6 OR 10 DIGIT CODE IF AVAILABLE — Example 5-4000 85300

Pancake Mixes section column headers:

- NUMBER OF OUNCES PER ITEM OR CON-TAINER
- TYPE OF MIX (✓ One Or Write In): DRY MIX — COMPLETE or INSTANT (add water or other liquid only), DRY MIX — REGULAR OR OLD FASHIONED (add eggs, shortening & liquid, etc.), FROZEN BATTER (THAW AND POUR), OTHER (Write In)
- KIND OF MIX: SUCH AS: BUTTER-MILK, REGULAR, WHEAT & SOYA, BUCKWHEAT, etc. (Write In)
- DOES MIX INCLUDE ANY SPECIAL FRUIT FLAVORS or SPICES? If yes, write in FRUIT or FLAVOR, such as BLUEBERRY, CIN-NAMON, etc. IF NO WRITE HERE
- MANUFACTURER'S CODE — WRITE IN ALL NUMBERS OF THIS 6 OR 10 DIGIT CODE IF AVAILABLE — Example 5-4000 85300

Other Baking Mixes section column headers:

- NUMBER OF POUNDS AND OUNCES PER PACKAGE
- KIND OF MIX (✓ One or Write In): BREAD, CORNBREAD, MUFFINS, BISCUITS, DINNER ROLLS, COOKIES, COFFEE CAKE, OTHER (Write In)
- COMPLETE FLAVOR FROM PACKAGE — SUCH AS: NUT, RAISIN, BANANA, WHOLE WHEAT, FRUIT, CHOC-OLATE CHIP, ETC. (Write In)
- MANUFACTURER'S CODE — WRITE IN ALL NUMBERS OF THIS 6 OR 10 DIGIT CODE IF AVAILABLE — Example 5-4000 85300

Each panel member records television-viewing behavior in a diary for a one- to four-week period.

Electronic Panels

Electronic panels are composed of households whose television viewing behavior is recorded electronically. Nielsen Media Research is the main organization active in this area. Until recently, Nielsen used a national sample of homes with TV sets that were wired to household meters. The meters were connected to a central computer by telephone line and automatically recorded when the set was turned on and the station to which it was turned (a separate sample reported individual viewing in diaries).

A major problem with audience measurements obtained from meters is that no information is provided on how many people, if any, are watching, and what their demographic characteristics are. A new kind of meter, called a people meter, has been developed to take care of this problem.[6] It has a remote control coupled to the television meter that allows each of the family members plus visitors (who also record their age and gender) to 'log on' when he or she begins viewing by punching an identifying button. This information is down loaded via a telephone line to a central computer where the demographics of the household members are stored. Thus, viewing by demographic segments can be determined. The person can "log off" by either pressing the same button or turning off the set. People meters appear to provide accurate viewing data. Panel members continue to use the meters properly over time, though there is continuing concern about the accuracy of children's viewing measured in this manner.[7]

The Nielsen television ratings are now based on a national probability sample of 4,000 households (with a complete turnover every 2 years) equipped with people meters. (They also use samples totaling approximately 100,000 households who keep a one-week viewing diary to estimate local viewing patterns in over 200 TV markets.)[8] Six European countries (using AGB's people meter system) are now using people meters, with plans set to launch the Nielsen system in Canada on 1989.[9]

Testing is now underway in both the United States and Europe on "passive" people meters. These meters will automatically sense who is in the room (based on a variety of technologies).[10]

Arbitron Ratings is also very active in television (and radio) ratings. Whereas Nielsen is best known for its national ratings, Arbitron focuses more on detailed ratings for local markets. Its ADI (area of dominant influence) designations are used throughout the research and advertising industries. An ADI is a geographic area in which stations located within the geographic area receive the preponderance of total viewing hours.

Arbitron relies primarily on a diary-based approach but uses television meters in 14 markets. It is expanding its use of people meters as well.

UPC Consumer Scanner Panels

A number of organizations, including SAMI/Burke, NPD/Nielsen, and Information Resources Inc. (IRI), have scanner-based panels in selected cities. There are two approaches used in such panels — automatic in-store data collection at checkout using the store's scanner system and at-home data collection using a hand-held scanner.

IRI is the largest supplier of consumer scanner panel data. Its panel consists of more than 100,000 households. The firm equips all supermarkets in a town or trading area of a city with UPC scanners. Panel members are recruited to match national and local demographic profiles. Substantial demographic and other background data is collected on each participating household. Each panel member is then provided an I.D. number that is entered at the checkout counter as the purchases are scanned. The purchase data are automatically transmitted to IRI's central computer for analysis.

The second approach to using scanners for data collection is being used by NPD/Nielsen in its new ScanTrack National Household Panel. (Nielsen is also developing 21 local market scanner panels with 57,000 household members using a methodology similar to IRI's.) The ScanTrack panel, which went on line in early 1989, consists of 15,000 households who use handheld scanners to record their packaged goods purchases from all outlets.

Compared to the automatic system used by IRI, the hand-held scanner system requires considerably more effort on the part of the respondent. Not only must the items be scanned at home, but store (once per trip), price (for the approximately 30 per cent of total items not purchased at a cooperating store that provides prices directly to NPD/Nielsen), and deal data must be entered manually. Inaccurate recall or checking of price information, items consumed before they are brought home, and unscanned purchases due to time pressures may affect the accuracy of this approach. However, validation studies indicate that these are not major problems. The system has the important advantage of allowing purchases from all types of stores to be scanned.

As we will see in the next section, UPC consumer scanner panels are increasingly being combined with electronic panels to create *single-source data*.

Single-Source Data

Single-source data are continuous data derived from the same respondent or household, covering at least television viewing and UPC product purchase information. In general, the data are collected electronically and also contain in-store data such as price level, coupon use, and so forth.[11] A complete system requires frequent in-store observation using an approach such as BOS (see Exhibit 5–6) to measure stock-outs, displays, and so forth. The advantages of such a system are substantial, as it can produce virtually real-time measures of advertising effectiveness, the effects of repetition, product changes, and so forth.[12]

A number of organizations have or are developing varying levels of single-source capability. IRI's BehaviorScan system is a 10,000-household subset of its scanner panel (discussed earlier) that has electronic monitoring of TV viewing. The NPD/Nielsen panel described earlier also has TV viewing monitored by meters in a 10,000-home subset of its at-home hand-held scanner panel. ScanAmerica currently operates a 600-household single-source panel in Denver, with a 5,000 member national panel scheduled. These systems, as

---

Exhibit 5-8 *Birch/Scarborough Single-Source Data*

Sample:

Random digit dialing, 2,000–10,000 adults per market with one adult randomly selected within each household (no substitutions). Six call backs at varying times. Spanish language interviews where appropriate.

Process:

— Initial interview collects newspaper, radio, magazine, product and retail information and demographics.

— Second interview collects additional product usage data plus repeat audience measurements of newspapers, radio, and magazines.

— Weekend radio interview conducted on Monday following initial interview.

— A self-administered 7-day personal television diary (and a product questionnaire if additional information is desired by subscribers in the market.)

— In some markets additional product and retail information is collected via a mail-out/mail-return booklet sent along with the TV diary.

Items Measured:

Media: — Daily and Sunday newspapers
— Weekly newspapers
— Television stations (including cable use)
— Radio stations
— Selected weekly and monthly magazines

Products:

— Automobile ownership

— Alcoholic beverages

— Restaurants

— Grocery expenditures

— Domestic and foreign travel

— Airline travel

— Banking and Finance

— Charge and credit cards

— Personal computers

— Audio, video and sound equipment

— Movie attendance

Population:

— Any use of purchase

— Heavy or frequent users (some categories)

— Retail store customers (department, discount, speciality, drug and grocery stores)

— Leisure time activities

— Demographic characteristics (e.g., income, occupation, education, etc.)

— Zip code and county breakouts

well as others under development, have substantial demographic and related data available on each household. In addition, they have varying capabilities for monitoring in-store and nontelevision marketing activities.

Birch/Scarborough Research provides single-source data on the top 30 markets using traditional interview and diary methods. The procedure is described in Exhibit 5–8.

Data Available from Commercial Surveys, Audits, and Panels

In the previous sections we described the characteristics of commercial surveys, audits, and panels. In this section we will highlight the information available from such sources.

Wholesale Sales

The SAMI Warehouse Withdrawal Service provides information on wholesale shipments of food and related items. These data allow monitoring of product category sales trends and market share trends, both nationally and in 54 major market areas. These data are less subject to short-term fluctuations due to local conditions than are data gathered at the retail level. However, they lag retail sales, do not cover direct store-delivered products, and provide only shipments data.

Retail Sales

Retail sales data are available from both audits and scanner-based retail panels. Scanner panels provide more current data at shorter time intervals than do audits. However, audits cover outlets not equipped with scanners.

Scanner data are particularly useful to both retailers and manufacturers for measuring the aggregate impact of coupons, in-store promotions, point-of-purchase displays, price discounts, and so forth. Table 5 – 1 illustrates the use of this type of data to analyze price promotions. Measuring only the sales of the promoted brand would lead a manager to the conclusion that the fifth (least) most popular brand should be promoted. However, an analysis of category sales reveals that sales increases of minor brands on sale come as a result of the cannibalization of the more popular brands. In contrast, price reductions on the leading brands appear to increase overall category sales.

Data and analyses such as those shown in Table 5 – 1 are particularly useful for retailers. PromotionScan, a tracking service based on IRI's retail panel, is particularly useful to manufacturers. In one application, a snack-food manufacturer was running a national promotional campaign with no regional variation. PromotionScan analysis quickly revealed strong regional variations in response to the promotion. The manufacturer was then able to reduce spending in low-response areas. The results were stable overall revenues with a 20 per cent reduction in promotion expenditures.[13]

Table 5 – 1 Sale Price Analysis Using Retail Scanner Data

Price Discount	Percentage Increase in Margarine Brand (Category) Sales				
	Leading Brand	2nd Leading Brand	3rd 3rd Leading Brand	4th 4th Leading Brand	5th Leading Brand
10%	50% (5%)	53% (5%)	51% (2%)	52% (1%)	63% (1%)
20%	137% (16%)	145% (14%)	141% (6%)	144% (6%)	182% (1%)
30%	296% (38%)	319% (35%)	307% (16%)	316% (16%)	425% (5%)

Source: R. C. Blattberg and W. R. Bishop Jr., "Make Sense and Dollars from Scan Data," *The Nielsen Researcher* (Spring 1987), 19.

Household Purchases

Data on household consumption are available from both diary- and scanner-based household panels. Household consumption data allows the firm to monitor shifts in an individual's or market segment's purchasing patterns over time. This allows the firm to evaluate the effects of both its own and its competitors' marketing activities on specific market segments. For example, if

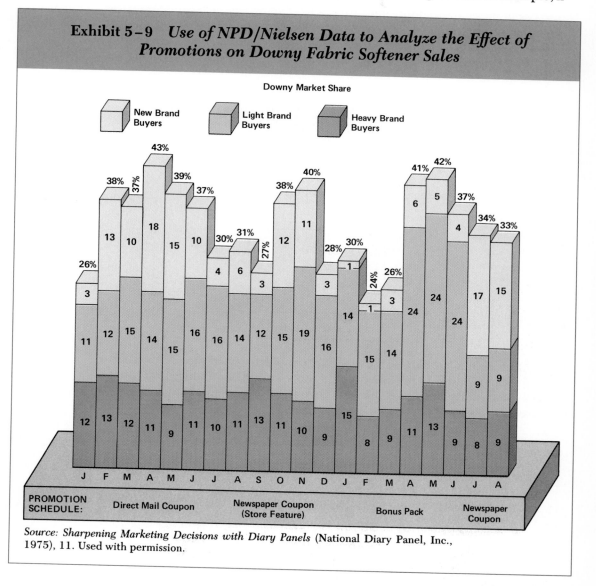

Exhibit 5–9 *Use of NPD/Nielsen Data to Analyze the Effect of Promotions on Downy Fabric Softener Sales*

Source: Sharpening Marketing Decisions with Diary Panels (National Diary Panel, Inc., 1975), 11. Used with permission.

a competitor introduces a larger package, the firm can tell what type (demographic and product usage characteristics) and how many people are switching to the new size. Exhibit 5–9 illustrates how NPD/Nielsen analyzed the impact of various promotional deals on new buyers, light-brand buyers, and heavy-brand buyers of Downy Fabric Softener.

Household panel data also serve as an important basis for forecasting the sales level or market share of a new product. A new product will often attract a number of purchasers simply because it is new. However, its ultimate success depends on how many of these initial purchasers become repeat purchasers. Exhibit 5–10 illustrates this problem and describes NPD/Nielsen's solution.

Exhibit 5–10 *Predicting New Product Sales Using NPD/ Nielsen Data*

The following graph shows Fruit Float's early share performance . . . by most measures an apparent success in the making in the $110,000,000 packaged pudding/whipped dessert market.

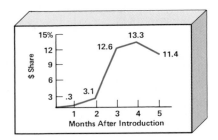

But, a detailed look at the composition of that early share indicated repeat purchases were slow to build; only strong continuing trial purchases supported sales . . . when trial purchases ceased, share declined dramatically.

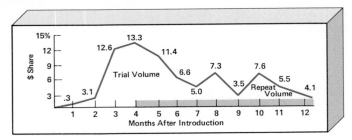

This could easily be seen even at 5 months when total share was broken apart into the contribution from new buyers (trial component) versus repurchases by earlier triers (repeat component):

COMPONENTS OF MARKET SHARE												
Period of	Share Contribution in Months After Introduction											
Initial Trial	1	2	3	4	5	6	7	8	9	10	11	12
1	.3	—	—	—	—	—	—	—	—	—	—	—
2		3.1	.7	.2	.2	.2	.2	.1	—	.1	—	.1
3			11.9	1.4	.5	—	—	.2	.1	.2	.1	—
4				11.7	1.7	.8	.2	.4	.2	.1	.1	.3
5					9.2	1.4	.8	.3	.1	.2	.1	.1
6						4.4	.8	.5	.2	.2	.1	.2
7							3.2	.8	.4	.4	.2	—
8								6.0	.9	.6	.4	.2
9									1.6	.3	.1	.1
10										5.5	.9	.5
11											3.4	.5
12												2.1
Total Share	.3	3.1	12.6	13.3	11.4	6.6	5.0	7.3	3.5	7.6	5.5	4.1
Trial Component	.3	3.1	11.9	11.7	9.2	4.4	3.2	6.0	1.6	5.5	3.4	2.1
Repeat Component	—	—	.7	1.6	2.4	2.2	1.8	2.3	1.9	2.1	2.0	2.0

While the poor repeat purchase volume in this example was easily spotted even in the above simplistic manner, most products require more sophisticated analysis to predict long run share. To do this, NPD uses three different forecasting models.

Source: Sharpening Marketing Decisions with Diary Panels (National Purchase Diary Panel, Inc., 1975), 13. Used with permission.

Media Usage

Given the billions spent on advertising, it is not surprising that substantial effort is expended to measure media usage. Exhibit 5–11 describes the major data sources available.

Exhibit 5–11 *Major Data Sources on Media Usage*

Media	Organization	Methodology
Newspapers	Simmons Market Research	National personal interviews (annual)
	Birch/Scarborough Research	Top market telephone interviews (annual)

129

Magazines	Standard Rate and Data	Semiannual circulation data
	Birch/Scarborough Research	Top market telephone interviews (annual)
	Simmons Market Research	National personal interview (annual)
	Starch INRA Hooper	Recall of readership of specific ads based on personal interviews of 100 or more of each gender
Radio	Arbitron	Top market periodic one-week diaries
	Simmons Market Research	National personal interview (annual)
Television	Nielsen	National people meter panel (can be combined with scanner panel data) and top market diaries
	NPD/Nielsen	Selected market television meters (can be combined with commercials aired and scanner panel data)
	Simmons	National two-week diary (annual)
	Arbitron	Top market (212) one-week diaries with television meters in 14 markets
	IRI	Selected market television meters (can be combined with scanner panel data
	Birch/Scarborough	Top market one-week diary (annual)
Billboards	Traffic Audit Bureau	Number of people passing specific locations
VCR	AGB	Integrated into its people-meter service

Attitudes/Knowledge/Behaviors

Commercial surveys, both periodic and panel-based, are the primary general sources of data on consumer attitudes, knowledge, and behavior. For example, a firm desiring to improve or alter its corporate image could engage in a variety of advertising and public relations programs in different regions of the country. Using one of the weekly shared-interview services, it could economically determine the relative impact on each approach over time.

MRCA provides a popular service for the food industry with its Menu Census. This service has the following characteristics:

— 2,000 households per year, containing over 5,500 members, based on rotating samples of 500 households per quarter

— Nationally representative samples — matched to U.S. Census figures for census regions, metro area size, household size, homemaker age, household income

— Diaries returned each day

— Each household reports the eatings of each household member for 14 consecutive days

— About 6 households start reporting each day of the year

— 77 diaries cover each day of the year

— All in-home and away-from-home food and beverage consumption is reported

— All ingredients and cooking agents used to prepare foods at home are included

— How dishes are prepared, including details on brand name, form as purchased, and packaging material

— Household demographics, household-member classifications, and attitudes, awareness and interests of the homemaker are provided

NPD Research provides a similar service known as NET (National Eating Trends). Another widely used service is The Monitor Survey offered by Yankelovich Clancy Shulman. Exhibit 5–12 provides a brief description of this service.

Using Commercial Surveys, Audits, and Panels

In this chapter we have briefly described only a few of the many services available to provide data that generally fall between secondary data and primary data. Such data often are not exactly what the researcher would prefer,

Exhibit 5-12 *The Monitor™ Service*

Based on an annual survey of 2,500 adults, this service provides:

1. Longitudinal tracking of over 50 social trends, tracked over past years to the present.

   Some of these trends (there are additions or deletions made from year to year) are:
   —Rejection of Authority
   —Return of Age and Experience
   —Commitment to Buy American
   —Search for Community
   —Need for Control
   —Reverence for Science
   —Responsiveness to Fantasy
   —Hunger for Feedback
   —Social Pluralism

2. Behavioral manifestations of these trends. For example:
   —Interest in regular performance of household chores and
   —Willingness to accept ad-hoc meal schedules (both related to the trend "Tolerance for Chaos and Disorder")
   —Belief that big business pays more attention to consumers these days and
   —Willingness to "beat the system" (both related to the trend "Belief in Consumer Power")
   —Relative guilt about buying products from foreign countries and
   —Perceptions of quality of American products (both related to the trend "Commitment to Buy American")

3. A detailed demographic question battery. Over 50 demographic variables including:
   —Standard demographics such as age, income-earning profile, age of youngest child
   —Education of respondent's parents
   —Household composition
   —Respondent's career information in depth, such as whether a wife's return to the work force represents a career to her or just a job.

4. Attitudinal segmentation of the population as an aid to understanding broad social trends

   The power of our testing and modeling produces a segmentation that is driven not by demographics—which would yield only an ordinary market segmentation—but by values. We currently identify 5 discrete types of people with discrete groupings of values.

Used with permission from Yankelovich Clancy Shulman.

due to timing, sample, or measurement characteristics. However, current or rapid availability and relatively low cost make such data very useful. Researchers need to be aware of those services relevant to their organization and to pursue their use actively where appropriate.

Review Questions

5.1. What is a *commercial survey?* A *periodic survey?* A *panel survey?* A *shared survey?*

5.2. Describe the *National Restaurant Market Index.*

5.3. What is an *interval panel?* What are the advantages and problems of surveys based on interval panels?

5.4. How does the NFO interval panel differ from the CMP interval panel?

5.5. What are the advantages of a *shared survey?*

5.6. What is an *audit?*

5.7. How does a *store audit* differ from a *product audit?*

5.8. What is a *retail distribution audit?*

5.9. What is a *panel?* A *continuous panel?*

5.10. Describe SAMI's *Census of Warehouse Shipments.*

5.11. What are *retail panels?* What are their advantages?

5.12. What is a *UPC bar code?* An *EPOS?*

5.13. What is a *consumer diary panel?* What are its advantages?

5.14. What are *consumer scanner panels?* What are their advantages?

5.15. How does IRI's approach to consumer scanner panels differ from Nielsen's?

5.16. What are *electronic panels?* What are their problems and benefits?

5.17. What is a *people meter?* Why has Nielsen switched to people meters?

5.18. What is meant by *single-source* data?

5.19. Describe two single-source data systems.

5.20. What are the primary commercial data sources available for:
  a. wholesale sales
  b. retail sales
  c. household consumption
  d. consumer attitudes, knowledge, or behaviors

5.21. What are the primary commercial data sources available on the use by consumers of:
  a. newspapers
  b. magazines
  c. radio
  d. television
  e. billboards

5.22. Describe the *Monitor Service.*

Discussion Questions/Problems

5.23. Do shared surveys generate primary or secondary data?

5.24. Describe how a brand manager could use Audits & Surveys National Restaurant Market Index (Exhibit 5–1).

5.25. What type of nonresponse error is likely to affect interval panel surveys? What can be done about this?

5.26. Describe three marketing problems for which *each* of the following would be an appropriate technique (12 problems in total):
   a. a periodic commercial survey
   b. a one-time interval panel survey
   c. a one-time shared survey
   d. a series of shared surveys

5.27. Describe three marketing problems for which each of the following would be an appropriate technique (15 in total)
   a. retail store audit
   b. wholesale shipments panel
   c. household diary panel
   d. household scanner panel
   e. single-source data

5.28. Given the advantages of scanner-generated data, is there a future for retail store audits?

5.29. Given the advantages of scanner-generated data, is there a future for household diary panels?

5.30. What problems do you see with the use of people meters?

5.31. Compared to retail level sales, what advantages would household level data offer a manufacturer evaluating a new flavor addition to a snack-food line?

5.32. Suggest three specific applications for the type of data generated by the Monitor Service (Exhibit 5–12).

Projects

5.33. Keep a record of your television viewing for two weeks. Have a friend do the same. How accurate is your record? How accurate do you think your friend's is? What could be done to improve the accuracy?

5.34. Keep a record of your radio listening for two weeks. Have a friend do the same. How accurate is your record? How accurate do you think your friend's is? What could be done to improve the accuracy?

5.35. Keep a record of the food and beverage you consume for two weeks. Have a friend do the same. How accurate is your record? How accurate do you think your friend's is? What could be done to improve the accuracy?

5.36. Keep a record of your personal grooming activities for two weeks. Have a friend do the same. How accurate is your record? How accurate do you think your friend's is? What could be done to improve the accuracy?

5.37. Interview one of the following people and ascertain the sources of media usage that he or she feels are most important.
   a. local radio station manager
   b. local television station manager
   c. local newspaper manager

5.38. Interview one of the following people and ascertain the sources of media usage that he or she feels are most important.
   a. media manager for a local ad agency
   b. advertising manager for a major department store
   c. marketing/advertising manager for a consumer goods manufacturer

References

[1] *Insights Into Consumer Behavior* (New York: The NPD Group, 1987), 8.

[2] J. Graham, "Bar Codes Becoming Universal," *Advertising Age*, April 18, 1988, 36.

[3] "Merchandise Ploys Effective? Scanners Know," *Marketing News*, January 4, 1985, 17.

[4] A detailed description of geodemographic segmentation systems and the PRIZM system in particular is in D. I. Hawkins, R. J. Best, and K. A. Coney, *Consumer Behavior* (Homewood, Ill.: Irwin/BPI, 1989), 415–426.

[5] For a discussion of VALS see ibid., 405–415.

[6] A. S. C. Ehrenberg and J. Wakshlag, "Repeat-Viewing with People Meters," *Journal of Advertising Research* (February 1987), 9–13: "Nielsen People Meter Service Launched," *Nielsen Newscast* (3, 1987); L. R. Stoddard, Jr., "The History of People Meters," *Journal of Advertising Research* (October 1987), 10–12; and P. Soong, "The Statistical Reliability of People Meter Ratings," *Journal of Advertising Research* (February 1988), 50–56.

[7] Ibid., "Tests Show That Accuracy of AGB People Meter High in Boston Area," *Marketing News*, March 14, 1986, 9; and J. A. Dimling, "How Will NTI in March 1989 Compare with NTI in March 1987?" *Nielsen Newscast* (Spring 1988), 2–8.

[8] *What TV Ratings Really Mean* (New York: A. C. Nielsen Company, 1987).

[9] C. Wilson, "People-meter Fight Hits France," *Marketing News*, January 25, 1988, 66.

[10] Ibid., and D. Lu and D. A. Kiewit, "Passive People Meters," *Journal of Advertising Research* (June 1987), 9–14.

[11] L. R. Stoddard, Jr., "Will Single Source Data Change Media Planning?" *Journal of Advertising Research* (April 1986), 13–15; P. Chouvou et al., "The Single-Source Concept," G. J. Eskin, "Applications of Electronic Single-Source Measurement Systems," W. J. McKenna, "ScanAmerica Buyer Graphic Ratings," all in *European Research* (#1, 1987), 4–11, 12–20, and 28–33.

[12] See M. J. Naples, "Media Research," *European Research* (#4, 1986), 186–96.

[13] J. Larkin, "Shifted Emphasis Cuts Costs," *InfoScan News* (November 1987), 7.

Survey Research

Automobile manufacturers interview visitors at major auto shows at learn of their reactions to new models and prototypes of new models. Traditionally, interviewers with questionnaires on clipboards would ask the questions and record the answers. After the show, the forms would be coded, the data tabulated, and, weeks later, a report would be prepared.

At the Fall 1984 Chicago Auto Show, Chevrolet used Demand Research Corp., to try a new approach. Approximately 800 attendees were recruited and asked to complete a self-administered questionnaire that was displayed on the monitor of an IBM PC. The responses were transmitted via phone line to a larger computer and a complete analysis was available shortly after the final interview was completed. The results indicated a need for a design change on a prototype of the Astro Van that was on display. The speed with which the responses were analyzed made such a change feasible.[1]

Survey research is the most common method of collecting primary data for marketing decisions. Surveys can provide data on attitudes, feelings, beliefs, past and intended behaviors, knowledge, ownership, personal characteristics, and other *descriptive* items. They also can provide evidence of *association* (individuals who report high income also report a high level of consumption of opera tickets). However, surveys can seldom prove *cause* (income may or may not cause opera ticket consumption).

Survey research is concerned with the administration of questionnaires (interviewing). In this chapter, a number of issues associated with administering a questionnaire are examined. First, the issues of degree of structure and degree of directness of the interview are addressed. Attention then moves to

137

the types of survey: personal, mail, computer, and telephone. The criteria relevant for judging which type of survey to use in a particular situation are described in some detail. Finally, an in-depth treatment of the problem of nonresponse error is provided.

The Nature of Survey Research

Survey research is the *systematic gathering of information from respondents for the purpose of understanding and/or predicting some aspect of the behavior of the population of interest.* As the term is typically used, it implies that the information has been gathered with some version of a questionnaire. Exhibit 6–1 illustrates the use of a survey to investigate consumer response to two proposed bank advertisements.

The survey researcher must be concerned with sampling, questionnaire design, questionnaire administration, and data analysis.[2] This portion of this chapter is concerned with questionnaire administration. Sampling, questionnaire design, and data analysis are covered in separate chapters.

The administration of a questionnaire to an individual or group of individuals is called an *interview*.

Exhibit 6–1 *Marine Midland Bank's Use of Mall-Intercept Interviews*

In March, Marine Midland Bank's advertising agency presented the management team with two different commercials to support Marine Midland's June introduction of an in-store banking system:

1. THE SERGEANT CONCEPT — The purpose of this spot was to tell viewers that the bank's customers now could do their everyday banking in supermarkets. To break through clutter and present an atypical bank commercial, a fast-paced, informative spot was designed using a stereotypical Marine Corps-like sergeant (playing off the bank's name and also tying in with the bank's slogan, "Tell It to the Marine") as the spokesman.

2. THE CASHCARD CONCEPT — The purpose of this spot was the same, but the straightforward message was presented in a gimmick-free manner. The video portion concentrated on the plastic card that provided access to the in-store banking facility. Animated graphics of the card gave way to a typical supermarket scene and the banking location.

Management was unable to agree on the best approach and asked the research department for assistance. A mall intercept survey was designed to provide the information. A mall intercept interview involves stopping shoppers in a shopping mall at random; determining if they have the characteristics of interest such as age, occupation, or prior product use; inviting them into the research firm's interviewing facilities that are located at the mall; and conducting the interview.

The two basic issues to be addressed in the study were:

1. Which ad concept communicates the in-store banking service more effectively?

2. Are there major negative attributes or problems with either approach?

In total, 400 interviews were conducted in two major New York cities. The sample was evenly distributed between the two test markets and two concepts. Each respondent evaluated only one ad.

To test the ad concepts, renderings of the commercials were prepared and slides were developed. The slides were presented to the respondents by projecting them on a screen in rapid sequence with a synchronized sound track. Each respondent was shown the commercial twice before the interviewer asked the questions, which took about 15 minutes.

Based on the results of this study, the following recommendations were made:

1. The sergeant concept should be used as the bank's creative strategy plan for introducing in-store banking.

2. The sergeant commercial should have more of a personal touch and a happy, pleasant environment so as to be more appealing to the target market.

3. Measures should be taken to alleviate the misconceptions and confusion that the service is accessed by credit cards.

Source: Adopted from A. K. Sen, "Bank Uses Mall-Intercept Interviews to Test Ad Concepts," *Marketing News*, January 22, 1982, 20.

Types of Interviews

Interviews are classified according to their degree of structure and directness. *Structure* refers to the amount of freedom the interviewer has in altering the questionnaire to meet the unique situation posed by each interview. *Directness* involves the extent to which the respondent is aware of (or is likely to be aware of) the nature and purpose of the survey.

Characteristics of Structured and Unstructured Interviews

As stated earlier, the degree of *structure* refers to the extent to which an interviewer is restricted to following the wording and instructions in a questionnaire. Structured interviews offer a number of advantages to the marketing researcher. Interviewer bias tends to be at a minimum in structured interviews. In addition, it is possible to utilize less skilled (and less expensive) interviewers with a structured format because their duties are basically confined to reading questions and recording answers.

These advantages of structured interviews may be purchased at the expense of richer or more complete information that skillful interviewers could elicit if allowed the freedom. Relatively unstructured interviews become more important in marketing surveys as *less* is known about the variables being investigated. Thus, unstructured techniques are used in exploratory surveys and for investigating complex or unstructured topic areas, such as personal values and purchase motivations. They should generally precede, and guide the development of, structured interviews.

Characteristics of Direct and Indirect Interviews

Direct interviewing, often referred to as *undisguised,* involves asking questions such that the respondent is aware of the underlying purpose of the survey. Most marketing surveys are relatively direct. That is, although the name of the sponsoring firm is frequently kept anonymous, the general area of interest is often obvious to the respondent.

Direct questions are generally easy for the respondent to answer, tend to have the same meaning across respondents, and have responses that are relatively easy to interpret. However, occasions may arise when respondents are either unable or unwilling to answer direct questions. For example, respondents may not be able to verbalize their subconscious reasons for purchases or they may not want to admit that certain purchases were made for socially unacceptable reasons. In these cases, some form of indirect interviewing is required.

Indirect interviewing, often referred to as *disguised,* involves asking questions such that the respondent does not know what the objective of the study is. A person who is asked to describe the "typical person" who rides a motorcycle to work may not be aware that the resulting description is a measure of his or her own attitudes toward motorcycles and this use of them.

Both structure and directness represent continuums rather than discrete categories. However, it is sometimes useful to categorize surveys based on which end of each continuum they are nearest. This leads to four types of interviews: *structured-direct, structured-indirect, unstructured-direct,* and *unstructured-indirect.*

140

Four Categories of Interviews

The *structured-direct* interview is the most commonly used technique in marketing surveys. It is simply a prespecified set of relatively direct or obvious questions. Virtually all mail and computer surveys are of this type, as are many telephone and personal surveys. Structured-direct techniques are used more often in the final stages of research projects than in the earlier, more exploratory stages. This type of interview requires extensive initial preparation but allows the use of less highly trained interviewers and interpreters.

Unstructured-direct interviews are frequently used in marketing research,

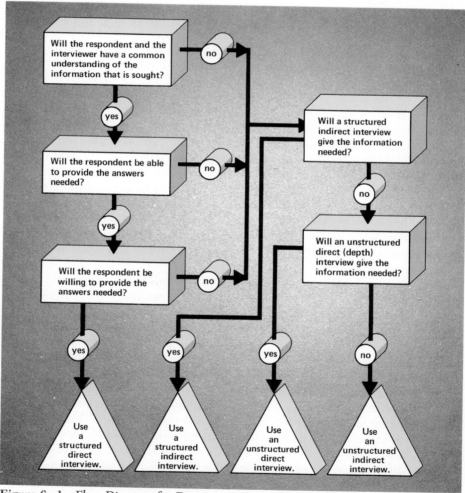

Figure 6–1   *Flow Diagram for Decision on Type of Interview to Use*

141

particularly in preliminary or exploratory research. The most common form of this approach is the *focus* group interview. *Structured-indirect* interviews are exemplified by the various projective techniques, such as word association and picture response. *Unstructured-indirect* interviews are seldom used in marketing research. The prototype example of this approach is the "psychiatrist's couch" interview.

Figure 6–1 is a flow diagram that illustrates the decisions leading to the selection of a type of interview.

Types of Surveys

Surveys are generally classified according to the method of communication used in the interviews: personal, telephone, mail, or computer. Figure 6–2 indicates the relative popularity of three of these techniques. Computer interviews are still uncommon. Each of the four methods is briefly described in the following sections:

Personal Interviews. *Personal interviews* are widely used in marketing research. In a personal interview, the interviewer asks the questions of the respondent in a face-to-face situation. The interview may take place at the respondent's home or at a central location, such as a shopping mall or a research office.

As Figure 6–2 indicates, *mall intercept interviews* (see Exhibit 6–1) are the predominant type of personal interview. The popularity of this type of personal interview is the result of its cost advantage over door-to-door interviewing, the ability to demonstrate products or use equipment that cannot be easily transported, greater supervision of interviewers, and less elapsed time required.[3]

Mall-intercept interviews involve stopping shoppers in a shopping mall at random, qualifying them if necessary, inviting them into the research firm's interviewing facilities that are located at the mall, and conducting the interview. Qualifying a respondent means ensuring that the respondent meets the sampling criteria. This could involve a quota sample where there is a desire to interview a given number of people with certain demographic characteristics such as age and gender. Or it could involve ensuring that all the respondents use the product category being investigated.

Shopping mall interviews generally take place inside special facilities in the center that are operated by a commercial research firm. These facilities make possible a variety of interview formats not available when the interviews are conducted door-to-door. Exhibit 6–2 describes the facilities available at a Market Facts, Inc., mall interview location.

Individuals who visit shopping malls are *not* representative of the entire population of the United States. In fact, a federal district judge required

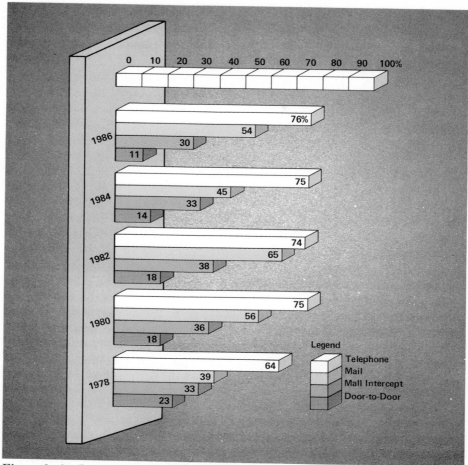

Figure 6–2   *Participation by Type of Interview°*
° *By individuals who participated in at least one survey in the past year.*

Source: B. J. Kyzr-Sheeley, "Results of Walker's 1986 Study Indicate Favorable Industry Image."
The Marketing Researcher (Vol 16, No. 3), 2.

Lorillard to withdraw a comparative advertising campaign for Triumph cigarettes which was based on mall intercept interviews and preference tests for this reason. After hearing testimony from market research experts, the judge stated: "I conclude that the percentages used, as derived from a mall intercept study, do not constitute national statistics." [4]

Whereas mall intercept interviews do not produce representative samples of the entire population, most applied research studies do not require such a sample. For many consumer products, shopping mall customers constitute a

Exhibit 6–2 *Facilities Available at a Market Facts, Inc.,*
Mall Interview Location

- Sound-conditioned interview rooms and booths
- Flexible areas for large displays
- Fully equipped kitchen with freezer storage
- Studio-quality monitoring system with three one-way mirrors, including kitchen observation
- Full-sound and closed-circuit TV monitors, cassette, reel-to-reel, and three-quarter-inch videotape recorders
- Focus group facilities
- Controlled track lighting
- Client conference room
- Twin vanity rooms
- INTERQUEST, an on-line CRT (computer) interviewing technique

major share of the market and therefore are an adequate sampling universe. In addition, careful control procedures can provide fairly representative samples.[5] (See Chapter 15.)

An additional problem with intercept interviews at malls where research firms maintain permanent facilities is "respondent burnout." That is, a significant portion of a given mall's customers shop at the mall regularly. Over time, these regular shoppers will be randomly selected into numerous studies. Both their willingness to cooperate and the nature of their responses will change as they participate in more and more studies.

Of course, intercept interviews are not limited to shopping malls. Increasingly, intercept interviews are conducted at locations relevant to the population of interest. For example, Burgoyne has conducted intercept interviews at specialty retail outlets such as pet stores, banks, fast food restaurants, truck stops, stadiums, movie theaters, golf courses, bowling alleys, and college campuses.

An emerging type of personal interviewing is the *in-store intercept.* In-store intercept interviews involve interviewing individuals inside retail outlets, generally immediately after they have purchased the product category in question. One version of this approach, the purchase intercept technique (PIT), is described in Exhibit 6–3.

Exhibit 6–3   *The Purchase Intercept Technique*

The purchase intercept technique (PIT) involves (1) observing shoppers purchasing the product category in a sample of stores, (2) recording relevant observational data such as brand(s) and size(s) purchased, and (3) interviewing the purchasers immediately to ascertain purchase motives, brands considered, and so forth.

This approach offers a number of advantages. First, the observational portion ensures accuracy in terms of brand and size purchased. This is a particularly important feature because consumers frequently are incorrect in reporting the last brand purchased. Second, the questions are presented while the decision is fresh in the respondent's mind. This not only improves recall but, since the questioning seems relevant, also results in high response rates. This is turn leads to a relatively low cost per completed interview. Third, there is no doubt that the actual purchaser is responding to the questions. Finally, the researcher can control, or at least measure, the actual purchase environment such as shelf facing and P.O.P. material.

This approach is particularly appropriate for items purchased infrequently and low-involvement products. In both cases, the closeness of the purchase and questioning enhances recall of the actual decision process used. It is also valuable when data are needed quickly on the impact of new marketing efforts by the firm or its competition. In addition, it can be used to generate a sample frame for subsequent detailed interviews.

The PIT approach has several weaknesses as well: (1) the sample is constrained to those who purchase during the time of the study, (2) the sample is limited to purchasers rather than users or deciders, (3) some stores will not allow in-store interviewing, (4) nonstore purchasers are excluded, and (5) it uses personal interviews and is subject to the problems associated with this form of data collection.

Source: S. H. McIntyre and S. D. F. G. Bender, "The Purchase Intercept Technique (PIT) in Comparison to Telephone and Mail Surveys," *Journal of Retailing* (Winter 1986), 364–383, and G. Meyers, "Consumers Offer 'Fresh' Purchase Data When Questioned in the Store" *Marketing News*, January 2, 1987, 28–29.

Telephone Interviews.   *Telephone interviews* involve the presentation of the questionnaire by telephone.[6] Low-priced WATS (Wide Area Telephone Service) lines have made nationwide telephone interviewing from a central location practical.

Computer-Assisted Telephone Interviewing (**CATI**) will eventually dominate telephone interviewing.[7] A CATI system involves programming a survey questionnaire directly into a computer. The telephone interviewer then reads the questions from a television-type screen and records the answer directly on the terminal keyboard or directly on the screen with a light pen.

The flexibility associated with the computer provides a number of advantages. Often the exact set of questions a respondent is to receive will depend on answers to earlier questions. For example, individuals who have a child under age three might receive one set of questions concerning food purchases whereas other individuals would receive a different set. The computer, in effect, allows the creation of an "individualized" questionnaire for each respondent based on answers to prior questions.

A second advantage is the ability of the computer to present different versions of the same question automatically. For example, when asking people to answer questions that have several stated alternatives, it is desirable to rotate the order in which the alternatives are presented. This is expensive if printed questionnaires are used, but is easy with a CATI system.

Another advantage of CATI systems is the ease and speed with which a "bad" question can be changed or a new question added. It is not uncommon to discover a poorly worded or missing question fairly early in a survey. If a printed questionnaire is being used, it is time-consuming and difficult to make changes. Again, however, it is easy to make such changes with CATI.

Data analysis is virtually instantaneous with a CATI system. Since the data are entered directly into the computer, an analysis can be produced at any time during the survey. These interim reports can be generated daily if desired. Interim reports may allow one to stop a survey if the "answer" becomes clear before the scheduled number of interviews has been completed. Final reports can also be produced rapidly.[8]

CATI systems are most appropriate for complex and/or large sample surveys. However, the substantial amount of "up-front" programming required reduces their value for other applications. In addition, the interviewers must have a high level of keyboard as well as interviewing skills.

Mail Interviews. *Mail interviews* may be delivered in any of several ways. Generally, they are mailed to the respondent and the completed questionnaire is returned by mail to the researcher. However, the forms can be left and/or picked up by company personnel. They can be also distributed by means of magazine and newspaper inserts or they can be attached to products. The warranty card attached to most consumer products serves as a useful source of survey data for many manufacturers. As Figure 6–2 indicates, mail interviews are widely used.

Computer Interviews. In a computer interview, the computer presents the questions to the respondents on a TV-type screen and respondents answer via a console.[9] This system reduces interviewer bias and interaction problems. In addition, it provides the same flexibility and speed advantages associated with the CATI systems described earlier. However, it does require the respondent to be willing and able to interact directly with the computer. Further, open-ended questions are seldom practical since many individuals cannot type.

Computer interviews are of two types. One type involves the deliberate selection of respondents in a door-to-door, shopping mall, or trade-show environment. Selected respondents are asked to participate and may be screened by the researcher or the computer. The second type involves placing the computer in an appropriate environment such as a shopping mall, retail store, or trade show along with a sign inviting participation. Respondents are self-selected and an interviewer or "host" need not be present.

Computer interviewing is beginning to gain acceptance. The popularity of mall-intercept interviews means that many interviews take place where PCs are easily accessible. Furthermore, the development of small portable PCs means that computer interviews can be conducted in a door-to-door situation.

Computer interviewing is most common in industrial and trade (distribution) applications. Trade shows are frequently used as locations for conducting interviews with engineers, purchasers, and other industrial respondents. For example, Converse Inc. conducted a computer interview "competitive per-

---

Exhibit 6–4 *Applications of Computer Interviewing*

- Keebler Co., Elmhurst, Ill., built traffic and collected data from a taste test of its new whole-grain wheat cracker at a National Restaurant show.

- Winnebago Industries Inc., Forest City, Iowa, sampled reaction to its plan to enter the licensed sporting-goods field with tents, canoes, life jackets, camp stoves, and the like at a National Sporting Goods Association show.

- Borg-Warner Acceptance Corp., Chicago, conducted an image and media-usage study about trade inventory financing at a National Association of Music Merchants show.

- Levi Strauss & Co., San Francisco, surveyed the trade's opinions of trends in active wear at a National Sporting Goods Association show.

- SmithKline Beckman Corp., Philadelphia, evaluated opinions about competitors in the diagnostic medical equipment market at a Health Industry Distributors Association show.

Source: B. Whalen, "On-site Computer Interviewing Yields Research Data Instantly," *Marketing News,* November 9, 1984, 17.

ception" analysis at a National Sporting Goods Association show. It found that the trade viewed Converse to be "strong" and Nike to be "weak" in distribution and product availability. Converse then ran trade ads stating the following:

> No one can beat a team with 11 fast distribution centers. In fact, in a survey conducted among dealers at the recent NSGA Show in Chicago, Converse ranked first with respect to "best delivery" among the leading brands. And since the results of fast turnaround are faster product turnover, that means increased sales and a higher return on your investment.[10]

Exhibit 6–4 provides additional illustrations of trade and industrial applications of computer interviewing.

Criteria for the Selection of a Survey Method

A number of criteria are relevant for judging which type of survey to use in a particular situation. These criteria are (1) *complexity*, (2) *required amount of data*, (3) *desired accuracy*, (4) *sample control*, (5) *time requirements*, (6) *acceptable level of nonresponse*, and (7) *cost*.

Complexity of the Questionnaire

Although researchers generally attempt to minimize complexity, some subject areas still require relatively complex questionnaires. For example, the sequence or number of questions asked often depends on the answer to previous questions. Consider the following questions:

2a. Have you ever read a copy of the evening *Tribune?*
    __ YES
    __ NO (GO TO Q. 3a)

   b. Did you happen to read or look into a weekday copy — that is, a Monday to Friday copy, of the *Tribune* during the past seven days?
    __ YES, HAVE READ
    __ NO, HAVE NOT READ
    __ (GO TO Q. 3a)
    __ DON'T KNOW (GO TO Q. 3a)

   c. *Not counting today,* when was the last time you read or looked into a weekday copy of the *Tribune?*
(IF TODAY, ASK:) And when was the last time before today?[11]
    __ YESTERDAY
    __ EARLIER THAN YESTERDAY
    __ DON'T KNOW

It would make very little sense to ask someone question 2b. if the response to question 2a. had been "No." A trained interviewer who has practiced administering a given questionnaire can handle such "skip" questions. Similarly, a computer can present such questions in the correct order, based on the respondent's earlier answers. However, a respondent, seeing a questionnaire of this type for the first time, can easily become confused or discouraged. Thus, computer, personal, and telephone interviews are better suited to collect this type of information than are mail interviews.

Other aspects of complexity also tend to favor the use of personal interviews. Visual cues are necessary for many projective techniques, such as the picture response. Multiple-choice questions often require a visual presentation of the alternatives because the respondent cannot remember more than a few when they are presented orally. However, most attitude scales can be administered via the phone.[12]

The telephone, and often mail, are inappropriate for studies that require the respondent to react to the actual product, advertising copy, package design, or other physical characteristics. Techniques that require relatively complex instructions are best administered by means of personal interviews. Similarly, if the response required by the technique is extensive, such as with many conjoint analysis studies, personal interviews are better.

Amount of Data

Closely related to the issue of complexity is the amount of data to be generated by a given questionnaire. The amount of data actually involves two separate issues: (1) *How much time will it take to complete the entire questionnaire?* and (2) *How much effort is required by the respondent to complete the questionnaire?*[13] For example, 1 open-ended question may take a respondent 5 minutes to answer, and a 25-item multiple-choice questionnaire may take the same length of time. Moreover, much more effort may go into writing down a 5-minute essay than in checking off choices on 25 multiple-choice questions.

Personal interviews can, in general, be longer than other types. Social motives play an important role in personal interviews. It would be "impolite" to terminate an interview with someone in a face-to-face situation. However, the refusal rate has been found to double (from 21 to 41 per cent) when either telephone or personal interviews last over five minutes.[14]

In addition, the amount of effort required of the respondents is generally less in a personal survey than in a mail survey and often less than in a computer or telephone survey. Answers to open-ended questions, responses to projective techniques, and other lengthy responses are recorded by the interviewer. This relieves the respondent of the tedious task of writing or typing answers. Both telephone and personal interviews share this advantage. However, personal interviews have the additional advantage of allowing the presentation of visual cues that can reduce the effort required by the respondent.

Telephone interviews are traditionally shorter than personal interviews. The ease of terminating a telephone conversation, coupled with the more suspicious nature of a telephone call, tends to limit the length of time a person will spend on a telephone.

Mail surveys are probably affected more by the type of questions than by the absolute length of the questionnaire. Open-ended questions require considerable effort on the part of the respondent, whereas an equally long multiple-choice response will take much less effort. The intuitive idea that short questionnaires will generate a higher response rate than longer questionnaires has *not* been supported by research.[15]

Accuracy of the Resultant Data

The accuracy of data obtained by surveys can be affected by a number of factors, such as interviewer effects, sampling effects, and effects caused by questionnaire design. In this section, we are concerned with errors induced by the survey method itself, particularly responses to sensitive questions and interviewer effects.

Sensitive Questions.   Personal interviews and, to a lesser extent, telephone interviews involve social interaction between the respondent and the interviewer. Therefore, there is concern that the respondent may not answer potentially embarrassing questions or questions with socially desirable responses accurately. Since mail and computer interviews reduce social interaction, it is often assumed that they will yield more accurate responses. However, research indicates that *well-constructed* and *well-administered* questionnaires will *generally* yield similar results, regardless of the method of administration, as shown in Table 6–1.[16]

Table 6–1   Proportion of Incorrect Responses by Survey Type°

| | | | *Topic* | | |
Survey Type	Registered to Vote	Own Library Card	Voted in Primary	Have Filed Bankruptcy	Have Been Charged with Drunken Driving
Personal	.15	.19	.39	.32	.47
Telephone	.17	.21	.31	.29	.46
Self-administered	.12	.18	.36	.32	.54

° Adapted from W. Locander, S. Sudman, and N. Bradburn, "An Investigation of Interviewer Method, Threat, and Response Distortion," *Journal of American Statistical Association* (June 1976), 271.

Interview Effects. The ability of interviewers to alter questions, their appearance, their manner of speaking, the intentional and unintentional cues provided, and the way they probe can be a disadvantage. It means that, in effect, each respondent may receive a slightly different interview.[17] Depending on the topic of the survey, the interviewer's social class, age, sex, race, authority, expectations, opinions, and voice *can* affect the results.[18]

The danger of interviewer effects is greatest in personal interviews. Telephone interviews are also subject to interviewer effects. Mail and computer surveys have minimal interviewer effects.

Questionnaire designs that minimize interviewer freedom also reduce the potential for interviewer bias. The most effective approach involves the skillful selection, training, and control of interviewers. However, after the most cost-effective design principles have been applied, some interviewer bias is apt to remain. This should be estimated subjectively or, preferably, statistically.[19]

One final problem that arises with the use of telephone and personal interviews is *interviewer cheating*. That is, for various reasons, interviewers may falsify all or parts of an interview. This is a severe enough problem that most commercial survey researchers engage in a process called *validation* or *verification*. For example, Sears requires that the local supervisor validate 10 per cent of each interviewer's calls and that the central office validate an additional 15 per cent.

Validation involves reinterviewing a sample of the population that completed the initial interview. In this reinterview, verification is sought that the interview took place and was conducted properly.

Other Error Sources. Other types of inaccuracies can have a differential impact on the different methods of administration. The respondent cannot seek clarification of confusing questions or terms when mail surveys are used. In a personal interview the interviewer can, by observing the respondent closely, be sure that the respondent understands the question. Another potential problem with mail questionnaires is that respondents can read the entire questionnaire prior to answering the questions or they can change answers to earlier questions after seeing later questions. This may result in less spontaneous and less revealing answers. Methods used to encourage individuals to respond to mail surveys such as prenotification, cover-letter messages, and follow-up contacts can reduce the accuracy of responses.[20] Such inducements may encourage "guessing" by uninformed respondents. However, such inducements do not necessarily reduce response accuracy. In fact, monetary inducements may *increase* response accuracy *if* the respondent can consult records such as insurance premiums or charge bills prior to responding.[21]

Sample Control

Each of the four interview techniques allows substantially different levels of control over *who* is interviewed. Personal and computer interviews offer the most *potential* for control over the sample. An explicit list of individuals or households is *not* required. Although such lists are desirable, various forms of area sampling can help the researcher to overcome most of the problems caused by the absence of a complete sampling frame (see Chapter 15). In addition, the researcher can control who is interviewed within the sampling unit and how much assistance from other members of the unit is permitted.

Controlling *who* within the household is interviewed can be expensive. If the purpose of the research is to investigate *household* behavior, such as appliance ownership, any available adult will probably be satisfactory. However, if the purpose is to investigate *individual* behavior, interviewing the most readily available adult within the household will often produce a biased sample. Thus, the researcher must randomly select from among those living at each household. The simplest means of selection is to interview the adult who last had (or next will have) a birthday.[22] The odds of *a* household member being at home are substantially larger than the odds of a *specific* household member being available. This means that there will be more "not-at-homes," which will increase interviewing costs substantially.

Evidence suggests that the potential for sample control in personal interviewing is seldom realized. A study conducted by the A. C. Nielsen Co. found serious bias in the sampling *execution* when personal interviews were used. A primary problem was the refusal of most interviewers to venture into strange neighborhoods in the evening.[23] This reduces contacts with single-parent families and families in which both spouses are employed.

Personal and computer interviews conducted in central locations, such as shopping malls, lose much of the control possible with home interviews because the interview is limited to the individuals who visit the shopping mall.

Telephone surveys are obviously limited to households with direct access to telephones. However, this is no longer a major restriction, as most businesses and U.S. households have a telephone. However, the fact that telephones are almost universally owned does not mean that lists of telephone numbers, such as telephone directories, are equally complete. Estimates of the percentage of phones not listed in a current telephone directory run as high as 60 per cent for some areas, with a national average of approximately 28 per cent.[24]

Unlisted phone numbers can be characterized as voluntarily unlisted and involuntarily unlisted. *Voluntarily unlisted* phone numbers are excluded at the owner's request. Voluntarily unlisted phone numbers are most common in urban areas and in the West. Research has shown significant differences between those with voluntarily unlisted numbers and those with listed numbers on such variables as ownership of luxury items and automobiles, housing characteristics, family composition, and other demographic and attitudinal variables.[25]

As the current telephone directory becomes older, the percentage of households with unlisted numbers increases because of new families moving into the area and others moving within the area. These *involuntarily unlisted* numbers generally consist of less than 10 per cent of all phones.

Random Digit Dialing. To ensure more representative samples, researchers generally utilize some form of *random digit dialing.* This technique requires that at least some of the digits of each sample phone number be generated randomly.

A primary problem with pure random digit dialing is that only about 20 per cent of all numbers within working prefixes are actually connected to home phones. Thus, four out of five calls will not reach a functioning number. A variety of techniques have been developed to minimize this problem. The most popular technique, *plus-one* or *add-a-digit,* simply requires the researcher to select a sample from an existing directory and add one to each number thus selected. Although the technique is more expensive than a sample selected directly from a directory,[26] and it has a higher refusal rate,[27] it produces a high contact rate and a fairly representative sample. A sophisticated version of this approach was found to reach 80 per cent working numbers of which only 4 per cent were business phones.[28]

Mail questionnaires require an explicit sampling frame composed of addresses, if not names and addresses. Such lists are generally unavailable for the general population. In fact, the telephone directory, or street directory where available, is generally used for this purpose. The problems associated with this type of sampling frame have already been described.

Lists of specialized groups are more readily available. For example, a bank can easily compile a mailing list of its current checking account customers. Often, specific mailing lists can be purchased from firms that specialize in this area. One catalog contains approximately 20,000 lists, many of which can be subdivided on a state-by-state, regional, or ZIP sequence basis.[29] However, even with a good mailing list, the researcher maintains only limited control over *who* at the mailing address completes the questionnaire. Different family members frequently provide divergent answers to the same question. Although researchers can address the questionnaire to a specific household member, they cannot be sure who completes the questionnaire.

Mailings to organizations have similar problems.[30] It is difficult to determine an individual's sphere of responsibility from his or her job title. Thus, in some firms the purchasing agent may set the criteria by which brands are chosen, whereas in other firms this is either a committee decision or it is made by the person who actually uses the product in question. Thus, a mailing addressed to a specific individual or job title may not reach the individual who is most relevant for the survey. In addition, busy executives may often pass on a questionnaire to others, who are not as qualified to complete it.

Time Requirements

Telephone surveys generally require the least total time for completion. In addition, it is generally easier to hire, train, control, and coordinate telephone interviewers. Therefore, the number of interviewers can often be expanded until any time constraint is satisfied.

The number of personal and computer interviewers can also be increased to reduce the total time required. However, problems with training, coordinating, and control tend to make this uneconomical after a certain point. Because "at-home" interviewers must travel between interviews, and often set up appointments, such interviews take substantially more time than telephone interviews. However, mall intercept interviews can be done fairly rapidly.

Mail surveys tend to take the longest time. Furthermore, there is relatively little the researcher can do to shorten this interval, except to reduce the number of follow-up attempts. It generally requires two weeks to receive most of the responses to a single mailing. A mail survey with only one follow-up mailing and no prenotification will require a minimum of three weeks for data collection.

Response Rate

The *response rate* refers to the percentage of the original sample that is interviewed.[31] The potential impact of a low response rate is so critical for survey research that it is treated in depth in a later section of this chapter.

Cost

The cost of the survey varies with the type of interview, the nature of the questionnaire, the response rate required, the geographic area covered, and the time at which the survey is made. However, personal interviews are generally much more expensive than the other approaches, particularly those conducted at the respondent's homes or offices. Intercept interviews are much more economical. Computer interviews involving the deliberate selection of respondents probably cost about the same as personal interviews. Computer interviews allowing self-selection cost much less.

One study found a random digit dialing telephone survey to cost (fieldwork and sampling) 20 to 25 per cent the cost of personal interviewing.[32] An A. C. Nielsen study found that "the average cost for interviewing time, supervision, and related expenses was 43 per cent higher for the personal interviewing than it was for the phone interviewing." [33] Telephone interviews are usually more expensive than those conducted by mail. However, for short interviews, this relationship may not hold. Cost considerations for selecting a survey approach must include not only the costs of initial contacts but also the costs of any callbacks, remailings, or added telephone calls designed to increase the response rate.

Which Method to Use?

Obviously, no one method of survey data collection is best for all situations. The specific information requirements, the information that can be provided by each method, and time and monetary constraints determine which approach to use. The primary consideration is which technique is capable of generating *appropriate information* from the *appropriate sample* at the *lowest cost*. Table 6–2 provides a summary of the general strengths of the four techniques. It must be emphasized that the ratings shown in the table are of a general nature and will not hold true in all situations.

Thus far we have been considering the techniques as though they were mutually exclusive. However, two or more of the techniques often may be combined in a single survey. This approach, if properly performed, may allow the weakness of each technique to be offset by the strengths of the others. The *lockbox* technique used in industrial research generally produces response rates above 60 per cent[34] while combining the advantages of mail and telephone interviews:

The respondent is sent a nice metal file box the size of a shoe box that is locked with a built-in three-digit combination lock. The box contains

Table 6–2 Strengths of the Four Survey Methods

Criterion	Mail	Telephone	Personal[a]	Computer[b]
1. Ability to handle complex questionnaires	Poor	Good	Excellent	Good
2. Ability to collect large amounts of data	Fair	Good	Excellent	Good
3a. Accuracy on "sensitive" questions	Good	Good	Fair	Good
3b. Control of interviewer effects	Excellent	Fair	Poor	Excellent
4. Degree of sample control	Fair	Excellent[c]	Fair	Fair
5. Time required	Poor	Excellent	Good	Good
6. Probable response rate	Fair	Fair	Fair	Fair
7. Cost	Good	Good	Fair	Fair

[a] Mall intercept interviews.
[b] Respondents deliberately selected at mall or trade show.
[c] Random-digit dialing.

interview materials such as flash cards. A cover letter explains the purpose of the survey and indicates that the lockbox is a gift. The letter also indicates that an interviewer will telephone in a few days and will provide the combination to the box. The respondent is told that the box is locked now because it contains interview materials and the researcher does not want to bias the respondent by providing an advance look at these materials. The actual interview is conducted by telephone.

Exhibit 6–5   *Tri-Met's Multimethod Consumer Survey*

Tri-Met (an urban bus company) used a combination of telephone and mail survey techniques in a ridership survey. Cost constraints ruled out at-home interviews. Mall intercept interviews were not practical because many bus riders did not visit shopping malls. "On-board" surveys were ruled out because of a desire to interview car drivers and "car poolers" as well as bus riders.

A standard mail survey was not feasible for two reasons. First, since only a very small percentage of the population rode the bus or car pooled to work, a huge random sample would be required. This would cost more than the study justified. Second, there was not enough time available for a sound series of follow-ups to a mail survey.

A telephone survey seemed to be the only practical method. It could be used quickly and could generate a quota sample (a fixed number of car drivers, car poolers, and bus riders). However, a very large amount of data was required from each respondent and some of these data were too complex to generate by telephone.

Therefore, a three-phase survey methodology was developed. Using plus-one dialing, a quota sample based on method of commuting to work was contacted. In the initial phone interview, several questions concerning commuting behavior were asked as were several nonsensitive demographic questions. The respondent was asked to provide his or her address, and a fairly lengthy and complex attitude questionnaire was *mailed* to each respondent.

The respondents were told that they should complete the questionnaire and keep it near the phone. In a few days they were recontacted by phone and asked to read their responses (generally attitude scale numbers) to the interviewer. They were then asked several additional questions, and the interview was completed.

This combination approach produced the required quota sample, a high response rate, and substantial amounts of complex information in a short time period at a reasonable cost.

However, the respondent removes any needed visual aids from the lockbox according to the interviewer's instructions.[35]

Exhibit 6–5 provides a detailed example of the use of a multimethod survey focused on consumers.

No matter which method of surveying is used, there is increasing concern with nonresponse. We will now examine this issue in some detail.

Nonresponse Error in Survey Research

Table 6–3 indicates the characteristics of respondents reached on each of a series of calls. As can be seen, a no call-back policy would have produced differences from those actually obtained. Differences of those magnitudes could lead the researcher to erroneous conclusions. Likewise, respondents in a survey of small businesses had actual average monthly phone bills of $134, whereas the actual monthly bills of nonrespondents averaged only $95.[36] Again, a potentially misleading difference exists.

Error caused by a difference between those who respond to a survey and those who do not is termed *nonresponse error*. Nonresponse can involve an entire questionnaire (refusal to answer any questions) or particular questions in the questionnaire (refusal to answer a subset of questions).[37] It is one of the most significant problems faced by the survey researcher.

Table 6–3 Response Variation by Call at Which Interviewed

| | Call at Which Interviewed | | | |
Behavior/Characteristic	First (N = 304)	Second (N = 114)	Third (N = 56)	Total Respondents (N = 474)
% Income > $25,000	31.5%	48.0%	64.8%	39.5%
% Male	36.8	41.2	57.1	40.3
% Democrat	40.8	34.1	19.6	36.7
% Voted for Democratic governor	53.8	43.0	57.1	51.7
% Feel President's economic policy is good	40.1	43.9	57.1	43.0
% Recalling a particular ad	24.1	27.2	37.5	26.4

Source: Adapted from J. C. Ward, B. Russick, and W. Rudelius, "A Test of Reducing Callbacks and Not-at-Home Bias in Personal Interviews by Weighting at-Home Respondents," *Journal of Marketing Research* (February 1985), 69.

Response rate is defined as *the number of completed interviews with responding units divided by the number of eligible responding units in the sample*.[38] In general, the lower the response rate to a survey, the higher is the *probability* of nonresponse error. However, a low response rate does not automatically mean that there has been nonresponse error.[39] Nonresponse error is a problem only when a difference between the respondents and the nonrespondents leads the researcher to an incorrect conclusion or decision.

Reducing Nonresponse in Telephone and Personal Surveys

Table 6 – 4 reveals the results of an analysis of almost 260,000 first-call attempts using the M/AIR/C Telno® System (a sophisticated random digit dialing system). As can be seen, less than one call in ten resulted in a completed interview with an adult (over 18). Approximately one third of the calls produced "no answer" and a similar percent were answered by someone under 18 with no one over 18 at home. Another 25 per cent were either nonworking numbers or business firms. Only one call in 10 reached an adult of either sex and 15 per cent of those contacted refused to participate in the interview.

Table 6 – 5 indicates the refusal rates for various types of personal and telephone interviews, based on almost 1.4 million respondent contacts by 46 research firms. Refusals ranged from 19 per cent to 56 per cent with an overall rate of 38 per cent.

An analysis of 182 commercial telephone surveys of consumers involving a total sample of over 1 million reached the following conclusions:

- A large percentage of potential respondents/households was never contacted. The median noncontact rate was 40 per cent.

Table 6 – 4 Results of First Call Attempt ($N = 259{,}088$)

Outcome	*Per Cent Occurring*
No answer	34.7%
No eligible person°	29.1
Nonworking number	20.3
Business	4.1
Busy	2.0
At home, eligible person	9.8
Refusal	1.4 (14.3)°°
Completion	8.4 (85.7)°°

° Any resident 18 years of age or older
°° Per cent *given* that an eligible person is at home
Source: R. A. Kerin and R. A. Peterson, "Scheduling Telephone Interviews," *Journal of Advertising Research* (May 1983), 44.

Table 6-5 Refusal Rates for Telephone and Personal Interviews

	Number	*Refusal Rate*
Total	1,387,000	38%
Telephone	926,000	30
Listed Number	553,000	25
Random Digit Dial	373,000	38
Personal	433,000	54
Mall	410,000	56
Other Intercept	10,000	29
Door-to-Door	13,000	19

Source: Your Opinion Counts (Chicago, IL: The Council of American Survey Research Organizations [CASRO]), 1986.

- Of those individuals contacted, slightly more than one in four refused participation. The median refusal rate was 28 per cent.
- Overall, response rates were low, with a median rate of 30 per cent for surveys in the data base.
- The low response rates were the result of controllable factors. In almost 40 per cent of the surveys, only one attempt was made to contact a potential respondent and rarely did research firms make a concerted attempt to convert reluctant respondents.[40]

Likewise, an analysis of almost 45,000 commercial mall intercept contacts found a refusal rate of 42 per cent.[41] At-home interviews also have substantially less than a 100 per cent response rate.[42] Thus, nonresponse error is a potential problem for telephone, personal, and computer interviews.

Not-at-homes and refusals are the major factors that reduce response rates. The major focus in reducing nonresponse in telephone and personal interview situations has centered on contacting the potential respondent. This was based on the belief that the social motives that are present in a face-to-face or verbal interaction situation operate to minimize refusals. However, there are increasing refusal rates in at-home personal interviews,[43] as well as high refusal rates in mall intercept interviews. Therefore, researchers must increasingly focus attention on gaining cooperation from, as well as making contact with, potential respondents.

Contacting Respondents

The percentage of not-at-homes in personal and telephone surveys can be reduced drastically with a series of *callbacks*. In general, the second round of calls will produce only slightly fewer contacts than the first call.

Table 6–6   Response Rate by Ring Policy

Number of Rings[a]	Per Cent of at-Home Reached
3	88.0%
4	96.7
5	99.2

[a] A 3-ring policy (ring, pause, ring, pause, ring) takes 16 seconds, while 5 rings require 30 seconds. *Source:* R. J. Smead and J. Wilcox, "Ring Policy in Telephone Surveys," *Public Opinion Quarterly* (Spring 1980), 115.

The minimum number of calls in most consumer surveys should be three. Callbacks should generally be made at varying times of the day and on different days of the week. There is, as one might suspect, a definite relationship between both the day of the week and the time of day and the completion rate of telephone and personal interviews.[44]

Commercial survey research firms vary widely in the number of times they allow a phone to ring before dialing the next number. Some allow only three rings, whereas others go as high as ten. One study indicates that five rings may be optimal, as shown in Table 6–6.

Motivating Respondents

Refusals are a problem in telephone and personal surveys.[45] Most refusals occur immediately after the introductory remarks of the interviewer. After they begin, very few interviews are terminated prior to completion.

An investigation of the effect of the *introductory remarks* on the response rate of telephone surveys concluded that "attempts to reduce refusals by manipulating the content of the introduction according to principles found successful with mail questionnaires produced no significant differences.[46]

However, *explicitly mentioning* the subject matter of the interview during the introduction lowers the refusal rate (38 per cent versus 42 per cent) although there are wide variations by *topic*.[47] Likewise, the *length of the interview* has a significant impact, as seen below:[48]

Length	Refusal Rate
5 minutes or less	21%
6–12 minutes	41
13 minutes or more	47

Gender of the interviewer does not appear to affect the refusal rate,[49] but characteristics of the interviewer's voice does.[50] *Prior notification* by letter lowers the refusal rate for telephone surveys.[51] Likewise, prior notification by telephone increased the cooperation rate to an at-home personal interview survey.[52] The *sponsor* of the survey affects telephone response rates with the rate being higher for university and charity sponsors than for commercial sponsors.[53]

The promise of a large *monetary incentive* ($10) was effective in generating a high response rate to a telephone survey that required respondents to agree to watch a specific television program.[54] However, the promise of $1.00 appeared to lower the response rate for a three-question telephone survey.[55] A $2.00 incentive was found to be a cost-effective means of increasing the response rate to a mall intercept interview.[56]

Attempts to gain cooperation for long or complicated interviews occasionally use the *foot-in-the-door technique.* This technique involves two stages. First, respondents are asked to complete a relatively short, simple questionnaire. Then, at a later time, they are asked to complete a more complex questionnaire on the same topic. Although this technique generally produces at least a small gain in the response rate, it is often not significant. Given the added expense this involves in telephone and personal interviews, concentrating on persuasion techniques and callbacks may provide a higher payoff.[57]

Refusal conversion or *persuasion* has been found to increase the overall response rate by an average of 7 per cent.[58] This involves not accepting a *no* response to a request for cooperation without making an additional plea. The additional plea can stress the importance of the respondent's opinions or the brevity of the questionnaire. It may also involve offering to recontact the individual at a more convenient time.

Finally, the *time of day* that contact is made appears to influence the refusal rate. Paradoxically, while evening is the optimal time to find respondents at home, it also generates the highest level of refusals.

Nonresponse in Mail Surveys

Predicting Response

Figure 6–3 shows the cumulative response rate to two mail surveys. Most mail surveys produce similar response patterns. However, the speed of response (slope of the curve) and ultimate percentage responding can vary widely.

Researchers can conduct small-scale preliminary mailings to a subsample of their target respondents. The observed curve can then be used to predict the number and timing of responses to the final survey. If a pilot study is not practical, perhaps because of time pressure, the observed response pattern to earlier similar surveys among similar respondents using similar response inducements can be used. Finally, it is possible, though less accurate, to predict

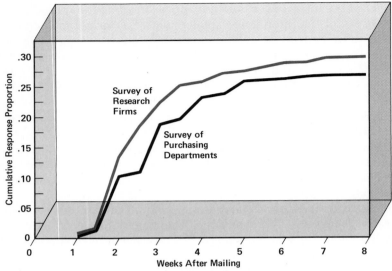

Figure 6–3   *Plots of Actual Response Patterns for Two Commercial Surveys*

Source: A. Parasuraman, "More on the Prediction of Mail Survey Response Rates," *Journal of Marketing Research* (May 1982), 263.

the overall curve using data from only the first few weeks.[59] Such predictions may provide an early indication of the need for additional follow-up efforts.

Reducing Nonresponse

Attempts to increase the response rate to mail surveys focus on increasing the potential respondents' motivation to reply. Two complementary approaches are frequently used. The first is to increase the motivation as much as possible in the initial contacts with respondents. The second approach is to remind the respondents through repeated mailings or other contacts.[60]

The initial response rate to a mail survey is strongly influenced by the respondents' *interest* in the subject matter of the survey. For example, one study found a range of refusal rates from 17 per cent to 53 per cent, depending on the topic.[61] Another study obtained a 54 per cent response rate with an "interesting" questionnaire compared to 31 per cent for a less interesting one.[62]

Interest level can cause a serious source of nonresponse bias in the survey results. Consider a firm that is evaluating the potential for introducing a new tennis elbow remedy. A survey is conducted to determine the incidence and severity of the problem among the general population. Those individuals most interested in tennis elbow, and thus most likely to respond to the survey, are probably currently suffering from the problem or have recently suffered from it. Therefore, initial returns are likely to overstate the incidence of the problem. This could easily lead the firm to the wrong conclusion concerning the size of the market.

Notification, such as an advance letter or telephone call, that informs the respondents that they will receive a questionnaire shortly and requests cooperation generally increases the response rate.[63] However, it does not necessarily increase the representativeness of those who respond.[64] Further, notification of commercial respondents does not appear to increase the response rate.[65]

The type of postage used has modest effects on the response rate. A number of researchers have concluded that, given the increased costs associated with first-class mail and hand-stamped envelopes, it is generally wiser to concentrate on other inducements.[66] However, a recent major analysis indicates that, compared to business reply postage, first class generates an additional 9 per cent response and is cost effective.[67]

As described earlier (see page 150), *the length of the questionnaire* does not appear to have a major impact on the response rate.

Prepaid monetary incentives cause substantial increases in response rates in both commercial and general public populations.[68] Although large incentives ($5.00 or more) have a stronger effect than smaller ones, there is little difference in response rates when the incentive is under $1.00. *Promised monetary incentives* of $1.00 or less do not appear to be effective in increasing response rates. Promised incentives of $2.00 appear to increase response rates substantially. However, equal or smaller prepaid incentives have much larger impacts.[69]

A prepaid incentive of $0.25 was more effective in generating a high response rate than was a *probabilistic incentive* of $100.00 (respondents' names were entered in a lottery with the winner receiving $100).[70]

Charity contributions are occasionally used as response inducements. Exhibit 6–6 illustrates how this approach was recently used by Time, Inc. The effectiveness of charity contributions in increasing response rates is not clear.[71]

The effect of *nonmonentary incentives* such as trading stamps and key rings varies. To be effective, the nonmentary incentive must be perceived as valuable *by the respondent.* However, financial incentives are generally easier to mail and more effective. For example, one study[72] produced the following response rates:

Incentive	Response Rate
None	14%
Pen	22%
25¢	39%

163

Exhibit 6–6 *Contribution to a Charitable Organization to Increase Response Rate as Used by Time, Inc.** *

I. Preliminary Post Card

> Dear TIME Subscriber:
>
> May we make a contribution to the charity of your choice?
>
> That's what **TIME** is prepared to do, if you will take just a few seconds of your time to complete a questionnaire we'll be sending you in a few days.
>
> Your participation in this survey is of considerable importance to us in making **TIME** as useful and informative as possible for you.
>
> I hope we can count on your response and I'm sure the charity of your choice will be most appreciative too.
>
> Ralph P. Davidson
> Publisher

II. Appearing immediately below the address on the outside of the envelope containing the questionnaire:

May we make a contribution to the charity of your choice?

III. From the cover letter:

The enclosed questionnaire will take only a short time to complete. We'll be very grateful for your help . . . and so, I'm sure, will the charity of your choice.

Because, for every 10,000 responses we receive from this survey, we will contribute $1,000 to charity.

With the full co-operation of subscribers like yourself, the contribution could reach $25,000.

Won't you please fill out the questionnaire now and send it back to me in the postpaid return envelope? Be sure to indicate to which organization you want the charitable contribution to go.

IV. From the questionnaire:

Please send a contribution for me to one of the following charities (please check only one):
1 ☐ *American Cancer Society*
2 ☐ *March of Dimes*
3 ☐ *Heart Fund*
4 ☐ *Muscular Dystrophy Association*

° Used with permission of Time, Inc.

Promises of a copy of the results of the survey do not appear to increase response rates even among industrial respondents.[73]

Physical characteristics of the questionnaire and cover letter appear to have very limited effects on the response rate.[74] The *degree of personalization* and the related variables *respondent anonymity* and assurances of *confidentiality* produce variable effects on both response rates and accuracy.[75] Personalization appears generally to increase response rates on nonsensitive issues, whereas assurances of anonymity or confidentiality are most effective on questionnaires dealing with personally important or sensitive issues. However, these effects are generally small.

The *identity of the survey sponsor* influences the response rate, with commercial sponsors generally receiving a lower response rate than noncommercial sponsors.[76]

The *type of appeal* used in the cover letter can take a number of approaches, such as *egoistic* (your opinion is important), *altruistic* (please help us), *social utility* (your opinion can help the community) or *negative* (if the questionnaire is not returned by a certain date, a telephone call or personal follow-up will result). Evidence indicates that the "best" appeal depends on the nature of the sponsor and purpose of the study;[77] though negative appeals appear to be dysfunctional.[78]

The *foot-in-the-door* technique described earlier involves gaining compliance with an initial easy task and then at a later time requesting assistance with a larger or more complex version of the same task. Thus, a researcher might attempt to gain responses to a simple postcard questionnaire. The respondents would then be sent a more complex questionnaire on the same topic. This approach does not appear to generate higher response rates than standard prenotification techniques.[79]

In addition to attempting to maximize the *initial* return of mail questionnaires, most mail surveys also utilize *follow-up contacts* to increase the overall response rate.[80] Follow-up contacts generally consist of a postcard or letter requesting the respondent to complete and return the questionnaire. Follow-up efforts are not limited to postcards or letters. The questionnaire may be sent again or telephone, telegraph, or personal contacts can be used to increase the response rate.

Summary on Methods to Increase Mail Survey Response Rates

Table 6–7 summarizes the effects that various approaches to reducing nonresponse to mail surveys appear to have. In any attempt to increase the total response rate to a survey, the researcher must try to balance the increased cost of each effort against the benefits of a more representative sample. The critical issue is how alike or different the respondents are from the nonrespondents on the variable(s) of concern. Methods of estimating the probable effect of nonresponse are described in the next section.

Strategies for Dealing with Nonresponse

The Federal Trade Commission (FTC) took action against Litton Industries, charging that surveys used in advertising for Litton microwave ovens "did not provide a reasonable basis for, or prove the claim of, the advertisement." Specifically, the FTC claimed that:

> The Litton surveys had a very high rate of nonresponse. However, Litton failed to determine whether there was a bias of nonresponse, that

Table 6–7   Summary of Factors Affecting Survey Response Rate

Factor	Effect
Limited Control	
Respondents' interest in topic	Strong
Questionnaire length	Limited
Identity of survey sponsor	Moderate
Full Control	
Preliminary notification	Moderate
Type of postage	Moderate
Monetary incentives	Strong
Nonmonetary gifts	Variable
Physical characteristics	Very limited
Degree of personalization	Variable
Anonymity and/or confidentiality	Variable
Type of appeal	Limited
Return deadlines	None
Follow-up contacts	Strong
Foot-in-the-door	Limited

is, whether the answers of nonrespondents would have differed significantly from those of respondents.[81]

Note that the complaint is *not* that the Litton survey had a low response rate. Rather, it is that Litton did not deal effectively with the error that could have resulted from the low response rate. In this section we discuss several means for dealing with potential nonresponse error.

After each successive wave of contacts with a particular group of potential respondents, the researcher should run a *sensitivity analysis*.[82] That is, one should ascertain how different the nonrespondents would have to be from the respondents in order to alter the decision one would make based on the data supplied by the current respondents. If the most extreme foreseeable answers by the nonrespondents would not alter the decision, no further efforts are required.

As an example, consider the decision rule: *If 20 per cent or more of the population appear favorable, we will introduce the new product.* A mail survey is launched and provides a 50 per cent return rate by the end of the second week. Of those responding, 44 per cent favor the new product. If the remaining 50 per cent of the potential respondents were unfavorable, the projected percentage of favorable attitudes would still be 22 per cent. Since this is more than the amount needed for a "go" decision, any attempt to generate additional responses would be a waste of resources. However, if the nonrespondents *could* alter the decision, the researcher should use one (or more) of the following techniques.

Subjective Estimates.   When it is no longer practical to increase the response rate, the researcher can estimate subjectively the nature and effect of the nonrespondents. That is, the researcher, based on experience and the nature of the survey, makes a subjective evaluation of the probable effects of the nonresponse error.

For example, the fact that those most interested in a product are most likely to return a mail questionnaire gives the researcher some confidence that nonrespondents are less interested in the topic than respondents. Similarly, the fact that young married couples with no children are at home less than couples with small children provides the researcher with a basis for evaluating some aspects of not-at-homes in personal or telephone interviews.

Imputation Estimates.   Imputation estimates involve imputing attributes to the nonrespondents based on the characteristics of the respondents.[83] These techniques can be used for missing respondents or for item nonresponse. For example, a respondent who fails to report income may be "assigned" the income of a respondent with similar demographic characteristics. This approach is used by the Census Bureau in the *Current Population Surveys*. A number of other imputation approaches to item nonresponse exist.[84] A common approach to differential nonresponse by groups defined by age, race, social class, and so forth is to weigh the responses of those who reply in a manner that offsets the nonresponse rate. This, of course, assumes that the nonrespondents in each group are similar to the respondents in each group and that the percentage of the population belonging to each group is known.

A commonly used method for adjusting for nonresponses (not-at-homes) for telephone and personal interview surveys is known as the *Politz-Simmons* method. This approach requires each respondent to estimate the percentage of times he or she has been at home at the time of the interview during the past several days or weeks. Those respondents who report that they are seldom home have their responses weighed more heavily than those who report generally being at home at the time of interview. This approach is based on the assumption that not-at-homes tend to be similar to those respondents who are seldom at home at the time of the interview but were at home on this occasion.

A recent test of this technique concluded that the benefits (small increases in accuracy) did not outweigh its costs in extra analysis and data collection.[85]

Trend Analysis. Trend analysis is similar to the imputation technique, except that the attributes of the nonrespondents are assumed to be similar to a projection of the trend shown between early and late respondents.

The data in Table 6–8 represent a fairly common finding when the results of several waves of a survey are compared to known characteristics of the total sample. As can be seen, each successive wave more closely resembles the final group of nonrespondents.

In Table 6–8, we can see that those responding to the second mailing owned only 84 per cent as many trees as those responding to the first mailing. Those responding to the third mailing owned 89 per cent as many trees as

Table 6–8 Using Trend in Responses to Estimate Nonresponses

	Response (in %)	Average No. of Fruit Trees	Percentage of Previous Wave's Response
First mailing	10	456	—
Second mailing	17	382	84%
Third mailing	14	340	89
Nonresponse	(59)	(290)	
Total	100	329	

Source: Adapted from L. Kish, *Survey Sampling* (New York: John Wiley & Sons, Inc., 1965), 545. Used with permission of the publisher.

Table 6–9 Variations in Median Income on Various Calls in a Survey

No. of Call at Which Interviewed	Median Income	No. of Interviews	Percentage of Previous Call's Income
1	$4188	427	
2	5880	391	140%
3	6010	232	102
4	6200	123	103
5	6010	77	97
6+	7443	59	124
All	$5598	1309	

Source: J. B. Lansing and J. N. Morgan, *Economic Survey Methods* (Ann Arbor: The University of Michigan Press, 1971), p. 161. Used with permission of the University of Michigan Press.

those responding to the second mailing. Therefore, one trend estimate would be that nonrespondents would own 94 per cent as many trees as those responding to the third mailing. This estimate, 320 trees, is then used *as if it were the value* (number of trees owned) *by the 59 per cent who did not respond when an overall average is calculated.*

Observe from Table 6–8 that the actual number of trees owned by the nonrespondents was 290 rather than the 320 estimated from the trend analysis. Although the trend estimate is in error, the error is less than it would have been had the nonrespondents been "ignored" (this would have resulted in an estimate of 389 trees per farm).

Unfortunately, we can never be sure that such trends will hold. Table 6–9 illustrates this problem. A trend estimate made after the second interview would have greatly overstated the final figure. In contrast, an estimate made after the fifth call would have underestimated the final results. Trend analysis should only be used when there are logical reasons to believe the trend will extend to the nonrespondents.

Measurement Using Subsamples.   Subsampling of nonrespondents, particularly when a mail survey was the original methodology, has been found effective in reducing nonresponse error. Concentrated attention on a subsample of nonrespondents, generally using telephone or personal interviews, can often yield a high response rate within that subsample. Using standard statistical procedures, the values obtained in the subsample can be projected to the entire group of nonrespondents and the overall survey results adjusted to take into account the nonrespondents. The primary drawback to this technique is the cost involved.

Review Questions

6.1. What is *survey research?*

6.2. What can be measured by surveys?

6.3. Can surveys prove causation?

6.4. What is meant by the *structure* of an interview?

6.5. What is meant by the *directness* of an interview?

6.6. What are the advantages and disadvantages of a *structured interview?*

6.7. What are the advantages and disadvantages of a *direct interview?*

6.8. Describe each of the following:
   a. *structured-direct interview*
   b. *unstructured-direct interview*
   c. *unstructured-indirect interview*
   d. *structured-indirect interview*

6.9. Define each of the following
   a. *personal interview*
   b. *mail interview*
   c. *telephone interview*
   d. *computer interview*

6.10. What is a *mall intercept interview?* What are its advantages and disadvantages?

6.11. Describe the Purchase Intercept Technique (PIT).

6.12. Which interview approach is most common?

6.13. What is meant by each of the following, and which interview method(s) deal with each one most effectively?
   a. *complexity of the questionnaire*
   b. *required amount of data*
   c. *accuracy*
   d. *sample control*
   e. *time requirements*
   f. *level of nonresponse*
   g. *cost*

6.14. What is meant by *interviewer effects?* How does one control for them?

6.15. What is a *validation* or *verification procedure?*

6.16. What are the two types of unlisted numbers?

6.17. What is meant by *random digit dialing? Plus one-dialing?*

6.18. What is a *CATI?*

6.19. What factors affect sample control for each of the interviewing techniques?

6.20. How many times should the phone ring in a telephone survey?

6.21. What is a typical response rate for phone interviews?

6.22. What is a typical refusal rate for phone interviews?

6.23. What is a typical refusal rate for mall intercept interviews?

6.24. What factors improve the response rate to phone interviews?

6.25. What factors improve the response rate to mall intercept interviews?

6.26. How can you predict the magnitude and timing of the response rate to a mail survey?

6.27. What factors affect the response rate to mail surveys?

6.28. What is a *sensitivity analysis*?

6.29. Describe each of the following as a means for dealing with nonresponse:
   a. *subjective estimate*
   b. *imputation estimate*
   c. *trend analysis*
   d. *subsample measurement*

6.30. What is the *Politz-Simmons method*? How effective is it?

Discussion Questions/Problems

6.31. How would you decide if a mall intercept interview approach is appropriate for a particular research project?

6.32. Why does a monetary gift enclosed with a questionnaire generally produce a higher response rate than the promise of a monetary gift if the questionnaire is returned?

6.33. Which survey method is best for the following situations?
   a. Administration of a complex attitude scale to measure the impact of a major new product launch by a competitor.
   b. Administration of a questionnaire on the viewing of "X-rated" movies on VCRs.
   c. Administration of a questionnaire to determine the number of people that had read a feature article in Sunday's paper.
   d. Administration of a questionnaire by a university to determine students' attitudes toward a proposed change in the core curriculum.

6.34. An attitude survey conducted via mail by a local school district obtained a 38 per cent response. How are the nonrespondents likely to differ from the respondents with respect to (a) attitudes and (b) voting behavior?

6.35. The following figures show the per cent of respondents having a favorable reaction to a new product on each successive wave of a telephone survey.

Wave	% Positive on this Wave	% of Total Sample Responding
1	42.9	32.2
2	52.7	25.8
3	58.1	13.1
4	64.3	6.0

A time deadline makes another wave of calls impossible. What should be the final estimate of the favorable percentage.

6.36. People tend to respond to surveys that deal with topics that interest them. How can this fact be used to increase the response rate from a mail survey of the general public on attitudes toward and usage of:
   a. furniture polish
   b. energy conservation
   c. automobile tires
   d. lawn fertilizer

6.37. Would you expect any nonresponse bias in the situations described in 6.36? Make a subjective estimate of the nature and extent of the bias if a 60 per cent response rate were obtained in each situation.

6.38. What biases, if any, might be introduced by offering to give respondents $10.00 upon receipt of the questionnaire? The purpose of the payment is to ensure a high response rate. Will it work?

6.39. The manager of a shopping center recently conducted a computer survey to provide information on the types of stores that should be sought for the center's new wing, which was under construction. Self administered computer terminals were placed near the entrances to the center. A large sign above each table said: "Help Us Plan the New Wing." The computers were left up for a two-week period. What type of errors are likely to be present in this study?

6.40. Describe and justify the survey methodology you would use in the following situations:
   a. A national survey to determine the reactions of males over age 50 with incomes above $30,000 per year toward a proposed new type of life insurance.
   b. A survey to determine the reaction of small business owners toward a new software package focused on cash flow management.
   c. A national survey of attitudes toward the social security system.
   d. A survey of middle-income individuals' reactions to new types of rugs.

6.41. Westinghouse Credit Corp. recently sent a survey to 3,512 chief executive officers and chief financial officers by mail. Half received $1.00 with the survey and half did not. The response rate to the 4 page questionnaire was 1.6 per cent without the incentive and 17.5 per cent with it.[86] What would you do?

Projects

6.42. Conduct a series of telephone interviews in your area to develop a guide for when to conduct telephone interviews.

6.43. Conduct a series of telephone interviews designed to develop a guide for when to conduct telephone interviews with students on your campus.

6.44. Design and conduct a telephone survey among students on your campus. The purpose of the survey should be to determine attitudes toward _____.

    a. drinking and driving
    b. smoking
    c. oral hygiene
    d. bananas
    e. tea
    f. VISA
    g. tax on stock dividends

6.45. As 6.44 but using "hall" intercept interviews.

6.46. Do 6.44 and 6.45 for the same product. Discuss any differences in the results.

6.47. Do 6.44 using the general population and plus-one dialing.

6.48. Conduct a telephone survey of adults 18 and older in your area. Determine if they have been interviewed in the past 12 months, how many times, on what topics, by what means, and their attitude toward the interviews.

References

[1] B. Whalen, "On-site Computer Interviewing Yields Research Data Instantly," *Marketing News*, November 9, 1984, 1.

[2] A good "how to" overview is P. L. Alreck and R. B. Settle, *The Survey Research Handbook* (Homewood, Ill.: Richard D. Irwin, Inc; 1985).

[3] See R. Gates and P. J. Soloman, "Research Using the Mall Intercept," *Journal of Advertising Research* (August/September 1982), 43–49.

[4] S. Harper, "Court Hits Lorillard's Triumph," *Advertising Age*, November 3, 1980, 95.

[5] S. Sudman, "Improving the Quality of Shopping Center Sampling," *Journal of Marketing Research* (November 1980), 423–431; E. Blair, "Sampling Issues in Trade Area Maps Drawn from Shopper Surveys," *Journal of Marketing* (Winter 1983), 98–106; A. J. Bush and J. F. Hair, Jr., "An Assessment of the Mall Intercept as a Data Collection Method," *Journal of Marketing Research* (May 1985), 158–167; and T. D. Dupont, "Do Frequent Mall Shoppers Distort Mall-Intercept Survey Results?" *Journal of Advertising Research* (August 1987), 45–51.

[6] For a system description see P. E. Green, P. K. Kedia, and R. S. Nikhil, *CAPPA* (Palo Alto: Scientific Press, 1985), and *ACRS* (Chicago: M/AIR/C Inc., 1985).

[7] See R. M. Mayeri, "Advanced Microcomputer to Revolutionalize Personal Interviewing," *Marketing News*, November 27, 1981, 5; and J. E. Rafael, "Self-administered CRT Interviews," *Marketing News*, November 9, 1984, 16.

[8] See J. H. Frey, *Survey Research by Telephone* (New York: Sage, 1983).

[9] See R. M. Groves and N. A. Mathiowetz, "Computer Assisted Telephone Interviewing," *Public Opinion Quarterly* (Spring 1984), 356–369; S. Kiesler and L. S. Sproull, "Response Effects on the Electronic Survey," *Public Opinion Quarterly* (Fall 1986), 402–13; and C. A. Higgins, T. P. Dimnik, and H. P. Greenwood, "The DISKQ Survey Method," *Journal of the Market Research Society* (October 1987), 437–45.

[10] B. Whalen, "On-site Interviewing Yields Research Data Instantly," *Marketing News,* November 9, 1984, 17.

[11] Taken from a survey conducted for a metropolitan newspaper by Belden Associates, Dallas, Texas. Used with permission.

[12] G. D. Upah and S. C. Cosmas, "The Use of Telephone Dials as Attitude Scales," *Journal of the Academy of Marketing Sciences* (Fall 1980), 416–426; and P. V. Miller, "Alternative Question Forms for Attitude Scale Questions on Telephone Interviews," *Public Opinion Quarterly* (Winter 1984), 766–778.

[13] See L. M. Sharp and J. Frankel, "Respondent Burden," *Public Opinion Quarterly* (Spring 1983), 36–53.

[14] *Your Opinion Counts* (Chicago: The Council of American Survey Research Organizations [CASRO], 1986), 18.

[15] C. S. Craig and J. M. McCann, "Item Nonresponse in Mail Surveys: Extent and Correlates," *Journal of Marketing Research* (May 1978), 285–289; and Sharp and Frankel, loc. cit.

[16] See F. M. Andrews, "Construct Validity and Error Components of Survey Measures," *Public Opinion Quarterly* (Summer 1984), 409–442; A. J. Bush and A. Parasuraman, "Assessing Response Quality," *Psychology & Marketing* (Fall/Winter 1984), 57–71; A. J. Bush and A. Parasuraman, "Mall Intercept versus Telephone-Interviewing Environment," *Journal of Advertising Research* (April/May 1985), 36–43; Bush and Hair, op. cit., 162–163; and Kiesler and Sproull, loc. cit.

[17] For overviews see M. Collins and B. Butcher, "Interviewer and Clustering Effects in an Attitude Survey," *Journal of Market Research Society* (January 1983), 39–58; C. Tucker, "Interviewer Effects in Telephone Surveys," *Public Opinion Quarterly* (Spring 1983), 84–95; and R. M. Groves and L. J. Magilavy, "Measuring and Explaining Interviewer Effects in Centralized Telephone Surveys," *Public Opinion Quarterly* (Fall 1986), 251–66.

[18] See B. Bailar, L. Bailey, and J. Stevens, "Measures of Interviewer Bias and Variance," *Journal of Marketing Research* (August 1977), 337–343; A. Barath and C. F. Cannell, "Effect of Interviewer's Voice Intonation," *Public Opinion Quarterly* (Fall 1976), 370–373; J. Freeman and E. W. Butler, "Some Sources of Interviewer Variance in Surveys," *Public Opinion Quarterly* (Spring 1976), 79–91; J. R. McKenzie, "An Investigation into Interviewer Effects in Market Research," *Journal of Marketing Research* (August 1977), 330–336; P. R. Cotter, J. Cohen, and P. B. Coulter, "Race-of-Interviewer Effects in Telephone Surveys," *Public Opinion Quarterly* (Summer 1982), 278–293; and E. Singer, M. R. Frankel, and M. B. Glassman, "The Effect of Interviewer Characteristics

and Expectations on Response," *Public Opinion Quarterly* (Spring 1983), 68–83.

[19] D. S. Tull and L. E. Richards, "What Can Be Done About Interviewer Bias?" in J. Sheth, *Research in Marketing,* 3d ed. (Greenwich, Conn.: JAI Press, 1980), 143–162, and Groves and Magilavy, loc. cit.

[20] K. C. Schneider, "Uninformed Response Rate in Survey Research," *Journal of Business Research* (April 1985), 153–162; and D. I. Hawkins, K. A. Coney, and D. W. Jackson, Jr., "The Impact of Monetary Inducement on Uninformed Response Error," *Journal of the Academy of Marketing Science* (Summer 1988), 30–35.

[21] S. W. McDaniel and C. P. Rao, "The Effect of Monetary Inducement on Mailed Questionnaire Response Quality," *Journal of Marketing Research* (May 1980), 265–268.

[22] R. Czaja, J. Blair, and J. P. Sebestik, "Respondent Selection in a Telephone Survey," *Journal of Marketing Research* (August 1982), 381–385; C. T. Salmon and J. S. Nichols, "The Next-Birthday Method of Respondent Selection," *Public Opinion Quarterly* (Summer 1983), 270–276; D. E. Hagan and C. M. Collier, "Must Respondent Selection Procedures for Telephone Surveys Be Invasive," *Public Opinion Quarterly* (Winter 1983), 547–556; and D. O'Rourke and J. Blair, "Improving Random Respondent Selection in Telephone Surveys," *Journal of Marketing Research* (November 1983), 428–432.

[23] E. Telser, "Data Exorcises Bias in Phone vs. Personal Interview Debate, But If You Can't Do It Right, Don't Do It at All," *Marketing News,* September 10, 1976, 6.

[24] "Unlisted Rate Rising Across Nation," *The Frame* Fall, 1988 (Fairfield, CT: Survey Sampling Inc)

[25] M. N. Segal and F. Hekmat, "Random Digit Dialing: A Comparison of Methods," *Journal of Advertising* (No. 4 1985), 36–43; "Dialing Selection Techniques: Random Digit vs. Directory," *Research on Research* (Chicago: Market Facts, Inc., No. 10, undated); P. E. Moberg, "Biases in Unlisted Phone Numbers," *Journal of Advertising Research* (September 1982), 51–55; and M. J. Krig, "Bias in a Directory Sample for a Mail Survey of Rural Households," *Public Opinion Quarterly* (Winter 1984), 801–806.

[26] W. Lyons and R. F. Durant, "Interviewer Costs Associated with the Use of Random Digit Dialing in Large Area Samples," *Journal of Marketing* (Summer 1980), 65–69; and "Dialing Selection," loc. cit.

[27] *Your Opinion Counts* (Chicago: The Council of American Survey Research Organizations [CASRO], 1986), 12.

[28] R. A. Kerin and R. A. Peterson, "Scheduling Telephone Interviews," *Journal of Advertising Research* (May 1983), 41–47; and Segal and Hekmat, loc. cit.

[29] *Catalog of Mailing Lists* (New York: F. S. Hofheimer, Inc., issued periodically); and *SRDS Direct Mail List Rates and Data* (New York: Standard Rate and Data Service), issued twice annually.

[30] See O. C. Ferrell, T. L. Childers, and R. W. Reukert, "Effects of Situational Factors on Mail Survey Response," in R. W. Belk et al., *1984 AMA Educators' Proceedings* (Chicago American Marketing Association, 1984), 364–367.

[31] F. Wiseman and M. Billington, "Comment on a Standard Definition of Response Rates," *Journal of Marketing Research* (August 1984), 336–338.

[32] A. J. Tuchfarber and W. R. Klecka, *Random Digit Dialing: Lowering the Cost of Victimization Surveys* (Washington, D.C.: The Police Foundation, 1976).

[33] Telser, loc. cit.

[34] D. M. Fitch, "Combination Technique Unlocks Hesitant Responses," *Marketing News,* January 4, 1988, 10.

[35] D. Schwartz, "Locked Box Combines Survey Methods Helps Ends Some Woes of Probing Industrial Field," *Marketing News,* January 27, 1978, 18.

[36] H. Assael and J. Keon, "Nonsampling vs. Sampling Errors in Survey Research," *Journal of Marketing* (Spring 1982), 114–123.

[37] See R. M. Durand, H. J. Guffey, Jr., and J. M. Planchon, "An Examination of the Random versus Nonrandom Nature of Item Omissions," *Journal of Marketing Research* (August 1983), 305–313; G. S. Omura, "Correlates of Item Nonresponse," *Journal of the Market Research Society* (October 1983), 321–330; J. R. Dickinson and E. Kirzner, "Questionnaire Item Omission as a Function of Within-Group Question Position," *Journal of Business Research* (February 1985), 71–75; and J. H. Leigh and C. R. Martin, Jr., "Don't Know Item Nonresponse in a Telephone Survey," *Journal of Marketing Research* (November 1987), 418–24.

[38] Wiseman and Billington, loc. cit.; and L. R. Frankel, "The Report of the CASRO Task Force on Response Rates," in T. Wiseman, *Improving Data Quality in Sample Surveys* (Cambridge, Mass.: Marketing Science Institute, 1982), 1–11.

[39] Assael and Keon, loc. cit.; and D. W. Finn, C. Wang, and C. W. Lamb, "An Examination of the Effects of Sample Composition Bias in a Mail Survey," *Journal of Market Research Society* (October 1983), 331–338.

[40] F. Wiseman, "Nonresponse in Consumer Surveys" in K. B. Monroe, *Advances in Consumer Research VII* (Provo: Association for Consumer Research, 1981), 267–269.

[41] Gates and Soloman, op. cit. See also F. Wiseman, M. Schafer, and R. Schafer, "An Experimental Test of the Effects of a Monetary Incentive in Central Location Interviewing," *Journal of Marketing Research* (November 1983), 439–442 and Bush and Hair, Jr., op. cit., 164.

[42] J. Goyder, "Face-to-Face Interviews and Mailed Questionnaires," *Public Opinion Quarterly* (Summer 1985), 234–252.

[43] C. G. Steeh, "Trends in Nonresponse Rates, 1952–1979," *Public Opinion Quarterly* (Winter 1981), 40–57.

[44] G. Vigderhous, "Scheduling Telephone Interviews," *Public Opinion Quarterly* (Summer 1981), 250–259; and R. A. Kerin and R. A. Peterson, "Scheduling Telephone Interviews," *Journal of Advertising Research* (May 1983), 44; and

M. F. Weeks, R. A. Kulka, and S. A. Pierson, "Optimal Call Scheduling for a Telephone Survey," *Public Opinion Quarterly* (Winter 1987), 540–49.

[45] J. M. Struebbe, J. B. Kernan, and T. J. Grogan, "The Refusal Problem in Telephone Surveys," *Journal of Marketing Research* (June 1986), 29–37.

[46] D. A. Dillman, J. G. Gallegos, and J. H. Frey, "Reducing Refusal Rates for Telephone Interviews," *Public Opinion Quarterly* (Spring 1976), 67.

[47] *Your Opinion Counts*, op. cit., 19–22.

[48] Ibid., p. 18.

[49] Dillman, Gallegos, and Frey, loc. cit.

[50] L. Oksenberg, L. Coleman, and C. F. Cannell, "Interviewers' Voices and Refusal Rates in Telephone Surveys," *Public Opinion Quarterly* (Spring 1986), 97–111.

[51] Dillman, Gallegos, and Frey, loc. cit., and M. W. Traugott, R. M. Groves, and J. M. Lepkowski, "Using Dual Frame Designs to Reduce Nonresponse in Telephone Surveys," *Public Opinion Quarterly* (Winter 1987), 522–39.

[52] J. W. Bergsten, M. F. Weeks, and F. A. Bryan, "Effects of an Advance Telephone Call," *Public Opinion Quarterly* (Fall 1984), 650–657.

[53] R. R. Harmon and A. J. Resnik, "The Impact of Sponsorship and Incentive on Survey Response Rates," in P. E. Murphy et al., *1983 AMA Educators' Proceedings* (American Marketing Association, 1983), 432–435.

[54] E. G. Goetz, T. R. Taylor, and F. L. Cook, "Promised Incentives in Media Research," *Journal of Marketing Research* (May 1984), 148–154.

[55] Harmon and Resnik, loc. cit.

[56] Wiseman, Schafer, and Schafer, op. cit.

[57] R. M. Groves and L. J. Magilavy, "Increasing Response Rates to Telephone Surveys: A Door in the Face for Foot-in-the-Door," *Public Opinion Quarterly* (Fall 1981), 346–358.

[58] Ibid.

[59] S. J. Huxley, "Predicting Response Speed in Mail Surveys," *Journal of Marketing Research* (February 1980), 63–68; R. W. Hill, "Using S-Shaped Curves to Predict Response Rates," *Journal of Marketing Research* (May 1981), 240–242; A. Parasuraman, "More on the Prediction of Mail Survey Response Rates," *Journal of Marketing Research* (May 1982), 263; D. W. Finn, "Response Speeds, Functions and Predictability in Mail Surveys," *Journal of Academy of Marketing Science* (Winter 1983), 61–70, and A. J. Nederhof, "European and North American Response Patterns in Mail Surveys," *Journal of Marketing Research Society* (January 1985), 55–63.

[60] See J. Yu and H. Cooper, "A Quantitative Review of Research Design Effects on Response Rates," *Journal of Marketing Research* (February 1983), 36–44; D. Jobber, "Improving Response Rates in Industrial Mail Surveys," *Industrial Marketing Management* (#3, 1986), 183–95; and B. J. Walker, W. Kirchmann, and J. S. Conant, "A Method to Improve Response to Industrial Mail Surveys," *Industrial Marketing Management* (#4 1987), 305–14.

[61] *Your Opinion Counts,* op. cit., 22.

[62] C. J. Dommeyer, "Does Response to an Offer of Mail Survey Results Interact with Questionnaire Interest?" *Journal of Marketing Research Society* (January 1985), 27–38. See also B. J. Kyzr-Sheeley, "Results of Walker's 1986 Survey," *The Marketing Researcher* (Vo. 16, No. 3), 4; and S. W. McDaniel, C. S. Madden, and P. Verille, "Do Topic Differences Affect Survey Non-Response?" *Journal of the Marketing Research Society* (January 1987), 55–66.

[63] C. T. Allen, C. D. Schewe, and G. Wijk, "More on Self-Perception Theory's Foot Technique in the Pre-Call/Mail Survey Setting," *Journal of Marketing Research* (November 1980), 498–502; and Yu and Cooper, op. cit.

[64] J. Chebat and J. Picard, "Prenotification of Respondents in Mailed Questionnaire Surveys," *International Journal of Research in Marketing* (#3, 1984), 235–239.

[65] D. Jobber and S. Sanderson, "The Effects of a Prior Letter and Coloured Questionnaire Paper," *Journal of the Marketing Research Society* (October 1984), 339–349; and M. M. Pressley and M. G. Dunn, "Inducing Response to Questionnaires Mailed to Commercial Populations," in R. F. Lusch et al., *1985 AMA Educators' Proceedings* (Chicago: American Marketing Association 1985), 356–361.

[66] K. F. McCrohan and L. S. Lowe, "A Cost/Benefit Approach to Postage Used on Mail Questionnaires," *Journal of Marketing* (Winter 1981), 130–133; H. J. Guffey, Jr., J. R. Harris, and M. M. Guffey, "Stamps Versus Postal Permits," *Journal of the Academy of Marketing Science* (Summer 1980), 234–242; and L. Harvey, "A Research Note on the Impact of Class-of-Mail on Response Rates," *Journal of the Marketing Research Society* (July 1986), 299–301.

[67] J. S. Armstrong and E. J. Lusk, "Return Postage in Mail Surveys," *Public Opinion Quarterly* (Summer 1987), 233–48.

[68] R. A. Hansen, "A Self-Perception Interpretation of the Effect of Monetary and Nonmonetary Incentives," *Journal of Marketing Research* (February 1980), 77–83; S. W. McDaniel and C. P. Rao, "The Effect of Monetary Inducement on Mailed Questionnaire Response Quality," *Journal of Marketing Research* (May 1980), 265–268; D. H. Furse, D. W. Stewart, and D. L. Rados, "Effects of Foot-in-the-Door, Cash Incentives, and Followups on Survey Response," *Journal of Marketing Research* (November 1981), 473–478; J. S. Mizes, E. L. Fleece, and C. Roos, "Incentives for Increasing Return Rates," *Public Opinion Quarterly* (Winter 1984), 794–800; "Using a Cash Incentive to Heighten Mail Survey Response," *Research on Research* (Chicago: Market Facts Inc., #39, undated); and P. R. White, "A Buck for Your Thoughts," *Marketing News,* March 14, 1988, 24.

[69] J. G. P. Paolillo and P. Lorenzi, "Monetary Incentives and Mail Questionnaire Response Rates," *Journal of Advertising* (#1, 1984), 46–48; and S. H. Berry and D. E. Kanouse, "Physician Response to a Mailed Survey," *Public Opinion Quarterly* (Spring 1987), 102–114.

[70] W. McDaniel and R. W. Jackson, "The Probabilistic Incentive in Mail Survey

Research," in R. W. Belk, *1984 AMA Educators' Proceedings* (Chicago: American Marketing Association, 1984), 372–375.

[71] D. H. Robertson and D. N. Bellenger, "A New Method of Increasing Mail Survey Responses: Contribution to Charity," *Journal of Marketing Research* (November 1978), 632–633; and D. H. Furse and D. W. Stewart, "Monetary Incentives versus Promised Contribution to Charity," *Journal of Marketing Research* (August 1982), 375–380.

[72] Hansen, op. cit. See also A. J. Nederhof, "The Effects of Material Incentives in Mail Surveys," *Public Opinion Quarterly* (Spring 1983), 103–111; and H. H. Friedman and N. Arenstein, "On Increasing the Rate of Response to Mail Surveys," *Journal of Consumer Marketing* (Summer 1983), 46–48.

[73] Dommeyer, op. cit.; and D. Jobber and S. Sanderson, "The Effect of Two Variables on Industrial Mail Survey Returns," *Industrial Marketing Management* (May 1985), 119–121.

[74] Yu and Cooper, loc. cit.; Jobber and Sanderson, ibid.; and T. L. Childers and S. J. Skinner, "Theoretical and Empirical Issues in the Identification of Survey Respondents," *Journal of Marketing Research Society* (January 1985), 39–53.

[75] L. L. Neider and P. K. Sugrue, "Addressing Procedures," *Journal of the Academy of Marketing Science* (Fall 1983), 455–460; R. D. Taylor and V. Blakney, "Response Rates, Item Omissions and Response Speed," in N. K. Malhotra, *Developments in Marketing Science* VIII (Academy of Marketing Science, 1984), 399–402; G. Albaum, "Do Source and Anonymity Affect Mail Survey Results," *Journal of the Academy of Marketing Science* (Fall 1987), 74–81; and G. C. Wunder and G. W. Wynn, "The Effects of Address Personalization and Mailed Questionnaire Response Rate, Time, and Quality," *Journal of Marketing Research Society* (January 1988), 95–101.

[76] A. A. Armenakis and W. L. Lett, "Sponsorship and Follow-Up Effects on Response Quality of Mail Surveys," *Journal of Business Research* (February 1982), 251–262; and Albaum, ibid.

[77] T. L. Childers, W. M. Pride, and O. C. Ferrell, "A Reassessment of the Effects of Appeals on Response to Mail Surveys," *Journal of Marketing Research* (August 1980), 365–370; J. Hornik, "Impact of Pre-Call Request Form and Gender Interaction on Response to a Mail Survey," *Journal of Marketing Research* (February 1982), 144–151; S. J. Skinner, A. J. Dubinsky, and T. N. Ingram, "Impact of Humor on Survey Responses," *Industrial Marketing Management* (April 1983). 139–143.

[78] C. J. Dommeyer, "The Effects of Negative Cover Letter Appeals on Mail Survey Response," *Journal of the Market Research Society* (October 1987), 445–51.

[79] A. L. Beaman et al., "Fifteen Years of Foot-in-the-Door Research," *Personality and Social Psychology Bulletin* (June 1983), 181–196. A slightly more favorable conclusion is E. F. Fern, K. B. Monroe, and R. A. Avila, "Effectiveness of Multiple Request Strategies," *Journal of Marketing Research* (May 1986), 144–52.

[80] T. A. Heberlein and R. Baumgartner, "Is a Questionnaire Necessary in a Second Mailing?," *Public Opinion Quarterly* (Spring 1981), 102–108; S. W. McDaniel

and C. P. Rao, "Response Quality" in K. Bernhardt et al., *The Changing Marketing Environment* (Chicago: AMA, 1981), 401–404; and P. J. O'Conner, G. L. Sullivan, and W. H. Jones, "An Evaluation of the Characteristics of Response Quality," in A. A. Mitchell, *Advances in Consumer Research IX* (Provo: Association for Consumer Research, 1982), 257–259.

[81] I. Roshwalb, "Recent Controversy in Washington: An FTC Case," in Monroe, op. cit., 277.

[82] See also D. K. Pearl and D. Fairley, "Testing for the Potential of Nonresponse Bias in Sample Surveys?" *Public Opinion Quarterly* (Winter 1985), 553–60.

[83] See T. Sharot, "Weighting Survey Results," *Journal of the Marketing Research Society* (July 1986), 269–84.

[84] V. Y. Pandit and Z. Khairullah, "Treatment of Item Nonresponse," in J. D. Lindquist, *Developments in Marketing Science VII* (Miami: Academy of Marketing Science, 1984), 435–437.

[85] J. C. Ward, B. Russick, and W. Rudelius, "Reducing Callbacks and Not-at-Home Bias in Personal Interviews," *Journal of Marketing Research* (February 1985), 66–73.

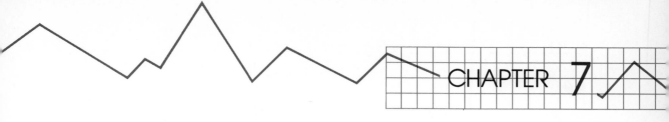

Experimentation

The American Heart Association uses direct mail as a major part of its fund-raising effort. A decision was made to develop and test alternative "teaser" lines for the outside of the fund solicitation envelopes. The six proposed envelopes are shown below and on page 182.

The current method that involved a plain envelope was used as a control. A large mailing of each type of envelope was sent to randomly selected prospects (individuals who had not given before) and donors (individuals who had given before). Donations were measured for each envelope type, and the results for prospects and donors were analyzed separately. Which was the best envelope?

(1)

(2)

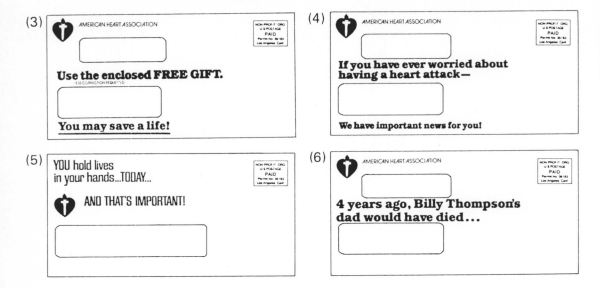

The American Heart Association study just described is an example of an *experiment.* Although we may not think of it as such, experimentation is a common part of our everyday lives. When we try on clothes, try a new route to school or work, or take a test drive in an automobile, we are engaged in experimentation.

Experimentation is also a common feature in the marketing activities of many firms: a grocer decides to use new point-of-purchase material to see how it works; a manufacturer offers an additional bonus for sales of certain products; an advertising agency compares the cost of a computer-generated media schedule with the cost of a schedule generated manually. All of these represent forms of experimentation.

Exhibit 7–1 describes a recent marketing experiment. Would you feel confident making a decision on the use of point-of-purchase displays based on this experiment? Why? The purpose of this chapter is to enable you to evaluate marketing experiments from a decision-making perspective.

The characteristics of a controlled experiment are described first. Then the various types of errors that might affect an experiment are analyzed. The third section of the chapter is devoted to a description of the more common types of experimental designs that have been developed to control or reduce experimental errors. Finally, *ex post facto* studies that resemble experiments are described. The environments — laboratory and field — in which experiments are conducted are examined in the next chapter.

Exhibit 7–1 *Olympia Beer Point-of-Purchase Display Impact Experiment*

The Point-of-Purchase Advertising Institute in cooperation with Olympia beer recently conducted a study to ascertain the impact of static and motion point-of-purchase displays on the sales of Olympia beer.° The displays were installed in twelve liquor stores and twelve supermarkets in two California cities with different demographics. Matching stores (stores in similar areas without displays) were used for control purposes. Sales were monitored for a four-week time period.

In the liquor stores, static displays increased sales by over 56 per cent compared to the control stores and motion displays produced a 107 per cent sales increase. In the food stores, static displays improved sales by 18 per cent over similar stores with no displays. Motion displays produced a 49 per cent sales gain. Market share followed a similar pattern in both types of outlet.

° Fieldwork was conducted by Product Acceptance & Research, Inc., Evansville, Indiana.
Source: Two Studies on the Effectiveness of Static and Motion Displays for the Brewing Industry (Point-of-Purchase Advertising Institute, Inc., undated), 1–2.

The Nature of Experimentation

Experimentation involves the manipulation of one or more variables by the experimenter in such a way that its effect on one or more other variables can be measured. A variable being manipulated is called the *independent variable.* In Exhibit 7–1, the point-of-purchase display is an independent variable. The envelope teaser line was the independent variable in the Heart Association study. A variable that will reflect the impact of the independent variable is called a *dependent variable.* Its level is at least partially dependent on the level or magnitude of the independent variable(s). Unit sales is the dependent variable in the point-of-purchase experiment, as is donations in the Heart Association experiment.

That portion of the sample or population that is exposed to a manipulation of the independent variable is known as a *treatment* group. Thus, the stores receiving the static point-of-purchase display and the stores receiving the motion point-of-purchase display are the two treatment groups in Exhibit 7–1. The six groups of prospects and the six groups of donors are the treatment groups in the fund-raising study.

A group in which the independent variable is unchanged is called the *control* group. Those stores receiving no display constitute the control group in the Olympia beer example, while those individuals receiving the plain envelope served as the control group in the Heart Association experiment.

In order to be confident that any change (or lack of change) in the dependent variable is caused by the independent variable, the researcher must measure or control the effects of other variables. This control is generally achieved by one of two methods, randomization or matching. *Randomization* involves randomly assigning subjects to treatment and control groups. This technique was used in the Heart Association study. *Matching* is the deliberate assignment of subjects to treatment and control groups to achieve balance on key dimensions. This was used in the point-of-purchase study. Both approaches attempt to ensure that the independent variable is the only variable that differs between the groups.

The purpose of the test involving Olympia beer was "to compare the difference in sales volume between no displays and a static display, and then to determine the impact of a static display versus a motion display." In other words, the experiment sought to establish the extent to which particular displays would *cause* a change in sales. Likewise, the Heart Association attempted to see if a teaser line on an envelope would *cause* an increase in donations. They found that envelope number two produced more donations than any other tested envelope.

Experimentation is oriented toward establishing and measuring causal relationships among the variables under consideration. Well-designed experiments are uniquely equipped to demonstrate causal relationships because they allow for or control other potential causal factors (extraneous variables). This is not possible with survey research or secondary data.

Types of Errors Affecting Experimental Results

Consider a retailer who has always charged $1.00 a unit for a particular product and has consistently sold 100 units per week. Curious about the effect of price level on sales, she increases the price to $1.20 a unit for a week and monitors sales. Sales drop to 50 units during the week. Price, in this example, is the independent variable and sales level is the dependent variable. Because sales changed, the retailer might be willing to conclude that price level does indeed affect sales level.

Before our retailer could reach such a conclusion, however, she would have to be sure that no other variable could have caused the change in sales. For example, if the area had had unusually bad weather, if the mass transit system had been closed because of a strike, or if a competitor had had a major sale, our retailer could not with any confidence attribute the cause of the sales

Table 7 – 1 Potential Sources of Experimental Error

I.   **Premeasurement:** Changes in the dependent variable that are solely the result of the effect of the initial measurement

II. **Interaction error:** An increase (or decrease) in the effect of the independent variable because of a sensitizing effect of the premeasure

III. **Maturation:** Biological or psychological processes that systematically vary with the passage of time, independent of specific external events, and affect the measurement of the dependent variable

IV. **History:** The impact of extraneous variables on the dependent variable

V.   **Instrumentation:** Changes in the measuring instrument over time

VI. **Selection:** Assignment of experimental units to groups such that the groups are initially unequal on the dependent variable or in the propensity to respond to the independent variable

VII. **Mortality:** The loss of a unique type of respondent from one of the experimental groups

VIII. **Reactive error:** Effect(s) on the dependent variable caused by the artificiality of the experimental situation and/or the behavior of the experimenter

IX. **Measurement timing:** Measuring the dependent variable at a point in time that will not reflect the actual effect of the independent variable(s)

X.   **Surrogate situation:** Using an experimental environment, a population, or a treatment that is different from the one that will be encountered in the actual situation.

decrease to the price increase. Thus, we must be concerned with potential errors that might affect the results of experiments.

In Table 7 – 1, 10 types of errors that can confound experimental results are described: (1) premeasurement, (2) interaction error, (3) maturation, (4) history, (5) instrumentation, (6) selection, (7) mortality, (8) reactive error, (9) measurement timing, and (10) surrogate situation. These potential errors are described in more detail in the following paragraphs.

Premeasurement Error

Assume that an interviewer knocks on your door and requests your cooperation for a marketing study. You agree and proceed to complete a questionnaire. The questions are concerned with a brand of soft drinks that you have heard of but have not tried. Shortly afterward, you describe the interview to a friend and the next day you try one of the firm's soft drinks.

Two weeks later the interviewer returns and asks you to complete another questionnaire. This questionnaire is an alternative form of the one you completed earlier. You have continued to consume the firm's soft drinks and the second questionnaire reflects both increased consumption and a more favorable attitude toward the brand.

What caused the shift in your behavior? Although the firm might have increased advertising, decreased price, altered the package design, or manipulated any of a number of other variables, the "cause" of your interest in and use of the product was the initial measurement. *Premeasurement effects occur anytime the taking of a measurement has a direct effect on performance in a subsequent measurement.*

Premeasurement is a major concern if the respondents realize they are being measured. However, if inanimate factors such as sales are being measured or if disguised measurement of human subjects is used, premeasurement no longer represents a potential error source and can be ignored.

Interaction Error

Interaction error occurs when a premeasure changes the respondents' sensitivity or responsiveness to the independent variable(s). This sensitizing effect is particularly important in studies involving attitudes, brand awareness, and opinions.

A group of individuals may be given a questionnaire containing several attitude scales concerned with a particular brand. These individuals are then likely to be particularly interested in, or sensitive to, advertisements and other activities involving this brand. Thus, an increase, decrease, or change in, say, advertising is more likely to be noticed and reacted to by these individuals than by a group who did not receive the initial questionnaire. This heightened sensitivity will often increase the effect of whatever change was made in the marketing variable and will be reflected in the postmeasurement.

It is important to note how interaction differs from direct premeasurement effects. In the example of direct premeasurement effects, the individual involved was never exposed to the independent variable. *All* of the change was caused by the initial measurement itself. In contrast, interaction does *not* require any *direct* effects from the initial measurement. It simply means that *the independent variable is more likely to be noticed and reacted to than it would be without the initial measurement.* Thus, premeasurement error occurs when the premeasurement, *by itself,* causes a change in the dependent variable. Interaction error occurs when the premeasurement *and the independent variable* have a unique, joint effect on the dependent variable. This distinction is important, as experimental designs that will control direct premeasurement effects will not necessarily control interaction effects.

Maturation

Maturation represents *biological* or *psychological processes that systematically vary with the passage of time, independent of specific external events.* Respondents may grow older, more tired, or thirstier between the pre- and postmeasurements.

For example, an experiment that begins at 1:00 P.M. and ends at 4:00 P.M. will begin with most of the respondents just having eaten and perhaps somewhat sleepy from lunch. By the time the experiment ends, the respondents will, on the average, be hungrier, thirstier (unless fluids were provided), less sleepy, and more fatigued. Maturation can also be a severe problem in those experiments that persist over months or years, such as market tests and experiments dealing with the physiological response to such products as toothpaste, cosmetics, and medications.

History

History is a somewhat confusing term. It does *not* refer to the occurrence of events prior to the experiment. Rather, *history refers to any variables or events, other than the one(s) manipulated by the experimenter, that occur between the pre- and postmeasures and affect the value of the dependent variable.* A soft drink bottler may measure its level of sales in a region, launch a promotional campaign for four weeks, and monitor sales levels during and immediately after the campaign. However, such factors as unusually heavy advertising by a competitor or unseasonably warm or cold weather could each produce (or nullify) a change in sales. These extraneous variables are referred to as "history" and represent one of the major concerns in experimental design.[1]

Instrumentation

Instrumentation refers to changes in the measuring instrument over time. These changes are most likely to occur when the measurement involves humans, either as observers or interviewers. Thus, during a premeasurement, interviewers may be highly interested in the research and may take great care in explaining instructions and recording observations. By the time the postmeasurements are taken, the interviewers may have lost most or all of their interest and involvement, and their explanations may be less thorough and their recording less precise. Alternatively, interviewers or observers may become more skilled with practice and perform better during the postmeasure.

Selection

In most experimental designs, at least two groups are formed. *Selection error occurs when the groups formed for purposes of the experiment are initially unequal with respect to the dependent variable or in the propensity to respond to the independent variable.*

    Random assignment to groups, the *matching* of subjects assigned to each, or *blocking* (this technique is described later) can minimize this problem. However, random assignment to groups still leaves the potential for selection error. In this case it would be similar to sampling error. Any time subjects volunteer for particular groups, regardless of the basis for making the decision — that is, time of day, location, pay, or other reasons — selection error may occur. For example, an experiment that requires three hours to complete and requires three groups could run one group from 9 to 12 in the morning, one group from 2 to 5 in the afternoon, and the third group from 7 to 10 in the evening. The experimenter could then request volunteers for each of these time periods. However, it is likely that people able and willing to volunteer for a morning session differ in a number of respects from those who come at a different time.

Statistical regression is a special form of selection error that can occur when individuals are assigned to experimental groups because of their scores on some measurement such as initial attitude toward a brand. If the initial measurement is not highly reliable, e.g., if the individual's scores are not very stable, the "high" score group is likely to score lower on average on a second measurement and the "low" score group is likely to score higher even if there has been no change in "real" attitude. This is because the high score group is more likely to contain individuals who scored higher than their actual feelings on the first test whereas the reverse is true for the low score group.[2]

Mortality

Mortality does not imply that some experiments reduce the population. Rather, *mortality refers to the differential loss (refusal or inability to continue in the experiment) of respondents from the various groups.* By a differential loss, we mean that some groups lose respondents that are different from those lost by other groups. If the experiment involves only one group, mortality error occurs when the respondents that remain in the study differ in responsiveness to the independent variable from those who withdraw.

Assume that a company has developed a new toothbrush that, although somewhat inconvenient to use, should reduce the incidence of cavities. A number of children, age eight to fifteen, are selected and randomly assigned to two groups, one of which will receive the new toothbrushes. The respondents in each group are given dental checkups and told to brush their teeth in their normal manner for the following year. During the year's time, both groups will lose some members because of moving, loss of interest, and so forth. This may not involve any mortality error because, if the sample is large enough, it will affect both groups more or less equally.

However, the treatment group with the new "inconvenient" toothbrush will lose some members because of this inconvenience. Furthermore, those remaining in the treatment group are likely to be more concerned about their teeth than those who quit. Therefore, by the end of the year, the treatment group will have a higher percentage of respondents who are concerned about their teeth. These respondents are likely to brush more often, eat fewer sweets, and generally take better care of their teeth than the control group.

This may be sufficient to cause a difference between the groups even if the new toothbrush itself has no effect.

Reactive Error

A reactive error occurs when the artificiality of the experimental situation or the behavior of the experimenter causes effects that emphasize, dampen, or alter any affects caused by the treatment variable. The reason for this is that human subjects do not respond passively to experimental situations. Rather, for some subjects at least, the experiment takes on aspects of a problem-solving experience in which the subject tries to discover the experimental hypothesis and then produce the anticipated behavior.

A reactive error cannot be controlled for by the experimental design. Rather, it must be controlled for by the structure of the experimental situation. Since reactive arrangements are most critical in laboratory experiments, a detailed discussion of the problem they pose is provided in the section on laboratory experiments.

Measurement Timing

We sometimes assume that the effect of any independent variable is both immediate and permanent. Thus, experiments occasionally manipulate an independent variable (price or advertising, for example), take an immediate measure of the dependent variable (sales), and then move on to the next problem. The danger in such an approach is that the immediate impact of the independent variable may be different from its long-range effect.

Errors of measurement timing occur when pre- or postmeasurements are made at an inappropriate time to indicate the effect of the experimental treatment. Consider the following example. Weekly sales of a product are measured in two equivalent groups of stores. Average sales in each group equal 100 units per week per store. The product is placed in a point-of-purchase display in one group (treatment group) and is left in its usual shelf location in the second group (control group) of stores. Sales are measured for each group during the first week of the point-of-purchase display. Average sales for the treatment group are 120 units compared to 105 for the control group. The point-of-purchase display appears to have caused an average sales increase of 15 units per store.

If the researcher stops here, however, an incorrect conclusion concerning the magnitude of the effect of the display may be reached. Measurements made after the first week or so of a point-of-purchase display typically show a decline in sales, often below the initial level. Thus, a part of the impact is simply a result of consumers stocking up on the product. Table 7–2 illustrates the general nature of these findings.[3]

The researcher must be certain that both the pre- and postmeasurements

Table 7-2 Effect of Measurement Timing on Point-of-Purchase Experiments

	Measurement (1)	Introduction of P-O-P	Measurement (2)	(3)	(4)	(5)
Point-of-purchase group	100	X	120	110	105	112
Control group	100		105	105	108	109

are made over a sufficient time period to indicate the effect of the independent variable.

Surrogate Situation

Surrogate situation errors occur when the environment, the population(s) sampled, and/or the treatments administered are different from those that will be encountered in the actual situation. A radio advertising copy test in which recall is measured after listening while driving an automobile simulator is clearly a surrogate for having the radio on while driving and may lead to substantial predictive errors of the effectiveness of radio advertising directed toward drivers.[4]

In market testing a potential change in price, the usual situation is that competitors are aware of the test and may either decide to do nothing or to "jam" the test by a promotional campaign or a price change of their own. In either case, if this is different from the action that the competitors would take in response to an actual price change, the results are a surrogate situation and consequent inaccurate data. Bristol-Myers test marketed its Clairol brand hair conditioner, *Small Miracle*, in what turned out to be a surrogate situation. When *Small Miracle* was initially tested, it had few major competitors and performed well in tests. However, as *Small Miracle* went national, so did Gillette's *Silkience* and S. C. Johnson & Son's *Enhance*. Thus, the market situation encountered by *Small Miracle* was substantially different from its test situation and it was not successful.[5]

Summary of Types of Experimental Errors

The ten types of experimental errors represent *potential* sources of error and do not necessarily affect all experiments. In general, experiments that utilize human respondents who are aware of some or all aspects of the experiment are most subject to these types of error. Those experiments that are concerned with nonhuman units, such as stores or geographic territories, are least subject to the various types of experimental error.

All of the various types of error, except reactive error, measurement timing, and surrogate situation, can be controlled for by the experimental design. In general, the more controls that are built into the design, the more costly the experiment becomes. In addition, a design that is very efficient in controlling for some types of errors may be relatively inefficient with respect to others. Therefore, experiments should be designed to control for those errors that are *most probable* and are believed to be *most serious* in a given situation, not for all potential sources of error.

Experimental Design

Experimental design involves obtaining the proper information within an acceptable accuracy range for a cost that does not exceed the value of the information. As we saw in the previous section, a number of potential errors exist that can adversely affect the accuracy of the data from an experiment. Figure 7–1 illustrates how experimental design is affected by these factors.

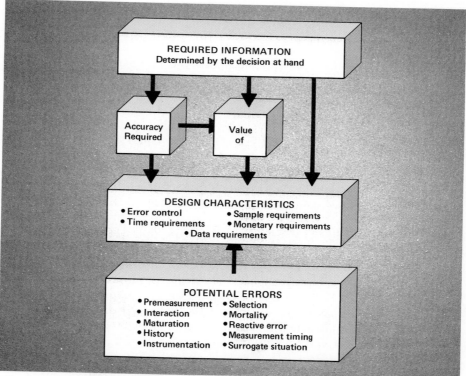

Figure 7–1   *Influences on Experimental Design*

Experimental designs can be categorized into two broad groups: *basic designs* that consider the impact of only one independent variable at a time, and *statistical designs* that allow the evaluation of the effect of more than one.

Before specific designs can be described, it is necessary to introduce the symbols that are used in their descriptions:

MB = *premeasurement:* a measurement made on the dependent variable before the introduction or manipulation of the independent variable

MA = *postmeasurement:* a measurement made on the dependent variable after or during the introduction or manipulation of the independent variable

X = *treatment:* the actual introduction or manipulation of the independent variable

R = designation that the group is selected randomly

Any symbol that is to the *right* if another symbol indicates that the activity represented occurred *after* the one to its left.

Basic Experimental Designs

After-Only Design

The *after-only* design involves manipulating the independent variable and following this with a postmeasurement, or

$$X \qquad MA$$

Ford Motor Co. spent $500,000 on an after-only experiment in Dallas and in San Diego. In this "experiment," women received engraved invitations to attend dealer showroom "parties" at which wine and cheese were served, the latest clothing fashions were displayed by models, and new Ford automobiles were shown in a "no pressure" situation. Subsequent purchases by those who attended the parties were one measure used to determine the "success" of the experiment.[6]

The Ford example is typical of most new-product test markets. While after-only designs are often used, their results are difficult to interpret and are subject to numerous errors. Suppose 1 per cent of the women attending a showroom "party" purchased a new Ford within six months after the party. What does this mean? Obviously, analyzing after-only experiments requires substantial market knowledge and subjective judgment. In addition, after-only studies do not control for such serious potential error sources as history, maturation, selection, and mortality. For example, a history error might have occurred if Chevrolet dealers had run special sales to coincide with Ford's "experiment." Therefore, after-only designs should be used with care.

Before-After Design

The before-after design is like the after-only design, except that it also involves a premeasurement:

$$MB \quad X \quad MA$$

The result of interest is the *difference* between the pre- and postmeasurements *(MA − MB)*. This comparison gives this design a considerable advantage over the after-only design. If no errors exist, the difference between the two measures is caused by the independent variable.

Unfortunately, the before-after design is subject to a number of experimental errors. *History, maturation, premeasurement, instrumentation, mortality,* and *interaction* all *may* affect the results of this design. However, if our experimental units are stores and we are measuring sales, the only source of error that is likely to be important is history.

Assume this approach is used to estimate the effect of a price increase on market share. The price of the leading brand of piecrust mix is increased by $.15 per box within a supermarket chain. The prices of the other three brands remain the same. Market share is measured both before and after the price change; it is found to drop 13 per cent.

Since history was not controlled for, attributing the market share decline to price involves judgment. The decline *may* have been caused by competitors' actions, quality-control problems, or other factors. The researcher may be willing to estimate subjectively the impact of any of these variables rather than go to the expense of adding a control group. However, the researcher must be alert to the possibility that extraneous variables caused the results, rather than the independent variable.

The before-after design occurs as a natural consequence of decision making. Prices are increased, packaging is altered, and commission systems are installed without the use of control groups. Before measures are compared to after measures and, after allowing judgmentally for the effects of other variables, the differences are attributed to the independent variable. However, unless the researcher is confident that extraneous variables are not operating, or that he or she can estimate their effects, before-after designs should be avoided.

Because they lack a control group and thus cannot control history effects, both after-only and before-after designs are often referred to as *quasi*-experimental designs.

Before-After with Control Design

The *before-after with control* design involves the addition of a control group to the before-after design:

$$R \quad MB_1 \quad X \quad MA_1$$
$$R \quad MB_2 \quad \quad MA_2$$

The addition of the control group allows for the control of all potential sources of experimental error, except *mortality* and *interaction.* For example, assume that a firm wishes to test the impact of a point-of-purchase display. Ten retail stores in the firm's trade area are selected at random for inclusion in the treatment group and ten are selected for the control group. Sales are measured in each group of stores before and after the introduction of the new point-of-purchase display. The *change* in sales between the two groups is compared. That is, the measure of interest is

$$(MB_1 - MA_1) - (MB_2 - MA_2)$$

This comparison controls for any initial inequalities between the sales of the two groups. Similarly, direct premeasurement effects are controlled. Both groups receive the premeasurement, and any changes caused by this should influence both postmeasures equally. In this example, premeasurement effects are unlikely to influence sales (unless the sales personnel suspect that *their* performance is being monitored). *History, maturation,* and *instrumentation* should also affect both treatment and control groups equally.

The before-after with control group design is subject to *interaction* effects. Suppose a researcher is interested in the effect on attitudes of a single direct-mail advertisement. A group of respondents is selected and a premeasurement administered to all of them. Half of the respondents then receive the direct-mail advertisement (treatment group) and half receive nothing (control group). One week after the advertisement is delivered, both groups of respondents are remeasured.

Any *direct* effect, that is, learning or attitude change, caused by the premeasurement should affect both groups equally. However, if the premeasure serves to increase the respondent's interest or curiosity in the brand, the treatment and the control group may be affected differently. Those respondents in the treatment group will receive a direct-mail advertisement from the firm that they may read simply because of the interest generated by the premeasurement.

The effect of the premeasurement (increased interest) *interacts* with the independent variable (advertisement) to influence the postmeasurement (change of attitude). The control group may also experience increased interest because of the premeasure. However, because the control group will not be exposed to the advertising, the increased interest will dissipate without influencing the postmeasurement of attitudes. The overall result of this is that any conclusions about the effects of the advertising campaign may only be generalized to individuals who have taken the premeasurement.

In cases where interaction is unlikely and control for history and selection errors is important, the before-after with control group design is the best design in terms of cost and error control. One example of this design involved a comparison of various channels of distribution for reaching low-volume accounts. Two treatment groups (mail-order and wholesale distributors) and one control group (the current distribution method — direct sales) were used:

$$
\begin{array}{cccc}
R & MB_1 & X_1 & MA_1 \\
R & MB_2 & X_2 & MA_2 \\
R & MB_3 & & MA_3
\end{array}
$$

The measures were of net profit contribution, so interaction was not a problem. The premeasurements were needed to ensure initial equality between the groups because small samples were used. The findings resulted in a shift to wholesale distributors for low-volume accounts.[7]

Simulated Before-After Design

The *simulated before-after design* was developed primarily to control for premeasurement and interaction errors in experiments dealing with attitudes and knowledge of human subjects. The design controls for these two errors by using separate groups for the pre- and postmeasurements:

$$
\begin{array}{cccc}
R & MB & & \\
R & & X & MA
\end{array}
$$

As in the before-after design, the measure of interest is the difference between *MA* and *MB*. Because different individuals receive the pre- and postmeasurements, there can be *no premeasurement* or *interaction effects*. However, the remaining problems associated with the standard before-after design, particularly *history*, remain.

This design is common in advertising research. A typical application of it involves giving a large sample of respondents a questionnaire to measure their attitude toward the product (premeasurement). An advertising campaign is then conducted (change in the independent variable). Finally, a *second* sample of respondents is given the same attitude questionnaire as the first group (postmeasurement). If the sampling is done properly and the two samples are large enough, they should be similar in terms of their initial attitude. Thus, any difference in the two scores can be attributed to the effects of the advertising campaign *and* any effects produced by history and maturation.[8]

After-Only with Control

The premeasurements in the before-after with control group design introduce the possibility of uncontrolled *interaction* effects. In addition, premeasurements generally cost money and may increase the artificiality of the overall situation. They are necessary whenever there is a reasonable probability that the treatment and control groups are not initially equivalent on the dependent variables. If it is likely that the groups are initially equal on the variable of interest, then there is no reason to go to the expense of a premeasurement. Instead, an *after-only with control* design can be used:

$$R \quad X_1 \quad MA_1$$
$$R \quad \qquad MA_2$$

This design explicitly controls for everything that the before-after with control design does except selection error. That is, even if random assignment is used, it is possible for the two groups to be initially unequal on the variable of interest. However, this design does eliminate the possibility of interaction. It is appropriate any time selection error is not likely to be a problem, such as when large random samples are used. It is uniquely appropriate when selection error is not a problem *and* interaction is. This design has been used recently to test the profitability of supermarket scanning data,[9] various formats for corrective advertisements,[10] different types of comparative advertisements,[11] and the effects of humor in radio advertising.[12]

After-only with control and before-after with control designs involving more than one level or version of the independent variable are sometimes called *completely randomized designs* (CRD). Such designs are subject to the same strengths and weaknesses as their simpler counterparts.

Solomon Four-Group Design

The *Solomon four-group design,* often called the *four-group six-study design,* consists of four groups, two treatment and two control, and six measurements, two premeasurements and four postmeasurements. An examination of the following diagram shows the overall design to consist of a before-after with control experiment and an after-only with control experiment run simultaneously:

$$R \quad MB_1 \quad X \quad MA_1$$
$$R \quad MB_2 \quad \quad MA_2$$
$$R \quad \qquad X \quad MA_3$$
$$R \quad \qquad \quad MA_4$$

The design explicitly controls for all sources of experimental error except *measurement timing, surrogate situation* and *reactive error,* which are not subject to control by designs. No single method of analysis makes use of all six measurements simultaneously. However direct estimates of the effect of interaction and selection, as well as other experimental errors, can be made by various between-group analyses.

Despite the virtues of this design, few instances of its use in applied marketing research have been reported.[13] The only time such an approach would be needed is when both selection error and interaction are likely to cause serious distortions of the data.

Conclusions Concerning Basic Designs

Table 7–3 summarizes the *potential* errors that may affect each design. A + indicates that the design controls for this type error; a − indicates that it is vulnerable to it; and 0 indicates that the error is independent of the type of design. Remember that *potential errors* are not the same as *actual errors*.

Statistical Designs

Statistical designs permit the measurement of the effects of more than one independent variable. They also allow the researcher to control for specific extraneous variables that may confound the results. Finally, statistical designs permit an economical design when more than one measurement will be conducted on each respondent.

Statistical designs are actually a means of structuring a series of basic experiments to allow statistical control and analysis of extraneous variables.

Table 7–3 Experimental Designs and Potential Errors°

	History	Maturation	Premeasurement	Instrumentation	Selection	Mortality	Interaction Error	Reactive Error	Measurement Timing	Surrogate Situation
1. *After-only*	−	−	+	+	−	−	+	0	0	0
2. *Before-after*	−	−	−	−	+	−	−	0	0	0
3. *Before-after with control*	+	+	+	+	+	−	−	0	0	0
4. *Simulated before-after*	−	−	+	−	−	+	+	0	0	0
5. *After-only with control*	+	+	+	+	−	−	+	0	0	0
6. *Solomon four-group*	+	+	+	+	+	+	+	0	0	0

° A + indicates that a method of controlling for the error is provided by the design; a − indicates no method of controlling is incorporated in the design; and an 0 indicates that the error is independent of the type of design.

That is, statistical designs are simply several basic experiments run simultaneously. Therefore, statistical designs are subject to the same errors that can affect the particular basic design that is being used in a given experiment.

Randomized Blocks Design

Completely randomized designs (CRD) are based on the assumptions that the experimental groups are initially similar on the dependent variable and that the members of these groups will react to the independent variable in a similar manner. These assumptions are frequently invalid.

Consider the following two experimental situations:

1. A field experiment to determine which of three price levels to use has a total of 27 stores available as experimental units. The sales volume of the stores ranges from $300,000 to $800,000 per month. Sales of the product in question tend to vary closely with total store sales. In this situation, a CRD would not be appropriate since the probability of randomly selecting equivalent samples would be small.

2. A laboratory experiment is to be conducted to decide on an advertising theme for a new liqueur. The primary issue is whether to use a masculine theme, a feminine theme, or a gender-free theme. Six advertisements are prepared that represent different positions along a masculine-feminine appeal dimension. Management suspects that the reaction to the advertisement will be strongly influenced by the gender of the respondent. Again, a CRD would not be appropriate since the gender effects could not be easily determined.

Randomized block designs (RBD) are appropriate for situations in which the researchers suspect that there is *one* major external variable, such as total sales or sex of the respondents, that might influence the results. Of course, one must be able to identify or measure this variable before one can utilize a RBD. In a RBD, the experimental units are *blocked,* that is, grouped or stratified, on the basis of the extraneous, or *blocking,* variable.

By ensuring that the various experimental and control groups are matched as closely as possible on the extraneous variable, we are assured that it affects all groups more or less equally. The principles and advantages of a RBD can be seen by reexamining the two research situations presented at the beginning of this section. In the first situation, the researcher was faced with the problem of selecting three groups from 27 stores with a wide range of sales. Total sales were believed to be an extraneous variable that could confound the experimental results. A RBD is appropriate since the stores can be grouped by sales level.

First, the stores are rank ordered in terms of sales. The total number of experimental units 27, is divided by the number of experimental groups, 3, to determine how many blocks are needed, 9. The experimental units are then systematically assigned to the 9 blocks such that the top 3 ranked stores are assigned to the first block, the second 3 to the second block, and so forth. Finally, one unit from each block is *randomly assigned to each of the treatment groups. Table 7–4 illustrates this process.*

This process was recently used to compare the effectiveness of nutritional point-of-purchase (P-O-P) signs, with standard P-O-P signs, and no P-O-P signs for vegetables. The researchers used a procedure exactly like that shown in Table 7–4. The results of the study indicated that neither type of P-O-P sign affected vegetable sales.[14]

In the situation involving the masculine versus feminine advertisements, the concern is somewhat different. In this situation, it is possible to secure a large enough group of men and women to assure adequate comparability of test and control groups. Rather than lack of comparability, the concern here is with isolating the effect of type of theme on the male and female subgroups as well as the total group. Again, an **RBD** represents an efficient approach.

Assume that a total sample of 800 males and 400 females is available. Individuals are assigned to blocks based on their gender, producing one block of 400 females and one block of 800 males. The individuals within each block are *randomly* assigned to treatment groups. The use of analysis of variance then allows the researcher to determine the impact of the commercial on the overall group as well as its effect on the male and female subgroups. The Heart Association study described at the beginning of the chapter used a

Table 7–4 RBD to Increase Experimental Precision

Block No.	Store Rank	Treatment Groups		
		X_1	X_2	X_3
1	1,2,3	3	2	1
2	4,5,6	4	5	6
3	7,8,9	9	7	8
4	10,11,12	10	11	12
5	13,14,15	14	13	15
6	16,17,18	17	18	16
7	19,20,21	20	19	21
8	22,23,24	22	23	24
9	25,26,27	25	26	27

similar RBD; prospects and donors served as the two blocking groups. Likewise, the study described in Exhibit 7–1 blocked on store type to allow the determination of any differential effects of P-O-P on the two types of outlets.

In general, RBDs are more useful than completely random designs because most marketing studies are affected by such extraneous variables as store type or size, region of the country, and sex, income, or social class of the respondent. The major shortcoming of RBDs is that they can only control for *one* extraneous variable. When there is a need to control for or block more than one variable, the researcher must utilize Latin square or factorial designs (although it is possible to block *within* blocks; that is, block by store type, and then block by size within store type).[15]

Latin Square Designs

Latin square designs allow the researcher to control statistically for two noninteracting extraneous variables in addition to the independent variable. This control is achieved by a blocking technique similar to that described in the previous section on randomized blocks designs.

This design requires that each extraneous or blocking variable be divided into an equal number of blocks or levels, such as drugstores, supermarkets, and discount stores. The independent variable must be divided into the same number of levels, such as high price, medium price, and low price. A Latin square design is shown in the form of a table with the rows representing the blocks on one extraneous variable and the columns representing the blocks on the other. The levels of the independent variable are then assigned to the cells in the table such that each level appears once, and only once, in each row and each column.

Latin square designs are described on the basis of the number of blocks on the extraneous variables. A design with three blocks is called a *3 × 3 Latin square*, four blocks is a *4 × 4 Latin square*, and so forth.

Suppose we wanted to test the impact on sales of three different price decreases for a personal care item. We suspect that the response may differ with the type of retail outlet — drugstore, supermarket, and discount store. In addition, we feel that sales may vary over the time of the experiment. How should we proceed?

The first step in constructing a Latin square design is to construct a table with the blocks on the extraneous variables associated with the rows and columns. Since we have three levels of the independent variable (price) and three levels of one blocking or control variable (store type), we need three levels of the remaining blocking variable (time). Then, we can construct a table as follows:

| | Store Type | | |
Time Period	Drug	Supermarket	Discount
1			
2			
3			

Next, we randomly assign the levels of the independent variable to the nine cells of the table, such that each of the three price levels is assigned once and only once to each row and each column.

This is, in fact, a simple procedure. The first step is to assign the three price levels randomly to each cell in row 1.

1	price 2	price 3	price 1

Next, price level 1 or 3 should be randomly assigned to row 2, column 1. Since price 2 is already in column 1, it is not eligible to appear there again.

1	price 2	price 3	price 1
2	price 1		

These four random assignments completely determine a 3 × 3 Latin square since the "once to each row and column" rule will automatically specify which treatment goes into each of the remaining cells:

| | Store Type | | |
Time Period	Drug	Supermarket	Discount
1	price 2	price 3	price 1
2	price 1	price 2	price 3
3	price 3	price 1	price 2

This table represents the 3×3 Latin square design. Now we must decide on which basic design to conduct in each cell of the square. Typically, a before-after or after-only (with or without control) design would be used. Suppose an after-only with control design is used. From 5 to 20 stores of each type would generally be involved. In this case, during the first time period (say two weeks), 5 drugstores would price the product at price *2*, 5 supermarket stores would be at price *3*, and 5 discount stores would be price *1*. Matched samples of 5 stores of each type would price at the current level. The average difference between the control and treatment stores in each cell would be recorded.

In the second time period the price levels would be shifted such that drugstores have price level *1*, supermarkets have price level *2*, and discount stores have price level *3*. The same measurement procedure would be used. Price levels would be shifted among store types once again for the third time period.

This design has the sales effect of each price level recorded once in each time period and once in each store type. Analysis would focus on which price level produced the most sales (or profits) and whether or not there were differential effects across store types.

Latin square designs are widely used in marketing research. They are especially useful in retail studies where the need to control for store type or size and time period is particularly acute. The Latin square design also allows the minimization of sample size by allowing the same experimental units to react to all the different levels of the independent variable.

Latin square designs suffer from several limitations. First, the requirement of an equal number of rows, columns, and treatment levels can sometimes pose problems for specific research tasks. For example, if we want to test four versions of a product and to control for time and store type, we must be able to isolate four store types. Furthermore, we must run the study for four time periods. If there are only three types of stores that carry this product, or if time is of critical importance, the Latin square must be altered.

Another drawback to the Latin square design is that only two extraneous variables can be controlled for at once. However, there is a relatively simple expansion of the technique, called a *Graeco-Latin square,* which permits the control of an additional variable.[16]

When several versions of a treatment variable, such as price, are applied to one control variable, such as a store; Latin square designs assume that there are no "carryover" effects from one condition to another. Thus, the design assumes that a low price in time period 1 will not affect the sales in time period 2 when a higher price is in effect. Clearly, such assumptions are not always valid, and there have been several versions of the Latin square design created to deal with this type of problem. One such version, called the *double changeover* design, consists of two standard Latin squares in which the sequence of treatments in the two squares is reversed.[17] Another approach is a short (one-week) "rest" period between the treatment time periods. During the rest period, price, advertising, or whatever the treatment variable is, is set at its normal or traditional level.[18]

A final weakness of the Latin square design is the restriction that the control variables cannot interact with each other or with the independent variable. As demonstrated in the next section, interaction between variables is fairly common in marketing.

Factorial Design

Factorial designs are used to measure the effect of two or more independent variables at various levels. They are particularly useful when there is some reason to believe that interaction might occur. *Interaction occurs when the simultaneous effect of two or more variables is different from the sum of their effects taken one at a time.* For example, an individual's favorite color might be gray and his favorite dessert might be ice cream. However, it does not follow that he would prefer gray ice cream.

Figure 7-2 illustrates two different types of interaction between gender and ad copy. In A, no interaction is present. Whereas males and females have different levels of "liking" for the ads, their relative liking does not change as the ad copy changes. In B, *ordinal interaction* is present. Both genders react to the ads in a similar manner, but to different degrees. In C, *disordinal interaction* occurs. Males and females have qualitatively different reactions to the different ads. Notice that failure to measure interaction would be particularly serious in this instance.

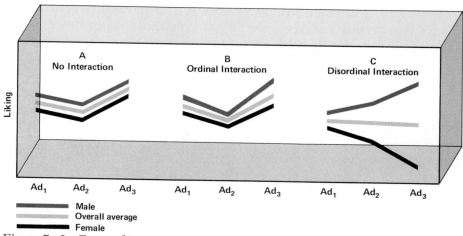

Figure 7-2 *Types of Interaction*

Interaction can involve any number of variables. Factorial designs coupled with analysis of variance statistical procedures (see Chapter 19) are required to measure interaction. Assume that we are testing a new carbonated fruit drink designed for the preteenage market. We need to decide how much carbonation and how much sweetener to put into the drink. Five levels of carbonation and five levels of sweetener cover the range of each of these variables.

How do we determine which combination of carbonation and sweetener to use? We could select one level of sweetener, add the five levels of carbonation to this level of sweetener, and have a group of preteenagers taste-test the resulting five combinations to select their favorite version. Then we could repeat this operation in reverse to determine the level of sweetener. Unfortunately, this approach does not take into account any interaction between the level of sweetener and the level of carbonation.

It is possible that low-carbonation drinks should be very sweet and high-carbonation drinks should not be very sweet. The most preferred combination might lie somewhere between these extremes. A factorial design can uncover this type of information.

In depicting a factorial design in a table, each level of one variable can represent a row and each level of another variable can represent a column. Factorial designs require a cell for every possible combination of treatment variables. Therefore, this example would require a table such as Table 7–5 with 5×5, or 25, cells. The hypothetical values in the cells shown in Table 7–5 represent the average rating assigned each combination by a random sample of 25 preteenagers (a total sample of $25 \times 25 = 625$). The rating scale ranged from 0 (strongly dislike) to 20 (strongly like).

Statistically, an analysis of variance can determine the effect on stated preference of carbonation level, sweetness, and the interaction between the two. Obviously, this is of great value in many research studies. However, the increase in measurement capabilities gained by using factorial designs is pur-

Table 7–5 5^2 Factorial Design

Carbonation Level	Sweetness				
	1	2	3	4	5
1	2	4	7	10	12
2	2	3	4	7	8
3	4	6	8	5	5
4	10	15	11	6	4
5	13	9	6	3	2

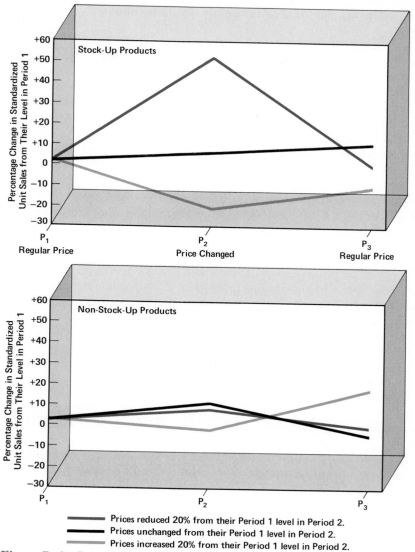

Figure 7–3 *Interaction in the Sales Response to Price Manipulations According to Product Type*

Source: D. S. Lituack, R. J. Calantone, and P. R. Warshaw, "An Examination of Short-Term Retail Grocery Price Effects," *Journal of Retailing," Fall 1985, 20–21.*

chased at the expense of greater complexity, more measurements, and higher costs.

For example, if a third variable were included in the example, such as color or flavoring, with five levels, the number of cells would increase to 125 and maintaining 25 observations per cell would require a sample of 3,125! The same three variables could be analyzed experimentally by means of a Latin square design with only 25 cells. However, the Latin square design will not detect interaction. Therefore, in cases where interaction is suspected, some form of a factorial design is required.[19]

A recent study investigated the sales impact of retail price changes on 72 supermarket items.[20] A 3 × 2 factorial design was used with three levels of price (normal, 20 per cent increase, 20 per cent decrease) and two levels of product type (subject to stocking-up and not subject to stocking-up). Figure 7-3 illustrates the results. As can be seen, very strong ordinal interaction occurs. Price changes have a major impact on stock-up items (decreases in price increase sales and vice-versa) but have virtually no impact on non-stock-up items. The strategy implications of these results are obvious.

The primary disadvantage of factorial designs is the large number of treatments required when there are more than a few variables or levels of each variable. These large numbers are required if all interactions and main effects are to be measured separately. However, in many situations, the researcher is interested in only a few of the possible interactions and main effects. In these cases, a *fractional factorial design* may be used. As the title suggests, these designs consist of only a portion of a full factorial design.[21]

Conclusions Concerning Experimental Designs

The preceding sections have described a number of experimental designs. These designs have ranged from the simple after-only design to factorial designs. No one design is *best*. The choice of the experimental design must balance cost constraints with accuracy requirements. Accuracy is related to the amount of error. However, we should not assume that the possibility of an experimental error means that the error *will* occur. It *is* possible that history will *not* bias the results in a before-after design, even though the design itself does not control for it. The researcher and the decision maker should apply judgment in deciding which errors represent sufficient potential danger to warrant additional outlays for control.

Figure 7-4 provides a very general guide for selecting an appropriate experimental design.

A research design that is similar to experimentation, but with the critical difference that the treatment and control group(s) are selected *after* the intro-

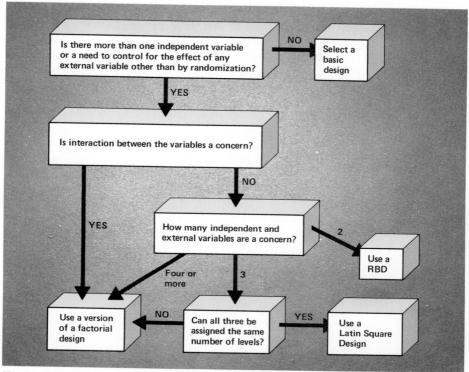

Figure 7-4   *General Guide to Selecting an Experimental Design*

duction of the potential causal variable, is the *ex post facto* design. Since it is often confused with a true experiment, its characteristics are described next.

Ex Post Facto Studies

Several department stores share details of their operations in order to improve their efficiency. A researcher selected one highly successful store and a relatively unsuccessful store. The study found "demographic differences and differences in self-confidence, aggressiveness, and fashion leadership" between the two stores' buyers. The researcher concluded that "balance in the buyer team and the discretion given to buyers may be two of the keys to success."[22]

The study described is an example of *ex post facto* research. In this type of research we start with "the present situation as an effect of some previously acting causal factors and attempt to trace back over an interval of time to some assumed causal complex of factors. . . ."[23] Thus, this study began with the

207

conditions "successful store" and "unsuccessful store" and examined one potential causative factor: characteristics of store buyers.

Ex post facto research is often treated as an experimental design. However, it does *not* meet the key characteristics of experimental designs: the researcher does *not* manipulate the independent variable nor control which subjects are exposed to the independent variable.

Exhibit 7–2   *National Cancer Institute of Canada: Study of Artificial Sweeteners and Cancer Using* Ex Post Facto *Methodology*

A Canadian study linking bladder cancer in humans to saccharin consumption was very influential in the FOA's decision to request a ban on the sale of saccharin.

The study involved a specific "case-control" methodology that is fairly common in medical studies of this type.° All reported nonrecurrent cases of primary bladder cancer in British Columbia, Nova Scotia, and Newfoundland served as one potential set of respondents. Of the 821 potential respondents, 632 participated in the study (56 had died, 65 refused to cooperate, 25 were too ill, and for 34 the attending physician refused permission). All participants were interviewed within six months of the diagnosis.

For *each* of the 632 "cases" participating in the study, a control (another individual) was included that was matched on sex, age (within ± five years), and neighborhood. A questionnaire was developed that included questions on demographic variables, residential history, use of nonpublic water supplies, occupational history, consumption of beverages and meats containing preservatives, medical history, use of analgesics, and smoking. The questionnaires were administered in the respondents' homes by trained interviewers.

An analysis of the resulting data on saccharin use and the incidence of bladder cancer revealed a statistically significant ($P = .01$) relationship. The final paragraph of the report concluded:

> Our results suggest a causal relation between saccharin use and bladder cancer in males, especially when they are considered in conjunction with results in animals.

° For a complete description of the study, see G. R. Howe et al., "Artificial Sweeteners and Human Bladder Cancer," *The Lancet*, September 17, 1977, 578–581.

Ex post facto projects are common and useful in marketing research.[24] They will continue to enjoy widespread utilization because they can provide *evidence* of causation in situations where experimentation is impractical or impossible. For example, *ex post facto* research provided the initial evidence that smoking cigarettes "causes" lung cancer. However, because the "smoker" and "nonsmoker" groups are self-selected, it was possible to suggest that some other factor, as yet unknown, "causes" or encourages *both* smoking and lung cancer. Exhibit 7 – 2 describes a controversial *ex post facto* study on the health effects of the consumption of artificial sweeteners.

Although frequently the only practical approach, *ex post facto* studies are not as desirable as experiments. They *cannot* be used to prove causation. Further, they are vulnerable to most of the errors described in the next section.

Review Questions

7.1. What does experimentation involve?

7.2. What do *ex post facto* studies involve?

7.3. Are *ex post facto* studies experiments? Why?

7.4. Describe and give an example of each of the following error types:
   a. premeasurement
   b. interaction error
   c. maturation
   d. history
   e. instrumentation
   f. selection
   g. mortality
   h. reactive error
   i. measurement timing
   j. surrogate situation

7.5. How does *premeasurement error* differ from *interaction error?*

7.6. Describe the following experimental designs using the appropriate symbols and indicate for which errors they control:
   a. after-only
   b. before-after
   c. simulated before-after
   d. before-after with control
   e. after-only with control
   f. Solomon 4-group

7.7. Is it always necessary to control for all types of experimental error? Why?

7.8. What is a *completely randomized design?*

7.9. How do *statistical* designs differ from *basic* designs?

7.10. What is the purpose of *randomization* and *matching* in experimental design?

7.11. What is *interaction?* How does *ordinal* interaction differ from *disordinal* interaction?

7.12. Describe each of the following designs:
   a. randomized block
   b. Latin square
   c. factorial

7.13. How do you decide which type of statistical design to use?

7.14. What is a *4 × 4 Latin square design?*

7.15. What is a *2 × 2 × 3 factorial design?*

7.16. What are the strengths and weaknesses of a *Latin square design?*

7.17. What are the strengths and weaknesses of a *factorial design?*

Discussion Questions/Problems

7.18. Why are simulated before-after designs sometimes used in field experiments on advertising effectiveness? What problems can arise in their use?

7.19. How will the increasing spread of UPC scanners affect marketing experiments?

7.20. Why is experimentation uniquely suited for determining causation?

7.21. Why is the Solomon four-group design seldom used in marketing studies?

7.22. Describe a specific situation for which you would recommend each of the following designs as being best (being sure to consider cost). Justify your answer.

a. after-only
b. before-after
c. after-only with control
d. before-after with control
e. simulated before-after with control

f. Solomon 4 group
g. randomized block
h. Latin square
i. factorial

7.23. Develop an alternative explanation for the results in Exhibit 7–2. How would you test your explanation?

7.24. Design an experiment to determine which of two colors for a new snack food are preferred by students on your campus.

7.25. Repeat 7.24 but introduce an explicit control for gender.

7.26. Repeat 7.24 but introduce explicit controls for gender and graduate/undergraduate status.

7.27. Repeat 7.24 but with five colors.

7.28. Repeat 7.25 but with five colors.

7.29. Repeat 7.26 but with five colors.

7.30. Repeat 7.26 but assume that you are concerned about the interaction between color and gender.

7.31. Develop a research design to provide information on each of the following hypotheses:

a. There is no difference between the percentage of families with total income between $25,000 and $30,000 that own vacation homes and the percentage of families with total income between $30,001 and $40,000 that own such homes.

b. A 10 per cent decrease in spot television advertising expenditures will not decrease sales.

7.32. How does one determine which experimental design to use?

7.33. What problems are encountered in experiments with human subjects that are not encountered in experiments with inanimate objects such as those a chemist might conduct?

7.34. Prosit is a regional beer with sales limited to three states, where it has always been popular among college students. The firm's management feels that Prosit is losing market share among students to several of the national brands. However, management currently has no exact measures of the students' attitudes or consumption patterns. Management is considering placing ads in the 93 college student newspapers in the area that accept such advertising. However, they are not sure how effective this would be. Design a study to test the effectiveness of this approach (assume that 2 versions of the advertisement are being considered).

Projects

7.35. Implement your design from problem _____ and write a managerial report on your results. What types of errors are most likely to have affected your results.

a. 7.24	d. 7.27	g. 7.30
b. 7.25	e. 7.28	
c. 7.26	f. 7.29	

7.36. Consult the latest issues of the *Journal of Marketing, Journal of Marketing Research,* or *Journal of Advertising Research.* Prepare and present to the class a description of an experiment reported in the journal. What errors may affect the results of the experiment?

References

[1] C. O'Herlihy, "Why Ad Experiments Fail," *Journal of Advertising Research* (February 1980), 53–58.

[2] For details see T. D. Cook and D. T. Campbell, *Quasi-Experimentation* (Rand McNally College Publishing Co., 1979), 52–53.

[3] See D. S. Lituack, R. J. Calantone, and P. R. Warshaw, "An Examination of Short-Term Retail Grocery Price Effects," *Journal of Retailing* (Fall 1985), 9–25.

[4] S. Collins and S. Jacobson, "A Pretest of Intrusiveness of Radio Commercials," *Journal of Advertising Research* (February 1978), 37–43.

[5] N. Giges, "No Miracle in Small Miracle: Story Behind Failure," *Advertising Age*, August 16, 1982, 76. See also L. Bogart and C. Lehman, "The Case of the 30-Second Commercial," *Journal of Advertising Research* (March 1983), 11–19.

[6] "Wine, Baubles, and Glamour Are Used to Help Lure Female Consumers to Ford's Showrooms," *Marketing News*, August 6, 1982, 1.

[7] C. H. Sevin, *Marketing Productivity Analysis* (New York: McGraw-Hill Book Company, Inc., 1965), 96–98. See also R. G. Chapman, "Assessing the Profitability of Retailer Couponing," *Journal of Retailing* (Spring 1986), 19–40.

[8] R. S. Winer, "Analysis of Advertising Experiments," *Journal of Advertising Research* (June 1980), 25–31.

[9] "Use of Scanning Data Improves Profitability in Supermarket Test," *Marketing News*, May 28, 1982, 10.

[10] R.J. Seminik, "Corrective Advertising: An Experimental Evaluation of Alternative Television Messages," *Journal of Advertising* (#3, 1980), 21–30.

[11] J. H. Murphy and M. S. Amundsen, "The Communications-Effectiveness of Comparative Advertising for a New Brand on Users of the Dominant Brand," *Journal of Advertising*, (#1, 1980), 14–20; and Z. S. Demirdjian, "Sales Effectiveness of Comparative Advertising," *Journal of Consumer Research* (December 1983), 362–5.

[12] C. P. Duncan and J. E. Nelson, "Effects of Humor in a Radio Advertising Experiment," *Journal of Advertising* (#2, 1985), 33–40.

[13] For an exception see R. W. Mizerski, N. K. Allison, and S. Calvert, "A Controlled Field Study of Corrective Advertising Using Multiple Exposures and a Commercial Medium," *Journal of Marketing Research* (August 1980), 341–348.

[14] D. D. Achabal, "The Effect of Nutrition P-O-P Signs" *Journal of Retailing* (Spring 1987), 9–24.

[15] Ibid.

[16] S. Banks, *Experimentation in Marketing* (New York: McGraw-Hill Book Co., Inc., 1965), 168–179.

[17] See ibid., Chap. 6; and G. T. McKinnon, J. P. Kelly, and E. D. Robinson, "Sales Effects of Point-of-Purchase In-Store Signing," *Journal of Retailing* (Summer 1981), 49–63.

[18] C. Paksog, J. B. Wilkinson, and J. B. Mason, "Learning and Carryover Effects in Retail Experimentation," *Journal of the Market Research Society* (April 1985), 109–129.

[19] A good example is J. B. Wilkinson, J. B. Mason, and C. H. Paksoy, "Assessing the Impact of Short-Term Supermarket Strategy Variables," *Journal of Marketing Research* (February 1982), 72–86.

[20] D. S. Lituack, R. J. Calantone, and P. R. Warshaw, "An Examination of Short-Term Retail Grocery Price Effects," *Journal of Retailing* (Fall 1985), 9–25. For

a more complex example see R. L. Earl and W. M. Pride, "The Effects of Advertisement Structure, Message Sidedness, Performance Test Results on Print Advertisement Informativeness," *Journal of Advertising* 3 (1980), 36–46.

[21] C. W. Holland and D. W. Cravens, "Fractional Factorial Experimental Designs in Marketing Research," *Journal of Marketing Research* (August 1973), 272, and P. E. Green, "On the Design of Choice Experiments Involving Multifactor Alternatives," *Journal of Consumer Research* (September 1974), 61–68.

[22] C. R. Martin, Jr., "The Contribution of the Professional Buyer to a Store's Success or Failure," *Journal of Retailing* (Summer 1973), 69–70.

[23] F. S. Chapin, *Experimental Designs in Sociological Research*, rev. ed. (New York: Harper & Row Publishers, Inc., 1955), 95.

[24] See M. Moriarty, "Feature Advertising-Price Interaction Effects in the Retail Environment," *Journal of Retailing* (Summer 1983) 80–98.

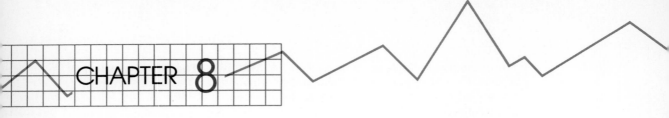

CHAPTER 8

Experimental Environment

Illinois Bell Telephone Co. recently developed an advertising program to increase local telephone use (measured by the number of local calls made). However, before launching the campaign, they wanted to be confident that the program would indeed increase local calls. Therefore, they conducted a field experiment.

The Test Market Group maintains a split cable facility in Moline and East Moline, Illinois. This facility allows the company to send specific commercials into some households and withhold them from others.

Two matched samples of 600 households each were used for the experiment. Local telephone use of each sample was monitored for 13 weeks to establish the before measure. Then the advertising campaign was presented to the treatment group at a level of 300 gross rating points (percentage of the audience reached × the number of times reached) per week for 38 weeks. The remaining sample, the control group, did not receive the advertising.

Over the 38-week period, the treatment group placed 7 per cent more calls than the control group (statistically significant at the .01 level of confidence). Further, this difference was slowly increasing throughout the 38-week test period.

Based on this experiment, Illinois Bell could estimate the economic value of advertising at this level throughout the region. Based on demographic and usage data on the 600 households in the experimental group, it could also determine the characteristics of those most responsive to the ad campaign. However, since only one level of advertising was tested (300 gross rating points), Illinois Bell does not know if this is the optimal level of advertising.[1]

The experiment conducted by Illinois Bell is a *before-after with control* experiment as described in the previous chapter. As noted in that chapter, all experimental designs are influenced by a number of controllable and uncontrollable factors. One of the major influences this research project must contend with is the experimental environment.

In the discussion in Chapter 7 of errors affecting experiments, the effect of the experimental environment (reactive error) was discussed briefly. This is a particularly severe problem for experiments using humans as the response group. To control for this type of error, we attempt to introduce as much realism into the study as possible.

Experimental environments can be classified according to the level of artificiality or realism that they contain. Artificiality involves eliciting behavior from the respondents in a situation that is different from the normal situation in which that behavior would occur. Thus, a taste test in which respondents are brought to a firm's product development laboratory, given three different versions of a soft drink in glasses labeled *L, M,* and *P,* and asked of which version, if any, they would like to receive a free carton, contains a high degree of artificiality.

At the other extreme, the three versions could be introduced into a number of stores or geographic areas accompanied by regular point-of-purchase displays, advertising, and pricing. Such an experiment is characterized by a high degree of realism.

The first study described represents a *laboratory experiment,* whereas the second represents a *field experiment.* Laboratory experiments are characterized by a relatively high degree of artificiality. Field experiments have a relatively high level of realism. A given experiment may fall anywhere along this artificiality-realism continuum. Those nearer the artificiality end are termed "laboratory" experiments and those nearer the realism end are termed "field" experiments. The Illinois Bell study was a field experiment. Each general type of experiment has its particular strengths and weaknesses as described in the following sections.

Laboratory Experiments

Laboratory experiments minimize the effects of history by "isolating the research in a physical situation apart from the routine of ordinary living and by manipulating one or more independent variables under rigorously specified, operationalized, and controlled conditions." [2] This degree of control is seldom possible in field experiments.

This isolation allows the researcher to be sure that the same experimental procedures will produce the same results if repeated with similar subjects. An advertisement that elicits a positive response from a subject group when viewed under strictly controlled laboratory conditions will elicit the same, or nearly the same, positive response when repeated with other groups of similar subjects in a similar laboratory setting.

However, the executive in charge of advertising is not concerned with the ability of the advertisement to elicit positive responses from other groups of respondents in a laboratory setting. The ultimate concern is the response of the market that is composed of individuals faced with real-world diversions, such as children wanting to play, noise from the television, and projects needing completion; and retailers and/or wholesalers who make stock level and promotional decisions.[3]

The ability of the results in an experimental situation to predict the results in the actual situation of interest to the researcher is called *predictive validity, generalizability,* or *external validity.*[4]

Exhibit 8–1 *Generalizability of a Laboratory Experiment for Oven Crock Baked Beans*

Green Giant developed a highly flavored version of baked beans which it labeled Oven Crock baked beans. According to an executive involved in the development: "We did a series of *blind taste tests* and had a significant winner over bland pork and beans by a 3-to-1 or 4-to-1 margin."

Blind taste tests are laboratory experiments in which consumers evaluate various versions of a product without knowing the brand name. In general, the consumption environment is strictly controlled so that time of day, accompanying foods, or individually added flavors cannot distort the results of the test. Thus, taste tests are generally highly replicable (similar subjects will prefer the same version each time the study is repeated).

However, Oven Crock was a "disaster" in test market. Surveys later showed that people who ate heavily flavored baked beans preferred to add their own "special" flavorings to the bland variety and therefore would not buy preflavored beans.

The physical control over external variables that the laboratory test provided did not exist in the test market situation. Once individuals could "spice up" their own beans, the preflavored variety was no longer preferred.

Source: L. Ingoassia, "A Matter of Taste," *Wall Street Journal,* February 26, 1980, 23.

Unfortunately, laboratory experiments are generally somewhat weak in generalizability. This weakness is a direct consequence of their primary strength. That is, the physical removal of most extraneous variables provides laboratory experiments with a high degree of *replicability* or *internal validity* at the same time that it limits their *generalizability*. Exhibit 8–1 provides an example of the problems this can cause.

Laboratory experiments tend to cost substantially less in terms of resources and time than field experiments. Further, they enable a company to minimize the chance that competitors will learn of its new ideas. This has led many researchers to utilize laboratory experiments in the early stages of their research projects when they are concerned with developing one or a limited number of advertisements or products. Then, if the costs and risks warrant it, these versions are subjected to further tests in field experiments. Appropriately designed laboratory experiments are also sometimes used as the final step before market introduction.[5]

Reactive Errors in Laboratory Experiments

The very nature of a laboratory experiment may cause the respondent to react to the situation itself, rather than to the independent variable (reactive error).[6] There are two aspects to reactive errors: the *experimental situation* and the *experimenter*.

Subjects do not remain passive in an experimental situation. They attempt to understand what is going on about them. In addition, they typically attempt to behave as "expected." If there are cues in the environment suggesting that a certain type of behavior is appropriate, many subjects will conform in order to be "good" subjects.

For example, a group of volunteers is brought to a room and given an attitude questionnaire that focuses on several products. The group then views a 30-minute tape of a television series with several commercials. One of the commercials relates to one of the products on the premeasure. A respondent may guess that an objective of the research is to try to change attitudes toward this product. If this occurs, the respondent is likely to comply.

The main control for errors of this type is to use creative environments and/or to design separate control conditions for suspected reactive arrangements.[7] In the example, a relatively neutral advertisement for the same product could be shown to one group. If the group's attitude is significantly more positive than that of a control group that saw no advertisement, it can be assumed that the reactive arrangements are causing at least some of the shift. Exhibit 8–2 illustrates an attempt to develop a realistic experimental environment in which to pretest package designs.

The effect of the *experimenter* is very similar to the influence of the personal interviewer in survey research. For example, nonverbal behaviors by

Exhibit 8-2 *The Pretesting Company's Laboratory Test Environment for Package Design Experiments*

A. Exposure to Advertising Campaign (where appropriate)

Each qualified respondent will be given six rough or finished advertisements on six different product categories (one being the test brand) and questioned on each ad's target message communication. This pre-exposure to advertising is only used where strong advertising support will be provided in the "real world" when introducing the new product or line extension.

B. Brand Examination While "Shopping"

Each respondent will be seated in front of a five and one-half foot diagonal rear projection screen and told that he/she is to photographically go "shopping" through a supermarket and to choose three different brands (first, second, and third choice) for three different product categories from the photographic "shelves." The respondent will have the ability to use the close-up panel, which will photographically bring any product chosen onshelf into a simulated one foot distance view. The respondent will be able to photographically go back and forth on any shelf, examining any product for as long or short a period as he/she desires. The respondent will not be aware that a computer is keeping an accurate measure of which products are being photographically approached and for what duration.

C. Measurements While "Shopping"

Each respondent will be tested in terms of how quickly he/she can find the test package in a real world setting, surrounded by competitive products on a life-size screen. The respondent will be told that he/she is about to see four shelf slides (one for each of the four product categories), one at a time. Each slide will show a product category in a natural shopping setting with full competitive surroundings. For each category, the slides may or may not actually contain the product to be found by the respondent. This is to prevent respondents from assuming that the test product is in view and quickly indicating the product has been "found."

As soon as the respondent believes he/she had identified the test product on shelf, he/she is to touch the product with a special pointer which will remove the slide from view and will record his/her reaction time. The respondent will then be asked to identify the test package, both for package design and copy.

D. Competitive Imagery Measurement

Each respondent will be asked to rate the ideal product for the test category on a customized list of attributes in terms of the importance of each attribute.

Consumer presses button on joystick to freeze slide of store shelf showing life-sized laundry-detergent packaging.

Respondent uses joystick to zoom in on four competitive brands. Enlargement allows subject to read product prices on shelf facings.

Source: The Pretesting Company (Englewood, New Jersey, undated). Used with permission.

experimenters have been found to influence subjects' preferences in a cola taste test even though the subjects were not aware of the influence.[8]

Experimenter effects can be limited by some of the same techniques used to reduce interviewer bias. For example, the experimenter should, to the extent possible, remain unaware of the hypotheses of the research. Of course, experimenters, like respondents, do not remain passive in an experimental situation. Therefore, it is likely that they will form hypotheses of their own early in the experiment. The best answer appears to be to use highly trained experimenters, to keep them uninformed about the research hypotheses, and to minimize their contact with the respondents. Tape recordings, written instructions, and other impersonal means of communication with respondents should be used whenever feasible.

Applications of Laboratory Experiments

Laboratory experiments are widely used in pretesting the impact of new or altered packages, advertisements, product concepts, and products. They are commonly used for evaluating pricing issues but are rarely used in assisting distribution decisions.

Package Tests. Packages must attract attention and convey information and image about the brand. Exhibit 8–2 illustrated one approach to conducting such experiments (various versions would be compared against each other or against the current package). Eye tracking and other physiological responses (see Chapter 14) are also used to test package designs.

Advertising Tests. The *tachistoscope* is a slide projector with adjustable projection speeds and levels of illumination. Ads can be flashed on a screen with exposure times down to a small fraction of a second — $\frac{1}{32}$, $\frac{1}{64}$ of a second if desired — with varying levels of light. Ads are tested to determine at which speeds elements such as the product, brand, and headline are recognized.

Tachistoscopic tests are widely used for copy testing. The nature of the technique effectively limits its application to the evaluation of print, outdoor, point-of-purchase, packages, and individual frames of TV ads. The ways in which one large advertiser uses tachistoscopic tests for ad evaluation, and the perceived advantages of his technique relative to other tests for this purpose, are described in Exhibit 8–3.

Another laboratory environment for testing television commercials is to simulate an exposure on television by showing the commercials with a new

Exhibit 8–3   *Evaluation of Advertisements at Sears, Roebuck & Co. Using the Tachistoscope* *

Uses of the Tachistoscope

1. *Screening a Number of Ads for Visual Impact*—20 to 30 ads are sequentially presented to a viewer using a T-Scope to control duration of exposure, which is usually seven-tenths-of-a-second. A second series of 20 to 30 ads is shown one-by-one. About half of the shots were seen earlier; the other half are new. Respondents are told that some of the ads they will now see were seen before. As they view each ad, the respondents are asked a recognition question (How certain are you that you saw this ad before?), and a series of rating scales. Using two or more sample cells, recognition scores can be adjusted by subtracting false recognition percentages. In this way, ads with the strongest visual impact are identified.

2. *Communication Tests*—An ad is shown at 0.7 seconds, 3 seconds, and for as long as the viewer likes. Questions about what the ad says and shows follows each viewing. In this way, we can determine if an ad is quickly communicating what is intended. Results on two or more ads can be easily compared, and norms for product identification, and other measures, established.

3. *Design Assessment*—A sign or package is shown at 0.7 seconds, sometimes longer, via the T-Scope, and viewers are asked to describe what they saw. Next, they are told they will see an array of signs or packages, usually six to nine items in a three-column two-row or 3×3 grid. Using the T-Scope as a reaction timer, the respondents are told to release the button, blackening the screen when they see the item they saw earlier. When that happens, they are shown a grid, and asked to tell where they saw the item. If they answer correctly, and only then, their time is counted. We learn what they cue on through the T-Scope exposure and how visually impactful the cue is. The test is usually carried out in black and white with one sample, and in color with another. This is done so the contributions of both color and design can be measured.

Advantages of Using the Tachistoscope

1. Behavioral measures are more sensitive than attitudinal ones, more reliable, less subject to regional variations, and more stable with smaller samples.

2. Marketing managers are less likely to challenge such objective data, and they readily understand it.

3. The T-Scope itself is a more reliable, portable, flexible, and accurate device than others used in physiological measurements of advertising effects.

° Provided by and used through the courtesy of Sears, Roebuck & Co.

television program to a theater audience. Pre- and postexposure attitudes and/or preferences are measured and the difference is taken as a measure of the effectiveness of the ad. One agency that conducts theater tests establishes pre-exposure preferences by offering each participant a choice of products before the showing, including those that are the subjects of the commercials they are about to see. A postshow offering is also made and changes in preferences are recorded.

Theater tests are conducted on new television commercials by about one-half of all large television advertisers. These tests have the advantage of being inexpensive and of providing a measure of the responses generated by the ad. Theater tests are conducted in a forced exposure setting, however, and so do not provide an indication of how well the ad attracts attention.

A variety of other laboratory environments are available for pretesting differing versions of print, radio, and television commercials. In general, these environments expose the commercials while the respondent is presumably focusing on the editorial or program content. Attitudes, affect, information recall, and/or purchase intentions are commonly used as the dependent variable(s). Before-after and after-only designs (either with an explicit control group or pre-established minimum "scores") are used. Focus groups and other in-depth questioning techniques are used to determine what the ad or package is communicating.

Pillsbury recently launched an advertising campaign for their new Crusty French Loaf using an Inspector Clouseau (the inspector portrayed by Peter Sellers in the Pink Panther movies) look-alike. Pretesting revealed that "the Clouseau character was so successful that he overshadowed the product . . . people tended to play back the character not the product." The commercial was revised to focus more on the product and the brand name. The revised version was successful in both the pretest situation and the market.[9]

Product Tests. Laboratory tests are widely used in the early stages of product development. Various versions of products that can be readily evaluated by consumers—such as foods, beverages, and most personal-care items—are routinely subjected to *blind* use tests (consumers rate performance without knowing the brand name) against each other and competitors. Procter & Gamble has a policy that no new product may be introduced unless it outperforms competitors in such a test.

While laboratory product tests such as taste tests offer a high degree of control over the consumption environment and produce data rapidly, they do not replicate the actual consumption environment. Exhibit 8–1 and the Coca-Cola example described at the beginning of Chapter 3 illustrate the problems this can cause.

Extended use tests, which are between a laboratory and field experiment, are frequently used as a follow-up to product taste tests or one-time use tests. In extended-use tests, consumers are given a supply of the product to use "normally" at home. While this method is still somewhat artificial (no purchase decision was made and there is pressure to use the product), it is substantially more realistic than a pure laboratory approach.

Field Experiments

Field experiments are characterized by a high degree of realism. The typical manner of obtaining this realism in marketing studies is to vary the independent variable in the marketplace. Unfortunately, field experiments are also characterized by a relative lack of control. This lack of control often extends to the independent variable as well as to extraneous variables.

For example, many field experiments require cooperation from wholesalers and/or retailers. However, this cooperation is often difficult to secure. Retailers who have a policy of price cutting may refuse to carry a product at the specified price, or they may be reluctant to assign prime shelf-facings to an untried product.[10]

Control of extraneous variables is even more difficult. Such factors as bad weather, strikes in pertinent industries, and campaigns by competitors are beyond the control of the researcher. In fact, such events may occur without the researcher becoming aware of them. The problem is compounded even further by the fact that these extraneous variables may affect some regions where the experiment is being conducted and not others.

This lack of control reduces the *replicability* or *internal validity* of field experiments. However, their "real world" setting tends to increase their *generalizability* or *external validity*. The strengths and weaknesses of this approach can be seen in field experiments of advertising copy.

Advertising Copy Field Tests

Day-after recall (DAR) is the most widely used method to field test television ads. The leading supplier of DAR copy tests, Burke Marketing Research, conducts tests for television commercials using the following research design:

1. *Nature of the exposure opportunity.* The opportunity for exposure is under natural (nonforced) conditions. An arrangement is made to have the test commercial shown in the sample cities in a prime-time (evening) slot.

2. *Sample.* A total of two hundred persons who had the TV set tuned to the program containing the test commercial are selected from the cities in which the test was conducted. Three cities typically are used for each test. After allowing for those persons who were out of the room, asleep, or changing channels at the time the test commercial was run, the remaining sample audience ranges from 135 to 155 in number. These persons are referred to as the *commercial audience.*

3. *Interviewing.* Respondents are interviewed by telephone the day after the airing of the test commercial. During this interview, viewers are asked to remember and describe as much of the commercial as they can. Recall is product- and brand-aided.

4. *Evaluative Criterion.* The percentage of persons in the commercial audience who remember and correctly describe one or more elements from the commercial is determined and compared to a recall norm. The norms for women are somewhat higher than for men. The norms at the end of 1985 were 23 per cent for women and 20 per cent for men, both for 30-second commercials. The women's norm was based on 1,365 tests conducted between 1981 and 1984, and the men's norm on 388 tests conducted during the same time period. Given the composition by sex of the 200 persons sampled, a weighted average norm (falling somewhere between 20 and 23 per cent) can be calculated for each DAR test. If the test ad score is higher than the weighted average norm, it is considered to be a better-than-average ad. If its score is lower than the norm, it is judged to be a poorer-than-average ad.[11]

The DAR method of copy testing receives better acceptance among advertisers than from advertising agencies. Agency personnel resist having their creative efforts judged by a number and by a method that provides no diagnostic information. In addition, at least one agency believes that the method discriminates in favor of commercials with rational appeals ("thinking" commercials) at the expense of those with emotional appeals ("feeling" commercials). (See Case III–3, "Foote, Cone & Belding, Inc.: Masked Recognition

Experiment," pp. 447–449, which describes the basis for this belief.)[12] Further, the relationship between recall or recognition and attitude change and purchase behavior is not well understood.

There is also no assurance that an ad that scores relatively high after one showing will hold up as well over the course of a campaign as one that initially had a lower score. Finally, brand and product category users tend to have higher recall than nonusers. (For an example see Exhibit 15–1, pp. 467.) For these and other reasons, electronic test markets, which are described shortly, are gaining popularity as a method of conducting experiments on advertising copy.

Test Marketing

Test marketing represents a particular type of field experiment that is often conducted in conjunction with the development of a new consumer product.[13] Test marketing involves the duplication of the planned national marketing program for a product in one or more limited geographical areas (usually cities). Often, differing levels of marketing mix variables are used in the test markets to help management isolate the best combination for the national introduction.

Test markets are not limited to new products. As shown in Exhibit 8–4, they can be used to evaluate price changes, new packages, variations in distribution channels, or alternative advertising strategies and levels. Governmental and social agencies are also active users of test marketing. For example, the Department of Agriculture used Madison, Wisconsin, and Knoxville, Tennessee, as test sites for a paid commercial campaign to steer schoolchildren and their parents toward healthy snacks.[14]

Although many types of products, as well as other aspects of the marketing mix, are frequently examined in test markets, durable goods are seldom tested in this manner. The fact that only a very small percentage of the total market (perhaps as low as 3 per cent) are potential purchasers of a durable good in a given year, coupled with the extremely high cost of tooling and production line changes, greatly limits the usefulness of such test markets. Exhibit 8–5 provides a description of a modified test market used by Amana Refrigeration for a refrigerator.

The two primary goals of most test market programs are the determination of market acceptance of the product and the testing of alternative marketing mixes.[15] A major additional value comes from alerting management to unsuspected problems and opportunities associated with the new product. For example, Stamford Marketing found that many purchasers of a new snack food placed the packages into their shopping carts upside-down. Since the package

Exhibit 8–4 *Recent Test Market Experiments*

1. K mart and Wendy's decided not to place Wendy's restaurants in K mart stores after a three-year test in Detroit.[a]

2. Colgate-Palmolive ran a four-month test of a teen fragrance called Maniac in Albany, Buffalo, and Rochester. Three different price levels were tested.[b]

3. Circle K convenience stores tested drop-off, overnight laundry service at its outlets in Tulsa.[c]

4. Neutrogena tested adding television advertising to existing print advertising for Neutrogena shampoo advertising in two Midwestern markets.[d]

5. The U.S. Travel and Tourism Administration is using West Germany as a test site for a proposed European advertising campaign.[e]

6. Del Monte tested the new aseptic package for its one-liter Hawaiian Punch in Marion, Indiana, and Pittsfield, Massachusetts.[f]

7. A group of California orange growers planned a test of generic advertising for oranges in 6 to 9 test markets. The test was expected to cost $500,000 ($320,000 for the advertising, $15,000 for trade promotion, $65,000 for production fees, and $100,000 for research expenses).[g]

8. Igloo Corp. tested the consumer awareness and sales impact of different levels of advertising expenditures. The test found that 600 gross rating points, compared to 150, produced a 75 per cent sales increase, compared to 25 per cent.[h]

[a] P. Strnad "K mart, Wendy's Drop Eatery Test," *Advertising Age* (March 28, 1988), 59.
[b] P. Sloan, "Manic Is Next Teen Fragrance," *Advertising Age* (November 3, 1986), 3.
[c] "Convenience Chain Testing New Service," *Marketing News* (June 19, 1988), 15.
[d] M. Magiera, "Neutrogena Faces TV Test," *Advertising Age* (October 19, 1988), 28.
[e] "New Beverages Are Brewing," *Advertising Age* (August 2, 1982), 14, 49.
[f] J. J. Honomichl, "N. W. Ayer writes Ticket for U.S. Tourism," *Advertising Age* (August 19, 1985), 3.
[g] "Orange Growers to Test Ads," *Advertising Age* (August 9, 1982), 61.
[h] T. Bayer, "Igloo Is Taking its Case to Consumer in Ad Drive," *Advertising Age* (June 21, 1982), 4.

was not designed for this, an unusual amount of compacting of the contents occurred and consumers were dissatisfied. A redesigned package has allowed a successful introduction.[16]

There are four basic types of market tests: *standard, controlled, electronic,* and *simulated.*

Exhibit 8–5 *Amana Refrigeration's Modified Test Market of a Refrigerator*

Amana Refrigeration, in conjunction with the Department of Energy, developed an energy-efficient refrigerator.

"With a product of this kind, final tooling can be in the order of $1,000,000 to $2,000,000," says Charles Mueller, manager of product planning at Amana. "We needed to have a good feeling about its acceptance." Amana manufactured prototypes of the unit, 25 of which were put into a field test market in stores in Norfolk, Va.

"Our goal was to find out both the consumer and distributor reaction. The refrigerator's price is higher than normal, so reaction to the higher cost vs. the models' payback — savings in electrical costs — was important. We also wanted to know what features were important to the consumer."

Consumers and dealers were not initially aware that the refrigerator they were buying was a prototype of a new product. After one month, Amana advised the purchasers of this and offered them the use of the refrigerators for one full year if they would monitor the models' performance each month. Not only would the full purchase price be refunded, but the customers would be given $100 toward the purchase of another refrigerator.

From the instore test, the company got feedback on the model's positioning to determine advertising emphasis, and also how it performed against the competition.

Working with the customers, Amana was able to make changes in the early design. For example, the thickness of the door was decreased to accommodate built-in installations.

Using the test market results, and with the refinements in place, Amana's Twin System refrigerator/freezer was rolled out nationally.

Source: G. Linda, "Those Test-Defying Goods," *Advertising Age,* February 22, 1982, M-36. Used with permission.

Standard Market Tests

A *standard market test* is one in which a small sample of market areas — usually cities — is selected and the product is sold through regular distribution channels, using one or more combinations of product, price, and promotional levels. Standard market tests are also used for price, package, and advertising testing.

Selecting the market areas for a standard test marketing program is obviously an important decision. Random sampling is seldom used. Rather, purposive selections are made based on the following general criteria: (1) they must be large enough to produce meaningful data but not so large as to be prohibitive in cost (the combination should comprise at least 2 per cent of the potential actual market to give projectable results); (2) they should have typical media availability and be self-contained from a media standpoint; (3) they should be demographically similar to the larger market area (region or entire United States); (4) the area should be a self-contained trading area, to avoid transhipments into and out of the area; (5) the areas should be representative with respect to competition; and (6) the combination of areas should allow testing under use conditions that are appropriate to the product (for example, both hard- and soft-water areas for a soap product, warm and cold climates for an all-weather tire). In addition, the firm needs to be aware of its "strength" in the test market area(s) relative to its strength nationally.

Test area selection is a particularly acute issue when more than one version of the product is to be tested. Not only must the areas meet criteria similar to those described but they must also be similar enough to each other to allow comparison of the various versions of the product.

A number of techniques can be used to assist the researcher in selecting both representative and equivalent test areas. However, most decisions as to which market to test in are based primarily on tradition and the researcher's judgment. Exhibit 8–6 provides a useful worksheet for structuring these judgments.

Brand sales are monitored through store audits, warehouse withdrawals, or, most commonly, UPC scanner data (see Chapter 5). Trial and repeat purchase rates, household penetration, substitution patterns, and use demographics are measured through existing or especially established household mail or scanner panels. Survey research can also be used for these purposes.

The length of time that a test market is conducted depends on the repurchase cycle for the product, the probability of a competitive response, the initial consumer response, and company philosophy. There is evidence that tests of new brands should run at least 10 months. Figure 8–1 illustrates the results of an analysis of 100 test markets that lasted at least 18 months. The final test market share was reached in 10 months 85 per cent of the time and 95 per cent of the time in 12 months.

Exhibit 8–6 *Test Market Selection Worksheet*

	1 St. Louis	2	3	4

I. PROJECTABILITY
  1. Market size – % of U.S. households in
     ADI
	1.29			

2. Demographic representation: Index U.S.
   Age – head of household: Under 35
                         35 – 54
                         55 and over
   Disposable Income: 0 – $14,999
                    $15,000 and over
   Ethnic composition: Spanish-American
                     Non-White
   Effective buying income/household
     in dollars
	94
	100
	105
	93
	107
	17
	100
	$17,623			

3. Media availability:
   Number of TV stations
   % Cable penetration
   Number of metro radio stations
     required for 50% share of adult
     listeners
   Number of daily newspapers in ADI
	6
	12
	5
	
	1			

4. Category/brand development:
   CDI
   BDI				

5. Geographic dispersion: Census area:	West North Central			

6. Sales-distribution representation:
   % ACV Expected
   (or now for company's other brands)				

7. Historical test market activity:
   Rank of use as test market during recent
     period (1977 – 1979)
	24th			

II. CONTROL 　1. Media isolation: 　　% spill-in 　　% spill-out	2% 5%				
2. Sales distribution spill-out/in: 　　% shipped outside ADI 　　% shipped into ADI	0% 0%				
3. Competitive balance: 　　(market share of major competitors 　　　indexed to national/regional). 　　1. 　　2. 　　3.					
III. MEASUREMENT 　　Availability of research services: 　　Warehouse withdrawals 　　Audits 　　Scanner item movement 　　Mail diary panel 　　Scanner consumer panel	SAMI Nielsen/ 　custom TRIM custom TRIM				
IV. COST 　　Estimated cost for period of the test	$_____				

ADI = Area of Dominant Influence
CDI = Category Development Index (How well established is the product category in this market compared to the national market)
BDI = Brand Development Index (How well established is the brand or firm in this market)
ACV = All-commodity Volume (% ACV for the firm should be similar to the national market.)
Source: E. M. Tauber, "Improve Test Market Selection with These Rules of Thumb," *Marketing News,* January 22, 1982, 8. Used with permission from the American Marketing Association.

Standard test marketing is not without its disadvantages. All of the comments made earlier concerning after-only designs apply to most test market situations. In addition, standard market tests take a long time. Not only do most tests run for 12 to 18 months, but the sales force must also spend 2 to 3 months selling the product through the distribution channel before the consumer test can begin.

In most test markets only two or three versions of the overall marketing mix are tested. Thus, the fact that the test versions do not prove successful (in terms of management's expectations) may not leave a clear-cut basis for eliminating other versions of the total product offering. Most organizations approach this problem by extensive consumer testing prior to test marketing. As a result of these preliminary tests, the researcher can often identify two to six versions of the total offering that appear most likely to succeed. These versions are then test marketed.

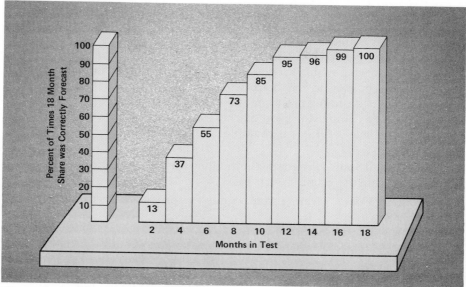

Figure 8–1 *Time and Test Market Accuracy*

Source: "The True Test of Test Marketing is Time," *Sales and Marketing Management*, March 14, 1983, 74.

In addition to the normal types of problems associated with experimental designs, and particularly after-only designs, test marketing faces two unique problems. First, firms routinely take direct actions, such as lowering their prices, increasing their advertising or even buying large quantities of the test product, to disrupt a competitor's test marketing program. This is commonly called *jamming*. Examples of such tactics include:

- Vick Chemical distorted test results for a new Colgate cough preparation by distributing 25,000 Nyquil samples into Colgate's two test markets.[17]

- Ralston Purina often hands out thousands of coupons for free five- or ten-pound bags of Purina Dog Chow in competitors' test areas.

- Competing toilet-paper producers disrupted American Can Co.'s test market of a pre-moistened toilet tissue by buying large quantities of the product.

- Chesebrough-Pond attempted to disrupt Procter & Gamble's test market of Wondra hand lotion in Milwaukee by offering huge discounts on its Vaseline Intensive Care lotion.[18]

- McDonald's "blew us away with promotion" when Wendy's tested a breakfast menu of biscuits and egg sandwiches.[19]

Another problem occurs when competitors successfully "read" a firm's test. Any market test is likely to alert competitors to the existence of the new product and its planned promotion. This allows competitors to begin to prepare their own versions of the product or to prepare other strategies. In addition, it is often possible for competitors to gain as much information from the test as the sponsoring firm because most test cities are included in various store auditing or scanning programs, to which many firms subscribe. An accurate reading of a competitor's test market may allow a firm to match or beat it to the national market. Recent examples of this include:

- Campbell Soup's Prego spaghetti sauce was beaten nationally by a similar product by Ragu.[20]
- General Foods' Maxim instant coffee was preceded by Nestle's Taster's Choice.
- Hills Bros. High Yield coffee was introduced nationally after Procter & Gamble's Folger's Flakes.
- Hunt-Wesson's Prima Salsa tomato sauce was beaten nationally by Chesebrough-Pond's Ragu Extra Thick & Zesty.
- Carnation's Ground Round dog food was preceded by General Foods' Gaines Complete.[21]
- Colgate-Palmolive's Fab 1 Shot beat Procter & Gamble's Tide brand version of a similar product to market.[22]

Concern over a competitor's beating it to the national market apparently influenced Carnation to go national without market testing its Come'n Get It dry dog food.[23] Other firms are also skipping tests. The chairman of National Presto explains his company's position:

We can't afford to spend the time test-marketing anymore. They'll start copying us too soon. So we're flying by the seat of our pants. It's gutsy as hell but the rewards are worth the risk.[24]

A final disadvantage of standard test marketing is its cost. The cost of standard market tests exceeds $1 million and sometimes runs as much as $10 million, with $3.5 million a typical figure. Tests of advertising campaigns cost over $1 million. The primary reason for their continued use is the high cost of new-product failure coupled with the difficulty of projecting new-product success (or other marketing mix changes) without standard test markets. It is estimated that three out of four products that are introduced after standard test markets succeed. In contrast, four out of five products introduced without standard test marketing fail.[25]

One reason for the accuracy of standard test markets is the fact that trade (retailer and/or wholesaler) support is also tested. Products or brands that cannot achieve sufficient shelf facings are unlikely to succeed even if consumers find them superior to those of the competition. The average supermarket stocks 14,000 items. In 1985, there were 2,200 new products and 2,700 line extensions introduced to supermarkets.[26] Obviously, supermarket managers cannot allocate shelf space to all new products. They allocate shelf space based on consumer demand, margin, handling costs, and fit with their overall product/brand mix. A standard test market is the only method that measures sales force and trade response on such key dimensions as:

- time to achieve target distribution levels
- actual versus planned distribution including stockouts
- actual pricing, shelf-space allocation, and so forth versus target
- "deal" levels and slotting allowances required to obtain distribution
- sales force involvement and committment

Major companies generally make the "test market-no test market" decision on a case-by-case basis rather than by following a strict policy. General Mills will skip test markets if simulated test markets and other pretests indicate that the risks of introducing a new product are negligible. Even then, General Mills often uses a regional rollout with the first region serving as somewhat of a test market. Quaker Oats and Kraft also evaluate the risks of national introduction against the cost of standard test markets on a case-by-case basis.[27] Procter & Gamble, which, until recently, conducted a market test on all new products as a matter of corporate policy, will now go national without a lengthy standard test market.[28]

Controlled-Store and Minimarket Tests

To overcome some of the problems associated with standard market tests, controlled-store and minimarket tests are being used with increasing frequency. In a standard market test, the product is distributed to the stores through the firm's regular distribution channels. In controlled-store and minimarket tests, a market research firm, such as Burgoyne or Ehrhart-Babic, handles all the warehousing, distribution, pricing, shelving, and stocking. The research firm typically pays a limited number of outlets to let it place the product in their stores.

In a controlled-store test a few outlets in several areas are utilized. A minimarket test involves enough outlets to represent a high percentage (Ehrhart-Babic uses 70 per cent) of the all-commodity sales volume in a relatively small community. In a controlled-store test, media advertising typically cannot be used because of the limited distribution of the product. The minimarket test overcomes this problem but increases the cost ($600,000 for an advertising test and $2,000,000 for a new product test) and visibility of the test.

Sales data are maintained by the research firm that is distributing the product. Existing or especially established household mail or UPC scanner panels can be used to provide trial- and repeat-purchase rates, household penetration, substitution patterns, and user demographics. Survey research can be used instead of panels or to supplement panel data.

These methods offer several important advantages over standard test markets. First, it is virtually impossible for competitors to "read" the test results since the research company is the only source of sales data. Second, the tests are somewhat less visible to competitors, though most controlled stores and minimarkets are actively observed. Third, they are substantially faster since there is no need to move the product through a distribution channel. Finally, they are much less expensive than standard test markets.

Unfortunately, this approach suffers from four drawbacks. First, the limited number of stores and/or the small size of the communities involved makes any projection of the results very difficult. Second, these tests do *not* allow an estimate of the level of support the trade will give a product. If wholesalers will not push the product, or if retailers will not give it shelf space, it will seldom succeed. These tests provide no information on this critical component. Third, it is sometimes difficult to duplicate planned national advertising programs. Finally, the fact that the research firm ensures near-optimal positioning in each store, no stockouts, adequate shelf-facings, correct use of point-of-purchase materials and so forth produces a situation very different from that typically encountered during the national introduction.

Sophisticated firms are minimizing these drawbacks. A critical element is to specify distribution, shelf-facings, and so forth at a level consistent with realistic expectations for the national introduction. Likewise, advertising expenditures in the minimarket are carefully constructed to match national levels. Projection from minimarket to national remains a problem, but use of historical data (relationships between past minimarket sales and subsequent national sales) and "what-if" analyses can provide some confidence.

Controlled-store tests and minimarkets are often used as a final check prior to standard test markets. At Andrew Jergens Co., the general policy is to conduct a controlled-store test to determine if the current version of a planned new product is worthy of a standard market test. In addition, Jergens uses simulated test markets to determine which products should go into controlled-store tests.[29] Other firms such as G. D. Searle & Co. (Equal sweetener) will go national directly from minimarket tests.[30]

In addition to testing new products, controlled store tests are rapidly gaining popularity as a means of testing price and promotional variables such as displays, coupons, cents-off, and so forth. A before-after with control or after-only with control design is generally used. Matched panels of stores rather than random allocation is also the norm. These tests are fast, inexpensive ($20,000 – $40,000), and realistic.

Electronic Test Markets

Electronic test markets (ETMs) have become an important part of test marketing. ETMs operate like minimarket tests, except that the research firm has (1) the ability to collect ongoing scanner-based sales data from the major food and drug outlets in the area, and (2) a UPC scanner-based household panel that also has its television viewing monitored electronically. In other words, the research firm has "single source" data capabilities (Chapter 5). In addition, the firm has the capability of sending differing commercials or differing frequencies of commercials to various households in the panel.[31]

Exhibit 8–7 describes Information Resources Inc.'s (IRI) BehaviorScan® ETM.[32] Although it is possible to use one of the BehaviorScan cities as a site for a standard test market, their rather small size generally precludes this (Eau Claire, Wis.; Midland, Tex.; Marion, Ind.; and Pittsfield, Mass. are typical cities). Instead, IRI handles the distribution as described in the exhibit.

Other organizations offering or developing ETM services include:

A. C. Nielsen's **ERIM** — (two locations, currently "on hold" with an uncertain future)[33]

SAMI/Burke's Ad Tel/View Scan (two locations, at-home wand scanners to measure purchases from nonscanner stores, monitoring of television viewing and ability to custom construct samples to receive different commercials. Two additional markets with split cable scanner capabilities. These markets allow less flexibility in designing samples to receive differing commercials.)[34]

Other single-source source data suppliers (see Chapter 5) such as Nielsen's ScanTrack, NPD/Nielsen's new panel, and Arbitron's ScanAmerica offer everything a full ETM does except the ability to target specific television commercials to specify panel households. They do, however, allow the measurement of television commercial exposure by individual households.

ETM's are used to test new products and, even more commonly, advertising levels and themes. They allow relatively precise measurement of individual household's purchasing and television-viewing behavior. They also provide reasonable control over individual household's television commercial exposure as well as receipt of direct mail ads and coupons. Their disadvantages are the same as those associated with minimarket tests, with additional concerns about the representativeness of the electronic diary panel (because of the high refusal rate of those asked to join such panels).

Exhibit 8–7 *Information Resources, Inc.'s (IRI) Behavior Scan® Minimarket System*

Currently available in 9 markets

- Covers 95 per cent of supermarket-sales volume in all 9 markets
- Covers 85 per cent of drugstore sales volume in 5 markets

Receives direct feedback from the UPC scanners

Maintains a panel of 3,000 households in each market

- Panel members have an ID number which is entered each time a purchase is made
- IRI maintains complete demographics and product usage data on each panel member
- IRI electronically monitors the television viewing of panel households

Controlled distribution

- IRI controls in-store distribution including shelf configuration, price, and point-of-purchase displays
- IRI monitors competitive activity daily on a store-by-store basis
- IRI monitors manufacturer and store coupon redemption by panel members

Allows test of various promotional activities

- Through proprietary technology, different television commercials can be sent to individual panel households. Groups can be formed based on past purchase behavior, demographics, or stores shopped.
- Direct mail, magazine, and newspaper inserts can be tested.

Feedback is rapid and cost efficient

- Scanner-based reports are available 4–6 weeks sooner than traditional reports
- Allows measures of trial and repeat, buying rate, loyalty, purchase cycles, brand shifting, buyer demographics, and response to market mix changes
- Generally costs about half of a standard test market

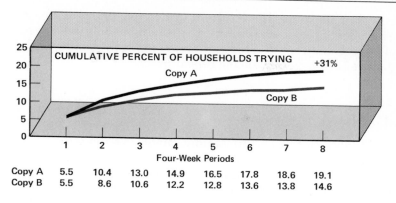

| Copy A | 5.5 | 10.4 | 13.0 | 14.9 | 16.5 | 17.8 | 18.6 | 19.1 |
| Copy B | 5.5 | 8.6 | 10.6 | 12.2 | 12.8 | 13.6 | 13.8 | 14.6 |

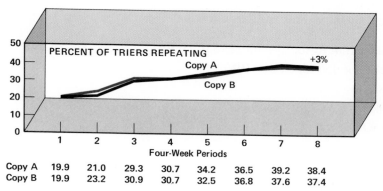

| Copy A | 19.9 | 21.0 | 29.3 | 30.7 | 34.2 | 36.5 | 39.2 | 38.4 |
| Copy B | 19.9 | 23.2 | 30.9 | 30.7 | 32.5 | 36.8 | 37.6 | 37.4 |

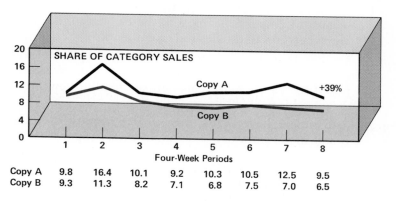

| Copy A | 9.8 | 16.4 | 10.1 | 9.2 | 10.3 | 10.5 | 12.5 | 9.5 |
| Copy B | 9.3 | 11.3 | 8.2 | 7.1 | 6.8 | 7.5 | 7.0 | 6.5 |

Figure 8–2 *Results of Testing Two Different Commercials for a New Brand Using IRI's BehaviorScan®*

Source: New Product Testing with Behaviorscan® (Chicago: Information Resources Inc., undated). Used with permission.

237

Figure 8–2 illustrates the results of testing two different advertisements for the introduction of a new product. The results not only indicate the superiority of copy **A**, but they also indicate that it works by gaining trial. Both ads are equally effective at influencing repeat purchases.

Simulated Test Markets

Simulated test markets (STM) are rapidly gaining in popularity.[35] STMs, often called laboratory tests or test-market simulations, involve mathematical estimates of market share based on initial consumer reactions to the new product. A number of private companies such as Pillsbury have their own STM systems. In addition, a number of consulting firms offer STM services. The primary firms and their systems are the following:[36]

Information Resources Inc. (ASSESSOR)

Elrick and Lavidge (COMP)

SAMI/Burke (BASES)

Yankelovich Clancy Shulman (Litmus)

BBDO (News)

STMs follow a similar basic procedure that is outlined in Figure 8–3 and that includes the following steps:

Step 1.   Potential respondents are contacted and "qualified." Qualified means the respondents must fit the demographics and/or usage characteristics of the desired target market.

Step 2.   Qualified respondents are invited to view a pilot television program, examine a proposed new magazine, or are otherwise exposed to one or more commercials for the new product in a disguised format.

Step 3.   Respondents are then given the opportunity to purchase the brand in a laboratory store or in a real supermarket through means such as coupon redemptions. The purchase situation generally requires the respondents to part with some of their own money to obtain the item.

Step 4.   The respondents take the purchased item(s) home and use it in a normal manner. They generally are not told that it is a test item or that they will be questioned later. The time allowed for usage depends on the "normal" consumption time for the product category.

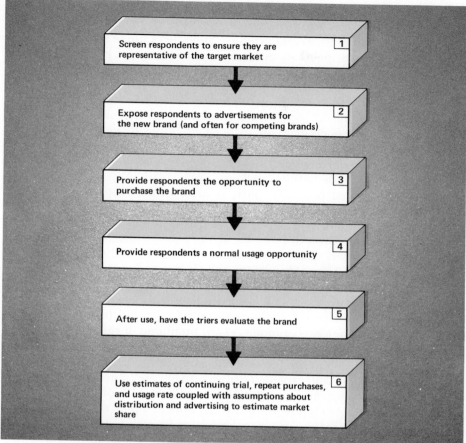

Figure 8–3 *Steps in Simulated Test Markets*

Step 5. Those respondents who purchased the test item are contacted and asked to evaluate its performance. This evaluation generally includes attitude measures and statements of repurchase intentions and likely usage rates. The evaluation may also include an opportunity to repurchase the item.

Step 6. The percentage of respondents who decide to try the new item is used to estimate the percentage of the target market population that would try the item *if* they were aware of the item and *if* it were available in the stores in which they shop. The firm's assumptions concerning advertising impact (target market awareness) and distribution are used with the "per cent trying" figure to estimate actual market trial. The after-use evaluations (attitudes, statements of repurchase intentions, or actual repurchases) are used to estimate the percentage of the triers who will continue to use the product. The rate of usage is estimated from either respondent estimates or knowledge of the product category, or both. These three estimates are then combined to estimate market share for the item.

It is clear from this description that substantial reliance is being placed on the behavior of respondents in an artificial situation. It seems intuitive that such behavior would differ from actual behavior in the marketplace. STMs do *not* assume that the behavior and attitudes displayed in the laboratory setting will be repeated exactly in the actual market. Instead, they rely on observed *relationships* between products' performances in the laboratory and their subsequent performances in actual market introductions.

An *extremely* simplified example will help make this process clear. Suppose 100 new products are run through the six-step procedure described and are then introduced in test markets or nationally. The researcher notices that in most cases, for every 10 people who try an item in the laboratory only 6 will try it in the actual market. Therefore, when product number 101 is tested and 40 per cent of the laboratory respondents try it, the researcher would project that 24 per cent (.60 times .40) of the target market would try it in an actual introduction. Although this example is *very* simplified, it reflects the general logic used in evaluating STM results.

STMs are fast, economical (generally costing under $100,000), confidential, easily controlled, and capable of substantial geographic spread. They do not measure trade response, competitors' reactions, or implementation difficulties. In addition, they are critically dependent upon the mathematical model used in the STM *and* on management estimates of total market size, advertising reach, distribution penetration, and similar variables.

Stimulated test markets appear to be accurate, particularly for product line extensions and "me-too" brands in well-established product categories. Unfortunately, there are few independent verifications of their accuracy[37] (only the companies that sponsor them have access to the data). However, client companies such as S. C. Johnson & Co. consistently report good results using STMs, although they warn, "We've conducted a number of validations and there is an error range that has to be weighed, which is why simulation is an educated indication, not a substitute for test marketing."[38]

STMs are generally used to determine if a product should go on to a controlled or standard test market. Pillsbury, for example, drops about one out of three products from consideration after Supertest (Pillsbury's STM). Further, Pillsbury takes the remaining products into market tests before going national. Pillsbury's logic behind this approach is: "There are too many risks. Even if you get a pretest volume that is great, how big is it, really? We use the

Supertest to get some feel, some perspective on how good the market is. The objective is to be more selective with what you take into test." [39]

However, other firms are increasingly going straight to national or regional rollouts after positive STM results. The Campbell Soup Company typifies many companies that are between these two extremes: "There are rare occasions when we would use a model and not do a conventional test market and commence introduction in a region of the country based on a simulation test. But about the only reason we would do that is to avoid the possibility of being preempted by a competitor. It also would have to be a situation where there wasn't a great investment in plant or equipment involved." [40]

Johnson & Johnson used an STM in a creative manner when a competitor introduced a new product that was positioned directly against its Reach toothbrush. Johnson & Johnson subjected the new product to an STM. The results indicated that the new product was not as much of a competitive threat as Johnson & Johnson had imagined. Therefore, the company was able to reduce its planned defensive campaign by $600,000.[41] Miles Labs used the same procedure to develop defensive strategy against Bristol-Myers' Dissolve.[42] The potential of this use of STMs is substantial enough that at least one company has developed an advanced simulation model for conducting such analyses.[43]

Review Questions

8.1. What is the difference between a *laboratory experiment* and a *field experiment?*

8.2. What are the strengths and weaknesses of laboratory experiments?

8.3. What is *predictive validity? External validity?*

8.4. What is *replicability? Internal validity?*

8.5. What are *reactive errors?* Why is this important for laboratory experiments?

8.6. How does one control for reactive errors?

8.7. What is a *tachistoscope?* How are they used in copy testing?

8.8. Describe how ads and packages are copy tested in laboratory settings.

8.9. What is an *extended use test?*

8.10. What is a *blind use test?*

8.11. What are the strengths and weaknesses of *field experiments?*

8.12. What is *DAR?* What problems are associated with this approach?

8.13. What is a *standard test market?*

8.14. What are the strengths and weaknesses of a standard test market?

8.15. What criteria are used in selecting an area for a standard test market?

8.16. In general, what is the minimum time a test market should last?

8.17. How does a *controlled-store test* differ from a *minimarket test?*

8.18. What are the advantages and disadvantages of *controlled-store* and *mini-market tests?*

8.19. What is an *electronic test market* (**ETM**)?

8.20. What are the strengths and weaknesses of ETMs?

8.21. Describe the BehaviorScan system.

8.22. What is a *simulated test market?*

8.23. What steps are involved in most simulated test markets?

8.24. What are the advantages and disadvantages of simulated test markets?

8.25. How is the output from STMs used?

Discussion Questions/Problems

8.26. What are the broad research methodology implications of Exhibit 8 – 1?

8.27. Design a laboratory experiment to test college students' reactions to _____ for a juice drink.
   a. three flavor levels
   b. three packages
   c. three brand names
   d. three advertising themes
   e. three price levels
   f. three point-of-purchase displays
   g. three different levels of advertising
   h. *c* and *d.*

8.28. How would your design for 8.27 deal with reactive error? What other error sources would concern you?

8.29. What problems exist with theater tests of advertising copy?

8.30. Evaluate the experimental environment and procedure described in Exhibit 8 – 2.

8.31. Evaluate the experimental environment and procedure described in Exhibit 8 – 3.

8.32. Is the lack of test marketing by durable-goods manufacturers wise? Why?

8.33. Although there is virtually no empirical evidence, it appears that the test marketing of industrial products is very rare. Why is this the case?

8.34. If you felt you had to use a standard test market, what steps could you take to minimize disruption by competitors?

8.35. Design a *field experiment* to test the general public's reactions to _____ for a juice drink.

      a. three flavor levels
      b. three packages
      c. three brand names
      d. three advertising themes
      e. three price levels
      f. three point-of-purchase displays
      g. three different levels of advertising
      h. *a.* and *e.*

8.36. To what extent do you think that people who know that their _____ behavior is being monitored change their behavior? In what ways?
      a. television viewing
      b. shopping

8.37. What factors would you consider in _____
      a. deciding whether to conduct a test market?
      b. deciding which type of test market to conduct?

Projects

8.38. Conduct the experiment you designed in 8.27a., b., c., d., e., f., g., or h. and report the results.

8.39. Interview three supermarket managers and determine their awareness of and attitudes toward test markets.

8.40. Design and conduct a field experiment on point-of-purchase display effectiveness with the cooperation of local retailers.

References

[1] J. Dodge, R. Lewis, and M. H. Zandell, "Illinois Bell Finds That Targetable TV Research Is the Right Number," *Marketing News,* January 4, 1988, 8.

[2] F. N. Kerlinger, *Foundations of Behavioral Research* (New York: Holt, Rinehart and Winston, Inc., 1973), 398.

[3] P. W. Farris and D. J. Reibstein, "Overcontrol in Advertising Experiments," *Journal of Advertising Research* (June/July 1984), 37–42.

[4] Excellent discussions of this issue are B. J. Calder, L. W. Phillips, and A. M. Tybout, "Designing Research for Application," *Journal of Consumer Research* (September 1981), 197–207; J. G. Lynch, Jr., "On the External Validity of Experiments in Consumer Research," and B. J. Calder, L. W. Phillips, and A. M. Tybout, "The Concept of External Validity," both in *Journal of Consumer Research* (December 1982), 225–239 and 240–244; and J. G. Lync, Jr., "The Role of External Validity in Theoretical Research," B. J. Calder, L. W. Phillips, and A. M. Tybout, "Beyond External Validity," and J. E. McGrath and D. Brin-

berg, "External Validity and the Research Process," all in *Journal of Consumer Research* (June 1983), 109–111, 112–114, and 115–124.

[5] See A. G. Sawyer, P. M. Worthing, and P. E. Sendak, "The Role of Laboratory Experiments to Test Marketing Strategies," *Journal of Marketing* (Summer 1979), 60–67; and M. J. Houston and M. L. Rothschild, "Policy-Related Experiments on Information Provision: A Normative Model and Explication," *Journal of Marketing Research* (November 1980), 432–449.

[6] See J. H. Barnes, Jr., and D. T. Seymour, "Experimenter Bias: Task, Tools, and Time," *Journal of the Academy of Marketing Science* (Winter 1980), 1–11.

[7] For another approach see J. Lim and J. O. Summers, "A Non-Experimental Investigation of Demand Artifacts in a Personal Selling Situation," *Journal of Marketing Research* (August 1984), 251–258.

[8] C. E. Brown et al., "The Effect of Experimenter Bias in a Cola Taste Test," *Psychology & Marketing* (Summer 1984), 21–26.

[9] "Revised Pillsbury Spot in the Pink," *Advertising Age*, February 13, 1986, 15.

[10] See R. D. Wilson, L. M. Newman, and M. Hastak, "On the Validity of Research Methods on Consumer Dealing Activity: An Analysis of Timing Issues," in N. Beckwith et al., *1979 Educators' Conference Proceedings* (Chicago: American Marketing Association, 1979), 41–46; Farris and Reibstein, loc. cit.; and "A Test the Sales Force Must Pass, Too," *Sales and Marketing Management*, March 14, 1983, 55–88.

[11] Taken from "Overview of the Burke Day-After-Recall Copy Testing Service," prepared by the Burke Agency, undated.

[12] H. A. Zielske, "Does Day-After Recall Penalize 'Feeling' Ads?" *Journal of Advertising Research* (February 1982), 1–2; S. M. Singh and M. L. Rothschild, "Recognition as a Measure of Learning from Television Commercials," *Journal of Marketing Research* (July 1983), 235–48; S. N. Singh and C. A. Cole, "Forced-Choice Recognition Test," *Journal of Advertising* (June 1985), 52–58; H. E. Krugman, "Low Recall and High Recognition of Advertising," *Journal of Advertising Research* (February 1986), 79–86; J. H. Leigh and A. Menon, "A Comparison of Alternative Recognition Measures of Advertising Effectiveness," *Journal of Advertising* (June 1986), 4–12, S. N. Singh and G. A. Churchill, Jr., "Using the Theory of Signal Detection to Improve Ad Recognition Testing," *Journal of Marketing Research* (October 1986), 327–36; and S. N. Singh and G. A. Churchill, Jr., "Response-Bias-Tree Recognition Test to Measure Advertising Effects," *Journal of Advertising Research* (June 1987), 23–35.

[13] See T. Karger, "Test Marketing as Dress Rehearsals," *The Journal of Consumer Marketing* (Fall 1985), 49–55. For excellent coverage of current test-market activities and problems see the special section in *Advertising Age* on test marketing that comes out in February of each year.

[14] "Students Get 1st Taste of Health Snacks Effort," *Advertising Age*, August 18, 1980, 61.

[15] See C. Narasimhan and S. K. Sen, "New Product Models for Test Market Data," *Journal of Marketing* (Winter 1983), 11–24.

[16] A. Helming, "Those Slings and Arrows!" *Advertising Age*, February 22, 1982, M-23.

[17] T. Angelus, "Experts' Choice: Top Test Markets, *Marketing/Communications* (May 1970), 29.

[18] N. Howard, "Fighting It Out in the Test Market," *Dun's Review* (June 1979), 69.

[19] R. Kreisman, "Wendy's Ready to Roll with Breakfast," *Advertising Age*, March 3, 1981, 3.

[20] B. G. Yorovich, "Competition Jumps the Gun," *Advertising Age*, February 9, 1981, S-20.

[21] J. Revett and L. Edwards, "Carnation Bites Back," *Advertising Age*, June 9, 1980, 78.

[22] L. Freeman, "Colgate P & G," *Advertising Age*, August 31, 1987, 1.

[23] "Tom Swift and His Electric Hamburger Cooker," *Forbes*, Octber 15, 1979, 112.

[24] L. Adler, "Test Marketing—Its Pitfalls," *Sales & Marketing Management* (March 15, 1982), 78.

[25] Ibid.

[26] A. M. Tarshis, "Natural Sell-In Avoids Pitfalls of Controlled Tests," *Marketing News*, October 24, 1986, 14.

[27] C. Lentini, "Whither Test Marketing?" *Advertising Age*, February 22, 1982, 40.

[28] J. B. Solomon, "P&G Rolls Out New Items at Faster Pace," *Wall Street Journal*, May 11, 1984, 33.

[29] "What's in Store," *Sales & Marketing Management*, (March 15, 1982), 60.

[30] E. Norris, "To Test or Not to Test is Seldom the Question," *Advertising Age*, February 20, 1984, M-10.

[31] E. Russell, Jr., "High-Tech Test Marketing at Campbell Soup Company," *The Journal of Consumer Marketing* (Winter 1986), 71–80.

[32] See R. Kreisman, "Buy the Numbers," *Inc.* (March 1985), 1.

[33] I. Teinowitz, "No-Go at Nielsen" *Advertising Age*, March 7, 1988, 12.

[34] L. Y. S. Lin and C. J. Kim, "Ad Tel," *European Research* (#1, 1987), 22–27.

[35] K. Higgins, "Simulated Test Marketing Winning Acceptance," *Marketing News*, March 1, 1985, 15; and R. Edel, "Lab-to-rollout Becoming More Traveled Test Path," *Advertising Age*, February 20, 1984, M-11.

[36] For an excellent discussion of this area and a comparison of four models see A. D. Shocker and W. G. Hall, "Pretest Market Models," *Journal of Product Innovation Management* (#3, 1986), 86–107.

[37] See A. J. Silk and G. L. Urban, "Pre-Test-Market Evaluation of New Packaged Goods," *Journal of Marketing Research* (May 1978), 171–191; P. Burger, C. H. Gundee, and R. Lavidge, "COMP," in Y. Wind, V, Mahajan, and R. N. Cardozo,

New Product Forecasting (Lexington, Mass.: Lexington Books, 1981), 269–84; L. G. Pringle, R. D. Wilson, and E. I. Brody, "NEWS," *Marketing Science* (Winter 1982), 1–30; G. L. Urban and G. M. Katz, "Pre-Test-Market Models," *Journal of Marketing Research* (August 1983), 221–234; and T. Watkins, "Do STM Models Work?" and P. Sampson, "Comment," both in *Journal of the Market Research Society* (July 1984), 255–256 and 256–258; D. M. Stayman and M. R. Hagerty, "Methodological Issues in Simulated Shopping Experiments," in E. C. Hirschman and M. B. Holbrook, *Advances in Consumer Research XII* (Association for Consumer Research, 1985), 173–176; and Shocker and Hall, ibid.

[38] "What's in Store," op. cit., 58.

[39] J. Alter, "Lab Simulations: No Shot in the Dark," *Advertising Age*, February 4, 1980, S-26.

[40] K. Higgins, loc. cit.

[41] D. N. Scott, "Test Market Simulation Evaluates New Products," *Marketing News*, January 22, 1982, 10.

[42] R. Edel, op. cit., M-43.

[43] R. Edel, "New Testing System to the Defense," *Advertising Age*, February 20, 1984, M-44; and P. Mimnaugh, "Reverse Simulation Preempts Competitors' Test Markets," *Marketing News*, June 19, 1987, 12.

CASE II–1 WEYERHAEUSER III — SECONDARY DATA

At this point, review Case I–2, Weyerhaeuser: Problem Definitions and Research Design (pages 68–70). That case indicates a number of areas where secondary data might prove useful. Utilize secondary data to provide information on the following issues. Also, describe any concerns you have about the accuracy, usefulness, or completeness of the data you find.

1. What are the past and projected sales of (1) building materials and (2) lumber products to the consumer repair and remodel market, broken down by DIYers and contractors?

2. What are the sales volumes of different types of outlets for (1) building materials and (2) lumber products for the DIY repair and remodel market? How are these changing over time?

3. What are the characteristics, including purchasing patterns and media habits, of DIYers.

4. Describe the competitive activities by lumber producers marketing to DIYers.

5. Describe the price sensitivity and the perceived price/quality relationship for products such as lumber.

CASE II–2 WEYERHAEUSER IV — ALTERNATIVE DATA SOURCES

Review Case I–2, Weyerhaeuser: Problem Definition and Research Design (pages 68–70). A variety of types of information could be collected to help management deal with both the general and specific decisions they face. In addition, there are a variety of means available to collect this data.

1. What data, if any, could audits and/or panels provide that would assist Weyerhaeuser? Describe precisely the data you would collect from each relevant service and specify how management would use such data in its decisions with respect to the DIY market. What concerns, if any, would you have about this data?

2. What data, if any, could a survey or surveys provide that would assist Weyerhaeuser? Develop a (or several if necessary) survey methodology to collect this data (provide a thorough description of your methodology). How would

you deal with nonresponse error? Justify your design in terms of data quality and costs.

3. What useful data, if any, could a laboratory experiment provide Weyerhaeuser? Develop one or more laboratory experiments to provide this data, giving complete details on the research design. How would reactive errors affect your results? What other concerns would you have about this data? Describe precisely how management would use your results.

4. What useful data, if any, could a field experiment provide Weyerhaeuser? Develop one or more field experiments using (1) standard test markets, (2) minimarkets, (3) controlled-store tests, (4) electronic test markets, and (5) simulated test markets. What concerns would you have with the data from each? How would management use the data from each? What is best? Why?

CASE II–3 WEYERHAEUSER V — SURVEY METHODOLOGY

Review Case I–2, Weyerhaeuser: Problem Definition and Research Design (pages 68–70). Weyerhaeuser management decided that the first priority was to determine the effects on the company image of sponsoring the television series, "This Old House." Secondary issues would be (1) the relationship between company image and price sensitivity, (2) the characteristics of DIYers, their homes, and their projects, and (3) the effect that sponsoring "This Old House" had on Owens-Corning's image.

Since the first priority was to measure the impact of sponsoring "This Old House," this issue dominated the others. It was decided that an annual survey of Weyerhaeuser's image among viewers and nonviewers of the program would be the best way to measure the effect of sponsorship over time. This would allow an annual evaluation of the desirability of continued sponsorship.

Because the season sponsored by Weyerhaeuser was to begin in early October and the decision to measure its effectiveness was not made until late August, speed was very important. Weyerhaeuser wished to obtain a set of image measures before the shows began, in order to assess changes due to sponsorship.

Prior research indicated that DIYers spending over $200 per year on projects were the primary part of the market. Approximately 10 per cent of all households were estimated to spend more than this per year. The questionnaire would not require the presentation of any visual aids or overly complex questions. The need for rapid response, limited questionnaire complexity, and the limited frequency of qualified respondents (which would require 10 or more household contacts for each qualified respondent even without nonrespondents) resulted in a telephone survey methodology.

Rather than use a national sample, Weyerhaeuser decided to conduct the surveys in Boston, Chicago, and Phoenix (see Case IV–1). Gilmore Research Group of Seattle conducted the surveys using random-digit dialing and three call backs at varying times and days.

The questionnaire was developed and pretested in-house with the final revision and format prepared in conjunction with Gilmore. Part of Gilmore's agreement with Weyerhaeuser is listed below:

Our costs are based on estimates that 10% of the population will qualify and that the interview is 10 to 11 minutes in length. We quoted a total fee of $XXXX° to complete 600 interviews, including the following services:

- Sample draw
- Questionnaire finalization and printing
- Data collection and quality control, including full-time supervision and monitoring, editing and clarification call backs, if necessary
- Long distance expense (calling will be done out of our WATS centers in Seattle and/or Omaha)
- Coding (listing of "others" and development of new code categories as needed)
- Data entry, together with 100% verification
- Data processing, resulting in one banner of cross-tab tables (up to 19 banner points). Additional banners run $250 each.
- Deliverables to include two copies of computer tables, a description of the sample disposition and incidence, and the actual questionnaires, if desired. If desired, data can also be provided on a diskette at no extra cost.

Our tentative schedule is:

- September 16 — Draft questionnaire to you
- September 18 to 21 — Into the field
- October 12 to 16 — Out of the field
- October 21 — Marginal dump of data, finalize processing specs

° Actual bid amount is omitted because of the competitive nature of such bids.

- October 29 — Computer cross-tab tables run
- October 30 — Printouts to you

1. Evaluate the survey methodology used and recommend appropriate improvements to this basic approach.
2. Assuming that either a few cities or a national sample could be used, what other survey approaches could be used? Develop, in detail, an alternative approach. Discuss the strengths and weaknesses of the alternative approach compared to the one used.

CASE II–4 SUBSTANTIATION OF BUFFERIN ADVERTISING CLAIM

The Bristol-Myers Company made an "establishment" claim (a claim asserted to have been established by a scientific test) in an advertisement that "*Bufferin's* laboratory test showed most of its pain reliever gets in the bloodstream 10 minutes sooner than plain aspirin." The Federal Trade Commission examined the proof offered by Bristol-Myers and was unconvinced that the claim was valid. The Commission issued a cease-and-desist order for the use of such a claim unless and until Bristol-Myers could substantiate, by conducting two well-controlled clinical experiments, that the claim was true.

The usual experimental design required by the Federal Trade Commission for over-the-counter pain relievers was called for in conducting the *Bufferin* tests. It is as follows:

1. Such proof must be in the form of two well-controlled clinical tests.
2. The tests must involve subjects who are experiencing the appropriate type of discomfort. In general, the appropriate type of pain is the pain for which the use of the drug is intended.
3. There should be a written protocol that describes the conduct of the study and its analysis.
4. Investigators who administer the test should be experienced, independent and adequately trained.

Bristol-Myers Company, Ted Bates & Co., Inc., and Young & Rubicam, Inc., *CCH Trade Regulation Reports,* Extra Edition, no. 604, July 19, 1983, and "Legal Developments in Marketing," *Journal of Marketing* (Spring 1984), 83, 84.

5. Test subjects must be randomly assigned to the treatment groups within the study.

6. Where possible, tests comparing two analgesics should also compare those drugs against a placebo.

7. The test should be a double-blind test so that neither the test subject nor the person administering the test is able to tell which treatment is being administered.

8. After the clinical tests are completed, the results should be analyzed to determine their clinical and statistical significance. A 95 per cent level of statistical significance is generally required.

9. A determination should be made whether a statistically significant difference between two drugs is clinically significant. A difference is of no clinical significance if scientists regard the difference as being so small as to be of no importance.

a. Comment on design requirements 2 through 8.

b. How do the design requirements differ from the requirements a manager might have if the objective were to see which of two versions of a new pain reliever to introduce to the market?

c. What other design requirements might the Federal Trade Commission (reasonably) have required? Explain.

CASE II–5 MARKET FACTS, INC.*

Market Facts, Inc., a marketing research agency, did a national telephone survey of a sample of 2,998 female heads of households whose telephone numbers were selected by random-digit dialing. The purpose of the study was to determine the attitudes toward, and advertising slogan recall of, beverages. As a means of determining what the effects of random-digit dialed versus directory-based sampling are, at the end of each interview the interviewer asked, "Is your telephone number listed or unlisted?"

Selected attitudinal data and the incidence of telephone listings by area and by demographic breakdown are as shown in the following tables.

* This case as a whole is based upon, and the tables and the quote it contains are taken directly from, P. C. Ellison, "Phone Directory Samples Just as Balanced as Samples from Computer Random Digit Dialing," *Marketing News*, January 11, 1980, 8.

Table 1 Incidence of Phone Listings

	Listed %	Unlisted %	No. of Respondents %
TOTAL U.S.	82	18	(2,998)
Metro	76	24	(1,651)
Non Metro	85	15	(1,347)
Region			
New England	87	13	(400)
Eastern	79	21	(650)
Central	86	14	(800)
Southern	83	17	(400)
Western	81	19	(750)
Metro			
New York	70	30	(400)
Metro Chicago	69	31	(400)
Metro Los Angeles	69	31	(400)

A conclusion by **MARKET FACTS** based on the findings of the study is as follows:

Interview samples drawn from directory-listed telephone numbers are just as representative and proportionate as those derived by computer-generated random-digit dialing.

This . . . study . . . found no significant differences in the samples of the two methods to justify the additional expense of the random-digit system.

The data show that there are apt to be significant demographic and attitudinal differences between households whose telephone numbers are listed and those households having unlisted numbers.

Nonetheless, the data suggest that when a comparison is made of "listed" households and total households (including listed and unlisted numbers), *there is no significant difference between these two groups on any demographic or attitudinal measure included in this study.*

The reason is quite simple. Unlisted telephone numbers comprise less than 20 per cent of total telephone-owning households. . . . Therefore, their effect is washed out when it is combined with the much larger number of households having listed numbers.

Since the listed sample does not differ significantly from the total

Table 2 Demographics (Summary)

	Total Sample %	Listed Telephone %	Unlisted Telephone %
Household Size (Mean Average)	3.0	3.0	3.1
Children Under 18 At Home	47	45	53
Age			
Under 35	35	33	49
35–54	34	34	32
55 and over	31	33	19
Mean Average	43	45	36
Marital Status			
Married	72	73	66
Single	11	10	15
Widowed/Divorced	18	17	19
Race			
White	87	90	75
Non-White	13	10	25
Income			
Under $10,000	28	28	31
$10,000 to $19,999	36	36	34
$20,000 or more	25	26	23
Refused	11	10	12
Median	$14,300	$14,400	$13,600
Education			
Less than High School	22	22	22
High School Graduate	38	37	41
College or Beyond	40	41	38
Employment			
Full Time	25	25	28
Part Time	12	12	11
Not Employed	63	63	61
(Number of Respondents)	(2,998)	(2,403)	(541)

sample, the data suggest that, for most studies, the selection of a sample based upon a random digit dialing technique *cannot* be economically justified. This is especially true if one is conducting a national study.

Do you agree with this conclusion? Explain.

Table 3 Selected Attitudinal Data

	Total Sample %	Listed Telephone %	Unlisted Telephone %
Some Beverage Perceptions:			
Coffee is best breakfast drink	16	17	12
Milk is good for any time of day	18	18	18
Orange Juice is best for quick energy	39	39	40
Soft Drink you personally like best	13	13	17
Milk gives you best value for the money	36	37	30
Orange Juice gives you best value for the money	23	23	28
Advertising Slogan Recall:			
National vegetable juice	59	59	58
National soft drink	33	34	33
National fruit juice	81	81	82
National ready to drink fruit drink	75	74	79
(Number of Respondents)	(2,998)	(2,403)	(541)

SECTION 3

Measurement Techniques in Marketing Research

Measurement is central to the process of obtaining data. How, and how well, the measurements in a research project are made are critical in determining whether the project will be a success.

Because of its centrality and importance, the first chapter of this section is devoted to a consideration of the underlying *measurement concepts.* What measurement is, by what scales measurements can be made, and the components and accuracy of measurements are each discussed in Chapter 9.

The next five chapters are each concerned with measurements within a marketing research context. The considerations involved in sound *questionnaire design* are the concern of Chapter 10 while Chapter 11 describes the techniques used in *direct measures of attitudes.* Chapter 12 covers *perceptual mapping* and *trade-off analyses,* two approaches for deriving attitude measures from simpler data. *Depth interviews* and *projective techniques,* often termed *qualitative research,* are the subjects of Chapter 13. Chapter 14 covers the rapidly evolving areas of *observation* and *physiological measures.*

CHAPTER 9

Measurement in
Marketing Research

Hanes Corp. suffered substantial losses on its *L'erin* cosmetics line. Although its initial marketing strategy was weak in several areas, marketing research contributed to its problems. According to the division head of *L'erin*, the company "listened to the consumer too much." Hanes conducted a substantial number of interviews with target market consumers. In the interviews, the women described their ideal cosmetic in functional rather than in emotional terms. They stated a desire for cosmetics that could be worn all day without much upkeep.

Based on this research, *L'erin* was launched with a strong logical advertising theme. The slogan, delivered by a "plain-Jane" model in an ordinary setting, was: "Put your face on and forget it." The results were $30 million in losses over the first few years. The company now uses a romantic theme with glamorous models and unusual settings.[1]

In this example, Hanes measured potential consumers' attitudes and based an important part of its marketing strategy on these measurements. Measurement is a familiar and common activity. College entrance examinations represent an attempt to measure an individual's potential to complete college successfully. An automobile speedometer measures how fast a car is going. Cooking recipes call for measures of the quantity of the various ingredients. Watches and calendars are used to measure the passage of time.

In this chapter, a discussion of the principles and problems involved in measurement as they apply to decision-oriented marketing research is presented. In the first section we attempt to clarify exactly what measurement is.

This is followed by a discussion of the distinction between the characteristic being measured and the actual measurement operations.

As the list of common measurements at the beginning of this section indicates, there are several *types* of measurement. One approach to classifying the various type scales used in measurement — *nominal, ordinal, interval,* and *ratio* scales — is described in the second section of this chapter.

As we know from our own experience, measurements are often not correct: the gasoline gauge shows a quarter of a tank when we run out of gas, or the 10 o'clock news comes on at 9:45, according to our clock. The *L'erin* cosmetic example illustrates how serious inaccurate measurements can be in a marketing situation.[2] Therefore, the third major section of this chapter is a discussion of measurement accuracy. The final section provides a recommended procedure for developing measuring instruments.

The Concept of Measurement

Measurement Defined

Measurement may be defined as *the assignment of numbers to characteristics of objects, persons, states, or events, according to rules.* What is measured is *not* the object, person, state, or event itself but some characteristic of it. When objects are counted, for example, we do not measure the object itself but only its characteristic of being present.[3] We never measure *people,* only their *age, height, weight,* or some other characteristic. A study to determine whether a higher percentage of males or females purchases a given product measures the *male-female* and *purchase-nonpurchaser* attributes of the persons sampled.

The term *number* in the definition of measurement does not always correspond to the usual meaning given this term by the nonresearcher. It does not necessarily mean numbers that can be added, subtracted, divided, or multiplied. Instead, it means that numbers are used as symbols to represent certain characteristics of the object. The nature of the meaning of the numbers — symbols — depends on the nature of the characteristics they are to represent and how they are to represent them. This issue is developed in some depth in the section on scales of measurement.

The most critical aspect of measurement is the creation of the rules that specify how the numbers are to be assigned to the characteristics to be measured. Once a measurement rule has been created and agreed on, the characteristics of events, persons, states, or objects are described in terms of it. Thus the statement: "Chrysler increased its market share by two percentage points during the past year," has a meaning that is common among those who know the measurement rule that is being applied. However, those who are not aware of the rule will not always be able to understand what has been measured.

This problem arises because the rules that specify *how* to assign the numbers to the characteristics to be measured are *arbitrary*. Numbers are assigned on the basis of created or invented rules, not as a result of some divine revelation or undeniable natural law. Consider the previous statement concerning Chrysler's market share. Is market share based on units sold or dollar sales? On factory shipments or retail sales? On worldwide sales or U.S. sales? On U.S. sales of domestically produced autos or on imports as well? Each of these alternatives implies *a different measurement rule*, and unless one knows which rule is being applied, a figure is not completely understandable.

Measurement and Reality

If measurement is a procedure performed to a set of arbitrary rules, how do we evaluate measurements? Can the *quality* of a measurement be measured? The answer to the latter question is a qualified yes. Two aspects of the quality of a measurement can be evaluated.

First, *we can evaluate the extent to which the measurement rule has been followed.* For example, a researcher may decide on a measurement rule and issue instructions to "count the total number of people who walk past the point-of-purchase display and the number of people who 'examine' the item." An assistant who counts only those who physically handle the item as "examiners" is applying one interpretation of the rule. A second assistant who includes those who look at the item as "examiners," applies another interpretation of the rule. A third assistant who fails to count a number of examiners because of distractions makes errors in applying the rule. The count of "examiners" of either the first or second assistant is in error because of misunderstanding the rule. The count of the third assistant is in error because of misapplication of the rule.

Second, *we can evaluate how closely the rule corresponds to some aspect of "reality."* The extent of the correspondence required depends on the purpose of the research. Consider the example shown in Table 9–1. There is a perfect correspondence between the characteristic *relative size,* or *rank,* as measured and as it actually exists. If the researcher is interested only in rank order, perhaps to decide in which market to concentrate marketing efforts, there is satisfactory correspondence. This is true despite the errors in measuring the exact size of market potential that served as the basis for deriving the ranks.

If the researcher is concerned with preparing a sales forecast based on the size of market potential, however, the correspondence to reality is probably insufficient for all except area *C*. Thus, it is possible to have a "good" measurement when one level of measurement is considered and a "bad" measurement when another level is considered. The rule of measurement in this case was

Table 9 – 1   Measurement and Reality

	Actual		Measured	
Area	Rank	Size	Rank	Size
A	1	24,800,000	1	29,600,000
B	2	16,500,000	2	25,300,000
C	3	15,200,000	3	14,900,000
D	4	12,100,000	4	6,300,000
E	5	1,700,000	5	4,900,000

adequate to determine rank but inadequate to determine absolute level. It is important that "good" measurements occur on those characteristics that will influence the decision.

Measurement and Concepts

A *concept* is simply *an invented name for a property of an object, person, state, or event.* The terms *construct* and *concept* are sometimes used interchangeably. We use concepts such as *sales, market share, attitude,* and *brand loyalty* to signify abstractions based on observations of numerous particular happenings. Concepts aid in thinking by subsuming a number of events under one heading.[4] Thus, the concept "car" refers to the generalization of the characteristics that all cars have in common. The concept *car* is closely related to a physical reality.

Many concepts in marketing research do not have such easily observed physical referents. It is impossible to point to a physical example of an *attitude, product image,* or *social class.* Therefore, particular attention must be devoted to defining precisely what is meant by a given concept. Two approaches are necessary to define a concept adequately: (1) *conceptual definition* and (2) *operational definition.*[5]

Conceptual Definitions

A *conceptual definition* (sometimes called a *constitutive definition*) *defines a concept in terms of other concepts.* It states the central idea or essence of the concept. Very often it is the equivalent of a definition found in a dictionary. A good conceptual definition clearly delineates the major characteristics of the concept and allows one to distinguish the concept from similar but different concepts. Consider "brand loyalty" as a concept. How do you define it? Under your definition, is one loyal to a brand if one consistently buys it because it is the only brand of the product that is available at the stores at which one shops? Is this individual brand loyal in the same sense as others who consistently select the same brand from among the many brands carried where they shop?

An adequate conceptual definition of brand loyalty should distinguish it from similar concepts such as "repeat purchasing behavior."

Operational Definitions

Once a conceptual definition has been established, an operational definition must be designed that will reflect accurately the major characteristics of the conceptual definition. An *operational definition describes the activities the researcher must complete in order to assign a value to the concept under consideration.* Concepts are abstractions; as such, they are not observable. Operational definitions translate the concept into one or more observable events. Thus, a conceptual definition should precede and guide the development of the operational definition.

Consider this conceptual definition of brand loyalty: "the preferential attitudinal and behavioral response toward one or more brands in a product category expressed over a period of time by a consumer (or buyer)."[6] Brand loyalty defined in this way can be measured in a number of different ways. However, it is sufficiently precise to rule out many commonly used operational definitions of brand loyalty. For example, an operational definition involving a purchase sequence in which brand loyalty is defined as X consecutive purchases (usually three or four) of one brand is often used. This operational definition is not adequate because it ignores the attitudinal component specified in the conceptual definition.

Table 9–2 shows a conceptual definition of social class and a number of operational definitions of this concept found in the marketing literature. Which of these operational definitions is best? The answer to this question depends on the purpose of the research project. The operational definition most related to the research question should be used.

Table 9–2 Conceptual and Operational Definitions of Social Class

Conceptual definition: Social classes are relatively permanent and homogeneous hierarchical divisions in a society into which individuals or families sharing similar values, lifestyles, interests, and behavior can be categorized.

Operational definitions:

1. Reputational: Individuals are assigned to social classes based on how people who know them rank them.
2. Sociometric: Individuals are placed into social classes based on those with whom they associate.
3. Subjective: Individuals are placed into social classes based on their self-ranking.
4. Objective: Individuals are placed in a social class based on their possession of some objective characteristic or combination of characteristics, such as occupation, education, and income.

As Table 9–2 indicates, it is possible, and in fact common, to have several operational definitions for the same concept. This fact requires us to specify clearly the operational definitions we are using. Such terms as *profit, social class*, and *market share* should be accompanied by precise operational definitions when used in a research context.

The final section of this chapter provides a step-by-step procedure for developing sound operational definitions for marketing concepts.

Scales of Measurement

In the preceding section, we saw that measurement consists of assigning numbers to characteristics of objects or events in such a way as to reflect some aspect of reality. The goal then is to assign numbers so that the properties of the numbers are the same as the properties of the objects or events that we are measuring. This implies that we have different kinds of numbers. A moment's reflection will indicate that this is indeed the case. In a large university or class you may be identified by your university ID card number or your seat number. A number used in this manner is very different from the number that represents your score on the final exam. And score on the final examination is different in nature from your final rank in the class.

It is useful to distinguish four different types of numbers or scales of measurement: *nominal, ordinal, interval,* and *ratio.* The rules for assigning numbers constitute the essential criteria for defining each scale. As we move from nominal to ratio scales, we must meet increasingly restrictive rules. As the rules become more restrictive, the kinds of arithmetic operations for which the numbers can be used are increased. Examine Exhibit 9–1 closely. Chances are you will not completely understand why three different results were obtained. The next few pages, which describe the four measurement scales, should resolve the mystery.

Nominal Measurements

Nominal scales are comprised of numbers used to categorize objects or events. Perhaps the most common example is when we assign a female the number 1 and a male the number 0. Numbers used in this manner differ significantly from those used in more conventional ways. We could just as easily have assigned the 0 to the females and the 1 to the males, or we could have used the symbols A and B or the terms "male" and "female." In fact, in the final research report, terms are generally substituted for numbers to describe nominal categories.

A nominally scaled number serves only as a label for a class or category. The objects in each class are viewed as equivalent with respect to the characteristic represented by the nominal number. In the example given, all those placed in

Exhibit 9–1 *Comparative Advertising, Measurement Scales, and Data Analysis*

Suppose you see an advertisement that claims that *Vital* capsules are 50 per cent more effective in easing tensions than the leading tranquilizer. As research director for the company that produces the leading tranquilizer, *Restease*, you immediately begin comparison tests. Using large sample sizes and a well-designed experiment, you have one group of individuals use *Vital* capsules and a second group use *Restease.* You then have each individual in each group rate the effectiveness of the brand they tried on a five-point scale as follows:

For easing tension, I found *Vital (Restease)* to be

_____ a.   Very effective
_____ b.   Effective
_____ c.   Neither effective nor ineffective
_____ d.   Ineffective
_____ e.   Very ineffective

For analysis, you decide to code the "very effective" response as $+2$; the "effective" response as $+1$; the "neither-nor" response as 0; the "ineffective" response as -1; and the "very ineffective" response as -2. This is a common way of coding data of this nature.

You calculate an average response for *Vital* and *Restease* and obtain scores of 1.2 and .8, respectively. Because the .4 difference is 50 per cent more than the .8 level obtained by your brand, you conclude that the claims for *Vital* are valid. Shortly after reaching this conclusion, one of your assistants, who was also analyzing the data, enters your office with the good news that *Vital* was viewed as only 10.5 per cent more effective than *Restease.* Immediately you examine his figures. He used the same data and made no computational mistakes. The only difference was that he assigned the "very ineffective" response at $+1$ and continued up to a $+5$ for the "very effective" response. This is also a widely used procedure.

Then, as you are puzzling over these results, another member of your department enters. She used the same approach as your assistant but assigned a $+5$ to "very ineffective" and a $+1$ to "very effective." Again, with no computational errors, she found *Vital* to be 18.2 per cent more effective. What do you conclude?

Source: Derived from B. Venkatesh, "Unthinking Data Interpretation Can Destroy Value of Research," *Marketing News,* January 27, 1978, 6, 9. Both brand names are completely fictitious.

Table 9–3 Restaurant Selection Criteria by Gender

	Gender		
Primary Reason	Male	Female	Total
Location	55	15	70
Menu	5	25	30
Total	60	40	100

category 0 would be regarded as equivalent in terms of "maleness"; those in category 1 would be equivalent in "femaleness." The number 1 *does not* imply a superior position to the number 0. The only rules involved are that *all members of a class* (every object that has a certain characteristic) *have the same number* and that *no two classes have the same number*.

An example of the use of nominal measurement is the case of a manager of a restaurant located in a shopping center who wants to determine whether noon customers select the establishment primarily because of its location or primarily because of its menu. The manager randomly selects and questions 100 customers and finds that 70 state that they eat there because of the location and 30 because of the menu. This represents a simple analysis using nominal data. The manager has formed a two-category scale, counted the number of cases in each category, and identified the modal category.

If our restaurant manager had also noted the gender of each respondent, he could array the data as shown in Table 9–3. Without doing a formal statistical analysis, it can be seen that females prefer the restaurant because of the menu and males prefer it because of the location.

Any arithmetic operations performed on nominally scaled data can only be carried out on the *count* in each category. Numbers assigned to represent the categories (1 for male, 0 for female, for example) cannot meaningfully be added, subtracted, multiplied, or divided.

A *mean* or a *median* cannot be calculated for nominal data. A *mode* can be used, however. In the example given, location was the modal reason for choosing the restaurant among the males and the menu was the modal reason among females. The *percentages* of items falling within each category also can be determined. A chi-square statistical test can be conducted to determine if differences between the numbers falling in the various catagories is likely to be the result of chance or randomness.

Ordinal Measurements

Ordinal scales represent numbers, letters, or other symbols used to rank items. Items can be classified not only as to whether they share some characteristic with another item but also whether they have more or less of this characteristic than some other object. However, ordinally scaled numbers do not provide information on how much more or less of the characteristic various items possess. For an example, refer to the "actual" column of Table 9–1, in which five markets are ranked in terms of market potential and their actual sales are indicated.

The rank order (ordinal) scale in Table 9–1 accurately indicates that area A is the largest market, B the next largest, and so forth. Thus, it is a sound measure of the relative size of the five areas. Note that the difference in rank between markets A and B is 1, as it is between markets B and C. However, the difference in sales between markets A and B is approximately $8 million, whereas the difference between markets B and C is approximately $1 million. Thus, ordinal data indicate the relative position of two or more items on some characteristic but *not* the *magnitude* of the differences between the items.

A significant amount of marketing research relies on ordinal measures. The most common usage of ordinal scales is in obtaining preference measurements. For example, a consumer or a sample of experts may be asked to rank preferences for several brands, flavors, or package designs. The following questions will produce ordinal data:

How would you rate the selection of goods offered for sale in Wards compared to the selection offered for sale in Sears?

( ) Better   ( ) The Same   ( ) Worse

Read the list of brands of gasoline on the card I just gave you. Tell me which brand you think has the highest quality. Now tell me the one you think is next highest in quality.
(Continue until all brands are named or until the respondent says she does not know the remaining brands. Record DK if she does not know the brand.)

(1) ——————   (3) ——————   (5) ——————
(2) ——————   (4) ——————

Suppose that Texaco is one of the brands of gasoline. Further suppose that the quality ratings it receives, as compared with four other brands from a sample of 500 car owners, are as follows:

Quality Rating	Number of Respondents Giving Rating to Texaco
1	100
2	200
3	100
4	50
5	50

What kind of descriptive statistics can be used on these data?

A *mode* or a *median* may be used, but not a *mean*. The modal quality rating is "2," as it is for the median. A mean should not be calculated because the differences between ordinal scaled values are not necessarily the same. The *percentages* of the total appearing in each rank may be calculated and are meaningful. The branch of statistics that deals with ordinal (and nominal) measurements is called *nonparametric statistics*.

Interval Measurements

Interval scales represent numbers used to rank items such that numerically equal distances on the scale represent equal distances in the property being measured. However, the location of the zero point is not fixed. Both the zero point and the unit of measurement are arbitrary. The most familiar examples of interval scales are the temperature scales, both centigrade and Fahrenheit. The same natural phenomenon, the freezing point of water, is assigned a different value on each scale, 0 on centigrade and 32 on Fahrenheit. The 0 position, therefore, is arbitrary. The difference in the volume of mercury is the same between 20 and 30 degrees centigrade and 40 and 50 degrees centigrade. Thus, the measure of the underlying phenomenon is made in equal units. A value on either scale can be converted to the other by using the formula $F = 32 + 9/5C$.

The most frequent form of interval measurement in marketing is *index numbers*. An index number is calculated by setting one number, such as sales, for a particular year equal to 100. This is known as the *base period* or *base value*. Other numbers for subsequent years are then expressed as percentages of the base value. The Department of Labor provides a consumer price index with 1967 as the base year (1985 = 320), whereas the Federal Reserve System uses 1977 as the base year for its industrial production index. Since any year or value, including a completely arbitrary value, can serve as the base value, index numbers have an arbitrary zero point and equal intervals between scale values.

Another common type of marketing research data generally treated as interval scale data is attitude measures. A Likert scale (described in Chapter 11), for example, requires the respondents to state their degree of agreement or disagreement with a statement by selecting a response from a list such as the following one:

1. Agree very strongly.
2. Agree fairly strongly.
3. Agree.
4. Undecided.

5. Disagree.
6. Disagree fairly strongly.
7. Disagree very strongly.

It is doubtful that the interval between each of these items is exactly equal. However, most researchers treat the data from such scales as if they were equal interval in nature since the results of most standard statistical techniques are not affected greatly by small deviations from the interval requirement.[7]

Table 9–4 Types of Measurement Scales

Scale	Basic Empirical Operations	Typical Usage	Typical Statistics[°]	
			Descriptive	Inferential
Nominal	Determination of equality	Classification: Male-female, purchaser-nonpurchaser, social class	Percentages, mode	Chi-square, binomial test
Ordinal	Determination of greater or less	Rankings: Preference data, market position, attitude measures, many psychological measures	Median	Mann-Whitney U, Friedman two-way ANOVA, rank-order correlation
Interval	Determination of equality of intervals	Index numbers, attitude measures, level of knowledge about brands	Mean, range, standard deviation	Product-moment correlation, T-test, factor analysis, ANOVA
Ratio	Determination of equality of ratios	Sales, units produced, number of customers, costs		Coefficient of variation

[°] All statistics applicable to a given scale are also applicable to any higher scale in the table. For example, all the statistics applicable to an ordinal scale are also applicable to interval and ratio scales.
Source: Adapted from S. S. Stevens, "On the Theory of Scales of Measurement," *Science*, June 7, 1946, 677–680.

Virtually the entire range of statistical analyses can be applied to interval scales. Such descriptive measures as the *mean, median, mode, range,* and *standard deviation* are applicable. *Bivariate correlation analyses, t-tests, analysis of variance tests,* and most multivariate techniques applied for purposes of drawing inferences can be used on intervally scaled data. However, as we saw in Exhibit 9–1, ratios calculated on interval data are not meaningful. A ratio —twice as much, 50 per cent more than, half as much—requires a ratio measurement scale.

Ratio Measurements

Ratio scales consist of numbers that rank items such that numerically equal distances on the scale represent equal distances in the property being measured *and* have a meaningful zero. In general, simple counting of any set of objects produces a ratio scale of the characteristic "existence." In this case, the number 0 has an absolute empirical meaning—none of the property being measured exists. Thus, such common measurements as *sales, costs, market potential, market share,* and *number of purchasers* are all made using ratio scales.

All descriptive measures and inferential techniques are applicable to ratio-scaled data. However, this produces only a minimal gain in analytic technique beyond those available for interval data. Table 9–4 provides a summary description of each of the four types of scales.

Components of Measurements

Suppose an individual has completed a 10-item questionnaire designed to measure overall attitude toward the Honda *Spree.* The score (number) for this measurement was 68. We can assume any scaling system, nominal through ratio. The question that the researcher must ask is: *What factors or characteristics are reflected in this score?*

In an ideal situation, there would be only one component in the score and this component would be a direct reflection of the characteristic of interest— the individual's attitude toward the *Spree.* Unfortunately, such a state of affairs is seldom achieved. For example, an analysis of 70 published studies found that, on average, 32 per cent of the variance between scores was random error, 26 per cent was due to the measurement approach and only 42 per cent reflected differences in the characteristic of interest.[8]

The researcher must, therefore, be concerned about the extent to which any single measurement reflects the characteristic under consideration versus other characteristics.

Table 9–5 summarizes the components that may be reflected in any given

Table 9–5 Components of Measurements

1. *True characteristic:* direct reflection of the characteristic of interest
2. *Additional stable characteristics of the respondent:* reflection of other permanent characteristics, such as social class or intelligence
3. *Short-term characteristics of the respondent:* reflection of temporary characteristics such as hunger, fatigue, or anger
4. *Situational characteristics:* reflection of the surroundings in which the measurement is taken
5. *Characteristics of the measurement process:* reflection of the interviewer, interviewing method, and the like
6. *Characteristics of the measuring instrument:* reflection of ambiguous or misleading questions
7. *Characteristics of the response process:* reflection of mistaken replies caused by checking the wrong response, and the like
8. *Characteristics of the analysis:* reflection of mistakes in coding, tabulating, and the like

measurement. As the table indicates, the characteristic of interest is only one of eight possible components of a measurement. The remaining components all constitute *measurement error* (sometimes referred to as *response error*). Each component of measurement error is described in the following paragraphs.

Reflection of Additional Stable Characteristics

Perhaps the most troublesome measurement error occurs when the *measurement reflects a stable characteristic of the object or event in addition to the one of interest to the researcher.* Thus, the score of 68 in the example may reflect the respondent's tendency to be agreeable by marking positive responses as well as the "true" attitude. Such "extraneous" variables as gender, education, and age have been found to be sources of bias in the measurement of attitudinal reactions to television commercials tested by the Leo Burnett Co.[9] As we saw earlier, Hanes developed an inappropriate advertising strategy for *L'erin* because it was misled by a tendency of the women it surveyed to describe cosmetic purchases in logical terms while (apparently) purchasing them on an emotional basis.

Temporary Characteristics of the Object

An equally common source of error is the *influence of short-term characteristics of the object.* Such factors as fatigue, health, hunger, and emotional state may influence the measure of other characteristics. In the attitude measure example, some of the "68" could reflect the fact that the respondent was in a bad mood because of a cold.

Researchers frequently assume that such temporary fluctuations are randomly distributed in their effect on the measurement and will cancel each other out. However, if such an assumption is made, it should be explicitly stated and justified.

Situational Characteristics

Many measurements that involve human subjects reflect both the true characteristic under consideration and *the characteristics under which the measurement is taken.* For example, husbands and wives tend to report one level of influence in a purchase decision if their spouses are present and another level if their spouses are absent. Location (store versus home) has been found to influence consumers' ability to discriminate between brands in a "blind" taste test.[10] However, other measures, such as recognition measures of television commercials, appear to be rather stable across measurement situations.[11]

Characteristics of the Measurement Process

The measurement also can include *influences from the method of gathering the data.* Gender, age, ethnic background, and style of dress of the interviewer have been shown to influence an individual's response patterns on certain questions. In addition, various methods of interviewing — telephone, mail, personal interview, and the like — sometimes alter response patterns.

Characteristics of the Measuring Instrument

Aspects of *the measuring instrument itself can cause constant or random errors.* Unclear instructions, ambiguous questions, confusing terms, irrelevant questions, and omitted questions can all introduce errors. For example, the term *dinner* causes some people to think of the noon meal and others to think of the evening meal. Our 68 score may not be an accurate reflection of overall attitude toward the *Spree* if a key dimension such as safety was omitted from the questionnaire.

Characteristics of the Response Process

Response errors are another reason why responses may not reflect the "true" characteristic accurately. For example, our respondent may have inadvertently checked a positive response when the intention was to check a negative one. Part of the score of 68 would be caused by this mistake, rather than by the true attitude.

Characteristics of the Analysis

Finally, *mistakes can occur in interpreting, coding, tabulating, and analyzing an individual's or a group's response.* In our attitude example, a keypuncher might punch an 8 rather than a 3 for one of the questions. Again, the 68 would be composed of an error component in addition to the characteristic of interest.

The measurement errors described are subject to varying degrees of control by the researcher.[12] The material in Chapters 10 through 14 provides explicit discussions of various approaches for controlling measurement error. The next section of this chapter describes the effect of the error components in terms of the accuracy of the measurement.

Measurement Accuracy

A measurement is a number designed to reflect some characteristic of an individual, object, or event. As such it is a specific observation or picture of this characteristic. Thus, we must keep in mind that a measurement is *not* the characteristic of interest but only an observation of it. Ideally, the observed measurement would be an exact representation of the true characteristic, or $M = C$ where M stands for the measurement and C stands for the true value of the characteristic being measured.

As we saw in the previous section, a number of errors tend to influence a measurement. Thus, the general situation is:

$$M = C + E, \text{ where } E = \text{errors.}$$

The smaller E is as a percentage of M, the more accurate is the measurement. Researchers should seek to achieve accuracy levels sufficient to solve the problem at hand while minimizing the cost of achieving the needed accuracy.

The terms *validity, reliability,* and *measurement accuracy* are often used interchangeably. For example, the vice-president of advertising and marketing services for Ralston Purina raised the following question concerning the Nielsen television audience information: "Is the information we're getting from a service like that . . . absolutely reliable and should we make million dollar decisions on every little point?"[13] However, in elaborating his concerns, it is clear that he is concerned about the total accuracy of the Nielsen data and not its reliability alone.

Although *validity, reliability,* and *accuracy* are often used interchangeably, each does have a specific meaning based on the type of measurement error that is present.[14] Measurement error can be either systematic or variable in its impact. A *systematic error,* also known as *bias,* is one that occurs in a consistent manner each time something is measured. In the Honda *Spree* example, a general tendency to respond favorably independent of one's true feeling (an additional stable characteristic) would occur each time that individual's attitude is measured. This would be a systematic error.

A *variable error* is one that occurs randomly each time something is measured. In the *Spree* example, a response that is less favorable than the true feeling because the respondent was in a bad mood (temporary characteristic) would *not* occur each time that individual's attitude is measured. In fact, an error in the opposite direction (overly favorable) would occur if the individual were in a very good mood. This represents a variable error.

The term *reliability* is used to refer to the degree of variable error in a measurement. We define *reliability* as the *the extent to which a measurement is free of variable errors.*[15] This is reflected when repeated measures of the same stable characteristic in the same objects show limited variation.

A common conceptual definition for validity is the extent to which the measure provides an accurate representation of what one is trying to measure. In this conceptual definition, validity includes both *systematic* and *variable* error components. However, it is more useful to limit the meaning of the term *validity* to refer to the degree of consistent or systematic error in a measurement. Therefore, we define *validity* as the *extent to which a measurement is free from systematic error.*

Measurement accuracy then is defined as *the extent to which a measurement is free from systematic and variable error.* Accuracy is the ultimate concern of the researcher since a lack of accuracy may lead to incorrect decisions. However, since systematic and variable errors are measured and controlled for in distinct ways, considering each separately under the concepts of reliability and validity is worthwhile. For example, the reliability of a score based on the sum of several similar items can be improved by increasing the number of items used to calculate the sum. The validity of the score is unaffected by this technique.[16]

Generalizability theory is a new, technical approach to assessing reliability and validity simultaneously.[17] While beyond the scope of this text, its focus on the purpose of the research and those aspects of the measurement process that require generalization suggests that it will evolve into a useful approach to measurement accuracy.

Reliability

Table 9–6 summarizes the major operational approaches to the estimation of reliability.[18] Each of these measures is discussed in some detail in the following paragraphs. No one approach is best; in fact, several different assessment approaches should generally be used.[19] The selection of one or more means of assessing a measure's reliability depends on the errors likely to be present and the cost of each assessment method in the situation at hand.

Test-Retest Reliability

Test-retest reliability estimates *are obtained by repeating the measurement using the same instrument under as nearly equivalent conditions as possible.*

Table 9 – 6   Approaches to Assessing Reliability

1. *Test-retest reliability:* applying the same measure to the same objects a second time.
2. *Alternative-forms reliability:* measuring the same objects by two instruments that are designed to be as nearly alike as possible.
3. *Internal-comparison reliability:* comparing the responses among the various items on a multiple-item index designed to measure a homogeneous concept.
4. *Scorer reliability:* comparing the scores assigned the same qualitative material by two or more judges.

The results of the two administrations are then compared and the degree of correspondence is determined. The greater the differences, the lower is the reliability.[20]

A number of practical and computational difficulties are involved in measuring test-retest reliability.[21] First, *some items can be measured only once.* It would not be possible, for example, to remeasure an individual's initial reaction to a new advertising slogan. Second, in many situations, *the initial measurement may alter the characteristic being measured.* Thus, an attitude survey may focus the individual's attention on the topic and cause new or different attitudes to be formed about it. Third, *there may be some form of a carryover effect from the first measure.* The retaking of a measure may produce boredom, anger, or attempts to remember the answers given on the initial measurement. Finally, *factors extraneous to the measuring process may cause shifts in the characteristic being measured.* A favorable experience with a brand during the period between the test and the retest might cause a shift in individual ratings of that brand, for example.

Alternative-Form Reliability

Alternative-form reliability estimates *are obtained by applying two "equivalent" forms of the measuring instrument to the same subjects.*[22] As in test-retest reliability, the results of the two instruments are compared on an item-by-item basis and the degree of similarity is determined. The basic logic is the same as in the test-retest approach. Two primary problems are associated with this approach. The first is the *extra time, expense, and trouble involved in obtaining two equivalent measures.* The second, and more important, is *the problem of constructing two truly equivalent forms.* Thus, a low degree of response similarity may reflect either an unreliable instrument or nonequivalent forms.

Internal-Comparison Reliability

Internal-comparison reliability *is estimated by the intercorrelation among the scores of the items on a multiple-item index.* All items on the index must be designed to measure precisely the same thing.[23] For example, measures of store image generally involve assessing a number of specific dimensions of the store, such as price level, merchandise, service, and location. Because these are somewhat independent, an internal-comparison measure of reliability is not appropriate across dimensions. However, it can be used *within* each dimension if several items are used to measure each dimension.

Split-half reliability is the simplest type of internal comparison. It is obtained by comparing the results of half the items on a multi-item measure with the results from the remaining items. The usual approach to split-half reliability involves dividing the total number of items into two groups on a random basis and computing a measure of similarity (a correlation coefficient — see Chapter 20).

A better approach to internal comparison is known as *coefficient alpha.* This measurement, in effect, produces the mean of all possible split-half coefficients resulting from different splittings of the measurement instrument.[24] Coefficient alpha can range from 0 to 1. A value of .6 or less is usually viewed as unsatisfactory.[25]

Scorer Reliability

Marketing researchers frequently rely on judgment to classify a consumer's response. This occurs, for example, when projective techniques, focus groups, observation, or open-ended questions are used. In these situations, the judges, or scorers, may be unreliable, rather than the instrument or respondent. To estimate the level of scorer reliability, *each scorer should have some of the items he or she scores judged independently by another scorer.* The correlation between the various judges is a measure of scorer reliability.[26]

Validity

Validity, like reliability, is concerned with error. However, it is *concerned with consistent or systematic error rather than variable error.* A valid measurement reflects only the characteristics of interest and random error. There are three basic types of validity: *content* validity, *construct* validity, and *criterion-related* validity (predictive and concurrent). These are defined in Table 9–7 and described in the following sections.[27]

Content Validity

Content validity estimates are essentially *systematic, but subjective, evaluations of the appropriateness of the measuring instrument for the task at hand.* The term *face validity* has a similar meaning. However, face validity generally refers to "nonexpert" judgments of individuals completing the instrument and/or executives who must approve its use. This does not mean that face

---

Table 9–7 Basic Approaches to Validity Assessment

I. *Content validation* involves assessing the representativeness or the sampling adequacy of the items contained in the measuring instrument.

II. *Criterion-related validation* involves inferring an individual's score or standing on some measurement, called a *criterion,* from the measurement at hand.

   a. *Concurrent validation* involves assessing the extent to which the obtained score may be used to estimate an individual's present standing with respect to some other variable.

   b. *Predictive validation* involves assessing the extent to which the obtained score may be used to estimate an individual's future standing with respect to the criterion variable.

III. *Construct validation* involves understanding the meaning of the obtained measurements.

---

validity is not important. Respondents may refuse to cooperate or may fail to treat seriously measurements that appear irrelevant to them. Managers may refuse to approve projects that utilize measurements lacking in face validity. Therefore, to the extent possible, researchers should strive for face validity.

The most common use of content validity is with multi-item measures. In this case, the researcher or some other individual or group of individuals assesses the representativeness, or sampling adequacy, of the included items in light of the purpose of the measuring instrument. Thus, an attitude scale designed to measure the overall attitude toward a shopping center would not be considered to have content validity if it omitted any major attributes such as location, layout, and so on. Content validation is the most common form of validation in applied marketing research.

Criterion-Related Validity

Criterion-related validity can take two forms, based on the time period involved: concurrent and predictive validity.

Concurrent validity is the extent to which one measure of a variable can be used to estimate an individual's current score on a different measure of the same, or a closely related, variable. For example, a researcher may be trying to relate social class to the use of savings and loan associations. In a pilot study, the researcher finds a useful relationship between attitudes toward savings and loan associations and social class, as defined by Warner's ISC scale. The researcher now wishes to test this relationship further in a national mail survey. Unfortunately, Warner's ISC is difficult to use in a mail survey. Therefore, the researcher develops brief verbal descriptions of each of Warner's six social classes. Respondents will be asked to indicate the social class that best describes their household. Prior to using this measure, the researcher should assess its concurrent validity with the standard ISC scale.

Predictive validity is the extent to which an individual's future level on some variable can be predicted by his or her performance on a current measurement of the same or a different variable. Predictive validity is the primary concern of the applied marketing researcher. Some of the predictive validity questions that confront marketing researchers are: (1) Will a measure of attitudes predict future purchases? (2) Will a measure of sales in a controlled store test predict future market share? (3) Will a measure of initial sales predict future sales? and (4) Will a measure of demographic characteristics of an area predict the success of a branch bank in the area?

Advertising researchers are trying to develop communications effects measures for use with storyboards that will accurately predict similar measures using "rough" commercials. Storyboards precede the development of commercials and cost substantially less than the $15,000 required to produce a rough commercial.[28] Thus, the economic benefits associated with a predictively valid measure of storyboard communications effects will be substantial.

Construct Validity

Construct validity — *understanding the factors that underlie the obtained measurement* — is the most complex form of validity. It involves more than just knowing how well a given measure works; it also involves knowing *why* it works. Construct validity requires that the researcher have a sound theory of the nature of the concept being measured and how it relates to other concepts.

A number of statistical approaches exist for assessing construct validity of which the most common is called the *multitrait-multimethod matrix* approach.[29] Although a detailed description of these techniques is beyond the scope of this text, they generally involve ensuring that the measure correlates positively with other measures of the same construct *(convergent validity)*, does not correlate with theoretically unrelated constructs *(discriminant validity)*, correlates in the theoretically predicted way with measures of different but related constructs *(nomological validity)*, and correlates highly with itself *(reliability)*.[30]

For example, suppose we develop a multi-item scale to measure the tendency to purchase prestige brands. Our theory suggests that this tendency is caused by three personality variables: low self-focus, high need for status, and high materialism. We believe that it is unrelated to brand loyalty and the tendency to purchase new products. Evidence of construct validity would exist if our scale:

- correlates highly with other measures of prestige brand preference such as reported purchases and classifications by friends (convergent validity);
- has a low correlation with the unrelated constructs *brand loyalty* and *tendency to purchase new products* (discriminant validity);

- has a low correlation with self-focus and high correlations with need for status and materialism (nomological validity); and
- has a high level of internal consistency (reliability).

Measurement Development

Suppose you need to develop a measurement for a particular concept such as brand image, customer satisfaction, or opinion leadership. How would you proceed? In this section we present a sound general method for developing such a measurement.

The proposed measurement development methodology is illustrated in Figure 9–1 and is discussed in the following paragraphs.[31]

Step 1. Specify domain of concept. This requires the development of a sound conceputal definition. It involves providing a conceptual answer to the question "Exactly what do we mean by (brand image, customer satisfaction, and the like)?" A careful literature review, discussions with knowledgeable individuals, and a thorough understanding of the management problem are useful aids in developing a sound conceptual definition.

Step 2. Generate sample of items. This step involves generating a list of specific items (questions, phrases, statements) for each dimension of the concept as defined in Step 1. A comprehensive literature review, discussion and/ or focus groups with key individuals (sales personnel, distributors, trade association officials, consumers), content analysis of product category advertising, and brainstorming are useful techniques at this stage. Once the list is generated, the individual items need to be edited for clarity.

Step 3. Collect data for measure purifying. The edited items should be placed in an appropriate format (questions, attitude scales, observations) and data collected from members of the target market of interest.

Step 4. Purify the measure. This basically involves eliminating those items that do not correlate highly with the total score for the overall measure or the specific dimensions with which they are associated. Coefficient alpha and factor analysis are useful techniques for this purpose.[32] As Figure 9–1 indicates, unsatisfactory results at this stage may require a reconsideration of the conceptual definition or the generation of additional sample items.

Step 5. Collect data for reliability and validity assessment. Once the measure has been satisfactorily purified (clearly unrelated items removed with several items remaining for each dimension of the concept), a new data set should be collected with the revised instrument.

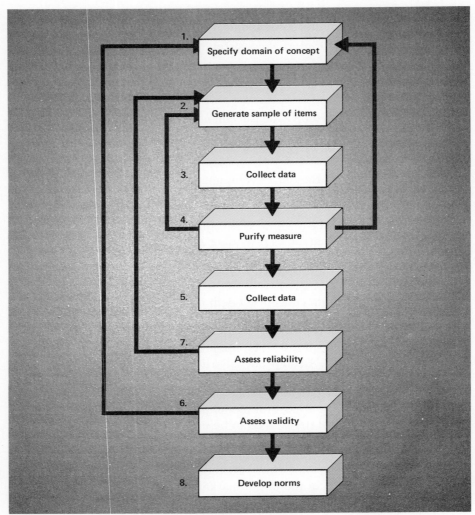

Figure 9–1 *Methodologies for Developing Sound Marketing Measures*

Source: Adopted from G. A. Churchill, Jr., "A Paradigm for Developing Better Measures of Marketing Constructs," *Journal of Marketing Research* (February 1979), 66. Used with permission from the American Marketing Association.

Step 6. Assess reliability. The new data set should be analyzed to test for reliability. To the extent possible, several different reliability assessments should be used. Unreliable items should be eliminated from the overall measurement instrument and, if necessary, replacement items should be generated.

Step 7. Assess validity. Once the reliability of the measurement has been established, its validity needs to be determined. Although any method of validation can be used, construct validation is preferred.

Step 8. Develop norms. Once a satisfactory measurement has been developed, it should be administered to various groups of people (demographic groups, users-nonusers, and so forth) and averages and variances determined. This will allow one to interpret better the meaning of a score obtained by an individual or group in a subsequent application of the instrument. Implementing this methodology fully may not be possible in some applied studies as a result of time and cost constraints, though it is economically justified in many cases. It is particularly valuable when the measurement will be used in multiple studies or will be repeated over time. In any case, it serves as a model that can be approximated in studies when one cannot justify the time or cost involved in complete implementation.

Review Questions

9.1. What is meant by *measurement?*

9.2. How can we evaluate measurements?

9.3. What is a *concept?*

9.4. What is the difference between a *conceptual* definition and an *operational* definition?

9.5. What is a *nominal* scale? What statistical techniques can be used with a nominal scale?

9.6. What is an *ordinal* scale? What statistical techniques can be used with an ordinal scale?

9.7. What is an *interval* scale? What statistical techniques can be used with an interval scale?

9.8. What is a *ratio* scale? What statistical techniques can be used with a ratio scale?

9.9. What measurement components can exist in any specific measurement?

9.10. Describe the measurement component *temporary characteristics of the object.*

9.11. Describe the measurement component *additional stable characteristics of the object.*

9.12. Describe the measurement component *situational characteristics.*

9.13. Describe the measurement component *characteristics of the measurement process.*

9.14. Describe the measurement component *characteristics of the measuring instrument.*

9.15. Describe the measurement component *characteristics of the response process.*

9.16. Describe the measurement component *characteristics of the analysis.*

9.17. How are the measurement accuracy, reliability, and validity related?

9.18. Describe each of the following:
a. Test-retest reliability
b. Alternative-forms reliability
c. Internal-comparison reliability
d. Split-half reliability
e. Coefficient alpha
f. Scorer reliability

9.19. What are the problems with test-retest reliability?

9.20. Describe each of the following:
a. Content validity
b. Face validity
c. Criterion-related validity
d. Concurrent validity
e. Predictive validity
f. Construct validity
g. Convergent validity
h. Discriminant validity
i. Nomological validity

9.21. What is the *multitrait-multimethod* approach?

9.22. Describe the procedure for developing a sound measure of a marketing concept.

Discussion Questions/Problems

9.23. For each of the following measurements, indicate whether a nominal, ordinal, interval, or ratio scale was used. Briefly explain why you believe your answer is correct.
a. A report indicating that Dannon is the largest-selling yogurt in the country
b. A report indicating that Pepsi has 20 per cent of total sales in a particular state
c. A report indicating that Pepsi sold fifty thousand cases during a special price promotion
d. A report classifying tofu as a basic food and thus exempt from sales tax.
e. A recommendation that milk be served at 48°F

9.24. What kind(s) of scale(s) is/are involved in the following statements? Is the analysis appropriate for the scale used?
a. "Many women need a calcium supplement. Two capsules of Calmight daily will correct the calcium deficiency of most women with a calcium deficiency."
b. "Our survey asked 500 men to rank the taste of McDonalds, Burger King, Dairy Queen, Wendy's, and Artic Circle hamburgers. The most preferred was given a rank of 5 and the least preferred a rank of 1. The mean rank for Wendy's was 3.7 and the modal rank was 3.0."

c. "Consumers ranked Classic Coke, Coke, Pepsi, and RC Cola in order of preference. Pepsi was twice as popular as RC Cola because the median for Pepsi was 3.2 and the median for RC was 1.6."

d. "When a sample of 500 customers was asked why they shopped at Sears, 210 listed service as the main reason. This was twice as many as the second most common reason, good prices. Thus, service is twice as important as price."

e. "Average per capita consumption is 4.2 bottles per month. Women consume twice as much as men do on a per capita basis."

9.25. Give one conceptual and two or more operational definitions for each of the following concepts:
   a. industrial product
   b. heavy user
   c. dissatisfied customer
   d. discount store

9.26. What measurement components do you think were or would be most important in the following situations?
   a. Your response to your date's question: "How did you like my new haircut?"
   b. Your scores on last term's finals.
   c. An audit of your clothing to determine your preferences for styles and brands.
   d. A telephone interview during Christmas season designed to measure cola preference.

9.27. In the Miss America Pageant, contestants are rated by each judge separately on a scale of 1 to 10 (10 highest) on talent, swimsuit appearance, evening gown appearance, and the results of an interview. These ratings are weighted one third for talent, one third for swimsuit appearance, one sixth for evening gown appearance, and one sixth for the interview. The weighted scores from each of these areas are first summed by judge and then for all judges. The contestant with the highest total score becomes the new Miss America.

   Ignoring for a moment any concerns you might have about the appropriateness of such a contest, comment on the assumptions implicit in this procedure with respect to:
   a. the scales involved
   b. interarea ratings by each judge
   c. intraarea ratings across judges
   d. the weights for the areas

9.28. As a manager, what indicators of measurement accuracy would you insist on in research reports?

9.29. Develop a series of index numbers using the following sales data:
   a. 1979 = 730,000
   b. 1980 = 835,000
   c. 1981 = 955,000
   d. 1982 = 985,000
   e. 1983 = 1,130,000
   f. 1984 = 1,200,000
   g. 1985 = 1,340,000
   h. 1986 = 1,250,000
   i. 1987 = 1,260,000
   j. 1988 = 1,310,000
   k. 1989 = 1,450,000
   l. 1990 = 1,300,000

281

Projects

9.30. Examine the marketing literature dealing with multiattribute attitude models. (Any recent consumer behavior text will describe the model and list additional references.) What type of validity has been stressed in this literature? What steps would you suggest to validate further these models?

9.31. Examine the marketing literature, and find and describe a marketing concept that has two or more distinct conceptual definitions.

9.32. Describe the assessment of reliability of the measurement instrument in a *recent* marketing study whose primary purpose did not relate to reliability assessment.

9.33. Describe the assessment of validity of the measurement instrument in a *recent* marketing study in which the primary purpose did not relate to validity assessment.

9.34. Using the procedure described in the text, develop a sound measurement for one of the following: (a) store image, (b) brand loyalty, (c) market share, (d) purchase satisfaction, (e) advertisement readership.

References

[1] B. Abrams, "Hanes Finds L'eggs Methods Don't Work with Cosmetics," *Wall Street Journal,* February 3, 1983, 33.

[2] For a detailed treatment of measurement in marketing see J. P. Peter and M. L. Ray, *Measurement Readings for Marketing Research* (Chicago: American Marketing Association, 1984).

[3] N. R. Campbell, "Symposium: Measurement and Its Importance for Philosophy," *Proc. Arist. Soc. Suppl.* (1938), 126 and J. C. Nunnally, *Psychometric Theory* (New York: McGraw-Hill Book Co., Inc., 1967), Chaps. 1, 5.

[4] C. Selltiz et al., *Research Methods in Social Relations,* rev. ed. (New York: Holt, Rinehart and Winston, Inc., 1959), 41.

[5] F. N. Kerlinger, *Foundations of Behavioral Research* (New York: Holt, Rinehart and Winston, 1973), 30–35.

[6] J. Engel et al., *Consumer Behavior* 4th ed. (New York: Holt, Rinehart and Winston, Inc., 1982), 570.

[7] J. W. Hanson and A. J. Rethans, "Developing Internal Scale Values Using the Normalized Rank Method: A Multiple Context, Multiple Group Methodology," in J. Olson, *Advances in Consumer Research VII* (Provo, Utah: Association for Consumer Research, 1980), 672–675; M. Traylor, "Ordinal and Interval Scaling," *Journal of the Market Research Society* (October 1983), 297–303; and M. R. Crask and R. J. Fox, "An Exploration of the Internal Properties of Three Commonly Used Research Scales," *Journal of the Market Research Society* (October 1987), 317–39.

[8] J. A. Cote and M. R. Buckley, "Estimating Trait, Method, and Error Variance," *Journal of Marketing Research* (August 1987), 315–18. See also H. Assael and J. Keon, "Nonsampling vs. Sampling Errors in Survey Research," *Journal of Marketing* (Spring 1982), 114–123.

[9] M. J. R. Schlinger, "Respondent Characteristics That Affect Copy-Test Attitude Scales," *Journal of Advertising Research* (February/March 1982), 29–35.

[10] R. D. Hill et al., "The Effects of Environment on Taste Discrimination of Bread Spreads," *Journal of Advertising,* (#3, 1981), 19–24.

[11] R. W. Mizerski, "Television Commercial Copy Testing with Recognition Measures," in P. E. Murphy, *1983 AMA Educators' Proceedings* (Chicago: American Marketing Association, 1983), 420–423.

[12] See J. Rothman, "Acceptance Checks for Ensuring Quality in Research," *Journal of the Market Research Society,* (#3, 1980), 192–204.

[13] W. M. Claggett, "Is the Info Reliable?" *Advertising Age,* October 15, 1979, S-8.

[14] For a technical discussion of the relationship of these concepts, see Kerlinger, op. cit., Chaps. 26 and 27.

[15] See L. A. Breedling, "On More Reliably Employing the Concept of 'Reliability,'" *Public Opinion Quarterly* (Fall 1974), 372–378. For other conceptual definitions of reliability see J. P. Peter, "Reliability: A Review of Psychometric Basics and Recent Marketing Practices," *Journal of Marketing Research* (February 1979), 6–17.

[16] G. A. Churchill, Jr., and J. P. Peter, "Research Design Effects on the Reliability of Rating Scales," *Journal of Marketing Research* (November 1984), 360–375; and W. O. Bearden, et al., "Reliability of Shortened Measures in Marketing Research," in R. W. Belk, *1984 AMA Educators' Proceedings* (Chicago: American Marketing Association, 1984) 392–397.

[17] J. O. Rentz, "Generalizability Theory," *Journal of Marketing Research* (February 1987), 19–28.

[18] See also Peter (1979), op. cit; and R. Parameswaran et al., "Measuring Reliability: A Comparison of Alternative Techniques," *Journal of Marketing Research* (February 1979), 18–25.

[19] G. Brooker, "On Selecting an Appropriate Measure of Reliability," in N. Beckwith et al., *1979 Educators' Conference Proceedings* (Chicago: American Marketing Association, 1979), 56–59; and Parameswaran et al., op. cit.

[20] For illustrations of this technique see A. S. Boote, "Reliability Testing of Psychographic Scales," *Journal of Advertising Research* (October 1981), 53–60; T. W. Leigh, D. B. MacKay, and J. O. Summers, "Reliability and Validity of Conjoint Analysis and Self-Explicated Weights," *Journal of Marketing Research* (November 1984), 456–462; and E. D. Jaffe and I. D. Nebenzahl, "Alternative Questionnaire Formats for Country Image Studies," *Journal of Marketing Research* (November 1984), 463–471.

[21] See A. Adams, "A Cautionary Note on the Reliability of Advertising Test-Retest Scores," *Journal of Advertising,* (#1, 1984), 41–45; and A. Adams, S. Mehrotra,

and S. Van Auken, "Reliability of Forced-Exposure Television Copytesting," *Journal of Advertising Research* (June/July 1983), 29–32.

[22] For illustrations see Jaffe and Nebenzahl, and M. N. Segal, "Alternate Form Conjoint Reliability," *Journal of Advertising* (#4, 1984), 31–38.

[23] See D. W. Gerbing and J. C. Anderson, "An Updated Paradigm for Scale Development Incorporating Unidimensionality and Its Assessment," *Journal of Marketing Research* (May 1988), 186–92.

[24] Peter (1979), op cit.; and G. Vigderhous, "Coefficient of Reliability Alpha," *Journal of Marketing Research* (May 1974), 194.

[25] Churchill and Peter, op. cit.

[26] R. T. Craig, "Generalization of Scott's Index of Intercoder Agreement," *Public Opinion Quarterly* (Summer 1981), 260–264 and J. P. McDonald, "Qualitative Data" in B. J. Walker, et al., *1982 Educators' Conference Proceedings* (Chicago: American Marketing Association, 1982), 435–438.

[27] This section is based on *Standards for Educational and Psychological Tests* (New York: American Psychological Association, 1974). See also Kerlinger, op. cit., Ch. 22. For attempts to validate marketing measures, see Peter and Ray, op. cit.

[28] E. M. Tauber, "Can We Test Storyboards?" *Journal of Advertising Research* (October/November 1983), 7.

[29] D. T. Campbell and D. W. Fiske, "Convergent and Discriminant Validation by the Multitrait-Multimethod Matrix," *Psychological Bulletin* (March 1959), 81–105; J. P. Peter, "Construct Validity: A Review of Basic Issues and Marketing Practices," *Journal of Marketing Research* (May 1981), 133–145; "Special Issue on Causal Modeling," *Journal of Marketing Research* (November 1982), 403–584; and J. P. Peter and G. A. Churchill, Jr., "Relationships Among Research Design Choices and Psychometric Properties of Rating Scales," *Journal of Marketing Research* (February 1986), 1–10.

[30] For a recent application see N. K. Malhotra, "Validity and Structural Reliability of Multidimensional Scaling," *Journal of Marketing Research* (May 1987), 164–73.

[31] Based on G. A. Churchill, Jr., "A Paradigm for Developing Better Measures of Marketing Constructs," *Journal of Marketing Research* (February 1979), 64–73. For applications see R. W. Ruekert and G. A. Churchill, Jr., "Reliability and Validity of Alternative Measures of Channel Member Satisfaction," *Journal of Marketing Research* (May 1984), 226–233; M. B. Traylor and W. B. Joseph, "Measuring Consumer Involvement in Products," *Psychology and Marketing* (Summer 1984), 65–77; T. A. Shimp and S. Sharma, "Consumer Ethnocentrism," *Journal of Marketing Research* (August 1987), 280–9; and A. Parasuraman, V. A. Zeithaml, and L. L. Berry, "SERVQUAL," *Journal of Retailing* (Spring 1988), 12–37.

[32] See Gerbing and Anderson, *"An Updated Paradigm."*

CHAPTER 10

Questionnaire Design

Burger King recently ran a series of commercials in which it claimed that its method of cooking hamburgers was preferred over McDonald's by three to one.[1] The question that was used to support this claim was: *Do you prefer your hamburgers flame-broiled or fried?* An independent researcher asked the "same" question a different way: *Do you prefer a hamburger that is grilled on a hot stainless-steel grill or cooked by passing the raw meat through an open gas flame?* This version of the question resulted in 53 per cent preferring McDonald's grilling process. When further description was added by noting that the gas-flame hamburgers are kept in a microwave oven before serving, the preference for grilled burgers was 85 per cent. Thus, three technically correct descriptions of cooking methods produced preferences ranging from 3 to 1 for Burger King to 5.5 to 1 for McDonald's.

Suppose we are curious about some aspect of another individual. Our curiosity could involve behavior, knowledge, personal characteristics, or attitudes. How would we satisfy this curiosity? For any one of a fairly wide range of topics, we would simply ask the individual to tell us the pertinent information. Most of us, at one time or another, have asked complete strangers for "the time." Most people consider this an entirely proper question and respond to it as freely and as accurately as possible.

There are other questions that we would hesitate to ask a stranger, or even a friend. Few of us would ask a stranger, "How much money do you have with you?" Even if we obtained an answer such as: "I left all my money at home," we would most likely suspect some distortion.

285

The point is that questioning is a common, everyday approach to obtaining information. There are, however, some types of information for which questioning is appropriate and other types for which it is less appropriate. Furthermore, as the opening example illustrates, *how* we ask questions is critically important.

The Nature of Questionnaire Design

A *questionnaire* is simply a formalized set of questions for eliciting information. As such, its function is measurement and it represents the most common

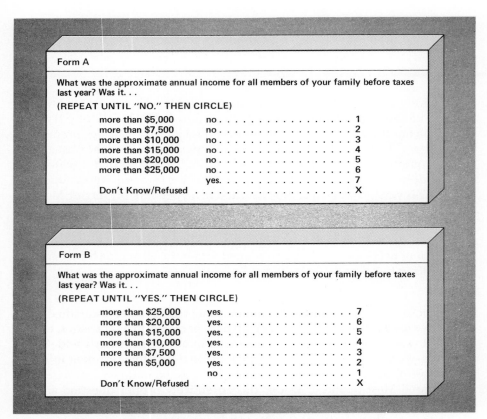

Figure 10–1   *Two Versions of an Income Question*

Source: Adapted from W. B. Locander and J. P. Burton, "The Effect of Question Form on Gathering Income Data by Telephone," *Journal of Marketing Research* (May 1976), 190. Used with permission.

form of measurement in marketing research. Although the questionnaire generally is associated with survey research, it is also frequently the measurement instrument in experimental designs as well. When a questionnaire is administered by means of the telephone or by a personal interviewer, it often is termed an *interview schedule,* or simply *schedule.* However, the term *questionnaire* is used throughout this text to refer to a list of questions, regardless of the means of administration.

The most critical concern in questionnaire construction is *measurement error.* For example, consider Figure 10–1, which shows two very similar versions of the same basic question. The median income reported in response to Form A was $12,711 compared to $17,184 for Form B! The Burger King-McDonald's questions described earlier produced equally dramatic differences.

Obviously, questionnaire construction is of critical importance. Only in rare instances will sampling error produce distortions as extreme as those just described. As a recent study concluded: "Random sampling error is a problem that has been solved. The major problem now is nonsampling error." [2]

Questionnaire design is a major source of nonsampling error. In the following pages, we provide a general guideline for questionnaire design. Although our discussion is based on the results of numerous studies and the accumulated experience of survey researchers, questionnaire design cannot yet be reduced to an exhaustive set of firm principles. Ultimately, a sound questionnaire requires applying *applicable principles, common sense, concern for the respondent, a clear concept of the needed information,* and *thorough pretesting.* Skill in designing questionnaires requires practice and is enhanced by experience in interviewing and editing completed questionnaires.

As Figure 10–2 indicates, questionnaire construction involves seven major decision areas: *(1) preliminary considerations, (2) question content, (3) question wording, (4) response format, (5) question sequence, (6) physical characteristics of the questionnaire,* and *(7) pretest.*

Although the seven decision areas are shown sequentially in Figure 10–2 and are discussed sequentially in the following sections, they are, in fact, interrelated. Not only do decisions made during the early stages influence the types of decisions that can be made later but decisions made during the final stages may compel the reconsideration of earlier choices. For example, decisions on question sequence will often influence the wording of the questions involved.

Software for personal computers is now available to assist in questionnaire design.[3] This software will automatically format various types of questions, provide instructions for answering, randomize response orders, and check for certain syntactical or logical errors. Although such software is a very useful aid, the researcher must still provide intelligent responses to the seven decision areas described.

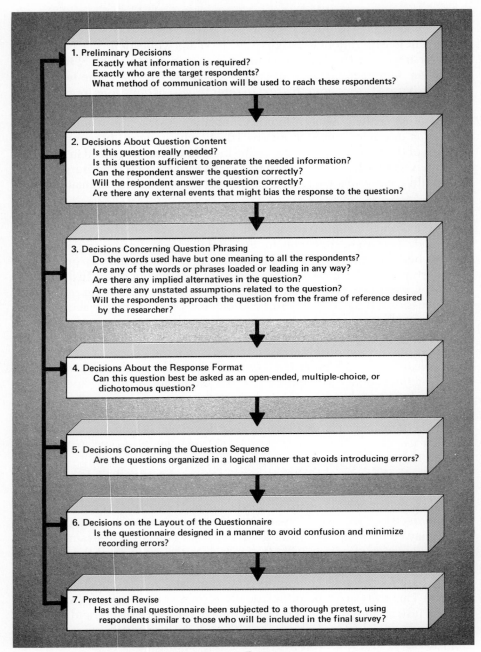

1. Preliminary Decisions
   Exactly what information is required?
   Exactly who are the target respondents?
   What method of communication will be used to reach these respondents?

2. Decisions About Question Content
   Is this question really needed?
   Is this question sufficient to generate the needed information?
   Can the respondent answer the question correctly?
   Will the respondent answer the question correctly?
   Are there any external events that might bias the response to the question?

3. Decisions Concerning Question Phrasing
   Do the words used have but one meaning to all the respondents?
   Are any of the words or phrases loaded or leading in any way?
   Are there any implied alternatives in the question?
   Are there any unstated assumptions related to the question?
   Will the respondents approach the question from the frame of reference desired
      by the researcher?

4. Decisions About the Response Format
   Can this question best be asked as an open-ended, multiple-choice, or
      dichotomous question?

5. Decisions Concerning the Question Sequence
   Are the questions organized in a logical manner that avoids introducing errors?

6. Decisions on the Layout of the Questionnaire
   Is the questionnaire designed in a manner to avoid confusion and minimize
      recording errors?

7. Pretest and Revise
   Has the final questionnaire been subjected to a thorough pretest, using
      respondents similar to those who will be included in the final survey?

Figure 10–2 *Questionnaire Construction Decisions*

Preliminary Decisions

Prior to constructing the actual questionnaire, the researcher must decide exactly *what information* is to be collected from *which respondents* by *what techniques*.

Required Information

We have already discussed the critical importance of clearly specifying exactly what information is needed (see Chapter 3). Obviously, data gained from a questionnaire are of limited value if they are on the wrong topic (surrogate information error) or if they are incomplete. The collection of data that are not required increases the cost of the project. The researcher must begin with a precise statement of what information is required to deal with the management problem at hand.

For example, Cases I–2 and II–3 describe Weyerhaeuser's interest in learning more about the do-it-yourself home repair and remodel market and the value of sponsoring "This Old House" on the Public Broadcasting Service. As described in these cases, a situation analysis resulted in the following objectives for the study:

1. to determine the effects on the company image of sponsoring "This Old House";
2. to discover the relationship between company image and price sensitivity;
3. to find out the characteristics of DIYers, their homes, and their projects; and
4. to discern the effect that sponsoring "This Old House" had on Owens-Corning's image.

The objectives for the study should lead to a list of informational items required. For example, it was decided that objective 3 required the following information:

a. respondents' gender, age, household size, stage in the household life cycle, social class, household income, ownership status, and tenure in current house
b. house age, size
c. last year's expenditures on DIY home improvement materials, last year's project descriptions, last year's lumber and building materials expenditures

Which Respondents?

It is also essential to have a clear idea of exactly who the respondents are to be. Questions that are appropriate for a group of college graduates might not be appropriate for a group of high school graduates. For example, a recent study found that "question understanding is systematically related to socioeconomic characteristics of respondents, and poor question understanding is associated with a high incidence of 'uncertain or no opinion' responses." [4]

In general, the more diversified the potential respondents, the more difficult it is to construct a sound questionnaire that is appropriate for the entire group.

Interview Technique

Finally, one needs to decide on the method or technique of administering the questionnaire prior to designing it. The nature of the decision involving which method of administration to use was described in Chapter 6. However, it may be necessary to alter the method of administration if attempts at designing an effective questionnaire for the initial method of administration are unsuccessful.

In addition, the researcher must be aware of the general approach that is to be taken with the respondents. This involves such issues as identification of the sponsor, what the respondents are told concerning the purpose of the research, and whether the respondents are to be treated anonymously.

Decisions About Question Content

Decisions concerning question content center on the general nature of the question and the information it is designed to produce, rather than on the form or specific wording of the question. Five major issues, or problem areas, are involved with question content. For each question, the researcher must ascertain *(1) the need for the data, (2) the ability of the question to produce the data, (3) the ability of the respondent to answer accurately, (4) the willingness of the respondent to answer accurately,* and *(5) the potential for external events to bias the answer.*

The Need for the Data Asked for by the Question

The preliminary decisions will result in a list of informational items required to solve the problem. The next task is to generate one or more questions for each information item.

In general, every question on a questionnaire should make a contribution to the information on which the recommendation(s) to management is based.

Therefore, the first question a researcher should ask about each question is: "Exactly how am I going to use the data generated by this question?" If a satisfactory answer cannot be provided, the question should *not* be retained on the questionnaire.

The best way to approach this problem is to make up responses (contrived) to each question, analyze the results, and ensure that the results of the analysis provide sufficient information for the resolution of the management problem. Questions that provide data not needed to resolve the management problem should be deleted from the questionnaire.

In certain situations we may ask questions that are not part of our planned analysis. It may occasionally be useful to ask a series of relatively neutral questions at the beginning of a questionnaire or interview in order to obtain respondent involvement and rapport prior to asking more sensitive or controversial questions. At other times, we may use questions that will not play an explicit role in our analysis to disguise the purpose or sponsorship of a study. People may exaggerate their positive feelings toward a store, brand, or company if they are aware that it is sponsoring the survey. Therefore, it is sometimes necessary to ask questions about competing brands or products, even though the information thus gained will not aid in the management decision.

Ability of the Question to Produce the Data

Once we have assured ourselves that the question is *necessary*, we must make sure that it is *sufficient*. That is, will this one question generate the information we need or should we use two or more separate questions? For example, many questions ask individuals to express choices or preferences. If the researcher is also interested in how *strongly* or *intensely* the respondent holds these views, a separate question should be asked to ascertain this: *"How strongly do you feel about this—very strongly, somewhat strongly, or not at all strongly?"*

The "double-barreled" question is one in which two or more questions are asked as one. Consider the question, *"Do you prefer a small, economy car or a larger, sporty car?"* Would a response of "larger, sporty car" mean that the individual preferred larger cars, sporty cars, or larger, sporty cars? *"Do you consider the Triumph TR-7 to be a fast, powerful car?"* suffers from the same problem. Two or more separate questions are required in such cases.

Questions that require the respondent to aggregate several sources of information in order to answer should generally be subdivided into several specific questions. For example, the question: *"What was your total family income before taxes last year?"* will produce a less accurate answer than a series of questions that focus on specific sources of income for each family member.

We must also be sure that the question will elicit sufficient information that is directly relevant to the purpose underlying the question. Suppose we want to measure the occupation of respondents to ascertain if high-status occupation groups ride the bus as frequently as low-status groups. Is the question *"What do you do for a living?"* sufficient for our purposes? An attempt to characterize the status associated with the response "I'm a salesperson" will indicate the inadequacy of this question for its stated purpose.

Ability of the Respondent to Answer Accurately

Once we are sure that our question is necessary and sufficient, we must consider the respondent's ability to provide an accurate answer. Inability to answer a question arises from three major sources: *(1) having never been exposed to the answer, (2) having been exposed to the answer but forgetting,* and *(3) being unable to verbalize the answer.* The first two categories are concerned primarily with "factual" information, whereas the third is concerned more with attitudes and motives.

Uninformed Respondents

Respondents are frequently asked questions on topics about which they are uninformed. "Uninformed" in this sense means that they have never known the answer to the question. A common example is to ask an individual's opinion about a product, store, or brand that he or she has literally "never heard of."

Uninformed respondents become a source of measurement error because of a reluctance by people to admit a lack of knowledge on a topic. This becomes particularly acute when the content or wording of the question implies that the individual *should* know the answer.

In one study, over 95 per cent of the respondents to a survey of lawyers and 97 per cent of the respondents to a survey of the general public expressed an opinion on the performance of the National Bureau of Consumer Complaints. One might question the validity of the opinions, however, in view of the fact that no such organization exists! Even with a "Don't Know" option in the response set, over half of the lawyers and three-fourths of the general public still expressed an opinion on the performance of the nonexistent agency.[5]

Respondents falsely reporting awareness or recognition of products, logos, advertisements or other specific stimuli in a survey is referred to as *spurious awareness* or *bogus recall.* One major research firm has established spurious awareness benchmarks for some product categories. Its studies indicate that around 8 per cent of the population will report awareness of nonexistent health and beauty products. Thus when awareness of an actual product is measured, the company will reduce reported awareness by 8 per cent.[6] Unfortunately, this percentage appears to vary rather widely by product category. For example, a recent study of bogus recall of advertising slogans found a range of 12 to 52 per cent depending on the nature of the bogus slogan.[7] Current evidence indicates that spurious awareness (1) is associated with demographic characteristics and with an "agreeing" or "yea-saying" response style, and (2) may distort attempts to analyze the causes of awareness as well as measures of the level of awareness.[8]

Any time there is a possibility that the respondent may not have knowledge of the information requested, an attempt should be made to verify this fact. The question, *"What is the current assessed value of your home?"* implies that the respondent should know the answer. This, in turn, will encourage guessing. The following sequence of questions will provide a much more interpretable response:

Are you aware of the current assessed value of your home? ____ *Yes* ____ *No*

*What do you think the current assessed value of your home is?*_____

How close to the actual assessed value do you think your estimate is:

____ $100   ____ $1,000   ____ $5,000   ____ $10,000   ____ $15,000
____ $25,000 ____ $50,000 ____ No idea

Forgetful Respondents

Another problem arises when respondents are forced to rely on memory for facts that they have been exposed to in the past. A simple test will indicate the delicate nature of memory. Answer the following questions from memory and then check the answers:

- How many pairs of shoes (of all types) do you own?
- How much money is in your wallet?
- How many soft drinks did you consume last week?

Most of us do not know the answer to one or more of these rather simple questions. Yet we confidently ask people to report not only on the last brand of peas purchased but also on why they purchased them and how many advertisements they had noticed about them.

Three aspects of forgetting are of concern to the researcher: (1) *omission*, which occurs when an individual is unable to recall an event that actually took place; (2) *telescoping*, which occurs when an individual remembers an event as occurring more recently than it actually occurred; and (3) *creation*, which occurs when an individual "remembers" an event that did not occur.[9]

Concern with all three types of forgetting increases with the length of the recall period. Recall periods as short as one week appear to create substantial telescoping effects. For example, one study found that "read in the last week" produced an average readership rate of 15.1 per cent for nine weekly maga-

Exhibit 10–1 *Measuring Purchase Incidence Rates*

Questionnaire Formats

I. One-step, direct question, three months

"Below are listed several products. Please 'X' each product you or anyone in your household *bought* in the PAST THREE MONTHS."

II. One-step, direct question, six months

"Below are listed several products. Please 'X' each product you or anyone in your household *bought* in the PAST SIX MONTHS."

III. Two-step, indirect question, multiple time periods

"Below are listed several products. Please 'X' each product you or anyone in your household *ever* bought. For each product ever bought, 'X' the box that best describes when the product was *purchased most recently.*
- ☐ Over 12 months ago
- ☐ 7–12 months ago
- ☐ 4–6 months ago
- ☐ within the past three months

(Note: The order of time periods was reversed on half the questionnaires.)

Results

| | *Per Cent Reporting Purchase by Question Format* | | | |
Product	*I*	*III (3 months)*	*II*	*III (6 months)*
White glue	46%	32%	54%	50%
Aspirin	68	57	73	72
Auto tires	32	24	39	39
Record Album	41	32	48	41
N =	800	800	800	800

Conclusion

The two-step, indirect approach appears to reduce telescoping and provides more accurate responses, particularly for shorter time periods.

Souce: "Measuring Purchase Incidence Rates," *Research on Research #5* (Chicago: Market Facts, Inc., undated).

zines. However, an appropriate aggregation of "read yesterday" reports on the same magazines produced an average readership of only 12 per cent (significantly different at $\alpha = .001$). Thus, the "last-week" measure was influenced by an apparent 26 per cent inflation in readership due to telescoping and/or creation.[10]

Telescoping and creation are minimized by using short recall periods. Exhibit 10–1 illustrates a question format that appears to reduce telescoping in reporting past behaviors. Attempts to minimize omission generally involve various levels of *aided recall*.

Questions that rely on *unaided recall* (questions that do not provide any clues to potential answers such as *"What brands did you consider before purchasing your current bicycle?"*) result in an understatement of *specific* events, such as brands in a choice set, shows watched, or small items purchased. In addition, more popular and known brands tend to be overstated in response to questions asking for this kind of information. For example, a respondent may vaguely remember seeing an advertisement for soup and so report seeing an advertisement for *Campbell's Soup*, as this is the only brand name that comes to mind.

Attempts to overcome problems with unaided recall focus on providing cues or aids to help the individual recall more accurately. *Aided recall* provides the respondents with descriptions of all or some aspects of the original events. The difference between an aided recall and an unaided recall question is similar to the difference between a multiple-choice and an essay examination question.

One measure of billboard advertising effectiveness would be to ask respondents to *"name or describe any billboards that you have noticed while commuting to and from work in the past week."* This would be unaided recall. A second way of measuring the effectiveness of billboard advertisements would be to present a list of product categories and ask the respondents to indicate whether they had noted billboards for each category and, if so, for which brands. A third approach would be to present a list of brand names for each product category and ask the respondents which, if any, of these brands were advertised on billboards along their route to work. Finally, a picture of a billboard for each brand could be shown and the respondents asked to identify those that appeared along their route to work.

The level of "aid" increases at each stage in this example and, in general, so will the number of billboards identified. Unfortunately, the number identified may exceed the number along the route the individual takes to work; even worse, the correspondence between those identified and those actually on the individual's route may not be perfect. In part this is caused by the fact that aided recall techniques reduce omissions but increase telescoping and creation. Exhibit 10–2 illustrates the effect that creation can have in aided recall studies.

Exhibit 10–2   *Time Inc.'s Test for Errors in Aided Recall Measures of Magazine Readership*

Time Inc. recently sponsored a test to detect creation error in a popular method of measuring magazine readership. The method employed in the test is based on that used by a syndicated research service, Market Research Institute. Their standard method of determining readership and frequency of readership is as follows:

(1) Each respondent is given a deck of approximately 160 cards. Each card contains, in black and white, the logo of a magazine. The respondent is instructed to sort the cards into three piles: "definitely have read in the past six months," "definitely have not read in the past six months," and "not sure."

(2) For each magazine in the "definitely read" and "not sure" piles, the respondent is asked how many out of four issues he/she usually reads.

(3) Next, the readership question is asked separately by publishing interval (seven days for weeklies, 14 for bimonthly, etc.): "Did you happen to read any of these publications in the last (*publishing interval*) days? That is, any copy in the days since (specific date), not including today?" The respondent again sorts the cards into the same three categories based on behavior during the last publishing interval.

To test for creation error, logos for 22 fictitious or otherwise unavailable magazines were placed in with 140 regular magazines. The 22 nonexistent magazines had between 0.6 per cent and 11.6 per cent of the respondents reporting that they "definitely have read" one or more issues in the past six months. Of these respondents, over 20 per cent reported that they usually read four out of four issues!

The readership during the publishing interval data also contained serious errors. Using standard projection techniques, the latest (nonexistent) issue of *Look* would have projected 6,690,000 readers. A nonexistent magazine, *Autocare*, would have projected almost 2,000,000 readers. Further, at least some aspects of the demographics of those who reported (inaccurately) reading the various magazines were consistent with the editorial content of the magazines (i.e., mostly males for *Autocare* and females for *Women's Weekly*). Thus, the errors do not appear to be random but reflect realistic errors of recall.

Source: Adapted from C. Schitler, "Remembered, But Never Read," *Advertising Age,* October 26, 1981, S. 14–15.

Informing respondents in aided-recall situations in advance that some of the items they will be shown are bogus may reduce creation. That is, in the billboard situation respondents could be told that they will be shown a number of billboards, *several of which are definitely not in the area,* and then asked which ones they recall seeing on their commute to or from work. In addition, creation sometimes can be adjusted for mathematically.[11]

The type and nature of aid provided has become a major controversy in measuring advertising impact (see Chapter 8, pages 224–225). Historically, unaided or limited aid recall measures have been used. However critics contend this discriminates against feeling-oriented ads in favor of content or factual ads. As a result, various recognition measures are gaining popularity. Recognition involves presenting portions of the ad without revealing the sponsor's identity. Respondents state whether they recognize the ad and, if so, who sponsored it.[12]

Inarticulate Respondents

Questions such as *"Why did you buy that style of car?"* or *"Why did you decide to shop here?"* cannot always be answered by the respondent. If we think carefully, each of us can remember instances when we made purchases for which we did not really understand our motives. We can also think of instances in which we probably purchased an object for some reason other than the one we admitted to ourselves.

We buy things from habit, for vanity, and other reasons of which we are not consciously aware. However, when we are asked *why* we buy a given product or brand we may respond with conventional reasons rather than the actual reasons. A researcher who accepts these conventional reasons is operating with substantial measurement error. A method for overcoming a respondent's inability to verbalize answers to particular questions involves *projective techniques* (See Chapter 13).

Willingness of the Respondent to Answer Accurately

Assuming that the respondent *can* answer the question, we must still assess the likelihood that he or she *will* answer it. A refusal to answer a question may take one of three forms. First, the respondent may refuse to answer the specific question or questions that offend and still complete the remainder of the questionnaire. This is called *item nonresponse.*[13]

Another effect of an improper question (from the respondent's viewpoint) is a refusal to complete the remainder of the questionnaire. In mail surveys, this generally results in a failure to return the questionnaire. In telephone interviews, it may result in a broken connection.

The third way of "refusing" to answer a question is through *distortion* — providing an incorrect answer deliberately. Thus, the respondent may avoid a particular question by providing acceptable but inaccurate information. This type of refusal is the most difficult of the three with which to deal because it is hard to detect.

Why would a respondent refuse to answer one or more questions accurately? There are at least three possible reasons. The information request may be perceived by the respondent as (1) *personal in nature* (2) *embarrassing,* or (3) *reflecting on prestige.*

Requests for Personal Information

Most people will provide answers to questions that they think are legitimate. By legitimate we mean that the questions are reasonable in light of the situation and the role of the person asking the question.

Unfortunately, some researchers seem to believe that a brief introduction and the fact that they are with a reputable marketing research firm (of which very few respondents will have heard) makes any question they wish to ask legitimate in the eyes of the respondent. Experience indicates that many respondents who have willingly answered a lengthy series of questions on purchasing and shopping patterns may balk when suddenly asked without an explanation for their income, age, occupation, or other data. A brief explanation of why a particular piece of information is required will often suffice: *"To help us understand how people in different age and income groups view the shopping process, we need to know . . ."*

Whenever it is practical and consistent with the information requirements, personal data should be requested in terms of broad categories rather than specific levels. In general, questions dealing with personal information should be placed near the end of the questionnaire. The expectation is that the rapport between the interviewer and the respondent, and/or the effort the respondent has already expended, will increase the probability that the respondent will provide the data. In addition, termination of the interview at this point is generally less harmful than if it occurs earlier. However, it should be emphasized that respondents will generally supply such personal data as age without distortion.[14]

Requests for Embarrassing Information

Answers to questions that ask for potentially embarrassing information are subject to distortion especially when personal or telephone interviews are used.[15] Questions on the consumption of alcoholic beverages, use of personal hygiene products, readership of certain magazines, and sexual or aggressive feelings aroused by particular advertisements are examples of topics on which questions are subject to refusals or distortions by the respondents.

Intuitively, it would seem that anonymity would enhance the likelihood that respondents would answer, and answer accurately, sensitive questions.

However, studies indicate that assurances of anonymity have little affect.[16] Two additional approaches to seeking potentially embarrassing information are the use of *counterbiasing statements* and *randomized response techniques.*

Counterbiasing Statements. Counterbiasing statements involve beginning a question with a statement that will make the potentially embarrassing responses seem common. For example, *"Recent studies have shown that a high percentage of males use their wives' cosmetics to hide blemishes. Have you used your wife's cosmetics in the past week?"* Another approach is to ask, *"When was the last time you used your wife's cosmetics?"* Both of these types of questions make it easier for the respondent to admit the potentially embarrassing behavior.

Counterbiasing effects can also be obtained by carefully structuring the response options to multiple-choice questions. Consider the following response sets for this question: *"Think back over the past month. About how many bottles or cans of beer did you drink at home each week?"*

Version I	Version II
—a. less than 6	—a. less than 6
—b. 6–11	—b. 6–11
—c. 12–17	—c. 12–17
—d. 18–23	—d. 18–23
—e. 24 or more	—e. 24–29
	—f. 30–35
	—g. 36–41
	—h. 42 or more

A test using similarly discrepant scales found that the extended-range version produced 47 per cent more individuals reporting a consumption level of 24 or more.[17]

By expanding the range of response items at the potentially embarrassing end of the scale, it is easier for respondents to admit a high level of consumption because this level seems more normal. However, not all respondents will be so inclined. Furthermore, counterbiasing questions may cause some to admit to behavior they did not engage in because it may suddenly seem embarrassing *not* to have engaged in the behavior.

Randomized Response Techniques. Another approach to overcoming nonresponse and measurement error caused by embarrassing questions is the randomized response technique.[18] It presents the respondent with two questions, one sensitive or potentially embarrassing, the other harmless or even meaningless. The respondent then flips a coin, looks at the last number on his or her Social Security card to see if it is odd or even, or in some other random manner selects which question to answer. The chosen question is then answered with a "yes" or "no," *without telling the researcher which question is being answered.*

The randomized response technique involves three elements:

1. a sensitive question to which the researcher desires a "yes" or "no" answer;

2. a neutral question which has known proportions of "yes" and "no" responses; and

3. a random means of assigning one of the questions to each respondent such that the question assigned a particular respondent is known only to that respondent, but the percentage of respondents assigned each question is known.

Consider the problem of the researcher who needs information on the number of employees who engage in shoplifting. It is unlikely that many employees would answer this question even if asked in an anonymous mail survey (because of a fear that the survey might not be truly anonymous). Therefore, the randomized response technique is appropriate. The two following questions could be used:

A. *"Have you taken anything from this store in the past four weeks without paying?"*

B. *"Was your mother born during the month of June?"*

The employees are instructed to check their Social Security cards. If the last two digits are 60 or above, they are to answer question A with the single word "yes" or "no," on a separate, blank card. If the last two digits are 59 or less, they are to answer the question B with a "yes" or "no" on the card. From these responses the researcher can estimate the percentage of employees who reported shoplifting in the previous four weeks. The appropriate formula is:

$$P(\text{yes}) = P(\text{Question A is chosen}) \cdot P(\text{Yes answer to question A})$$
$$+ P(\text{Question B is chosen}) \cdot P(\text{Yes answer to question B})$$

If we receive "yes" replies from say 16 per cent, we can compute the best estimate of the percentage of employees who reported that they engaged in shoplifting. From census data we determine that 10 per cent of the U.S. population was born in June. The formula then contains only one unknown — the percentage of respondents who answered "yes" to the sensitive question:

$$.16 = (.4)(X) + (.6)(.1)$$
$$.10 = .4X$$
$$x = .25$$

Thus, we can estimate that 25 per cent of those who answered the sensitive question answered positively. This technique has been used successfully in telephone, mail, and personal interview settings and for a variety of question types. However, it does not always generate accurate data.

Requests for "Prestige" or "Normative" Information

Prestige-oriented questions, such as those dealing with education obtained, income earned, or amount of time spent in reading newspapers, typically produce answers with an upward bias. For example, readership of high-prestige magazines is frequently overstated and readership of low-prestige magazines is often understated when self-report techniques are utilized. The reported consumption of both "negative" products, such as alcoholic beverages, and "positive" products, such as milk, is also subject to distortion.

Similarly, questions with a normative or socially accepted answer tend to have a consistent bias toward social norms. For example, surveys generally indicate strong support for educational television; yet, relatively few people consistently watch education channels, according to research using observational techniques.

When possible, it is best to avoid questions with prestige or normative answers. When unavoidable, counterbiasing statements can sometimes be used to reduce measurement error. Careful wording and frequent pleas for candor, coupled with explanations of why candor is needed, can also reduce measurement error on these questions. Sometimes normative answers can be eliminated in the question itself: *"Other than nutrition, why do you serve . . . ?"*

Indirect questions can be employed. For example, *"Have you read _____ (the latest nonfiction best-seller)?"* will probably result in an overstatement of the number of readers. An indirect approach such as *"Do you intend to read _____?"* allows those who have not a graceful way to say so by indicating that they intend to read it. Those who say they do not intend to read the book can then be asked why. Those who have already read the book can then so indicate. This approach will often produce a more accurate measurement than the more direct approach.

The Effect of External Events

A final issue involving question content is error caused by factors outside of the questionnaire itself. The time at which a question is asked is such a variable. A traffic planning commission was considering the need for bicycle paths. A questionnaire was designed and mailed to a sample of the population. One question asked for information on bicycle riding during the past week, which, in and of itself, was a reasonable question. However, the questionnaire was sent out after a week of particularly bad weather. Therefore, the bicycle-usage figures were most likely much less than would have been obtained had the weather been normal the preceding week.

For topics that are likely to be influenced by external events, particularly unpredictable external events such as weather, questions should generally be situation-free (e.g., ''in a typical week'' rather than ''last week'').

Decisions About Question Phrasing

Question phrasing is the translation of the desired question content into words and phrases that can be understood easily and clearly by the respondents. In general, questions should be as simple and straightforward as possible.

The primary concern with question phrasing is to ensure that the respondents and the researcher assign exactly the same meaning to the question. There are five general issues involved in question phrasing; *(1) Are the words, singularly and in total, understandable to the respondents? (2) Are the words biased or "loaded" in any respect? (3) Are all the alternatives involved in the questions clearly stated? (4) Are any assumptions implied by the question clearly stated? and (5) What frame of reference is the respondent being asked to assume?*

The Meaning of Words

Most of us would agree that questions designed for 8-year-olds should have a simpler vocabulary than questions designed for adult respondents. The researcher must take the vocabulary skills of the intended respondent group into account when designing a question.[19] Such terms as *innovations, psychographics,* and *advertising medium* should be used only when dealing with specialized respondent groups.

Unfortunately, common words sometimes create equally serious problems. *"How many members are there in your family?"* Does family mean nuclear family? If so, will it have the same meaning to all respondents? Is a grandmother, aunt, or the spouse of one of the children that lives with the nuclear family to be counted? The word *kind* can cause similar problems. *"What kind of razor do you use?"* will result in some respondents identifying the type (safety or electric) whereas others will name brands.

Which of the following questions do you think will produce the highest level of reported new-product interest?

"Would you be interested in buying any of these products?"

"Which, if any, of these products would you be interested in buying?"

Fifty-three per cent of a sample gave a positive response to the first question, whereas 64 per cent did so for the second question.[20]

Even more critical problems can be introduced when the same term takes on different meanings to different groups of people.[21] In some regions of the United States, middle- and upper-class individuals apply the term "dinner" to the evening meal and refer to the noon meal as "lunch." However, working-class families tend to call the evening meal "supper" and the noon meal "dinner." Therefore, a question eliciting information about eating habits at "dinner" would receive evening meal information from one group and noon meal information from the other. If social class were then used as a classification variable, the two groups would most likely report vastly different eating habits at "dinner."

How do we ensure that the words we select are likely to be clear to our respondents? A good first step is to consult an up-to-date dictionary and a thesaurus and ask the following six questions of each word (including the common ones, whose meaning may seem obvious to us):

1. Does it mean what we intend?
2. Does it have any other meanings?
3. If so, does the context make the intended meaning clear?
4. Does the word have more than one pronunciation?
5. Is there any word of similar pronunciation with which it might be confused?
6. Is a simpler word or phrase suggested?

The meaning of some terms are vague to most respondents. Alternative terms may be equally confusing. After substantial pretesting, a government health survey included a diagram indicating the location of the abdomen as attempts at verbal descriptions proved fruitless.[22]

It is important to remember that the objective is an understandable question, not a group of understandable words. Sometimes seeking the simplest terms results in a more complex question. Of the following two "identical" questions, which is easier to understand?[23]

Should the state sales tax on prescription drugs be reduced from 5 per cent to 1 percent?

Should the state sales tax on those medicines that can only be bought under a doctor's order be lowered so that people would pay 1 cent tax instead of 5 cents tax for every dollar spent on such medicine?

Most words have similar meanings to most people. Responses to most questions will remain stable when similar words are substituted for each other. Unfortunately, this is not *always* the case, so close attention to question phrasing is required.[24]

Biased Words and Leading Questions

Biased, or loaded, words and phrases are emotionally colored and suggest an automatic feeling of approval or disapproval. Leading questions suggest what the answer should be or indicate the researcher's own point of view.

Consider the following questions: *"Do you think the United States should allow public speeches against democracy?"* and *"Do you think the United States should forbid public speeches against democracy?"* Will they lead to the same conclusions? Slightly less than half (44 per cent) of a sample said *no* (not allow) in response to the first question. However, only one-fourth (28 per cent) of a similar sample said "yes" (forbid) to the second question.[25] Thus, it appears that the word *forbid* and/or the word *allow* induce bias.

Studies consistently find that about 60 per cent of those responding favor increased spending/assistance for the *poor*. However, when the word poor is replaced by the term *welfare*, less than 25 per cent support increased spending.[26] Likewise, a study found 67 per cent opposed to a constitutional amendment "prohibiting abortions" while 50 per cent were in favor of one "protecting the life of the unborn."[27]

Biased phrases are difficult to deal with because phrases that are neutral to one group may be emotionally charged to another. Phrases such as *luxury items* and *leisure time* are neutral to many people, yet carry negative overtones to others. This fact illustrates the need to pretest with respondents who are as similar as possible to those people who will be included in the final survey.

"Do you think that General Motors is doing everything possible to reduce air pollution from the cars it manufactures?" is a loaded question. General Motors is not doing "everything possible" in this area. This does not mean that it is not doing everything *reasonable*. Few firms or individuals ever do "all that is possible." The use of phrases such as *everything possible* (or its opposite, *anything*) tend to produce biased responses.

Different ways of identifying the same organization can affect the response to the organization. The data in Table 10–1 were collected by the market research division of Procter & Gamble Company to illustrate this point.

Table 10–1 Level of Confidence in Different American Institutions, Using Different Terms

Institution	Great Deal of Confidence	Moderate Confidence	No Confidence
Army, Navy, and Air Force	63%	31%	6%
The Military	48	45	7
Military leaders	21	59	20
Established religion	50	41	9
Organized religion	35	49	16
Business	20	73	7
Big business	12	62	26
Organized labor	21	53	26
Big labor	7	66	27
U.S. presidency	30	53	17
Executive branch of federal government	18	62	20

Source: adapted from S. M. Lipset, "The Wavering Polls," *The Public Interest* (Spring 1976), 83.

The use of examples to clarify a question can sometimes introduce a bias. *"Do you believe that people should eat at least one leafy vegetable such as spinach each day?"* will produce different answers than *"Do you believe that people should eat at least one leafy vegetable such as lettuce each day?"* The answers to the first question posed will reflect, in part, the respondents' perceptions of spinach, whereas answers to the second question will reflect their perceptions of lettuce.

Implied Alternatives

Making an implied alternative explicit frequently, but not always, increases the percentage of people choosing that alternative. For example, the following question:

> *"If there is a serious fuel shortage this winter, do you think there should be a law requiring people to lower the heat in their homes?"*

produced 38.3 per cent in favor of the law. Adding the phrase, *"or do you oppose such a law?"* reduced the percentage in favor of the law to 29.4. Adding the phrase, *"or do you think this should be left to individual families to decide?"* produced 25.9 per cent in favor of the law.[28] Clearly, both the presence and nature of stated alternatives can influence responses.

Implied Assumptions

Questions are frequently asked in such a way that the answer depends on assumptions about factors outside the question itself.[29] *"Are you in favor of curtailing the amount of advertising allowed on television?"* will elicit differing responses, depending on the respondents' assumptions concerning the effects this might have on the quantity and quality of television programming. A more effective way of wording the question would be *"Are you in favor of curtailing the amount of advertising allowed on television if this would have* (such and such an effect) *on television programming?"*

Failure to state essential assumptions often produces (not always accidentally) inflated estimates of the public's demand for various products, social programs, or services. One more example should make the importance of this issue clear: *"Are you in favor of requiring all new refrigerators to be built with the most effective insulation available as an energy conservation measure?"* will elicit substantially more positive responses in that form than it will when *"even though it will mean a 25 per cent increase in the retail price of the refrigerator"* is added.

Frame of Reference

The wording of the question will often determine which frame of reference or viewpoint the respondent will assume. Consider the following versions of a question to be answered by recent claimants of an automobile insurance company.

Does Allstate provide satisfactory or unsatisfactory settlement of claims?

Do you believe that Allstate provides satisfactory or unsatisfactory settlement of claims?

Were you satisfied or unsatisfied with Allstate's settlement of your recent claim?

Each of these versions provides the respondent with a somewhat different frame of reference. The first version calls for an objective answer that may include the respondent's perceptions of other people's standards for claim settlement and how adequately Allstate meets these expectations. The third question involves only the individual's own standards and perceptions of the firm's reaction to his or her last claim. The second question probably elicits responses somewhere between the first and the third. Which question is best depends upon the purposes of the research.[30]

Frame of reference can be influenced by a variety of factors including preceding questions (see the section on Decisions about the Question Sequence, pages 313–315) and other brands or objects mentioned in the question. Figure 10–3 illustrates the impact that different comparator groups had on perceptions of Chevrolet Nova's gas mileage.

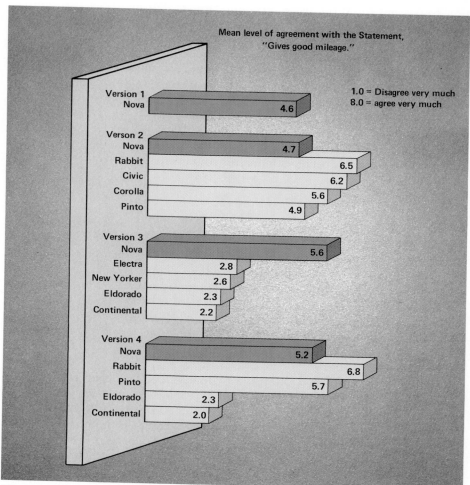

Figure 10–3   *Frame of Reference and Product Performance Ratings*

$n \cong$ approximately 800 of each version

Source: "Brand Perceptions: Relative vs. Absolute Ratings," *Research on Research* 6 (Chicago: Market Facts, Inc., undated).

307

Decisions About the Response Format

"Who do you think will win the Super Bowl this year?" "Who do you think will win the Super Bowl this year, the Cowboys, the Bears, or the Forty-Niners?" "Do you think the Cowboys will win the Super Bowl this year?" These three questions represent the three basic response formats that questions can assume. The first question is an example of an *open* or *open-ended* question. The respondent is free to choose any response deemed appropriate, within the limits implied by the question. The second question is an example of a *multiple-choice* response format. Here the respondent must select from among three or more prespecified responses. The final question represents a *dichotomous* question. Multiple-choice and dichotomous questions are often referred to as *closed* questions.

The decision as to which form of question to use must be based on the objective for the particular question. Each has its particular uses, advantages, and disadvantages.[31] Most questionnaires contain all three types of questions.

Open-Ended Questions

Open-ended questions leave the respondent free to offer any replies that seem appropriate in light of the question.

The degree of openness will vary from question to question. The question *"What do you think about cigarettes?"* allows almost total freedom to the respondent who may discuss cigarettes in general, particular brands, advertising slogans, health issues, ethics, and a host of other issues. The question *"What brand of cigarettes do you generally smoke?"* offers much less freedom. In this case, the respondent is constrained (we hope) to merely naming the brand generally smoked.

Advantages of Open-Ended Questions. Open-ended questions do not influence the respondent with a prestated set of response categories. Thus, opinions can be expressed that are quite divergent from what the researcher expected or what others had expressed. Related to this is the fact that open-ended questions elicit a wide variety of responses. These properties make open-ended questions particularly suitable for exploratory and problem-identification research.

Open-ended questions can provide the researcher with a basis for judging the actual values and views of the respondents that are often difficult to capture with more structured techniques. This "feel" for the quality of the information can be conveyed in the final report by the inclusion of quotes from representative responses. Finally, respondents generally like to have at least a few opportunities to express themselves openly.

Disadvantages of Open-Ended Questions. Open-ended questions should be limited on self-administered questionnaires because most respondents will seldom write elaborate answers. Furthermore, these questions are subject to two important sources of error. First, they may measure *respondent articulateness.* Some respondents will answer clearly and in depth on almost any topic, whereas others, who may have equal knowledge, may be more reluctant to express themselves.

A second source of error is *interviewer effects.* Interviewers will vary in their ability to record the respondents' answers, in their intensity of probing, and in their objectivity.

An additional problem with open-ended questions is that except for very small surveys, the responses must eventually be coded or categorized.[32] Few researchers can read 1,000 responses to an open-ended question and understand all of the ramifications of the data. If the interviewers record the answers verbatim, or nearly so, the time and cost of coding becomes a sizeable portion of the total cost of the research.

As an alternative to central coding, each interviewer can code or categorize the respondent's answer without showing the respondent the list of response alternatives. This technique is generally called *precoding.* The interviewer has, in effect, a multiple-choice question that is presented to the respondent as an open-ended question. The interviewer must then select the appropriate response category based on the respondent's verbal reply. Thus, the question *"Which brand of cigarettes did you last purchase?"* can be treated as open-ended by the respondent, but the interviewer may, instead of recording the response, have a list of the most popular brands and simply check which brand the respondent names, or an "other" category.

Multiple-Choice Questions

Do European, Japanese, or American cars represent the highest level of workmanship?

Do you plan to buy a new refrigerator in the next 6 months?

—— Definitely Yes —— Probably Yes —— Probably No
—— Definitely No

What was the brand name of the last soft drink you purchased?

—— Pepsi —— Diet Pepsi —— Classic Coke —— Coke —— Diet Coke
—— 7-Up —— Diet 7-Up —— Sprite —— Slice —— Fresca —— Other

These questions represent versions of the multiple-choice question. The essential feature of a multiple-choice question is that it presents, either in the question proper or immediately following the question, the list of possible answers from which the respondent must choose.

Advantages of Multiple-Choice Questions. Multiple-choice questions offer a number of advantages over open-ended questions. They are generally easier for both the interviewer and the respondent. Indeed, they are almost essential for securing adequate cooperation in self-administered surveys. They also tend to reduce interviewer bias and bias caused by varying levels of respondent articulateness. In addition, tabulation and analysis are much simpler. Multiple-choice questions have an advantage over dichotomous questions whenever the answer naturally involves more than two choices or when some measure of gradation or degree is desired.

Disadvantages of Multiple-Choice Questions. The development of a sound set of multiple-choice questions (or dichotomous questions) requires considerable effort. In addition, showing the respondents the list of potential answers can cause several types of distortion in the resulting data.

If all possible alternatives are not listed, no information can be gained on the omitted alternatives. Even if an *"Other (Specify)"* category is included, there is a strong tendency for respondents to choose from among those alternatives listed. This may occur simply because one of the alternatives sounds familiar or logical, and not because it is the proper answer to the question. Alternatives that the respondent had not thought about before may be selected over alternatives that would have been thought of independently. This particular feature may be good or bad, depending on the precise purpose of the question.

Number of Alternatives. A crucial issue in multiple-choice questions is how many alternatives to list. The standard answer to this question is that "each alternative should appear only once and all possible alternatives should be included." However, it is frequently impractical to include all possible alternatives. A list of all possible brands of cigarettes, for example, would have to include not only American brands but also all foreign brands that are available in local tobacco shops. A researcher is seldom interested in those brands or alternatives that only a few people will select. Therefore, the general approach is to list the more prevalent choices and an "Other" category, which is often accompanied by a "Please specify" and a short space to write in the answer. If the original list somehow excluded a major alternative, the "Other" category may uncover it.

Alternatives also may be omitted when one alternative would overwhelm the others and hide valuable information. Thus, one might ask, *"Aside from honesty, which of the following characteristics is most important for a politician?"* This is also a good way to avoid receiving socially acceptable answers, rather than those that are perhaps more germane: *"Not considering patriotism and support for the U.S. economy, which of the following reasons best justifies purchasing products made in the United States?"*

Finally, as discussed in the section on counterbiasing statements (p. 299), enough alternatives must be presented to reflect adequately the full range of potential behaviors. This is particularly important when sensitive or normative behaviors such as drinking, exercise, newspaper readership, and television viewing are being measured.

Balanced or Unbalanced Alternatives. Another important issue concerns the number of alternatives on each side of an issue. For example, consider the following two lists of alternatives for the same question:

Is Sears' advertising truthful or misleading?
—— Extremely misleading
—— Very misleading
—— Somewhat misleading
—— Neither misleading nor truthful
—— Truthful

versus

Is Sears' advertising truthful or misleading?
—— Extremely truthful
—— Very truthful
—— Somewhat truthful
—— Neither truthful nor misleading
—— Misleading

The results obtained from the two sets of response categories will differ significantly. Although the preceding example is an extreme one, it is not difficult to find cases where a high degree of imbalance exists. Unless there is a specific reason (such as evidence that all respondents will respond on one side of the issue) to do otherwise, a balanced set of alternatives should be presented.

Position Bias. Which of the two alternative response sets to the following question will produce the highest percent reporting that they eat out "much more often" than last year? Or, will both sets produce similar results? The two versions of the questionnaire were administered by mail to over 750 respondents each.

Compared to a year ago, my household eats at a restaurant:

Version A	Version B
—— Much more often	—— Much less often
—— Somewhat more often	—— Somewhat less often
—— About as often	—— About as often
—— Somewhat less often	—— Somewhat more often
—— Much less often	—— Much more often

Version A produced twice as many "much more often" responses than version B (10 per cent versus 5 per cent). Similar results were obtained for questions on television viewing and the use of home repair professionals versus doing-it-yourself.[33]

It has been found that if three or four relatively long or complex alternatives are read to the respondents, there will be a bias in favor of the last alternative. However, if the alternatives are presented visually and all at the same time, the bias shifts to the alternative appearing at the top of the list.[34]

A list of numbers, such as amount of money spent, and estimates of facts, such as the number of outlets in a given chain store, is subject to a middle-position bias. That is, respondents tend to select those values that are near the middle of the range presented.

This type of error can become especially critical when there is no "correct" answer and the researcher is merely attempting to ascertain some fact that should be unique to each respondent. For example, suppose the researcher, interested in the number of trips to the grocery store that a group of respondents makes in an "average" week, constructs a multiple-choice question to measure this. The researcher's judgment is that the average is two trips per week and very few people make more than four trips. Therefore, the alternatives are "less than one," "one," "two," "three," and "four or more." The natural tendency of people to select the middle position will tend to confirm the hypothesis, even though it may be incorrect.

The labeling of alternatives can influence the respondent's choice. Coney found a strong preference for the alternative labeled A in a set of alternatives labeled A, B, C, and D. This label preference was not present when the alternatives were labeled H, L, M, and P.[35] Table 10–2 contains a "favorableness" index of all the letters in the alphabet.

Table 10–2   Favorableness Index for the Alphabet°

Letter	Index°	Letter	Index°	Letter	Index°
A	116	J	61	S	82
B	92	K	49	T	68
C	73	L	71	U	14
D	53	M	78	V	20
E	64	N	44	W	38
F	12	O	50	X	−08
G	56	P	44	Y	25
H	51	Q	−08	Z	−03
I	54	R	65		

° The higher the index, the more favorably the letter is viewed.
Source: Adapted from G. J. Spagna, "Questionnaires: Which Approach Do You Use?" *Journal of Advertising Research* (February/March 1984), 70.

A *split-ballot* technique—using multiple versions of the questionnaire with responses subject to position bias—will minimize, but not eliminate these effects.[36]

Dichotomous Questions

Dichotomous questions, which represent an extreme form of the mulitple-choice question, allow only two responses; such as "yes-no," "agree-dis-agree," "male-female," and "did-did not." Often the two categories are supplemented by a neutral category such as "don't know," "no opinion," "both," or "neither."

Advantages of Dichotomous Qustions. The advantages of the dichotomous question are similar to those of the multiple-choice question. It is particularly well suited for determining certain points of fact, such as *"Did you purchase a new model car in the past year?"* and other clear-cut issues on which the respondents are likely to hold well crystallized views.

Disadvantages of Dichotomous Questions. The critical point in the decision on whether to use a dichotomous question is the extent to which the respon-dent group approaches the issue in dichotomous terms. Although decisions themselves can often be broken down into a series of "yes-no" type responses, the thought process that leads up to them may be characterized by "maybes," "ifs," and "probablys." A simple dichotomous question, such as "Do you plan to purchase a new car within the next three months?" may elicit "yes" from one individual and "no" from another. Yet, both individuals may "plan" to buy a car *if* they get a promotion. Furthermore, each may be equally likely to receive the promotion. However, the optimistic individual responds with "yes" and the pessimistic one responds with "no."

The form in which agree-disagree dichotomous statements are presented can also affect the results. The statement *"Individuals* are more to blame than *social conditions* for crime and lawlessness in this country," produced a 59.6 per cent level of agreement. Only 43.2 per cent of a matched sample disagreed with the opposite statement: *"Social conditions* are more to blame than *indi-viduals* for crime and lawlessness in this country."[37] Again, a split-ballot tech-nique seems required.

Decisions About the Question Sequence

Question sequence, the specific order in which the respondents receive the questions, is a potential source of error.[38] As in other areas of questionnaire design, no unalterable rules are available. However, a number of general guidelines will reduce the probability of generating measurement error caused by the sequence of the questions.

The first questions should be simple, objective, and interesting. If the respondents cannot answer the first questions easily, or if they find them uninteresting, they may refuse to complete the remainder of the questionnaire. Similarly, if the questions arouse suspicions in any way, such as causing the impression that the interview really may be a sales call, respondents may distort the answers to later questions. Therefore, it is essential that the first few questions relax and reassure the respondent.

In general, *the overall questionnaire should move from topic to topic in a logical manner, with all questions on one topic being completed before the respondent moves to the next.* Questions that are difficult to answer or that ask for controversial or sensitive information should be placed near the end of the questionnaire. By this time, the interviewer, if one is being used, will have had ample opportunity to establish rapport with the respondent. Furthermore, the respondent, having put forth the effort to answer the preceding questions, will be more likely to feel committed to completing the questionnaire. In addition, any suspicion or resentment caused by these questions will not influence the answers to preceding questions.

Initial questions should avoid providing a biased frame of reference or suggesting answers to following questions. Within groups of questions on a given topic, general questions should be asked first and more specific ones later. Consider the two following questions: *"How many miles per gallon does your present car get?"* and *"What things would you like to see improved in your car?"* If these questions are asked in the order presented, gas economy will be mentioned many more times in the second question that it would if the order were reversed.[39]

Preceding questions may not only indicate the answer to following questions, but they also may set the frame of reference or point of view that the respondent uses in answering following questions. For example, a recent survey required respondents to state their preference for American versus foreign cars following one of three sets of prior questions:

- neutral — no automobile-related questions preceded the preference question,
- pro-American — questions concerning attributes on which American cars perform well preceded the preference question,
- pro-import — questions concerning attributes on which imports perform well preceded the preference question.

The pro-American point of reference produced a 59 per cent preference for American cars; neutral produced 52 per cent for American cars; and pro-import produced 42 per cent for American cars.[40]

Finally, there is evidence that response quality declines near the end of long questionnaires.[41] This suggests the need to use several versions of long questionnaires with differing question groups located at the end. Fortunately, computer technology makes it possible to prepare multiple versions of questionnaires relatively inexpensively.

Physical Characteristics of the Questionnaire

The physical characteristics of the questionnaire should be designed to make it easy to use.

The first and most important objective is to minimize the possibility of recording mistakes. Exhibit 10–3 illustrates the effect that a confusing layout had on a questionnaire administered by Market Facts of Canada, Ltd.

The questionnaire must be designed so that the interviewer or respondent can easily move from one question to the next. This is particularly important when *skip* or *branching* instructions are involved. These instructions require

Exhibit 10–3 *Impact of Questionnaire Layout*

Form A of a question was used in a regular wave of Market Facts of Canada Ltd.'s Consumer Mail Panel. The households were known to have one or more of the products mentioned in the question.

Form A

IMPORTANT: FOR EACH TYPE, *IF* YOU HAVE MORE THAN ONE, ANSWER FOR THE NEWEST

3a) What make or brand is it?

	Product X	*Product Y*	*Product Z*
Brand A	( )1	( )1	( )1
Brand B	( )2	( )2	( )2
Brand C	( )3	( )3	( )3
Brand D	( )4	( )4	( )4
Brand E	( )5	( )5	( )5
Brand F	( )6	( )6	( )6
Brand G	( )7	( )7	( )7
Other brand (SPECIFY)	_____	_____	_____

The year before, Brand G had had 67, 39, and 55 per cent ownership reported across the three products, and Brand F had had 5, 1, and 8 per cent ownership. This year the results were 47, 27, and 35 per cent, and 30, 18, and 27 per cent respectively. The client, Brand G, found changes of these magnitudes unbelievable.

Telephone contracts with some reported Brand F owners indicated that they were, in reality, Brand G owners. Therefore, the question was revised into form B and readministered.

Form B

3. What make or brand is the newest one?

	Product X	*Product Y*	*Product Z*
Brand A	( )1	( )1	( )1
Brand B	( )2	( )2	( )2
Brand C	( )3	( )3	( )3
Brand D	( )4	( )4	( )4
Brand E	( )5	( )5	( )5
Brand F	( )6	( )6	( )6
Brand G	( )7	( )7	( )7
Other brand . . .	( )8	( )8	( )8

The revised version produced Brand G ownership percentages of 71, 41, and 58, whereas Brand F percentages dropped to 3, 2, and 3! It appears that the respondents noticed that Brand G was the next-to-last option (just above "other brand") and therefore looked for the next-to-last response box to check. However, in Form A the next-to-last response box was associated with Brand F because the *Other brand* option did not have a response category to mark. This error was eliminated by the Form B question.

Source: Adapted from C. S. Mayer and C. Piper, "A Note on the Importance of Layout in Self-Administered Questionnaires," *Journal of Marketing Research* (August 1982), 390–391. The questions are reproduced with permission from the American Marketing Association.

the respondent to answer different following questions based on the answer to the current question.

Branching instructions have been found to confuse respondents in mail surveys and should be avoided if possible.[42] However, branching is common and useful in telephone and personal interview situations where experienced interviewers can easily follow even rather difficult branching instructions, such as those shown in Exhibit 10–4.

In self-administered questionnaires, particularly mail surveys, appearance is an important variable in securing cooperation from the respondent. In general, self-administered questionnaires should be printed on quality paper using an open format and type that is easy to read.

Exhibit 10–4 *Branching Instructions in a Telephone Questionnaire*

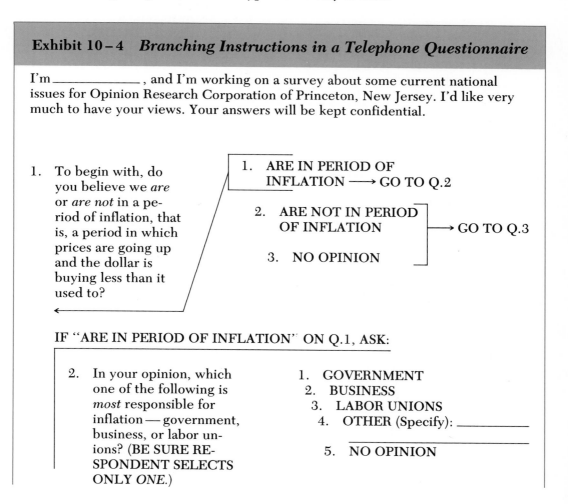

I'm _____ , and I'm working on a survey about some current national issues for Opinion Research Corporation of Princeton, New Jersey. I'd like very much to have your views. Your answers will be kept confidential.

1. To begin with, do you believe we *are* or *are not* in a period of inflation, that is, a period in which prices are going up and the dollar is buying less than it used to?

   1. ARE IN PERIOD OF INFLATION ⟶ GO TO Q.2

   2. ARE NOT IN PERIOD OF INFLATION

   3. NO OPINION

   ⟶ GO TO Q.3

IF "ARE IN PERIOD OF INFLATION" ON Q.1, ASK:

2. In your opinion, which one of the following is *most* responsible for inflation — government, business, or labor unions? (BE SURE RESPONDENT SELECTS ONLY *ONE*.)

   1. GOVERNMENT
   2. BUSINESS
   3. LABOR UNIONS
   4. OTHER (Specify): _____
   5. NO OPINION

3. Do you believe the country as a whole *is* or *is not* making economic progress?

    1. IS MAKING PROGRESS ⟶ GO TO Q.4
    2. IS NOT MAKING PROGRESS ⟶ GO TO Q.5
    3. NO OPINION ⟶ GO TO Q.6

IF "IS MAKING PROGRESS" ON Q.3, ASK:

4. Which of the following do you think contributes *most* to economic progress in this country — government, business, or labor unions? (BE SURE RESPONDENT SELECTS ONLY *ONE*.)

    1. GOVERNMENT
    2. BUSINESS
    3. LABOR UNIONS
    4. OTHER (Specify): _____
        _____
    5. NO OPINION

IF "IS NOT MAKING PROGRESS" ON Q.3, ASK:

5. Which one of the following do you think is *most* responsible for the lack of economic progress in this country — government, business, or labor unions? (BE SURE RESPONDENT SELECTS ONLY *ONE*.)

    1. GOVERNMENT
    2. BUSINESS
    3. LABOR UNIONS
    4. OTHER (Specify): _____
        _____
    5. NO OPINION

6. Do you believe that the personal freedoms of Americans *are* or *are not* being threatened?

    1. ARE BEING THREATENED ⟶ GO TO Q.7
    2. ARE NOT BEING THREATENED ⟶ GO TO Q.8
    3. NO OPINION

Used with permission from Opinion Research Corporation.

Decisions About the Pretest

Burke Marketing Research designed a study to determine the extent and nature of consumer use of barbecue-style sauces at home.[43] One of the questions to be used on this questionnaire was:

In just the past 2 months, what types of barbecued foods have you eaten which were prepared at home?

However, during pretesting, it became clear that many respondents defined barbecued food as food cooked outside on a charcoal grill, *not* food cooked with barbecue sauce. This led to this question being revised to:

In just the past 2 months, what types of food have you eaten which were prepared at home using a barbecue sauce?

Only on rare occasions and for specific, explicit reasons should a questionnaire be administered without a *thorough* pretest.[44] A pretest requires five types of decisions. First, *what items should be pretested?* Obviously, one would want to be alert for problems with any aspect of the questionnaire such as layout, question sequence, branching instructions, word meaning, and question difficulty. However, in most questionnaires some question areas and sequences are of little concern because they have been presented in previous surveys and are very straightforward. Other areas are unique and more ambiguous and should receive the most attention.

Second, *how should the pretest be conducted?* At least part of the pretest should involve administering the questionnaire in the same manner planned for the final survey. This allows the researcher to discover which questions are likely to be skipped or refused in the actual administration, the likely range of responses, the use of "other" categories, and so forth.

In addition to a standard administration of the questionnaire, a *debriefing* and/or a *protocol* analysis should be conducted. In a *debriefing,* some of the pretest respondents are interviewed after they have completed the questionnaire. These respondents are asked to explain *why* they answered each question as they did, to state what each question meant to them, and to describe any problems or uncertainties they had in completing the questionnaire. A *protocol analysis* requires the respondent to "think aloud" while completing the questionnaire. The interviewer notes areas of confusion and terms with differing meanings among respondents.

Third, *who should conduct the pretest?* Telephone and personal pretest interviews should generally be conducted by several regular staff interviewers. Part of the purpose of the pretest is to discover problems for and with the interviewers. In addition, using regular interviewers allows a check on response rates and time per interview. This, in turn, allows a check on cost estimates.

In addition, the project director and/or the person charged with developing the questionnaire should conduct several interviews. Since it is the project director whose questions are being checked and who is responsible for the final report, he or she should be actively involved in testing and revising the questionnaire.

Fourth, *which respondents should be involved in the pretest?* The respondents should be as similar as possible to the target respondents.

Fifth, *how many respondents should be used?* There is no set answer to this question. A sufficient number of respondents should be used to satisfy the similarity-to-target-respondents consideration just described. Thus, the more varied the target respondents, the larger the pretest should be. Likewise, the more complex and unique the questionnaire, the larger the sample should be.

Pretesting questionnaires is a critical activity that should be conducted prior to administering any but a completely routine questionnaire.

Review Questions

10.1.   What is a *questionnaire?*

10.2.   What is the most critical problem or concern in questionnaire design?

10.3.   What are the steps in questionnaire design?

10.4.   What are the preliminary decisions that must be made before a questionnaire can be constructed?

10.5.   What are the five major issues, or problem areas, involved with question content?

10.6.   What is the best way to ascertain the need for the information generated by a question?

10.7.   Why would one put questions on a questionnaire that are not relevent to the management problem at hand?

10.8.   What is a *double-barreled question?*

10.9.   What factors can reduce the ability of a respondent to answer a question accurately?

10.10.   What is an *uninformed respondent?*

10.11.   Describe the three aspects of forgetting that concern researchers.

10.12.   What counteracts the tendency to forget?

10.13.   What are the advantages and disadvantages of *unaided recall?*

10.14.   What are the advantages and disadvantages of *aided recall?*

10.15. What affects the willingness of respondents to answer accurately?

10.16. How can one secure "embarrassing" information from respondents?

10.17. What are *counterbiasing statements?*

10.18. Describe the *randomized response technique.*

10.19. How should one request normative or prestige information?

10.20. How can external events affect the response to questions?

10.21. What are the five general issues involved in question phrasing?

10.22. What is a leading question?

10.23. What is an *implied alternative?*

10.24. What is an *implied assumption?*

10.25. What is meant by *frame of reference?*

10.26. What are the advantages and disadvantages of *open-ended questions?*

10.27. What are the advantages and disadvantages of *multiple-choice questions?*

10.28. What are the advantages and disadvantages of *dichotomous questions?*

10.29. How many alternatives should be used in a *multiple-choice question?*

10.30. What is meant by *position bias* with respect to multiple-choice questions?

10.31. What are "branching" and "skip" instructions?

10.32. What are the five decisions involved in a pretest?

Discussion Questions/Problems/Projects

10.33. Develop five *double-barreled* questions and corrected versions of each.

10.34. Develop two unaided recall questions of relevance to marketing. Develop three aided recall questions to replace each of the unaided questions. Have each aided recall question contain a different level of aid.

10.35. Develop a question for "unsafe sex" using the randomized response technique.

10.36. Develop a question on consumption of cigarettes for children aged 13 to 15 using a counterbiasing statement.

10.37. How would you select the response categories for a multiple-choice question on:
   a. weekly consumption of soft drinks
   b. favorite soft drink
   c. preferred radio station
   d. most important attributes in an automobile
   e. hours spent exercising per week
   f. hours spent watching television per week

10.38. Evaluate the following questions. The intended respondent group is shown in parentheses prior to the question.

a. (Airline passengers) *What kind of work do you do?*
1. ___ Professional, Technical
2. ___ Business, Managerial
3. ___ Clerical, Office, Sales
4. ___ Government, Military
5. ___ Housewife
6. ___ Other Employed
7. ___ Retired
8. ___ Student
9. ___ Other Nonemployed

b. (Random sample, "primary grocery shopper") *Approximately how much did you spend for groceries IN THE PAST 7 DAYS?*
___ Under $30 ___ $30 to $50 ___ $50 to $70 ___ Over $70

c. (As above) *Has anyone in your household bought ready to eat food at a drive-in restaurant IN THE PAST 30 DAYS?* ___ Yes ___ No

d. (Adults, random) *Describe the last shoe advertisement you remember seeing.*

e. (Adults, random) *Which shoe stores does your spouse shop at for dress shoes?*

f. (Adults, random) *Do you ever go shopping solely to purchase shoes?*

g. (Adults, random) *Which is most important to you when you buy a pair of shoes*
___ Style ___ Quality ___ Price ___ Service

h. (Telephone subscribers) *During the past month, when making local calls, did you reach any wrong numbers?*
___ Very often
___ Fairly often
___ Seldom
___ No

i. (Adults, random) *Have you ever seen a forest after a fire?*

j. (Bus riders) *If two improvements could be made in LTD (local bus company) service, which of the following would you select? (Check only two).*
___ Newer, better buses
___ More routes on additional streets
___ More frequent service
___ More shelters, benches, and information displays
___ Fewer transfers
___ Less travel time (more direct routes)
___ Fewer route and schedule changes
___ Earlier and later bus service
___ Other (specify) _____

k. (Adults, random) *In addition to providing the raw materials for thousands of wood and paper products consumers need, our national forests* *bring in about 500 million dollars a year to the U.S. Treasury from sales of government timber. Forestry experts say this could be doubled to a billion dollars a year through better forest management methods without loss of forest land. Do you think the U.S. Forest Service should try to increase the yield and sales of timber from our national forests, or should it continue to preserve these trees in their natural state?*

1. Increase the yield and sales of timber
2. Continue to preserve these trees in their natural state
3. No opinion

10.39. In an attempt to determine the extent of employee shoplifting, the following question was administered to a sample of 600 employees of a large regional department store chain:

If the last two digits of your Social Security number are 40 or above, answer question A. If the last two digits of your Social Security number are 39 or below, answer question B. The answers should consist of only "yes" or "no" and should be written on the separate blank card provided you. You are not to write your name or any other information on the card. When you have answered the question, place the card in the box at the entrance to the cafeteria.

Question A: *"Have you taken any merchandise from this store since the first of the year without paying for it?"*

Question B: *"Were you born in August?"*

Employee records indicate that 11 per cent of the employees were born in August. Eighteen per cent of those sampled answered yes on the card. What per cent of the employees would you estimate have engaged in shoplifting since the first of the year? Show all work.

10.40. Develop a questionnaire to measure the reactions of families who acquired a compact disc player for Christmas. Assume that the questionnaire will be administered on January 15 by mail to a nationwide sample (a mail panel has been used for initial screening so the sample frame is composed of qualified respondents).

10.41. Which version of the Burger King question described at the beginning of the chapter provides the most accurate information? Why?

10.42. Why do Form A and Form B in Figure 10–1 produce such dramatically different results?

10.43. How would you explain the results shown in Table 10–1?

10.44. How would you explain the results shown in Table 10–2?

Projects

10.45. Develop, pretest, and revise a telephone questionnaire that will allow you to estimate:

    a. the total amount of soft drinks consumed per week by full-time students on your campus

    b. the amount of money spent per day on soft drinks by the student body

    c. the top 10 brands of soft drinks in terms of amount of money spent by (1) all students, (2) by undergraduates, (3) by graduates, (4) by women, (5) by men, and (6) by those with incomes above the median. Describe the major areas of concern you have with your revised questionnaire.

10.46. As 10.45 but for mail interviews.

10.47. As 10.45 but for personal interviews.

10.48. As 10.45 but for contraceptives.

10.49. As 10.46 but for contraceptives.

10.50. As 10.47 but for contraceptives.

10.51. Develop, pretest, and revise questionnaires to elicit information on the following topics from (1) first-graders, (2) high school sophomores, (3) college seniors.

    a. Food preferences and dislikes and the underlying reasons for these likes and dislikes

    b. Opinions about the seriousness of the "green house" effects

    c. Opinions about music and how many hours a week the respondent spends listening to music.

10.52. Develop, pretest, and revise a telephone questionnaire to measure the television-viewing habits of students on your campus. What were your major concerns in developing this questionnaire?

References

[1] "Have it your way with research," *Advertising Age*, April 4, 1983, 16.

[2] H. Assael and J. Keon, "Nonsampling vs. Sampling Errors in Survey Research," *Journal of Marketing* (Spring 1982), 118.

[3] P. E. Green, P. K. Kedia, and R. S. Nikhil, *CAPPA* (Palo Alto, Calif.: The Scientific Press, 1985).

[4] R. A. Peterson, R. A. Kerin, and M. Sabertehrani, "Question Understanding in Self-Report Data," in B. J. Walker et al., *An Assessment of Marketing Thought and Practice* (Chicago: American Marketing Association, 1982), 426–429. See also M. C. Macklin, "Do Children Understand TV Ads?" *Journal of Advertising Research* (February/March 1983), 63–70.

[5] D. I. Hawkins and K. A. Coney, "Uninformed Response Error in Survey Research," *Journal of Marketing Research* (August 1981), 373. See also G. F. Bishop, R. W. Oldendick, and A. J. Tuchfarber, "Effects of Filter Questions in Public Opinion Surveys," *Public Opinion Quarterly* (Winter 1983), 528–546; K. C. Schneider, "Uninformed Response Rates in Survey Research," *Journal of*

Business Research (April 1985), 153–162; G. F. Bishop, A. F.Tuchfarber, and R. W. Oldendick, "Opinions on Fictitious Issues," *Public Opinion Quarterly*, (Summer 1986), 240–50; and D. I. Hawkins, K. A. Coney, and D. W. Jackson, Jr., "The Impact of Monetary Inducement on Uninformed Response Error," *Journal of the Academy of Marketing Science* (Summer 1988), 30–35.

[6] R. Goydon, "Phantom Products," *Forbes,* May 21, 1984, 292.

[7] M. Glassman and J. B. Ford, "An Empirical Investigation of Bogus Recall," *Journal of the Academy of Marketing Science* (Fall 1988), 38–41.

[8] R. E. Goldsmith, "Personality and Uninformed Response Error," *The Journal of Social Psychology* (February 1986), 37–45; R. E. Goldsmith, J. D. White, and H. Walters, "Explanations for Spurious Response in Survey Research," *Business and Economic Review* (Summer 1988), 93–104; and R. E. Goldsmith, "Spurious Response Error in a New Product Survey," *Journal of Business Research* (December 1988), 271–81.

[9] S. Sudman, A. Finn, and L. Lannom, "The Use of Bounded Recall Procedures in Single Interviews," *Public Opinion Quarterly* (Summer 1984), 520–524. For a broader conceptualization see E. Blair and S. Burton, "Cognitive Processes Used by Survey Respondents to Answer Behavioral Frequency Questions," *Journal of Consumer Research* (September 1987), 280–88.

[10] W. A. Cook, "Telescoping and Memory's Other Tricks," *Journal of Advertising Research* (February 1987), 5–8. See also B. Walstra, "Validating the First-Time-Read-Yesterday Method," *Journal of the Market Research Society* (April 1986), 157–73.

[11] See S. N. Singh and C. A. Cole, "Forced Choice Recognition Tests" *Journal of Advertising* (#3, 1985), 52–58; J. H. Leigh and A. Menon, "A Comparison of Alternative Recognition Measures of Advertising Effectiveness," *Journal of Advertising* (#3, 1986), 4–12; S. N. Singh and G. A. Churchill, Jr., "Response-Bias-Free Recognition Tests to Measure Advertising Effects," *Journal of Advertising Research* (June 1987), 23–36; and S. N. Singh, M. L. Rothschild, and G. A. Churchill, Jr., "Recognition Versus Recall as Measures of Television Commercial Forgetting," *Journal of Marketing Research* (February 1988), 72–80.

[12] Ibid; and H. E. Krugman, "Low Recall and High Recognition of Advertising," *Journal of Advertising Research* (February 1986), 79–86.

[13] See G. S. Omura, "Correlates of Item Nonresponse," *Journal of the Market Research Society* (October 1983), 321–330; and S. Presser, "Is Inaccuracy on Factual Survey Items Item-Specific or Respondent-Specific?" *Public Opinion Quarterly* (Spring 1984), 344–355.

[14] See J. N. Sheth, A. LeClaire, Jr., and D. Wachspress, "Impact of Asking Race Information in Mail Surveys," *Journal of Marketing* (Winter 1980), 67–70; and R. A. Peterson, "Asking the Age Question: A Research Note," *Public Opinion Quarterly* (Spring 1984), 379–383.

[15] N. M. Bradburn et al., "Question Threat and Response Bias," *Public Opinion Quarterly* (Summer 1978), 221–246. See also R. A. Peterson and R. A. Kerin,

"The Quality of Self-Report Data: Review and Synthesis," in B. M. Enis and K. J. Roering, *Review of Marketing 1981* (Chicago: American Marketing Association, 1981), 5–20; and J. H. Malrin and J. M. Moskowitz, "Anonymous versus Identifiable Self-Reports," *Public Opinion Quarterly* (Winter 1983), 557–66.

[16] P. E. Downs and J. R. Kerr, "Recent Evidence on the Relationship Between Anonymity and Response Variables for Mail Surveys," *Journal of the Academy of Marketing Science* (Spring 1986), 72–82; J. H. Frey," An Experiment with a Confidentiality Reminder in a Telephone Survey," *Public Opinion Quarterly* (Summer 1986), 267–69; and G. Albaum, "Do Source and Anonymity Affect Mail Survey Results." *Journal of the Academy of Marketing Science* (Fall 1987), 74–81.

[17] A. D. Cox and R. L. Johnson, "Bias in Behavioral Self-Reports," in T. A. Shimp, ed., *1986 AMA Educator's Conference Proceedings* (Chicago: American Marketing Association, 1986), 387–92; and N. Schwarz et al., "Response Scales," *Public Opinion Quarterly* (Fall 1985), 388–95.

[18] C. W. Lamb, Jr., and D. E. Stem, Jr., "An Empirical Validation of the Randomized Response Technique," *Journal of Marketing Research* (November 1978), 616–621; Sudman and Bradburn op. cit.; M. D. Geurts, "Using a Randomized Response Research Design to Eliminate Non-Response and Response Biases in Business Research," *Journal of the Academy of Marketing Science* (Spring 1980), 83–91; D. E. Stem, Jr., W. T. Chao, and R. K. Steinhorst, "A Randomization Dance for Mail Survey Applications of the Randomized Response Model," in R. P. Bagozzi et al., *Marketing in the 80's* (Chicago: American Marketing Association, 1980), 320–323, and D. E. Stem, Jr., and R. K. Steinhorst, "Telephone Interview and Mail Questionnaire Applications of the Randomized Response Model," *Journal of the American Statistical Association* (September 1984), 555–564.

[19] See N. Webb, "Levels of Adult Numeracy," and P. Shepherd, "Literacy and Numeracy and Their Implications for Survey Research," both in *Journal of the Market Research Society* (April 1984), 129–139 and 147–158.

[20] R. R. Batsell and Y. Wind, "Product Testing: Current Methods and Needed Developments," *Journal of the Market Research Society*, 2 (1980), 129. See also O. D. Duncan and H. Schuman, "Effects of Question Wording and Context, *Journal of the American Statistical Association* (June 1980), 269–275; and T. W. Smith, "Qualifications to Generalized Absolutes," *Public Opinion Quarterly* (Summer 1981), 224–230.

[21] P. Billins, "Research or R'search;" and P. Robinson, "Language in Data Collection," both in *Journal of the Market Research Society* (April 1984), 141–145, and 159–169.

[22] R. Jaroslovsky, "What's On Your Mind, America?" *Psychology Today* (July 1988), 57.

[23] Taken from D. A. Dillman, *Mail and Telephone Surveys* (New York: John Wiley & Sons, 1978), 98.

[24] J. O'Brien, "How Do Market Researchers Ask Questions?" *Journal of the Market Research Society* (April 1984), 93–107.

[25] H. Schuman and S. Presser, "Question Wording as an Independent Variable in Survey Analysis," *Sociological Methods and Research* (November 1977), 155; Schuman and Presser, *Questions and Answers,* op. cit; and H. J. Hippler and N. Schwarz, "Not Forbidding Isn't Allowing," *Public Opinion Quarterly* (Spring 1986), 87–96.

[26] T. W. Smith, "That Which We Call Welfare By Any Other Name Would Smell Sweeter," *Public Opinion Quarterly* (Spring 1987), 75–83.

[27] S. Budiansky, "The Numbers Racket," *U.S. News & World Report,* July 11, 1988, 44.

[28] Schuman and Presser, *Questions & Answers* op. cit., 181, 186. See also G. F. Bishop, R. W. Oldendick, and A. J. Tuchfarber, "Effects of Presenting One Versus Two Sides of an Issue in Survey Questions," *Public Opinion Quarterly* (Spring 1982), 69–85; E. Noelle-Neumann and B. Worcester, "International Opinion Research," *European Research* (July 1984), 124–131; and G. F. Bishop, "Experiments with the Middle Response Alternative in Survey Questions," *Public Opinion Quarterly* (Summer 1987), 220–32.

[29] See Schuman and Presser, *Questions & Answers*, op. cit.; and Noelle-Neumann and Worcester, ibid.

[30] See F. M. Andrews, "Construct Validity and Error Components of Survey Measures," *Public Opinion Quarterly* (Summer 1984), 409–442. See also E. D. Jaffe and I. D. Nebenzahl, "Alternative Questionnaire Formats for Country Image Studies," *Journal of Marketing Research* (November 1984), 463–471.

[31] S. Seiberling, S. Taylor, and M. Ursic, "Open-Ended Question v. Rating Scale," in *Developments in Marketing Science: Proceedings of the Seventh Annual Conference of the Academy of Marketing Science, 1983, Vol. 6,* Conference of the Academy of Marketing Science, ed. by John C. Rogers, III (Ann Arbor, Mich.: Books on Demand), 440–445; G. J. Spagna, "Questionnaires: Which Approach Do You Use," *Journal of Advertising Research* (February/March 1984), 67–70; and Schuman and Presser, *Questions & Answers,* op. cit.

[32] See S. Jones, "Listening to Complexity," *Journal of the Market Research Society* (January 1981), 26–39; and C. McDonald "Coding Open-Ended Answers with the Help of a Computer," *Journal of the Market Research Society* (January 1982), 9–27.

[33] "An Examination of Order Bias" *Research on Research,* #1, (Chicago: Market Facts Inc, undated).

[34] See J. A. Krosnick and D. F. Alwin, "An Evaluation of a Cognitive Theory of Response-Order Effects in Survey Measurement," *Public Opinion Quarterly* (Summer 1987), 201–19.

[35] K. A. Coney, "Order-Bias: The Special Case of Letter Preference," *Public Opinion Quarterly* (Fall 1977), 385–388. See also Spagna, op. cit.

[36] See N. J. Blunch, "Position Bias in Multiple-Choice Questions," *Journal of Marketing Research* (May 1984), 216–220.

[37] Schuman and Presser, "Question Wording," loc. cit.

[38] See, L. Sigelman, "Question-Order Effects on Presidential Popularity" *Public Opinion Quarterly* (Summer 1981), 199–207; S. G. McFarland, "Effects of Question Order on Survey Responses," *Public Opinion Quarterly* (Summer 1981), 208–215; H. Schuman, G. Kalton, and J. Ludwig, "Context and Contiguity in Survey Questionnaires," *Public Opinion Quarterly* (Spring 1983), 112–115; I. Crespi and D. Morris, "Question Order Effect," *Public Opinion Quarterly* (Fall 1984), 578–591; and S. Schröder, "Toward a Theory of How People Answer Questions," *European Research* (April 1985), 82–90.

[39] Jaroslovsky, op. cit., 58.

[40] Spagna, op. cit. See also N. D. Rothwell and A. M. Rustemeyer, "Studies of Census Mail Questionnaires," *Journal of Marketing Research* (August 1975), 405.

[41] A. R. Herzog and J. C. Bachman, "Effects of Questionnaire Length on Response Quality," *Public Opinion Quarterly* (Winter 1981), 549–559; Andrews, op. cit.; and J. R. Dickinson and E. Kirzner, "Questionnaire Item Omission as a Function of Within-Group Question Position," *Journal of Business Research* (February 1985), 71–75.

[42] D. J. Messmer and D. T. Seymour, "The Effects of Branching on Item Nonresponse," *Public Opinion Quarterly* (Summer 1982), 270–271.

[43] A. B. Blankenship, *Professional Telephone Surveys* (New York: McGraw Hill Book Company, Inc., 1977), 105.

[44] See R. N. Zelnio and J. P. Gagnon, "The Construction and Testing of an Image Questionnaire," *Journal of the Academy of Marketing Science* (Summer 1981), 288–299; and S. D. Hunt, R. D. Sparkman, Jr., and J. B. Wilcox, "The Pretest in Survey Research: Issues and Preliminary Findings," *Journal of Marketing Research* (May 1982), 269–273.

CHAPTER 11

Direct Response
Attitude Scales

The U.S. Army has a recruitment budget of $182 million. This budget has to generate 780,000 sales — new enlistments or reenlistments — each year. The Army competes with private industry and educational institutions for skilled young people. Marketing research has played an important role in the success of the army's recruiting efforts.

For example, attitude surveys in the late 1970s and early 1980s revealed a continuing "anti-Vietnam backlash" against the military. In response, the army developed the "Be all you can be" campaign. It focused on personal growth and adventure while avoiding direct references to military activities. Instead, it emphasizes the high-technology career training available in the army. As a result of a study of attitudes toward recruiting incentives, the army modified key aspects of its recruitment strategy. To appeal to individuals interested in higher education, a $15,200 continuing education benefit for two-year enlistees was developed.

An army spokesperson summarizes the basic research problem facing the Army:

> Every year it's a different cohort that we're dealing with in terms of high school students who are graduating. Three years from now, we're going to be trying to convince the present population of 9th graders to come into the military vs. choosing to go to college or other employment opportunities.

> The problem is those 9th graders have a certain mindset. It's affected by what's happening today, and that may affect how we have to deal with

329

them three years from now — and that could be a change from how we have to deal with today's high school seniors.[1]

The "mindsets" or attitudes of consumers are of critical importance to those who wish to influence consumers. An attitude is *an enduring organization of cognitive, affective, and behavioral components and processes with respect to some aspect of the individual's world.* That is, attitude is generally conceived of as having three components: (1) a *cognitive* component — a person's beliefs or information about the object; (2) an *affective* component — a person's feelings of like or dislike concerning the object; and (3) a *behavioral* component — action tendencies or predispositions toward the object.

A substantial proportion of all marketing effort is designed to influence the attitudes of consumers and intermediaries. Therefore, marketing managers frequently require information on attitudes and changes in attitudes induced by marketing activities.

In this chapter, we focus on attitude scales that attempt to measure directly an individual's attitude or a component of the attitude. That is, the individual is required to explicitly state his or her attitude on the scale being used. These responses are then analyzed as direct reflections of attitudes or attitude components. We refer to these as *direct response attitude scales.*

Our treatment of self-report attitude scales is divided into two major areas. The first of these is called *rating scales.* In this section, we discuss the construction of scales used to measure single dimensions of components of attitudes, such as the pleasantness of a taste. In the second section, we describe several of the more common *attitude scales,* which are combinations of rating scales designed to measure several or all aspects of an individual's attitude toward an object. Thus, although the division is somewhat arbitrary, we can say that attitude scales are composed of two or more rating scales.

Rating Scales

The use of a rating scale requires the rater to place an attribute of the object being rated at some point along a numerically valued continuum or in one of a numerically ordered series of categories. Rating scales can focus on: (1) overall attitude toward an object, such as *Pepsi Free;* (2) the degree to which an object contains a particular attribute, such as sweetness; (3) one's feelings toward an attribute, as in liking the taste, or (4) the importance attached to an attribute, such as the absence of caffeine.

Since individuals' evaluations of *specific* product attributes are influenced by the brand's reputation, measures of specific functional attributes, such as taste, are generally performed with the brand name removed. Such tests or comparisons are referred to as *blind* tests.

Noncomparative Rating Scales

With a noncomparative rating scale, the respondent is not provided with a standard to use in assigning the rating. If asked to rate a product, the respondent does so based on whatever standards seem appropriate. The researcher does not provide a comparison point such as an "average brand" or "your favorite brand." Noncomparative scales are often referred to as *monadic* scales since only one brand or product is evaluated. Such tests are common at the product-concept testing stage of the new product development process.[2]

A standard monadic concept test involves a sample of 200 to 400 persons, with personal interviews conducted at a shopping center or in the respondents' homes. Each respondent is presented with the concept in written, pictorial, or in finished print or television ad form for evaluation. The most popular evaluative question used involves intention to purchase. Here is a typical example:

After having (read the concept statement, seen the ad) *if this product were available at your* (supermarket, drugstore) *how likely are you to buy it? Would you say that you*
□ *would definitely buy it*
□ *would probably buy it*
□ *might or might not buy it*
□ *would probably not buy it*
□ *would definitely not buy it*

An 11-point scale similar to the following is sometimes used in lieu of the 5-point scale.

10 *Certain, practically certain (99 in 100)*
9 *Almost sure (9 in 10)*
8 *Very probably (8 in 10)*
7 *Probable (7 in 10)*
6 *Good possibility (6 in 10)*
5 *Fairly good possibility (5 in 10)*
4 *Fair possibility (4 in 10)*
3 *Some possibility (3 in 10)*
2 *Slight possibility (2 in 10)*
1 *Very slight possibility (1 in 10)*
0 *No chance, almost no chance (1 in 100)*

The order of appearance of the alternatives can be reversed on half of the questionnaires to avoid position bias.

The *top box score*—the percentage of respondents who mark the most favorable rating possible—is the one most often used for predictive purposes.

If an 11-point scale is used, the percentage of respondents who mark one of the two most favorable ratings is usually used as the 'top box' score.

These scores are used in one of two ways. Given a history of top box scores on similar products that were subsequently introduced, norms can be established to separate the "winning" from the "losing" product concepts. If, for example, past experience indicates that a top box score of "30" (30 per cent of the respondents marked the most favorable rating) was necessary for the products (whose concepts were tested) to be successful when introduced, this score can be established as the norm for deciding to continue or discontinue product development.

The "top box" score can also be used to estimate the initial trial rate or volume. Methods for doing this range from the very simple (the percentage of respondents marking the top box will also be the percentage who will try the product) to the fairly sophisticated (the Bases I system that makes allowances for seasonality, product category biases in top box scores, distribution buildup, and so forth).

Graphic Noncomparative Rating Scales

A *graphic noncomparative rating scale*, sometimes referred to as a *continuous rating scale*, requires the respondent to indicate the rating assigned by placing a mark at the appropriate point on a line that runs from one extreme of the attitude in question to the other. Two versions of a graphic rating scale are presented here.

Overall, how would you rate the taste of Pepsi Free?

Excellent ——————————————————————— *Very poor*

Overall, how would you rate the taste of Pepsi Free?

Probably the best	*Very good. I like it*	*All right Neither good nor bad*	*Not at all good. I do not like it*	*Probably the worst*

| 1 | 2 | 3 | 4 | 5 | 6 | 7 | 8 | 9 | 10 | 11 | 12 | 13 | 14 | 15 |

As may be seen from the examples, the researcher may or may not choose to provide *scale points* (that is, numbers and/or brief descriptions along the continuum). If such aids are provided, the purpose is to assist the respondents in localizing their rating, rather than to provide distinct categories. *After* the respondent has indicated an attitude by placing a mark on the line, the researcher divides the line into as many categories as desired and assigns the individual a score based on the category into which the mark falls. These scores are typically analyzed as interval data.

Although graphic rating scales are easy to construct, they are not as reliable as itemized scales and little additional information is gained.[3] Thus it is not surprising that they are seldom used in marketing research.

Itemized Noncomparative Rating Scales

Itemized rating scales require the rater to select one of a limited number of categories that are ordered in terms of their scale positions. Exhibit 11–1

Exhibit 11–1 Alternative itemized Rating Scales Designed to Measure Product/Service Satisfaction

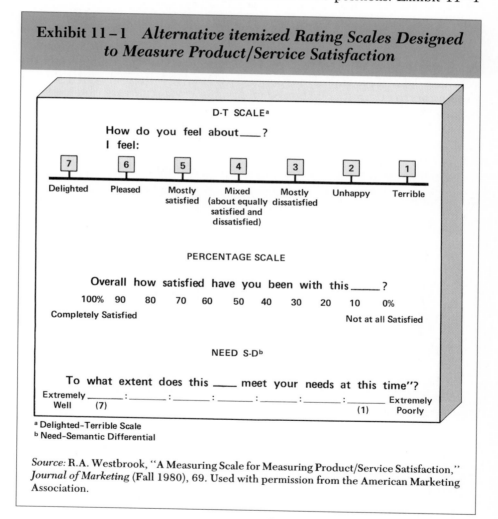

a Delighted–Terrible Scale
b Need–Semantic Differential

Source: R.A. Westbrook, "A Measuring Scale for Measuring Product/Service Satisfaction," *Journal of Marketing* (Fall 1980), 69. Used with permission from the American Marketing Association.

illustrates three itemized rating scales that have been developed to measure satisfaction with a product or service.

Itemized rating scales are widely used in marketing research and are the basic building blocks for the more complex attitude scales. Therefore, we examine the issues surrounding the use of itemized rating scales in some detail.

Nature and Degree of Verbal Description in Itemized Rating Scales. Scale categories can have verbal descriptions associated with them, as does the D-T Scale in Exhibit 11 – 1, or they may be numerical, such as the Percentage Scale in the exhibit. They may even be a completely unlabeled (except for the end points) series of categories, such as the Need S-D Scale in the exhibit.

The presence and nature of verbal category descriptions have an effect on the responses.[4] Somewhat surprisingly, providing a verbal description for *each* category does not necessarily improve the accuracy or the reliability of the resultant data.[5] Techniques have been developed to assign values to category descriptors to ensure that balanced or equal interval scales are obtained, and several lists of category descriptors and their associated values are available.[6]

Instead of verbal descriptions, pictures have been used for special respondent groups. Exhibit 11 – 2 illustrates a ''smiling face'' scale that was successfully used with children as young as five.[7] A scale similar to this was used by Gillette in developing the marketing mix for PrestoMagiX (a toy).

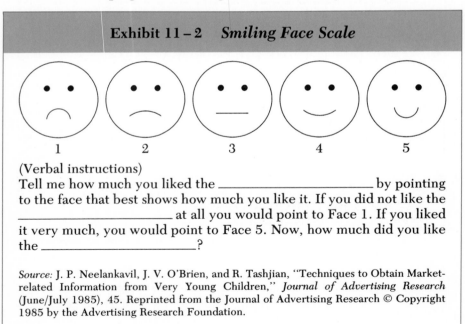

Exhibit 11 – 2   *Smiling Face Scale*

1   2   3   4   5

(Verbal instructions)
Tell me how much you liked the _____ by pointing to the face that best shows how much you like it. If you did not like the _____ at all you would point to Face 1. If you liked it very much, you would point to Face 5. Now, how much did you like the _____?

Source: J. P. Neelankavil, J. V. O'Brien, and R. Tashjian, ''Techniques to Obtain Market-related Information from Very Young Children,'' *Journal of Advertising Research* (June/July 1985), 45. Reprinted from the Journal of Advertising Research © Copyright 1985 by the Advertising Research Foundation.

The Number of Categories. Any number of categories may be created, depending on the nature of the attitude being investigated. Rating scales should generally have between 5 and 10 response categories, though the measurement task may indicate a larger or smaller number.[8] For example, 11 category 0–10 scales have been found to work well in telephone interviews.[9] If several scale items are to be added together to produce a single score for an individual, 5 categories are generally adequate. When the focus is on discriminating attributes of various products or brands, more categories should be used, particularly if the respondents are interested in the scaling task and have detailed knowledge of the attributes.[10]

Balanced Versus Unbalanced Alternatives. The researcher also must decide whether to use a *balanced* or *unbalanced* set of categories.[11] A *balanced* scale provides an equal number of favorable and unfavorable categories. The decision to use a balanced scale should hinge on the type of information desired and the assumed distribution of attitudes in the population being studied. In a study of current consumers of a firm's brand, it may be reasonable to assume that most of the consumers have a favorable *overall* attitude toward the brand (this would *not* be a safe assumption if we were measuring attitudes toward specific attributes). In this case, an unbalanced scale with more favorable categories than unfavorable categories might provide more useful information.

Odd or Even Number of Categories. The issue of an *odd* or *even* number of scale categories is a relevant issue when balanced scales (equal number of favorable and unfavorable categories) are being constructed. If an odd number

Table 11–1   Variation in Responses to Different Neutral Points (in %)

	Strongly agree	Agree	Undecided	Disagree	Strongly disagree	
1.	18.9	47.9	15.4	14.8	3.0	
	Strongly agree	Agree	Disagree	Strongly disagree	Undecided	
2.	21.4	48.9	21.3	4.7	3.8	
	Strongly agree	Agree	Disagree	Strongly disagree		
3.	23.2	51.8	20.9	4.2		
	Strongly agree	Agree	Neutral	Disagree	Strongly disagree	Undecided
4.	16.3	42.2	26.9	10.8	3.0	0.8

Source: E. A. Holdaway, "Different Response Categories and Questionnaire Response Patterns," *Journal of Experimental Education* (Winter 1971), 59. Used with permission.

of scale items is used, the middle item is generally designated as a neutral point. As Table 11–1 indicates, the presence, position, and labeling of a neutral category can have a major impact on response.[12]

Table 11–2 indicates that, in a study involving over 3,000 female heads of households, inclusion of a neutral middle position in a purchase intent scale affected primarily the adjacent positions. Further, this impact was asymmetrical, with the neutral position drawing disproportionately from the "probably will not buy" response category. However, in several of the situations shown in the table, the "top box" ("definitely will buy") is also affected by the inclusion of a neutral category. This response category is the one most widely used by marketing researchers, particularly for product-concept tests. Thus, care must be taken when comparing results from different studies if one study used a neutral point and the other did not.

Proponents of even-numbered categories prefer to avoid neutral points, arguing that attitudes cannot be neutral and that individuals should be forced to indicate some degree of favorableness or unfavorableness. However, in

Table 11–2 Impact of Neutral Middle Position on Purchase Intent Measures

| | | Time Period/Product | | | | | |
| | | In Next 30 Days | | | In Next 7 Days | | |
Response	Number of Categories	Toothbrush	Flashlight Battery	Light Bulb	Pie Filling	Movie Ticket	Frozen Pizza
Definitely	4	16%	21%	26%	16%	13%	15%
will buy	5	19	23	28	16	14	15
Probably	4	23	28	30	22	15	17
will buy	5	27	35	35	30	20	23
Might or might not buy	5	22	25	22	26	25	21
Probably will not buy	4	19	15	11	19	21	18
	5	33	28	24	33	39	31
Definitely will not buy	4	20	11	11	17	26	29
	5	21	14	13	21	27	31

Source: "Measuring Purchase Intent," *Research on Research* 2 (Chicago: Market Facts Inc., updated), 1.

many issues, consumers may indeed be neutral and should be allowed to express that neutrality. Thus, the resolution of the odd/even question depends on whether at least some of the respondents may indeed be neutral on the topic being measured.

Forced Versus Nonforced Scales. Another issue of importance with rating scales is the use of *forced* versus *nonforced scales.* A forced scale requires the respondent to indicate an attitude on the item. In this situation, respondents often mark the midpoint of a scale when in fact they have no attitude on the object or characteristic being rated. If a sufficient portion of the sample has no attitude on a topic, utilization of the midpoint in this manner will distort measures of central tendency and variance. On those occasions when the researcher expects a portion of the respondents to have no opinion, as opposed to merely being reluctant to reveal it, more accurate data may be obtained by providing a "no opinion" or "no knowledge" type category.[13]

Conclusions on Itemized Rating Scales

Itemized rating scales are the most common means of measuring attitudes. There is no one "best" format for itemized rating scales. Instead, rating scales must be adjusted to the nature of the information required and the characteristics of the respondents. With this warning in mind, Table 11 – 3 summarizes our *general* recommendations on each of the key decision areas, while Figure 11 – 1 provides examples of a variety of types of itemized rating scales.

Table 11 – 3 Summary of General Recommendations on Itemized Rating Scales

Issue	General Recommendation
1. Verbal category descriptions	Use precise descriptions for at least some categories.
2. Number of categories	5 when several scales are to be summed for 1 score, and up to 9 when attributes are being compared across objects by interested, knowledgeable respondents.
3. Balanced or unbalanced	Balanced unless it is known that the respondents' attitudes are unbalanced, e.g., all favorable.
4. Odd or even categories	Odd if respondents could feel neutral, even if this is unlikely.
5. Forced or nonforced choice	Nonforced unless it is likely that all respondents will have knowledge on the issue.

Figure 11–1 *Examples of Itemized Rating Scales°*

1. Balanced, forced-choice, odd-interval scale focusing on an attitude toward a specific attribute.

   How do you like the taste of Classic Coke?

Like it very much	Like it	Neither like nor dislike it	Dislike it	Strongly dislike it
_____	_____	_____	_____	_____

2. Balanced, forced-choice, even-interval scale focusing on an overall attitude.

   Overall, how would you rate Ultra Bright toothpaste:

Extremely good	Very good	Somewhat good	Somewhat bad	Very bad	Extremely bad
_____	_____	_____	_____	_____	_____

3. Unbalanced, forced-choice, odd-interval scale focusing on an overall attitude.

   What is your reaction to this advertisement?

Enthusiastic	Very favorable	Favorable	Neutral	Unfavorable
_____	_____	_____	_____	_____

4. Balanced, nonforced, odd-interval scale focusing on a specific attribute.

   How would you rate the friendliness of the sales personnel at Sears' downtown store?

Very friendly	Moderately friendly	Slightly friendly	Neither friendly nor unfriendly	Slightly unfriendly	Moderately unfriendly	Very unfriendly	Don't know
_____	_____	_____	_____	_____	_____	_____	_____

° When used in a written format, the scales may appear either horizontally, as shown in this table, or vertically. In general, the particular layout can be based on how the scale will best fit on the questionnaire.

Comparative Rating Scales

In the graphic and itemized rating scales described previously, the rater evaluates the object without direct reference to a specified standard. This means that different respondents may be applying different standards or reference points. When asked to rate the overall quality of a particular brand, some respondents may compare it to their ideal brand, others to their current brand, and still others to their perception of the average brand. Therefore, when the researcher wants to ensure that all respondents are approaching the rating task from the same known reference point, some version of a comparative rating scale should be used. It is for this reason that comparative scales are generally required to substantiate comparative advertising claims.[14] However, the brand(s) or other standards used for comparison have a major impact on the evaluation given the brand of interest.[15]

Graphic and Itemized Comparative Rating Scales

Noncomparative graphic and itemized rating scales can be converted to comparative scales by simply introducing a comparison point. Often it is not even necessary to change the category descriptions. The following examples should make clear the nature of comparative graphic and itemized rating scales.

Compared to the soft drink I generally drink, Classic Coke is:

Vastly superior	Neither superior nor inferior	Vastly inferior

How do you like the taste of "new" Coke compared to Classic Coke?

Like it much more	Like it more	Like it about the same	Like it less	Like it much less	Don't know
___	___	___	___	___	___

The usage of comparative graphic and itemized rating scales parallels that of their noncomparative counterparts. That is, comparative graphic scales are infrequently used in marketing research, whereas comparative itemized scales are widely used. The issues and recommendations discussed under noncomparative scales also apply to comparative scales.

Pairwise Measures of Preference and Discrimination

Suppose a firm wants to reduce the cost of its beverage product by lowering its sugar content. However, it does not want consumers to notice any taste difference. Therefore, it must determine how much of a reduction it can obtain without affecting the noticeable taste of the product. Problems such as this one require measures of consumers' ability to discriminate between brands or product versions.

Another common problem confronting marketers is to decide which of two similar product versions to introduce. A related problem is whether consumers prefer a new product to a leading competitor's product (or vice-versa). Problems such as these require measures both of consumers' ability to discriminate between similar products and of their preference for one of the products.[16]

Paired Comparisons. The use of the *paired comparison technique involves presenting the respondent with two objects at a time and requiring the selection of one of the two according to some criterion.* Thus, the respondent must make a

Table 11–4 Proportions Preferring Brand I (top of table) to Brand J (side of table)

	A	B	C	D	E
A	—	.81	.68	.26	.37
B	.19	—	.28	.08	.14
C	.32	.72	—	.15	.26
D	.74	.92	.85	—	.57
E	.63	.86	.74	.43	—

series of judgments of the nature: A tastes better than B; overall, B is better than A; or A is more important than B.

Each respondent must compare all possible pairs of objects. If the researcher is interested in 5 brands ($n = 5$), there will be 10 comparisons [$n(n - 1)/2$]. If there are 10 brands, the number of required comparisons increases to 45. Furthermore, there must be a comparison for each attribute of interest. Thus, if we are interested in 10 brands and 5 attributes, our respondents will each be required to make 225 comparisons. Thus, paired comparisons are generally limited to one attribute such as overall preference or two or three brands on multiple attributes.

Table 11–4 presents the output generated by comparing 5 brands on one attribute. This output can be analyzed in a number of ways. A simple visual inspection reveals that brand B is preferred over each other brand (81 per cent preferred B to A; 72 per cent preferred B to C; 92 per cent preferred B to D; and 86 per cent preferred B to E). Visual analysis can also provide the basis for judging the rank order of the 5 brands. The data in Table 11–4 can also be converted into an interval scale through the application of Thurstone's law of comparative judgment.[17]

Double-Paired Comparison.   Paired comparison tests generally force the respondent to choose one item over the other. However, there are many cases when a significant portion of the respondents cannot distinguish one version from the other. Even when provided a "no preference" option, many of these "nondiscriminators" will express a preference. Obviously, this confounds the measure of preference.

A *double-paired comparison* test attempts to measure both discrimination and preference simultaneously. Respondents are provided four objects to compare consisting of two identical samples of Product A and two identical samples of Product B. The respondents are *not* told that there are only two products involved. Instead, they are required to rank order all four "brands." Those who can discriminate should rank both samples of the preferred product version over the two samples from the less preferred version. Those who do not, cannot clearly discriminate between the two products.

This approach places considerable demands on the respondents and is therefore limited to a relatively few brands or product versions (each pair of which requires a separate test).

Consistent Preference Discrimination Test. Another approach to measuring discrimination and preference simultaneously is known as *consistent preference discrimination testing*. This technique requires the subject to repeat the paired comparison task several times (generally 4 to 8). Consider a 7-Up versus Sprite blind (unlabeled) taste test. If a person cannot discriminate between the two, a series of 8 paired comparisons will generally result in each brand "winning" approximately half the time. A person who can discriminate between the brands should consistently prefer one over the other.

Triangle Discrimination and Triangle Preference Tests. The *triangle discrimination test* and the *triangle preference test* are conducted in the same manner as the paired-comparison test except that the respondent has two samples of one product and one of the other. In the triangle discrimination test, the respondent simply identifies the version that differs from the other two. No measure of preference is taken. Those who can differentiate then respond to additional preference and attitude questions.

The triangle preference test, sometimes referred to as *preference ranking*, asks the respondent to rank order the three brands. Those who can discriminate should rank the odd brand either first or third. Thus, both discrimination and preference is measured.

Double Triangle Discrimination and Double Triangle Preference Tests. These tests are identical to the versions described, except that a second triangle test is performed in which the minority version in the first trial is the majority version in the second.[18]

It is a common practice to consider only those consumers who correctly chose the unique version on *both* trials as "discriminators." However, pure guessing should result in $\frac{1}{9}$ of the respondents being correct on both trials ($\frac{1}{3}$ should guess correctly on the first trial and $\frac{1}{3}$ of these should guess correctly on the second). Therefore, estimates of the percentage of the population that can discriminate must be adjusted to control for correct guessing.[19] Similar adjustments are required for all the discrimination measures if forced choice measures are used.

Response Latency. Response latency, the time delay before a respondent answers a question, indicates the respondent's certainty or confidence in the answer. It has been found to be a useful indicator of "guessing" responses to factual questions.[20] However, the most common use of response latency is with paired comparisons. When used in conjunction with a paired-comparison preference test, the faster the choice is made, the stronger is the preference for the chosen brand.[21]

Response latency preference measures are particularly useful in telephone surveys since (1) they are unobtrusive, (2) automated equipment can make the measurements, and (3) more complex scales such as rank order and constant sum are difficult to administer via telephone. These advantages have led duPont's marketing research department to use response latency in a major corporate image telephone survey.

Response latency times and brand selections can be converted into a scale known as the affective value distance (AVD) scale.[22] This indicates the degree to which one brand or product version is preferred over another. Exhibit 11–3 illustrates the output of this approach. Respondents saw a television program with several commercials. Some saw a *Coke* commercial that was known to be successful, others saw a Heinz catsup commercial that was known to be unsuccessful, and a final group saw neither commercial. After viewing the program, the respondents performed a paired-comparison preference task with response latencies measured for 5 brands of cola and 5 brands of catsup. As Exhibit 11–3 indicates, this technique clearly reflected the effects of the two commercials.

Rank Order Rating Scale

The *rank order method requires the respondent to rank a set of objects according to some criterion.* Thus, a respondent may be asked to rank 5 brands of a snack food based on overall preference, flavor, saltiness, or package design. This approach, like the paired-comparison approach, is purely comparative in nature. An individual may rank 10 brands in descending order of preference and still "dislike" the brand rated as 1 because the ranking is based solely on the individual's reactions to the *set of objects presented for evaluation.* For example, a brand might be ranked number 5 when compared with brands A, B, C, and D and yet be ranked first when compared to brands E, F, G, and H. Therefore, it is essential that the researcher include all the relevant competing brands, product versions, or advertisements in the comparison set.

The rank order method is widely used to measure preference for both brands and attributes. It forces respondents to discriminate among the relevant objects and does so in a manner closer to the actual shopping environment than does the paired-comparison technique. It is also substantially less time-consuming than paired comparisons. Ranking 10 items is considerably faster and easier for most people than making the 45 judgments required to generate paired comparison data for 10 brands. The instructions for ranking are also

Exhibit 11–3 *Response Latency Measures of Advertising Impact*

AVD Scale Scores*

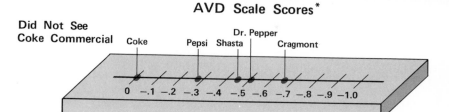

Did Not See
Coke Commercial

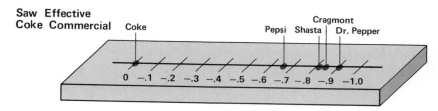

Saw Effective
Coke Commercial

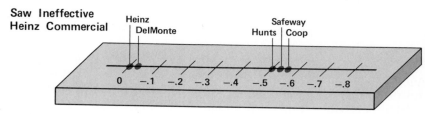

Saw Ineffective
Heinz Commercial

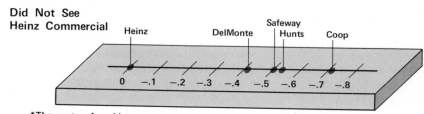

Did Not See
Heinz Commercial

*The most preferred is set at zero, lesser preferred items have negative scores.

Source: J. MacLachlan and J. G. Myers, "Using Response Latency to Identify Commercials That Motivate," *Journal of Advertising Research* (October/November 1983), 54. Reprinted from the Journal of Advertising Research © Copyright 1983, by the Advertising Research Foundation.

easily understood by most individuals, a fact that makes it useful for self-administered questionnaires where more complex instructions may reduce the response rate or increase measurement error.

The major shortcoming of the technique is that it produces only ordinal data. As discussed in Chapter 9, the number of statistical analyses permissible with ordinal data is limited. For example, we cannot calculate a *mean* from rank order data; a *median* must be used instead.

The Constant Sum Scale

The constant sum scale requires the respondent to divide a constant sum, generally 10 or 100, among two or more objects or attributes in order to reflect the respondent's relative preference for each object, the importance of the attribute, or the degree to which an object contains each attribute. In personal interview situations, physical objects such as pennies or chips are often used to aid the respondents with the allocation task.

The constant sum technique can be used for two objects at a time (paired comparison) or more than two objects at a time (quadric comparison).

Most common applications in marketing involve quadric comparisons. In these situations, the respondent is asked to divide the 100 points among *all* the brands or attributes under consideration. The resulting values can be averaged across individuals to produce an *approximate* interval scale value for the brands or attributes being considered.

The value of the constant sum approach can be seen in the following example. Suppose a sample of respondents from a target market is requested to rank order several automobile characteristics with 1 being more important. Assume the individual ranks are similar and produce the following median ranks for each attribute:

Price	1
Economy	2
Dependability	3
Safety	4
Comfort	5
Style	6

A constant sum measure of the importance of the same attributes could be obtained from the following procedure:

Divide 100 points among the characteristics listed so that the division will reflect how important each characteristic is to you in your selection of a new automobile.

Economy
Style
Comfort
Safety
Price
Dependability ____
    Total   *100*

All three of the following groups' average responses to the constant sum scale would be consistent with the rank order results just described:

	Group A	Group B	Group C
Price	35	20	65
Economy	30	18	9
Dependability	20	17	8
Safety	10	16	7
Comfort	3	15	6
Style	2	14	5
	100	100	100

However, with rank order data, the researcher has no way of knowing if price is of overwhelming importance (Group C); part of a general, strong concern for overall cost (Group A); or not much more important than other attributes (Group B). Constant sum data provide such evidence.

Individuals will occasionally misassign points such that the total is more than, or less than, 100. This can be adjusted for by dividing each point allocation by the actual total and multiplying the result by 100.

Attitude Scales

Attitude scales are carefully constructed sets of rating scales designed to measure one or more aspects of an individual's attitude toward some object. The individual's responses to the various scales may be summed to provide a single attitude score for the individual. Or, more commonly, the responses to each scale item or subgroup of scale items may be examined independently of the other scale items.

The development of a sound attitude scale follows the procedures outlined in Chapter 9 (pages 277–279).

Three unique forms of the itemized rating scale are commonly used to construct attitude scales in applied marketing research studies. These are known as *Likert scales, semantic differential scales,* and *Stapel scales.*[23] These scale types and their use in attitude scales are discussed in some detail in the following sections. Since these are versions of the itemized rating scale, we must keep in mind the various issues and problems associated with itemized rating scales.

The Semantic Differential Scale

The *semantic differential scale* is the most frequently used attitude scaling device in marketing research.[24] In its most common form, it requires the respondent to rate the attitude object on a number of itemized, seven-point rating scales bounded at each end by one of two bipolar adjectives. For example:

Camaro Z28

	1	2	3	4	5	6	7	
Fast	___	___	X	___	___	___	___	Slow
Plain	___	___	___	___	___	X	___	Stylish
Large	___	___	___	X	___	___	___	Small
Inexpensive	___	___	___	___	X	___	___	Expensive

The instructions indicate that the respondent is to mark the blank that best indicates how accurately one or the other term describes or fits the attitude object. The end positions indicate "extremely," the next pair indicate "very," the middlemost pair indicate "somewhat," and the middle position indicates "neither-nor." Thus, the respondent in the example described the Camaro Z28 as somewhat fast, extremely stylish, somewhat expensive, and neither large nor small.

The widespread use of the semantic differential has promoted a number of attempts to improve the format in which it is presented to respondents. The most common alteration is to have the respondent rate two or more brands or stores on the *same scales* (as shown below). This approach is referred to as the *upgraded semantic differential* or the *graphic positioning scale.*[25] It takes less space than the standard semantic differential and appears to give similar results.

Camaro Z28 (Z)
Ford Escort GT (F)
Plymouth Laser (L)
Ideal sports car (I)

	1	2	3	4	5	6	7	
Fast	___	FZ	I	L	___	___	___	Slow
Plain	___	___	___	Z	___	LF	I	Stylish
Large	___	___	Z	___	IL	F	___	Small
Inexpensive	___	___	___	F	L	IZ	___	Expensive

A recently tested enhancement of this scale is known as the *numerical comparative scale* and is shown below. The instructions are similar to those for the semantic differential, except that the respondent records the category number for each concept being measured beside each scale. An initial test indicates that, in a mail survey, it provides a response rate comparable to the graphic positioning scale but with an increased questionnaire completion rate and higher data quality.[26]

		Camaro Z28	Ford Escort GT	Plymouth Laser	Ideal Sports Car
Fast	1 2 3 4 5 6 7 Slow	2	3	4	2
Plain	1 2 3 4 5 6 7 Stylish	6	7	5	7
Large	1 2 3 4 5 6 7 Small	4	6	5	5
Inexpensive	1 2 3 4 5 6 7 Expensive	4	4	5	6

Semantic differential data can be analyzed in a number of ways. The versatility is increased by the widely accepted assumption that the resultant data are interval in nature. Two general approaches to analysis are of interest to us — aggregate analysis and profile analysis. The first step in either approach is to assign each interval a value of 1 through 7. For aggregate analysis, it is essential (and helpful for profile analysis) that the larger numbers are consistently assigned to the blanks nearer the more favorable terms.

Aggregate analysis requires that the scores across all adjective pairs be summed for *each individual*. Each individual is thus assigned a summated score. The individual or group of individuals can then be compared to other individuals on the basis of their total scores, or two or more objects (products, brands, or stores) can be compared for the same group of individuals. Aggregate analysis is most useful for predicting preference or brand share. However, disaggregate, or profile analysis, appears to provide more useful data for marketing decision making.

Profile analysis involves computing the mean, or median, value assigned to each adjective pair for an object by a specified group. This profile can then be compared with the profile of another object, an "ideal" version of the object, or another group. Figure 11–2 provides an example of a profile comparison of two retail department stores. Both stores would receive similar aggregate scores. However, these profiles are quite different, even though both are favorable. Store B is at a disadvantage in terms of "price," "service," "helpful employees," "pleasantness," and "friendliness." All of these factors except price appear to be related to the store personnel and the general manner of their dealing with customers. Store A is at a disadvantage with regard to "quality," "selection," and "modernness." These factors seem to be related primarily to product-line decisions.

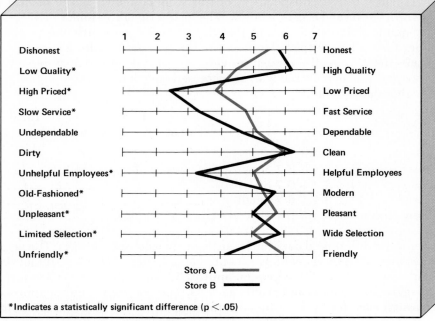

Figure 11–2 *Profile Analysis Using Semantic Differential Data*

Profile analysis is used to isolate strong and weak attributes of products, brands, stores, and so forth. Marketing strategies are then devised to offset weak attributes and/or to capitalize on strong ones. For example, General Motors has used profile analysis of a 35-item semantic differential to develop advertising strategies. Container Corporation of America has used profile analysis to evaluate direct mail approaches. General Electric has used the semantic differential to isolate attributes of persuasive appliance advertisements.

Stapel Scale

The *Stapel scale* is a simplified version of the semantic differential. The standard Stapel scale is a unipolar, 10-interval rating scale with values ranging from +5 to −5. However, any number of values can be used. Unlike the semantic differential, the scale values are used to indicate how accurately *one* adjective describes the concept in question.

Figure 11–3 shows the format of the Stapel scale as it is presented to respondents. The respondent is instructed to indicate how accurately (or inaccurately) each term describes the concept by selecting a numerical re-

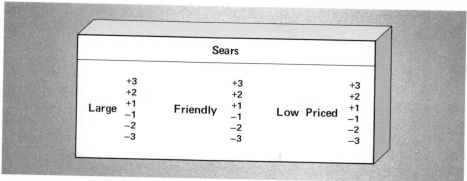

Figure 11–3 *Format of the Stapel Scale*

sponse category. The higher the numerical response category, the more the term describes the concept.

The advantages of this technique lie in the ease of administration and the absence of any need to pretest the adjectives or phrases to ensure true bipolarity. In addition, the Stapel scale can be administered over the telephone.[27]

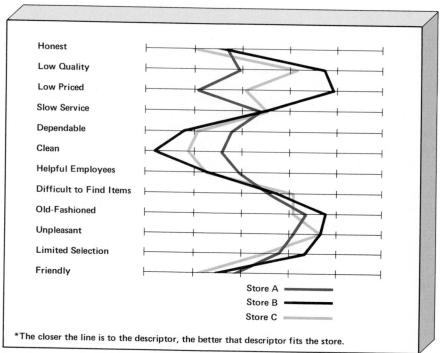

Figure 11–4 *Comparative Profiles—Stapel Scale*

The Stapel scale produces results similar to the semantic differential[28] and the results can be analyzed in the same ways. Figure 11–4 presents a visual profile analysis of three stores using six-point Stapel scale data.

Likert Scales

Likert scales, sometimes referred to as *summated scales,* require a respondent to indicate a degree of agreement or disagreement with each of a series of statements related to the attitude object such as:

1. Macy's is one of the most attractive stores in town.
   ____Strongly ____Agree ____ Neither agree ____Disagree ____ Strongly
       agree   nor disagree   disagree

2. The service at Macy's is *not* satisfactory.
   ____Strongly ____Agree ____ Neither agree ____Disagree ____ Strongly
       agree   nor disagree   disagree

3. The service at a retail store is very important to me.
   ____Strongly ____Agree ____ Neither agree ____Disagree ____ Strongly
       agree   nor disagree   disagree

To analyze responses to a Likert scale, each response category is assigned a numerical value. These examples could be assigned values, such as strongly agree = 1 through strongly disagree = 5, or the scoring could be reversed, or a −2 through +2 system could be used.

Like the semantic differential and Stapel scales, Likert scales can be analyzed on an item-by-item basis (profile analysis), or they can be summed to form a single score for each individual. If a summated approach is used, the scoring system for *each* item must be such that a high (or low) score *consistently* reflects a favorable response. Thus, for statement 1, *strongly agree* might be assigned a 5 and *strongly disagree* a 1. If so, the reverse would be required for statement 2.

The Likert scale offers a number of advantages. First, it is relatively easy to construct and administer. The instructions that must accompany the scale are easily understood, which makes the technique useful for mail surveys of the general population as well as in personal interviews with children.[29] It can also be used in telephone surveys. It does, however, take longer to complete than Stapel or semantic differential scales.

Which Scale to Use?

The preceding pages describe a number of techniques, all of which purport to measure some aspect of attitudes. In addition to these techniques, numerous less well-known techniques and various versions and alterations of the popular scales are available.

When various scaling techniques have been compared, the results generally have been equivalent across the techniques.[30] Therefore, the selection of a scaling technique depends upon the information requirements of the problem, the characteristics of the respondents, the proposed means of administration, and the cost of each technique. In general, multiple measures should be used. That is, no matter what type of scale is used, whenever it is practical, several scale items should be used to measure each object, attribute, belief, or preference under consideration. Summing these several items will provide a more accurate measurement than a single measurement.

Review Questions

11.1. What is a *rating scale?*

11.2. What is an *attitude scale?*

11.3. What is a *noncomparative rating scale?*

11.4. What is a *monadic scale?*

11.5. What is a *blind* test?

11.6. What is a *graphic rating scale?*

11.7. What is an *itemized rating scale?*

11.8. What are the major issues or decisions involved in constructing an itemized rating scale?

11.9. Does the presence and nature of verbal description affect the response to itemized rating scales?

11.10. How many categories should be used in itemized rating scales?

11.11. What factors affect the appropriate number of categories to use with itemized rating scales?

11.12. What is meant by *balanced* versus *unbalanced alternatives?*

11.13. Should an *odd* or *even* number of response categories be used? Why?

11.14. Should *forced* or *nonforced* scales be used? Why?

11.15. What is a *comparative rating scale?*

11.16. What is a *paired comparison?*

11.17. What is a *double paired comparison?*

11.18. What is *consistent preference discrimination testing?*

11.19. How does a *triangle discrimination test* differ from a *triangle preference test?*

11.20. What is a *double triangle discrimination test?*

11.21. What is *response latency?* How does it relate to paired comparison preference tests?

11.22. What is the *rank order rating scale?* What are its advantages and disadvantages?

11.23. What is the *constant sum scale?* What are its advantages and disadvantages?

11.24. How do you construct an *attitude scale?*

11.25. Describe the *semantic differential scale.*

11.26. Describe the *graphic positioning scale (upgraded semantic differential scale).*

11.27. Describe the *numerical comparative scale.*

11.28. What is meant by *profile analysis?*

11.29. Describe the *Stapel scale.*

11.30. What are the advantages of the Stapel scale?

11.31. Describe the *Likert scale.*

11.32. What are the advantages of the Likert scale?

11.33. What criteria influence which scale should be used?

Discussion Questions

11.34. Assuming the stores in Figure 11−2 are attempting to sell to the same market using the same basic approach (products, advertising, and price), what are the managerial implications of this figure for store A? Store B?

11.35. Assuming the stores in Figure 11−4 are attempting to sell to the same market using the same basic approach (products, advertising, and price), what are the managerial implications of this figure for store A? Store B? Store C?

11.36. ''A product could receive the highest median rank on a rank order scale of all brands available in the market and still have virtually no sales.'' Explain how this could occur. Could a paired-comparison technique overcome the problem?

11.37. Develop an attitude scale to measure the following groups' attitude toward (1) math, (2) drugs, or (3) Michael Jackson.
   a. Children age 4−6
   b. Children age 10−12
   c. Children age 14−16
   d. Parents
   e. Grade-school teachers

11.38. Develop _____ to measure college students' attitudes toward three pizza outlets. Measure their overall liking; their beliefs about relevant attributes and the importance they attach to each of these attributes. Assume a personal interview format.

      a. noncomparative graphic rating scales
      b. noncomparative itemized rating scales
      c. comparative graphic rating scales
      d. comparative itemized rating scales
      e. paired comparisons
      f. rank order scales
      g. constant sum scales
      h. semantic differential scales
      i. Stapel scales
      j. Likert scales

11.39. Develop a set of items (adjectives, phrases, and the like) for use in a semantic differential or Stapel scale to study the image college students have of
      a. their university or college
      b. the U.S. President
      c. IBM
      d. Honda Spree

Projects

11.40. Use the (a) semantic differential, (b) Stapel scale, and (c) Likert scale to measure a sample of 10 students' attitudes toward (1) football, (2) marketing as a career, (3) Chinese food, (4) motorcycles, (5) beer. Use a separate sample for each technique.

11.41. Conduct a double triangle discrimination test on the following products using a sample of 20 students. Follow each by a paired comparison preference test using a constant sum (100 points) expression of preference. Analyze the constant sum preferences of those who correctly discriminated 0, 1, and 2 times separately.
      a. Pepsi versus Pepsi Free
      b. Classic Coke versus Diet Coke
      c. Pepsi versus Classic Coke

11.42. For 3 different samples of 20 students each, use (a) paired comparison, (b) rank order scale, and (c) constant sum scale to measure preferences for 6 popular TV shows. What do you conclude?

11.43. As 11.42, but use only one sample of 20 students.

11.44. Implement 11.38 using a sample of 30 students.

References

[1] "Today's Army Relying on Marketing Research," *Marketing News*, July 6, 1984, 1.

[2] W. M. Moore, "Concept Testing," *Journal of Business Research*, 10 (1982), 279–294.

[3] A. O. Grigg, "Some Problems Concerning the Use of Rating Scales for Visual Assessment," *Journal of the Market Research Society* (January 1980), 29–43; and L. W. Friedman and H. H. Friedman, "Comparison of Itemised vs. Graphic Rating Scales," *Journal of the Market Research Society* (July 1986), 285–90. For a different view see D. S. Tillinghast, "Direct Magnitude Estimation Scales in Public Opinion Surveys," *Public Opinion Quarterly* (Fall 1980), 377–84; and S. I. Lampert, "The Attitude Pollimeter: A New Attitude Scaling Device," *Journal of Marketing Research* (November 1979), 578–82.

[4] H. H. Friedman and J. R. Leefer, "Label Versus Position in Rating Scales," *Journal of the Academy of Marketing Science* (Spring 1981), 88–92.

[5] F. M. Andrews, "Construct Validity and Error Components of Survey Measures," *Public Opinion Quarterly* (Summer 1984), 432; and G. A. Churchill, Jr., and J. P. Peter, "Research Design Effects on the Reliability of Rating Scales," *Journal of Marketing Research* (November 1984), 365–366.

[6] C. B. Schertzer and J. B. Kernan, "More on the Robustness of Response Scales," *Journal of the Market Research Society* (October 1985), 261–82; and M. R. Crask and R. J. Fox, "An Exploration of the Internal Properties of Three Commonly Used Marketing Research Scales," *Journal of the Market Research Society* (July 1987), 317–339.

[7] J. P. Neelankavil, J. V. O'Brien, and R. Tashjain, "Techniques to Obtain Market-related Information from Very Young Children," *Journal of Advertising Research* (June/July 1985), 41–47. See also M. C. Macklin, "Do Children Understand TV Ads?" *Journal of Advertising Research* (February/March 1983), 63–70.

[8] See F. D. Reynolds and J. Neter, "How Many Categories for Respondent Classification," and R. J. Lawrence, "Reply," both in *Journal of the Market Research Society* (October 1982), 345–346 and 346–348; G. J. Spagna, "Questionnaires: Which Approach Do You Use." *Journal of Advertising Research* (February/March 1984), 67–70; M. M. Givon and Z. Shapira, "Response to Rating Scalings," *Journal of Marketing Research* (November 1984), 410–419; and D. E. Stem, Jr., and S. Noazin, "The Effects of Number of Objects and Scale Positions on Graphic Position Scale Reliability," in R. F. Lusch et al., *1985 AMA Educators' Proceedings* (Chicago: American Marketing Association, 1985), 370–372.

[9] B. Loken, et al., "The Use of 0–10 Scales in Telephone Surveys," *Journal of the Market Research Society* (July 1987), 353–362.

[10] J. H. Leigh and C. R. Martin, Jr., "'Don't Know' Item Nonresponse in a Telephone Survey," *Journal of Marketing Research* (November 1987), 418–24.

[11] See H. Schuman and S. Presser, *Questions and Answers in Attitude Surveys* (New York: Academic Press, 1981), 179–201.

[12] See Schuman and Presser, ibid., 161–178; Andrews, op. cit., 432; Churchill, Jr., and Peter, op. cit., 366; and Spagna, loc. cit.

[13] D. I. Hawkins and K. A. Coney, "Uninformed Response Error in Survey Research," *Journal of Marketing Research* (August 1981), 370–374; Schuman and

Presser, op. cit., 113–160; G. F. Bishop, R. W. Oldendick, and A. J. Tuchfarber, "Effects of Filter Questions in Public Opinion Surveys," *Public Opinion Quarterly* (Winter 1983), 528–546; K. C. Schneider, "Uninformed Response Rate in Survey Research," *Journal of Business Research* (April 1985), 153–162; R. W. Mizerski, J. B. Freiden, and R. C. Green, Jr., "The Effect of the 'Don't know' Option on TV Ad Claim Recognition Tests," in *Advances in Consumer Research X* (Association for Consumer Research, 1983), 283–287; and G. F. Bishop, R. W. Oldendick, and A. Tuchfarber, "What Must My Interest in Politics Be If I Told You 'I Don't Know,'" *Public Opinion Quarterly* (Summer 1984), 510–519.

[14] B. Buchanan, "Can You Pass the Comparative Ad Challenge?" *Harvard Business Review* (July/August 1985), 108.

[15] See "Brand Perceptions: Relative vs. Absolute Ratings," *Research on Research #6* (Chicago: Market Facts Inc., undated). The primary findings are reproduced in Figure 8–3 of this text.

[16] For an excellent discussion of these issues see R. M. Johnson, "Simultaneous Measurement of Discrimination and Preference," *Research on Research #33* (Chicago: Market Facts Inc., undated); B. Buchanan, M. Givon, and A. Goldman, "Measurement of Discrimination Ability in Taste Tests," *Journal of Marketing Research* (May 1987), 154–63; B. S. Buchanan and D. G. Morrison, "Taste Tests," *Psychology and Marketing* (Spring 1984), 69–91; and B. S. Buchanan and D. G. Morrison, "Measuring Simple Preferences," *Marketing Science* (Spring 1985), 93–109.

[17] P. E. Green, D. S. Tull and G. Albaum, *Research for Marketing Decisions* (Englewood Cliffs, Prentice-Hall, Inc., 1988); 292–98.

[18] H. R. Moskowitz, B. Jacobs, and N. Firtle, "Discrimination Testing and Product Decisions," *Journal of Marketing Research* (February 1980), 84–90.

[19] D. G. Morrison, "Triangle Taste Tests: Are the Subjects Who Respond Correctly Lucky or Good?" *Journal of Marketing* (Summer 1981), 111–119.

[20] J. MacLachlan, J. Czepiel, and P. LaBarbera, "Implementation of Response Latency," *Journal of Marketing Research* (November 1979), 573–577.

[21] T. T. Tyebjee, "Response Latency: A New Measure for Scaling Brand Preference," *Journal of Marketing Research* (February 1979), 96–101; and D. A. Aaker et al., "On Using Response Latency to Measure Preference," *Journal of Marketing Research* (May 1980), 237–244.

[22] J. MacLachlan and J. G. Myers, "Using Response Latency to Identify Commercials That Motivate," *Journal of Advertising Research* (October/November 1983), 51–57. See also W. J. Burroughs and R. A. Feinberg, "Using Response Latency to Assess Spokesperson Effectiveness," *Journal of Consumer Research* (September 1987), 295–99.

[23] Three other well-known scales are widely used in social science research but only rarely in marketing research. For a discussion of the Q-sort, see F. N. Kerlinger, *Foundations of Behavioral Research* (New York: Holt, Rinehart and Winston, Inc., 1973), 582–600; the Guttman technique, see A. Edwards, *Tech-

niques of Attitude Scale Construction (New York: Appleton-Century-Crofts, 1957), 172–200; the Thurstone scale, see L. L. Thurstone, *The Measurement of Values* (Chicago: University of Chicago Press, 1959).

[24] For details see C. Osgood, G. Suci, and P. Tannenbaum, *The Measurement of Meaning* (Chicago: University of Illinois Press, 1957).

[25] See R. H. Evans, "The Upgraded Semantic Differential: a Further Test," *Journal of the Market Research Society* 2 (1980), 143–147; J. E. Swan and C. M. Futrell, "Increasing the Efficiency of the Retailer's Image Study," *Journal of the Academy of Marketing Science* (Winter 1980), 51–57; and D. E. Stem and S. Noazin, "Effects of Number of Objects and Scale Positions on Graphic Position Scale Reliability," in R. F. Lusch, *1985 AMA Educators' Proceedings* (Chicago: American Marketing Association, 1985), 370–372.

[26] L. L. Golden, G. Albaum, and M. Zimmer, "The Numerical Comparative Scale," *Journal of Retailing* (Winter 1987), 393–410.

[27] D. I. Hawkins, G. Albaum, and R. Best, "Stapel Scale or Semantic Differential in Marketing Research?" *Journal of Marketing Research* (August 1974), 318–322. See also G. D. Upah and S. C. Cosmas, "The Use of Telephone Dials as Attitude Scales," *Journal of the Academy of Marketing Science* (Fall 1980), 416–426.

[28] Hawkins et al., loc. cit.; and D. Menezes and S. Chandra, "Differentiating between Store Images," in J. C. Rogers, III, *Developments in Marketing Science VI* (Academy of Marketing Science, 1983), 437–439.

[29] G. Riecken and A. C. Samli, "Measuring Children's Attitudes Toward Television Commercials: Extension and Replication," *Journal of Consumer Research* (June 1981), 57–61.

[30] Hawkins et al., loc. cit.; R. I. Haley and P. B. Case, "Testing Thirteen Attitude Scales for Agreement and Brand Discrimination," *Journal of Marketing* (Fall 1979), 20–32; Lampert, loc. cit.; D. Menezes and N. Elbert, "Alternate Semantic Scaling Formats for Measuring Store Image," *Journal of Marketing Research* (February 1979), 80–87; Menezes and Elbert, loc. cit.; and Churchill, Jr., and Peter, op. cit., 365.

CHAPTER 12

Derived Attitude Scales

Sunbeam Appliance Company (SAC) recently decided to revamp a number of their small appliance product lines. For each line, management needed to make three decisions:

- What models should be in the line?
- What should their physical appearance be?
- What should their performance characteristics be?

SAC undertook the following four-phase research procedure to help answer these questions for each product line:

1. *A Consumer Usage and Attitude Survey* to determine how and for what purpose products in the product category are used, frequency of use, brand ownership, brand awareness, and attitudes towards the appliance. The results of this part of the process are useful for product and advertising planning.

2. *A Consumer Attribute and Benefit Survey* to obtain importance ratings of product attributes and benefits along with their perceived presence or absence in each of the products of the key competitive brands including SAC. This data provides the basis for identifying "need gaps" where the perceived benefits are not being supplied by the existing brands.

3. *A Conjoint Analysis Study* to produce the data from which the structure of consumers' preferences for different product features is determined

357

via the conjoint measurement technique. This structure of preferences is then used as an input into the fourth step of the procedure.

4. *Product Line Simulations* where various possible versions of the SAC product line are described and their shares of the market are predicted from the structure of consumers' preferences. The market share generated by each version of the product line is used to determine the best configuration for SAC's redesigned product line.

When the study was initiated, SAC's food processor line was composed of 2 versions of each of three basic models, making a total of 6 items in the line. The food processor market consists of 3 price categories: less than $60; $60 to $125; and over $125. Sunbeam had 1 model in the lower range and 2 in the mid range. The 6 models had less than a 10 per cent unit share, placing SAC fifth behind Cuisinart, General Electric, Hamilton Beach, and Moulinex. A primary motivation for the product-line redesign was to increase market share.

The food processor project began with a series of group interviews to learn consumers' thoughts and feelings about food processors, their attributes and benefits, the uses they made of food processors, and their preferences regarding features. The interviews provided an opportunity for SAC's research people to learn the vocabulary consumers use when they talk about and think about food processors. This was intended to allow the questionnaires and interviewers used in the conjoint data collection to use words and phrases regarding food processors that the responding consumers could understand.

Based on this exploratory work, 12 attributes, each with two or three possible levels (i.e., 3 prices, 2 bowl types, 2 bowl shapes, 3 motor sizes, etc.), were identified as relevant. These attributes and levels could be combined to produce 69,984 different food processor configurations! Obviously, consumers could not directly evaluate each combination. Therefore, a conjoint analysis using an orthogonal array of only 27 combinations was used. Target market consumers merely rank-ordered combination pictorial and verbal descriptions of these 27 models in terms of their preferences. Based on this rank order data, the analysis program could estimate the value each consumer assigned to each level of each attribute (termed *utility functions*). Thus, each consumer's relative preference for *any* of the 69,984 possible models could be estimated.

More than 500 consumers completed the preference task and their utility functions were calculated. Then, consumers with similar utility functions were identified mathematically. The results produced four market segments. For example, one segment was labeled the *Cheap and Large* segment because of the importance its members place on large bowl capacity and low price.

Next, the 32 leading food processor models were identified and their level on each of the 12 attributes determined. A simulation was run, using the utility functions of the 500 respondents and applying the assumption that each respondent would "buy" the actual brand with the highest total utility score. These simulated sales were converted to simulated market shares and compared to actual market shares. They corresponded almost perfectly with the actual shares.

The next step was to place various sets of new combinations of SAC processors into the simulations to isolate a set that would optimize total SAC share. As a result, all the old models were dropped and three new models were introduced, one in each of the price points. Within a year of the change, SAC moved into fourth place in share despite having only half the line items of a year earlier.[1]

In this example, consumers were *not* asked how much value or utility they assigned to different levels of various attributes. Instead, these utilities were derived mathematically from the consumers' preference rankings of specially constructed product descriptions. In this chapter, we will describe a variety of approaches to this problem under the general heading of *conjoint analysis*.

In conjoint analysis, the researcher attempts to determine the relative value consumers assign to specific levels of product attributes, without directly asking the consumer about the value of individual attributes. These techniques require the researcher to prespecify both the attributes and levels to be tested. At other times, the researcher is interested in determining how many and which attributes consumers use to evaluate brands and/or how various brands are viewed based on these attributes. Again, there are often reasons why direct questioning is not appropriate. A variety of mathematical techniques exist for deriving *perceptual maps* of product categories. This topic constitutes the second section of this chapter.

Conjoint Analysis[2]

Recall from the last chapter that consumers are often asked to rate or describe their ideal version of a product, store, service, advertisement, or other object on a semantic differential, Stapel, or Likert scale. A major problem with these procedures is that for many attributes more (or less) is always better. Thus, consumers want extremely powerful, fast, stylish, reliable, and safe automobiles that provide extremely high gas mileage and have very low price tags. Unfortunately, such combinations are rarely possible in actuality. In the marketplace, consumers must make trade-offs between power and gas mileage, between style and initial price, and so forth. Rating scales are poorly equipped to measure such trade-offs.

Rankings provide the primary direct approach for measuring trade-offs. Thus, simple rank orderings of product attributes, various versions of the paired-comparison technique, or the constant sum scale are used to measure consumers' stated importance of specific attributes. While useful, these techniques suffer from a variety of weaknesses when used to estimate consumers' willingness to trade varying levels of different attributes. First, they are based on stated importance levels rather than on importance levels based on observations of choice behavior. Thus, normative responses rather than actual ones are a problem. For example, consumers often state that price and quality are more important than image or status, yet people consistently purchase high-status brands when lower-priced brands of equivalent quality are available.

Another problem is that these measures do not effectively deal with attribute levels. That is, a consumer may state that price is less important than capacity for a popcorn popper. Does this mean that this consumer would pay $25.00 for a three-quart popper rather than $15.00 for a two-quart popper? Or would he or she only pay a $5.00 differential?

Conjoint analysis is a set of techniques designed to measure (1) the importance individual consumers attach to each attribute and (2) their degree of preference for each level of each attribute.[3] Further, preferences for each level of each attribute are calculated in a manner that allows direct comparisons of an individual's preferences across attributes. That is, the method allows determination of a consumer's willingness to trade a 10 per cent price premium for a 12-month longer warranty or 15 per cent greater gas mileage.

Suppose a firm were interested in introducing a new cat food designed to meet the nutritional needs of cats with kittens. Management is concerned with 5 attributes that may affect the cat owner's willingness to try the product: (1) *form* (dry, moist, canned); (2) *brand name* (MamaCat, Formula 9, Plus); (3) *price* ($.55, $.65, $.75); (4) *endorsement* from a veterinarian association (yes, no); and (5) a *money-back guarantee* if not satisfied (yes, no). Which combination of these attributes will produce the highest level of trial? Which attributes are most important? Will consumers be willing to pay $.75 rather than $.65 if the brand has an endorsement, all other things equal? We will use this problem to illustrate the uses and issues involved in conjoint analysis.

Data Collection Approaches for Conjoint Analysis

A fundamental procedural decision in conjoint analysis is whether to use *full profile* or a *pairwise procedure* for data collection.

Pairwise Approach to Conjoint Data Collection

The pairwise procedure presents the respondents with a set of matrixes representing all possible attribute pairs, with the levels of one attribute appearing on the X axis and the levels of the other attribute appearing on the Y axis. Two of the 10 (N(N-1)/2) matrices required for the cat food problem are:

	Price		
	$.55	$.65	$.75
Dry			
Form Moist			
Canned			

	Guarantee	
	Yes	No
Dry		
Form Moist		
Canned		

Respondents are instructed to rank-order each combination (cell) in each table to reflect their preference or purchase likelihood. Thus, individual **A** below is very price-sensitive relative to form and prefers moist over canned and canned over dry. In contrast, individual **B** is somewhat price sensitive but will trade off price to an extent to obtain a desired form (the numbers in the cells represent the respondents' stated preference rankings with 1 being most preferred).

Individual A

	$.55	$.65	$.75
Dry	3	6	9
Form Moist	1	4	7
Canned	2	5	8

Individual B

	$.55	$.65	$.75
Dry	4	7	9
Form Moist	1	2	5
Canned	3	6	8

After the respondent completes all 10 matrices, the analytical task of the researcher is to derive a set of numbers, called *utilities* or *part-worths*, that, when assigned to each level of each attribute, will reproduce the rank orders in each table. Thus, for individual **A**, the sum of the part-worths for a price level of $.55 and moist form should be greater than the sum of the combination of any other two levels of these attributes, the sum of the part-worths for $.55 and canned form should be second, and so forth. Appropriate analytical techniques are described in the next section.

Although it was initially widely used, the pairwise approach is rapidly losing favor in applied research studies. One reason for its early popularity was the ease of designing the study compared to that of the full profile alternative. The researcher simply prepares matrices of all possible attribute pairs. Unfortunately, ease for the researcher may mean tedium for the respondent. In our rather simple example, the respondent must complete 10 matrices while making 55 trade-off judgments. Not only is this a rather tiresome task, but it is also unrealistic. Consumers seldom make brand choices after going through such a structured, abstract approach. Instead, they confront products with all attributes simultaneously visible and choose from among the available combinations. Full profile conjoint represents this process more realistically.

Full Profile Conjoint

Full profile conjoint involves presenting the respondent with a set of product descriptions such that each description contains information on the level of each attribute. In our example, the researcher could develop descriptions of the 108 ($3 \times 3 \times 3 \times 2 \times 2 = 108$) possible product versions and ask the respondents to react to each. However, this would be a difficult and time-consuming task for both the researcher and the respondents. Fortunately, a *fractional factorial orthogonal array* (an experimental design in which the combinations to be tested are selected in such a way that the independent contributions of all five factors are balanced) can be used to simplify the

Table 12–1 Attribute Combinations for Evaluation of a Cat Food

No.	Form	Name	Price	Endorse-ment	Guarantee	Respondent's Evaluation Ranking	Rating
1	Canned	MamaCat	$.75	No	Yes	12	50
2	Canned	Formula 9	.55	Yes	No	7	78
3	Canned	Plus	.65	No	No	9	66
4	Dry	MamaCat	.75	Yes	No	18	15
5	Dry	Formula 9	.55	No	Yes	8	72
6	Dry	Plus	.65	No	No	15	32
7	Moist	MamaCat	.55	No	No	4	90
8	Moist	Formula 9	.65	Yes	No	6	80
9	Moist	Plus	.75	No	Yes	5	84
10	Canned	MamaCat	.65	No	No	10	52
11	Canned	Formula 9	.75	No	No	16	28
12	Canned	Plus	.55	Yes	Yes	1°	95
13	Dry	MamaCat	.55	No	No	13	42
14	Dry	Formula 9	.65	No	Yes	11	50
15	Dry	Plus	.75	Yes	No	17	20
16	Moist	MamaCat	.65	Yes	Yes	2	92
17	Moist	Formula 9	.75	No	No	14	38
18	Moist	Plus	.55	No	No	3	90

° Most preferred.

situation.[4] In this case, only 18 of the possible 108 combinations are required, as shown in Table 12-1. Orthogonal arrays are difficult to design and in practice are done via computer software[5] or manually based on published prototype designs.[6]

The respondents either rank-order the resulting product descriptions or rate them on a relevant dimension such as preference or purchase likelihood.[7] It is important to note that it is *the overall offering (physical product, name, price, and so on) that is ranked or rated*. The respondent does *not* make a separate evaluation of the individual attributes of the product. Table 12-1 indicates the "likelihood of trial" ranking and rating (on a 1-100 scale), given each of the 18 versions in the example by one respondent.

Again, the analytical task is to determine the part-worths or utilities of each level of each attribute such that adding the part-worths for the levels contained in the 18 versions will reproduce the rank order or ratings as stated by the respondent directly. Thus, in our example in Table 12-1, the part-worths associated with canned form, Plus name, $.55 price, and both an endorsement and a money-back guarantee should sum to a larger number than any other combination tested.

Selecting Attributes and Attribute Levels

The results of a conjoint analysis depend on the attributes and attribute levels selected for inclusion. The attributes selected depend on the purpose of the study. However, they should generally be variables that the manager can alter and that affect consumers' choices or preferences.[8] Since the complexity of the experimental design and the burden on the respondent increases with the number of attributes, studies should generally be limited to fewer than 10 attributes, with 6 or 7 being common. Not only does the number of attributes affect the complexity of the experimental design, but their range and realism influence the credibility of the task to the respondent.

The levels selected for each attribute should be as few as possible while still covering the key decision points. Some attributes have finite, discrete levels (such as canned, moist, or dry cat food). In our example, liquid cat food could be added, but *only* if it represents an alternative the company is considering producing. It would not be wise to omit any of the remaining form options because we cannot assume that their values lie on a straight line (are linearly related). Other variables, such as price, do not have such clear-cut levels. There are 21 price levels between $.55 and $.75 inclusive. It is natural to select the highest and lowest levels being considered. The number of levels to select between these points is based on the researcher's estimate of the linearity of the utility function for the variable in question. For a completely linear function only the two extreme levels need to be selected. The less certain the researcher is of the nature of the function between the extremes, the more intermediate levels he or she should include.

Data Collection Procedures

Data collection for pairwise conjoint studies requires respondents to complete the matrixes described earlier. These are presented directly to the respondent, generally with an example of how to complete one.

Full profile conjoint studies require that complete descriptions of the product on the relevant attributes be presented to the respondent. The presentation format can range from cards, as shown in Exhibit 12 – 1, to drawings, also shown in the Exhibit, to actual products, pictures, ads for the product, and

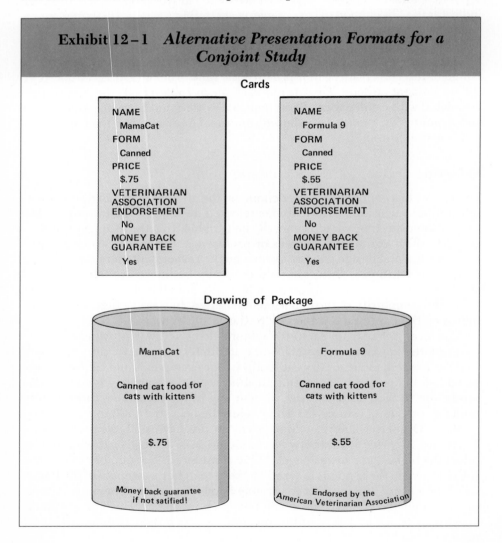

Exhibit 12 – 1 *Alternative Presentation Formats for a Conjoint Study*

Cards

NAME	NAME
MamaCat	Formula 9
FORM	FORM
Canned	Canned
PRICE	PRICE
$.75	$.55
VETERINARIAN ASSOCIATION ENDORSEMENT	VETERINARIAN ASSOCIATION ENDORSEMENT
No	No
MONEY BACK GUARANTEE	MONEY BACK GUARANTEE
Yes	Yes

Drawing of Package

MamaCat

Canned cat food for cats with kittens

$.75

Money back guarantee if not satified!

Formula 9

Canned cat food for cats with kittens

$.55

Endorsed by the American Veterinarian Association

so on. In general, the more realistic the stimuli, the more confidence one can have in the results.

Respondents are asked to rate each item on a scale (1–10, 1–100 are common) to reflect their liking or purchase probability. Or, they are asked to rank order the items on similar criteria.

Analysis of Conjoint Data

A variety of approaches are available for analyzing conjoint data. The three most common approaches are **LINMAP**, **MONANOVA**, and dummy-variable regression. The three approaches generally produce similar results. LINMAP[9] utilizes a linear programming approach and assumes that the rank-ordering or rating responses are ordinal in nature (see Chapter 9). MONANOVA[10] is an analysis of variance technique (see Chapter 19) which also assumes only ordinal data. Dummy-variable regression analysis is standard least squares regression analysis (see Chapter 20), using effects coding to create the dummy variables.

Since regression is the most widely used analytical approach, we describe it in some detail in Appendix C. The analysis process produces an estimate of the value or utility that each level of each attribute has for each respondent. These are referred to as *part-worths*. *Part-worths* are scaled so that the utility of different levels of different attributes can be directly compared. The part-worths for the respondent rank-order data in our example are shown in Table 12–2. These were calculated using dummy variable regression analysis (Appendix C). Figure 12–1 displays the same results in standard graphic form.

Table 12–2 Part-Worths for a Cat Food

I. Form			IV. Endorsement	
Dry	−4.17		Yes	.75
Moist	3.83		No	−.75
Canned	.33			
			V. Guarantee	
II. Name			Yes	2.25
MamaCat	−.33		No	−2.25
Formula 9	−.84			
Plus	1.17			
III. Price				
$.55	3.50			
.65	.67			
.75	−4.17			

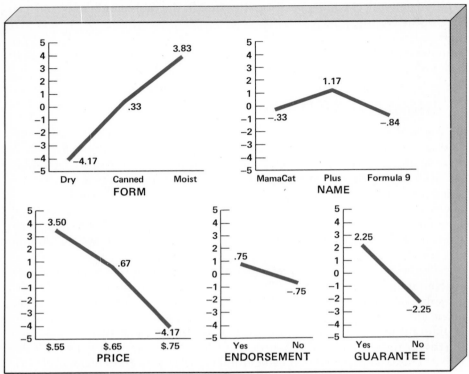

Figure 12-1   *Graphic Display of Attribute Utilities for Cat Food*

Table 12–2 and Figure 12–1 indicate that *moist* is the preferred form, *Plus* is the preferred name, the *lower price* is preferred, and both the *endorsement* and the *guarantee* are desired. It is also clear that some attributes are more important than others. Moving from no endorsement to endorsement increases the total utility by only 1.5. However, moving from the highest price considered to the lowest will increase utility by 7.67. Thus, the firm need not be too concerned with the endorsement but should pay considerable attention to pricing policy.

This logic is used to calculate the relative importance of each attribute (the methodology is described in Appendix C). In our example, the following relative importance scores can be calculated:

Form	.34
Name	.08
Price	.32
Endorsement	.06
Guarantee	.19

These importance measures should be interpreted carefully, as they are heavily influenced by the levels chosen to represent the attributes.[11] Thus, adding a very high or low price level would increase the relative importance of price.

The ability to assign a value to any possible combination of attributes or to compare directly a consumer's willingness to trade high levels of one attribute for lower levels of another makes this technique particularly useful. For example, the most preferred combination of attributes is number 12 (see Table 12–1). Could any of the 90 combinations that the respondent did not evaluate (108 possible, minus 18 compared) be preferred to combination 12? The answer is "yes," based on the following analysis. The total utility of combination 12 is currently 8.33. If the form were to be changed from canned to moist, and all other attributes were left unchanged, the total utility would increase to 11.83. Thus, because of the special nature of the experimental design, combinations not evaluated by the respondents can also be analyzed.

Consider another question posed when we first presented this example — "Will consumers be willing to pay $.75 rather than $.65 if the brand has an endorsement, all other things equal?" The answer is *no*. Moving from $.65 to $.75 reduces utility by 4.84, while adding an endorsement increases utility by 1.50, for a net decrease of 3.34.

Issues in Conjoint Analysis

Although conjoint analysis is widely used and is gaining popularity rapidly, a number of issues are involved in its use.

Is Conjoint Analysis Appropriate?

In addition to the need for the type of information that conjoint analysis provides, several other factors influence its appropriateness. The product, service, advertisement, or other item being evaluated must be realistically decomposable into a set of basic attributes. Perfumes and other image-based products are less amenable to conjoint analysis than are more function-based products. Likewise, conjoint analysis works better for moderate- to high-involvement products than for low-involvement, habitual purchases.

The method requires the researcher to describe the various alternative attribute combinations either verbally, pictorially, or with actual versions of the items. If creating the actual item is required, for example to test various television commercials using celebrity spokespersons and humor, the cost can be prohibitive.

The various factorial combinations of the attribute levels must be believable to the respondents. Thus, a high price/high-status brand/low-quality product combination might not be believable and could therefore distort the overall results.

Are the Attributes Independent?

An assumption behind conjoint analysis as normally conducted is that the attributes are more or less independent as perceived by the respondents. The use of existing brand names is a focus of concern in this area. Established brand names convey images of quality, reliability, price, service, and so forth. Thus, if the name Honda appears in conjunction with "frequent repairs," the respondent may ignore the stated repair information because of an established belief about Honda's reliability.

Should Price Be Used as an Attribute?

Practitioners are divided on the issue of using price in conjoint analysis studies. In many situations, mention of price adds realism and allows the manager to evaluate the pricing implications of product and service changes. However, price is often used as an indicator of quality, particularly for image items and items for which it is difficult to determine quality. If the quality of such a product is explicitly stated in the research design and price is also included, the importance of price can be understated compared to actuality.

At other times, the inclusion of the price will focus more attention on it than is likely in the actual purchase situation. For example, many consumers purchase greeting cards without examining the price. If price is used in a conjoint study of greeting cards, the respondent's attention is drawn to it, and this feature is likely to appear more important than it actually is.

If, and How, Should Utilities Be Aggregated Across Respondents?

Conjoint analysis programs produce part-worths for *each* respondent for each level of each attribute. However, these should not be averaged across individuals to determine the average utility for each level of each attribute. Before we calculate such averages, we need to be sure that segments with unique utilities do not exist. Consider the following example:

Utility for Forum

Respondent	Moist	Canned	Dry
A	.80	.10	−.90
B	.70	.05	−.75
C	−.85	.20	.65
D	−.95	.00	.95
E	−.10	.20	−.10
Average	−.08	.11	−.03

If this example represented the utility distribution of the market, we might be misled into introducing the canned version for which 20 per cent of the market

368

had a slight preference. In actuality, we should introduce either, or both moist or dry, each of which is strongly preferred by 40 per cent of the market. Therefore, we should be sure we have homogeneous groups before averaging across respondents. This can be done by using a technique such as cluster analysis first.[12]

For some applications, it is not desirable to aggregate utilities across individuals. Often, marketers want to estimate the market share implications of one or more new or altered products introduced by either their firm or their competition. In such a case, a model or simulation is designed so that each customer will purchase the brand whose attribute combination provides the highest total utility to that customer. Then each existing brand and proposed new or altered brand is described in terms of the relevant attributes. The computer model simulates the choice process of each individual, based on his or her unique utility functions and the market share of each alternative is calculated. This approach was used by Sunbeam in our opening example.

Applications of Conjoint Analysis

Carnation routinely uses conjoint analysis in developing advertisements, Sunbeam used it to redesign all its small appliance lines, Weyerhaeuser has used it to assist in pricing and branding decisions, Hallmark Cards for designing cards and puzzles, General Electric in the design of industrial products. The list goes on. Each year, numerous conjoint studies are conducted,[13] both in-house and by research firms such as Total Research Corporation. Use of the method will undoubtedly spread as software programs become more widely available.

Conjoint's primary advantage is its ability to estimate consumers' willingness to trade off varying levels of one attribute for another based on a relatively simple (low-effort) data collection procedure. This is extremely valuable in designing products, advertisements, programs, and so on, as well as in discovering unique market segments. In addition to immediate managerial benefits in terms of improved marketing programs, conjoint analysis provides increased understanding of why consumers have certain preferences. If managers use conjoint output as systematic inputs into a formal or informal model of consumer behavior for their product, substantial long-run gains in understanding may occur.

The danger with conjoint analysis is that it may be used naïvely without considering the issues discussed earlier. In particular, users should be concerned about, or avoid:

1. Making any inferences beyond the range of attribute levels tested. In our example, the manager must *not* assume that a price of $.45 would add even more utility. At some unknown price point, consumers might conclude the product is low quality and not buy it. This is true for all attributes tested.

2. Assuming that the calculated importance level for an attribute reflects its actual importance. A low level of importance simply means that the attribute levels tested were viewed similarly. In our example, name had a low importance score because the three names did not affect preference. This could occur if "name" is of *critical* importance but three equally desirable (or undesirable) names are tested.

3. Predicting market response if key attributes are missing. Conjoint analysis allows the construction of an optimal combination of *the attributes tested.* Untested attributes may completely distort the predicted results. In our example, the cat food's aroma, appearance, taste (from the cat's perspective), package design, and a host of other variables will influence sales but are not tested in the conjoint study.

Perceptual Mapping

Perceptual mapping encompasses a variety of mathematical approaches designed to place or describe consumers' perceptions of brands or other objects on one or a series of "spatial maps" such that the relationship between brands can be easily seen. Suppose you were asked to locate Dr. Pepper, Classic Coke, Tab, Diet Coke, Sprite, 7-Up and your "ideal" soft drink on the two dimensional map below. Chances are you could do so without much difficulty.

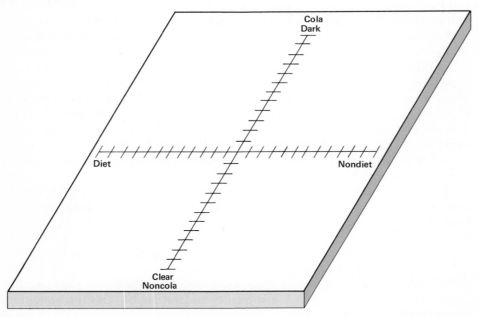

Even with such a simple procedure, valuable information would be obtained if you represented a sizeable market segment. For example, brands located close together would be in direct competition and brands closest to your ideal brand would probably get most of your business. Of course, this assumes that (1) the two dimensions are the only two relevant to your purchase, and (2) our simple measurement system accurately reflects your perceptions and desires.

Perceptual mapping techniques are designed to accomplish four major tasks related to the two assumptions just described:

1. to determine the number of dimensions consumers use to distinguish between or choose from among products, packages, and so forth;
2. to provide insights into the nature or characteristics of these dimensions;
3. to locate brands or other objects on these dimensions as consumers perceive them; and
4. to determine the preferred location of a brand on each of the relevant dimensions.

As Figure 12–2 indicates, there are two major approaches to creating perceptual maps—attribute-based and nonattribute-based—each of which can be further subdivided. While there are fundamental differences among

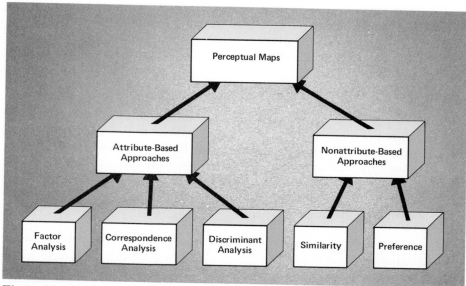

Figure 12–2 *Basic Approaches to Generating Perceptual Maps*

the assumptions underlying each approach, each attempts to derive mathematically the structure of a consumer's psychological view of a product category (or other stimulus domain). That is, the approaches seek to map the structure of consumers' perceptions of both existing and ideal products without having the consumer do so directly.

Attribute-Based Perceptual Maps

Attribute-based approaches require respondents to evaluate a set of brands or other objects on a large number of attributes.[14] This is typically done using semantic differential or Likert scales, as described in the previous chapter. The fundamental assumption of attribute-based techniques is that respondent ratings or judgments about specific attributes are manifestations of the underlying or latent dimensions that consumers use to distinguish between brands. Thus, attributes such as helpful salespersons, good service, friendly, and easy-to-return merchandise may represent a dimension such as "easy to do business with," which consumers use to compare outlets.

Both psychological theory and empirical tests indicate that the assumption that consumers use relatively few dimensions to compare brands or objects is valid. However, in order for attribute-based approaches to isolate the complete set of underlying dimensions, the set of attributes that the researcher provides to the consumer must be complete. For example, consumers may use *ease of access* as a dimension in comparing supermarkets. This dimension could be reflected by such attributes as "ample parking," "no traffic congestion," and "close by." If these or similar attributes are not included on the semantic differential, the underlying dimensions cannot be recovered.

We will describe the three attribute-based perceptual mapping techniques — factor analysis, discriminant analysis, and correspondence analysis.

Factor Analysis

Factor analysis is a set of mathematical techniques designed to analyze the interrelationships among a large number of variables such as consumer ratings of numerous product attributes and to explain these variables in terms of their common underlying dimensions (factors). A more detailed coverage of factor analysis procedures is provided in Chapter 20 (pages 627–631). Here we will describe the use of factor analysis output to construct perceptual maps.

The basic process is:

1. Respondents rate each of n brands or other objects on each of i attributes.

2. A computerized factor analysis program using this data and judgmental decisions by the researcher (see pages 628–630) isolates j dimensions called *factors* (generally 2–5). A *factor loading* score indicates

the nature of the association between each attribute and each factor. A measure of the variance in the original data explained by that factor is also provided. This is often interpreted (with caution) as an indicator of the importance of that factor.

3. The computer program provides a *factor score* for each individual for each brand. This represents the position of that brand on the underlying dimension as seen by that individual.

4. The average factor scores across individuals for each brand are used to position the brands in the perceptual map, with the factors serving as axes. Thus, it is important that the respondents have reasonably similar perceptions of the brand set.

5. The original attributes (or a subset of the more important or interesting ones) are incorporated into the map as lines or vectors such that the direction of the line indicates the nature of its association with each of the factors and the length of the line represents the strength of that association.

We will illustrate these steps with a *very* simple example. Suppose a segment of consumers have rated 11 brands of beer using a 10-point rating scale on the dimensions shown in Table 12–3. Table 12–3 also shows the factor loadings

Table 12–3 Factor Loadings for a Beer Study

Attributes	*Factor Loadings*		
	I	*II*	*III*
Masculine	.52	.21	−.10
Expensive	.14	.91	−.32
Strong	.83	.12	−.08
Filling	.52	.08	−.13
Light	−.67	.34	.20
Low Quality	−.08	−.67	.16
Exclusive	.32	.24	−.62
High Status	.02	.79	−.27
Malty	.52	−.18	−.01
Pale	−.67	−.16	.22
Popular	−.21	.03	.88
Thirst-quenching	.21	.02	.32
Young	−.26	−.04	.45
Thin	−.58	.05	.18
Convenient	−.16	.11	.62
Eigen value	5.91	4.86	1.44
Explained Variance	39.4	32.4	6.67

derived from a 3-factor principal component factor analysis and the variance explained by each component. Together, the 3 factors explain over 80 per cent of the variance in the original consumer ratings.

Table 12–4 contains the average factor scores for each of the 11 brands rated by the consumers. Figure 12–3 places each of these brands in a two-dimensional perceptual map based on the first two factors by using the two factor scores as coordinates. Seven of the 15 attributes are also shown on the map by using their factor loadings as coordinates. Two additional maps — one for Factors I and III and one for Factors II and III — would provide a complete set for this solution.

It would have been possible to include the location of one or more segment's ideal or preferred brands on this map by a variety of means. The simplest would be to include "your ideal brand" as one of the original set of brands rated by the respondents. This would produce a set of factor scores for each individual's "ideal brand." These sets of factor scores would then be grouped such that individuals with similar ideal brands would be considered a market segment. The average factor scores of each segment would be used to place each segment's ideal brand on the map. This is generally done using circles such that the size of the circle is proportional to the size of the segment represented by that ideal point.

This approach is subject to the problems described at the beginning of this chapter, particularly the "more-is-better" problem. However, there are occasions such as this one where the method could work reasonably well because most of the attributes measured do not imply that more (or less) is better. Nonetheless, ideal brand descriptions developed in this manner should be used with caution and should be verified with such techniques as conjoint

Table 12–4 Average Factor Scores for a Beer Study

	Factor		
	I	II	III
1. Amstel Light	−1.40	1.82	−.63
2. Budweiser	.87	.43	1.42
3. Bud Lite	−.65	.56	1.01
4. Coors	−.45	.12	.68
5. Coors Lite	−1.93	.06	.18
6. Corona	−.21	1.32	1.05
7. Michelob	1.13	1.68	−.52
8. Miller	−.21	−.21	.25
9. Miller Lite	−1.01	.19	.45
10. Pabst	.21	−.85	.30
11. Samuel Adams	1.87	1.15	−1.60

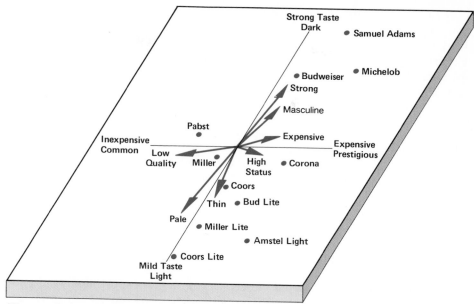

Figure 12–3 *Two-Dimensional Perceptual Map from a Beer Study*

analysis if possible. A special computer program, **PREFMAP**, described later in this chapter, is a better alternative.

An examination of Tables 12 – 3, 12 – 4, and Figure 12 – 3 reveals the value of this approach even without the inclusion of ideal points. Among the many insights about this segment of consumers are (1) they evaluate beers in terms of strong/mild taste, prestige, and popularity, (2) Coors is viewed similarly to Lite beers, and (3) Corona has obtained success by finding a unique product position. Of course, a complete analysis would involve all relevant competitors and market segments.

Discriminant Analysis

As stated, factor analysis attempts to reduce a data set to a set of underlying dimensions that are interpretable and to explain the variance in the original data set. Discriminant analysis seeks to generate dimensions that will separate the brands or objects as much as possible. While somewhat complex to calculate, the procedure in discriminant analysis is roughly analogous to that described for factor analysis.[15] In general, factor analysis appears to produce richer solutions and is more widely used.[16]

Correspondence Analysis

Both factor analysis and discriminant analysis require that the attribute evaluations be interval (or at least "near" interval data). However, a substantial

amount of marketing data is nominal or ordinal in nature: a car has airconditioning or does not have airconditioning, a respondent is male or female, a
drink is too sweet, just right, or not sweet enough, blue is preferred to red
which is preferred to green, and so on. Such nominal and ordinal data are often
accompanied by interval data on other attributes.

Correspondence analysis allows the creation of perceptual maps using
categorical data as well as mixed data sets (nominal, ordinal, and/or interval).[17]
While the computations are complex, personal computer software is rapidly
becoming available and correspondence analysis has gained widespread acceptance.[18]

An example from a study of automobiles indicates the value of this technique. A manufacturer was evaluating potential revisions of both its base
model and its premier model of a particular line. The firm had nominal data
(applies/does not apply) on a large number of attributes for the two current
models and mock-ups of the proposed new models.

A correspondence analysis produced the perceptual map shown in Exhibit
12–2. The two axes were labeled sporty/practical and comfort/performance.
This indicates that these respondents view sporty and practical as incompati-
ble or as trade offs. That is, a car viewed as very high in sportiness would not
also be viewed as highly practical. The same is true for comfort and performance.

The perceptual map also indicates the location of the two existing and the
two revised models in relationship to the two perceptual dimensions. As can
be seen, relative to the current models, the proposed models are viewed as
substantially more comfortable and less performance oriented.

Nonattribute Based Perceptual Maps (MDS)

As we saw in the previous section, attribute-based perceptual maps are derived by having respondents evaluate brands or objects on numerous attributes; then, various mathematical procedures are applied to uncover the
underlying dimensions consumers use to evaluate the brands. These procedures are relatively straightforward, use readily available software, and generally produce dimensions that are easy to name and understand. Unfortunately,
they require the researcher to develop a complete set of attributes *in advance*
and they force respondents to consider attributes representing dimensions
that they might not normally use.

Nonattribute based techniques are generally referred to as *multidimensional scaling (MDS)*.[19] In fact, MDS is occasionally used to refer to both
attribute and nonattribute-based approaches. However, we will restrict our
use to nonattribute mapping techniques.

MDS overcomes the weaknesses associated with the attribute-based approaches. In MDS, consumers do *not* rate brands on individual attributes.

Exhibit 12-2 Correspondence Analysis of a Proposed Automobile Model Revision

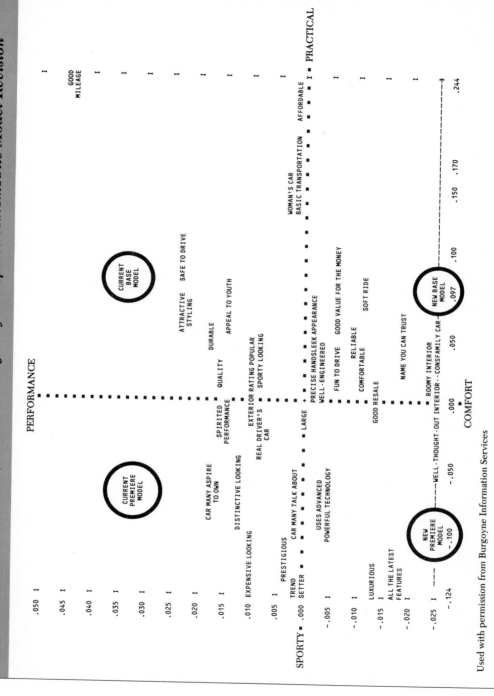

Used with permission from Burgoyne Information Services

Instead, they rate brands in terms of similarity or, less frequently, preference. A computer program then derives the number of dimensions and the location of each brand on each dimension that would be required to duplicate the consumer's similarity or preference judgments (an example presented shortly will make this clearer). Thus, the researcher does *not* supply the attributes in advance and the respondents use their normal, implicit criteria in making their judgments.

These advantages are acquired at the expense of dimensions that are more difficult to name and understand. In addition, special computer programs based on rather esoteric mathematical procedures are required. While these programs are increasingly available for PC's, the sophisticated nature of the underlying mathematics increases the likelihood that they will be used inappropriately. Finally, although the researcher need not supply any attributes, a comprehensive set of brands or other subjects is required.

A Simple MDS Example

Whereas marketers use MDS to understand consumers' *perceptions* of the relationships between brands, firms, or other objects of interest, we can illustrate the process more clearly by using a concrete example. The lower left half of Table 12–5 presents the approximate straightline distances (air miles) between 10 European cities. This represents a form of similarities data where cities closest together are more similar in terms of distance than are cities that are further apart.

If we put this data into an MDS program, would we be able to produce a two-dimensional map that duplicates these cities' positions in Europe? The answer is yes. In fact, a virtually error-free duplication would result. Notice that the input data in this case are distances in miles. These data are at least interval in nature and so are termed *metric*. MDS techniques that require metric input are termed *metric multidimensional scaling* techniques. The out-

Table 12–5 Straightline Distances Between European Cities

	Amst	Berlin	Brussels	Gibrlt	London	Madrid	Munich	Oslo	Paris	Rome
Amsterdam		9	1	41	5	33	12	17	6	27
Berlin	360		11	43	19	39	8	15	16	25
Brussels	110	405		38	3	29	10	21	2	24
Gibralter	1230	1455	1125		37	7	40	45	35	36
London	225	580	200	1090		26	18	23	4	32
Madrid	920	1165	820	305	785		34	44	20	31
Munich	415	310	375	1200	570	925		28	13	14
Oslo	565	520	675	1795	720	1485	815		30	42
Paris	265	550	165	960	210	655	425	835		22
Rome	805	735	730	1035	890	850	435	1250	690	

put of such techniques, the coordinates of objects on multiple dimensions, is also metric.

The upper right half of Table 12–5 replaces the metric input table with an ordinal table. That is, all the pairs of cities are now rank ordered in terms of their closeness, with Amsterdam-Brussels being closest and Gibralter-Oslo being furthest apart. If ordinal or *nonmetric* input data such as these are used, then a *nonmetric multidimensional scaling* technique must be used. Metric and nonmetric techniques generally provide similar solutions. Since nonmetric data are generally easier to collect, nonmetric MDS techniques are most common in marketing.

We can illustrate the MDS process using the ordinal data in Table 12–5. We start by constructing an arbitrary scale using one dimension and placing Amsterdam (Am), Brussels (Br), and London (Lo) on the scale such that the distance between Amsterdam and Brussels is less than the distance between Amsterdam and London or London and Brussels *and* the distance between Amsterdam and London is more than the distance between London and Brussels:

	Am	Br	Lo	

−10 −9 −8 −7 −6 −5 −4 −3 −2 −1 0 1 2 3 4 5 6 7 8 9 10

Now we need to add Paris (Pa) to the scale in a manner that will preserve the following order in terms of closeness of pairs (based on Table 12–5): Am/Br, Pa/Br, Lo/Br, Lo/Pa, Am/Lo, Am/Pa. This cannot be done in one dimension. However, adding a second dimension makes it possible:

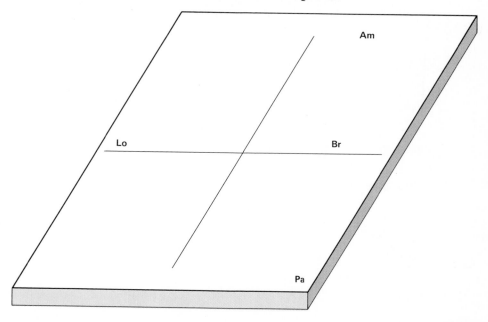

Unfortunately, even though the map just presented looks reasonable, a virtually infinite number of configurations could be derived that would preserve the original rank order relationships of 4 cities or other objects in a two-dimension space. However, as we add cities, the number of possible two-dimensional configurations is reduced and our MDS map will increasingly resemble a map of Europe. Figure 12–4 illustrates the relative positions of the 10 cities in Table 12–5 as derived from the ordinal data using the SYSTAT MDS program.[20]

Figure 12–4 *European City Locations Based on an MDS Analysis of Rank Order Distances*

Obviously there is little value in using sophisticated techniques to map a known reality. MDS techniques are useful to marketers for deriving psychological or perceptual maps. For marketers, consumers' perceptions of reality count as much as "objective" reality, because consumers' behaviors are based on their perceptions. For example, if asked to rank the distance between pairs of cities, a European manager might perceive distance in terms of ability to drive versus fly, customs-clearance requirements, distance of the airport from town, frequency of flights, traffic congestion, and so forth. Thus, a traveler might rate Gibralter and Madrid to be furthest apart due to the absence of direct flights between the two cities. Such "distortions" would produce a very different map from that given in Figure 12–4. However, this perceptual map would be the one that would influence the individual's travel behavior.

Joint Space Maps

The maps shown in Figures 12–3 and 12–4 are *simple space* maps because only one set of objects are rated and displayed. At times, it is desirable to create *joint space* maps in which distinct sets of objects are scaled simultaneously, particularly brands and consumer preferences.

While Figure 12–3 reveals a number of very useful insights into the structure of the beer market as represented by 11 beer brands, it does not provide any direct guidance about where a brand *should* be positioned to attract a particular consumer or market segment. As discussed earlier, it is possible with attribute-based approaches to have consumers rate their ideal brand along with the actual brands. Consumers would generally consume those brands perceived to be most similar to the ideal brand. Unfortunately, direct scaling of ideal points is subject to the numerous measurement problems previously described. Further, such a process is possible only with attribute-based scaling procedures.

A variety of alternative approaches exist for scaling individual or average (for segments) ideal points on perceptual maps using preference data. An extremely simplified example will make the logic if not the process of this approach clear. Suppose an individual rank-ordered his or her preferences for the 11 brands used to create Figure 12–3 as follows (1 being most preferred): (1) Michelob, (2) Corona, (3) Budweiser, (4) Bud Lite, (5) Amstel Lite, (6) Samuel Adams, (7) Coors, (8) Miller, (9) Miller Lite. (10) Pabst, and (11) Coors Lite. The basic task, then, is to locate a point on Figure 12–3 such that the distances from this point will preserve the rank order of preferences. That is, Michelob should be closest to the ideal point, Corona second closest, and so forth. The point I_1 in Figure 12–5, satisfies this requirement. If I_1 represented a segment of reasonable size, it would suggest positioning a brand as very prestigious and somewhat stronger than Corona but milder than Michelob. What preference ranking and marketing strategy are implied by I_2 in Figure 12–5?

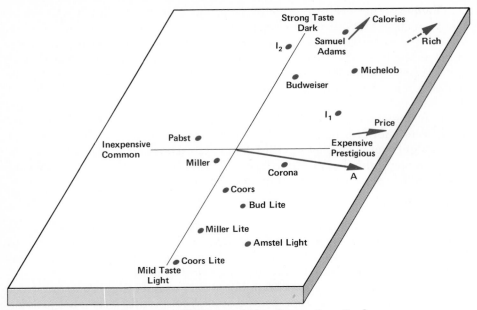

Figure 12-5   *Two-Dimensional Perceptual Map from a Beer Study*

The actual techniques that are used to locate ideal points are substantially more complex than implied by the above description, but the logic is similar. There are two fundamental approaches to generating ideal points and two types of ideal points. *Internal analysis* generates ideal points from the same preference data that is used to generate the object space. These techniques are adopted when the original data matrix is based on preferences rather than on similarities. This approach is generally inferior to external analysis.

External analysis involves plotting preferences in a multidimensional space derived independently from the preference measures. This was the approach we used in placing the ideal point in Figure 12-5. PREFMAP, a popular program for external analyses, is described in Table 12-6.

Preferences can be plotted as either ideal points or as directional vectors. Vectors represent a "preferred direction" for an individual or segment. Thus, vector A in Figure 12-5 indicates that preference increases sharply with prestige and that it increases somewhat with mild taste. Vectors are simpler than ideal points and are appropriate in "more-is-better" situations such as those involving fuel economy and safety. However, for many consumers "more status" in a beverage or other product is good up to a point; after that point, increases in status become undesirable. In such situations, ideal points rather than vectors should be used.

It is also possible to place external scales onto perceptual maps derived by either MDS or attribute-based techniques. These scales can be objective —

Table 12–6   Popular MDS Programs

ALSCAL is a versatile program that is part of the SAS system. It will handle metric and nonmetric input data and can create joint space maps based on internal analysis. It can handle individual differences in perceptions. It can also take attribute ratings (i.e., semantic differential scales) on a set of brands and convert these into similarities data for subsequent analysis.

INDSCAL is a widely used program based on similarities data. It can evaluate individual differences in perceptions. It produces simple space maps.

MDPREF is based on preference data. It can produce joint space maps indicating preference vectors for individual consumers (or segments), using internal analysis and dimension coordinates for objects.

MDSCAL 5M is a versatile program with a number of scaling options. It uses metric or nonmetric similarities data. It can also generate internal analysis ideal points and joint space maps.

TORSCA 9 is a nonmetric similarities based program that can input ranks or estimates of similarities.

KYST is a blend of **TORSCA 9** and **MDSCAL 5M**. It will handle both metric and nonmetric input data. It can generate joint space maps using internal analysis.

PREFMAP takes a known spatial configuration of brands or other objects (derived from other MDS or attribute-based programs) and maps either preference vectors or ideal points onto the original map based on preference rankings.

PROFIT also starts with a known spatial map of brands derived by either **MDS** or attribute-based measures. It then maps vectors of independently scaled concepts (objective or subjective product characteristics) onto the same map.

such as calories, price, acidity, or advertising expenditures in our example. Or, they can be subjective, for example semantic differential scales measuring attributes such as masculine-feminine, strong-weak, bitter-sweet, and so forth.

These scales are generally shown on maps as the end points of vectors arrayed around the outer edges of the map. Different colors or dotted and solid arrows can be used to distinguish objective versus subjective vectors. The direction of the arrow can be interpreted as a measure of the correlation or fit of the concept represented by the arrow with the dimensions of the map.

The three scale vectors shown in Figure 12–5 reveal that the objective scale *price* is closely related to the prestige dimension and that *calories* is fairly closely related to the strong taste dimension. The subjective evaluation *rich* is related to both strong taste and prestige, though more closely with strong taste. **PROFIT** is the most commonly used program for fitting external scales onto perceptual maps (see Table 12–6).

MDS Programs

MDS analyses require computer programs. Fortunately, a wide array of such programs are now available in PC as well as mainframe versions.[21] Table 12–6 provides very brief descriptions of several widely used programs. While the software for many of these are quite user friendly, MDS is a complex procedure based on a number of assumptions. One is generally well advised to secure expert advice when using these techniques.

Issues in Using MDS

A variety of issues are involved in using MDS. Several of the more important ones are described in this section.

Inputs.   The input for an MDS analysis can be similarities or preferences data. With *preference data,* consumers rank brands in terms of their preference for them. The theory underlying MDS analyses of preference data is that brands near each other in a preference rating are similar on the dimensions a consumer uses in forming those preferences.

Preference-based models will thus provide dimensions related to preference or choice. These may well be different from, and fewer than, those used to compare brands in a nonevaluative manner. Thus, a "price" shopper may prefer brands based solely on relative price (one dimension) but may perceive numerous other dimensions that distinguish brands.

Similarities data are likely to reveal more comprehensive structures, and they are most widely used. It should be noted that *dissimilarities data,* a term also widely used, is simply the inverse of similarities data.

Another input-related issue involves the number of brands or objects that should be evaluated. The more objects evaluated, the more precisely the derived map will reflect the actual perceptions. However, increasing the number of brands greatly increases the burden on respondents. For example, rank ordering the similarity of 8 brands would require ranking 28 pairs of brands from most to least similar. Adding just 3 more brands doubles the task to 55 pairs to rank! The formula is:

$$\frac{N(N-1)}{2}$$

A general rule of thumb is that there should be a minimum of 3 objects for every dimension that one might uncover. Thus, a 4-dimensional solution should be based on an evaluation of at least 12 brands.

Scaling Method.   Selection of the scaling method and the input method are interdependent. However, a variety of scaling methods exist for most input formats. The selected method depends on the assumptions being made about the nature of the perceptions and preferences involved, availability of software, sample sizes, and other technical features.

Number of Dimensions.   Most MDS programs will extract any number of dimensions from 1 to $N - 1$, where N is the number of objects being evaluated. The general objective is to achieve a good fit (reproduce the original rank ordering or other input data as closely as possible using the interbrand distances on the map), using as few dimensions as possible. Fit will generally improve with each added dimension.

In practice, researchers often produce solutions in 1 through 4 or 5 dimensions. The best number of dimensions may then be determined subjectively as the map that provides the best interpretation (fits theory or simply "makes sense"). It is preferable to use statistical measures of fit instead of, or in conjunction with, subjective evaluations.

Some MDS techniques such as ALSCAL provide an *R-square* measure of fit, which is interpreted in the same manner for the MDS solution as it is in regression analysis. That is, it is a value between 0 and 1 that reflects the proportion of variance in the original data set explained by the MDS solution.

Other MDS programs use *stress* as a measure of fit. There are several ways to calculate stress. However, smaller values are better. With Kruskal's stress measure (a common one), stress above .1 is not acceptable and a level below .05 is desirable. The Kruskal stress for Figure 12–4 is .00042. A one-dimension solution produced an unacceptable stress level of .15.

Naming/Understanding Dimensions.   It is sometimes very difficult to understand the nature of a dimension. The first approach is to look at the positions of various brands on each dimension. This works perfectly for Figure 12–4 and reasonably well for Figure 12–5. However, the process is often more difficult than is implied by these two examples, particularly when more than two dimensions are derived.

Scaling independently collected subjective and objective measures of the brands onto the same map via PROFIT (Table 12–6) can provide very useful insights into the nature of each dimension. However, it is important to be aware that the labels applied to dimensions are subjective. Reasonable researchers sometimes provide sharply differing labels for the same map.

Aggregation.   The various MDS programs differ in *if* and *how* they handle individual variations in perceptions. In general, it is best to aggregate the perceptual data prior to the MDS analysis. That is, the similarities or preference data from the sample should be analyzed (generally via cluster analysis) to form groups with relatively homogeneous perceptions. Then a separate MDS analysis should be conducted for each group, using the average perceptions of the group. In fact, this approach is one way in which MDS is used to identify and understand market segments.

Conclusions on Perceptual Mapping

Perceptual mapping has been used in marketing research since the early 1970s. However, the rapid diffusion of computer power and software is exploding its use today.[22] It offers tremendous power as an aid to understanding consumer perceptions.

Review Questions

12.1. What is *conjoint analysis?*

12.2. What is the purpose of conjoint analysis? What advantages does it have over direct approaches?

12.3. How can conjoint analysis be used to assess a consumer's preference level for a combination of attributes that he or she has not evaluated?

12.4. What is the difference between *full profile* and *pairwise* conjoint analysis? What is superior? Why?

12.5. What is a *utility* or *part-worth?*

12.6. What is a *fractional factorial orthogonal array?*

12.7. What do consumers evaluate in a full profile conjoint study?

12.8. How does one select the attributes to include in a conjoint study?

12.9. How does one determine the levels of each attribute to use in a conjoint study?

12.10. Describe *effects coding* for dummy variable regression analysis (Appendix C).

12.11. How does one calculate and interpret *attribute importance scores* in conjoint analysis?

12.12. How do you determine if conjoint analysis is the appropriate technique for a given problem?

12.13. Why do the attributes tested in a conjoint study need to be relatively independent?

12.14. What issues arise concerning *price* as an attribute in a conjoint study?

12.15. How do you determine if, and how, to aggregate utilities across respondents?

12.16. How is conjoint output used to estimate market share?

12.17. What is *perceptual mapping?* What is it used for?

12.18. What is the difference between *attribute-based* and *nonattribute-based* perceptual maps?

12.19. What is *factor analysis?* How is it used to create a perceptual map?

12.20. What is a *factor?* a *factor score?* a *factor loading?*

12.21. How can one locate *ideal points* on an attribute-based perceptual map?

12.22. What is *discriminant analysis?*

12.23. What is *correspondence analysis?*

12.24. What is *multidimensional scaling* (MDS)? What is it used for?

12.25. What advantages and disadvantages does MDS have compared to attribute-based approaches?

12.26. What is the difference between *metric* and *nonmetric* multidimensional scaling?

12.27. What is the difference between *simple space* maps and *joint space* maps?

12.28. What is the difference between *internal analysis* and *external analysis* for creating joint space maps? Which is generally superior?

12.29. What is the difference between an *ideal point* and a *preference vector*? When is each appropriate?

12.30. How can one map externally scaled features into a perceptual map?

12.31. What are the differences among *similarities data, dissimilarities data,* and *preference data?* Which is generally superior for MDS applications?

12.32. Briefly describe ALSCAL, INDSCAL, MDPREF, PREFMAP, and PROFIT.

12.33. How many objects should be included in an MDS study?

12.34. How do you determine how many dimensions to use in an MDS solution?

12.35. How do you name the dimensions in an MDS solution?

12.36. When and how do you aggregate perceptions in MDS studies?

Discussion Questions/Problems

12.37. Develop a product concept with at least 5 attributes, with 2 to 4 levels each. Develop a complete set of pairwise tables and complete them. How much effort was involved in completing the tables? What, if any, measurement errors would concern you if you used this methodology?

12.38. Develop a product concept of interest, with the same number of attributes and levels as the cat food example in the text. Using the cat food example as a model, develop a full profile stimulus set. Rank order this set in terms of your preferences. What, if any, measurement errors would concern you if you used this methodology?

12.39. Code your response to 12–38 using effects coding for dummy variable regression analysis (Appendix C). Make up a reasonable output and provide a complete interpretation.

12.40. Provide a complete interpretation of Table 12–2 and Figure 12–1.

12.41. Provide a complete interpretation of Tables 12–3, 12–4, and Figure 12–3.

12.42. Are attribute-based or nonattribute-based approaches to perceptual mapping superior? Why?

12.43. Provide a complete interpretation of Figure 12–5.

12.44. How do you think MDS techniques are most likely to be misused?

Projects

12.45. Analyze the data from 12–39 and prepare a brief managerial report, assuming your responses are typical for a market segment.

12.46. Repeat 12–38, having two fellow students rank the combinations. Analyze their responses via dummy variable regression analysis. Discuss the resulting utility profiles with them.

12.47. Check your mainframe and microcomputer centers. Prepare brief descriptions of the various _____ programs available on your campus.
  a. conjoint
  b. MDS

12.48. Select a product category of interest, with at least 10 brands familiar to students. Using a sample of one, collect semantic differential data on each brand, similarities data, and preference data.
  a. construct an attribute-based simple space map and interpret it.
  b. construct a similarities-based **MDS** simple space map and interpret it.
  c. construct a preference-based **MDS** simple space map and interpret it.
  d. using external analysis, add a preference vector to *a, b,* and *c.* Interpret the results.
  e. using external analysis, add an ideal point to *a, b,* and *c.* Show the results.
  f. using **PROFIT** (or another relevant technique), plot the semantic differential items onto b and c and interpret the results.

12.49. Repeat 12–48, using the following fruits: (1) apple, (2) banana, (3) peach, (4) pear, (5) plum, (6) orange, (7) nectarine, (8) tangerine, (9) kiwi, (10) papaya, (11) mango.

References

[1] A. L. Page and H. F. Rosenbaum, "Redesigning Product Lines with Conjoint Analysis," *Journal of Product Innovation Management* (#4, 1987), 120–37.

[2] This section is based on an unpublished paper by David Santee of Hallmark Cards, and J. Morton and H. J. Devine, Jr., "How to Diagnose What Buyers Really Want," *Business Marketing* (October 1985), 71–83.

[3] For a comparison of conjoint with other attribute importance measures see J. Jaccard, D. Brinberg, and L. J. Ackerman, "Assessing Attribute Importance," *Journal of Consumer Research* (March 1986), 463–68.

[4] See P. E. Green, "On the Design of Experiments Involving Multiattribute Alternatives," *Journal of Consumer Research* (September 1974), 61.

[5] See *Conjoint Designer* (New York: Bretton-Clark, 1985).

[6] S. Addelman, "Orthogonal Main-Effect Plans for Asymmetrical Factorial Experiments," *Technometrics* (#1 1962), 21–46.

[7] For issues on this area, see R. K. Teas, "Magnitude Scaling of the Dependent Variable in Decompositional Multiattribute Preference Models," *Journal of the Academy of Marketing Science* (Fall 1987), 64–73.

[8] See R. Kohli, "Assessing Attribute Significance in Conjoint Analysis," *Journal of Marketing Research* (May 1988), 123–33.

[9] V. Srinivasan and A. D. Shocker, *LINMAP Version IV — User's Manual* (Nashville, Tenn.: Vanderbilt University, 1981).

[10] See P. E. Green and V. R. Rao, "Conjoint Measurement of Quantifying Judgement Data," *Journal of Marketing Research* (August 1971), 355–65.

[11] See P. E. Green, A. M. Krieger, and P. Bansal, "Completely Unacceptable Levels in Conjoint Analysis," *Journal of Marketing Research* (August 1988) 293–300.

[12] For differing approaches see N. E. Marr, "A Method for the Aggregation of the Results in a Conjoint Measurement Study," *European Research* (November 1987), 257–63; and W. A. Kamakura, "A Least Squares Procedure for Benefit Segmentation with Conjoint Experiments," *Journal of Marketing Research* (May 1988), 157–67.

[13] A survey of applications is P. Catlin and D. R. Wittink, "Commercial Use of Conjoint Analysis," *Journal of Marketing* (Summer 1982), 44–53. Detailed application examples are in D. Tantiwong and P. C. Wilton, "Understanding Food Store Preferences Among the Elderly Using Hybrid Conjoint Measurement Models," *Journal of Retailing* (Winter 1985), 35–64; L. P. June and S. L. J. Smith, "Service Attributes and Situational Effects On Customer Preferences for Restaurant Dining," *Journal of Travel Research* (Fall 1987), 20–27; and P. E. Green and A. M. Krieger, "A Consumer-Based Approach to Designing Product Line Extensions," *Journal of Product Innovation Management* (#4, 1987), 21–32.

[14] This portion of this chapter is based on D. A. Aaker, "Multidimensional Scaling," in D. A. Aaker, *Multivariate Analysis in Marketing* (Palo Alto, Calif.: *The Scientific Press*, 1981) 185–192; and J. F. Hair, Jr., R. E. Anderson, and R. L. Tatham, *Multivariate Data Analysis*, (New York: Macmillan Publishing Co., 1987), 233–61.

[15] See Hair, Anderson, and Tatham, op. cit., 73–144; and D. R. Lehmann, *Market Research and Analysis* (Homewood, Ill.: Irwin, 1989), 691–95.

[16] See J. R. Hauser and F. S. Koppelman, "Alternative Perceptual Mapping Techniques," *Journal of Marketing Research* (November 1979), 495–506.

[17] D. L. Hoffman and G. R. Franke, "Correspondence Analysis," *Journal of Marketing Research* (August 1986), 213–27.

[18] For software, see S. Smith, *PC-MDS: Multidimensional Scaling and Conjoint Analysis Version 4.1* (Provo, Utah 1987).

[19] This section is based heavily on Hair, Anderson, and Tatham, op. cit., 349–370; and P. E. Green and Y. Wind, *Multiattribute Decisions in Marketing* (Hinsdale, Ill.: The Dryden Press, 1973). An excellent detailed treatment of the topic with software is P. E. Green, F. J. Carmone, Jr., and S. M. Smith, *Multidimensional*

Scaling (Boston: Allyn and Bacon, 1989). See also M. L. Davidson, *Multidimensional Scaling* (New York: Wiley-Interscience, 1985), and S. S. Schiffman, M. L. Reynolds, and F. W. Young, *Introduction to Multidimensional Scaling* (New York: Academic Press, 1981).

[20] L. Wilkinson, *SYSTAT* (Evanston, Ill.: SYSTAT, 1986).

[21] Software program descriptions and software are available in S. Smith, *PC-MDS: Multidimensional Scaling and Conjoint Analysis, Version 4.1,* (Provo, Utah, 1987); and Green, Carmone, and Smith, op. cit. Descriptions and comparisons of programs are available in A. P. M. Coxon, *The User's Guide to Multidimensional Scaling* (London: Heinemann Educational Books, 1982).

[22] A review of applications is L. G. Cooper, "A Review of Multidimensional Scaling in Marketing Research," *Applied Psychological Measurement* (Fall 1983), 427–50.

CHAPTER 13

Qualitative Research

The marketing department of Curlee Clothing undertook a major marketing research effort to help management evaluate current advertising and product strategy. As part of this effort, it brought together various groups of 6 or 7 young men with similar demographic characteristics, such as college students, blue-collar workers, or sales representatives. These groups were placed in comfortable surroundings, provided refreshments, and asked to discuss clothing in terms of why and how they purchased it, their likes and dislikes, and so forth. Each session was taped and analyzed.

Management anticipated that the discussions would focus on styles, prices, quality, and perhaps advertising. However, what emerged from each session was a critical discussion of the retail sales personnel. Most of the individuals, once relaxed, expressed a feeling of insecurity in purchasing men's fashion-oriented clothing. This insecurity was coupled with a distrust of both the intentions and competence of the retail salesperson. As a result of these findings, Curlee embarked on a major effort at training the retail sales personnel through specially prepared films and training sessions.

The most common method of obtaining information about the behavior, attitudes, and other characteristics of people is to ask them. In Chapters 10 and 11 we were concerned with the preparation of structured, direct questionnaires for that purpose.

It is not always possible, or desirable, to use direct questioning to obtain information. People may be either *unwilling* or *unable* to give answers to questions they consider to be an invasion of their privacy, that adversely affect their self-perception or prestige, that are embarrassing, that concern motivations that they do not fully understand or cannot verbalize, or for other reasons. Therefore, additional approaches to obtaining such information may be necessary.

Depth interviews and *projective techniques* are frequently used by marketing researchers when direct questioning is impractical, more costly, or less accurate. These techniques, generally referred to as qualitative research, are described in this chapter.[1]

Depth Interviews

Depth interviews can involve one respondent and one interviewer or they may involve a small group (8 to 15 respondents) and an interviewer. The latter are called *focus group interviews,* and the former are termed *individual depth interviews* or *one-on-ones.* Groups of 4 or 5 are often referred to as *minigroup interviews.*

Of the three "types" of depth interviews—*individual, minigroup,* and *focus group*—the focus group is by far the most popular. In fact, until recently, focus groups were virtually the only type of depth interview being used by marketing researchers. However, both individual and minigroup interviews are gaining greater usage.[2]

Individual Depth Interviews

Individual depth interviews typically require 30–45 minutes. The interviewer does not have a specific set of prespecified questions that must be asked according to the order imposed by a questionnaire. Instead, there is freedom to create questions, to probe those responses that appear relevant, and generally to try to develop the best set of data in any way practical. However, the interviewer must follow one rule: one must not consciously try to affect the content of the answers given by the respondent. The respondent must feel free to reply to the various questions, probes, and other, more subtle, ways of encouraging responses in the manner deemed most appropriate.

In addition to the relatively direct pursuit of detailed information as described, Durgee recommends three questioning techniques for use in individual depth interviews.[3] *Laddering* involves having respondents identify attributes that distinguish brands by asking questions such as "In what way is Pepsi different from Classic Coke and Dr. Pepper?" Each distinguishing attribute is then probed to determine why it is important or meaningful. These reasons are then probed to determine why they are important, and so forth. The purpose is to uncover the "network of meanings" associated with the product, brand, or concept.[4]

Hidden-issue questioning focuses on individual respondents' feelings about sensitive issues such as wanting to have an affair or having a desire for power. Analysis focuses on common underlying themes across respondents. These themes can then be used to guide advertising development. *Symbolic questioning* requires respondents to describe the opposites of the product/activity of interest or a specific attribute of the product/activity. For example, a segment might describe the opposite of beer as skim milk—thin, flat, watery, nonalcoholic, staid, healthy, but almost medicinal. This suggests that beer is perceived as lively, full, rich, fun, but not entirely good for you, which further suggests guilt about consuming it. Another segment might consider the opposite of beer to be fine wine—sophisticated, glamorous, upscale, expensive, subtle, and consumed primarily with excellent food. This suggests that they view beer as unsophisticated, common, inexpensive, straightforward, and inappropriate with good food. Obviously, these two segments would require dramatically different marketing approaches.

Individual depth interviews have been found to generate more and higher quality ideas on a per respondent basis than either focus or mini groups.[5] They are particularly appropriate when:

1. detailed probing of an individual's behavior, attitudes, or needs is required;
2. the subject matter under discussion is likely to be of a highly confidential nature (e.g., personal investments);
3. the subject matter is of an emotionally charged or embarrassing nature;
4. certain strong, socially acceptable norms exist (e.g., baby feeding) and the need to conform in a group discussion may influence responses;
5. where highly detailed (step-by-step) understanding of complicated behavior or decision-making patterns (e.g., planning the family holiday) are required; or
6. the interviews are with professional people or with people on the subject of their jobs (e.g., finance directors).

For example, one-on-one interviews were conducted for Merrill Lynch with individuals who make large financial investments.[6] This research revealed that the "Bullish on America" advertising theme that stressed patriotism did not appeal to this group. The heavy investor wanted an investment firm that would help him or her achieve larger financial gains. Merrill Lynch changed its advertising content and used a new theme—"A breed apart." It is quite possible that in a group setting these respondents would not have revealed the importance of financial gain relative to patriotism.

Exhibit 13–1 *Individual Depth Interviews in a High Technology Environment*

U.S. WEST, one of the seven regional telephone operating companies formed after the break-up of AT&T, launched a major research project to help it understand the evolving communications needs of its customers. One customer group of interest was composed of the large, sophisticated business and government users. These organizations viewed voice and data communications as either a key competitive tool or as a central cost center.

The initial phase of the research project involved specification of a population of such firms based on billings, growth, industry characteristics, and the judgment of industry experts. Next, a judgment sample of firms was selected to represent the relevant range of industries, firm size, communications applications, and in-house communications expertise.

The third phase involved extensive semistructured telephone interviews with the selected firms to identify the key participants in the evaluation of the firm's communications needs. Titles such as telecommunications manager, data communications manager, and information systems manager were most common, but a wide array of other job titles such as controller also appeared.

The one-to-two hour interviews took place at the respondent's location, either in his or her office or a conference room. The respondent was frequently assisted by one to four assistants such as engineers and computer scientists.

The interview involved a long semistructured questionnaire that served as a guideline, but the interviewer was not bound to follow it. The interview team consisted of a highly trained interviewer (graduate degree, extensive interviewing experience, experience with the telecommunications industry), an engineer or other technical person from U.S. WEST, and a member of the U.S. WEST research project team.

Each member of the interviewing team took notes during the interview and wrote out a long summary of his or her impressions and conclusions following the interview. The summary followed the format of the semistructured questionnaire to provide comparability across interviews. The interviews were also tape recorded so that additional notes and quotes could be taken. Finally, most respondents agreed to respond to telephone inquiries to clear up any uncertainty as the interviews were being analyzed.

One-on-ones are very common in industrial research. Exhibit 13–1 describes a particularly complicated industrial survey that used this approach.

At least one consulting firm is successfully conducting depth interviews by telephone. Using skilled interviewers, the firm has respondents tell stories about both typical and atypical times they have used a certain product. The interviewer probes for additional details concerning the story (how did you feel? how were you dressed? what else was happening?). A series of such interviews revealed that chicken and cooking chicken has strong, warm associations with home and family:

> I have such happy memories of the big family picnics on Labor Day. There was such excitement and anticipation. I remember my mother frying chicken all day in the kitchen, just enormous platters full. Everyone brought fried chicken, but she always made extra because hers was the best; the crustiest, the crispiest. She fried chicken from morning to night and would be just worn out, but it was worth it. The picnics were at my uncle's out in the country near Nashville. She put out picnic tables under the elm trees and everyone just ate and ate: potato salad, chicken, green beans, fried corn, cole slaw, baked beans, pecan pie. I want to convey those good memories to my son, and I always feel that way when I make my mother's fried chicken for him.[7]

Such associations provide useful information for product positioning and advertising decisions.

A vice-president of Elrick and Lavidge, a major consulting firm, describes the advantages and disadvantages of individual depth interviews as follows:

> Compared with group interviews, individual in-depth interviews can provide more detail, point out personal preferences and idiosyncrasies, and describe subtleties, nuances and shades of difference that are masked in the group setting. Such results cannot however be accomplished within the time and cost parameters generally associated with focus group studies. Interviewing 35 individuals in a series of four groups takes approximately one-fourth the time required to conduct one-on-ones with that same number on an individual basis.[8]

Another factor that must be considered when conducting individual in-depth studies is interviewer burn-out. No matter how experienced or intrepid the interviewer/discussion leader, it is not often possible to complete more than 4 or 5 hour-long interviews in one day without sacrificing quality.

It also should be kept in mind that whatever is said must be analyzed;[9] stimulus overload can also take place once the interviews are completed and the conversations are compiled.

Focus Group Interviews

The standard focus group interview involves 8 to 12 individuals. Normally, each group is designed to reflect the characteristics of a particular market segment. Exhibit 13–2 illustrates the importance of including groups from each major market segment. The respondents are selected according to the relevant sampling plan and meet at a central location that generally has facilities for taping and/or filming the interviews. The discussion itself is "led" by a moderator. The moderator attempts to develop 3 stages in the 1.5- to 3-hour interview: (1) establish rapport with the group, structure the rules of group interaction, and set objectives; (2) attempt to provoke intense discussion in the relevant areas; and (3) attempt to summarize the group's responses to determine the extent of agreement.

In general, either the moderator or a second person prepares a summary of each session after analyzing the session's transcript.

The following procedure is followed at one marketing research agency:

- Employ a relatively formal setting: a conference table in a large office within the agency (or similar facilities in other cities).

- Employ a one-way mirror and/or videotape, and overhead microphones which are connected to an audio recording system and to a loudspeaker in the observation room behind the mirror.

- Conduct panels of, typically, 10–12 consumers, using the following format:
  —After panelists enter and seat themselves and are given refreshments, there is a short *warm-up,* during which everyone including the moderator, introduces him(her)self to the rest of the group and "ground rules" for the interview are stated.
  —This is followed by a *predisposition* discussion, which concerns itself with the contexts in which the product is *bought, used,* and *thought about.* This will include general reactions to advertising in the product area generally.
  —We then introduce *materials:* concepts, rough or finished creative executions, products, etc., and ask panelists first to *write,* privately, their immediate reactions to each of the materials, and then to *discuss* it. This pattern of "write, then talk" is continued until all materials have been exposed.
  —After all materials have been discussed individually, there is usually a collective and comparative discussion of everything exposed to the respondents.
  —The discussion ends with the *wrap-up:* a summary statement of what panelists think the group as a whole has expressed during the interview.

—Before leaving, panelists complete a brief demographic question-naire and a self-administered projective instrument (drawings and stories).[10]

Focus group interviews can be applied to (1) basic-need studies for product idea creation, (2) new product idea or concept exploration, (3) product positioning studies, (4) advertising and communications research, (5) background studies on consumers' frames of reference, (6) establishment of consumer vocabulary as a preliminary step in questionnaire development, and (7) determination of attitudes and behaviors.

LKP International, a large advertising agency, uses what it terms *modular research* in designing advertisements. Modular research involves presenting every element that might appear in a particular advertisement to a focus group for a discussion of its appropriateness. For example, before LKP launched its Prego spaghetti sauce campaign, it used focus groups to identify the details of the setting—from room to pot to people—that would be most effective. Among other things, LKP learned that steel gourmet kitchens and formal dining rooms were inappropriate for the preparation and consumption of spaghetti.[11]

Exhibit 13–2 *Focus Group Discussions on Bread Consumption*

Four focus groups were held on bread consumption. The groups consisted of individuals who made most of the bread purchases for their households. The groups were organized by type of bread consumed. The following differing reactions of two groups indicate the importance of having separate focus groups from each major market segment.

Group 1 (Wheat-bread consumers, primarily middle-class)

Speaker	Comment	Group Reactions
Moderator:	Let's take just a minute and let me ask you one final question. Is there any advice that you would give a bakery about bread?	Several folding napkins, picking up coffee cups. It is at the end of the session.
Gayle (responding quickly):	Tell us more about what you put in and why.	All except Billie stop their preparations.

Joan (emphatically):	Yeah!	General nodding agreement but no one speaks.
Moderator:	More educational materials?	
Gayle:	Even if it was just posted in the bakery so you could just look. It wouldn't have to be on the package.	General nodding agreement from group.
Lori:	Give us a primer to tell us what all those long complicated words mean.	
Joan:	A lot of times, it will say "no preservatives" and then you read a lot of these words that you don't understand. The layman doesn't know. Those are not common words in my vocabulary.	Light laughter accompanied by nods of agreement.
Susan:	I think it would be nice to have just a little pamphlet that you could read. That they could tack it up there.	Billie looks at doors, others remain attentive.
Gayle:	I'd like to know that it is a real necessity that they add all those nonartificial preservatives. I understand that a smaller bakery like that (referring to a small local bakery discussed earlier) is selling things on a bigger turnover rate and not baking in such large quantities. I suppose that is why they don't have to add any preservatives at all.	Joan nods and starts to speak but Patty speaks first.
Patty:	A variety of sizes would be good. Maybe make this a smaller loaf too because when I am by myself I have to put half of it in the freezer.	The discussion shifts to package size, then to price. The session lasts about 5 more minutes.

Group 2   (White-bread consumers, primarily working-class)

		It is at the end of the session. Moderator has made several probes for "advice" for bakeries. Additional information has *not* been mentioned. The group is not particularly restless but is rather passive.
Moderator:	What about more information? Are any of you interested in bakeries doing more to educate you in terms of what all these things on the labels mean?	Several shrugs, no one speaks.
Moderator:	Would that be of interest to anybody?	Moderator looks around the room at the participants who appear to be thinking about the question.
Doug:	Don't they put their address on it for people who are interested in wanting to know more?	After a pause.
Moderator:	So you wouldn't be interested?	Sylvia and Ann nod, others seem uninterested.
Doug:	It just seeems like that most people who are interested in knowing more usually write.	A brief pause.
Moderator:	So no one here thinks that would be a good idea?	Most of the group nods.
Doris:	Would it be possible to find out why they don't identify McKenzie Farm bread as being made by Williams? It just says on the label: baked for McKenzie Farm bakery.	Group interest perks up somewhat.
Moderator:	That is a concern to you?	General discussion of private labels follows. Session ends after 10 more minutes.

Focus groups played a major role in the development of Fisher-Price's line of preschool playwear. Group members were mothers with children less than 6 years of age. The topics discussed were children's clothing and dressing children. The discussions revealed deep dissatisfaction with many of the functional aspects of children's clothing, particularly zippers, buckles, buttons, and other features that made it difficult for children to dress themselves. As one researcher summarized:"Oshkosh overalls are beautifully designed but kids being toilet trained need to be Houdini to get out of them." The new Fisher-Price line has Velcro fasteners, padded knees and elbows, extra-long shirttails, and cuffs that can be lowered as kids grow.[12]

Focus groups are also useful in industrial research. Weyerhaeuser has used such groups to analyze the purchasing process and problems encountered by building contractors. U.S. WEST used them in an analysis of demand for a new property maintenance service for "technologically sophisticated" buildings. This research revealed dramatic differences in the problems and needs confronting managers of public buildings (such as cities and universities) and managers of private buildings (such as IBM).

Advantages of Focus Groups

The interaction process induced by the group situation produces a number of *potential* advantages.[13] Each individual is able to expand and refine their opinions in the interactions with the other members. This process provides more detailed and accurate information than could be derived from each separately.

A group interview situation is generally more exciting and offers more *stimulation* to the participants than a standard depth interview. This heightened interest and excitement makes more meaningful comments likely. In addition, the *security* of being in a crowd encourages some members to speak out when they otherwise would not. Because any questions raised by the moderator are to the group as a whole rather than to individuals, the answers contain a degree of *spontaneity* not produced by other techniques. Furthermore, individuals are not under any pressure to "make up" answers to questions.

Focus groups can be used successfully with young children.[14] Such groups are also particularly valuable with adults in developing countries where literacy rates are low and survey research is difficult.[15]

A final, major advantage of focus groups is that executives often observe the interview (from behind mirrors) or watch films of the interviews. For many executives, this is their only "direct" contact with customers (dealers, suppliers, or whomever the research focuses on). This helps provide a "feel" for the market that is beyond the scope of the more quantitative approaches. Unfortunately, this dramatic impact causes some executives to place too much reliance on focus group results.

Disadvantages of Focus Group Interviews

Given these benefits, it is not surprising that focus group interviews are widely used. However, a number of disadvantages are associated with focus groups.[16] Since focus group interviews last 1.5 to 3 hours and take place at a central location, securing cooperation from a random sample is difficult. Those who attend group interviews and actively participate in them are likely to be different in many respects from those who do not. Participants may "play games" in the group setting,[17] go along with the group rather than express their own opinions, or otherwise provide inaccurate or incomplete information. One vocal person with a strong opinion on the topic being discussed may alter the expressed views of the group substantially.

The moderator can introduce serious biases in the interview by shifting topics too rapidly, verbally or nonverbally encouraging certain answers, failing to cover specific areas, and so forth. Focus groups are expensive on a per-respondent basis. Securing a sample, paying the participants, using a central location, and paying trained interviewers and analysts generally costs over $2,000 per group.

The combined effects of potential nonresponse errors, small sample sizes caused by high costs, abnormal behavior by participants, and the potential for interviewer effects makes generalization from a few focus groups to the larger population a risky undertaking. Unfortunately, many researchers and managers do make such generalizations. This tendency to generalize without adequate concern for the potential errors is a serious problem.

Focus groups, although widely used, remain controversial. Chrysler Corporation conducts over 13 thousand interviews a year, "many" of which are focus group interviews. In contrast, a research manager of Ford discounts focus groups, claiming that they "generate random, top-of-the-head remarks instead of substantive suggestions and ideas."[18]

Minigroups

Minigroups consist of a moderator and 4 or 5 respondents rather than the 8 to 12 used in most focus groups. They are used when the issue being investigated requires more extensive probing than is possible in a larger group.

Minigroups do not allow the collection of as confidential or highly sensitive data as might be possible in an individual depth interview. However, they do allow the researcher to obtain substantial depth of response on the topics that are covered. Further, the intimacy of the small group often allows discussion of quite sensitive issues. For example, Predictor, a home pregnancy test marketer, used minigroups, each composed of five women closely matched in terms of age and life cycle, to develop advertising for its product. The minigroups proved as effective as earlier one-on-ones and were more cost effective.[19]

The advantages and disadvantages of minigroups are similar to those of standard focus groups, but on a smaller scale.

Projective Techniques

Projective techniques are based on the theory that the description of vague objects requires interpretation, and this interpretation can only be based on the individual's own background, attitudes, and values. The more vague or ambiguous the object to be described, the more one must reveal of oneself in order to complete the description.

The following general categories of projective techniques are described: *association, completion, construction,* and *expression.* All of these techniques have been adopted from clinical psychology. Marketing researchers have tended to use these techniques out of context and to expect more from them than they were designed to deliver. However, when properly used, projective techniques can provide useful data.[20]

Association Techniques

Association techniques require the subject to respond to the presentation of a stimulus with the first thing or things that come to mind. The *word association* technique requires the respondent to give the first word or thought that comes to mind after the researcher presents a word or phrase. In *free word association,* only the first word or thought is required. In *successive word association,* the respondent is asked to give a series of words or thoughts that occur after hearing a given word. The respondent is generally read a number of relatively neutral terms to establish the technique. Then the words of interest to the researcher are presented, each separated by several neutral terms. The order of presentation of the key words is randomized to prevent any position or order bias from affecting the results.

The most common approach to analyzing the resulting data is to analyze the frequency with which a particular word or category of word (favorable, unfavorable, neutral) is given in response to the word of interest to the researcher.

Word association techniques are used in testing potential brand names and occasionally for measuring attitudes about particular products, product attributes, brands, packages, or advertisements.

Compton Advertising uses a version of this approach that it refers to as a *benefit chain.* A product, brand, or product description is shown to the respondent, who names all the benefits that possession or use of that product might provide. Then, for each benefit mentioned, the respondent is asked to name two other benefits. Then, for each of these benefits, the respondent is asked to name two more benefits. This continues until the respondent is unable to name additional benefits.

For example, a respondent might mention "fewer colds" as a benefit of taking a daily vitamin. When asked the benefit of fewer colds, one respondent might identify "more efficient at work" and "more energy." Another might name "more skiing" and "fewer problems dating."

A similar approach is to use the terms generated in either a free or successive word association task as the stimulus words in a second round of associations. For example, the term *soap* generates relatively few associations. Among these are *clean* and *fresh*. Clean and fresh, however, generate additional responses such as *free, relaxed, unhindered, nature, country,* and *sensual.*[21] The value of information of this type for product positioning and advertising is apparent.

Completion Techniques

Completion techniques require the respondent to complete an incomplete stimulus. Two types of completion techniques are of interest to marketing researchers — *sentence completion* and *story completion.*

Sentence completion, as the name implies, involves requiring the respondent to complete a sentence. To some extent, it merely rephrases an open-ended question. For example, the questions "What kind of people prefer filter cigarettes?" and "People who prefer filter cigarettes are _____" represent two approaches to the same information. However, in direct questioning, respondents are giving *their* answers. In most sentence-completion tests, the respondents are asked to complete the sentence with *a* phrase. Generally they are told to use the first thought that comes to mind or "anything that makes sense." Because the individual is not required directly to associate himself or herself with the answer, "conscious" and "subconscious" defenses are more likely to be relaxed and allow a more revealing answer. For example, a study of smokers obtained the following results using direct questioning and sentence completion:

> The majority gave responses [to direct questions] such as, "Pleasure is more important than health," "Moderation is OK," "I like to smoke." One gets the impression that smokers are not dissatisfied with their lot. However, in a portion of the study involving sentence-completion tests, smokers responded to the question, "People who never smoke are _____," with comments such as "better off," "happier," "smarter," "wiser, more informed." To the question, "Teenagers who smoke are _____," smokers responded with, "foolish," "crazy," "uninformed," "stupid," "showing off," "immature," "wrong."[22]

Clearly, the impression one gets from the sentence completion test is that smokers are anxious, uncomfortable, dissonant, and dissatisfied with their habit. This is quite different from the results obtained with the open-ended question. This finding was further supported in other phases of the study, indicating that it is probably the more valid of the findings.

Story completion is an expanded version of sentence completion. As the name suggests, part of a story is told and the respondent is asked to complete it. In a study on the role of husbands and wives in the purchase of furniture, for example, the respondents could be presented a story that included a visit to a furniture store and a disagreement as to which brand to purchase. The respondents would be asked to complete the story. Because respondents do not know how the people in the story will react, they must create the end of the story based on their own experiences and attitudes.

Consider a manufacturer who introduces a major appliance innovation that generates a great deal of consumer interest but few sales. A story could be created about a couple who were interested in the product but did not purchase it. The respondents would then be asked to complete the story, beginning as the couple were driving home after looking at the product, with one saying to the other: "That whidgit was nice, but. . . ." This would serve to direct the remainder of the story along the lines of interest to the researcher.

Construction Techniques

Construction techniques require the respondent to produce or construct something, generally a story, dialogue, or description. They are similar to completion techniques except that less initial structure is provided.

Cartoon techniques present cartoon-type drawings of one or more people in a particular situation. One or more of the individuals are shown with a sentence in bubble form above their heads and one of the others is shown with a blank bubble that the respondent is to "fill in."

Instead of having the bubble show replies or comments, it can be drawn to indicate the unspoken thoughts of one or more of the characters. This device allows the respondent to avoid any restraints that might be felt against having even a cartoon character *speak,* as opposed to *think,* certain thoughts. Exhibit 13–3 illustrates both approaches. Other opening phrases could include such statements as: "My boyfriend bought a new Honda," "The Joneses are building a new swimming pool," "We are thinking about carpeting the living room," and the like. The reply and "unspoken" thoughts of the other person would be supplied by the respondent.

The basic idea in this technique is the same as in other projective techniques. The individual is allowed to "project" any "subconscious" or socially unacceptable general feelings onto the cartoon character. The analysis is the same as it is for word association and sentence completion.

Exhibit 13-3   *Cartoon Technique*

Third-person techniques allow the respondent to project their attitudes onto some vague third person. This third person is generally "an average woman," "your neighbors," "the guys where you work," "most doctors," or the like. Thus, instead of asking the respondent why he or she did something or what he or she thinks about something, the researcher asks what friends, neighbors, or the average person thinks about the issue.

The following quote illustrates the theory and use of this technique:

Realizing that consumers might not want to admit spending on luxuries when many believe they should be scrimping, BBDO (Batton, Barton, Durstine & Osborne, a large advertising agency) first asked what they thought others were splurging on. The agency believes these figures are more indicative of what respondents were spending themselves than what they said about their own behavior.

For example, 30 per cent said they thought others were buying major appliances while only 17 per cent said they themselves were. For movies, 29 per cent said others were splurging while only 13 per cent admitted they themselves were.[23]

A useful version of this technique is to provide a description of a set of an individual's possessions, purchases, or activities and ask the respondents to describe the individual's personality, interests, or other characteristics of interest. The respondent's feelings toward the items on the list will be reflected

Exhibit 13–4 *An Application of the Picture Response Technique*

Instructions

Now make up a story about who these people are and what's going on. Make up any kind of story you want. (Probe with:) How does each one feel about what they are doing? What (else) are they saying to each other? Why? What happens afterward — how does it turn out for them in the long run?

A Response

The woman buys a wig because the salesgirl suggests a change is what she needs. Getting home, the woman shows her family the wig and they laugh at her. She gets mad and tells them she is going to change, she is not going to let them bully her around any more. She has confidence in her new self. Her motto becomes: "Never worry about today, just live it."

Study Conclusions

The wig has become an important symbol (as well, in effect, as a working tool) of a woman's right to change her identity if and when she sees fit. The wig is symbolic of her declaration of feminine independence.

Source: Social Research, Inc., *A Study of Working-Class Women in a Changing World* (Chicago: Social Research, Inc., 1973), Appendix II, p. 22. Used with permission.

in the description of the owner. Haire provides a now classic example of the use of this technique.[24] When instant coffee was first introduced, many housewives refused to use the product. When questioned why, the standard response was "It doesn't taste good." Haire, who was not willing to accept such a surface reason, prepared two brief shopping lists. The lists were identical except that one contained "Nescafé instant coffee" and the other "Maxwell House coffee (drop grind)." One group of 100 women was given one list and a second group received the second list. Each woman was asked to "write a brief description of the personality and character" of the woman who would purchase the set of items on the list.

The differences in the descriptions provided by the two lists (which differed only in the type of coffee) were both striking and revealing. The hypothetical woman whose shopping list contained drip grind coffee was described as being more or less average. In contrast, the woman with instant coffee on her shopping list was characterized as being lazier, more of a spendthrift, and not as good a cook. These responses were more revealing about the women's attitudes toward instant coffee than the "I don't like the taste" response generated by direct questions.[25]

Picture response, another useful construction technique, involves using pictures to elicit stories. These pictures are usually relatively vague, so that the respondent must use his or her imagination to describe what is occurring. Exhibit 13–4 shows a version of this technique, used by a research firm in a study of the attitudes of working-class women. A similar study revealed four stereotypes of dried soup users: (1) a creative person; (2) a practical, modern person; (3) a lazy or indifferent person; and (4) a deprived person.[26]

Exhibit 13–5 *Psychological Motivations, Inc., Use of Role Playing in a Focus Group Context*

Problem

Schenley has a premium brand of Canadian whiskey called O.F.C.. Sales of the brand were considerably below par. Past marketing efforts for O.F.C. were generally unsuccessful or short lived. The client gave us the open-ended assignment: "See what you can recommend."

Approach and Results

We conducted a series of focus group sessions among people who consumed at least three drinks of Canadian whiskey per week. During the sessions we asked a volunteer to role play a bottle of O.F.C. Canadian Whiskey. After the initial laughter and disclaimers ("I'm a person and not a bottle of booze") the volunteer settled into the task. We handed him a bottle of O.F.C. to help him along.

Starting from the very general, we asked the gentleman what his name was. "Pastor Bushman," he replied. Our moderator reminded him that he was role playing. "Excuse me," he said, "My name is O.F.C.." From there the discussion proceeded.

Eventually, we asked our bottle of O.F.C. to tell us what his fears were. He confided that he was afraid no one liked him; that no one could really get to know him, since he did not have a name.

The role play continued and, after awhile, we asked our bottle of O.F.C. to tell us what he would like to have most. He quickly responded, "A *real* name."

We then observed that this participant was closely examining the O.F.C. bottle in his hand. We asked, "What are you thinking about?" He explained, "I see this product is both distilled and bottled in Valley Rand, Canada. That's the French Canadian area of Quebec. Why not call the product 'French Canadian?' You know, like 'Canadian Club?' " Our moderator probed further: "And what do we do with the 'O'?" "Use it; call it 'Old French Canadian!' "

We played this back to several other groups and observed that it immediately caught on. The client and its agency likewise recognized the potential.

Today, O.F.C. is being test marketed as Old French Canadian. The results, thus far, are encouraging.

Source: Supplied by Dr. H. Clarke Noyes, Psychological Motivations Incorporated, Dobbs Ferry, New York. Used with permission.

Expressive Techniques

Role playing is the only expressive technique utilized to any extent by marketing researchers. In *role playing,* the consumer is asked to *assume the role or behavior of an object or another person,* such as a sales representative for a particular department store. The role-playing customer can then be asked to try to sell a given product to a number of different "consumers" who raise varying objections. The means by which the role player attempts to overcome these objections can reveal a great deal about his or her attitudes. Another version of the technique involves studying the role-player's approach to shoppers from various social class backgrounds. This could reveal the role player's attitudes on what type of people "should" shop at the store in question. Exhibit 13–5 describes an example of role playing.

Problems and Promise of Projective Techniques

As projective techniques generally require personal interviews with highly trained interviewers and interpreters to evaluate the responses, they tend to be very expensive. This, in turn, has led to small sample sizes that increase the probability of substantial sampling error. Furthermore, the reliance on small samples often has been accompanied by nonprobability selection procedures. Thus, selection error is also likely to be present. These potential errors are not an integral aspect of the technique. They have become associated with projective techniques because of the costs and the predispositions of some of the practitioners, not because of the techniques themselves. These problems can be minimized with proper sampling.

Nonresponse is more serious. Some of the projective techniques require the respondents to engage in behavior that may well seem strange to them. This is particularly true for techniques such as role playing. Therefore, it is reasonable to assume that those who agree to participate differ in a number of ways from those who refuse to participate. This is a strong argument for testing the findings generated by projective techniques with other techniques that may permit a more representative sample to be taken.

Measurement error is also a serious issue with respect to projective techniques. The possibility of interpreter bias is obvious. The responses to all except the word association techniques are open-ended. The opportunity for error in attempting to decide what a fairly vague and contradictory story or phrase means is great.

The typical approach to analyzing the responses of all the techniques is to look for common, underlying themes. Each stimulus type (Ford, Plymouth) or respondent group (blue-collar, white-collar) is scored based on the percentage of the respondents who mention the key theme. This can be developed into a relatively efficient and reliable scoring system.

Projective techniques are a valuable and useful marketing research tool. For example, Exhibit 13–6 illustrates how Kane, Bortree & Associates, Inc., used unfinished scenarios (story completion) to develop a successful new product concept. As the examples presented indicate, they can help to uncover information not available through direct questioning or observation. They are particularly useful in the exploratory stages of research. They can generate hypotheses for further testing and provide attribute lists and terms

---

Exhibit 13–6   Using Unfinished Scenarios (Story Completion) in a Focus Group to Develop New Product Concepts

Kane, Bortree & Associates find *Unfinished Scenarios* to be a particularly effective technique. A description of an open-ended situation is read aloud to focus group respondents, who complete the story in their own words in writing. Individual answers are then discussed as a group, and specific issues are probed by the moderator.

In an effort to learn about consumers' changing drinking patterns for Seagram's, we used the following unfinished scenario:

> There are so few choices if you want something light, said Liz. I get tired of Perrier but don't want a heavy drink. I wish . . .

Respondents' answers led us to believe that there was a growing desire for a light drink with more taste. Women in particular were bored with the limited selection available, especially white wine and Perrier. Other scenarios were used to explore other pertinent issues, such as the following to explore image:

> Sarah hadn't seen Jane for a long time. She seemed very sophisticated and self-assured these days. At the bar she ordered. . . .

Completions of this scenario by female groups had Jane most often ordering a glass of wine. Women felt that this selection reflected her higher level of knowledge and sophistication.

Based on our learning through these and other scenarios, we developed the concept for a wine-based beverage with a twist of citrus to liven it up. The result: Taylor California Cellar's Chablis with a Twist.

Source: Kane, Bortree & Associates, Inc., New York, New York.

for more structured techniques, such as the semantic differential. The results of projective techniques can also be used directly for decision making. However, the techniques are complex and should not be used naïvely.

Review Questions

13.1.   Describe each of the following types of *depth interviews*, including appropriate uses and advantages and disadvantages:
      a. one-on-one
      b. minigroup
      c. focus group

13.2.   What is *laddering*?

13.3.   What is *hidden-issue questioning*?

13.4.   What is *symbolic questioning*?

13.5.   What are the stages of a focus group interview?

13.6.   Describe and give examples of each of the following types of projective techniques:
      a. association
      b. completion
      c. construction
      d. expression.

13.7.   How does *free word association* differ from *successive word association*?

13.8.   How does a *cartoon* technique differ from a *picture-response* technique?

13.9.   How do *third-person* techniques differ from *sentence-completion* techniques?

13.10.   What is *role playing*?

Discussion Questions/Problems

13.11.   Develop a projective technique to determine students' attitudes toward cheating on exams.

13.12.   Under what conditions would individual depth interviews be more appropriate than projective techniques? Less appropriate? Under what conditions should both be used?

13.13.   Evaluate the procedure used in Exhibit 13–1.

13.14.   What conclusions does Exhibit 13–2 suggest?

13.15.   Evaluate the procedure described in Exhibit 13–5.

13.16.   What techniques would you use to help develop a campaign to reduce drinking and driving by college students? Why would you choose these methods?

13.17. Would your answer to 13.16 change if the target audience were (a) young blue-collar workers or (b) professionals such as doctors, lawyers, and managers? Why?

13.18. Would minigroups or individual depth interviews provide better data on college students' attitudes toward cheating on exams?

Projects

13.19. Using the third-person technique and the cartoon technique, conduct a series of interviews of students on drinking and driving. Do you believe the students' responses reflect their own behavior? Why?

13.20. Select a product from the list below. Administer each of the following techniques to 5 fellow students (different students for each technique) to develop an idea of their feelings toward the selected product: (a) successive word association, (b) sentence or story completion, (c) cartoon, and (d) third person.
    i. contraceptives
    ii. wine
    iii. bread
    iv. compact disc players
    v. Chinese food

13.21. Conduct a *focus group* interview with 8 students not in this class on the purchase and consumption of (a) wine, (b) contraceptives, or (c) bread. Write a report based on your results.

13.22. Conduct an interview as in 13.21 but use a *minigroup.*

13.23. Conduct an interview as in 13.21 but use two *one-on-one* interviews.

13.24. Implement 13.11 with a sample of 10 students.

References

[1] For a discussion of the issues surrounding qualitative research see A. J. Kover, "The Legitimacy of Qualitative Research," *Journal of Advertising Research* (January 1983), 49–50; G. Greenway and G. deGroot, "The Qualitative-Quantitative Dilemma," *Journal of the Market Research Society* (April 1983), 147–164; L. Fuller, "Use of Panels for Qualitative Research," *Journal of the Market Research Society* (July 1984), 209–220; K. M. Wallace, "The Use and Value of Qualitative Research Studies," *Industrial Marketing Management* (August 1984), 181–185; P. Sampson, "Qualitative Research in Europe," *European Research* (October 1985), 163–169; G. deGroot, "Qualitative Research," *European Research* (#3, 1986), 136–141; and R. Bartos, "Qualitative Research"; C. Overholser, "Quality, Quantity, and Thinking Real Hard"; W. D. Wells, "Truth and Consequences"; W. T. Moran, "The Science of Qualitative Re-

search''; all in *Journal of Advertising Research* (June 1986); and D. T. Seymour, *Marketing Research: Qualitative Methods for the Marketing Professional* (Probus Publishing Co., 1988)

2 M. S. Payne, "Resurgence of In-Depth Interviewing Leads to Better Qualitative Research," *Marketing Today* (Elrick and Lavidge, 1, 1984); and H. Sokolow, "In-depth Interviews Increasing in Importance," *Marketing News,* September 13, 1985, 26.

3 J. T. Durgee, "Depth-Interview Techniques for Creative Advertising," *Journal of Advertising Research* (December 1985), 29–37.

4 T. Reynolds and J. Gutman, "Advertising Is Image Management," *Journal of Advertising Research* (February 1984), 27–37.

5 E. F. Fern, "The Use of Focus Groups for Idea Generation," *Journal of Marketing Research* (February 1982), 1–13.

6 J. T. Plummer, "Emotions Important for Successful Advertising," *Marketing News,* April 12, 1985, 18.

7 J. Langer, "Story Time Is Alternate Research Technique," *Marketing News,* September 13, 1985, 19.

8 M. S. Payne, "Individual in-Depth Interviews Can Provide More Details than Groups," *Marketing Today* (Elrick and Lavidge, 1982).

9 See S. Griggs, "Analysing Qualitative Data," *Journal of the Market Research Society* (January 1987), 15–34; and C. J. Fedder, "Listening to Qualitative Research," *Journal of Advertising Research* (December 1985), 57–59.

10 J. Templeton, "Presearch as Giraffe: An Identity Crisis," in B. L. Anderson, *Advances in Consumer Research III* (Provo: Association for Consumer Research, 1976), 443. Additional details on the conduct of focus group interviews are available in M. R. Lautman, "Focus Groups"; L. Percy, "Using Qualitative Focus Groups"; and W. A. Cook, "Turning Focus Groups Inside Out"; all in A. A. Mitchell, *Advances in Consumer Research IX* (Association for Consumer Research, 1982), 52–56; 57–61; and 62–64; J. L. Welch, "Researching Marketing Problems and Opportunities with Focus Groups," *Industrial Marketing Management* (1985), 245–53; E. F. McQuarrie and S. H. McIntyre, "Focus Groups and the Development of New Products by Technology Driven Companies," *Journal of Product Innovation Management* (#1, 1986), 40–47; and J. Durgee, "New Product Ideas from Focus Groups," *Journal of Consumer Marketing* (Fall 1987), 57–65.

11 "How an Agency Lifted Its Admakers' Creativity," *Business Week,* November 30, 1981, 114.

12 R. Alsop, "Fisher-Price Banks on Name," *Wall Street Journal,* August 2, 1984, 23. Additional applied examples are described in K. K. Cox, J. B. Higgenbotham, and J. Burton, "Applications of Focus Group Interviews in Marketing," *Journal of Marketing* (January 1976), 77–80; D. T. Seymour, "3-Stage Focus Groups Used to Develop New Bank Product," *Marketing News,* September 17, 1982, 11; and R. J. Cohen, "Computer-Enhanced Qualitative Research," *Journal of Advertising Research* (June/July 1985), 48–52.

[13] For contradictory evidence see Fern, "The Use of Focus Groups," loc. cit.

[14] W. J. McDonald, "Approaches to Group Research with Children," *Journal of the Academy of Marketing Science* (Fall 1982), 490–499.

[15] M. Goodyear, "Qualitative Research in Developing Countries," *Journal of the Market Research Society* (April 1982), 86–96.

[16] D. T. Seymour, "Focus Groups and the Development of New Products by Technologically Driven Companies," *Journal of Product Innovation Management* (#4 1987), 50–54.

[17] R. Langmaid and B. Ross, "Games Respondents Play," *Journal of the Market Research Society* (July 1984), 221–229.

[18] "Panelists Provide a Glimpse of Automotive Marketing Research," *Marketing News*, September 30, 1983, 3.

[19] H. Mulholland, "Advertising Home Pregnancy Tests," *European Research* (November 1987), 242–247.

[20] S. J. Levy, "Interpretation Is the Essence of Projective Research Techniques," *Marketing News*, September 28, 1984, 1.

[21] Langer, op. cit., 24.

[22] H. H. Kassarjian, "Projective Methods," in R. Ferber, *Handbook of Marketing Research* (New York: McGraw-Hill Book Company, Inc., 1974), 3·85–3·100.

[23] N. Giges, "Inflation Doesn't Deflate Luxury Spending," January 23, 1980, 1.

[24] M. Haire, "Projective Techniques in Marketing Research," *Journal of Marketing* (April 1950), 649–656; see also D. H. Robertson and R. W. Joselyn, "Projective Techniques in Research," *Journal of Advertising Research* (October 1974), 27–31; and G. S. Lane and G. L. Watson, "A Canadian Replication of Mason Haire's 'Shopping List' Study," *Journal of the Academy of Marketing Science* (Winter 1975), 48–59.

[25] See also L. N. Reid and L. Buchanan, "A Shopping List Experiment of the Impact of Advertising on Brand Images," *Journal of Advertising* (Spring 1979), 26–28; and C. Anderson, "The Validity of Haire's Shopping List Projective Technique," *Journal of Marketing Research* (November 1978), 644–649.

[26] Levy, op. cit., 20.

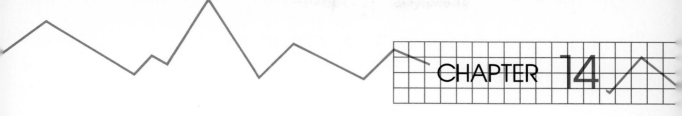

CHAPTER 14

Observation and Physiological Measures

The Park Avenue offices of the Clairol Products division of Bristol-Myers house something called the Consumer Research Forum, a test salon at which Clairol tries out all kinds of hair-care items on women volunteers.

Staffers watch the women through a one-way mirror as they shampoo, condition, or color their hair with Bristol-Myers, and competing products. The volunteers, who realize they are testing products, are given a free hair styling for their help.

In return, the company gets some idea of how consumers react to products and learns whether they understand and correctly follow label directions. It sometimes also obtains "verbatims," or favorable comments from the volunteers that can be used in advertising.

An observational study in this facility of women using the hair conditioner *Small Miracle* prior to its introduction predicted failure. The observers noticed that it caused fine, thin hair to stick together. Standard research, including an in-home use test by more than 1,000 women, did not uncover this weakness. Despite the warning from the observational study, *Small Miracle* was introduced and became a commercial failure.[1]

This example indicates the potential value of observation of consumers' behaviors. Monitoring individual's physiological changes, a specialized type of observation, offers equally valuable insights. Both of these approaches are described in this chapter.

415

Observation

Some time ago a well-known British ice cream manufacturer was concerned that sales of some of its products in neighborhood shops were not achieving the levels that had been expected from children's enthusiasm for these products as measured through interviews. A direct-observation study in a sample of shops revealed why. The ice cream was kept in top-loading refrigerators with sides that were so high that many of the children could not see in to pick out the products they wanted. Nor did the young children ask for the product by name. A picture display was devised for the side of the cabinet to enable the children to recognize each product and to indicate their choice by pointing to it. Sales increased substantially.[2]

Informal observation is a common means of collecting relevant marketing information. The manufacturer notices changes in competitors' advertising, the product manager observes changes in competitors' prices, and the retail manager notices long lines forming around a register. The list of common, day-to-day observations that provide useful information to marketing managers is virtually endless.

However, casual observation, like casual questioning, is likely to produce excessive measurement error. The purpose of this section is to describe "scientific" observation, as opposed to casual observation.

General Characteristics of the Observational Approach

Conditions for Use

Before observation can be used in applied marketing research, three minimum conditions must be met. First, the *data must be accessible* to observation. Motivations, attitudes, and other "internal" conditions cannot be readily observed. However, it is possible to make inferences about attitudes and motivations from behavior that can be observed. For example, facial expressions have been used as an indicator of babies' preferences for various food flavorings.

Nonetheless, attitudes are not well suited for measurement by observation. Nor are a host of private or intimate activities such as dressing, eating, worshiping, or playing with one's children.

A second condition is that the *behavior must be repetitive, frequent, or otherwise predictable.* Although it is possible to observe infrequent, unpredictable occurrences, the amount of time that would have to be spent waiting would be excessive for most purposes.

Finally, an *event must cover a reasonably short time span.* To observe the entire decision-making process that a couple might go through as it considers purchasing a new home could easily take months, if not years. The time and monetary costs associated with this are beyond the value of most applied studies. Thus, we are usually restricted to observing activities that can be completed in a relatively short time span or to observing phases, such as store visits, of activities with a longer time span.

Reasons for Preferring Observational Data

The fact that a given type of data *can* be gathered by observational techniques does not imply that it *should* be gathered by such techniques. There are two conditions under which observational techniques are preferred over alternative methods. In some cases, *observation is the only technique that can be used to collect accurate information.* Two of the most obvious examples are food or toy preferences among children who cannot yet talk and pet food preferences.

For example, before it developed advertising copy, the creative group from Paper Mate's advertising agency observed children playing with a proposed new toy. Exhibit 14–1 describes the federally mandated observational study required for child-resistant packaging. Major pet food manufacturers maintain extensive testing centers in which the reactions of animals to new and reformulated pet foods are observed.

At times people are not aware of, cannot remember, or will not admit to certain behaviors. For example, many retailers monitor their competitors' prices and advertising efforts. In this way, they can remain informed despite the fact that the competitors would not voluntarily supply them with this information.[3]

A study of the influence of various family members in purchase decisions found that children were rarely described as influential in verbal reports. However, observational studies found that most of the children had a substantial level of influence.[4]

Observational studies of garbage have found that individuals tend to underreport beer consumption and to overreport milk and beef consumption in verbal reports.[5] Thus, observational studies can sometimes provide more accurate data than other methods.

The second reason for preferring observational data is that in some situations the *relationship between the accuracy of the data and the cost of the data is more favorable for observation than for other techniques.* For example, traffic counts, both of in-store and external traffic, can often be made by means of observational techniques more accurately and for less expense than using some other technique such as a survey.

The preceding discussion should not be interpreted as meaning that observation techniques are in competition with other approaches. On the contrary, observation techniques can supplement and complement other techniques. When used in combination with other techniques, each approach can serve as a check on the results obtained by the other.

Exhibit 14–1 *Requirements for an Observational Study of Child-Resistant Packaging*

(1) Use 200 children between the ages of 42 and 51 months inclusive, evenly distributed by age and sex, to test the ability of the special packaging to resist opening by children. The even age distribution shall be determined by having 20 children (plus or minus 10 per cent) whose nearest age is 42 months, 20 whose nearest age is 43 months, 20 at 44 months, etc., up to and including 20 at 51 months of age. There should be no more than a 10 per cent preponderance of either sex in each age group. The children selected should be healthy and normal and should have no obvious physical or mental handicap.

(2) The children shall be divided into groups of two each. The testing shall be done in a location that is familiar to the children; for example, their customary nursery school or regular kindergarten. No child shall test more than two special packages, and each package shall be of a different type. For each test, the paired children shall receive the same special packaging simultaneously. When more than one special packaging is being tested, they shall be presented to the paired children in random order, and this order shall be recorded. The special packaging, each test unit of which, if appropriate, has previously been opened and properly resecured by the tester, shall be given to each of the two children with a request for them to open it. Each child shall be allowed up to 5 minutes to open the special packaging. For those children unable to open the special packaging after the first 5 minutes, a single visual demonstration, without verbal explanation, shall be given by the demonstrator. A second 5 minutes shall then be allowed for opening the special packaging. If a child fails to use his teeth to open the special packaging during the first 5 minutes, the demonstrator shall instruct him, before the start of the second 5-minute period, that he is permitted to use his teeth if he wishes.

Source: Consumer Product Safety Commission, "1700.20 Testing Procedure for Special Packaging," *Title 16-Commercial Practices*, updated, 580–581.

Sampling Problems

Sampling for observational techniques poses some unique problems. Consider the sampling process involved in observing consumer reactions to a point-of-purchase display. It would not be practical to take a probability sample of consumers and follow them until they pass the display. Instead, the researcher must sample the stores that contain the displays and also sample (or take a census of) the times of the day, week, and month during which observations will be made. Then, during the selected time period, all, or some proportion, of those who pass the display are observed.

Types of Observational Approaches

There are five basic dimensions along which observational approaches can vary: (1) *natural or contrived situation*, (2) *open or disguised observation*, (3) *structured or unstructured observation*, (4) *direct or indirect observation*, and (5) *human or mechanical observers*. These five dimensions are not dichotomous; they represent continuums. That is, a situation is more or less natural, and more or less open, rather than being natural *or* contrived, open *or* disguised.

Natural Versus Contrived Situation

The researcher who sits near the entrance to a restaurant and notes how many couples, groups of couples, or families of various sizes enter during specified time periods is operating in a natural situation. Nothing has been done to encourage or restrain people from entering. It is likely that those entering the restaurant view the situation as being natural in every way.

Unfortunately, many behaviors that a researcher might like to observe occur so seldom or under such specialized conditions that it is impractical for the researcher to attempt to observe them in the natural state. Exhibit 14–2 provides an example of a contrived situation, in which the "applicant" was a trained observer with no intention of opening an account at the bank. This is a widely used research technique in the retailing area that is known as *service shopping* or *mystery shopper* programs.

Service shopping is offered by a variety of research firms. It is used by retailers and service firms to analyze their performance in serving customers relative to key competitors. Manufacturers use these services to evaluate how their brand is displayed by retailers and sold by retail personnel. In mystery-shopper programs, the respondent is unlikely to notice the contrived nature of the study. At other times, the research objective requires a contrived situation that is completely obvious. For example, a researcher might need to control precisely the length of time a message designed for a billboard is shown to a respondent. A common approach requires the respondent to look into a rather large machine (a tachistoscope) while the "billboard" is shown. This would be a contrived situation that would be noticeable to the respondent. Exhibit 14–3 describes an obviously contrived situation.

419

Exhibit 14–2 *An Example of Contrived Observation**

Bank: Competitor B
Location: Cranston   Time: 10:20 A.M.
Clerk: Mrs. L.   Account: Savings

I entered the bank and approached a teller, Miss I., and asked who I would see to find out about a savings account. She said I should see Mrs. L., indicating her. Mrs. L. had a customer at her desk, so the teller suggested I have a seat and wait. She said, "There's a pamphlet on savings accounts on the rack over there you might like to look over while you're waiting." I thanked her, took a pamphlet, and sat down. After about two minutes Mrs. L. was free and I told her I was interested in a savings account. She took out a pamphlet and said, "I see you have one of these; maybe it would be best if we go through it together." She then went over each type of savings plan offered, adding comments on each that were not in the brochure. She told me I could save by mail or come in to the office and gave me their hours. She also mentioned that if I had a checking account I could have money saved automatically. I said I did not have a checking account, so she went over them fully, giving me literature. At the end she said, "We're a full service bank — we have loans, safe deposit boxes, even a credit card!" I had already told her I wouldn't be opening anything "until payday." She said, "Right over where you got that first brochure, we have literature on all our services; why don't you take one of each and look them over, and come back and see me on payday?"

Mrs. L. was extremely knowledgeable, well organized, and very pleasant.

Source: Specialized Marketing Services for the Banking Industry. A special report by Bank Marketing Group, a division of Sheldon Spencer Associates, Inc., Warwick, Rhode Island. Used with permission.

Open Versus Disguised Observation

The example presented in Exhibit 14–2 was basically a disguised approach. Had the teller known she was under observation, she would probably have altered her behavior in some manner. One-way mirrors, observers dressed as stock clerks, and hidden cameras are a few of many ways that are used to prevent respondents from becoming aware that they are being observed.

It is not always possible to prevent the respondent from being aware of the observer. For example, in observing a sales representative's behavior on sales calls, it would be difficult to remain effectively disguised. Similarly, in labora-

420

Exhibit 14-3 *Observation of Television Commercial Viewing*

The Pretesting Company maintains a "Simulated Network" facility in eight shopping-mall locations as well as portable versions. The firm inserts test commercials (usually two versions for each test) into videotapes of actual network TV programs. Subjects are recruited to match the client's target market and are told they are to evaluate TV programs.

The participants watch a standard television set for 12 minutes. Each respondent has a remote-control changer and can switch channels, and thus avoid commercials, at will. The test commercials are shown twice, at five minute intervals. A computer insures that each respondent is exposed to each test commercial and records if the commercial is viewed or not. A variety of before and after measures of attitude, purchase intention, and brand and commercial liking are made.

While the technique is used primarily for proprietary commercial testing, a number of general findings have begun to emerge. For example, "forced exposure" testing of commercials in focus group settings often produces high scores for fact based, hard data commercials. However, these same commercials are frequently "zapped" in the more realistic "Simulated Network."

Source: The Pretesting Company Inc., Englewood, New Jersey. Used with permission.

---

tory studies disguise is seldom practical. A meter attached to a radio or a television set that records when and to what station a set is tuned is a form of another observation method that cannot be used in a disguised form. Our opening example described an open observation system used by Bristol-Myers.

The known presence of an observer offers the same potential for error as the presence of an interviewer in survey research. Observers may vary in how "obviously present" they are. A meter attached to a television set is relatively unobtrusive, whereas the presence of an observer who travels with a sales representative is obvious. The magnitude of observer effects is probably closely related to how obvious the observer is to the subject. Therefore, it seems wise always to minimize the presence of the observer to the extent possible. Notice that this was done in our opening example, even though the women knew that they were being observed. Likewise, the respondents in Exhibit 14-3 were not aware that their commercial viewing was being recorded.

Exhibit 14–4 *An Example of a Structured Observation Report Form**

Bank _____   Date _____
Location _____   Time _____
Teller _____   Transaction _____

Appearance
  Well groomed   Yes _____ No _____

Behavior
  Chewing gum or eating _____
  Smoking _____
  Personal conversations:
    with customer _____
    with other employees _____
    on telephone _____
  Other poor behavior _____

Window
  Nameplate visible   Yes _____ No _____
  Loose cash or checks   Yes _____ No _____
  Cluttered work area   Yes _____ No _____
  Personal belongings visible   Yes _____ No _____

Transactions (General)
  Waited on immediately   Yes _____ No _____
    If no, waited (_____) minutes
      presence acknowledged   Yes _____ No _____
      teller was:
        helping customer _____
        talking with employee:
          business _____
          personal _____
        working:
          at station _____
          at back counter _____
          at drive-in window _____
        other _____

* *Source: Specialized Marketing Services for the Banking Industry.* A special report by Bank Marketing Group, a division of Sheldon Spencer Associates, Inc., Warwick, Rhode Island. Used with permission.

Structured Versus Unstructured Observation

In structured observation, the observer knows in advance precisely which aspects of the situation are to be observed or recorded. All other behaviors are to be "ignored." Exhibit 14–4 provides an example of part of a form for use in a structured observation. Note that the form specifies the behaviors that are to be observed.

Highly structured observations typically require a considerable amount of inference on the part of the observer. For example, in Exhibit 14–4 the observer is required to note whether the teller is well groomed. This is a judgment task that is influenced by personal tastes. However, well-trained observers can achieve a high degree of agreement as to the category in which a given individual should be placed.

Completely unstructured observation places no restriction on what the observer should note. Thus, an observer for a department store might be told to mingle with the shoppers and notice whatever seems relevant. Completely unstructured observation is often useful in exploratory research.

Direct Versus Indirect Observation

We can generally observe current behavior directly. That is, if we are interested in purchasing behavior, we can observe people actually making purchases. Most of the examples described so far have focused on direct observation. However, to observe other types of behavior, such as past behavior, we must turn to some record of the behavior or indirect observation. That is, we must observe the effects or results of the behavior rather than the behavior itself.

One type of indirect observation is the examination of *archives,* or secondary sources. This type of observation is so critical to applied research that Chapter 4 was devoted to it. Another type of indirect observation involves *physical traces.* Physical traces are physical evidence of past behavior, such as empty packages. Analysis of garbage from various areas of a community has been used to infer consumption of a variety of products.[6]

Another use of physical traces is known as the *pantry audit.* In a pantry audit, respondents' homes are examined (with the owners' permission) for the presence and quantity of prespecified items. The basic assumption of this approach is that possession is related to purchase and/or usage. Unfortunately, this is often a tenuous assumption. For example, one of the authors has had a bottle of Ouzo (a Greek liqueur) in his pantry for several years, and it is likely to remain there for several more. To infer that this product is liked or consumed because of its presence would be incorrect.

Human Versus Mechanical Observations

Most of the examples and discussions thus far have emphasized human observers. However, it is sometimes both possible and desirable to replace the human observer with some form of mechanical observer. This may be done for accuracy, cost, or functional reasons.

Traffic counts of automobiles can generally be performed more accurately and for less expense by machine than by human observers. Even these machines are subject to some error. One of the authors remembers being in a group as a teenager that took great delight in finding traffic counters and driving back and forth across them.

Mechanical devices may also be used when it would be functionally impossible to use human observers. It would not generally be possible, for example, to have human observers monitor a family's television viewing habits. However, the television meter used by Nielsen does this effectively.

An electric utility group found that fuel-use projections based in part on survey research reports of where people set their home-heating thermostats were not sufficiently accurate. A research firm focused unobtrusive video cameras on the thermostats in 150 homes. The findings were quite revealing:

> People might say they kept the things at 68 degrees, but it turned out that they fiddled with them all day. Older relatives and kids—especially teen-agers—tended to turn them up, and so did cleaning ladies. Even visitors did it. In a lot of homes, it was guerrilla warfare over the thermostat between the person who paid the bill and everyone else.[7]

Time-lapse photography is proving very useful in analyzing in-store traffic flows and the effect of point-of-purchase displays.[8] In addition, measures of physiological reactions to advertisements, package designs, and the like rely on mechanical observers that can "observe" or measure changes which are beyond the capabilities of human observers. These physiological measures have become so important in marketing research that the next major section of this chapter is devoted to them.

Physiological Measures

Physiological measures are direct observations of physical responses to a stimulus such as an advertisement. These responses may be controllable, as are eye movements, or uncontrollable, as is the galvanic skin response. Physiological measures are used for the same reasons that other observations are used: to obtain more accurate or more economical data. Since physiological measures generally cost more than verbal reports, they are used when it is felt that respondents cannot or will not provide accurate verbal responses.[9]

Brain-Wave Analysis

The human brain emits a number of electrical "signals" that can be monitored. Some of the signals reflect the level of interest the respondent has in whatever stimulus he or she is confronted with.[10] Thus, brain waves may indicate a respondent's interest in a commercial, package, or product. By carefully controlling which aspects of the commercial or package are shown, the researcher can measure interest in the components of the stimulus.

Both the left and the right hemispheres of the brain produce brain waves. The level of brain waves being emitted by each side is an indication of how actively involved that side of the brain is with the stimulus at hand. This is useful to the marketing researcher because of *hemispheral lateralization* — the fact that humans have specialized activities for each side of the brain. The left hemisphere of the brain deals with verbal, sequential, and rational activities; the right side of the brain specializes in pictorial, time free, and emotional responses. Much of the activity of the right brain is not "available" to the individual for verbal reporting.[11]

Brain-wave analysis offers the potential of evaluating the interest generated by a commercial or package and the nature — emotional or rational — of that interest.[12] A consulting firm in this area, Neuro-Communication Research Laboratories, breaks commercials down into 5-second "epochs." The degree of right and left hemisphere activity is recorded for each epoch. Exhibit 14-5 shows the brain-wave patterns elicited by an award-winning commercial. The first 20-seconds (epochs 1-4) presented a problem. The left (analytical) hemisphere was actively seeking solutions during this portion of the commercial. The solution to the problem (a brand) was presented in epoch 5. This produced a strong right hemisphere or emotional response. The final epoch presented brand information that elicited a high level of left brain, or rational processing.

This type of analysis offers obvious benefits to anyone wishing to communicate with consumers. For example, a commercial designed primarily to elicit a positive emotional response should produce right hemisphere activity. Failure to do so indicates an ineffective message presentation.

One weakness of brain-wave research is the artificial environment in which the measurements take place. These studies are generally conducted in a research laboratory and involve a forced exposure to the advertisement or package while the respondent is literally wired to a machine. An individual may respond differently in the hectic environment of the supermarket than he or she would in a quiet research facility. Of course, any technique short of test marketing suffers from this problem to some degree.

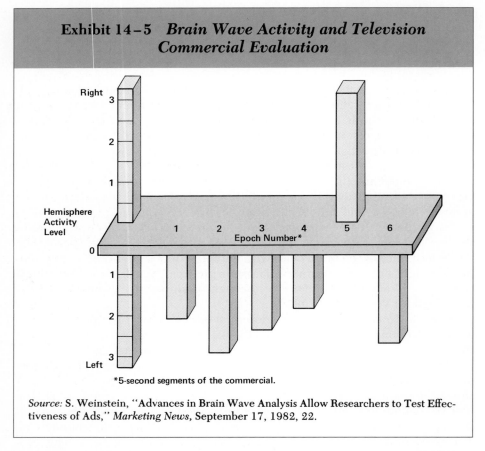

Exhibit 14–5 *Brain Wave Activity and Television Commercial Evaluation*

Right

Hemisphere Activity Level

Epoch Number*

Left

*5-second segments of the commercial.

Source: S. Weinstein, "Advances in Brain Wave Analysis Allow Researchers to Test Effectiveness of Ads," *Marketing News,* September 17, 1982, 22.

Unfortunately, there are other complex theoretical and methodological issues associated with brain-wave analysis.[13] Until additional basic research is completed, this technique will not be widely used.

Eye Tracking

Computer/video technology allows researchers to record movements of the eye in relation to a stimulus, such as a package or commercial.[14] This allows the determination of the order and amount of time an individual spends looking at the various parts of an advertisement or package, or which of two competing stimuli receives the most attention.

The procedure involves the respondent sitting in a chair and reading magazines, observing television commercials or slides of print advertisements, billboards, packages, shelf facings, point-of-purchase displays, and the like. For all except television commercials and billboard tests, the respondents control how long they view each scene. An eye-tracking device sends an undetectable beam of filtered light which is reflected off the respondent's eyes. This reflected beam represents the visual focal point and can be superimposed on whatever is being viewed. These data are stored in computer memory that allows a complete analysis of the viewing sequence. Portable, inconspicuous equipment is now available, as shown in Exhibit 14–6.

Knowing the time spent on viewing an advertisement or package, the sequence in which it was examined, and which elements were examined has obvious value. For example, Samantha Eggar appeared in a conservative dress in a television commercial for RCA Colortrack. Eye tracking (Exhibit 14–7) indicated that viewers focused substantial attention on the product. Seventy-two hours later, brand-name recall was 36 per cent. In contrast, a similar

Exhibit 14–6   *The Pretesting Company's People Reader Eye Camera*

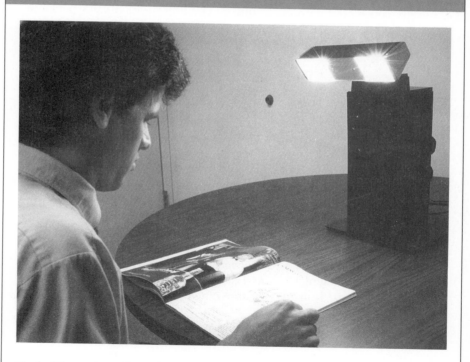

Used with permission from The Pretesting Company Inc., Englewood, New Jersey.

Perception Research Services, Inc. (PRS) is a research agency that specializes in the use of physiological measures. A description of its research design using eye cameras to evaluate package changes follows.

1. Test Materials

To simulate a competitive environment for the viewer, PRS uses an actual store for photographing test packages. Packages are photographed in an actual display alongside major competition. Packages are rotated on the shelf so positioning will not bias results. 35 mm slides are used for testing purposes.

2. Sample

PRS recommends that all interviewing be conducted with target market respondents as defined by the advertiser and agency. Interviewing is generally conducted with one hundred (100) participants per package.

3. Research Procedure

Screening:

PRS interviewers approach respondents at central location facilities (shopping malls). Screening questions are administered, though care is taken to disguise the nature of the test.

Shelf Impact:

The participant is seated at the PRS eye-tracking recorder. He or she views a screen onto which 35 mm slides the test material will be projected. These slides include a series of in-store displays which simulate a walk through a store. The participant is instructed that she will see a series of displays that she might normally encounter during a shopping trip to a specific outlet, i.e., supermarket, drugstore, liquor store, etc. She controls the viewing time, and is told to take as much or as little time with each scene as desired. Eye movements are recorded for the test scene.

Eye tracking determines precisely what a respondent looks at in a display and in what order she notes the individual packages. More specifically, PRS can report how quickly each brand draws attention, the number of times a consumer looks at a particular package, and the total time she spends with the facings on the shelf.

PRS can evaluate packaging for different brands with the same individual, thus conserving time and cost in maintaining a consistent audience sample from one brand or package to the next.

After the respondent has been exposed to the store walk-through, recall questioning is administered. This provides insight into the ability of the packaging to register brand name.

Package Readability:

Respondents are presented close-up pictures of packages including the test design for a time period voluntarily controlled by the participant. Eye movements are tracked to determine the extent to which each element on the package (brand name, product type, illustration, ingredient content, etc.) is noted, the speed of noting, sequence of viewing (i.e., element seen first, second, etc.), incidence of copy readership, and time spent with each element. Importantly, eye tracking documents those elements quickly bypassed or totally overlooked.

Recall questions are administered to determine the saliency of package components.

Verbal Interview:

Participants are now shown the actual package or a slide, if prototypes are not available. A comprehensive interview is administered, generally covering the following areas:

Aesthetic Appeal: Does the consumer like the package? Is it pleasant to look at?

Brand Image Connotations: The kinds of images generated for the product are important.

Functional Characteristics: Most packages do more than identify and promote the product. In use, they protect the product from contamination or damage and provide a convenient means of storing and dispensing.

Likes and Dislikes: Open-ended questioning offers the consumer an opportunity to convey spontaneous reactions to the package and product.

Purchase Interest: Responses to this line of questioning demonstrate degrees of commitment or resistance to product trial.

Product Usage and Demographics: Questioning during the verbal interview typically concludes with specified product usage and demographic information.

Source: E. Young, *Multidimensional Communications Research* (Perception Research Services, Inc., undated), 3. Used with permission.

commercial used Linda Day George dressed in a "revealing" gown. Eye tracking showed that most attention was focused on Ms. George, and subsequent brand name recall was only 9 per cent. Similar results were obtained when Catherine Deneuve appeared in a low-cut dress to advertise Lincoln-Mercury.[15]

Exhibit 14–7 describes how one firm uses eye tracking to evaluate package designs (Exhibit 8–2 described another firm's use of a similar methodology for the same problem). Notice that eye tracking is used in combination with verbal interviews. Eye tracking measures *what* is attended to; it does not measure *why*. Thus, a package could attract attention and still be inappropriate for the product. However, eye tracking has been found to predict both stated interest and sales.[16]

Eye tracking has become widely accepted among consumer packaged-good marketers. It is used to evaluate all aspects of advertisements and packages as well as related variables such as ad location within a magazine and on a page. As technological advances continue, eye tracking may become a standard pretest for marketing communications.

Other Physiological Measures

A number of other physiological measures are occasionally used by marketing researchers.

The *psychogalvanometer* measures emotional reactions to various stimuli by measuring changes in the rate of perspiration. Because this reaction is beyond the control of the subject, there is no chance for the respondent to deliberately distort the response. Through the use of this device, researchers can determine whether subjects have an emotional reaction to various slogans, brand names, or advertisements. Unfortunately, the machine provides only limited information about the nature of the response and it is seldom used in marketing research.

Walt Wesley Associates, a consulting firm, used psychogalvanometer measurements to determine why one advertisement for V-8 juice was successful, whereas a similar advertisement was not. By testing the response to various elements of the advertisements, the firm found that "the ad with the high emotional punch, the ad which sold cases and cases of V-8, showed only the product display. The weak ads added a drawing of a housewife holding the horn of plenty. The resultant split attention between the woman and the product display killed the appetite appeal of the illustration and the ad died in the market."[17]

Voice pitch analysis examines changes in the relative vibration frequency of the voice to measure emotion or stress. Voice pitch analysis has been used to evaluate emotional responses to packages, brands, new products, and commercials. A potential advantage of voice analysis is that it may be able to determine which verbal responses reflect an emotional commitment and which are merely low-involvement responses.

Unfortunately, at this stage of its development, voice pitch analysis suffers from a number of technical (measurement instrument) difficulties. In addition, there is limited empirical as well as theoretical knowledge linking voice to different emotions. For these reasons, voice pitch analysis is not yet widely used.[18]

Review Questions

14.1. What conditions must be met before *observation* can be used in applied marketing research?

14.2. Under what conditions are observational techniques preferred over other methods?

14.3. Why is sampling complicated for observational studies?

14.4. Describe each of the following dimensions of an observational study:
   a. natural/contrived situation
   b. open/disguised observation
   c. structured/unstructured observation
   d. direct/indirect observation
   e. human/mechanical observers

14.5. Describe *brain-wave analysis* and how it can be of use to marketing managers.

14.6. Describe *eye tracking* and how it can be of use to marketing managers.

14.7. Describe the information provided by the *psychogalvanometer*. Of what value is it to marketing researchers?

14.8. What is *voice pitch analysis?* Of what value is it to marketing researchers?

Discussion Questions/Problems

14.9. Self-reports of beer consumption indicate substantially lower consumption levels than indicated by an analysis of the same household's garbage. What factors could account for this?

14.10. A national retail chain has 1,500 outlets. The stores are located in all types of neighborhoods and are open from 10:00 A.M. until 9:00. P.M., 6 days per week. Management would like to test reactions to a new point-of-purchase display. The display is large, brightly colored, and has several moving parts. Design an observational study of the display, including:
   a. the sampling plan
   b. details on each of the 5 dimensions involved in an observational study
   c. other research technique(s), if any, that would be more suitable for this problem.

14.11. Design an observation approach for evaluating the relative effectiveness of the service at two competing fast food chains.

14.12. Will physiological measures become common in marketing research by 1998? Justify your response.

14.13. What advantages would be associated with combining brain-wave analysis and eye tracking?

14.14. If you were manager of _____, what observational studies, if any, would you want to have conducted on a regular basis? On a sporadic basis?
a. McDonalds
b. K mart
c. Gleem toothpaste
d. G.E. dishwashers

14.15. For what kinds of products is an analysis of garbage likely to be useful? What kinds of errors would you expect to arise in garbage analysis that are not present in self reports? What kinds of errors would you expect to arise in self reports that are not present in garbage analysis?

14.16. Compare Exhibits 14–7 and 8–2. Which approach is best? Why?

14.17. Evaluate the procedure in Exhibit 14–1.

14.18. Evaluate the procedure in Exhibit 14–3.

14.19. Evaluate the form in Exhibit 14–4.

14.20. If you were manager of _____, how would you use eye tracking?
a. McDonalds
b. K mart
c. Gleem toothpaste
d. G.E. dishwashers

Projects

14.21. Observe shoppers purchasing _____. What hypotheses or insights have you gained from this observation?
a. fresh vegetables
b. shoes
c. flowers
d. records
e. paperback books

14.22. Implement 14.11 and report the results.

14.23. Form a group of three. Develop a form similar to the one in Exhibit 14–4 for a store type of interest. Enter the store and observe the same behaviors. Complete the form without discussing it with your colleagues. Explain any differences in your group's responses.

References

[1] N. Giges, "No Miracle in Small Miracle: Story behind Clairol Failure," *Advertising Age*, August 16, 1982, 76.

[2] J. Richer, "Observation, Ethology and Marketing Research," *European Research* (January 1981), 22.

[3] See L. M. Fuld, *Competitor Intelligence* (New York: John Wiley, 1985).

[4] C. K. Atkins, "Observation of Parent-Child Interaction in Supermarket Decision-Making," *Journal of Marketing* (October 1978), 41–45.

[5] W. L. Rathje, W. W. Hughes, and S. L. Jernigan, "The Science of Garbage: Following the Consumer Through His Garbage Can," in W. Locander, *1976 Business Proceedings* (Chicago: American Marketing Association, 1976), 56–64.

[6] *Ibid.*

[7] F. C. Klein, "Researcher Probes Consumers Using Anthropological Skills," *Wall Street Journal*, July 7, 1983, 23.

[8] R. Kurtz, "On-Site's Cameras Focus on the Retail Marketplace," *Marketing News*, November 9, 1984, 46.

[9] Discussion of the theoretical linkage between physiological responses and cognitive or verbal responses can be found in W. Kroeber-Riel, "Activation Research: Psychobiological Approaches in Consumer Research," *Journal of Consumer Research* (March 1979), 240–250; M. J. Ryan, "Psychobiology and Consumer Research: A Problem of Construct Validity," and W. Kroeber-Riel, "Rejoinder," *Journal of Consumer Research* (June 1980), 92–95, 96–98; M. J. Ryan, "Achieving Correspondence Among Cognitive Processes and Physiological Measures," in A. A. Mitchell, *Advances in Consumer Research IX* (Provo: Association for Consumer Research, 1982), 170–72; and J. T. Cacioppo and R. E. Petty, "Physiological Responses and Advertising Effects," *Psychology and Marketing* (Summer 1985), 115–26.

[10] See S. Weinstein, "Brain Wave Analysis: The Beginning and Future of Package Design Research," in W. Stern, *Handbook of Package Design Research* (New York: John Wiley & Sons, Inc., 1981), 492–504.

[11] See F. Hansen, "Hemispheral Lateralization: Implications for Understanding Consumer Behavior," *Journal of Consumer Research* (June 1981), 23–36; and S. Weinstein, "A Review of Brain Hemisphere Research," *Journal of Advertising Research* (June/July, 1982), 59–63.

[12] S. Weinstein, C. Weinstein, and R. Drozdenko, "Brain Wave Analysis," *Psychology & Marketing* (Spring 1984), 17–42.

[13] W. A. Katz, "A Critique of Split-Brain Theory," *Journal of Advertising Research* (April/May 1983), 63–66; S. Weinstein, R. Drozdenko, and C. Weinstein, "Advertising Evaluation Using Brain-Wave Measures," *Journal of Advertising Research* (April/May, 1984), 67–70; D. W. Stewart, "Physiological Measurement of Advertising Effects," *Psychology and Marketing* (Spring 1984), 43–48; J. S.

Nevid, "Methodological Considerations," *Psychology and Marketing* (Summer 1984), 5–19; and Cacioppo and Petty, loc. cit.

[14] E. C. Young, "Determining Conspicuity and Shelf Impact through Eye Movement Tracking" in Stern, op. cit., 535–542; J. Treistman and J. P. Gregg, "Visual, Verbal, and Sales Responses to Print Ads," *Journal of Advertising Research* (August 1979); B. Whalen, "Eye Tracking Technology to Replace Day-After Recall by '84," and E. Young, "Use Eye Tracking Technology to Create Clutter-Breaking Ads," both in *Marketing News,* November 27, 1981; 18 and 19 respectively; and " 'Real-World' Device Sheds New Light on Ad Readership Tests," *Marketing News,* June 5, 1987, 1.

[15] *What the Eye Does Not See, the Mind Does Not Remember* (Telecom Research, Inc., undated).

[16] Treistman and Gregg, loc. cit.

[17] "Psychogalvanometer Testing 'Most Predictive,' " *Marketing News,* June 16, 1981, 11. See also P. J. Watson and R. J. Gatchel, "Autonomic Measures of Advertising," *Journal of Advertising Research,* June 1979, 15–26.

[18] N. J. Nighswonger and C. R. Martin, Jr., "On Using Voice Analysis in Marketing Research," *Journal of Marketing Research* (August 1981), 350–355; G. A. Brickman, "VOPAN: Voice Pitch Analysis in Testing Packaging Alternatives," in Stern, op. cit., 543–551; G. A. Brickman, "Uses of Voice-Pitch Analysis," *Journal of Advertising Research* (April 1980), 69–73; R. G. Nelson and D. Schwartz, "Voice-Pitch Analysis," *Journal of Advertising Research* (October 1979), 55–59; and J. Grant and D. E. Allmon, "Voice Stress Analyzer Is a Marketing Research Tool," *Marketing News,* January 4, 1988, 22.

CASE III–1 WEYERHAEUSER VI: QUESTIONNAIRE DESIGN AND ATTITUDE MEASUREMENT

Review Cases I–2 and II–3 (pages 68–70 and 248–250). Weyerhaeuser designed a questionnaire to provide an initial benchmark measurement of the company's image among viewers and nonviewers of "This Old House." Secondary objectives were to obtain data on (1) the relationship between company image and price sensitivity, (2) the characteristics of DIYers, their homes, and their projects, and (3) the effect that sponsoring "This Old House" had on Owens-Cornings' image.

The questionnaire is reproduced below (see Case IV–1 for the sampling plan). Questions on Georgia-Pacific were included to provide a comparison point and to allow a measure of differential image change over time between viewers and nonviewers of "This Old House." Questions on Owens-Corning were included to allow an assessment of the impact of sponsoring "This Old House" on that company's image. Questions on Stanley Tools were included because other research had indicated that it was one of the most respected brands among DIYers. Having Stanley's scores on the same items as Weyerhaeuser would indicate reasonable target objectives. These responses could also be used to analyze the relationship between image and price sensitivity.

There was a strong desire to keep the questionnaire under 10 minutes to increase the response rate, be considerate to respondents, and control interviewing costs.

Evaluate the questionnaire, making changes, additions, and deletions as appropriate.

GILMORE RESEARCH GROUP
1100 OLIVE WAY, SUITE 250
SEATTLE, WA 98101-1840

RESP. #:_____ 1–3

"THIS OLD HOUSE" SURVEY

TEL.#: (___) ___-____ DATE:_____
           AC

INTERVIEWER:_____ ID #:_____ 4–6

STOP TIME:_____ TOTAL TIME:_____ 7–8

START TIME:_____ MALE 1

FEMALE 2 9

OTHER QUOTA INFORMATION		
Area:		
	Viewer	Non-Viewer
Boston	1	4
Chicago	2	5
Phoenix	3	6

10

Hello, I'm _____ of Gilmore Research Group, a national marketing research firm. We're conducting a brief survey of do-it-yourselfers who have recently completed a home improvement project.

1a. Have you personally done a do-it-yourself home improvement project in 1987?

SKIP TO Q.2 ←——— Yes   1

ASK Q.1b ←——— ⎡ No   2
                ⎣ Don't know/Refused   3   11

1b. Has anyone else in your household been involved in such a project this year?

ASK TO SPEAK WITH THAT PERSON, ←—— Yes   1
ARRANGE A CALL-BACK IF
REQUIRED

THANK & TERMINATE ←——— ⎡ No   2
                       ⎣ Don't know/Refused   3

(2nd PERSON INTRODUCTION:) I'm _____ from Gilmore Research Group. We're conducting a brief survey of do-it-yourselfers. I understand that you have personally done a do-it-yourself home improvement project this year.

2. Approximately how much would you estimate you spent on materials for do-it-yourself home improvement projects in 1987?
(PROBE:) We're not interested in an <u>exact</u> amount, just your best estimate.

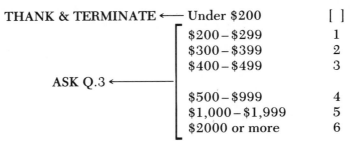

THANK & TERMINATE ←—— Under $200   [ ]

⎡ $200 – $299   1
| $300 – $399   2
| $400 – $499   3
ASK Q.3 ←——— |
| $500 – $999   4
| $1,000 – $1,999   5
⎣ $2000 or more   6

(PROBE:)

We're not interested in an <u>exact</u> ←————[Don't know/Refused   7   <u>12</u>
amount, just your best estimate.
(IF STILL UNABLE, THANK & TERMINATE)

3a. Are you aware of any <u>television programs</u> designed to provide assistance and information on home improvement projects for do-it-yourselfers?

PROBE FOR NAMES. DO NOT READ.

SKIP TO Q.4 ←———— "This Old House"   1

                 ⌈ Other (SPECIFY):

ASK Q.3b ←————   ————————————————   2
                 ————————————————   2
               ⌊ Don't know/Aware of none/Refused   3   13

3b. Are you aware of a program on PBS called "This Old House"?

ASK Q.4 ←—— Yes   1

CHECK NON-VIEWER QUOTA. ←⌈ No   2
IF QUOTA UNFILLED, ASK Q.4;   ⌊ Don't know/Refused   3   14
IF QUOTA FILLED, THANK & TERMINATE.

4. How often, if at all, would you say you watch "This Old House" during a typical winter or spring month? DO NOT READ.

NON-VIEWER: TERMINATE IF   ←—— Less than once/Never   1
QUOTA FULL   ⌈ Once   2
                              | 1 – 2 times   3
                                | Twice   4
ASK Q.5 ←———— | 2 – 3 times   5
                                | 3 times   6
                                | 3 – 4 times   7
                                ⌊ 4 or more times   8

(PROBE:) What is your best guess?   ←—— Don't know/Refused   9   15
       (IF STILL DON'T KNOW, COUNT AS
NON-VIEWER & TERMINATE IF QUOTA FULL.)

5. Which company sponsors "This Old House"? DO NOT READ. CIRCLE <u>ALL</u> RESPONSES.

                                 Owens-Corning   1
                                   Georgia Pacific   2
                                   Stanley   3
                                   Weyerhaeuser   4
                                   Other (SPECIFY):
                                   ————————————   5
                                   Don't know/Refused   6   16–20

6. Thinking back to the home improvement work you have done in 1987, could you please briefly describe the do-it-yourself projects you have done?

_____

_____ 21 – 28

_____

OFFICE USE ONLY:

Attic, converted to room	01	Kitchen, remodeled	25
Basement, converted to room	02	Landscaping	26
Bathroom, remodeled	03	Minor projects (bird feeder,	
Bathroom, cabinets	04	toys, etc.)	27
Bedroom, remodeled	05		
		Painted, exterior	28
Carpet, installed	06	Painted, room(s)	29
Carport, added	07	Paneled a room	30
Carport, converted to garage	08	Roof, repaired/replaced	31
Carport, converted to room	09	Shelving, added	32
Ceiling, replaced/repaired	10		
		Siding, added	33
Decking, added	11	Siding, replaced	34
Decking, repaired	12	Weatherproofing	35
Den, remodeled	13	Other	36
Door, replaced	14	Don't know/Refused	37
Fence, added	15		
		Added categories (during	
Fence, repaired	16	the survey)	
Flooring, repaired/replaced	17	Wallpaper	38
Furniture, built	18	Other plumbing	39
Garage, added	19	Other electrical	40
Garage, converted to room	20	Windows	41
		Addition to house/other	
Garage door, replaced	21	building	42
Insulation, installed	22	Patio	43
Kitchen cabinets, added	23	Walls/wallboard	44
Kitchen cabinets, replaced	24		

7. Excluding paint and tools, what is the most you have spent on <u>lumber and building materials</u> for any one single do-it-yourself project this year? (**DO NOT READ.**)

Under $25	1
$25 – $49	2
$50 – $99	3
$100 – $199	4

$200–$499	5	
$500–$999	6	
$1,000 or more	7	
(PROBE:) What is your best estimate? ←——— Don't know/Refused	8	29

8a. When you think of major companies that make products for do-it-your-self home improvement projects; including paint, tools, and other products; what is the company name that first comes to mind? **DO NOT READ.**

8b. What others? **PROBE FOR: UP TO 6 NAMES.**

	(CC 30–31)	(32–33)	(34–35)	(36–37)	(38–39)	(40–41)
	Q.8a			Q.8b Mentioned		
	1st	2nd	3rd	4th	5th	6th
Anderson	01	01	01	01	01	01
Armstrong	02	02	02	02	02	02
B & D	03	03	03	03	03	03
Boise Cascade	04	04	04	04	04	04
Borden	05	05	05	05	05	05
Champion	06	06	06	06	06	06
Dutch Boy	07	07	07	07	07	07
Georgia-Pacific	08	08	08	08	08	08
Glidden	09	09	09	09	09	09
Kohler	10	10	10	10	10	10
Masonite	11	11	11	11	11	11
Moen	12	12	12	12	12	12
Olympic	13	13	13	13	13	13
Owens-Corning	14	14	14	14	14	14
Peerless	15	15	15	15	15	15
Pittsburgh Plate Glass (PPG)	16	16	16	16	16	16
Sears	17	17	17	17	17	17
Sherwin-Williams	18	18	18	18	18	18
Stanley	19	19	19	19	19	19
Wagner	20	20	20	20	20	20
Weyerhaeuser	21	21	21	21	21	21
Other (**SPECIFY:**)						
_____	22	22	22	22	22	22
_____	22	22	22	22	22	22
_____	22	22	22	22	22	22
_____	22	22	22	22	22	22
_____	22	22	22	22	22	22
_____	22	22	22	22	22	22
Don't know/Refused	23	23	23	23	23	23

| None/No other | 24 | 24 | 24 | 24 | 24 | 24 |

SKIP TO Q.9

9. I'll name four major companies. For each, please tell me what products that company provides for do-it-yourself projects.
First, (ROTATE, START AT RED "X").
What products does (RED "X") provide to do-it-yourselfers for home improvement projects? DO NOT READ.
Next . . . REPEAT FOR OTHER THREE NAMES.

(BLANK 78–79)
(IND 80/1)
(DUP 1–3)

	(CC 42–53) [ ]	(54–65) [ ] Georgia-	(66–77) [ ] Stanley	(4–15) [ ] Owens-
	Weyerhaeuser	Pacific	Tools	Corning
Cabinets	01	01	01	01
Doors	02	02	02	02
Glue, sealers and related items	03	03	03	03
Insulation	04	04	04	04
Lumber (2×4, studs, etc.)	05	05	05	05
Nails and related items	06	06	06	06
Paint	07	07	07	07
Paint stain	08	08	08	08
Paneling	09	09	09	09
Plywood	10	10	10	10
Power tools	11	11	11	11
Sheetrock	12	12	12	12
Shelving	13	13	13	13
Tile	14	14	14	14
Tools	15	15	15	15
Treated lumber	16	16	16	16
Wood	17	17	17	17
Other (SPECIFY:)				
_____	18	18	18	18
_____	18	18	18	18
_____	18	18	18	18
_____	18	18	18	18
Don't know/Refused	19	19	19	19

Added categories (during the survey)

Roofing/shingles	20	20	20	20
Siding	21	21	21	21
Fiberglass	22	22	22	22

10. Now I would like you to rate <u>(ROTATE, START AT RED "X")</u> on several characteristics. (EACH RESONDENT WILL RATE WEYERHAEUSER AND <u>ONE</u> OTHER BRAND.)

    Use a 10-point scale where "10" means that <u>(NAME)</u> scores "very high" on that characteristic and a "1" means that it scores "very low." You can use any number between "1" and "10" to rate <u>(NAME)</u> on these characteristics.

    First, <u>(RED "X" PHRASE).</u> How would you rate <u>(NAME)</u> on <u>(PHRASE)</u>? REPEAT FOR ALL a–1:

	Very Low								Very High	DK/Ref.	
[ ] Weyerhaeuser												
( ) a. High quality products	01	02	03	04	05	06	07	08	09	10	11	16–17
( ) b. Useful advertising	01	02	03	04	05	06	07	08	09	10	11	18–19
( ) c. Low price	01	02	03	04	05	06	07	08	09	10	11	20–21
( ) d. Care about their customers	01	02	03	04	05	06	07	08	09	10	11	22–23
( ) e. Good value	01	02	03	04	05	06	07	08	09	10	11	24–25
( ) f. Honest and trustworthy	01	02	03	04	05	06	07	08	09	10	11	26–27
( ) g. High quality packaging	01	02	03	04	05	06	07	08	09	10	11	28–29
( ) h. Stand behind their products	01	02	03	04	05	06	07	08	09	10	11	30–31
( ) i. Provide design services for customers	01	02	03	04	05	06	07	08	09	10	11	32–33
( ) j. Offer a satisfaction guarantee	01	02	03	04	05	06	07	08	09	10	11	34–35
( ) k. Worth 10% more than others	01	02	03	04	05	06	07	08	09	10	11	36–37
( ) l. Complete product line	01	02	03	04	05	06	07	08	09	10	11	38–39

[ ] Other (READ RED-CHECKED, <u>ONLY</u>:)	[ ] (1) Georgia Pacific				[ ] (2) Stanley Tools				[ ] (3) Owens-Corning			40
( ) a. High quality products	01	02	03	04	05	06	07	08	09	10	11	41–42
( ) b. Useful advertising	01	02	03	04	05	06	07	08	09	10	11	43–44
( ) c. Low price	01	02	03	04	05	06	07	08	09	10	11	45–46
( ) d. Care about their customers	01	02	03	04	05	06	07	08	09	10	11	47–48

441

( ) e.	Good value	01	02	03	04	05	06	07	08	09	10	11	49–50
( ) f.	Honest and trustworthy	01	02	03	04	05	06	07	08	09	10	11	51–52
( ) g.	High quality packaging	01	02	03	04	05	06	07	08	09	10	11	53–54
( ) h.	Stand behind their products	01	02	03	04	05	06	07	08	09	10	11	55–56
( ) i.	Provide design services for customers	01	02	03	04	05	06	07	08	09	10	11	57–58
( ) j.	Offer a satisfaction guarantee	01	02	03	04	05	06	07	08	09	10	11	59–60
( ) k.	Worth 10% more than others	01	02	03	04	05	06	07	08	09	10	11	61–62
( ) l.	Complete product line	01	02	03	04	05	06	07	08	09	10	11	63–64

11. Finally, I'd like to ask a few questions about you and your house so that we can better understand the types of people and houses that are involved in various do-it-yourself projects.
Do you own or rent your home?

Own	1	
Rent	2	
Refused	3	65

12. About how long have you lived in this house?
RECORD: _____

OFFICE USE ONLY:		
Under 1 year	1	
1–4 years	2	
5–9 years	3	
10–14 years	4	
15 or more years	5	
Refused	6	66

13. About how old is this house?
RECORD: _____

OFFICE USE ONLY:		
Less than 1 year	1	
1–4 years	2	
5–9 years	3	
10–14 years	4	
15–19 years	5	
20–24 years	6	
25+ years	7	
Refused	8	67
Don't know	9	

14. About how many square feet are there? **RECORD:** _____

<u>OFFICE USE ONLY</u>:

Less than 750	1	
750–999	2	
1,000–1,499	3	
1,500–1,999	4	
2,000–2,499	5	
2,500–2,999	6	
3,000–3,499	7	
3,500–3,999	8	
4,000+	9	
Refused	0	68
Don't know	A	

15. How many people live in this house? **DO NOT READ.**

One	1	
Two	2	
Three	3	
Four	4	
Five	5	
Six	6	
Seven or more	7	
Refused	8	69

16a. Does anyone under 18 live in the house?

ASK Q.16b ←——— Yes   1

SKIP TO Q.17 ←——— No   2

Refused   3   70

16b. How old is the youngest person in the house? **RECORD:** _____

17. What is your approximate age . . . **READ 01–10:**

18–24	01
25–29	02
30–34	03
35–39	04
40–44	05
45–49	06
50–54	07
55–59	08
60–64	09
65 or over	10
Refused	11 71–72

443

18. What is your occupation? **IF RETIRED, PROBE FOR PRIOR OCCU-PATION AND NOTE** "Retired."

OFFICE USE ONLY:

Houseperson	1	
Student	2	
Retired	3	
Employed	4	
Refused	5	73

(Employed):

Low-skill, blue-collar/Manual labor	1	
High-skill, blue-collar worker/Technical	2	
Low-skill, white-collar/Sales	3	
High-skill white-collar/Sales/Low-level management	4	
Managerial/Professional	5	
Refused	6	74

19. And finally, what is your total household income (before taxes) . . . READ 1–9:

Less than $10,000	1	
$10,000–$19,999	2	
$20,000–$29,999	3	
$30,000–$39,999	4	
$40,000–$49,999	5	
$50,000–$69,999	6	
$70,000–$99,999	7	
$100,000–$124,999	8	
$125,000 or over	9	
Refused	0	75

20. RECORD:

MALE	1	
FEMALE	2	76

In case my supervisor needs to verify this call, may I have your first name, please?   BLANK 77–79
                                                                                                        END 80/2

_____

This concludes my questions. Thank you very much.

CASE III–2 PRICE PREMIUM, WARRANTY, AND BRAND NAME STUDY

A major firm involved in the food industry was interested in the potential for branding various vegetables that are generally sold as unbranded commodities (potatoes, tomatoes, lettuce, and celery). A primary objective was to determine if a price premium could be generated for branded vegetables with consistent high quality. Specifically, management wanted to determine how much of a price premium, if any, customers would pay for various brand names and types of guarantee. The brand names and guarantee levels of interest were as follows:

- Brand: none, Del Monte, Carnation, Green Giant
- Guarantee: none, satisfaction guaranteed, refund if not satisfied, replace if not satisfied

It was decided to test these value-added features against three price levels: average market price, 10 per cent above market, and 20 per cent above market. Price was set in actual dollar amounts to reflect these conditions.

A conjoint analysis approach was used. Six hundred store-intercept interviews were conducted in Rochester, Detroit, and San Francisco during November. Respondents were stopped as they left a supermarket and were offered a $5.00 gift certificate redeemable in the store for participating in the 15-minute survey. Only individuals who were the primary grocery shoppers for their household and who purchased at least one of the four vegetables at least twice a month were included. Various times of the day (week days and week-ends) were randomly selected to enhance the representativeness of the sample. Two stores from 2 different chains were used in each city.

The firm's ad agency prepared realistic 8 × 11 inch newspaper ads for each combination of attributes (1 price level, 1 brand name condition, and 1 guarantee condition) specified by the full profile conjoint design. This resulted in 16 ads for each vegetable.

Each respondent was asked to rank order the ads in terms of preference for the advertised product for each of two vegetable categories. In addition, a variety of background and attitude questions were asked. The instructions for the conjoint task are as follows:

We would like you to rank several vegetables. Each vegetable features several characteristics such as price, guarantee and brand.

(PRESENT ONE SET OF CARDS FROM PAIR TO RESPONDENT)

445

Each product characteristic is described on these cards. There are 16 cards describing 16 combinations of product characteristics. Please take your time and look them over.

Divide the cards into 3 piles. In the *LEFT* pile, place the ones you like the *most.* In the *RIGHT* pile, place the ones you like the *least.* In the *MIDDLE,* place the cards you are not sure about.

Now, take the pile on the *left* (the ones you liked the most) and rank them, putting those cards with the characteristics you are most favorable to on *top* of the pile, down to the least favorite on the bottom.

(REPEAT INSTRUCTIONS FOR OTHER TWO PILES. CHECK TO MAKE SURE RESPONDENT UNDERSTANDS PROCEDURE. RECORD PROFILE NUMBER FROM THE FRONT OF CARDS IN RANK ORDER BELOW, PROCEEDING FROM TOP TO BOTTOM OF EACH PILE.)

WRITE IN CARD COLOR & PRODUCT NUMBER BELOW

CARD COLORS	RANK ORDER
YELLOW = potatoes	LEFT PILE (LIKED MOST)
BLUE = tomatoes	MIDDLE PILE (NOT SURE)
PINK = lettuce	RIGHT PILE (LIKED LEAST)
GRAY = celery	

PRESENT NEXT SET OF CARDS TO RESPONDENT AND REPEAT INSTRUCTIONS

_____ 37 _____ 70
(WRITE IN CARD COLOR & PRODUCT NUMBER)   (WRITE IN CARD COLOR & PRODUCT NUMBER)

LIKE MOST
1. _____ 38 – 39   _____ 71 – 72
2. _____ 40 – 41   _____ 73 – 74
3. _____ 42 – 43   _____ 75 – 76
4. _____ 44 – 45   _____ 77 – 78
5. _____ 46 – 47   _____ 5 – 6
6. _____ 48 – 49   _____ 7 – 8
7. _____ 50 – 51   _____ 9 – 10
8. _____ 52 – 53   _____ 11 – 12

9.	——— 54–55	———	13–14
10.	——— 56–57	———	15–16
11.	——— 58–59	———	17–18
12.	——— 60–61	———	19–20
13.	——— 62–63	———	21–22
14.	——— 64–65	———	23–24
15.	——— 66–67	———	25–26
LIKE LEAST 16.	——— 68–69	———	27–28

1. Evaluate this use of conjoint analysis.
2. Evaluate the research design used, and suggest specific improvements as required.
3. What additional data would you collect? Why? How would you use it?
4. Develop a set of part-worth figures that would indicate:
   a. high brand impact, low price sensitivity, low guarantee sensitivity
   b. low brand impact, high price sensitivity, modest guarantee sensitivity

CASE III–3 FOOTE, CONE, & BELDING, INC.: MASKED RECOGNITION EXPERIMENT*

A question that advertisers have pondered for many years is "Will my brand's advertising have a better chance for sales success if it is *rational* and appeals to the *logic* of my prospect, or will it do better if it appeals to the *emotions?*"

Emotional appeal commercials ("feeling" commercials) almost always score lower in day-after-recall tests than do rational appeal commercials ("thinking" commercials). This could be the result of one, or both, of two causes: it may be that emotional appeals are less memorable than rational appeals, and that the day-after-recall (DAR) tests scores correctly reflect this difference, or it may be that the way DAR tests typically are conducted unfairly discriminates against emotional appeal commercials.

Research department personnel at the Foote, Cone & Belding advertising agency believed that DAR tests might be unfairly discriminatory. Typical DAR tests require the respondent to verbalize a recognizable part of the advertising message. This, they speculated, can be difficult when the ad's appeal is pri-

* The material for this case was provided by Foote, Cone & Belding, Inc. and is used with the agency's permission.

447

3 "thinking" commercials

3 "feeling" commercials

marily emotional. Based on this possible explanation of the persistent **DAR** score difference, a decision was made to conduct a recall experiment in which verbalization of one or more copy points was not required, and to see how the scores of "thinking" and "feeling" commercials compared.

The measure of recall that was decided upon for the experiment was a "masked recognition" score. A "masked" commercial is a regular commercial with the brand name erased from the sound track and blanked out of the video. Otherwise, nothing is altered. The subject is shown the "masked" commercial the day after she saw the regular commercial with nothing blocked out. She is asked if she can identify the brand in the masked commercial. The proportion who are able to do so correctly comprises the score for the commercial.

Three "thinking" and three "feeling" commercials, all judged to have been well executed, were selected from among 39 video commercials produced by Foote, Cone & Belding. All six commercials selected represented regularly advertised brands, were of interest to women, and had received little exposure. Frames from these commercials are shown above.

The six selected commercials were used on cable television in Grand Rapids, Michigan and San Diego, California. A preselected sample of 400 women, aged 18 to 49, agreed to watch a 30-minute situation comedy on which three of the commercials appeared.

The sample of 400 was divided into four subsamples of 100 women each. Subsample 1 and 2 women were exposed to the "thinking" commercials A, D, and F. Subsample 3 and 4 women were shown the "feeling" commercials B, C, and E.

On the following day, all the women were interviewed. Subsample 1 women were interviewed using standard **DAR** techniques (as described on page 224). Subsample 2 women were interviewed after seeing the masked version of the commercials and asked to identify the brand of the product involved. As an extra accuracy measure, subsample 2 women were also shown masked versions of commercials B, C, and E — ones they had not seen on the preceding day — and false recognition scores for each woman were subtracted from her correct identification score.

The same pattern was followed for subsamples 3 and 4. The overall exposure and test assignments by subsample is shown in the following box.

Subsample 1 100 Women	Subsample 2 100 Women	Subsample 3 100 Women	Subsample 4 100 Women
Standard Day- After Recall Measurement Commercial A Commercial D Commercial F	Masked Recognition Measurement Commercial A Commercial D Commercial F Commercial B° Commercial C° Commercial E°	Standard Day- After Recall Measurement Commercial B Commercial C Commercial E	Masked Recognition Measurement Commercial B Commercial C Commercial E Commercial A° Commercial C° Commercial E°

° Shown in masked form only and only on the following day. False identification scores were used to reduce correct identification scores.

Masked recognition scores on the average were 19 per cent greater than DAR scores for the three "thinking" commercials. Masked recognition was 68 per cent greater than DAR for the three "feeling" commercials. The findings led FCB agency personnel to conclude that masked recognition is a truer measure of actual remembering than asking people to verbalize their recollection of a commercial. They believe this becomes particularly significant on emotional — "feeling" — commercials.

1. How would you describe the design used in the experiment (e.g., before-after with control, 4-group 6-study, and so on)?

2. What are the major strengths of the design? What are the major weaknesses? Explain.

3. Do you agree with the FCB contention that "masked recognition is a truer measure of actual remembering than asking people to verbalize their recollection of a commercial?" Why or why not? (Note: In answering question 3 you may find reference to the following articles helpful: J. Alter, "Skeptics Descend on FCB Recall Study," *Advertising Age*, May 25, 1981, 14; and R. B. Zajonc, "Feeling and Thinking: Preferences Need No Inferences," *American Psychologist*, 35 (1980), 151–175.)

CASE III−4 BRX INTERMEDIA COMPARISON TEST: A PROPOSED RESEARCH DESIGN FOR TESTING THE RELATIVE EFFECTIVENESS OF MEDIA*

The management of **BRX**, Inc., a marketing research agency in Rochester, New York, was convinced that there was a substantial need for valid measurements of the relative effectiveness of a specific set of advertisements across the print, television, radio, and billboard media. Acting upon this belief, the agency devised the following method of intermedia comparisons and proposed it to its clients.

The BRX Process for Intermedia Comparisons: A Proposal

The Experimental Design

We propose to test the relative effectiveness of different media for a single ad that has been adapted for use in each medium involved. To do so we intend to select, in a shopping mall that has a research facility, separate samples of approximately 200 consumers for each medium that is selected. The tests will be conducted on an "after only" basis because we believe that "before" measurements tend to lead to potential biases. A control group that is not exposed to any of the ads can also be used if desired.

To disguise the fact that we are conducting tests on advertising, the sample consumers will be told that they will be participating in a "product" test. The ad in the test will be presented in such a way that the consumers can view, look, or listen to it or not depending upon their interest and the attention-getting ability of the ad. Each respondent will have the opportunity for three exposures to the ad in his or her test.

We intend to interview respondents immediately after they are exposed to the test advertisement. The basic criterion measures for evaluating relative effectiveness will be brand awareness, attitude toward the brand, pertinent values or goals related to product category usage, and beliefs about the brand leading to and from these goals. No reference will be made to the exposure situation, at least until after the key measures have been taken.

---

* The material presented in this case is adopted from "The BRX Process for Inter-Media Comparisons Proposal," prepared by BRX, Inc. It is used with the company's permission.

Exposure Opportunities

We intend to place each respondent in one of four test situations depending upon whether we are testing TV commercials, radio commercials, print ads, or billboards.

Television

If we are testing TV commercials for a brand, we propose to use a TV monitor that will be showing a public service film. The same test commercial would be spliced into the film at two-minute intervals so that an eleven-minute segment of programming would contain three repeats of the same commercial. The TV monitor would be situated so that respondents could look at it while they were seated in the waiting room. Some magazines would also be available for them to peruse. Prior to the "pseudo" product test and exposure, demographic and product usage data would be obtained. No mention would be made of the television set, the program, or the commercials. The respondent would be told that the few minutes' wait was necessary for us to prepare the material for testing.

Radio

In the case of testing a radio commercial, we would simply be playing music with three tapes of the identical commercial spliced in at two-minute intervals. The respondent, in this situation also, would have the opportunity to be exposed to three advertisements in the ten minutes in which he or she would be waiting. Again, demographic and product usage data would be obtained prior to exposure to the product test. As before, there would also be magazines available. No mention would be made of the radio program or the commercial. (It should be noted that in testing radio commercials we can systematically vary the context from popular music to acid rock to classical music or to news.)

Print Media

In the case of print the procedure is somewhat more involved. While the respondents are in the waiting room, we tell them that their task is going to be to match product samples with brand names and that, in order to help them make this match, we are first going to show them advertisements for each of the brands. At this point, we present them with a folder full of advertisements. When we open the folder we note that "accidentally" there are advertisements from other tests along with ads at which we are asking them to look. Of course, these accidental ads are, in fact, the real test ads. Here again, the respondent would have the opportunity to be exposed to three of the same test ads intermixed with the "ads we wanted her to examine."

451

Outdoor

The procedure for testing billboards is different from that used for TV, radio or print, although the time and number of exposures are held constant. (Regardless of whether we are talking about TV, radio, print, or billboard, an overriding concern is keeping the time period and the number of exposure opportunities constant.) We ask respondents to participate in a "driver safety test" using a Link Trainer type device. This test simply entails "driving" along a road lined with three billboards featuring the same advertisement. We make no mention of these billboards to the respondent.

1. List as many implicit assumptions involved in this proposed research design as you can.
2. Provide a brief evaluation of the validity of each assumption.
3. Give an overall evaluation of the likely
   a. validity, and
   b. reliability
   of the proposed research design.

CASE III−5 UNITED STATES POSTAL SERVICE TEST MARKET OF THE INDIAN HEAD PENNY STAMP

The United States Postal Service (USPS) planned to issue a 150-subject postage stamp in 150 units per sheet form on January 11. The stamp, Indian Head Penny, would be smaller in size than the standard postage stamp currently in the system. Because of the unusual size of this new issue, the stamp was to be test marketed to determine the degree of public acceptance. An annual savings of approximately $500,000 in material costs could be realized in the production of prime rate sheet stamps should a smaller size be adopted.

Background

The standard postage stamp measures .75 × .87 inches and is produced with 100 stamps to a sheet. The Indian Head Penny stamp measured .66 × .83 inches and had 150 stamps to the same size sheet. The stamps were to be test marketed in five selected cities, one in each postal region, from January to May, the probable month of the next postage rate increase. The stamps were also to be available at each of the approximately 100 stamp-collecting centers and at the Philatelic Sales Branch in Washington, D.C., for a minimum of one year for the benefit of collectors.

There were two basic reasons for the study. The primary reason was related to customer perception and the introduction of a change of this nature. Although acceptance problems were not anticipated, a national introduction of the smaller stamp without prior testing could appear to be an arbitrary move by the USPS. Therefore, the study was conducted and its results taken seriously. The second reason for the study was to discover any unanticipated problems with the acceptance or use of the smaller stamps.

Procedure

An initial quantity of the Indian Head Penny stamp was delivered to each of the test cities. These stamps were sold in lieu of the current American Flag over Independence Hall and the Eagle and Shield sheet postage stamps, unless the customers specifically requested the Flag and Eagle sheet stamps. No minimum purchase was required for orders placed at the Philatelic Sales Branch; however, the sale of plate numbers and marginal markings were restricted to full sheets.

The testing took place in two segments. The first segment was to determine the reaction of the philatelist and others who did not purchase their stamps through regular post office windows. During the first two weeks after issuance of this stamp, handout questionnaires were given to purchasers of this smaller-sized stamp in all of the approximately one hundred USPS philatelic centers and included in orders processed by the Philatelic Sales Branch in Washington, D.C. During the two-week test period, each Philatelic Center received approximately 150 questionnaires to be given to stamp collectors, until either the supply was exhausted or the two-week survey period ended. The questionnaire used in this first segment is shown in Exhibit A.

The second segment of the test was conducted by telephone interview in each of the five cities in which the new 150-stamp sheets were distributed. The telephone interviews were conducted twice during the five-month test period. A target of one hundred small-stamp purchasers were interviewed from each city for each survey. The selection of respondents was made through a random dial technique and geared toward adult householders, of which an equal number were male and female. The questionnaire used for the telephone survey is shown in Exhibit B.

Exhibit A 150 Stamp Sheet Survey Stamp Collector Questionnaire

POST OFFICE STATION/BRANCH AND ZIP CODE   YOUR ZIP CODE   DATE

Dear Postal Customer:

We would like your opinion about the new smaller stamp which you just purchased. Please complete this questionnaire, then fold, seal, and drop it in the nearest mailbox. NO POSTAGE IS REQUIRED.

1. How many of the new smaller size stamps did your purchase?

   (1) _____ full sheets   (2) _____ single stamps
       (16–17)   (18–19)

2. A. Did you purchase the new smaller size stamp for (Please check):

   (1) ☐ Your personal use   (3) ☐ Collection purposes[20]
   (2) ☐ Business use   (4) ☐ Other reasons (Specify)

   B. If you purchased these stamps for collection purposes, about how many will be saved? _____ (21–23)
      number saved

3. Did you purchase your stamps:

   (1) ☐ In person at a philatelic sales center   (2) ☐ By mail from the Philatelic Sales Branch in
         or post office?   Washington, D.C.?[24]

4. How did you first become aware of the new smaller stamps? Did you:

   (1) ☐ See them in a news release or stamp   (2) ☐ Hear about them from a friend or acquaintance[25]
         journal article
   (3) ☐ Receive them when purchasing postage stamps at the post office without knowing that a new smaller stamp had
         been issued.
   (4) ☐ Other (Specify)

5. What do you like about the new smaller size stamps _____   ( ) 26–27
                                                                                        ( ) 28–29

6. What do you dislike about the new smaller size stamps? _____   ( ) 30–31
   _____   ( ) 32–33

7. Have you applied any of the new smaller stamps on mail matter?

   (1) ☐ Yes   (2) ☐ No (If "No," go to question number 9)[34]

8. A. Compared to regular size stamps, how would you rate the way in which the new smaller stamps separated? Do the
      smaller stamps separate:

(3) ☐ More difficult. [35] Why do you say that? _____ $\left.\begin{array}{l}\\\\\end{array}\right\}$[36-37]

(4) ☐ Did not need to separate. $\left.\begin{array}{l}\end{array}\right\}$[38-39]

B. Compared to regular size stamps, how would you rate the way the new smaller stamps adhere to the mail matter? Do the smaller stamps adhere:

(1) ☐ Easier   (3) ☐ More difficult. [40] Why do you say that? _____ $\left(\begin{array}{l}\end{array}\right.$[41-42]

(2) ☐ About the same _____ $\left(\begin{array}{l}\end{array}\right.$[43-44]

9. The next time that you purchase stamps, will you request more stamps of this same size?

(1) ☐ Yes   (2) ☐ No (Why not?) _____   (3) ☐ No preference[45]

10. Do you collect U.S. Mint Stamps?

(1) ☐ Yes   (2) ☐ No (If "No," go to question number 15)[46]

11. How long have you been a collector of U.S. Mint Stamps? _____ $\left(\begin{array}{l}\end{array}\right.$[47-48]

12. How frequently do you purchase U.S. Mint Stamps? _____ $\left(\begin{array}{l}\end{array}\right.$[49-50]

13. On the average, how much do you spend each time you purchase U.S. Mint Stamps? \$ _____ [51-53]

14. Do you primarily collect (Check ALL that apply):

(1) ☐ Plate Blocks   (3) ☐ Strips   (5) ☐ Other (Specify)[54]
(2) ☐ Full sheets   (4) ☐ Single Stamps   _____

15. What is your sex?

(1) ☐ Male   (2) ☐ Female[55]

16. Which represents your age group?

(1) ☐ Under 13   (3) ☐ 18-35   (5) ☐ Over 55[56]
(2) ☐ 13-17   (4) ☐ 36-55

17. What is the highest level of education that you have obtained?

(1) ☐ 8th Grade or Less   (3) ☐ High School Graduate   (5) ☐ College Graduate[57]
(2) ☐ Some High School   (4) ☐ Some College   (6) ☐ Post-Graduate

18. Which represents the range of your total family income?

(1) ☐ up to \$9,999   (3) ☐ \$15,000-\$19,999   (5) ☐ \$25,000-\$29,999[58]
(2) ☐ \$10,000-\$14,999   (4) ☐ \$20,000-\$24,999   (6) ☐ \$30,000 or more

THANK YOU FOR YOUR COOPERATION

PS Form 5079-X

GPO 925-434

455

Exhibit B *150 Stamp Sheet Survey Telephone Questionnaire*

Study # _____
Interviewer _____
Date _____
Time Start _____ Time End _____
ID # _____

INTERVIEWER: ASK TO SPEAK TO AN ADULT MEMBER OF THE HOUSEHOLD.

Hello, my name is _____ of _____.

We are conducting a survey among purchasers of postage stamps.

1. About how long ago did you purchase any U.S. Postage Stamps?
   Time or Date _____

(INTERVIEWER: IF PURCHASE DATA WAS PRIOR TO DISTRIBUTION OF 150 STAMP SHEET—JANUARY 11, TERMINATE INTERVIEW.)

2a. What types of stamps did you purchase? (READ AND CHECK UNDER "PURCHASED")
   FOR EACH TYPE PURCHASED ASK . . .

2b. How many (TYPE) did you purchase? (RECORD UNDER "NUMBER")
   (PROBE IF NECESSARY)

	2a. Purchased (Yes)	(No)	2b. Number
Sheets	_____	_____	_____
Coils	_____	_____	_____
Singles	_____	_____	_____
Books	_____	_____	_____
Other . . . SPECIFY	_____	_____	_____

3. Recently, the Postal Service issued a new smaller size stamp which is available in your area. Are you aware of this new smaller stamp?
   _____a) YES   _____b) NO . . . SKIP TO Q. 16

4. Were any of the stamps that you purchased the new smaller sized postage stamps?
   _____a) YES . . . GO TO Q. 6   _____b) NO

5. What was your reason for *not* purchasing the smaller size stamp?
   _____
   _____
   _____

   GO TO Q. 16

6. At present, this new small stamp is available only in sheet form. It does not come in books or coils. How many of the new smaller size stamps have you purchased in total?
   _____Full Sheets   _____Single Stamps

7. a. Did you purchase the new smaller size stamp for:
   (CHECK ALL THAT APPLY)
   _____1) Your personal use
   _____2) Business use
   _____3) Collection purposes
   _____4) Other reasons SPECIFY _____

   b. If you purchased these stamps for collection purposes, about how many will be saved?
   _____Number saved

8. The new smaller stamp is available only in selected cities, including (RESPONDENT'S CITY). Did you purchase your stamps:
   _____a) In person at a post office
   _____b) By mail from the Philatelic Sales Branch in Washington, D.C.
   _____c) Other . . . SPECIFY _____

9. I'd like to know how you first became aware of the new smaller stamps? Did you:

_____a) See them in a news release or stamp journal article
_____b) Hear about them from a friend or acquaintance
_____c) Receive them when purchasing postage stamps at a post office without knowing that a new smaller stamp had been issued
_____d) Other . . . SPECIFY_____

10. What do you *like* about the new smaller size stamps?_____
_____
_____
_____
_____

11. What do you *dislike* about the new smaller size stamps?_____
_____
_____
_____

12. Have you applied any of the smaller size stamps on mail matter?
_____a) YES   _____b) NO . . . GO TO Q. 15

13. Compared to regular size stamps, how would you rate the way in which the new smaller stamps separated? Do the smaller stamps separate:
_____a) Easier
_____b) About the same
_____c) More difficult . . . Why do you say that?_____
_____
_____
_____d) Did not need to separate

14. Compared to regular size stamps, how would you rate the way the new smaller stamps adhere to the mail matter? Do the smaller stamps adhere:
_____a) Easier
_____b) About the same
_____c) More difficult . . . Why do you say that?_____
_____
_____

15. The next time that you purchase stamps will you request more of the same size?
_____a) Yes   _____b) No . . . Why not?
_____c) No Preference   _____
_____

16. Do you collect U.S. Mint Stamps:
_____a) Yes   _____b) No . . . GO TO Q. 21

17. How long have you been a collector of U.S. Mint Stamps?_____

18. How frequently do you purchase U.S. Mint Stamps:_____

19. On the average, how much do you spend each time you purchase U.S. Mint Stamps?
$_____

20. Do you primarily collect: (CHECK *ALL* THAT APPLY)
_____a) Plate Blocks   _____d) Single Stamps
_____b) Full Sheets   _____e) Other
_____c) Strips   SPECIFY_____

21. What is your sex? _____a) Male   _____b) Female

22. Which represents your age group?
_____a) 18–35   _____b) 36–55   _____c) over 55

23. What is the highest level of education that you have obtained?
_____a) 8th grade or less   _____d) Some college
_____b) Some high school   _____e) College graduate
_____c) High school graduate _____f) Post-graduate college

24. Which represents the range of your total family income?
_____a) Up to $9,999   _____d) $20,000–$24,999
_____b) $10,000–$14,999   _____e) $25,000–$29,999
_____c) $15,000–$19,999   _____f) $30,000 or more

Thank you for your cooperation.

457

Action to Be Taken

In the event that public acceptance of a new smaller-sized stamp proved to be favorable, consideration was to be given to producing the regular prime rate sheet stamp in the new smaller size.

1. Evaluate the methodology used.
2. Evaluate the questionnaires.
3. Will the study provide the required data?

SECTION 4

Sampling and Data Analysis

Sampling and data analysis each play an important role in the research project. Without a sound sampling plan and a suitable sample size, the data will be collected from neither the proper respondents nor the appropriate number of them. And inadequate or inappropriate data analysis can negate the efforts going into an otherwise soundly designed and competently conducted project.

The first two chapters of this section are concerned with sampling. Chapter 15 deals with devising the *sampling plan*, and then putting it into effect. Determining the appropriate size *of the sample* is the subject of Chapter 16.

The next five chapters are devoted to data analysis. *Data reduction*, the process of getting the data ready for analysis, and *statistical estimation* are the subjects of Chapter 17. Hypothesis tests involving one variable are considered in Chapter 18. Multivariate hypothesis tests are the concern of Chapter 19, while measures of association between variables are covered in Chapter 20.

Sales forecasting is a pervasive activity that is central to marketing, production, and financial planning. It is the subject of Chapter 21.

CHAPTER 15

Sampling and Research: The Sampling Process

The following are sampling situations arising from actual research projects:

- *The president of Frontier Stoves, a wood stove manufacturer, asked the person in charge of marketing research for the company to conduct focus-group interviews of blue-collar, white-collar, and managerial/professional owners of wood stoves to determine what they see as the principal benefits and problems arising from the use of stoves.*

- *Elrick and Lavidge, a research agency, has interviewing facilities located in 19 shopping malls throughout the United States. A client wanted a mall-intercept sample of adult women selected to obtain information about preferences concerning alternative formulations of a proposed new food product.*

- *A manufacturer and marketer of home permanent preparations, the Toni Company, decided to commission a national survey on the electronic media viewing/listening and reading habits of women.*

The persons who designed the sampling plans for each of these research situations had to answer the two basic questions involved in every sample design: "What kind of sample should we take?" and "How large should it be?"

Sampling is a necessary and inescapable part of human affairs. Each of us samples and is sampled regularly. We sample the kind of performance and riding characteristics we can expect of a car we are considering buying by a test drive, the quality of the food and the service at a restaurant by a first meal, and how likely we are to become friends with an acquaintance by a first

461

meeting. We are parts of groups that are sampled to select juries, express a preference from among political candidates, state opinions on issues, and record which television shows we watch and products we buy.

If all possible information needed to solve a problem could be collected, there would be no need to sample. We can rarely do this, however, because of limitations on the amount we can afford to spend and on the available time, or for other reasons. We, therefore, must take samples.

This chapter begins with a discussion of the reasons for sampling. The steps in the sampling process are then discussed, including a description of the various types of samples that may be taken, and the principal factors involved in their selection. The sampling process actually used in each of the situations described at the beginning of this chapter is then discussed.

Census Versus Sample

It is sometimes possible and practicable to take a *census;* that is, to measure each element in the group or population of interest. Surveys of industrial consumers or of distributors of consumer products are frequently in the form of a census. More often than not, however, it is impractical, or even impossible, to take a census. The reasons involve considerations of *cost, time, accuracy,* and *the destructive nature of the measurement.*

Cost and Census Versus Sample

Cost is an obvious constraint on the determination of whether a census should be taken. If information is desired on grocery purchase and use behavior (frequencies and amounts of purchase of each product category, average amount kept at home, and the like) and the population of interest is all households in the United States, the cost will preclude a census being taken. The budget for the 1980 Decennial Census of Population was more than $1 billion. As an approximation of the cost of a census of households to obtain the information on groceries, it is apparent that this cost would far exceed any conceivable value of such information for a marketer of this type of product. A sample is the only logical way of obtaining new data from a population of this size.

If one needed information on a proposed new product for use on commercial airlines, however, a census might be a highly practical solution. There are only about 25 major airlines in the United States and, if this were the population of interest, the cost of taking a census might well be less than the value of the information obtained.

462

Time and Census Versus Sample

The kind of cost we have just considered is an *outlay* cost. The time involved in obtaining information from either a census or a sample involves the possibility of also incurring an *opportunity* cost. That is, delaying the decision until information is obtained may result in a smaller gain or a larger loss than would have been the case from making the same decision earlier. The opportunity to make more (or save more, as the case may be) is, therefore, foregone.

Even if a census of households to obtain information on grocery purchase and use behavior were practical from a cost standpoint, it might not be so when the time required to conduct the census is considered. Data collection for the 1980 Decennial Census in the United States was begun in April 1980, and yet the detailed characteristics of the population were not published until early 1983. Most of the kinds of decisions made by business firms need to be made in less time than that.

Accuracy and Census Versus Sample

A study using a census, by definition, contains no sampling error. It may contain any of the other types of error described in Chapter 3. A study using a sample may involve sampling error in addition to the other types of error. Therefore, *other things being equal,* a census will provide more accurate data than a sample.

However, it is sometimes possible, given the same expenditure of time and money, to reduce the nonsampling errors in a sample relative to those in a census to the point at which the sum of the sampling and nonsampling errors of the sample are *less* than the nonsampling error alone in the census. When this is the case, *it is possible to obtain a more accurate measurement from a sample than from a census.* This involves the concept of error trade-off discussed in Chapter 3.

It has been argued that a more accurate estimate of the population of the United States could be made from a sample than from a census. Taking a census of population on a "mail out – mail back" basis requires that the names and addresses of almost 80 million households be obtained, census questionnaires mailed, and interviews conducted of those not responding. The questionnaires are sent to a population whose median number of school years completed is 10.6, and whose median reading level is perhaps that of the 6th or 7th grade. The potential for errors in the questionnaires returned is therefore high.

Approximately 275 thousand temporary interviewers have to be recruited, trained, and supervised to conduct interviews at those households that did not return questionnaires. The interviewers must be taught how to read maps, ask questions, and record information. The potential for error from missed assignments, poor interviewing, nonresponse, and faulty recording is large.

As examples, people interviewed by census takers have reported afterward that they thought they had been visited by a representative of the Internal Revenue Service, a man from the county assessor's office, or a termite inspector. Open and unbiased responses seem unlikely in such situations. Because of these and other problems, the 1980 census undercounted the population of the United States by an estimated 2.2 million people. This is the equivalent of not including a city the size of Baltimore in the census.

With those kinds of problems, it is understandable how it could be argued that, given careful selection, training, and supervision of interviewers, nonsampling errors in a sample of the population could be reduced to the point at which the overall population estimate would be more accurate than one obtained from a census. In fact, samples are used for much of the data gathered by the Bureau of the Census and, in some cases, sample data are used to check the accuracy of data collected in censuses.

It is not always possible to reduce nonsampling error by an amount sufficient to compensate for sampling error. In the case of the company needing an evaluation of a potential new product for use by the major U.S. domestic airlines, this may not be the case. Given a total population of 25 airlines, missing just one of them raises the possibility of a sampling error in the estimation of the market potential for the product an average of 4 per cent. It is unlikely that significant reductions could be made in the other types of errors by the expenditure of the funds freed by changing from a census to a sample in a case such as this.

Destructive Nature of the Measurement

Measurements are sometimes destructive in nature. When they are, it is apparent that taking a census would usually defeat the purpose of the measurement. If one were producing firecrackers, electrical fuses, or grass seed, performing a functional use test on all products for quality-control purposes would not be considered from an economic standpoint. A sample is then the only practical choice. On the other hand, if light bulbs, bicycles, or electrical appliances are to be tested, a 100 per cent sample (census) may be entirely reasonable.

The Sampling Process

We have discussed briefly *why* samples are taken; it is now appropriate to consider *how* they are taken. The sampling process consists of seven sequen-

Table 15-1 Steps in the Sampling Process

Step	Description
1. Define the population	The population is defined in terms of (a) element, (b) units, (c) extent, and (d) time.
2. Specify sampling frame	The means of representing the elements of the population — for example, telephone book, map, or city directory — are described.
3. Specify sampling unit	The unit for sampling — for example, city block, company, or household — is selected. The sampling unit may contain one or several population elements.
4. Specify sampling method	The method by which the sampling units are to be selected is described.
5. Determine sample size	The number of elements of the population to be sampled is chosen.
6. Specify sampling plan	The operational procedures for selection of the sampling units are selected.
7. Select the sample	The office and fieldwork necessary for the selection of the sample are carried out.

tial steps. These steps are listed and a brief summary description is given in Table 15-1, and a more detailed treatment of each step of the sampling process is given in the sections that follow.

Step 1. Define the Population

The population for a survey of purchasing agents might be defined as "all purchasing agents in companies and government agencies that have bought any of our products in the last three years." The population for a price survey might be defined as "the price of each competitive brand in supermarkets in the Cleveland sales territory during the period July 15-30."

To be complete, a population must be defined in terms of *elements, sampling units, extent* and *time.* In relation to these constituent parts, the population of purchasing agents is

(element)	purchasing agents in
(sampling unit)	companies and governmental agencies that have
(extent)	bought any of our products
(time)	in the last three years.

Similarly, the population for the price survey is defined as

(element)	price of each competitive brand
(sampling unit)	in supermarkets
(extent)	in the Cleveland sales territory
(time)	during the period July 15–30.

Eliminating any one of these specifications leaves an incomplete definition of the population that is to be sampled.

Defining a population incorrectly may render the results of the study meaningless or even misleading for the decision at hand. For example, the population for a study of the eating habits of single persons was defined as

(element)	All persons 18 years of age or older who live by themselves and are shopping in
(sampling unit)	supermarkets
(extent)	in Los Angeles, California
(time)	during the week of January 18–24.

One of the findings of the research was that "singles do not eat meals away from home as frequently as previously thought."[1] This result could hardly have come as a surprise given that the singles interviewed were all shopping in supermarkets. If the interviews had been conducted in restaurants, the finding would almost certainly have been that "singles eat meals away from home *more* frequently than previously thought." What the finding would have been on this issue if a probability sample of all singles had been taken is not known.

It is sometimes difficult to define the population properly. For example, how would you define the population for a survey to determine the best features to develop for a children's cereal, a large telecommunications system, a station wagon, a marketing research textbook, or a frozen dessert? To define any of these populations properly, one would have to know the role played by each family or organizational member in the purchase and consumption of the product, as well as what types of families and/or organizations constitute the primary market. At times, a research project is required to define the population before the study for which it is to be used can begin.

Exhibit 15–1 illustrates how misspecifying a population almost led Johnson & Johnson into making an incorrect advertising decision.

Step 2. Specify the Sampling Frame

If a probability sample is to be taken, a *sampling frame* is required. A *sampling frame is a means of representing the elements of the population.* A sampling frame may be a telephone book, a city directory, an employee roster, a listing of all students attending a university, or a list of all possible phone numbers.

Maps also serve frequently as sampling frames. A sample of areas within a city may be taken and another sample of households may then be taken within each area. City blocks are sometimes sampled and all households on each sample block are included. A sampling of street intersections may be taken and interviewers given instructions as to how to take "random walks" from the intersection and select the households to be interviewed.

A perfect sampling frame is one in which *every element of the population is*

Exhibit 15–1   *The Effect of Population Specification on Day-After-Recall Measures of Advertising Effectiveness*

Day-after-recall (DAR) is one of the most popular methods for copy testing television commercials. The method involves running the commercial on the air and telephoning a random sample of individuals the next day to determine their recall of the copy of the commercial. A recall score is computed as the percentage of those watching television when the commercial was aired who can recall some aspect of the commercial. Substantial evidence suggests that recall is not strongly affected by product usage. The following results were obtained from an analysis of 611 DAR studies.

	Recall Scores	
Total	*Product Users*	*Product Nonusers*
24	26	21

Based on evidence of this nature and the high cost of sampling only users, the population for most DAR studies is defined as all adults (or males or females) at homes with telephones who were at a television set when the commercial was aired. This approach was used by Johnson & Johnson to test two commercials for a skin-conditioning product. The results were:

	Recall Score
Commercial A	14
Commercial B	15
Norm	23

The norm represents the average recall score for commercials this length (30 seconds).

Based on these results, neither commercial would be used. However, the commercials were also tested in a theater test (people are brought to a theater to view programs that contain the commercials). The theater test used a sample composed primarily of product category users. Using a somewhat different measure of copy effectiveness, the following results were obtained:

	Effectiveness Score
Commercial A	20
Commercial B	12
Norm	8

Using this sample and measurement technique, both commercials could be used but A is clearly superior.

Given these conflicting results, Johnson & Johnson retested commercial A on a DAR basis with a sample selected from a universe defined as "purchasers of any brand in the product category in the past year." A third DAR test was conducted on a sample selected from a universe defined as "users of any brand in the product category in the past month." The results were:

	Recall Score
Total audience	14
Past year purchasers	47
Past month users	59
Norm	23

Clearly, measured recall for some types of commercials depends on the specification of the population. Since the Johnson & Johnson campaign was designed to influence current product users, relying on the normal population specification for DAR tests would have caused the company to make the wrong decision.

Source: Derived from C. L. Hodock, "Copy Testing and Strategic Positioning," *Journal of Advertising Research* (February 1980), 33–38.

represented once but only once. The listing of stock prices in the *Wall Street Journal* provides a perfect frame for sampling listed stocks on the New York Stock Exchange. Examples of perfect frames are rare, however, when one is interested in sampling from any appreciable segment of a human population.

Probably the most widely used frame for sampling human populations is the telephone book. Although over 97 per cent of the households in the United States have telephones,[2] the distribution of telephone ownership is not even across all groups. Low-income, rural, and inner-city homes constitute the primary source of homes without telephones. In addition, many homes with telephones do not have their numbers listed in the telephone directory. For the United States as a whole, an estimate from one study is that 28 per cent of the households have unlisted telephone numbers with rates above 60 per cent in some metropolitan areas.[3]

People with unlisted telephone numbers tend to live in metropolitan areas, be younger, and have a somewhat lower income, and are more likely to be single than those with listed numbers. Single women who live alone often have unlisted numbers for security reasons. Nonwhites are about three times as likely to have an unlisted number as are whites (see Chapter 6, and Case II – 5). In contrast, middle income and affluent households with children are likely to have multiple phone numbers, a factor that enhances their likelihood of inclusion in a telephone book based sample.

These omissions and dual listings may lead to *frame errors* in a study in which the telephone book is used as a sampling frame. This is true of city directories, maps, census tract information, or any other listing or representation of a population that is incomplete or out of date. Unfortunately, some frame error is probably unavoidable in most surveys of human populations. Exhibit 15 – 2 describes Survey Sampling, Inc.'s procedure for developing a sampling frame for random digit dialing samples (see Chapter 6, page 153).

One does not need a sampling frame to take a nonprobability sample. Samples of people taken on a convenience basis or by *referral* or by any of the other techniques for taking nonprobability samples discussed later in this chapter do not require a sampling frame. Rather, sampling units are selected on the basis of judgment or convenience, given that they each have the characteristics, if any, that are specified (including sex, age, education level, ownership or nonownership of a product).

Step 3. Specify Sampling Unit

The sampling unit is the basic unit containing the elements of the population to be sampled. It may be the element itself or a unit in which the element is contained. For example, if one wanted a sample of males over 13 years of age, it might be possible to sample them directly. In this case, the sampling unit would be identical with the element. However, it might be easier to select

Exhibit 15–2   *Survey Sampling, Inc.'s Sample Frame for Random Digit Dialed Surveys*

By starting out with an extensive cleaning and validation process, we can ensure that all phone numbers in our database are assigned to the correct area code and fall within an appropriate set of ZIP codes. Once this cleaning has been done, we determine working blocks.

A block is defined as the first two digits of a phone number within an exchange. The phone number 226-7558 falls within block 75 of exchange 226. A working block is a block which contains at least three listed residential telephone numbers. Nonworking blocks — those with zero, one, or two listed numbers, are eliminated from consideration in our database, as many of these turn out to be data entry errors.

Currently, there are estimated to be 87 million households in the United States. About 93% of these households have telephones, projecting to a national telephone household base of 80.9 million. AT&T currently reports 36,827 exchanges nationally, projecting to 368.27 million possible telephone numbers.

Only 31,530 of these exchanges contain valid residential listings, projecting to 315.5 million possible phone numbers. If all the blocks within these exchanges were considered eligible for random digit samples, the incidence would be 25.6% (not very efficient).

To improve this incidence, our first step is to eliminate from the universe of potential numbers those blocks with less than three listed telephone numbers. Currently, this represents approximately 1.76 million blocks.

That means that almost 56% of all blocks in active exchanges are inactive. By limiting the universe to working blocks only, 139 million potential numbers, the incidence of reaching a working residential number is raised to 58%. This incidence is further improved to 62% after eliminating the 9.2 million business phone numbers listed in our Yellow Page data base.

There are, on average, 43 listed numbers per active block. The median, however, is between 53 and 54 numbers per block. While the ratio of listed to unlisted phones may vary greatly from one exchange to another, there is no evidence that telephone companies assign unlisted numbers differently than they assign listed numbers.

Therefore, by weighing each working block in an exchange in proportion to its share of the listed phones in that exchange, the overall incidence of working residential phones can be raised by as much as 10 points.

Used with permission from Survey Sampling, Inc.

households as the sampling unit and interview all males over 13 years of age in each household. Here the sampling unit and the population element are not the same.

The sampling unit selected is often dependent upon the sampling frame. If a relatively complete and accurate listing of elements is available — a register of purchasing agents, for example — one may well want to sample them directly. If no such register is available, one may need to sample companies as the basic sampling unit.

The selection of the sampling unit is also partially dependent upon the overall design of the project. A mail questionnaire requires a sampling unit of an address (name if available). If it is conducted at the home, a personal interview also requires an address (or a means of selecting the address by the interviewer). A telephone interview necessarily requires that the sampling unit be a telephone number.

In both in-home personal interviews and telephone interviews, a further specification of the sampling unit is required. Should the person who happens to answer the doorbell or the telephone be interviewed; or, in multiple-person households, should there be a purposive selection made from the persons residing there? Interviewing whomever happens to be at home will underrepresent employed persons, individuals who travel, persons who eat out frequently, and others who are seldom at home. It will overrepresent the elderly, the chronically ill, the nonemployed, mothers with small children, and others who spend more than the average amount of time at home. Therefore, for surveys in which a random sample of the adult population is desired, a random selection must be made from the adult residents of each household. The "next birthday" method (see Chapter 6, p. 152) is the simplest method to use to select one adult from a household at random. It requires only that the interviewer ask which adult in the household has the next birthday and interview that person.

Step 4. Selection of Sampling Method

The sampling method is the way the sample units are to be selected. Five basic choices must be made in deciding on a sampling method:

> *probability versus nonprobability,*
> *single unit versus cluster of units,*
> *unstratified versus stratified,*
> *equal unit probability versus unequal unit probability,* and
> *single stage versus multistage.*

The five choices listed are not meant to be exhaustive. Other decisions may be required (sequential versus nonsequential sampling, and sampling without

471

replacement versus sampling with replacement, for example). However, the five listed choices are the most important ones in the sampling of human populations, and we limit our consideration to these choices.

Probability Versus Nonprobability Sampling

We have listed the most crucial decision first: the choice of a probability versus a nonprobability selection procedure. *A probability sample is one in which the sampling units are selected by chance and for which there is a known chance of each unit being selected. A nonprobability sample is one in which chance selection procedures are not used.*

Probability Samples. Probability samples are selected by use of a stable, independent data-generating process. The table of random numbers in Appendix I is the result of the use of such a process. Tables of random numbers such as this are commonly used for selecting the sampling units to be included in a probability sample.

Suppose a major oil company wants to sample its credit card holders to test a "travel club" program by sending promotional flyers with the next billing to the customer. Further suppose that the first seven numbers on the card identify each customer.

A probability sample could be taken by starting at a preselected place in a table of random numbers and selecting seven-digit numbers by a designated procedure. The preselected place in the table might be, for example, the top right-hand corner of Appendix I if one were using the table in this book. An example of an appropriate procedure for selecting seven-digit random numbers would be to take each seven digits in sequence as one moves down the right-hand column, go to the top of the adjoining column, move down it, and so forth.

This would result in a particular kind of random sample being taken. It is known as a *simple random sample* (often abbreviated as *srs*) and, in addition to being a *probability* sample, it would have the characteristics of consisting of *single units,* each of which was drawn from an *unstratified* population with an *equal probability of each unit's being selected* by a *single-stage* procedure. It is a frequently used sampling technique.

It should be emphasized that a probability sample does not ensure a *representative* sample. If an *srs* of 100 students were taken from the students on your campus, for example, it is possible that the sample selected would consist of 100 sophomore men. This sample obviously would not be representative of the total student body demographically, and probably not so in most other respects.

Nonprobability Samples. Several kinds of nonprobability samples are in common use. They include *convenience, judgment, quota,* and *purposive* samples.

472

Convenience Samples. A *convenience* sample is one in which the only criterion for selecting the sampling units is the convenience of the sampler. An example of convenience sampling is the testing by food product manufacturers of potential new products by adding them to the menu of the company cafeteria. A potential new cake mix, for example, can be tested by adding it to the dessert section and noting how well it sells relative to the other kinds of cake offered.

Convenience samples are often used in exploratory situations when there is a need to get only an approximation of the actual value quickly and inexpensively. Commonly used convenience samples are associates, friends, family members, and "passers by." Such samples are often used in the pretest phase of a study, such as pretesting a questionnaire.

Convenience samples contain unknown amounts of both variable and systematic selection errors. These errors can be very large when compared to the variable error in an *srs* of the same size. This possibility should be considered both before and after using convenience samples.

Judgment Samples. A *judgment* sample is one in which there is an attempt to draw a representative sample of the population using judgmental selection procedures. An example is a sample of addresses taken by a municipal agency to which questionnaires on bicycle-riding habits were sent. A judgment sample was taken after researchers looked at traffic maps of the city, considered the tax assessment on houses and apartment buildings (per unit), and kept the location of schools and parks in mind.

Judgment samples are common in industrial marketing research. In this environment, very small samples of lead users, key accounts, or technologically sophisticated firms or individuals are regularly used to test new product/ service concepts, pricing programs, and so forth.

The amount of variable and systematic selection error present in a judgment sample depends upon the degree of expertise of the person making the selection. These errors *can* be substantially less than the variable error present in an *srs* of the same size, particularly if the sample is small. In test-market situations in which the new product is to be introduced in a small number of cities (usually two to four), the selection of cities is almost always made on a judgmental basis. Anyone who has a general knowledge of the product and of cities in the United States is likely to choose a more representative sample than would be selected by a random process. As sample size increases, however, judgment becomes less trustworthy compared to random selection procedures.

Quota Samples. A *quota* sample is one selected purposively in such a way that the demographic characteristics of interest are represented in the sample in the same proportion as they are in the population. If one were selecting a quota sample of persons for a use test of pizza-flavored catsup, for example, one might want to control by ethnic background, age, income, and geographic location. That is, the sample taken would have the same proportion of people in each income bracket, ethnic group, age group, and geographic area as the population. Quota samples are widely used in consumer panels.

The controls used in quota samples of human populations (1) *must be available and should be recent*, (2) *should be easy for the interviewer to classify by*, (3) *should be closely related to the variables being measured in the study*, and (4) *should be kept to a reasonable number so as not to produce too many cells.* Each possible set of controls produces a separate *cell* in a quota sample. If the selection of respondents is controlled by five income brackets, three ethnic backgrounds, four age brackets, and six areas, for example, there would be $5 \times 3 \times 4 \times 6 = 360$ different cells in the sample. The interviewers would have trouble filling the quota assigned to many of these cells, and the costs of taking the sample would rise as a result.

The number of cells is not the only concern in designing a low-cost quota sample; the rate of occurrence, or percentage, of persons eligible to fill each cell — the *incidence* for each cell — can also increase costs. For example, suppose that in a study of cold cereals a quota sample is being used for which one of the cells calls for "female heads of households aged 25–44." Of women between the ages of 18 and 54 — women who might reasonably be approached to see if they quality — approximately 14 per cent are heads of households between the ages of 25 and 44. This means that on the average about 7 women would have to be approached to obtain one qualified respondent.

In addition to meeting this requirement, however, suppose that the following requirements must also be met for a potential respondent to qualify:

— has eaten a cold, ready-to-eat cereal in the past two weeks (about 60 per cent of all women 18–54);

— has no known dietary restrictions, diabetes, or food allergies (about 90 per cent of all women 18–54);

— no one in the household is employed by the advertising agency, marketing research company, or the cereal manufacturer (about 98 per cent of all women aged 18–54 in the city where the study is being conducted;

— has not participated in a marketing research study in the last three months (about 95 per cent of all women 18–54).[4]

The incidence of women between the ages of 25 and 44 that would qualify for the cell could therefore be estimated to be as follows:

.14	×	.60	×	.90
female heads of households in age group 25–44		eaten any cold cereal in past two weeks		no known dietary restrictions, diabetes, allergies

$\times$	.98	$\times$	.95	$=$	.07
	no one employed by advertising agency, marketing research company, or cereal manufacturer		not participated in marketing research study in past three months		incidence for cell

On the average, therefore, about 14 women would have to be approached in order to obtain one qualified respondent — 7 more than if the controls had been limited to the female head of household aged 25 – 44 designation.

The fact that a quota sample resembles a proportional stratified probability sample (this type of sample is discussed later in the chapter) should not be used for concluding that the variances of the two are the same. In a study of the results of election polls, it was found that the standard error of the quota samples used averaged about one-and-one quarter times that of an equivalent sized *srs*. Sizeable selection errors can arise from the way interviewers select the persons to fill the quota for each cell, incorrect information on the proportions of the population in each of the control variables, biases in the relationship of the control variables to the variables being measured, and from other sources.[5]

Quota samples are usually "validated" after they are taken. The process of validation involves a comparison of the sample and the population with respect to characteristics *not* used as control variables. In a quota sample taken to form a consumer panel for which income, education, and age were used as control variables, for example, a comparison of the panel and the population might be made with respect to such characteristics as average number of children, the occupation of the chief wage earner, and home ownership. If the panel differed significantly from the population with respect to any of these characteristics, it would be an indication of potential bias in the selection procedures. Similarity with respect to the validating characteristics does not necessarily mean the absence of other kinds of bias, however.

Purposive Samples. A purposive sample is one that is purposefully chosen to be nonrepresentative, to achieve some specific objective(s). The most common approach is to follow the procedure just described for a quota sample but to overrepresent some cells. In practice, purposive samples are often referred to (incorrectly) as quota samples.

An example of a purposive sample would be study by a cosmetics firm of a new line of make-up for women with darker complexions. One issue is whether the line might be appropriately positioned as unique for Hispanic or black women. Therefore, the initial mall intercept interviews were set at 75 Hispanic, 75 black, and 75 Anglo women.

Purposive samples frequently "overrepresent" heavy users, frequent viewers, potential users, and small population groups. Obviously, results from such samples cannot be generalized to the larger population without appropriate weighting. Even then, the cautions required for quota samples still apply.

The Choice Between Probability and Nonprobability Samples. The choice between probability and nonprobability samples is based on the *cost versus value* principle. We want to take whichever kind of sample yields the greatest margin of value over cost.

No one would question this principle; the problems come in applying it. The real question at issue is, "How can I estimate with a reasonable degree of confidence whether a probability sample will give more or give less value for its cost than a nonprobability sample?"

This question cannot be answered fully. The following factors are to be considered in estimating relative value, however.

1. *What kind of information is needed — averages and/or proportions or projectable totals?*
   Do we need to know only the proportion of users and/or the average amount used, or do we need to estimate the overall market share and/or the total market for the product?

2. *What kind of error tolerance does the problem allow?*
   Does the problem require highly accurate estimates of population values?

3. *How large are the nonsampling errors likely to be?*
   How sizeable are the population specification, frame, selection, nonresponse, surrogate information, measurement, and experimental errors likely to be?

4. *How homogeneous is the population with respect to the variables we want to measure?*
   Is the variation likely to be low among the sampling units, or will it be high?

5. *What is the expected cost of errors in the sample information?*
   What is the cost to me if the average(s)/proportion(s) I obtain from the data are above the error tolerance on the high side? The low side?

Generally speaking, the need for *projectable totals, low allowable errors, high population heterogeneity, small nonsampling errors, and high expected costs of errors* favors the use of probability sampling. A tight error tolerance means that the elimination of selection bias and the ability to calculate sampling error become more important considerations in the selection of the sampling plan; and so favor a probability sample. Small nonsampling errors likewise favor probability samples: the sampling error becomes relatively more important the smaller the other errors are. The more diversified and heterogeneous the population is, the greater is the need to assure representativeness through a probability sampling procedure.

Single-Unit Versus Cluster Sampling

In *single-unit sampling,* each sampling unit is selected separately; in *cluster sampling* the units are selected in groups. If the unit is a household, for example, single-unit sampling would require that each household be selected separately. One form of cluster sampling would be to change the sampling unit to city blocks and to take every household on each block selected.

The choice between single-unit and cluster sampling is again an economic tug-of-war between cost and value. Cluster sampling usually costs less (and often substantially less) per sampling unit than does single-unit sampling. For samples of the same size, the sampling error for a cluster sample will usually be greater than that of a single-unit sample because of less within-cluster variability than for the population as a whole.

Consider a sample of 100 households to be selected for personal interviews. If selected on a single-unit basis, they will most likely be scattered around the city. This will increase the chance of getting a representative cross-section of the various ethnic groups, social classes, and so on. In contrast, a cluster sample in which 10 blocks are selected and 10 households interviewed on each block will be likely to miss more of the social groups since members of social groups tend to live near each other. The costs of personal interviews per unit in a cluster sample will be low, however, because of the close proximity of the units in each cluster. Low error tolerance, high population heterogeneity, and high expected costs of errors all favor single-unit sampling.

Unstratified Versus Stratified Sampling

A *stratum* in a population is a segment of that population having one or more common characteristics. It might be an age stratum (age 35–49), an income stratum (all families with incomes over $50,000 per year), or a part of the population identified with some other characteristic of interest.

Stratified sampling involves treating each stratum as a separate subpopulation for sampling purposes. If the head-of-household age strata "18–34," "35–49," "50 and over" are of interest in a study on household furnishings, each of these age groups could be treated separately for sampling purposes. That is, the total population could be divided into age groups and a separate sample drawn from each group.

The reasons for stratifying a population for sampling purposes are: (1) it may be administratively convenient (if one wanted to take a sample of customers of a bank, for example, it would probably be more convenient to take separate subsamples from each of the lists of checking account customers, saving account customers, mortgagees, etc. than to merge all of the lists to take an unstratified sample); (2) one may want estimates of the means, proportions, or other parameters of strata in the population (if one were sampling users of a product, one might well want to know the mean consumption for each of the segments that comprise the market, for example); and (3) the required sample size for a well-designed, stratified sample will usually be smaller than for a well-designed, unstratified sample.

The saving in the size of the sample, although still obtaining the same level of sampling error as a nonstratified sample, may not be intuitively obvious but is easily explained. In the household furnishings study referred to previously, the age group 18–34 is that of family formation and initial acquisition of most furnishings; age 35–44 is the time of replacement of original purchases and acquisition of more marginal items; and age 50 and over is generally a time of limited purchasing of any kind of furnishings. To the extent that these generalizations hold, the households falling within each of these strata should be more like each other than they are to those in any other stratum.

The greater the degree to which this within-stratum similarity holds, the smaller is the sample size required in each stratum to provide information about that stratum. Consider the extreme case in which all units in each stratum are *identical*. If this were true, a sample of *one* would be all that was required from each stratum to give complete information on the subpopulation of interest. Thus, the more homogeneous each stratum is with respect to the variable of interest, the smaller is the sample required.

The primary reason that stratified samples are not used more widely is the difficulty of obtaining adequate sample frames. A stratified sample requires that members of each stratum be selected *randomly* from that stratum. Thus, a separate sampling frame is required for each stratum. In the household furnishing example, it is unlikely that separate sample frames for individuals in each of the age groups exists for the general population.

Equal Unit Probability Versus Unequal Unit Probability Sampling

"Most of the gross errors of bad sampling are violations of simple common sense. The methods of good sampling are not obvious to common sense."[6] One of the methods of good sampling that is intuitively not obvious is that it is often better to have *unequal* probabilities of selection. The example of the household furnishing study just described affords an example.

Suppose we are interested in the average amount spent on household furnishings by families in each of the age strata. It seems reasonable to assume that the variation in expenditures of the 18–34 and the 35–49 age group households are likely to be higher than those for the 50-and-over group. If this is the case, it is more efficient statistically to take a smaller sample of the 50-and-overs and allocate part of its proportionate share to the two groups with the higher variation in purchase amounts.

Stated differently, it is only when we have no reason to believe that the variation (variance) is different among the strata that we would take a proportional sample and thus give an equal chance of representation to each sampling unit.

Single Stage Versus Multistage Sampling

The number of stages involved in the sampling method is partially a function of the kind of sampling frame available. If a perfect frame were always available complete with all the associated information one might want for purposes of clustering and/or stratifying, there would be far fewer multistage samples taken than there are now. In practice, it is not uncommon to have a first-stage area sample of, say, census tracts, followed by a second-stage sample of blocks, and completed with a systematic sample of households within each block. These stages would not be necessary if a complete listing of households were available.

Multistage samples are sometimes taken for economic reasons, however. In interviewing human populations it is almost always less expensive to interview groups of respondents that are located close to each other than those that are dispersed. This may dictate a first-stage sample of cities and towns, followed by a second-stage sample of firms or households.

Step 5. Determination of the Sample Size

The determination of the proper sample size has traditionally been taught by one method in statistics classes and often practiced by an entirely different approach in the field. The reason for this is that traditional sampling theory generally ignores the concept of the cost versus the value of the information to be provided by various sized samples. Practitioners have been forced to deal with the realities of sampling economics regardless of whether theory recognizes them.

The problem of determination of sample size is dealt with in the next chapter.

Step 6. Specify Sampling Plan

The *sampling plan* involves the specification of how each of the decisions made thus far is to be implemented. It may have been decided that the household will be the element and the block the sampling unit. How is a household defined operationally? How is the interviewer to be instructed to distinguish between families and households in instances where two families and some distant relatives of one of them are sharing the same apartment? How is the interviewer to be instructed to take a systematic sample of households on the block? What should the interviewer do when a housing unit selected is vacant?

Exhibit 15–3 *Special Situations Encountered in Systematic Sampling by Circling a Block**

In the instructions that follow, reference is made to follow your route around a "block." In cities this will be a city block. In rural areas, a "block" is a segment of land surrounded by roads.

1. If you come to a dead end along your route, proceed down the opposite side of the street, road, or alley, traveling in the other direction. Continue making right turns, where possible, calling at every third occupied dwelling.

2. If you go all the way around a block and return to the starting address without completing four interviews in listed telephone homes, attempt an interview at the starting address. (This should seldom be necessary.)

3. If you work an entire block and do not complete the required interviews, proceed to the dwelling on the opposite side of the street (or rural route) that is *nearest* the starting address. Treat it as the next address on your Area Location Sheet and interview that house only if the address appears next to an "X" on your sheet. If it does not, continue your interviewing to the left of that address. Always follow the right turn rule.

4. If there are no dwellings on the street or road opposite the starting address for an area, circle the block opposite the starting address, following the right turn rule. (This means that you will circle the block following a clockwise direction.) Attempt interviews at every third dwelling along this route.

5. If, after circling the adjacent block opposite the starting address, you do not complete the necessary interviews, take the next block found, *following a clockwise direction.*

6. If the third block does not yield the dwellings necessary to complete your assignment, proceed to as many blocks as necessary to find the required dwellings; these blocks follow a clockwise path around the primary block.

* Reprinted from an actual interviewer guide by permission of Belden Associates, Dallas, Texas. The complete guide was over 30 pages long and contained maps and other aids for the interviewer.

What is the callback procedure for households at which no one is at home? What age and/or sex of respondents speaking for the household are acceptable?

An example of a part of a sampling plan for a systematic sample is provided in Exhibit 15–3. The special situations that are shown in the exhibit represent problems that an interviewer might encounter in "starting with the first occupied dwelling unit to the left of the preliminary address, attempt to interview every third occupied dwelling unit in the block until four completed interviews are obtained in homes with listed phone numbers."

Step 7. Select the Sample

The final step in the sampling process is the actual selection of the sample elements. This requires a substantial amount of office and fieldwork, particularly if personal interviews are involved. Many of the difficulties encountered in this stage were described in the chapter on surveys, generally because it is the interviewer who completes this stage of the process.

Sampling Situations

In this section we describe the kinds of samples taken, and the reasons for their choice, in the three sampling situations described at the beginning of the chapter.

Frontier Stoves. *The president of Frontier Stoves, a wood stove manufacturer, asked the person in charge of marketing research for the company to conduct focus-group interviews of blue-collar, white-collar, and managerial/professional owners of wood stoves to determine what they see as the principal benefits and problems arising from the use of wood stoves.*

The benefits from focus group research are primarily those of indicating attitudes and beliefs, and perhaps suggesting new courses of action, rather than to provide statistically reliable, projectable responses. One of the requirements for a successful focus-group interview is to have reasonably outgoing, verbal persons who will respond to questions and participate in group discussions. For this reason, sample members for focus groups, however they are selected initially, usually require prequalification.

The samples for the Frontier Stove focus groups were contacted initially on a probabilistic basis but were selected on a purposive basis. Since the incidence of wood stove owners is low, efficiency dictated that a list of owners be obtained to use as a sampling frame. At the time the samples for the focus groups were taken, the city in which Frontier was located had an ordinance requiring permits to operate a wood stove. A list of permit holders was obtained and households were called randomly until the forty-eight sample households necessary to provide participants for six focus groups (one adult member from each household, eight persons per focus group, two focus groups each from the blue-collar, white-collar, and managerial/professional social classes) were selected. Selection involved verification that the wood stove was still owned, open-ended questions on the benefits of it were asked to assess how verbal the respondents were. If they qualified on these counts and were willing to participate, demographic data were obtained to determine to which focus group they should be assigned.

The initial selection method used was a variation of simple random sampling called *systematic sampling* with elements of purposive sampling. It involved obtaining a sampling frame, picking a random starting point, and, beginning there, taking every *k*th unit in the frame. If Frontier were interested in taking a 2 per cent sample of the permit holders, for example, a random starting point between 01 and 50 would have been taken, and, starting there, every 50th name would have been selected. In the more general case, *k* is equal to the total number of units *N* divided by the sample size in units *n*, or $k = N/n$.

In the sampling situation, the steps in the sampling process were handled as follows:

1. Define the population — *(element)* adult member of *(sampling unit)* households holding a wood stove permit *(extent)* in the area covered by the ordinance *(time)* in the week at which the focus groups took place

2. Specify sampling frame — List of permit holders

3. Specify sampling unit — Individual households holding permits

4. Specify sampling method — Systematic random sampling of households with prequalification of one adult member. Later assignment to specific focus groups based on social class. (The prequalification and later assignment to social class-based focus groups makes this a purposive sample since the managerial/professional group was overrepresented. Had representation matched the population, it would have been a quota sample.)

5. Determine sample size	48 (2 focus groups each from blue-collar, white-collar, and managerial/professional social classes, 8 persons per focus group)
6. Specify sampling plan	Select households. Prequalify an adult member by calling and determining that (a) a wood stove is still owned, (b) the person is sufficiently verbal, (c) he or she is willing to participate, and (d) the demographic characteristics match a need in one or more focus groups.
7. Select the sample	Obtain the list of permit holders, select a starting point, determine the value of k, take every kth unit, and prequalify as in (6).

Elrick and Lavidge. *Elrick and Lavidge, a research agency, has interviewing facilities located in 19 shopping malls throughout the United States. A client wanted a mall-intercept quota sample of 250 adult women (18 years of age or older) selected to obtain information about preferences concerning alternative formulations of a proposed new food product.*

One of the most frequently used methods of collecting data is to interview a sample of respondents in a shopping center. It is (relatively) inexpensive and provides the opportunity for new products, packages, and advertisements to be displayed and tested, capabilities that are not present in telephone interviews.

Unless the sampling plan is devised carefully, however, the results of mall-intercept sampling are subject to potentially large selection biases. These biases result from variations in the demographic composition of shoppers from that of the population as a whole by shopping center, by day and time of day, and by location in the shopping center, as well as the biases that potentially arise from how individual shoppers are selected. Elrick and Lavidge uses the following generally accepted methods to reduce the biases that could result from each of these causes:

1. Selection of the shopping center. The client decided that one of the Elrick and Lavidge mall facilities in Chicago would be acceptable from a bias standpoint and would keep the costs of the study down.

2. Allowance for unrepresentative demographic composition of shoppers. Data indicate that persons aged 25 to 54, women, and unemployed persons make more than a proportional number of visits to shopping centers. There is wide variation among persons in each of these groups with respect to the number of visits to a shopping mall in

any given time period. Those people who visit shopping malls most often have a higher than proportional probability of being selected in any given sample. This unrepresentative demographic composition can be allowed for by taking a quota sample. The allowance for the number of visits can be made by obtaining information from the respondent on frequency of visits and either (i) weighting responses appropriately or (ii) subsampling respondents on the basis of frequency.[7]

3. Allowance for location within the center. Buses typically stop at only one or two of several entrances. Those shoppers who arrive by bus are likely to have different demographic characteristics (be less affluent, for example) than those who drive to the center. The simplest adjustment procedure is to station an interviewer or interviewers at every entrance and instruct them to select every kth customer who enters. If this is not feasible, entrances can be sampled with equal probability and every kth customer is interviewed at the selected entrances.

4. Allowance for variation in demographic composition of shoppers by day and time of day. The characteristics of shoppers vary by season, by day of the week, by time of day, by whether there are sales, and by weather.

How can allowance be made for these variations? The season in which the study is to be taken presumably will have been decided upon and so can be ignored as a source of bias insofar as the sample design is concerned. Day of the week and time of day variations can be allowed for by taking a probability sample. If a shopping center is open from 10:00 A.M. to 9:00 P.M. 7 days a week, there are 77 1-hour periods or 154 $\frac{1}{2}$-hour periods to be sampled. The length of the time period chosen should depend upon the length of the interview and other administrative considerations. The time periods should be selected with a probability proportionate to the number of customers visiting then (necessitating information from a prior count) and the probability of each customer being selected within the time period should be inverse to that probability.

Adjustments for sales and weather effects typically have to be made in terms of the quantity visiting rather than for differences in composition. Sampling rates are adjusted downward to allow for a larger number of shoppers because of a sale, for example, or adjusted upward to allow for a lower number resulting from a snowstorm.

5. Instructions for selecting respondents. If every kth person is to be selected, a continuing count has to be taken during the sample time period. Unambiguous rules have to be established to ensure that the count is accurate if potential biases are to be avoided.

A line, or lines, at intersections of corridors, need to be specified as the point(s) to be crossed before a person becomes eligible for selection. Rules for how to select persons from ties (persons crossing the line simultaneously as, for example, two or more persons shopping together) need to be specified. ("Select the person who is farthest north who meets the characteristics of the cell in the quota to be added to next," is an example of such a rule.)

This sampling situation can be summarized as follows:

1.	Define the population	*(element)* women 18 years of age or older in *(sampling unit)* a shopping mall *(extent)* in suburban Chicago *(time)* during the time (days and hours) of the survey
2.	Specify sampling frame	Locations within the mall, specific points at each location
3.	Specify sampling unit	Women 18 years of age or older
4.	Specify sampling method	A multistage method that involves (1) selecting the shopping mall, (2) selecting a sample of locations within the mall, (3) selecting times (days and hours), and (4) selecting a quota sample of women at those locations at those times
5.	Determine sample size	250 women
6.	Specify sampling plan	Using the shopping mall in which Elrick and Lavidge have an interviewing facility, select women passing these points (points designated) during these times (hours designated), on these days (days designated) until quotas are filled.
7.	Selection of the sample	Follow plan in (6) qualifying women by whether or not they meet quota requirements

The Toni Company. *A manufacturer and marketer of women's home permanents, the Toni Company, decided to commission a national survey on electronic media viewing/listening and reading habits of women. The sampling plan and the actual selection and interviewing were done by a marketing research agency.*

The sampling plan decided upon was a relatively complicated one. The following steps were used:

Definition of population	The population was defined as white females; 15 years and older *(element)* in households *(unit)*, in the continental United States *(extent)* during the month the sample was taken *(time)*.
Sampling frame used	Three frames were used: (1) a list of the counties and (2) the Standard Metropolitan Statistical Areas (SMSA) in the continental U.S. with (3) maps of the counties/metropolitan areas selected.
Sampling unit used	Households
Sampling method used	*Probability*

A sampling of 228 counties was taken. When a sample county was part of an SMSA, it was used in lieu of the county.

Individual blocks and country segments were then selected by probability sampling methods.

Single unit selection was used. A systematic sample of households was taken from each block. A systematic procedure for selecting households from road intersection starting points was devised for the country open segments.

The population was *unstratified*. However, age group and geographic area comparisons were made with census data to determine the representativeness of the sample.

Unequal probability of element selection was used. For example, in the metropolitan areas of the Northeast, where the company had high per capita sales, one woman was interviewed for (approximately) every 15,600 women. In the metropolitan areas of the South Atlantic states, where per capita sales were lower, one woman was interviewed for each 3,900 women.

The sample was a *multistage* design: County/SMSA to block or open country segment and then systematic selection of households.

Desired sample size	A sample of 6,000 women was specified.
Sampling plan	An entire notebook of materials was prepared and used for training interviewers and field supervisors.
Selection of the sample	Only 5,493 of the interviews were actually completed. A quota sample of 500 cases was added to make up the deficit. The quotas stipulated were such as to compensate in age groups that were underrepresented and to provide added cases in subgroups in which special analyses were desired.

A final point needs to be made about sampling in practice as opposed to sampling in theory: *judgment has to be exercised at every step of the sampling procedure.* As the sampling situations just described illustrate, at each of the steps in devising and carrying out the sampling plan many alternatives are available from which to choose. Someone had to make the choices and, although objective criteria were available for some of these choices, the final decisions were at least partially dependent on the judgment of the person(s) who made the decisions. The sample taken can be no better than the quality of the judgments made.

Review Questions

15.1. What are the reasons a *sample* is usually preferable to a *census?*

15.2. What are the steps in the *sampling process?*

15.3. What are the necessary parts of the definition of a *population?*

15.4. What is a *sampling frame?*

15.5. What are the five basic choices that can be made among sampling methods?

15.6. What is a *probability* sample?

15.7. What is a
   a. *convenience* sample?
   b. *quota* sample?
   c. *judgment* sample?
   d. *purposive* sample?

15.8. What are the major factors to consider in *choosing between a probability and a nonprobability sample?*

15.9. What is a *stratum* in the population?

15.10. What is a *cluster* of sampling units?

15.11. What is the *incidence* for a cell in a sample?

Discussion Questions/Problems

15.12. Would you expect that a carefully designed and well executed plan for a sample of households would yield a better, or worse, sample of adults of the general population than on an equally well-designed and executed mall-intercept sampling plan? Why?

15.13. Evaluate the procedure described in Exhibit 15–3.

15.14. Describe three decisional situations in which a census might be preferable to a sample. Explain why this would be the case in each instance.

15.15. Why are judgment samples common in industrial research?

15.16. Trade shows and industry conferences are common locations for intercept interviews in industrial research. What sampling issues does this fact pose?

15.17. Assume that the sample size for each of the following paired choices of sampling methods is the same. Given that, state which you think would be
   i. less costly
   ii. have the lower sampling variance:
      a. quota vs. stratified
      b. simple random vs. systematic
      c. convenience vs. purposive
      d. cluster vs. simple random
   Explain your reasoning in each case.

15.18. How would you define the population from which to select a sample for a survey for
   a. a design for a tricycle for children age 3–6
   b. a station wagon costing $17,000
   c. an office-automation system for small offices (7 to 20 secretaries and assistants)
   d. an integrated data/voice communications system for multibuilding office and manufacturing sites
   e. course offerings at the business school for the next academic year
   f. the effectiveness of an ad campaign aimed at reducing drinking and driving.

15.19. Suppose a quota sample was desired for each of the surveys described in question 15.18. How would you go about deciding which controls to use for each survey?

15.20. Suppose that each of the surveys described in question 15.18 are to involve personal interviews.
   a. What sampling frame(s) would you use for each survey?
   b. How would you go about selecting the sample for each survey?

15.21. Suppose you were asked to design a probability sample to obtain the names and addresses of 100 students on your campus for a taste test of a new soft drink. Describe how you would proceed through the first six steps in Table 15–1.

15.22. A local retailer has asked you to select a sample of 50 "fashion leaders." These leaders will be paid $20 each to "evaluate" the store's layout and merchandise selection. The store carries men's and women's clothing. Describe the sampling process you would use.

15.23. A quota sample is being developed for use in forming a 5,000-member national consumer panel of pet owners. What quota variables and levels of variables should be used, and how many persons should be included in each cell?

15.24. For each situation below, critique the method used and suggest alternatives you consider better where appropriate:
  a. To study attitudes toward a fast-food chain, interviewers were stationed in the parking lots of the chain and questioned all those willing to answer.
  b. In studying the results of a screening method for credit card applications for a department store, folders of applicants were selected at a fixed interval beginning at the front of each file drawer.
  c. To develop information on the *purchasers* of its new video game, *Space Cowboys,* the manufacturer made the activation of the product warranty conditional upon the receipt of the warranty card, which also contained a short questionnaire.

15.25. Suppose that mall-intercept interviews are to be made in a regional U.S. shopping mall of male sport car owners between the ages of 25 and 44 who live in households with annual incomes of $25,000 or more. Further suppose that 3.7 per cent of all U.S. males aged 25–44 own sport cars, and 58.1 per cent of all U.S. males aged 25–44 live in households with incomes of $25,000 per year or more. Assuming independence between sport car ownership and income, what would you expect to be the percentage of males between the ages 25–44 approached in the mall that are found to be qualified to be interviewed?

Projects

15.26. Determine the cell sizes for a 500-person quota sample of students on your campus, given the following quota variables (a) gender (b) classification (freshman, sophomore, junior, senior, graduate) (c) full time or part time, and (d) domestic or foreign.

15.27. Develop a sample of classes from which you will select 5 members each who will provide a representative sample of your university.

15.28. A firm wishes to estimate the number of VCR players being used by
  a. business firms
  b. nonprofit organizations
  c. service organizations
  d. retailers
  e. households

in your state. Using material available from your university library, develop a sampling plan that uses a stratified random sample. Justify your selection of strata.

References

[1] "Single People Are Traditional Grocery Shoppers: Survey," *Marketing News*, July 10, 1981, 6. The *extent* and *time* of the population definition given are illustrative rather than actual.

[2] *Statistical Abstract of the United States*, U.S. Government Printing Office, 1985, 542.

[3] "Unlisted Rate Rising Across Nation," *The Frame* (Fairfield, Connecticut: Survey Sampling, Inc., Fall 1988), 1.

[4] Adapted from K. G. Lee, "Incidence Is a Key Element," *Marketing News*, September 13, 1985, 50.

[5] See L. J. Kish, *Survey Sampling* (New York: John Wiley & Sons, Inc., 1965), 562–566, for a discussion of errors that can be present in quota sample measurements.

[6] Quoted from a privately circulated manuscript written by H. V. Roberts.

[7] The weighting assigned will be equal to the inverse of the frequency of visits. Those who had not visited any other time during the period (except the present visit) have a weighting of 1, those who had visited one other time a weighting of $\frac{1}{2}$, those visiting two other times a weighting of $\frac{1}{3}$, and so forth. The subsampling procedure is similar. The sampling rate would be 100 per cent of those initially selected who had not visited any other time during the period, 50 per cent of those who had visited one other time, and so forth. For a critical discussion of this issue, see T. D. Dupont, "Do Frequent Mall Shoppers Distort Mall-Intercept Survey Results?" *Journal of Advertising Research* (August 1987), 45–51.

CHAPTER 16

Sample Size Determination

In 1985, Statistical Research, the company that for a number of years has provided the RADAR® syndicated measurement of listener share of radio networks, increased the size of its national (U.S.) random-digit dialed telephone sample from 6,000 to 8,000. The increase in sample size was for two reasons: (1) advertisers have begun to demand finer demographic breakdowns of the listeners by network; and (2) the number of radio networks has increased faster than the total number of listeners has increased, and so a smaller average sample of listeners per network was being obtained.

A calculation of the sample size that the company decided would meet advertiser objectives, and not exceed its cost objectives, is given later in this chapter.

An inescapable part of taking a sample is determining what size it should be. At least six different methods of determining sample size are used in marketing research. These are (1) *unaided judgment,* (2) *all you can afford,* (3) *the average for samples for similar studies,* (4) *required size per cell,* (5) *use of a traditional statistical model,* and (6) *use of a Bayesian statistical model.*[1]

These methods are listed in (rough) order of increasing sophistication. In terms of usage, one has no trouble finding examples of sample size being determined by the two least sophisticated methods, *unaided judgment* and *all-you-can-afford,* even though these methods have little to recommend them. A more credible method is to take the same size as *the average for samples for similar studies,* but this too is suspect as it relies on other persons' decisions that were made on sets of considerations that are often not disclosed. To the credit of the profession, the more sophisticated methods, *required size per cell* and *use of a traditional statistical model,* are much more widely used. The last method, *use of a Bayesian statistical model,* is not commonly used in marketing research.

We briefly describe each of these methods and then turn to a more detailed discussion of the use of traditional statistical models in the determination of the size of probability samples. This discussion is introduced by a description (and simulation) of a sampling distribution. Sample size determination for both estimation and hypothesis testing problems is discussed.

We then discuss the problems and techniques involved in determining the size of *nonprobability* samples.

Methods of Determining Sample Size

Unaided Judgment

It is not unusual to hear a client for a research project say, "I want a sample of 50 (or 100 or 200) persons for this study." When the client is asked why he or she thinks this is the appropriate sample size, not an uncommon response is "For this problem that is about the size we need."

This arbitrary approach to arriving at sample size gives no explicit consideration to either the likely *precision* of the sample results or the *cost* of obtaining them, characteristics in which any client should have an interest. It is an approach to be avoided.

All-You-Can-Afford

In this method, a budget for the project is set by some (generally unspecified) process and, after the estimated fixed costs of designing the project, preparing a questionnaire (if required), analyzing the data, and preparing the report are deducted, the remainder of the budget is allocated to sampling. Dividing this remaining amount by the estimated cost per sampling unit gives the sample size.

This method concentrates on the cost of the information to the exclusion of concern about its value. Although cost always has to be considered in any systematic approach to sample size determination, one also needs to give consideration to how much the information to be provided by the sample will be worth. This approach produces sample sizes that are larger than required as well as sizes that are smaller than optimal.

Average Size for Samples for Similar Studies

The sample sizes reported in several hundred studies are shown in Table 16–1.[2] Depending upon the number of subgroup analyses to be run, national

492

Table 16–1 Typical Sample Sizes for Studies of Human and Institutional Populations

	People or Households		Institutions	
Number of Subgroup Analyses	National	Regional or Special	National	Regional or Special
None or Few	1,000–1,500	200–500	200–500	50–200
Average	1,500–2,500	500–1,000	500–1,000	200–1,000
Many	2,500+	1,000+	1,000+	1,000+

studies of individuals or households had samples ranging in size from 1,000 to 2,500 or more, and regional studies had samples of 200 to 1,000 or more. National samples of institutions (companies, for example) ranged in size from 200 to 1,000 or more, and regional or special studies from 50 to 500 or more. The sample sizes for institutional studies tended to be smaller because of the use of stratified sampling and because the sample frequently comprised a large fraction of the total population.

These typical sample sizes can be used as an initial aid in deciding what size sample to take, but not as a substitute for formal judgment.

Required Size Per Cell

This method of determining sample size can be used on *stratified random* and on *quota* samples. For example, in a study of the attitudes and preferences with respect to fast food establishments in a local marketing area it was decided that information was desired for two occupational groups (blue-collar and white-collar/managerial-professional) and for each of four age groups (12–17, 18–24, 35–44, and 45 and over). This resulted in $2 \times 4 = 8$ sample cells. A sample size of 30 was needed per cell for the types of statistical analyses that were to be conducted. The overall sample size was therefore $8 \times 30 = 240$.

Generally, as shown in Table 16–1, the larger the number of cells the larger the sample will be. Sudman recommends that the sample should be large enough so that "there are 100 or more units in each category of the major breakdowns and a minimum of 20 to 50 in the minor breakdowns (cells)." [3]

Use of a Traditional Statistical Model

If you have taken one or more courses in inferential statistics, you will have already been introduced to the traditional statistical formulas for determining the size of probability samples. Although the formula varies depending upon the type of sample to be taken, it always incorporates three common variables:

(1) an estimate of the *variance in the population* from which the sample is to be drawn, (2) the *error from sampling* that the researcher will allow, and (3) the desired *level of confidence* that the actual sampling error will be within the allowable limits.

The statistical models for simple random sampling for estimation of proportions and of means, and for hypothesis tests of proportions and of means, are discussed later in the chapter. The comparable models for stratified and for cluster samples are discussed in Appendix **B**.

Use of a Bayesian Statistical Model

The Bayesian model involves finding the difference between the expected value of the information to be provided by the sample and the cost of taking the sample for each potential sample size. This difference is known as the *expected net gain from sampling* (ENGS). The sample size with the largest *positive* ENGS is chosen. (If all sample sizes have negative ENGSs, no sample is taken).[4]

The Bayesian model is not as widely used as the traditional statistical models for determining sample size, even though it incorporates the cost of sampling and the traditional models do not. The reasons for the relatively infrequent use of the Bayesian model are related to the greater complexity and perceived difficulty of making the estimates required for the Bayesian model as compared to the traditional models.

The next section of the chapter provides a more extensive discussion of the traditional statistical formulas for determining sample size. These formulas are each based on a *sampling distribution*, which is considered first.

The Sampling Distribution

Sampling theory rests on the concept of a *sampling distribution*. Having a basic understanding of what a sampling distribution is and how it is used removes much of the mystery from sampling theory. If the sampling distribution is itself somewhat mysterious, the rest of sampling theory is almost certain to be so.

To help understand the concept of a sampling distribution, we illustrate a *sampling distribution of the mean* by drawing samples from a population of 1,250 sales invoices from a local retailer's Easter sale catalog. We use simple random samples of size $n = 50$ from this population for the illustration.

A sampling distribution of the mean *is the relative frequency distribution of the means of all possible samples of size n taken from a population of size N.*[5] The definition specifies that *all* possible samples of size n from population size N should be taken, and the mean of *each* sample be calculated and plotted in a relative frequency distribution. With a sample of size 50 from a population of size 1,250, this would require approximately 2×10^{91} samples. Because such an undertaking is possible in theory but not in practice, we have to settle for a more modest number of samples in our illustration.

Illustration of Sampling Distribution of the Mean

Five hundred simple random samples of size 50 were taken from 1,250 invoices whose values ranged from $1 to $100, and the mean was calculated for *each* sample. These sample means were sorted into intervals based on their values. The resulting frequency distribution is shown in Table 16–2.

The relative frequencies in column 2 of Table 16–2 were calculated by dividing the absolute number in each interval (the figure in column 1) by the total number of samples taken, 500. Thus, a relative frequency for a class (interval) in this example is nothing more than the number of times means with values falling within the class limits occurred *relative* to the total number of means.

A relative frequency, then, is a measure of a *probability*. If one were asked to predict the probability of a random sample of size 50 taken from this population having a mean between $50.00 to $51.99, the best estimate would be .22, based on the table. That is, we would expect about 2 out of every 10

Table 16–2 Frequencies and Relative Frequencies of 500 Sample Means

	Column 1	Column 2
	Frequency of Sample Means	Relative Frequency of Sample Means
$38.00–39.99	1	1/500 = .002
40.00–41.99	2	2/500 = .004
42.00–43.99	17	17/500 = .034
44.00–45.99	39	39/500 = .078
46.00–47.99	52	52/500 = .104
48.00–49.99	85	85/500 = .170
50.00–51.99	110	110/500 = .220
52.00–53.99	77	77/500 = .154
54.00–55.99	64	64/500 = .128
56.00–57.99	37	37/500 = .074
58.00–59.99	10	10/500 = .020
60.00–61.99	4	4/500 = .008
62.00–63.99	2	2/500 = .004
Total	500	1.000

simple random samples of size 50 drawn from this population to have a mean within this range.

The relative frequencies in Table 16–2 are shown in a histogram in Figure 16–1. A normal curve is shown in the same figure. It may be seen that the relative frequency distribution is very close to being normally distributed. Had *all* possible samples been drawn rather than only 500, it *would* have been normally distributed. The normal curve in Figure 16–1 is the *sampling distribution of the mean* for the sampling problem with which we are working. A sampling distribution of the mean for *simple random* samples that are large (30 or more) has

1. *a normal distribution*
2. *a mean equal to the population (M)*
3. *a standard deviation, called the standard error of the mean ($\sigma_{\bar{x}}$), that is equal to the population standard deviation (σ) divided by the square root of the sample size ($\sqrt{n}$). This is,*

$$\sigma_{\bar{x}} = \frac{\sigma}{\sqrt{n}} \qquad (16-1)$$

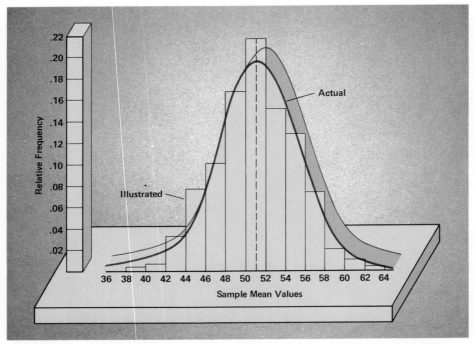

Figure 16–1 *Illustrated and Actual Sampling Distribution of the Mean for Sales Invoice Problem (n = 50)*

The only reason that a *standard error of the mean* is called that instead of a standard deviation is to indicate that it applies to a *distribution of sample means* and not to a single sample or a population.

A basic characteristic of a sampling distribution is that the area under it between any two points can be calculated so long as each point is defined by the number of standard errors it is away from the mean. The number of standard errors a point is away from the mean is referred to as *the Z value* for that point. For example, the areas under one side of the curve between the mean and points that have Z values of 1.0, 2.0, and 3.0, respectively, are as follows:

Z value (number of standard errors)	area under the curve from the mean to the point defined by the Z value
1.0	0.3413
2.0	0.4772
3.0	0.4986

(A complete table of areas under the normal curve is given in Appendix D.)

Thus, the area between the population mean (M) and a sample mean ($\bar{x}$) that is one standard error to the right of the mean ($Z = +1.0$) is 0.3413. This area is shown as the shaded area in Figure 16–2.

The dollar value for one standard error in the sales invoice problem is \$3.97. It is calculated from the values for the standard deviation ($\sigma = \$28.06$) and the sample size ($n = 50$) as follows:

$$\sigma_{\bar{x}} = \frac{\sigma}{\sqrt{n}} = \frac{\$28.06}{\sqrt{50}} = \$3.97.$$

Thus, the dollar values shown in Figure 16–2 for the mean and one standard deviation to the right of it in the sales invoice problem are as follows:

$$M = \$50.97, \text{ and}$$
$$M + 1.0\sigma_{\bar{x}} = \$50.97 + \$3.97 = \$54.94.$$

The area between two points under a sampling distribution is a *probability*. In our example, if we took all possible samples of size 50 from the population, the relative frequency of occurrence of those with means falling from \$50.97 to \$54.94 would be .3413. That is, slightly more than one third of them would fall between \$50.97 and \$54.94.

The fact that the *relative frequency* of occurrence of *all possible* samples of size 50 with a mean of plus (or minus) one standard error from the population

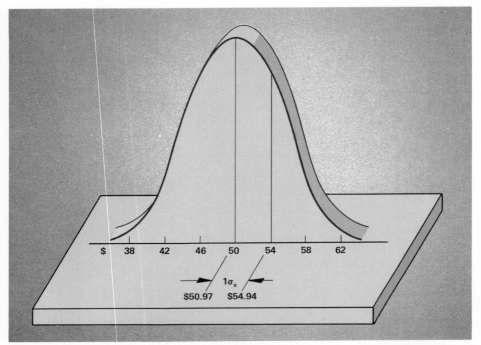

Figure 16–2 *Determination of Probability of Getting a Sample Mean with a Value of $50.97 to $54.94*

mean is .3413 means that the *probability* of *one* sample with a mean falling within this range is .3413 (or 34.13 per cent). That is, if we know the population mean and the standard error, we know that the probability of any given sample mean being within one standard error $(Z = 1.0)$ on one side of the population mean is .3413. We can determine the comparable probability for any Z value (number of standard errors) from the table of areas under the normal curve.

Statistical Estimation and the Sampling Distribution of the Mean

In statistical estimation problems involving the mean, we want to estimate a *population mean* that *we do not know* from a sample mean that *we do know.* Two kinds of estimates of a population mean may be made, *point* and *interval.*

A *point estimate* of the mean is an estimate involving only a single value. If a random sample is taken, the sample mean is the best estimate that can be made from the sample data. If we have taken a random sample of 50 invoices from the population of 1,250 sales invoices and want to estimate the population mean, we simply use the sample mean as the best guess, or estimate, of the value of the population mean.

A visual examination of the sampling distribution of the mean in Figure

498

16–2 shows that the mean of a *srs* of size 50 is likely to be quite close to the actual population mean. Most of the sample means are clustered near the center of the sampling distribution; that is, near the true mean. But the mean of a particular *srs* of size 50 could be any one of the sample means in the distribution, and some are a substantial distance from the true mean. The distance between the sample value and the true value of the mean is the *sampling error*.

Increasing sample size will reduce the potential sampling error, because as sample size increases, the sampling distribution becomes clustered more closely around the true population value. Or, stated differently, *the standard error of the mean becomes smaller as the sample size increases.* This can be seen easily by examining formula 16–1.

The fact that point estimates based on sample means are seldom *exactly* correct makes the *interval estimate* quite useful. As the name implies, it is an estimate concerning an interval, or range of values. A statement of the probability that the interval will enclose the true value of the mean is also given. This probability is called a *confidence coefficient* and the interval is called a *confidence interval*.

An interval estimate of the mean is arrived at by the following procedure. A sample is taken and the sample mean is calculated. We know that this sample mean falls somewhere within the sampling distribution, but not at what location. We do know, however, that there is a probability of .3413 (34.13 per cent) that it lies within one standard error above and a probability of .3413 (34.13 per cent) that it lies within one standard error below the actual population mean. We may, therefore, make an interval estimate that *allows us to be 68.26 per cent confident* (34.13 + 34.13 per cent) *that the population mean (M) lies within the interval formed by the sample mean ($\bar{x}$) plus one standard error ($\sigma_{\bar{x}}$) and the sample mean minus one standard error.*

In symbols this confidence interval may be shown as

$$\bar{x} - 1.0\sigma_{\bar{x}} \leq M \leq \bar{x} + 1.0\sigma_{\bar{x}}$$

The 68.26 per cent is the *confidence coefficient* of the estimate.

We may extend the interval to be more confident that the true value of the population mean is enclosed by the estimating process. We might enlarge the interval to plus or minus two standard errors. Reference to Appendix D indicates that the appropriate confidence coefficient is 95.44 per cent. Although we are more confident of our interval estimate now, it is a larger interval and, therefore, may not be as useful. The same observation applies to the estimate formed by the sample mean and three standard errors on either side (99.74 per cent confidence coefficient).

The question may be asked, "This seems all right if you know the value of the standard deviation of the population. But what do you do when you don't know that either?" One answer is that you may estimate it from the sample. If we let $\hat{\sigma}$ stand for an *estimate* of the standard deviation of the population and *s* represent the sample standard deviation, an estimate is given by

$$\hat{\sigma} = s, \text{ where } s = \sqrt{\frac{\sum_{i=1}^{n}(x_i - \bar{x})^2}{n - 1}} \qquad (16\text{-}2)$$

The Sampling Distribution of the Proportion

Researchers are often interested in proportions (percentages) as well as in means. For example, marketers are concerned about the percentage of magazine readers who remember a specific advertisement, the percentage of a group that prefers brand A over brand B, and so on. Therefore, marketing researchers are often dealing with proportions and, of necessity, with the sampling distribution of the proportion.

A *sampling distribution of the proportion is the relative frequency distribution of the proportion (p) of all possible samples of size n taken from a population of size N.*[6] The same basic reasoning used to determine the sampling distribution of the mean applies to the sampling distribution of the proportion. A sampling distribution of a proportion for a simple random sample has a

1. *normal distribution*
2. *a mean equal to the population proportion (P)*
3. *a standard error (σ_p) equal to*

$$\sigma_p = \sqrt{\frac{P(1 - P)}{n}} \qquad (16\text{-}3)$$

The estimated standard error of the proportion (given a large sample size that is a small proportion of the population) is

$$\hat{\sigma}_p = \sqrt{\frac{p(1 - p)}{n - 1}} \qquad (16\text{-}4)$$

where p represents the sample proportion.

Having briefly reviewed the critical concept of the sampling distribution, we now turn our attention to how this concept can be used in the determination of sample size.

Traditional Statistical Methods of Determining Sample Size

Determination of Sample Size in Problems Involving Estimation

Specifications Required for Estimation Problems Involving Means

Suppose an estimate of the mean dollar amount per invoice is required for a decision concerning the continuation of the direct mail campaign that generated the invoices. A simple random sample is to be taken from the 1,250 invoices described earlier to make the estimate. What information is needed before a calculation of the sample size can be made?

Three kinds of specifications have to be made before the sample size necessary to estimate the population mean can be determined. These are

1. *Specification of error (e) that can be allowed*—how close must the estimate be (how accurate do we need to be)?
2. *Specification of confidence coefficient*—what level of confidence is required that the actual sampling error does not exceed that specified (how sure do we want to be that we have achieved our desired accuracy)?
3. *Estimate of the standard deviation (σ)*—what is the standard deviation of the population (how "spread out" or diverse is the population)?

The first two of these specifications are matters of judgment involving the *use* of the data. The questions of "How much error in the estimate is acceptable?" and "How confident do you want to be that the error really isn't any greater than that?" need to be raised.

Suppose that, after discussing these questions, it is decided that the allowable error is ±$8.00 and that a confidence level of 90 per cent is desired.

The third specification, the estimate of the standard deviation of the population, is the responsibility of the analyst. Estimates of the standard deviation sometimes are available from previous studies. Most government agencies that collect data report means and deviations.[7] Standard deviations are either available directly or can be calculated for such demographic and other variables as personal income, corporate income, age, education, labor rates, housing values, and most other information collected and reported by the Bureau of the Census, Bureau of Labor Statistics, and other government agencies. Exhibit 16–1 provides estimates of variances (σ^2) associated with rating scales commonly used in marketing research.

If other sources are not available for estimating the standard deviation, one can sometimes design the sampling plan so that a small sample is taken for that purpose. The sample standard deviation is calculated and used to estimate the population standard deviation and the final sample size is determined. The initial sample is included as a part of the total sample so that the only loss is the extra time involved.

Assume that, based on past studies, we estimate the standard deviation of the population of invoice values to be $28.90. With the allowable error already set at $8.00 and the confidence coefficient at 90 per cent, all the specifications needed to calculate sample size are complete.

Exhibit 16–1   *Estimating Variances for Rating Scales Used in Marketing Research*

Rating scales are "doubly-bounded": on a 5-point scale, for instance, responses cannot be less than 1 or greater than 5. This constraint leads to a relationship between the mean and the variance. For example, if a sample mean is 4.6 on a 5-point scale, then there must be a large proportion of responses of "5" and it follows that the variance must be relatively small. On the other hand, if the mean is near 3.0, the variance can be potentially much greater. The nature of the relationship between the mean and the variance depends on the number of scale points and on the "shape" of the distribution of responses (e.g., approximately normal or symmetrically "clustered" around some central scale value, or skewed, or uniformly spread among the scale values). By considering the types of distribution shapes typically encountered in practice, it is possible to estimate variances for use in calculating sample size requirements for a given number of scale points.

Ranges of variances likely to be encountered for various numbers of scale points are shown below. The low end of the range is the approximate variance when data values tend to be concentrated around some middle point of the scale, as in a normal distribution. The high end of the range is the variance that would be obtained if responses were uniformly spread across the scale points. Although it is possible to encounter distributions with larger variances than those listed (such as distributions with modes at both ends of the scale), such data are rare.

In most cases, data obtained using rating scales tend to be more uniformly spread out than in a normal distribution. Hence, in order to arrive at conservative sample size estimates — i.e., sample sizes that are *at least* large enough to accomplish the stated objectives — it is advisable to use a variance estimate at or near the high end of the range listed.

Number of Scale Points	Typical Range of Variances
4	0.7 – 1.3
5	1.2 – 2
6	2 – 3
7	2.5 – 4
10	3 – 7

Source: "Sample Sizes for Analyses of Means and Proportions," *Research on Research* (Chicago: Market Facts, Inc., undated), 37.

Calculation of Sample Size in Estimation Problems Involving Means

The three specifications are related in the following way:

$$\frac{\text{number of standard errors}}{\text{implied by confidence coefficient}} = \frac{\text{allowable error}}{\text{standard error}}$$

or in symbols,

$$Z = \frac{e}{\dfrac{\sigma}{\sqrt{n}}} \qquad\qquad (16-5)$$

The only unknown variable is the sample size.

This equation is the direct result of the logic of the sampling distribution. We know that the sample mean ($\bar{x}$) lies somewhere on the sampling distribution, which has as its mean the population mean ($\overline{M}$). In order to be 90 per cent confident that the population mean will be included, we must construct an interval that will include the population mean in all cases except those in which the sample mean happens to fall in the last 5 per cent of the area at the two ends of the distribution. This interval is shown in Figure 16-3.

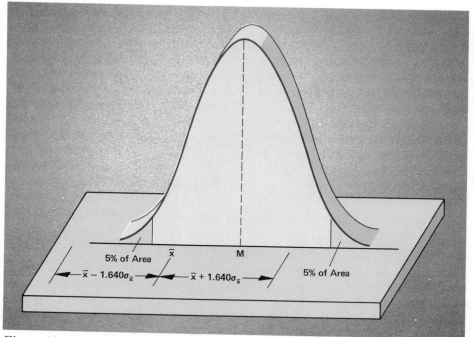

Figure 16-3 Sampling Distribution and 90 Per Cent Confidence Interval—Estimate of Mean

What is the number of standard errors (Z) required to give a 90 per cent level of confidence? Reference to Appendix D indicates that 1.64 standard errors cover 45 per cent of one side of the sampling distribution; $M \pm 1.64\sigma_{\bar{x}}$ covers 90 per cent of the entire distribution.

The calculation remains. Substituting in the equation 16–5 we obtain a required simple random sample size of 35 as follows

$$Z = \frac{e}{\dfrac{\sigma}{\sqrt{n}}}$$

$$1.64 = \frac{\$8.00}{\dfrac{\$28.90}{\sqrt{n}}}$$

$$\sqrt{n} = \frac{\$28.90 \times 1.64}{\$8.00} = 5.92$$

$$n = 35$$

A simpler formula for the size of simple random samples can be derived from equation 16–5. It is

$$n = \frac{Z^2\sigma^2}{e^2} \qquad (16-6)$$

This formula can be used for calculating sample size without the requirement of doing the algebraic manipulations required if equation 16–5 is used.[8]

For many problems, we need to set the allowable error in relation to the mean rather than in absolute terms. That is, we may want to avoid an error any larger than, say, 1 or 5 or 10 per cent of the mean. It, therefore, makes sense to set the tolerable error in these terms. This is known as the *relative allowable error* and is denoted by the letter R. Mathematically, R is equal to the allowable error divided by the mean, or

$$R = \frac{e}{M} = \text{relative allowable error}$$

The standard deviation may also be estimated relative to the mean. The relative standard error is called the *coefficient of variation* and is denoted by the letter C. Mathematically, C is equal to the standard deviation divided by the mean, or

$$C = \frac{\sigma}{M} = \text{coefficient of variation}$$

Expressing the allowable error and the standard deviation in relative rather than in absolute terms permits equation 16–6 to be shown as

$$n = \frac{Z^2 C^2}{R^2} \qquad\qquad (16-7)$$

This equation is used as the basis for a sample size *nomograph* for mean estimation problems. This nomograph allows one to read off the sample size rather than having to calculate it. It is shown in Figure 16–4.

As an example of the use of the nomograph, assume that a sample size is to be determined for a simple random sample for a situation in which it has been specified that (1) *the allowable error is to be no more than 20 per cent of the population mean, or R* = .20; (2) *the confidence level is to be 95 per cent; and* (3) *the standard deviation of the population is estimated to be 65 per cent of the mean, or C* = .65. By placing a ruler on the values R = .20 and C = .65, the sample size can be read off where it crosses the column of sample sizes for a 95 per cent confidence level. It is found that n = 40.

Specifications Required for Estimation Problems Involving Proportions

Suppose an estimate of the proportion of invoices that have dollar amounts of $20.00 or less is to be made. A simple random sample is to be taken from the population of 1,250 invoices described earlier. What additional information is needed before one can determine the sample size to take?

The specifications that must be made to determine the sample size for an estimation problem involving a proportion are very similar to those for the mean. They are

1. *Specification of error (e) that can be allowed*—how close must the estimate be?
2. *Specification of confidence coefficient*—what level of confidence is required that the actual sampling error does not exceed that specified?
3. *Estimate of population proportion (P̂) using prior information*—what is the approximate or estimated population proportion?

The reasoning for these specifications and the methods of obtaining them are the same as that for the mean. They, along with the sample size, collectively determine the sampling distribution for the problem. Because sample size is the only remaining unknown, it can be calculated.

As was the case with the sample mean, the three specifications are related as follows:

$$\frac{\text{number of standard errors implied}}{\text{by confidence coefficient}} = \frac{\text{allowable error}}{\text{standard error}}$$

The formula for the estimated standard error of the proportion is

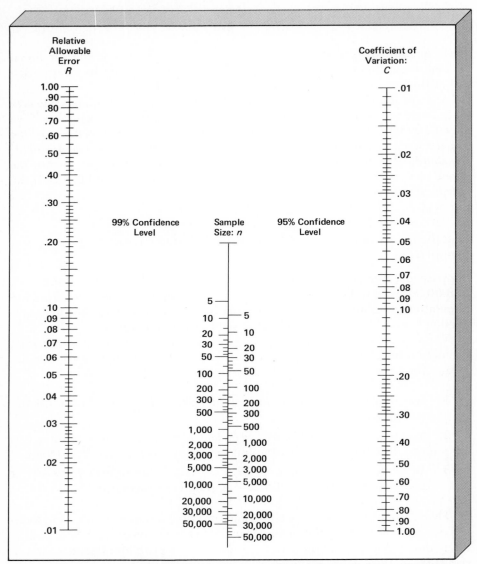

Figure 16–4 *Nomograph for Determining Size of a Simple Random Sample in Estimation Problems of the Mean—Infinite Population (Used with the permission and through the courtesy of Audits and Surveys, Inc.)*

$$\hat{\sigma}_{\mathbf{P}} = \sqrt{\frac{\hat{P}(1.0 - \hat{P})}{n}}$$

The relation among specifications may be shown symbolically as

$$Z = \frac{e}{\sqrt{\dfrac{\hat{P}(1.0 - \hat{P})}{n}}} \qquad (16-8)$$

Because the logic for this relationship is the same as it is for problems involving estimation of means, we do not repeat it here. The calculation of sample size can also be made in the same way.[9]

The formula for determining n directly is

$$n = \frac{Z^2[\hat{P}(1.0 - \hat{P})]}{(e)^2} \qquad (16-9)$$

The sample size required for estimating the proportion of invoices with dollar amounts of $20.00 or less where the specification of *error that can be allowed* (e) is .08 (8 percentage points), *the confidence level* is 95.4 per cent (thus, $Z = 2.0$) and the estimate of the *population proportion* is $P = .20$ (20.0 per cent) is

$$n = \frac{2^2[.20(1.0 - .20)]}{(.08)^2}$$

$$= \frac{4[.16]}{.0064}$$

$$= 100$$

Figure 16–5 may also be used for determining the (simple random) sample size after the necessary specifications have been made for a problem involving estimation of a proportion. Determine the sample size for the problem stated using the nomograph and see if the answer is the same.

So far we have been discussing sample size determination for estimating the proportion of sample elements that have an attribute. Because we can only classify each element into one or two categories — either it has the attribute or it does not — the population from which the sample is drawn is called a *binomial* population.

Estimates of proportions from this kind of population are very common in marketing research. Every question on a survey questionnaire that requires a "yes" or "no," or "agree" or "disagree," or some other dichotomous response involves a binomial estimation problem. Such basic information as "user" – "nonuser" of the product class; "know of the brand" – "do not know of the brand;" "tried the brand" – "have not tried the brand;" "use the brand" – "do not use the brand;" is also binomial.

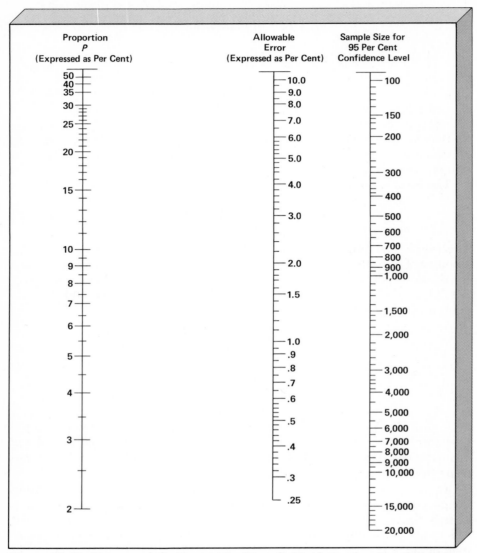

Figure 16–5 *Nomograph for Determining Size of a Simple Random Sample in Estimation Problems of the Proportion — Infinite Population (Used with the permission and through the courtesy of Audits and Surveys, Inc.)*

Sample Size Determination for SRS Samples for Multinomial Problems

We are also frequently interested in obtaining estimates from *multinomial* populations. A multinomial population is one in which each element can be classified into one of more than two categories. All multiple-choice questions involve multinomial populations. Estimating the proportion of users of each of three or more brands of a product or the proportion of listeners to each of the eighteen U.S. networks of radio stations during a given 15-minute period during the day are examples in marketing research.

In such cases, if the specifications of error that can be allowed (e) and of the confidence coefficient are to apply to the estimates of proportions for each of the several categories (rather than to only two of them, as it would if it were a binomial estimation problem), a *larger* sample will have to be taken than if the population were a binomial one. This is because three or more proportions are being estimated simultaneously and the estimates are such that the error in one of them affects the error in one or more of the others.

The direct determination of sample size for estimates of proportions from multinomial populations involves a somewhat complicated set of calculations. Fortunately, however, a table is available that permits conversion of the sample size that would be used if the estimate were to be treated as if it were to be made from a binomial population to the one that is appropriate for the multinomial population.[10] This table (Table 16–3) and a set of procedures for using it are described shortly. To illustrate the use of the table, suppose we want to estimate the proportion of all users of a product class who use brand **A**, brand **B**, and brand **O** (all other brands). The steps in the procedure to determine the appropriate sample size are:

1. *Specify the allowable error (e) that is applicable to each proportion to be estimated.*
   Assume that the proportion of users of brand **A**, brand **B**, and brand **O** are each to have an allowable error of ±.05.
2. *Specify the confidence coefficient for the estimates.*
   Assume a 95 per cent level of confidence (Z = 1.96)
3. *Using prior information, estimate the population proportion for each item.*

Table 16–3   Factors for Converting Binomial Sample Size to Multinomial Sample Size

Confidence Coefficient	No. of Proportions to Be Estimated					
	3	*4*	*5*	*10*	*15*	*20*
95 per cent	1.53	1.66	1.73	2.05	2.37	2.53
90 per cent	1.71	1.84	2.04	2.44	2.76	2.91

Source: Adapted from R. D. Tortora, "A Note on Sample Size Estimations for Multinomial Populations," *The American Statistician* (August 1978), p. 101.

Assume the following estimates for the brands:

Brand A	$\hat{P}_A = .30$
Brand B	$\hat{P}_B = .20$
Brand O	$\hat{P}_O = \underline{.50}$
	1.00

4. *Calculate the sample size that would be required for the estimate of the proportion for each item if the population were treated as if it were binomial.*

    If brand A were the only brand of interest, the sample size (ignoring the finite population correction) would be

    $$n_A = \frac{Z^2[\hat{P}_A(1.0 - \hat{P}_A)]}{(e)^2}$$

    $$= \frac{1.96^2[.30(1.0 - .30)]}{.05^2}$$

    $$= 323$$

    For brand B, the sample size (calculated in the same way) is

    $$n_B = 246$$

    and for Brand O

    $$n_O = 385$$

    Note: If the same confidence coefficient is used for the estimate of the population proportion for each of the items, one need calculate only the sample size for the item whose estimated population proportion is closest to (or equal to) .50. This sample size will always be the largest because the product $\hat{P}_i (1 - \hat{P}_i)$ in the numerator becomes larger as $\hat{P}_i$ approaches .50. Observe that this is the case in this example: $\hat{P}_O = .50$ and n_O is larger than either n_A or n_B.

5. *Multiply the largest sample size obtained in step 4 by the appropriate conversion factor from Table 16–3. The result is the proper sample size for the estimates to be made from the multinomial population.*

    The number of brands whose proportion is to be estimated is three, and the confidence coefficient is set at 95 per cent. The conversion factor from Table 16–2 is therefore 1.53, and

    $$n = 1.53 \times 385 = 589$$

    Calculating the sample size for the estimated share of listeners for each of the eighteen U.S. radio networks was a multinomial problem. The calculation is shown in Exhibit 16–2.

Exhibit 16–2 *Calculation of Sample Size for Radio Audience Measurement — Statistical Research, Inc.*

Statistical Research Inc. measures and reports U.S. radio audiences overall and for each of 18 radio networks through its **RADAR**® syndicated service. It sells these data to the networks and to advertising agencies and large advertisers for use in media planning, selling, and buying.

The company measures radio listening by a sample of persons within households selected by random digit dialing and interviewed by telephone. One member 12 years of age or older is selected at random from each sample household. The respondent is asked to report his or her radio listening by daypart — 15-minute intervals are the basic measurement period — for the last 24 hours. A call is made each day for a week and listening data are reported by the sample household member. After weighting to reflect the probability of selection and to make the sample more representative geographically and demographically, the listening data are analyzed and reported for a variety of demographic characteristics and market areas.

In determining sample size, a company providing syndicated survey information has to balance the needs of customers for information that is as accurate and timely as possible against the costs of sampling. The sample size that is finally decided upon is inevitably a compromise between these two considerations. The procedure used in reaching this compromise is to (1) decide on (reasonable) desirable accuracy and confidence level requirements and use them to calculate sample sizes for those estimates that are considered to be the more important ones; (2) from among these calculated sample sizes determine the largest one required; (3) estimate the cost of using a sample of that size; (4) decide if that cost is acceptable; and (5) if it is, use that sample size. If it is not, start again at step (1) with somewhat lower accuracy and/or confidence level requirements.

We illustrate part of this procedure with a calculation of sample size for the Fall 1984 – Spring 1985 radio audience measurements. It is concerned with the estimate of the share of audience for each of the radio networks. These estimates are of obvious use to media planners in deciding with which networks to place ads, and the planners would like them to be as accurate as possible.

This is a *multinomial* estimation problem and so the procedure described on pp. 508 – 510 is appropriate for determining sample size. That is, one determines the largest sample size that would be required if it were being treated as a binomial estimation problem, and multiplies that sample size by a factor obtained from Table 16–3. The largest sample treating it as a *binomial* estimation problem will be required to estimate the audience share of the network with the largest share. Earlier surveys have shown the largest network share to be about 10 per cent ($p = 0.10$). If the tolerable error is set at 0.015 ($e = 0.015$), and the confidence level at 96 per cent (a confidence coefficient of $Z = 1.96$), the sample size treating the estimation as a *binomial* problem is found to be

$$n = \frac{Z^2[p(1 - p)]}{e^2}$$

$$= \frac{1.96^2[0.10(1 - 0.10)]}{0.015^2}$$

$$= 1,536$$

(This estimate assumes that the effect on sample size of the weighting of sample member responses is negligible.)

Applying the factor of 2.46 (interpolated from Table 16–2) to convert it to a *multinomial* estimation problem, the final sample size becomes

$$n = 2.46 \times 1,536 = 3,780$$

This is one calculation made as part of the first of the steps described above in deciding what sample size to take. This sample size turned out to be smaller than that needed for other estimates. The economics of the situation were also such as to allow a larger sample. The sample size actually used was 7,990.

Source: Statistical Research, Inc.

Sample Size Determination for Non-SRS Random Samples in Problems Involving Estimation

Thus far we have considered only simple random samples (srs) in the determination of the size sample to take. The reasons for limiting the discussion to simple random samples are two: (1) it is the simplest of all the methods, and (2) the principles that apply to it are applicable to all methods of probability sampling.

The complexities of determining the proper size of a several-stage sample of a human population involving areas, strata, and clusters are well beyond the scope of this book. In Appendix B a discussion is given of the determination of the sample size for stratified random and for cluster samples for purposes of estimating the mean or a proportion for a population.

Determination of Sample Size in Problems Involving Hypothesis Testing

A major oil company sells low-priced durable items (clock radios, typewriters, binoculars, and the like) by direct mail to its credit card holders. The mailing piece is sent out with the monthly statements. Those customers who decide to buy the item each month do so by returning a card on which their name, address, and credit card number are already entered.

Approximately 3.5 per cent of those receiving the mailing place an order. Initial research indicated that a larger, high-quality and more expensive mailer would increase the order rate to 5 per cent, which would more than cover the added costs. However, since the initial research did not involve actual purchases, several executives remained convinced that the new mailer would have no impact on sales. They felt that the product, brand, and price determined sales and that any mailer that clearly displayed these attributes would be effective.

The research director recommended that the company run a market test consisting of an item judged to be representative of those the company sold through the program. It was recommended further that the test be run using order rates of 3.5 and 5.0 per cent; if 3.5 per cent were the estimated average order rate, the idea should be dropped. If 5.0 per cent turned out to be the indicated rate, the company should proceed with the new mailer.

How large a simple random sample of credit card holders should be taken?

Specification Required and Calculation of Sample Size for Hypothesis Testing Problems Involving Proportions

In order to determine the sample size in a hypothesis testing problem involving proportions, the following specifications must be made:

1. *the hypotheses to be tested;*
2. *the level of sampling error permitted in the test of each hypothesis.*

The Hypothesis to Be Tested.   A *null* and an *alternate hypothesis* are involved in each hypothesis test. A *null hypothesis*, designated by H_0, *is one that, if accepted, will result in no opinion being formed and/or action being taken that is different from any currently held or being used.* The null hypothesis in the problem just described is

$$H_0: \text{order rate} = 3.5\%$$

If it is accepted, the program being considered will not be initiated.

The *alternate hypothesis*, designated by H_1, *is one that will lead to opinions being formed and/or actions being taken that are different from those currently held or being used.* The alternate hypothesis here is

$$H_1: \text{order rate} = 5.0\%$$

Although the null hypothesis is always explicitly stated, this is sometimes not true of the alternate hypothesis. In those instances when the alternative hypothesis is not stated, it is understood that it consists of all values of the proportion not reserved by the null hypothesis. In this situation, if the alternate hypothesis were not explicitly stated, it would be understood that it would be

$$H_1: \text{order rate} > 3.5\%$$

The Level of Sampling Error Permitted in the Test of Each Hypothesis. Two types of error can be made in hypothesis-testing problems. An error is made when the null hypothesis is true but the conclusion is reached that the alternate hypothesis should be accepted. This is known as a *type I error*. A *type II error* is made when the alternate hypothesis is true but the null hypothesis is accepted. The two possible states, along with the two possible conclusions about them, are shown in Table 16–4.

The probability of making a type I error is designated as α (alpha) and of making a type II error as β (beta). These errors are commonly specified at the .10, .05, or .01 levels, although there is nothing other than convention to recommend these values over others that could be chosen. In fact, naive acceptance of such conventional levels can lead to serious errors in applied research. In this problem we assume that $\alpha = .15$ and $\beta = .05$.

The specification of the hypotheses to be tested and the allowable error probabilities result in the testing situation shown in Figure 16–6. The α and β levels specified result in a rejection region for H_0 and H_1, respectively. The boundary of each region is common and defines a *critical value* in the test. Any sample value higher than the critical value in our example means that H_1 will be accepted; any lower sample value will result in H_0 being accepted.

The determination of the Z values associated with α and β, designated as Z_α and Z_β, respectively, is similar to that of the Z values associated with a confidence coefficient in an estimation problem. The distance to the critical value

Table 16–4 Conclusions and Errors

Conclusion	H_0 Is True	H_1 Is True
Accept H_0	Correct conclusion	Type II error
Accept H_1	Type I error	Correct conclusion

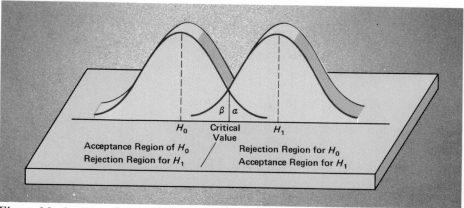

Figure 16–6   *Test of H_0 and H_1*

from the center of the sampling distribution is $Z_\alpha \sigma_{p0}$ for the null hypothesis distribution and $Z_\beta \sigma_{p1}$ for the alternate hypothesis distribution.

We can see from Figure 16–7 that this distance covers one half of the total area of the distribution minus α. If $\alpha = .15$, then .35 (35 per cent) of the curve is covered by $Z_\alpha \sigma_{p0}$. Looking in Appendix D we find that the corresponding Z value is $Z_\alpha = 1.04$. The Z_β value is 1.64.

We have now specified all that is required to determine the sample size for the problem being considered.

From the specifications that have been made we can determine the appropriate sample size using the formula

$$n = \frac{[Z_\alpha \sqrt{P_0(1.0 - P_0)} + Z_\beta \sqrt{P_1(1.0 - P_1)}]^2}{(P_1 - P_0)^2} \qquad (16–10)$$

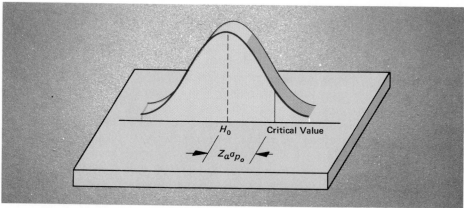

Figure 16–7   *Distance of Critical Value — Null Hypothesis Distribution*

Substituting the specifications made earlier, we obtain

$$n = \frac{[1.04\sqrt{0.35(1.0 - .035)} + 1.64\sqrt{.05(1.0 - .05)}]^2}{(.05 - .035)^2}$$

$$n = 1,338$$

Specifications Required and Calculation of Sample Size for Hypothesis-Testing Problems Involving Means

For hypothesis-testing problems involving means, the following specifications are required:

1. *the hypothesis to be tested*
2. *the level of sampling error permitted in the test of each hypothesis*
3. *the standard deviation of the population.*

These specifications are the counterparts of those required for problems involving proportions.

The logic of the calculation of sampling size in mean problems is the same as that for proportions. The equation determining the sample size in mean problems is

$$n = \frac{(Z_\alpha + Z_\beta)^2 \sigma^2}{(M_1 - M_0)^2} \qquad (16\text{-}11)$$

Several Sample Sizes Must be Calculated for Most Survey Research Studies — Largest Is Ruling

In most survey research projects there are questions on the questionnaire that, when the answers are analyzed, involve proportions *(Do you own a microwave oven? At which of the following supermarkets have you shopped in the past two weeks?)* and other questions that involve means *(On the average, how many times a week would you say you use your microwave oven? At how many different supermarkets would you say you shop during an average month?)* The answers to these questions are almost always analyzed to provide estimates of population values. They are also often used to test hypotheses.

Thus, the usual situation is that more than one sample size has to be calculated. When this occurs, the *largest* sample size should be taken. Reflecting for a moment will indicate that this is the only way that the specifications concerning allowable error and confidence level can be met for the estimate or hypothesis test that requires the largest sample.

516

Sample Size, Incidence and Nonresponse[11]

Our discussion of sample size determination thus far has ignored incidence and nonresponse. *Incidence,* as described in the previous chapter, is the percentage of individuals who have the traits necessary to be included in a survey. Such traits include product category user, male, viewed program, or a host of other variables. *Nonresponse,* as described in Chapter 6, refers to the percentage of respondents who refuse to participate in a survey or who cannot be contacted.

The formulas we have described are based on a population of qualified respondents with a 100 per cent response rate. Suppose you need to conduct a mail survey of owners of aquariums. Using the formulas described previously, you calculate a required sample size of 200. However, previous research indicates that only 8 per cent of all households have aquariums. Further, the mail panel company you are using estimates a 75 per cent response rate to your questionnaire. How many questionnaires do you mail out?

A simple approach is to use the formula:

$$\text{Initial sample size} = \text{required response} \div (\text{incidence} \times \text{response rate})$$
$$= 200 \div (.08 \times .75)$$
$$= 3{,}333$$

However, this will yield 200 or more qualified responses only about half the time. A formula for determining the required initial sample size to achieve an obtained sample size with a specified level of confidence is as follows:

$$IS = \frac{2X + Z(ZQ + \sqrt{(ZQ)^2 + 4XQ})}{2P} \qquad (16-12)$$

where IS = Initial sample

X = required sample (number of people with characteristic of interest) minus .5
$$= 200 - .5 = 199.5;$$

P = the incidence (proportion) for the characteristic times the estimated response rate $= .08 \times .75 = .06$;

$Q = 1 - P = 1 - .06 = .94$;

C = the desired probability or confidence that the initial sample will produce the desired sample, say .90 for this case; and

Z = the value that exceeds $100(C)\%$ of the standard normal distribution = 1.282 (from Appendix D).

Thus, for this example, where $ZQ = (1.282)(.94) = 1.205$

$$IS = \frac{2(199.5) + 1.282(1.205 + \sqrt{1.205^2 + 4(199.5)(.94)})}{2(.06)}$$

$$= 3{,}631$$

Thus, an initial sample of 3,631 will produce 200 or more qualified aquarium owners 90 per cent of the time. This relatively small (9 per cent) increase in the initial sample size over the number calculated by the more traditional approach greatly increases the probability of obtaining a sample as large or larger than the one required (from .5 to .9).

Review Questions

16.1.   What are *six* different methods of *determining sample size?*

16.2.   What is a *sampling distribution of the mean?*

16.3.   What is the difference between a *population standard deviation* and a *standard error of the mean?*

16.4.   What is the formula for the *standard error of the mean* for a simple random sample?

16.5.   What is a *point estimate* of the mean? An *interval estimate* of the mean?

16.6.   What is a *confidence coefficient?*

16.7.   What is a *confidence interval?*

16.8.   What is a *sampling distribution of the proportion?*

16.9.   What is the formula for the *standard error of the proportion* for a simple random sample?

16.10.   What are the specifications that must be made in order to determine the sample size required to estimate the population mean using a *simple random sample?*

16.11.   What are the specifications that must be made in order to determine the sample size required to estimate the population proportion using a *simple random sample?*

16.12.   What is the formula for the sample size for an estimate of the population mean using a simple random sample?

16.13.   What is the formula for the sample size for an estimate of the population proportion using a simple random sample?

16.14.   What is the *relative allowable error?*

16.15.   What is the *coefficient of variation?*

16.16.   What is a *binomial* population? A *multinomial* population?

16.17.   Does an estimate of the proportions of a multinomial population require a smaller or a larger sample size than that for an estimate of the proportions of a binomial population, given that the allowable error and the confidence coefficient are the same? Why?

16.18.   What are the specifications that are necessary to determine the sample size of a simple random sample for a *hypothesis-testing problem* involving population proportions?

16.19. What is the formula for the sample size for a simple random sample for a *test of hypotheses* concerning population proportions?

16.20. What are the specifications that are necessary to determine the sample size for a simple random sample for a *hypothesis-testing problem* involving the population mean?

16.21. What is the formula for the sample size for a *simple random sample* for a test of hypotheses concerning population means?

16.22. Why is it often necessary to make more than one sample size calculation for a survey? If more than one is calculated, which is used? Why?

16.23. How do incidence and response rate affect the requirements for initial sample size?

16.24. What is the formula to determine initial sample size, taking into account incidence, response rate, and desired confidence that the required confidence level will be obtained?

Discussion Questions/Problems

16.25. Suppose that there is a population of 20 users of an industrial raw material. The mean of the sampling distribution of the mean for a simple random sample of size $n = 3$ of the amount of the material used last year is 1,000 lbs. The mean of the amount of the same material used last year by the 20 companies is 1,150 lbs. What conclusion(s) can you draw concerning the difference in the two means? Explain.

16.26. Recently a Congressional committee investigating television ratings in the U.S. stated its belief that the samples of households on which ratings are based are far too small for a country with more than 80 million households. The sample used by the research agencies that provided the ratings is typically in the range of 1,000 to 1,500 households. Would Congress have less cause for concern about the sample size if the number of households were 8 million instead of 80 million? Why or why not?

16.27. The American Testing Institute provides both static and dynamic tests of automobile characteristics and performance. Such tests are used for comparison advertising and advertising documentation purposes. Static tests are measures of relatively uniform characteristics such as head room or leg room. Dynamic tests involve performance characteristics such as acceleration, braking, handling, and so forth. According to the firm's president, a valid dynamic test requires a minimum sample size of five cars of each model tested.[12]
What assumptions about the performance characteristics of cars are implied by this statement?

16.28. It can be argued that in most applied problems involving the determination of the sample size for a hypothesis test α should be *larger* than β. What is the basis for this assertion? Do you agree or disagree with it?

16.29. A simple random sample is to be taken from a population of 50,000 sales invoices to estimate the mean amount per invoice. Suppose that the population mean is actually $6,000 and the standard deviation of the population is $1,500. The allowable error is set at $200 and the confidence coefficient at 90 per cent.

    a. What size sample is required? (You may ignore the finite population correction factor.)

    b. Suppose the sample means turns out to be 6,302. What is the interval estimate?

16.30. The A. C. Nielsen Company would like to estimate the proportion of TV sets tuned to ABC, CBS, NBC, and to all other programs during the Tuesday evening 6:00–6:30 P.M. time slot. It plans to use the data from the meters on TV sets in a panel of randomly selected households. Suppose it sets the allowable error at ±1 per cent for each network and for the "all other" programs with a confidence level of 95 per cent. Further suppose that it estimates the population proportions to be as follows:

$$P(\text{ABC}) = .18, \ P(\text{CBS}) = .20, \ P(\text{NBC})$$
$$= .22, \text{ and } P(\text{all other}) = .40$$

What size sample should it take?

16.31. The management of a large supermarket chain is considering adding a generic brand of canned fruits and vegetables. It would add the generic brand if it were to obtain as much as a 10 per cent share of canned fruit and vegetable sales and would be unwilling to add the brand if it were to get as little as a 6 per cent share. The chain decides to run a controlled store test using randomly selected stores in its chain. The alpha and beta errors are set at $\alpha = .15$, $\beta = .05$.

How many stores should be selected for the test? (Ignore the finite population correction factor.)

16.32. Assume that a sequential monadic taste test of new Coke vs. regular Coke is to be conducted by Coca-Cola USA. The analyst designing the taste test has recommended that if the estimated preference is 60 per cent or more for new Coke it should be introduced; if it is 50 per cent or less it should be dropped. He has further recommended that the risk of making a Type I error be set at .20 and the risk of making a Type II error at .01.

    a. Do the analyst's recommendations for the Type I and Type II errors seem reasonable to you? Why or why not?

    b. What size simple random sample should be taken if the analyst's recommendations are accepted?

    c. The Coca-Cola USA management actually required a total sample of 190,000 persons in the taste tests it had conducted before deciding to introduce the new Coke formulation. What does this suggest about the risks of making a Type I and a Type II error that the management was willing to assume?

Projects

16.33. Form a project group with three other members of your class. Design a sampling plan and conduct an observational study of brands of soft drinks purchased at a large supermarket. Design the study so that the allowable error is $e = P - p = \pm.05$ with a confidence level of 90 per cent ($Z = \pm 1.64$) for each of what you believe to be the three leading brands plus an "all other" category.

16.34. Form a project group with three other members of your class. Design a sampling plan and a questionnaire and conduct a poll among the students on your campus to determine the per cent that plan to go directly into graduate school after graduation from their undergraduate program. Design the sample so that the allowable error is $e = P - p = \pm.02$ with a confidence level of 95.4 per cent ($Z = \pm 2.0$).

References

[1] Sequential sampling is a method also used for determining sample size, but is used primarily in quality-control applications. The size of the sample taken varies depending upon the cumulated results as the sampling proceeds.

[2] S. Sudman, *Applied Sampling* (New York: Academic Press, 1976), 87.

[3] Ibid., 30.

[4] For a discussion and illustration of the use of the Bayesian statistical model in determining sample size, see Sudman, op. cit. 88–104.

[5] This definition assumes that the sampling is from a population of finite rather than infinite size. This is usually the situation in marketing and, if the sampling is from an infinite population, presents no conceptual problem.

[6] This definition also assumes that the sampling is from a population of finite size.

[7] A formula for calculating the standard deviation from a frequency table is

$$\sigma = \sqrt{\frac{\sum_{i=1}^{h} f_i(x_i - M)^2}{N}}$$

where h is the number of classes, x_i is the midpoint of class i, f_i is the frequency of class i, N is the size of the population, and M is the population mean.

[8] These formulas assume an infinite rather than a finite population. If the population is finite and sample size calculated by equation 16–6 is 5 per cent or more of the population, it is larger than necessary. In such cases, the formula that should be used for calculating sample size is

$$n = \frac{\hat{\sigma}^2}{\dfrac{e^2}{Z^2} + \dfrac{\hat{\sigma}^2}{N}}$$

[9] These formulas assume an infinite rather than a finite population. If the population is finite and sample size calculated by equation 16–9 is 5 per cent or more of the population, it is larger than necessary. In such cases, the formula that should be used for calculating the sample size is

$$n = \frac{\hat{P}(1 - \hat{P})}{\dfrac{(e)^2}{Z^2} + \dfrac{\hat{P}(1 - \hat{P})}{N}}$$

[10] The method for calculating the sample size directly and the conversion table are given in R. D. Tortora, "A Note on Sample Size Estimation for Multinomial Problems," *The American Statistician* (August 1978), 100–102.

[11] This section is based on "Estimating Sample Sizes for Mailouts," *Research on Research* (Chicago: Market Facts Inc., undated), #32.

[12] Based on "How Company Tests Comparative Auto Claims," *Advertising Age*, October 2, 1978, 28.

CHAPTER 17

Data Reduction
and Estimation

Sauce Study. In a survey for a new sauce product a semantic differential scale was used in which participants had to rate, among other attributes, their preference with respect to the degree of hotness for this type of sauce. After the survey was completed, the analyst calculated the mean rating and found that it was very close to the middle of the scale which had "very mild" and "very hot" as its bipolar adjectives. This served to confirm the prior expectations of the client that most people liked a sauce that was neither too mild nor too hot.[1]

Taste Test of Different Types of Vinegars. While analyzing data from paired comparison blind taste tests of vinegars (wine based versus apple-juice based, wine based versus synthetically produced, and apple-juice based versus synthetically produced), an analyst discovered that approximately 15 per cent of the respondents had reported preferences that appeared to be logically inconsistent. About 9 per cent of the persons taking the test had reported that they preferred vinegars that were wine based to apple-juice based, and those synthetically produced to wine based, but also that they preferred those that were apple-juice based to those synthetically produced. Another 6 per cent indicated a preference for apple based to wine based, and wine based to synthetically produced, but synthetically produced to apple based. Both of these sets of preferences were logically inconsistent so long as it was assumed that (a) the respondents could discriminate among the tastes of the various types of vinegars, and (b) ties in taste preferences were not allowed. (The taste discriminating ability of the respondents was not tested but ties were not allowed.)

The analyst planned to run cross tabulations of the most preferred and least preferred vinegar types against the levels of various demographic variables (sex, age, income, etc.) and decided he could not include these results (since they were ambiguous as to which kind of vinegar was most and least preferred). For this reason he decided to discard the data. He stated in the report of the project that these responses were discarded because of "respondent error."

Market Test of Mexican Prepared Food.   A company that manufactures and sells ethnic foods was market testing a new Mexican prepared food. The test had been running for some months and both the overall trial and repeat purchase rates were so low that the company management had decided to discontinue the test and drop the product.

Three test markets were being used, of which Pittsburgh was one. An analyst noticed that trial and repeat there was much higher than in either of the other two cities. Since she knew that the Mexican population in Pittsburgh was proportionately no higher than in the other test cities, she was curious as to why this result was the case. She asked the diary panel service that was providing information on individual household purchases to run a tabulation of purchases by Pittsburgh households by a number of demographic variables, including the ethnic origin of the household head.

To her surprise, she discovered that Polish households were heavy trial and repeat purchasers of the product, whereas Mexican and other ethnic origin households were not.

The way the raw data from a research project are prepared for analysis and the manner in which the summarizing and descriptive statistics are calculated can often make a substantial difference in the usefulness of the report. The examples just given illustrate the effects of both good and bad practices in these early stages of data analysis. (The effects of what was done in each case are reported later in the appropriate section of the chapter.)

Data become useful only after they are analyzed. *Data analysis involves converting a series of observations (data) into descriptive statements about variables and/or inferences about relationships among variables.* Put more simply, *data analysis provides answers to questions we might want to ask of a set of data.* Some examples:

How many pairs of jeans does the average teenager buy per year?

Do boys or girls buy more jeans?

Is there a relationship between social class and brands of jeans bought?

Do social class, sex, age, and geographic region combine in some way to influence jean buying?

To answer questions such as these, analyses of a set of observations are required. It is the objective of this and the next three chapters to acquaint you with the process of data analysis—the means of having observations answer questions.

In this chapter, we deal with *data reduction*, which refers to *the process of getting the data ready for analysis and the calculation of summarizing or descriptive statistics. Estimation* techniques are also discussed in this chapter. Estimation techniques involve inferring the value of some group (called a *population*) from a subset of that group (a *sample*). Since virtually all marketing studies involve samples, estimation techniques are very important.

An Example Involving New Product Research

In this section, we present a very simplified example of a set of observations to illustrate the data reduction, estimation, bivariate association, and hypothesis test procedures described in this and the following 3 chapters. The example is simpler than most marketing research studies. That is, it involves a smaller sample size, fewer variables, and "cleaner" data. However, this simplicity makes it easier to visualize and follow the procedures being described.

A regional soft drink firm is concerned about its ability to remain viable in the face of strong competition from national brands. The firm is currently evaluating a number of options, including the introduction of a nonalcoholic carbonated apple cider. Preliminary research has been completed, and the company is now conducting a series of taste and preference tests among several potential market segments.

One market segment of interest is the college student market. As a means of examining the nature and extent of potential student demand for the product, the firm commissioned a small "pilot" experiment using students from a state university in the area (26,000 students). The experiment and the data collected in conjunction with it were designed to determine a number of different things:

1. The percentage of males, females, and all students who consume a carbonated beverage at least one day a week.
2. The amount of carbonated beverages consumed per week by males, females, and all students.
3. The importance of price in general to students.
4. The importance to students of image or status for publicly used items.
5. The taste reaction of male and female students to the new product.

6. The relative preference by male and female students for this product compared to four potential competitors.

7. The likelihood of purchasing the product by males, females, and all students.

8. Which of two brand names is better for the product.

9. The differences in reactions between males and females to the product and the brand names.

It was decided that the study would involve a sample of 100 students. To provide a sampling frame, a list of all students registered at the university was generated. Approximately sixty per cent of the students were male. A random sample of 100 students produced 60 male and 40 female respondents. Had the sample produced a disproportionate per cent of one gender, it would be necessary to weight the responses differentiately. These procedures are described later.

The selected students completed a questionnaire dealing with their demographics, attitudes toward a variety of beverages, and beverage-consumption patterns. Then the selected students tasted the new beverage.

Half of each group (30 males and 20 females) tasted the beverage with the label *Bravo* while the other half tasted the identical beverage labeled *Delight*. The students then rated the taste of the product, ranked its overall appeal compared to four competitors, stated their likelihood of purchasing the product, and finally chose either a six-pack of the version they tasted or $3 as a payment for their participation in the study.

Table 17–1 contains some of the questions used in the study and Table 17–2 contains the responses to these questions.

Data Reduction

The steps involved in the reduction of data are *(1) field controls, (2) editing, (3) coding, (4) transcribing, (5) generating new variables,* and *(6) calculating summarizing statistics.* The first five of these steps are concerned with developing a basic data array that is as complete and as error-free as possible. The last step involves calculations made from the array.

A *basic data array* is a table comprised of the value of each variable for each sample unit. Table 17–2 is the basic array for the beverage study described in the previous section. It consists of the values for 15 variables for 100 subjects, or a total of 1,500 measurements. This is a small data array compared to those encountered in most marketing studies.

Table 17 – 1 Selected Questions and Measurements from the Student Beverage Preference Study

1. Gender: _____ (1) Male _____ (2) Female
2. Age: _____
3. How many bottles, cans, and/or glasses of carbonated beverages do you drink in a typical week?_____
4. How many days in a typical week do you drink at least one carbonated beverage?_____
5. How important is price to you when you purchase beverages?
   (1) Extremely Important __ (2) Very Important __ (3) Somewhat Important __
   (4) Neither Important Nor Unimportant __ (5) Somewhat Unimportant __
   (6) Very Unimportant __ (7) Extremely Unimportant __
6. How important is the quality image of a brand to you when you purchase beverages?
   (1) Extremely Important __ (2) Very Important __ (3) Somewhat Important __
   (4) Neither Important Nor Unimportant __ (5) Somewhat Unimportant __
   (6) Very Unimportant __ (7) Extremely Unimportant __
7. Having tasted Bravo (Delight), indicate how much you like its taste by assigning 0 to 100 points, where 0 indicates extreme dislike, 50 indicates indifference (neither like nor dislike), and 100 indicates extreme liking. (Use any value between 0 and 100) _____
8. Please rank the following five brands in order of your overall preference. Let a "1" represent your most preferred brand and a "5" your least preferred brand. No ties, please. *(Note: the order of the brands shown was rotated across the questionnaires.)*
   Rank
   _____ a. Perrier (or similar brands)
   _____ b. Coke (or similar brands)
   _____ c. 7-Up (or similar brands)
   _____ d. Hi-C (or other fruit drinks)
   _____ e. Bravo (Delight)
9. Please indicate the likelihood or probability that you would purchase six or more bottles of Bravo (Delight) per month if it were available for $3.00 per six-pack. Indicate by allocating 100 points such that 0 indicates that there is no possibility that you would purchase the product, 50 indicates that you are equally likely to purchase or not purchase the product, and 100 indicates certainty that you would purchase the product. (Use *any* number between 0 and 100) _____
10. As an expression of our appreciation for your assistance, you may have either $3.00 or a six-pack of Bravo (Delight). Which would you prefer?
    _____ (1) $3.00 _____ (2) Bravo (Delight)
Completed by Editor
   Respondent # _____
   Treatment: _____ (1) Bravo _____ (2) Delight

Table 17–2 Responses to Selected Questions and Measurements from a Beverage Preference Test

Respondent #	Treatment #	Gender	Age	Bottles Consumed per Week	Day's Consumed per Week	Price Importance	Image Importance	Taste Reaction	Rank This Brand	Rank Brand A	Rank Brand B	Rank Brand C	Rank Brand D	Purchase Probability	Choice
1	1	1	21	1	1	2	6	45	4	2	5	1	3	30	1
2	1	1	21	0	0	7	4	90	1	2	5	4	3	100	2
3	1	1	23	3	1	4	6	50	4	3	5	2	1	15	1
4	1	1	20	12	4	2	2	65	4	2	3	1	5	30	2
5	1	1	25	0	0	6	5	62	2	3	5	1	4	80	1
6	1	1	19	24	5	1	1	60	3	1	2	5	4	0	1
7	1	1	19	0	0	1	5	56	2	5	4	1	3	50	2
8	1	1	45	36	5	5	1	72	1	2	5	4	3	75	1
9	1	1	22	18	4	3	4	62	3	4	5	2	1	50	1
10	1	1	38	6	4	7	6	35	5	1	2	4	3	0	1
11	1	1	18	12	4	2	1	60	2	1	3	5	4	20	1
12	1	1	19	0	0	7	1	60	1	2	4	3	5	50	1
13	1	1	27	24	5	7	1	64	2	3	5	1	4	80	1
14	1	1	21	10	3	1	6	70	2	1	5	3	4	90	2
15	1	1	20	18	4	7	4	54	3	4	5	1	2	0	1
16	1	1	23	12	3	2	7	40	3	2	4	1	5	50	2
17	1	1	19	24	5	7	3	58	3	1	2	4	5	20	1
18	1	1	20	0	0	4	4	66	2	1	3	5	4	100	2
19	1	1	21	0	0	1	7	70	1	2	4	3	5	90	2
20	1	1	19	12	4	6	1	58	2	3	4	5	1	50	1
21	1	1	21	18	4	2	7	62	3	1	2	5	4	50	2
22	1	1	19	2	1	6	5	35	5	3	4	2	1	0	1
23	1	1	23	0	0	4	6	56	3	4	5	1	2	50	1
24	1	1	19	12	4	4	4	70	2	3	5	1	4	30	2
25	1	1	41	24	5	7	1	58	2	1	5	4	3	80	1
26	1	1	20	12	3	7	4	45	4	2	5	3	1	100	2
27	1	1	26	36	5	1	6	90	1	2	4	5	3	75	1
28	1	1	21	0	0	7	4	60	2	5	3	4	1	20	1
29	1	1	19	0	0	2	1	65	2	1	5	3	4	90	2
30	1	1	24	8	4	1	5	60	1	2	4	3	5	0	1
31	1	2	22	1	1	6	1	60	5	3	2	4	1	60	1
32	1	2	18	0	0	7	4	70	2	1	3	4	5	70	1
33	1	2	24	0	0	4	5	59	3	1	5	4	2	20	1
34	1	2	20	12	5	2	7	67	1	2	4	3	5	100	2

Table 17-2 Responses to Selected Questions and Measurements from a Beverage Preference Test *(Continued)*

Respondent #	Treatment #	Gender	Age	Bottles Consumed per Week	Day's Consumed per Week	Price Importance	Image Importance	Taste Reaction	Rank This Brand	Rank Brand A	Rank Brand B	Rank Brand C	Rank Brand D	Purchase Probability	Choice
35	1	2	19	8	4	7	2	30	5	3	4	1	2	0	1
36	1	2	20	0	0	6	3	62	3	2	4	1	5	50	1
37	1	2	24	2	1	1	7	65	2	3	5	1	4	0	1
38	1	2	19	12	4	4	4	72	3	2	5	4	1	20	1
39	1	2	22	0	0	1	3	85	1	2	3	5	4	90	2
40	1	2	20	18	6	5	3	66	4	1	5	2	3	0	1
41	1	2	31	6	1	2	5	58	2	1	4	3	5	90	2
42	1	2	21	0	0	7	2	64	2	3	4	1	5	75	1
43	1	2	18	0	0	2	6	65	3	1	4	2	5	0	1
44	1	2	29	12	7	6	2	69	1	2	5	4	3	100	1
45	1	2	32	0	0	1	7	85	2	1	5	3	4	100	2
46	1	2	24	6	2	2	7	70	1	2	5	3	4	50	2
47	1	2	20	0	0	6	6	61	3	2	1	4	5	20	1
48	1	2	28	6	3	5	5	63	3	1	5	2	4	0	1
49	1	2	19	0	0	7	6	65	2	3	1	4	5	90	1
50	1	2	27	0	0	1	6	71	2	4	3	5	1	50	2
51	2	1	21	12	2	4	3	35	5	4	3	1	2	0	1
52	2	1	20	6	3	7	2	38	4	1	5	3	2	10	1
53	2	1	22	42	6	3	3	46	4	1	3	2	5	0	1
54	2	1	18	0	0	6	2	52	2	1	5	4	3	50	1
55	2	1	19	1	1	2	5	45	2	4	3	5	1	60	2
56	2	1	23	10	4	2	6	41	3	1	5	2	4	75	2
57	2	1	24	0	0	7	1	25	5	3	2	1	4	0	1
58	2	1	19	18	2	4	7	36	2	1	4	5	3	100	2
59	2	1	21	0	0	7	3	44	4	2	5	1	3	0	1
60	2	1	22	0	0	1	4	80	1	2	3	4	5	100	2
61	2	1	20	2	2	5	4	42	2	1	4	3	5	50	1
62	2	1	26	0	0	2	7	39	3	2	1	5	4	0	2
63	2	1	21	10	4	7	3	40	3	1	5	4	2	0	1
64	2	1	23	12	3	4	1	38	4	2	5	1	3	10	1
65	2	1	18	18	3	1	6	28	5	4	2	3	1	0	1
66	2	1	22	0	0	6	3	40	5	1	3	4	2	0	1
67	2	1	20	12	4	2	6	42	2	3	4	1	5	50	2
68	2	1	20	6	2	2	7	34	4	3	5	2	1	0	1

Table 17–2 Responses to Selected Questions and Measurements from a Beverage Preference Test *(Continued)*

Respondent #	Treatment #	Gender	Age	Bottles Consumed per Week	Day's Consumed per Week	Price Importance	Image Importance	Taste Reaction	Rank This Brand	Rank Brand A	Rank Brand B	Rank Brand C	Rank Brand D	Purchase Probability	Choice
69	2	1	19	12	4	6	2	25	5	1	4	2	3	0	1
70	2	1	21	0	0	7	2	35	4	2	5	1	3	10	1
71	2	1	20	6	2	3	3	34	4	1	5	2	3	50	1
72	2	1	18	2	1	2	6	39	4	2	5	1	3	75	2
73	2	1	23	40	5	7	1	42	2	1	4	3	5	0	1
74	2	1	25	0	0	1	4	25	5	1	3	4	2	10	1
75	2	1	20	12	4	7	3	46	2	3	5	4	1	0	1
76	2	1	19	0	0	5	2	40	4	3	2	1	5	0	1
77	2	1	22	10	4	7	7	75	1	4	5	3	2	0	1
78	2	1	21	18	3	2	6	36	5	2	3	1	4	100	2
79	2	1	19	12	3	6	2	45	2	4	1	5	3	0	1
80	2	1	21	0	0	4	3	38	3	1	4	2	5	50	2
81	2	2	23	72	7	1	6	85	2	1	3	5	4	100	2
82	2	2	28	12	4	4	2	95	1	3	5	2	4	90	2
83	2	2	19	6	4	5	4	90	3	2	5	1	4	0	1
84	2	2	38	1	1	3	5	80	2	5	3	4	1	90	1
85	2	2	21	6	2	6	7	77	1	2	3	4	5	50	1
86	2	2	18	0	0	4	3	81	3	1	5	2	4	50	2
87	2	2	52	0	0	1	2	79	2	1	4	3	5	75	2
88	2	2	21	6	1	3	2	87	1	3	4	2	5	90	2
89	2	2	20	0	0	7	1	50	5	2	4	1	3	0	1
90	2	2	35	18	3	1	7	87	2	1	3	5	4	50	2
91	2	2	19	0	0	4	4	90	1	4	5	2	3	100	2
92	2	2	23	0	0	7	2	85	1	3	2	5	4	90	1
93	2	2	20	6	2	6	2	60	3	1	4	2	5	50	2
94	2	2	19	0	0	7	7	30	5	2	3	1	4	0	1
95	2	2	22	0	0	1	4	80	2	1	5	4	3	100	2
96	2	2	20	1	1	7	1	78	3	2	4	5	1	50	1
97	2	2	18	0	0	4	4	92	1	3	4	2	5	90	2
98	2	2	21	0	0	1	6	86	1	2	5	3	4	75	2
99	2	2	20	0	0	6	4	96	1	2	3	4	5	100	1
100	2	2	19	12	3	2	3	87	4	1	5	3	2	0	1

Field Controls

Field controls are *procedures designed to minimize errors during the actual collection of data.* These controls involve ensuring that the sampling, data collection, and measurement tasks are carried out as specified. Since most fieldwork is conducted by firms that specialize in such activities, it is frequently beyond the direct control of the sponsoring company. That is, even corporations with large research departments generally subcontract interviewing, observation, and many experiments to research suppliers. However, there is substantial concern over the quality of work performed by these suppliers.[2]

Sound field controls require both monitoring and validation procedures. As discussed in the next sections, editing field materials as they are received can also serve as a form of field control. *Monitoring* is the observation of field work by supervisors or project directors as it occurs. Monitoring is common in central location telephone interviewing. In such situations a supervisor will "listen in" on several interviews by each interviewer. Unfortunately, such direct monitoring is seldom used in other telephone interview situations, or in personal interviews.

Validation involves checking the accuracy of fieldwork after it has been conducted. Validation is particularly important in survey research where the temptation for interviewer cheating may be present.

Survey research validation involves a supervisor or a separate interviewer recontacting a sample of respondents (generally 10 to 20 per cent) from each interviewer's list of completed interviews. The purpose is to ensure that the interview took place and that the respondent was asked all the questions on the questionnaire. The second objective is achieved by asking the respondent to verify his or her answers to several questions taken from different parts of the questionnaire.

Effective field controls and editing require several variables in addition to the variables required by the research problem. Every sample unit should be assigned a number and the result of the contact attempt(s) recorded. Contact attempts can result in completed interviews, refusals, or noncontacts. The time of each contact attempt should also be recorded. This allows a validation of noncontact and refusal responses. Although noncontacts and refusals are not entered as part of the basic data array, it is important to have a record of them so that the potential for nonresponse bias can be estimated.

Every sample unit in a study involving more than one interviewer or observer should also have the *interviewer code* attached to its record. This allows an analysis of interviewer variations that can indicate potential problems such as interviewer bias. It also makes it possible to contact an interviewer to seek clarification of handwriting or other confusing responses.

Each completed interview should be assigned a *respondent number.* Often the respondent number is the same as the *sequence number* in which the completed interviews were received. The first three columns in Table 17–2 are the respondent numbers from the beverage experiment.

Editing

The responsibility of the editor is to ensure that the data requested are *present, readable,* and *accurate.* Unfortunately, many questionnaires are precoded and are entered directly into computer processing with little or no editorial analysis. Although this approach can save time and money, it often produces less accurate data. Data entry operators must decide what to do with unclear responses, missing data, or inconsistent responses. If the questionnaire is not precoded, clerical assistants may be assigned the task of transcribing questionnaire responses onto code sheets. Like data entry operators, the assistants are seldom trained to deal with editorial tasks.

Unless the questionnaire and analysis are very simple, or the responses are being entered directly into the computer in CATI (Computer Assisted Telephone Interviewing) systems, an editor should examine every completed questionnaire before it is transcribed onto disks or magnetic tape. In addition, after the data are entered into the computer, computer editing should be conducted.

Missing Data

It is very common for a questionnaire to be returned with one or more specific questions unanswered. This is known as *item nonresponse.* The editor must decide what to do about such missing data.[3] Often it is possible and desirable to use the data "as are." That is, the unanswered questions are assigned a missing data code, perhaps a blank or a -9, and entered into the computer along with the other observations.

When multivariate analyses are being conducted, it is generally necessary to exclude completely any respondent with missing data on *any* variable in the analysis. Since this often reduces sample size significantly, all major computer programs have an option that assigns missing data some version of the average value for that variable.

On occasion, the editor can have respondents recontacted to collect key bits of missing information. Alternatively, *plug values,* values developed in advance to use for missing data, can be used. For example, an editor could have a list of the average salaries associated with a wide array of occupations. One of these values could be used for respondents who reported their occupations but not their incomes. Such values can also be developed from the data base itself.

Questions such as question 8 in Table 17–1 often produce only partial answers. Respondents often refuse to rank brands or products with which they are not familiar. If a respondent were to rank only four of the five brands in question 8, the editor would have to decide if the unranked brand should be assigned a "5" indicating "least liked" or a missing data code or perhaps another value indicating that the brand was unfamiliar to the respondent.

Some questionnaires contain more missing data than others. The editor must decide how much and what types of missing data constitute sufficient grounds for "tossing" or deleting the entire questionnaire.

Ambiguous Answers

Many questionnaires contain one or more responses whose meaning is not clear. This occurs even in questionnaires composed entirely of "closed" questions. Question 3 in Table 17–1 requests the respondent to provide a numerical answer. However, answers similar to the following will also appear a significant number of times:

"I almost never drink carbonated drinks, but when I do I usually have several."

"10–15 Cokes and several fruit drinks."

"12 if you count mixed drinks."

"6-summer, 0-winter."

The editor must assign values to responses such as these. Question 8 in Table 17–1 requests a rank order of five brands without ties. Some respondents will assign tied ranks anyway. Again the editor must determine how to break ties (generally randomly or systematically in a manner designed to minimize bias).

Suppose a respondent answered "0" to question 3 in Table 17–1 and "3" to Question 4. Both answers cannot be correct. Again, the editor must decide whether to "guess" which answer is correct based on other responses in the questionnaire, to discard the entire questionnaire, to treat both answers as missing data, to recontact the respondent, or to take other relevant action.

Other kinds of ambiguities with which editors must deal are illegible responses and marks between response categories.

Before changing or discarding seemingly ambiguous or logically inconsistent data, the editor should consider the possibility that there may be a significant underlying cause for the problem. This turned out to be the case with the 15 per cent of the participants who gave responses of the $A > B$, $B > C$, but $C > A$ variety in the vinegar taste test described at the beginning of the chapter. (Responses of this kind are known as being *intransitive*.) Whereas the analyst had discarded the data originally on the basis of respondent error, management raised questions later about why such a large proportion of the data was in error. During the discussion, the possibility was suggested that since the participants had not been tested to determine if they could discriminate among the tastes of the various kinds of vinegars, and since ties had not been allowed, the intransitive responses might have been the result of those participants not having recognizable preferences in taste. As a result, a small study was made to see if people could in fact discriminate among the tastes of the three types of vinegars. About 20 per cent could not. Those respondents unable to discriminate in taste could be considered to have no taste preference among the three types of vinegar.

Accuracy/Quality

As editors review a series of questionnaires, they should note suspect responses. Respondents will sometimes rush through questionnaires in an almost random manner. This tends to produce a number of inconsistent responses such as a high-income category and a low-paying job category, or unawareness of a brand that is also reported as frequently used. Questionnaires containing such inconsistencies should be examined carefully and deleted from the data base if it appears that the respondents were haphazard in completing them.

Editors should also be alert for inconsistencies between the responses obtained by different interviewers. Such inconsistencies may be expected if the interviewers are contacting different respondent groups, such as in distinct geographic areas. However, they may also reflect interviewer bias, question interpretation, interviewer quality, or even interviewer cheating. Thus, the cause of inconsistencies between interviewers should be determined as rapidly as possible. For this reason, interviews should be turned in and edited daily, if practical.

Finally, editors should be alert to individual questions that are frequently left unanswered or that produce ambiguous responses. Such questions can sometimes be altered to improve response quality during the interview.

Exhibit 17–1 provides four general guidelines for editing.

Computer Editing. Computer editing can be used instead of, or preferably in addition to, manual editing.[4] The computer can be instructed to examine each set of coded responses for values that lie outside the permissible range, or for conflicting responses to similar questions. The respondent number associated with the problem measurement is printed out as is an indication of the nature of the problem (e.g., for respondent 044 an "8" is coded for question 5 and it has only seven response categories). The editor or supervisor can then check the original questionnaire and take the appropriate action.

The computer can supply prespecified "plugs" for missing data or it can calculate values for missing data based on the responses in the overall data array. It can also be used to run checks for variations in responses between

---

Exhibit 17–1 *Editing Procedures*

1. *Interviews Should Be Turned in and Edited Promptly.* With prompt receipt and editing, missing, illegible, and ambiguous data can be identified quickly and referred to the interviewer while the interview is still recent. It may enable instructions to be given to the interviewers to obtain additional information that the editing process discloses is needed.

2. *Editors Should Be Assigned Interviews by Interviewer.* The better an editor knows the recording style and the handwriting of an interviewer, the better the interpretation of the data on the questionnaire. It is also easier to discover instances of interviewer bias or cheating if this procedure is followed.

3. *Editors Should Make Changes by Crossing Out or Transferring Data Rather Than by Erasing.* The original data should be preserved for future reference if required. Changes made in the data on the questionnaire should be in colored pencil so that they are easily identifiable as editorial entries.

4. *When More Than One Editor Is Used, Editing Instructions Should Be Prepared.* Editing requires extensive use of judgment. Whenever possible, however, instructions should be developed to reduce the amount of editorial judgment required. Agreement among editors on the general procedures to be used for such editorial problems as supplying missing data, checking for internal inconsistency, and treating ambiguous responses will provide greater consistency in the editing of the data when more than one editor is involved.

---

interviewers. Computer editing is relatively inexpensive and should generally be used in addition to manual editing. It offers the additional advantage of being able to detect some coding and data entry errors.

Coding

Although coding may also be done by the editor, it is a separate step, which involves *establishing categories* and *assigning data to them*.

Establishing Categories

Categories for the answers to multiple-choice or dichotomous questions are established at the time the question is formulated. These procedures were described in Chapter 10. Open-ended questions may also have response categories established at the time they are formulated. However, it is common to create some or all of the response categories to open-ended questions after at least some of the questionnaires have been returned.

Since almost all marketing studies are analyzed by computer, each category must be assigned a numerical value (alphabetic codes are rarely used). Thus, in Table 17–2, Male was assigned the value "1" and Female, the value "2." It is important that a category be available for every response, which often requires the use of a "catch-all" category such as "Other." Likewise, it is important to have a specified category for nonresponses or missing data.

Three fairly common category values are assigned for missing data, the most common of which is the value "blank." That is, no value is assigned to missing data. However, this can cause a problem, as some analytical programs "read" blanks as zeros. Thus, if the responses to a question (such as number 3 in Table 17–1) contain both 0 responses and missing data (no response), some analytical programs will treat the missing data as zeros.

Another common approach to dealing with missing data involves the use of a constant such as -9 that will not be one of the legitimate response values. A -9 could be used for missing data for all of the questions in Table 17–1. A third approach is to assign the missing data category a value that is one number larger than the largest response value. Thus, missing data to question 1 in Table 17–1 (largest response value = 2) would be assigned a 3, whereas it would be assigned an 8 for question 5 (largest response value = 7).

Assigning Data to Categories

After categories have been established and questionnaires or other measuring instruments have been completed by at least some respondents, the observations must be assigned to categories.

Many questionnaires, particularly those administered by telephone or personal interview, are *precoded*. That is, appropriate category values and column numbers are listed on the questionnaire. Had question 3 in Table 17–1 been precoded according to the input format shown, it would have taken the following form:

3. *How many bottles, cans, and/or glasses of beer do you consume in a typical week?* _____ 8–9

The 8–9 to the right of the question indicates that the response should be entered into the eighth and ninth columns. By reserving only two spaces for the response, the researcher is assuming that 99 is the largest response which will be obtained. Should someone report an amount larger than this, it will have to be coded as a 99, or the entire coding system would have to be restructured.

Exhibit 17–2 *Coding an Open-End Question*

A consumer survey conducted by the Institute for Social Research°
contained the questions.

C19 *Do you (or your family) do any of your own repair work on cars?*
_____ Yes _____ No (go to Section D)
(If yes)
C20 *What kind of work have you done on your cars in the last year?*

_____

_____

The Codebook for question C20 gave the following codes and examples for each:

Code	Example of Answer for Code
5	*Yes, complex repairs that usually take a skilled mechanic (rebuilt engine or transmission).*
4	*Yes, extensive repairs taking much skill (rings, valves, bearings), install factory rebuilt engine, king pins, ball joints, transmission work, motor work, or "I do anything that needs doing."*
3	*Yes, some skill required (brakes, wheel bearings, exhaust system, starter).*
2	*Yes, some skill (tune-up, points, plugs, adjust carburetor, fuel pump).*
1	*Yes, little or no skill, mostly maintenance (oil change, greasing, tire switching, touch-up painting).*
0	*Inappropriate, family does not have car, does no repair work.*
9	*Answer not given whether repairs were done or what kind of repairs.*
7	*Yes, but not in the last year.°*

How should the following replies be coded? (All indicated yes to C19.)
(a) "My car has been running fine the past year, but I completely overhauled the motor in the washing machine."
(b) "I put in a new tape deck."
(c) "My husband and I made and installed new rugs for the floor."
(d) "I've changed the oil in my car a few times. I also helped my cousin overhaul his car's engine."
(e) "I always give it a tune-up every year."
(f) "I changed a flat last spring."
(g) "I took the carburetor off, but I had a mechanic overhaul it before I put it back in."
(h) "I do all the repairs, but it hasn't needed anything recently."

° J. B. Lansing and J. N. Morgan, *Economic Survey Methods* (Institute for Social Research, 1971), 247. Copyright © 1971 by the University of Michigan; reprinted by permission of the publisher, the Survey Research Center of the Institute for Social Research.

Postcoding involves the same procedure as precoding except that it is done after the questionnaires are received. The advantage of postcoding is that the range of responses to the open-end questions are known before category values are assigned and columns reserved.

Coding open-ended responses is difficult and requires sound instructions to ensure consistency between coders.[5] Because of the complexity involved, a *codebook*, which provides explicit instructions for coding each variable and indicates the columns to be used for each response, should be developed. Exhibit 17-2 illustrates codebook instructions as well as the difficulty that one may encounter in following these instructions.

It is not uncommon to have questionnaires coded independently by two persons to reduce errors. One marketing research agency routinely has each coder's work double coded by supervisors "to keep coding errors below 1 per cent."[6]

Transcription of Data

Transcription of data is the process of physically transferring data from the measuring instruments onto magnetic tape or disk, or directly into the computer. Other methods that are sometimes used include the use of *mark-sensed questionnaires* and *optical scanning*. Mark sensing requires that the answer be recorded by marking it with a special pencil in an area that is coded for that answer; a machine "reads" the answer by sensing the area in which it is recorded. An elaborate system named FOSDIC (Foto-Electric Sensing Device for Input to Computers) using this principle was designed for and is used by the Bureau of the Census for the transcription of census data.

Optical scanning involves direct machine "reading" of alphanumeric codes and transcription onto cards, magnetic tape, or disk. These methods are usually too expensive and awkward to use except for very large or repeated studies in which the same collection form is used. Consumer panels, buyer intention surveys, and the Census of Population are examples of field studies in which automated transcription processes are used.

Data entry via a keyboard to magnetic tape or disk or directly into the computer will normally be used in a sample survey.

Available analytical programs have varying data entry requirements. As shown in Table 17-2, the basic data array is a matrix, where rows typically represent respondents (or cases) and columns represent values of variables. The variable values may be entered into the computer with each value separated by a comma, a blank space, or nothing. If nothing is used to separate the numbers (an increasingly uncommon approach), a "read" or format command tells the computer which columns are to be grouped together to form a single number.

Generating New Variables

It is often necessary to create new variables as a part of the analysis procedure. Although several kinds of such variables are possible, only the four most commonly used are discussed here.

First, *new variables are often generated from combinations of other variables in the data.* For example, data on a person's age, marital status, and presence and age of children may be combined to generate a new variable called "stage in the family life cycle." Or, measures of household consumption of a product such as bread or milk may be combined with measures of household size to produce *per person* consumption measures. The computer can be instructed to create such variables and to add them to the basic data array.

Second, *it may be desirable to collect intervally scaled data as such and later assign them to classes.* Family income is often collected in dollars, for example, and later classified by a convenient number of income brackets or deciles. The coder can classify by brackets but would have to examine the entire income array to code by decile. A new variable generated by the computer, *income decile*, is the usual way this is done.

Third, *new variables may be added from secondary data.* It may be desirable to add such information as the median level of income, education, and employment in the county of residence of the respondent to be used in the analysis.

Fourth, *transforming the data into another functional form* may be desirable. An example is transforming intervally scaled data into logarithmic form for use in certain kinds of analyses.[7]

Tabulation of Frequency Distributions and Calculations of Summarizing Statistics for Each Variable

Unless the research project is a very small one — involving a limited number of respondents, only a few items of information collected from each respondent, or both — it will be tabulated and the data analyzed by computer. A large (and growing) number of computer programs with differing capabilities are available for these purposes. Since the same program will typically be used for tabulation and analysis of the data, it is important for the analyst to choose a program that is suited to the overall needs of the project.

Statistical Computer Programs

There have been two distinct phases in the use of computers in tabulating and analyzing marketing research data. The first was the period from the early 1950s through the early 1980s when virtually all the statistical work done on a marketing research project was carried out on a mainframe computer.

The development and marketing of micro and personal computers in the early 1980s brought about the second phase of computer usage in marketing research. After that time, the reduction and analysis of research data was no longer tied to the mainframe computer; many packaged programs as well as a large number of individual programs became available for the micro, and so the analyst gained the capability of conducting the analyses for most projects on the computer sitting on his or her desk. Many research agencies now provide the data from a project to the client, either by telephone or on a diskette, so that a researcher there can also run analyses if desired.[8]

There are many packaged statistical programs available for use on microcomputers as well. A special version of MARKSTAT[9] designed for this text was used for the calculations to follow unless otherwise noted. The data array from Table 17–2 as well as data from other problems and cases in this text are

---

Exhibit 17–3 *MARKSTAT: Statistical Analysis for Marketing Research*

EQUIPMENT REQUIRED:	IBM PC or compatible with 256K RAM
ANALYTICAL CAPABILITIES:	**Variable Transformations** (add a constant; multiply or divide by a constant; lead or lag a variable; calculate a 1st difference or a per cent 1st difference; take a natural, inverse natural, or base 10 log; raise to a power; calculate the Z score, the LOGIT, or an index for a variable; add, subtract, multiply, or divide 2 variables; sort a series of variables; categorize a variable; select a variable based on an index)
	Create Data (time variable, evenly or normally distributed random variables)
	Tables/Graphs (cross plots, histograms, time series plots, table of values)
	Summary Statistics (number of data points, high and low value, range, mean, median, standard deviation, coefficient of variation, skewness, kurtosis, and absolute, relative, adjusted relative, adjusted cumulative frequency distributions)
	Cross Tabulations (2 variables with up to 9 levels each; provides chi-square, probability, phi, Crammer's V, and the contingency coefficient)

Confidence Intervals (large and small sample means and proportions)

Univariate Hypotheses Tests (sample mean, variance, proportion to a standard; 2 sample means, variances, or proportions; several proportions)

ANOVA (one- and two-way)

Correlation Analysis (Pearson product-moment, Spearman rank-order, Kendall rank order, point-biserial correlation)

Regression Analysis (multiple variables)

Curve Fitting (linear, exponential, power function, logarithmic, inverse v, inverse t, inverse t and V, S-shaped)

Autocorrelation Analysis, Seasonality, and Cycles

Exponential Smoothing

CAPACITY: 25 variables with up to 500 observations per variable

A special version designed to accompany this text has the data from the relevant case and problems included: P. J. LaPlaca, MARKSTAT (New York: Macmillan, 1990)

already inputed onto the MARKSTAT disk. Exhibit 17–3 describes the capabilities and limitations of this software.

Tabulation of Frequency Distributions

The tabulation process starts with the preparation of the *basic data array*. As described earlier, this involves preparing a table comprised of the value for each variable for each sample unit. Table 17–2 shows the basic data array for the beverage study we are using as an example.

The next steps in the tabulation process are the preparation of *one-way* and *n-way* frequency distributions.

One-Way Frequency Distributions. Examine the responses to the image importance question shown in Table 17–2. Is it easy for you to understand what these responses mean? The odds are that it is not. Imagine how much more difficult it would be to develop a "feel" for the data if there were 1,000 respondents instead of 100! Now examine Table 17–3, which represents a one-way frequency distribution of the same data from the MARKSTAT program. The frequency distribution provides a much more concise portrayal of the data.

Table 17–3 One-Way Frequency Distribution and Summary Statistics

Frequency Distribution for Variable Image Importance

Value	Label	Absolute Frequency	Relative Frequency	Adjusted Relative Frequency	Cumulative Adjusted Frequency
1	Extremely Im	14	0.1400	0.1400	0.1400
2		15	0.1500	0.1500	0.2900
3		14	0.1400	0.1400	0.4300
4		17	0.1700	0.1700	0.6000
5		9	0.0900	0.0900	0.6900
6		17	0.1700	0.1700	0.8600
7	Extremely Un	14	0.1400	0.1400	1.0000
	Missing Data	0	0.0000		
	Total	100	1.0000	1.0000	

Number of data points = 100
Number of valid points = 100
Lowest value = 1.000
Highest value = 7.000
Range = 6.000

Mean = 3.990
Standard deviation = 2.018
Median = 4.000

The absolute frequency is simply the number of respondents who provided that particular value (14 respondents gave image an importance rating of 3). The *relative frequency* is the percentage of all respondents who provide a particular value (14 per cent of the respondents — 14/100 — gave image an importance rating of 3). The *adjusted relative frequency* is the same as the relative frequency except that any nonrespondents have been removed from the analysis.

The *cumulative frequency* is generally expressed as a per cent, though it can be expressed as an absolute value. It is the percentage of all respondents who provide a response equal to or less than a particular value (43 per cent of the respondents — 43/100 — gave image an importance rating of *3 or less*).

When categorical data are being analyzed, all of the categories are normally used in the construction of a frequency distribution. However, if there are a large number of categories, or if interval or ratio data are involved, it is useful to group the responses into a smaller set of categories. For example, the 100 respondents in Table 17–2 provided 46 different values in response to the taste-reaction question. A frequency distribution with 46 responses for 100 respondents would do little to clarify the nature of the response.

In such situations, the researcher may use a smaller number of categories determined either *a priori* or by the distribution of the data. For example, in the taste-reaction case, we might specify 10 categories of equal range of response starting at 1 – 10 and continuing through 91 – 100. Or, the computer could construct 10 categories with an equal number of responses in each (deciles).

A *one-way* frequency distribution is a frequency distribution for a single variable. It is also called a *simple tabulation* and is to be distinguished from a *two-way* or *n-way* frequency distribution (two variables, *n* variables). These *n*-way frequency distributions, one form of which is known as *cross tabulations*, and another form as *banners*, are described next.

Cross Tabulations. Cross tabulation involves constructing a table so that one can see how respondents with a given value on one variable responded to one or more other variables. Constructing a two-way cross tabulation involves the following steps:

1. On the horizontal axis list the value or name for each category of the first variable.
2. On the vertical axis list the value or name for each category of the second variable.
3. For each respondent, locate the category on the horizontal axis that corresponds to his or her response.

Table 17 – 4 Cross Tabulation of Selected Individual Respondents

CHOICE

		MONEY (1)	PRODUCT (2)	TOTAL
T R E A T M E N T	B R A N D	**BRAVO**	"1" "22"	"4" "21"	4
		DELIGHT	"42" "61"	"41" "62"	4
		TOTAL	4	4	8

4. Then find the value on the vertical axis that corresponds to his or her response on the second variable.

5. Record a *1* in the cell where the two values intersect.

6. Count the *1*'s in each cell.

Suppose we are interested in examining the relationship between the choice of money or product and the brand name of the beverage sample tasted by the respondent. First we would place the two categories for choice on the horizontal axis and the two brand names on the vertical axis, to form four cells of a table. The table and the assignment of respondents 1, 4, 21, 22, 41, 42, 61, and 62 are shown in Table 17–4.

Table 17–5 shows the cross tabulation for all 100 respondents as produced by the MARKSTAT program. A visual examination of this table indicates that (1) most respondents chose option 1 — money, and (2) the brand name may have affected this choice.

MARKSTAT, like most other programs that produce cross tabulations, calculates and prints percentages for each cell of the table. Two different bases are used for the percentages in each cell — the percentage that the frequency

Table 17–5   Cross Tabulation of All Respondents

	CHOICE		
BRAND	Money (1)	Product (2)	Total
Bravo No. Col. % Row %	33 52.0 66.0	17 46.0 34.0	50 50.0
Delight No. Col. % Row %	30 48.0 60.0	20 54.0 40.0	50 50.0
Total Row %	63 63.0	37 37.0	100 100.00%

in that cell is of the frequency for the row in which it appears, and the percentage that the frequency in that cell is of the frequency of the column in which it appears.

In drawing interpretations with respect to potential causal relationships, one will want to use either the row- or the column-based percentage, *whichever is calculated across the levels (or categories) of the dependent variable.* In using Table 17–5 for example, we would be interested in determining whether tasting the beverage labeled *Bravo* or tasting the one labeled *Delight* (the *independent* variable) had any apparent effect on whether money or product was chosen (the *dependent* variable). Applying the rule just stated, we would want to use the *row* percentages in Table 17–5 since they are calculated across the two categories of the dependent variable. We find that for *Bravo* the percentage that chose 'money' (66 per cent) was higher than the percentage for *Delight* that chose 'money' (60 per cent). Thus, it appears that the brand label of the sample tested *may* have had a causal relationship with the 'money' versus 'product' choice made.

It is perhaps unnecessary to warn that even if an apparent association is found between levels of the independent and dependent variables it may be the result only of chance, or of some third variable that affects both the other two. For example, the analyst for the ethnic food company who discovered through a cross-tab that there was a high trial and repeat purchase rate among Polish households for the Mexican prepared food product being test marketed could have been observing a chance association, or possibly viewing the result of an aggressive retailer or two in the Polish section of the city. Investigation proved that the association was a causal one, however; the Mexican food product happened to be very similar in taste to a Polish product that was priced considerably higher. The company subsequently brought out a brand positioned as a Polish ethnic food and marketed it very successfully.

Banners. *Banners* are a way of displaying several cross tabulations in one table. In a banner, the values for a variable of interest (preferably a dependent variable) are arrayed down the first column on the left and the values of potentially associated variables are arrayed in columns to the right in the table.

An example of a banner from the beverage study is given in Table 17–6. The values of the variable of interest, the number of points assigned for taste on a 0–100 scale, are arrayed in five categories in the first column. The cross tabulated values for variables that could be associated with taste — beverage name, gender and age of the taster, bottles of soft drinks consumed per week, and reported purchase probabilities of *Bravo* and *Delight* — are arrayed in columns to the right. (As we shall see shortly, some of these variables should *not* have been included in this banner. Before reading the next three paragraphs, can you tell which ones — and why?)

Banners are widely used, especially in reports prepared by research agencies. Banners allow data to be presented concisely so as to give a depth to the

Table 17–6 Example of Banner Format for Question 7: Having Tasted Bravo/Delight, Indicate How Much You Like Its Taste by Assigning 0 to 100 Points Where 0 Indicates Extreme Dislike, 50 Indicates Indifference (Neither Like nor Dislike), and 100 Indicates Extreme Liking. (Use Any Value Between 0 and 100).

Number of Points Assigned	Total Sample	Brand		Gender		Age		
		Bravo	Delight	Females	Males	18–24	25–34	35 or Over
	100 (100%)	50 (100%)	50 (100%)	40 (100%)	60 (100%)	83 (100%)	11 (100%)	6 (100%)
0–20	0 (0%)	0 (0%)	0 (0%)	0 (0%)	0 (0%)	0 (0%)	0 (0%)	0 (0%)
21–40	23 (23%)	4 (8%)	19 (38%)	2 (5%)	21 (35%)	20 (24%)	2 (18%)	1 (16.7%)
41–60	29 (29%)	17 (34%)	12 (24%)	5 (12.5%)	24 (40%)	27 (32.5%)	1 (9%)	1 (16.7%)
61–80	32 (32%)	25 (50%)	7 (14%)	19 (47.5%)	13 (21.7%)	24 (29%)	5 (46%)	3 (50%)
81–100	16 (16%)	4 (8%)	12 (24%)	14 (35%)	2 (3.3%)	12 (14.5%)	3 (27%)	1 (16.7%)

data displayed in the table that is not possible with the display of a single cross tabulation. Percentages for each cell based on the column total are usually supplied. When the variable of interest is the dependent variable, these percentages will then be calculated across it, the proper direction for use in drawing inferences for potential causal relationships.

For example, in Table 17–6 the number of points assigned for taste may depend upon the name of the beverage tasted, and the gender, age, and number of bottles consumed per week by the taster. Therefore, taste is the dependent variable and the cell percentages ought to be calculated across it. A glance at Table 17–6 will indicate that this is the way they were in fact calculated.

Variables may be dependent in some cross tabulations and independent in others, however. For example, the reported purchase probabilities for *Bravo* and *Delight* will very likely depend upon taste, rather than the reverse. For the cross tabulations of points assigned for taste with these variables, therefore, taste is the *independent* variable. Since the purchase probabilities for *Bravo* and *Delight* are dependent variables in these cross tabulations, the cell percentages for the purchase probabilities ought to be calculated across them, rather than across the taste variable, as in Table 17–6. To do this it is necessary to display the cross tabulation of points assigned for taste and the purchase probabilities for *Bravo* and *Delight* in other tables (or banners) in which the percentages can be calculated properly.

Table 17–6 Example of Banner Format for Question 7: Having Tasted Bravo/Delight, Indicate How Much You Like Its Taste by Assigning 0 to 100 Points Where 0 Indicates Extreme Dislike, 50 Indicates Indifference (Neither Like nor Dislike), and 100 Indicates Extreme Liking. (Use Any Value Between 0 and 100). (continued).

Bottles Consumed Per Week				Purchase Probability-Bravo				Purchase Probability-Delight			
0	1–10	11–20	>20	0–25	26–50	51–75	76–100	0–25	26–50	51–75	76–100
39	27	25	9	39	11	5	8	1	12	5	19
(100%)	(100%)	(100%)	(100%)	(100%)	(100%)	(100%)	(100%)	(100%)	(100%)	(100%)	(100%)
0	0	0	0	0	0	0	0	0	0	0	0
(0%)	(0%)	(0%)	(0%)	(0%)	(0%)	(0%)	(0%)	(0%)	(0%)	(0%)	(0%)
8	8	7	0	16	1	0	0	1	2	1	2
(20.5%)	(30%)	(28%)	(0%)	(41%)	(9.1%)	(0%)	(0%)	(100%)	(16.7%)	(20%)	(10.5%)
8	9	7	5	14	6	1	1	0	3	2	2
(20.5%)	(33%)	(28%)	(55.5%)	(36%)	(54.5%)	(20%)	(12.5%)	(0%)	(25%)	(40%)	(10.5%)
14	8	8	2	7	4	3	5	0	5	1	7
(36%)	(30%)	(32%)	(22.25%)	(18%)	(36.4%)	(60%)	(62.5%)	(0%)	(41.6%)	(20%)	(37%)
9	2	3	2	2	0	1	2	0	2	1	8
(23%)	(7%)	(12%)	(22.25%)	(5%)	(0%)	(20%)	(25%)	(0%)	(16.7%)	(20%)	(42%)

Banners are not without other limitations and disadvantages as well.[10] To reduce space requirements, categories of the independent variables are often combined, resulting in the display of a reduced data set. Marginal row totals are often left out for each independent variable as another means of conserving space. Since banners present what amounts to a series of two-way cross tabulations, examining covariation effects of two or more of the independent variables on the dependent variable is not possible — a 3-way (or n-way) cross tabulation is necessary for that purpose.

Summarizing Statistics

There are two major kinds of summarizing statistics. The first provides measures of the midpoint of the distribution and is known as *measures of central tendency*. The second gives an indication of the amount of variation in the data comprising the distribution and is known as *measures of dispersion*.

Measures of Central Tendency. The three primary measures of central tendency are the *arithmetic mean*, the *median*, and the *mode*.

The *arithmetic mean* should be computed only from intervally or ratio scaled data. It is obtained by adding all the observations and dividing the sum by the number of observations. When the exact value of each observation is known, this is a simple process. Often, however, arithmetic means must be calculated from absolute frequency distributions. In these cases, the midpoint of each category is multiplied by the number of observations in that category, the resultant category values are summed, and the total is divided by the total number of observations, or:

$$\bar{x} = \frac{\sum_{i=1}^{h} f_i x_i}{n} \qquad (17-1)$$

where f_i = the frequency of the ith class
$\quad x_i$ = the mid point of that class
$\quad h$ = the number of classes
$\quad n$ = the total number of observations

The *median,* which requires only ordinal data, is obtained by finding the value below which 50 per cent of the observations lie. If cumulative frequencies were calculated for the data array, it would be the value for which the cumulative frequency was 50 per cent.

The *mode,* requiring only nominal data, is found by determining the value that appears most frequently. In a relative frequency distribution, the mode is the class that has the highest frequency. Data can have more than one mode if two or more values tie for most frequent appearance. For example, the data in Table 17–3 are bimodal, with the values *4* and *6* each appearing 17 times.

The three measures will *not* be the same for distributions of values that are not symmetrical and, when different, they are useful for different purposes. For obtaining an *estimate of a population total,* the sample *arithmetic mean* times the number of population units provides the best estimate. One could estimate the total amount of carbonated beverages consumed per week on the campus in our example by multiplying the arithmetic mean for the sample by the total population.

If one wants an *estimate of the most representative amount,* the *mode* should be used. Suppose we wanted to determine the most common or typical number of days per week that consumers in the study consumed a carbonated beverage. The modal value would be best for this purpose. If we want an average that is *unaffected by extremes,* the *median* is the best estimator. The median is a better measure of average income than either the mean or the mode, for example, because the distribution of incomes is asymmetrical and a few large incomes distort the mean.

In our example, using an arithmetic mean to reflect average consumption by females who consumed carbonated beverages would be misleading. Weekly consumption reported by those who consume such products was

1, 12, 8, 2, 12, 18, 6, 12, 6, 6, 72, 12, 6, 1, 6, 6, 18, 6, 1, 12

The arithmetic mean is 11.2, which exceeds the consumption of all but eight of the respondents. In contrast, the median is 6 (as is the mode). The arithmetic mean is severely distorted by the single respondent who reported very heavy usage (ignoring this respondent changes the arithmetic mean from 11.2 to 7.9).

Measures of Dispersion.   The *standard deviation, variance,* and *range* are common measures of how "spread out" the data are. The smaller these three values are, the more compact are the data.

The formula for the standard deviation of a sample calculated from an array of the sample data is[11]

$$s = \sqrt{\frac{\sum_{i=1}^{n} (x_i - \bar{x})^2}{n - 1}} \qquad (17\text{--}2)$$

s = sample standard deviation
x_i = the value of the ith observation
$\bar{x}$ = the sample mean, and
n = the sample size

The *variance,* the square of the standard deviation, is found by the same formula with the square-root sign removed. The *range* is equal to the maximum minus the minimum value in the data array.

Calculating the mean of a data set without determining its distribution can sometimes lead to mistaken interpretations. The example given at the beginning of this chapter of the data developed from a survey concerning a new sauce product illustrates this point. The mean preference for 'hotness' of the sauce turned out to be about halfway between very mild and very hot. This was what the management of the company expected the survey data would show

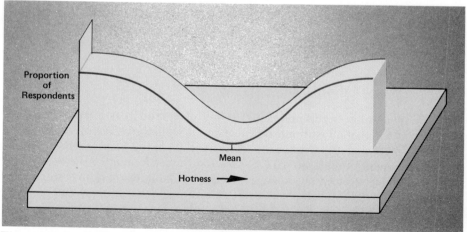

Figure 17–1   *Preferences for Degree of Hotness in a Sauce*

and so, if the distribution of the responses on the hotness scale had not been reported, a sauce with a medium degree of hotness would have been introduced. The distribution of the responses indicated that preferences were really as shown in Figure 17–1, however; bimodal with roughly one-half of the respondents preferring a mild sauce and the other half a hot sauce. The company therefore introduced two sauces, one mild and one hot, rather than only one with a medium degree of hotness.[12] The message is clear: *always examine the distribution of the data in addition to measures of central tendency*.

Statistical Estimation

Statistical estimation involves the estimation of a *population value we do not know* from a *sample value we do know.* Estimates of the mean amount of a product bought per person per time period, the market share of a brand, or the proportion of outlets that carry the brand are common estimates used in making marketing decisions.

As was pointed out in Chapter 16, there are two kinds of estimation procedures, *point estimation* and *interval estimation.* A brief review and illustration of each of these procedures is useful here. Estimation is based on the sampling distribution; therefore, it would be wise to review the treatment of that concept in the previous chapter. If you do not have a sound understanding of the concept of a sampling distribution, you will not fully understand either estimation or hypothesis testing procedures.

Point Estimation

A *point estimate* is a single number, or point, that is used to estimate a population value of interest. A point estimate may be made for any population value, but the estimates most commonly made are for the *mean* and the *proportion* of the population.

Point Estimates of Population Means

The management group in our example was interested in estimating the average taste rating that all students on the campus would give the product if they were to taste it with the *Bravo* label. The average of the 50 students (30 male and 20 female) in the sample is 62.1. This unadjusted average is the best single estimate of the population mean when either a simple random sample or a proportional stratified sample is used. A nonproportional stratified sample, which is quite common in marketing research requires an adjustment.[13]

To ensure that you understand this procedure, verify that the point estimate for the average number of bottles consumed per week based on the 50 students who tasted the Bravo brand is 8.14.

Point Estimates of Population Proportions

Management also wanted to estimate the proportion of students that consume a carbonated beverage at least once per week. The overall sample proportion is 61.0 (the number of students reporting this level of consumption divided by the total number of students). Again, this is the best estimate for a simple random sample or a proportional stratified sample, but a nonproportional stratified sample would require an adjustment.[14]

Interval Estimation

An *interval estimate* consists of *two points between which the population value is estimated to lie with some stated level of confidence.* Rather than report to management that the estimated proportion of consumers is .61, as shown previously, it is possible and preferable to report: "There is a 90 per cent probability that the proportion of the population that consumes a carbonated beverage at least once a week is between .51 and .71." In this section, we describe how to construct such intervals.

Interval Estimate of the Mean: n = 30 or Larger

How is an interval estimate of the mean made? Recall from the discussion in Chapter 16 that an interval estimate with a specified level of confidence is obtained from an interval formed by the two points,

$$\bar{x} - Z\sigma_{\bar{x}} = \text{lower point and}$$
$$\bar{x} + Z\sigma_{\bar{x}} = \text{upper point}$$

where Z represents the number of standard errors for the desired confidence level and $\sigma_{\bar{x}}$ is the size of the standard error. A confidence level of 68 per cent is obtained when $Z = 1.0$, 90 per cent when $Z = 1.64$, and 95 per cent when $Z = 1.96$ (see Appendix D). Each Z value gives the indicated level of confidence because that percentage of the samples that could be taken (of that size from that population) would have means falling between the lower and upper ends of the interval formed using that Z value.

Remember that $\sigma_{\bar{x}}$, the standard error of the mean, is the standard deviation of the distribution of all possible sample means of a simple random sample of a given size from a given population. It can be calculated by dividing the *population* standard deviation by the square root of the sample size (see equation 16.1). If the population standard deviation is not known, $\sigma_{\bar{x}}$ can be estimated by using the sample standard deviation. When $\sigma_{\bar{x}}$ is estimated from sample data, it is written as $\hat{\sigma}_{\bar{x}}$. Thus,

$$\hat{\sigma}_{\bar{x}} = \frac{\hat{\sigma}}{\sqrt{n}} \qquad\qquad (17\text{--}3)$$

where

$$\hat{\sigma} = s = \text{sample standard deviation.}$$

Suppose we want to estimate the average weekly consumption of carbonated beverages per male student with 68 per cent and 95 per cent confidence intervals. How would we proceed?

1. The sample mean is calculated as $\bar{x} = 9.75$.
2. The sample standard deviation is determined using equation 17.2. This gives us a value of 10.78.
3. This value is divided by the square root of the sample size to provide the standard error of the mean:

$$\sqrt{60} = 7.75$$
$$\hat{\sigma}_{\bar{x}} = 10.78/7.75 = 1.39$$

4. The appropriate number of standard errors are placed around the estimated mean to create the desired confidence interval:

68% confidence interval	95% confidence interval
$\bar{x} \pm 1.0 \, \hat{\sigma}_{\bar{x}} = 9.75 \pm 1.0(1.39)$	$\bar{x} \pm 1.96 \, \hat{\sigma}_{\bar{x}} = 9.75 \pm 1.96(1.39)$
$= 8.36 - 11.14$	$= 7.03 - 12.47$

Notice that the 95 per cent confidence interval is substantially larger than the 68 per cent confidence interval. It makes intuitive sense that one would be more confident that the correct value would fall within a wider interval. (To ensure that you understand the procedure, verify that the 68 per cent confidence interval for average female consumption per week is 3.7 to 7.5.)

Equation 17–3 is designed for a simple random sample. An estimate based on a stratified sample would follow exactly the same procedure *except* that a different formula for calculating the estimated standard error of the mean would be required. The formula is

$$\hat{\sigma}_{\bar{x}_{st}} = \sqrt{\sum_{h=1}^{k} W_h^2 \frac{S_h^2}{n_h}} \qquad (17\text{–}4)$$

where h = each stratum sampled
       W_h = the percentage of the population in stratum h
       S_h = the sample standard deviation from stratum h
       n_h = the sample size taken from stratum h

Interval Estimate of the Mean: n Less than 30

For an interval estimate in which the sample size is less than 30 and for which the sample standard deviation, s, is used to estimate the population standard deviation, $\hat{\sigma}$, the sampling distribution is no longer normal. Because the distribution of the Z statistic is normal, it is not applicable in small sample situations. The Student t distribution is used instead of the normal distribution when the sample size is less than 30. The t statistic is calculated and used in the same way as the Z statistic, except that the values for areas of the sampling distribution are looked up in a different table (see Appendix E).

The t distribution changes as the sample size changes. Therefore, when using Appendix E, we must find a t value based on the number of *degrees of freedom* (df) in our sample. The df in this situation is equal to $n - 1$. Thus, the t value for a 90 per cent confidence interval with a sample size of 20 (19 degrees of freedom) is 1.729. This value would be used exactly the same as the Z value for a 90 per cent confidence interval as described in the preceding section.

Interval Estimate of a Proportion

Interval estimation for proportions is carried out by a procedure similar to that for means. The estimated standard error of the proportion, $\hat{\sigma}_p$, must be determined; then the interval is formed around the sample proportion such that

$$p - Z\hat{\sigma}_p = \text{lower point, and}$$

$$p + Z\hat{\sigma}_p = \text{upper point}$$

where $Z =$ the number of standard errors for the desired confidence level.

When the sample is an srs and the population proportion is known, the formula for the standard error of the proportion is

$$\sigma_p = \sqrt{\frac{P(1 - P)}{n - 1}} \qquad (17\text{--}5)$$

If the population proportion is not known, it can be estimated from the sample proportion p and the estimated standard error, $\hat{\sigma}_p$, found from the formula

$$\hat{\sigma}_p = \sqrt{\frac{p(1 - p)}{n - 1}} \qquad (17\text{--}6)$$

If the sample is a stratified random sample, the estimated standard error is the weighted average of the estimated stratum standard errors, or

$$\hat{\sigma}_{p_{st}} = \sqrt{\sum_{h=1}^{k} W_h^2 \frac{p_h(1 - p_h)}{n_h - 1}} \qquad (17\text{--}7)$$

Management wanted to estimate with a 90 per cent confidence interval the proportion of males and the proportion of females that drink a carbonated beverage at least once a week. The procedure for males would be:

1. Calculate the sample proportion: $p = .68$
2. Calculate the estimated standard error:

$$\hat{\sigma}_p = \sqrt{\frac{.68(.32)}{60 - 1}}$$
$$= .06$$

3. The appropriate number of standard errors are placed around the sample proportion to create the desired confidence interval:

$$p \pm 1.64\hat{\sigma}_p = .68 \pm 1.64(.06)$$
$$= .58 \text{ to } .78$$

To ensure that you understand this process, verify that the 90 per cent confidence interval for the proportion of females who consume at least one carbonated beverage per week is .37 to .63.

The Population for Which the Point and Interval Estimates Are Valid

The description given in the early part of this chapter of the situation from which the example we have been using is drawn stipulated that (a) the sample is a simple random sample drawn from (b) the students at a state university. The point and interval estimates are therefore strictly valid only for the students at that university at the time the sample was drawn.

It is not unusual for the analyst or for the client to extend, by judgment, the population to which the findings of a study apply. In mall intercept surveys, for example, only a few nonrandomly selected malls may be involved. Strictly speaking, the results can be projected only to the population of shoppers at those malls. However, it is probably the rule, rather than the exception, that the results will be *assumed* to be projectable to the total population of shoppers in the area (state, region, entire country) of interest, and for the time period in which action based on the findings is to be taken. Similarly, it would not be out of the ordinary for the management of the soft drink firm to assume that the findings of the study of the students at the one university are projectable to the entire population of college/university students in the region in which the company markets its products, and that they are valid for the time period during which the company's actions based on the findings will affect that market.

Recognizing that the population actually sampled may in fact not be the same as the one to which the findings are being projected, is this an acceptable procedure? The answer is a qualified yes. It is a fully acceptable procedure so long as the management (a) recognizes that an extension to a different population is being made, and (b) believes that the population actually sampled is not sufficiently different from the one to which the results are being projected to cause the sample results to be misleading.

554

Review Questions

17.1. What are the steps involved in *data reduction?*

17.2. What is the purpose of *field controls?*

17.3. What do sound field controls require?

17.4. Describe *monitoring and validation* as field controls.

17.5. What variables in addition to the variables required by the research problem are often necessary for field controls and editing?

17.6. Why is an *interviewer code* useful?

17.7. What is the purpose of *editing?*

17.8. In what ways can one deal with *missing data?*

17.9. How can editors assess the accuracy/quality of questionnaire data?

17.10. What is *computer editing?*

17.11. Why should questionnaires be turned in and edited promptly?

17.12. What is meant by *coding?*

17.13. What is *precoding? Postcoding?*

17.14. What is a *codebook?*

17.15. What is meant by *transcription of data?* How is this usually done?

17.16. What is *FOSDIC?*

17.17. Why are new variables generated?

17.18. What is a *one-way frequency distribution?*

17.19. How does the *absolute frequency* differ from the *relative frequency* in a one-way frequency distribution?

17.20. What are *cross tabulations?*

17.21. What is the appropriate direction in which to calculate percentages in the cells of a two-way cross tabulation if one is interested in investigating the possibility of a causal relationship between the independent and the dependent variable?

17.22. What is a *banner?*

17.23. When would you use a ———— to describe the central tendency of a distribution?
a. mean
b. median
c. mode

17.24. Describe each of the following:
a. standard deviation
b. variance
c. range

17.25. How would you calculate a point estimate for a population mean from a simple random sample? A population proportion?

17.26. Would your answer to 17.25 change if a nonproportional stratified sample were used?

17.27. What is an *interval estimate?*

17.28. What is a *Z value?*

17.29. What is a *t value?*

17.30. When is a *t* table used?

Discussion Questions/Problems

17.31. a. Develop instructions for coding the response to *"What* is the occupation of each adult in the household?" by whether the response is (i) *blue collar,* (ii) *white collar,* or (iii) *managerial-professional.*

b. Using your instructions, how should the following occupations be coded? (i) marine sergeant, (ii) race car driver, (iii) filling station manager, (iv) housewife, (v) marketing research consultant, (vi) substitute teacher, (vii) police detective

c. Devise a rule using additional information on the questionnaire to help resolve confusing job descriptions.

17.32. "The mean is generally meaningless in marketing research." Comment on this remark (ignoring the quality of the pun).

17.33. A multinational firm has developed a new product that is particularly appropriate for use in developing countries. In order to meet the firm's sales potential requirements, the product will be introduced *only* in those countries with one million or more households with an average annual income of $720 or more. Initial research uncovers the following data. In which country or countries, if any, should the product be introduced? In which countries should the product *not* be introduced?

Annual Household Income

Country	Mean	Median	Mode	Variance	No. of Households
A	$1,200	$614	$400–500	$1,540	5,000,000
B	770	718	600–700	468	3,500,000
C	806	504	400–500	600	2,700,000
D	930	780	600–700	900	2,000,000
E	1,034	620	500–600	1,048	1,900,000

17.34. Precode the following questions and develop the codebook. Assume that this is the order in which the questions will appear on the questionnaire and that the first three columns of the code sheet are to be used for the respondent code.

a. _____ Male _____ Female
b. Marital status: _____
c. What is your occupation? _____
d. How often do you engage in rigorous physical exercise for more than 15 consecutive minutes?
e. Why do you engage (or not engage) in rigorous physical exercise?

17.35. Refer to Tables 17–1 and 17–2 to perform the following tasks.
a. Prepare a one-way frequency distribution and summary statistics for
  i. age: entire sample
  ii. age: males and females separately
  iii. bottles consumed per week: entire sample
  iv. bottles consumed per week: males and females separately
  v. price importance: entire sample
  vi. price importance: males and females separately
  vii. rank brand C: entire sample
  viii. rank brand C: males and females separately
  ix. choice: entire sample
  x. choice: males and females separately
b. Prepare a two-way cross tabulation using
  i. gender and image importance
  ii. price importance and image importance
  iii. choice and rank this brand
  iv. taste reaction and treatment
c. Prepare a banner from the data in b(i) and b(ii) with gender and price importance on the horizontal axis and image importance on the vertical axis.
d. Prepare a point estimate and a 99 per cent confidence interval for:
  i. the average age of the students
  ii. the average age of males and females separately
  iii. the average taste reaction of all students
  iv. the average taste reaction of males and females separately
  v. image importance (assume interval data) for all students
  vi. image importance (assume interval data): males and females separately

17.36. Perform the tasks specified in 17.35(d) but with a 80 per cent confidence level.

17.37. Repeat 17.35(d) ii, iv, and vi using only those students receiving treatment 1 (Bravo).

17.38. Prepare a point estimate and a 99 per cent confidence interval for
a. the proportion of students tasting Bravo who choose Bravo rather than money.
b. the proportion of students tasting Delight who choose Delight rather than money.

c. Repeat (a) for males and females separately.

d. Repeat (b) for males and females separately.

e. the percentage who assigned price importance a "1."

17.39. Repeat 17.38 using a 80 per cent confidence interval.

Project

17.40. Pick three frequently purchased products and survey students on your campus concerning their purchase levels. Estimate total expenditures on these products by students registered on your campus during the 9-month school year. Prepare separate estimates for (a) male/female, (b) graduate/undergraduate, and (c) overall.

References

[1] Reported in Elrick and Lavidge Inc., "How to Mislead Product Planners, Or Marketing Research Mistakes to Avoid," *Marketing Today,* No. 2, 1984.

[2] See H. R. Beegle, "How Does Field Rate?" *Advertising Age,* October 20, 1980, p. S-18–S-26; J. Rothman, "Acceptance Checks for Ensuring Quality Research," *Journal of the Market Research Society* (August 1980), 192–204; and "Field Service Workers Criticized by Research Suppliers, Clients," "Clients, Suppliers, Field Services Tell Expectations of One Another," and "Need Honesty, Better Quality from Research Suppliers, Field Services," all in *Marketing News,* September 18, 1981, 2, 3, and 4 respectively.

[3] See D. W. Stewart, "Filling the Gap: A Review of the Missing Data Problem," in B. J. Walker et al., *An Assessment of Marketing Thought and Practice* (Chicago: American Marketing Association, 1982), 395–399.

[4] See I. P. Fellegi and D. Holt, "A Systematic Approach to Automatic Edit and Imputation," *Journal of the American Statistical Association* (March 1976), 17–35, and B. D. Hodges III and T. J. Cosse, "Computer Code, Edit Open-ended Questions to Improve Survey Accuracy and Efficiency," *Marketing News,* January 21, 1983, 10.

[5] C. Coke, "Update: Data Mechanization and Coding Now," *Journal of the Market Research Society,* 1 (1982), 75–76; J. P. McDonald, "Assessing Intercoder Reliability and Resolving Discrepancies," in Walker, op. cit., 435–438; and Hodges and Cosse, op. cit., 1983.

[6] Statement in an Audits and Surveys, Inc., advertisement appearing in the *Journal of Marketing,* July 1976, 6.

[7] See, for example, W. S. DeSarbo and D. K. Hildebrand, "A Marketers' Guide to Log-Linear Models for Qualitative Data Analysis," *Journal of Marketing* (Summer 1980), 40–51.

[8] Walker Research is one such agency. It offers options of providing diskettes for and/or communication links with customer PC's with " . . . raw data, tabulated data, raw data in spreadsheet form, or spreadsheet formatted tables." *The Marketing Researcher,* Walker Research, Inc. (Summer 1985), 1.

[9] P. J. LaPlaca, *MARKSTAT* (New York: Macmillan, 1990).

[10] R. Maguire and T. C. Wilson, "Banners or Cross-Tabs? Before Deciding, Weigh Data-Format Pros, Cons," *Marketing News,* May 13, 1983, 10.

[11] The formula for the sample standard deviation calculated from data in a frequency distribution is

$$s = \sqrt{\frac{\sum_{i=1}^{h} f_i(x_i - \bar{x})^2}{n - 1}}$$

where f_i = the frequency of the ith class, x_i = the midpoint of the ith class, h = the number of classes, and all of the other symbols are the same as the formula for arrayed data.

[12] Elrick and Lavidge, op. cit.

[13] The correction simply involves computing the weighted average of the sample means of the groups where the weights equal each group's percentage of the total population, or

$$\bar{x} = \sum_{i=1}^{n} W_i \bar{x}_i$$

[14] The corrected sample proportion can be found by the following formula, using the same weights derived to correct the sample mean:

$$p = \sum_{i=1}^{n} W_i p_i$$

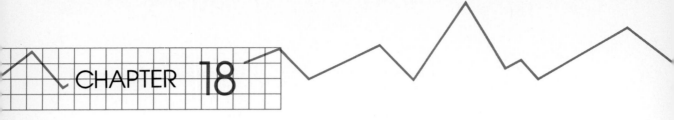

CHAPTER 18

Univariate Hypothesis Tests

In a paired-comparison taste test of *Classic Coke*, new *Coke*, and *Pepsi-Cola* (Case IV – 4: *Classic Coke* vs. New *Coke* vs. *Pepsi-Cola*; pp. 681), 78 respondents reported the following preferences:

New *Coke* preferred to *Classic Coke*   54
Classic Coke preferred to new *Coke*   <u>24</u>
   <u>78</u>

Pepsi-Cola preferred to *Classic Coke*   52
Classic Coke preferred to *Pepsi-Cola*   <u>26</u>
   <u>78</u>

Pepsi-Cola preferred to new *Coke*   42
New *Coke* preferred to *Pepsi-Cola*   <u>36</u>
   <u>78</u>

It seems clear from the data that both new *Coke* and *Pepsi-Cola* are preferred to *Classic Coke* by a rather wide margin. It is less clear, however, whether the narrow lead of *Pepsi-Cola* over new *Coke* (42 to 36) represents a genuine, if slight, overall preference for *Pepsi-Cola,* or is the result of sampling variation.

As indicated at the beginning of Chapter 17, statistical techniques are simply ways of asking questions of a set of data. In this chapter, we examine statistical approaches to a particular type of question:
Is the difference between one or more sample values and one or more other

values likely to be the result of random characteristics of the sample or of some other factor?

Answering this type of question generally involves some form of a hypothesis test.

Chapter 16 provided a description of the nature of hypothesis tests. It will be recalled that the purpose of a hypothesis test is to determine the probability that the difference between the value of a variable as estimated from a sample and the value of that same variable as estimated from another sample, or as specified by management, is the result of random characteristics of the sample.

As was indicated in Chapter 16, random samples are not always *representative* samples. Thus, one could randomly select 40 names from a student directory and obtain a sample of 40 females, even though 50 per cent of the students listed in the directory were males. Therefore, when samples are used, it is necessary to calculate the probability that the observed results are based on random sampling error.

Selecting an appropriate statistical technique for hypothesis testing requires the answers to five questions:

1. Are the effects of more than one variable being examined?
2. Are the data *ratio, interval, ordinal,* or *nominal?*
3. How many groups are to be compared?
4. Are the samples from the group(s) to be compared independent? (Does the selection of a sample element from one population limit the sample elements that can be selected from the second population?)
5. How large are the samples that were taken?

If the effects of more than one variable are of interest, a multivariate hypothesis test must be used. Such tests are common and are described in the next chapter. In this chapter, we limit our discussion of hypothesis tests to those that focus on one variable. These are called *univariate tests.*

Table 18–1 indicates some of the appropriate techniques for testing hypotheses based on the answers to the last four questions. We briefly describe the more widely used of these techniques.[1] Where appropriate, we illustrate their computation and application using the example from Chapter 17.

Hypothesis Tests Requiring Interval Data

As indicated in Chapter 9, techniques that are appropriate for lower levels of measurement, such as nominal and ordinal scales, can be applied to higher

Table 18-1 Univariate Statistical Techniques

Level of Data	No. of Samples	Independent Samples?	Sample Size	Appropriate Statistical Techniques
Interval	1	N.A.°	≥ 30	Z test
Interval	1	N.A.	< 30	t test
Interval	2	Yes	≥ 30	Z test
Interval	2	Yes	< 30	t test
Interval	2	No	a	t_r test
Interval	2+	Yes	a	One-way ANOVA
Interval	2+	No	a	t tests of all pairs
Ordinal	1	N.A.	a	Kolmogorov-Smirnov one-sample test
Ordinal	2	Yes	a	Mann-Whitney U, median test, Kolmogorov-Smirnov two-sample test
Ordinal	2	No	a	Sign test, Wilcoxon matched-pairs
Ordinal	2+	Yes	a	Kruskal-Wallis one-way ANOVA
Ordinal	2+	No	a	Friedman two-way ANOVA
Nominal	1	N.A.	a	Binomial test, χ^2 one-sample test
Nominal	2	Yes	a	Fisher test, χ^2 two-sample test
Nominal	2	No	a	McNemar test
Nominal	2+	Yes	a	χ^2 k-sample test
Nominal	2+	No	a	Cochran Q test

° N.A. = Not Applicable.
a Sample size is not a determinant of the appropriate technique.

levels such as ratio and interval. The reverse is not true. Since there are no commonly used techniques that require ratio data, we begin our discussion with techniques requiring interval data.

Test of a Sample Mean, One Sample: $n \geq 30$

The management of the firm in our example (pages 525–527) believed that the average consumption of carbonated beverages per female student per week was more than four bottles. If the consumption were found to be this high, the firm would test a product positioning strategy designed specifically for females. However, the firm wants to be "very" sure that actual average consumption is over four bottles per week before developing and testing this strategy. The average consumption found in the sample was 5.58 bottles per week. Can management be "very" sure that overall consumption by females is over 4 bottles per week?

As discussed in Chapter 16, three specifications are necessary in hypothesis tests of a single mean against a null hypothesis:

1. *the hypothesis to be tested;*
2. *the level of sampling error (alpha, or α) permitted in the test; and*
3. *the standard error of the mean for the sample size taken.*

The hypothesis was developed by management. As analysts, we need to restate the hypothesis in its null form; that is, that the average consumption was no more than four bottles, glasses, or cans per week. This is written formally as:

$$H_0: M \geq 4 \text{ bottles, glasses, or cans per female per week}$$

The desire to be "very" sure that the mean female consumption is indeed above 4 bottles we will interpret to mean a chance of being wrong as a result of a sampling error of no more than .05 (an α of .05). All that remains is to calculate $\hat{\sigma}_{\bar{x}}$, by the use of equation 17–3. The steps to be performed are:

1. *Determine the sample standard deviation using equation 17–2:*

$$s = \sqrt{\frac{\sum\limits_{i=1}^{n}(x_i - \bar{x})^2}{n-1}} = 12.0$$

2. *Divide this deviation by the square root of the sample size:*

$$\hat{\sigma}_{\bar{x}} = \frac{12.0}{\sqrt{40}} = 1.9$$

The value of the mean specified in the null hypothesis, the α value, and $\hat{\sigma}_{\bar{x}}$ are combined to create a *rejection region* for H_0. This is done by assuming that the mean specified in the null is the mean of the sampling distribution (a normal distribution). The rejection region is any value outside the *critical value* created by moving the number of standard errors from the mean required by the alpha level chosen. The required number of standard errors (Z values) required by various alpha levels can be determined from Appendix D (Area Under the Normal Curve). Any sample value (mean) lower than the critical value in this case indicates that H_0 should be accepted.

This test is illustrated for our problem in Figure 18–1. The distance to the critical value from the mean of the sampling distribution as specified by the null hypothesis ($M \leq 4.00$) is

$$Z_\alpha \hat{\sigma}_{\bar{x}} = 1.64 \ (1.90) = 3.12$$

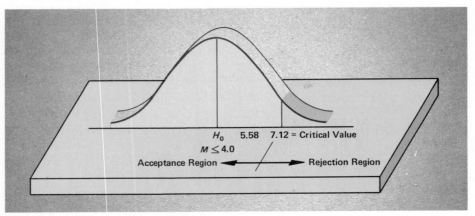

Figure 18–1   *Test of Hypothesis* H_0: $M \leq 4.0$

The critical value is then

$$M + Z_\alpha \hat\sigma_{\bar{x}} = 4.00 + 3.12 = 7.12$$

The critical value is greater than the sample value of 5.58 and so *the null hypothesis is accepted.* That is, management cannot be "very" sure that females consume an average of more than four bottles per week.

A natural question for a manager to ask, given these results is: "O.K. I can't be *very sure* that these results are due to sampling error. What is the exact probability that they are indeed caused by sampling variation?"

This probability is determined by finding the shaded area of the sampling distribution shown in Figure 18–2. To find this area, the Z value for the

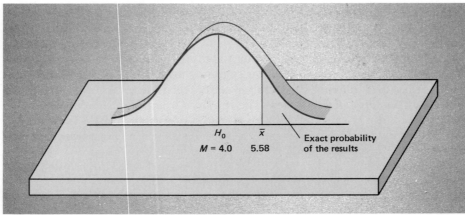

Figure 18–2   *Probability That* H_0 *Is True*

distance of the sample mean from the hypothesized mean is calculated and the area of the sampling distribution excluded by this value is determined from Appendix D. Or

$$Z = \frac{|M - \bar{x}|}{\hat{\sigma}_{\bar{x}}} \qquad (18-1)$$

$$Z = \frac{|4.00 - 5.58|}{1.90} = .83$$

The probability corresponding to this Z value is .20. Stated another way, our test has shown that (1) given the sample size used and (2) given the variance in consumption in our sample, we would obtain a sample consumption value of 5.58 or larger 20 per cent of the time *if the actual population mean were 4.0.* In a decisional context, there may be a substantially different interpretation given to the conclusion, "there is a 20 per cent chance we would obtain these results if the null hypothesis is correct" than to the conclusion, "the null hypothesis is accepted." For this reason, the exact probability should always be reported in decisional research projects.

You should be sure that you understand this procedure by verifying that the exact probability associated with H_0: $M \leq 6.00$ for male consumers is .0036 (where M refers to the mean number of bottles consumed per week).

Our discussion has centered on *one-tailed* tests, that is, our hypothesis specified the direction of the anticipated difference (*more than* four glasses per week). Occasionally, we need to test for differences in either direction (more or less than four glasses per week). This would be a *two-tailed test* because values in either tail of the normal distribution could lead to the rejection of the null. The basic procedures are identical except that two critical values are required, i.e.

$$\text{higher critical value} = M + Z_\alpha \hat{\sigma}_{\bar{x}}$$
$$\text{lower critical value} = M - Z_\alpha \hat{\sigma}_{\bar{x}} \qquad (18-2)$$

The Z values would also reflect the fact that both ends of the distribution are involved. That is, an α level of .05 would require a Z value that would cut off 2.5 per cent of the area under the normal curve at each end ($Z = 1.96$).

Test of a Proportion, One Sample

The hypothesis test of a proportion follows the same logic and procedure as a test of a mean. The only difference is that the estimated standard error of the proportion, $\hat{\sigma}_p$, is used instead of the estimated standard error of the mean ($\hat{\sigma}_{\bar{x}}$).

Management believed that more than 50 per cent of college males would consume six or more glasses of carbonated beverages per week. If so, the firm would develop an extensive strategy aimed at males. Again, management wants to be "very" sure that the actual percentage is at least this high before developing the program. An examination of Table 17–2 reveals that 58 per cent (35/60) of the males reported a consumption rate of six glasses or more per week. The following procedure is employed.

1. *Specify the null hypothesis:*
   H_0: $P \leq .50$

2. *Specify the level of sampling error allowed:*
   $\alpha =$ "very" sure, use .05; thus $Z = 1.64$

3. *Calculate the estimated standard error using the p specified in the null hypothesis:*

$$\hat{\sigma}_p = \sqrt{\frac{P(1-P)}{n-1}} = \sqrt{\frac{.50(1-.50)}{60-1}} = .065$$

4. *Calculate the critical value:*
   critical value $= .50 + (1.64).065 = .61$

5. *Since the observed value, .58, is less than the critical value, the null hypothesis cannot be rejected.* That is, we cannot, with a .05 confidence level, conclude that the null hypothesis is false.

6. However, as stated earlier, in decisional research we should also report the exact probability. *This involves calculating the Z value for the distance the sample proportion is from the null hypothesis proportion and looking up in Appendix D the area of the sampling distribution excluded by this value.* This calculation is

$$Z = \frac{|P - p|}{\hat{\sigma}_p} = \frac{.08}{.065} = 1.23 \qquad (18-3)$$

A Z value of 1.23 cuts off about 11 per cent of one tail of the distribution. Thus, given our sample size, we would obtain by chance a sample proportion of .58 or larger *if the actual population proportion were* .50 about 11 per cent of the time.

Assuming that a simple random sample was taken in the taste test described at the beginning of this chapter involving *Pepsi-Cola, Classic Coke,* and new *Coke,* we can use this same procedure to test whether the slight edge that *Pepsi-Cola* had over new *Coke* (42 to 36, $p_{Pepsi} = 42/78 = .54$) could reasonably be attributed to sampling variation rather than an actual preference in taste. The null hypothesis in the test is that there is no difference in preference between *Pepsi* and new *Coke,* or

$$H_0: P_{Pepsi} = P_{new\,Coke} = .50.$$

If we run a one-tailed test and set the allowable sampling error at $\alpha = .05$, the critical value turns out to be .63 (critical value $= .50 + (1.64)(.08) = .63$). Since the observed value of p_{Pepsi} was .54, less than the critical value, the null hypothesis cannot be rejected. By calculating the Z value and looking up the area in Appendix D, we find that sampling variation could be expected to provide a difference in the observed value of p_{Pepsi} this large or larger if P_{Pepsi} were actually .50 about 31 per cent of the time. (You should verify this figure to make sure you understand the procedure.)

A two-tailed test of a proportion would be conducted in the same manner as a two-tailed test of a mean.

Test of a Mean, One Sample: $n < 30$

The Z test used in the initial section on a hypothesis test of the mean is based on the sampling distribution of the mean being normally distributed. For samples less than 30, this is not the case. Instead, the sampling distribution of the mean follows one of the student t distributions. There is a unique student t distribution for every sample size. As the sample size increases, the t distribution increasingly resembles the normal distribution.

The appropriate t distribution to use is determined by the *degrees of freedom*, or *df*. For a hypothesis test of a single mean, the degrees of freedom are one less than the sample size $(n - 1)$. A table of t distributions is provided in Appendix E.

Hypothesis tests of a mean with a sample of less than 30 are conducted in exactly the same manner as those involving larger samples, except that a t value and the t distribution are used instead of a Z value and the normal distribution.

We illustrate this procedure by testing management's feeling that the 30 males who tasted Bravo would assign the Bravo brand an average taste rating greater than 50. From Table 17–2 we calculate the sample mean of these 30 males as 59.93 and the sample standard deviation as 12.65. The following steps are required:

1. *Specify the null hypothesis:*
   H_0: $M \leq 50.00$

2. *Specify the level of sampling error allowed:*
   let $\alpha = .05$, thus t for 29 $df = 1.70$

3. *Calculate the estimated standard error:*

$$\hat{\sigma}_{\bar{x}} = \frac{s}{\sqrt{n}} = \frac{12.65}{\sqrt{30}} = 2.31$$

4. *Calculate the critical value:*
   critical value $= 50 + 1.70(2.31) = 53.62$

5. *Since the sample value (59.93) is larger than the critical value (53.62), we can reject the null hypothesis that the average taste rating is 50.00 or less.*

6. *The exact probability given our sample results is calculated:*

$$t = \frac{|M - \bar{x}|}{\hat{\sigma}_{\bar{x}}} = \frac{9.93}{2.31} = 4.30$$

The area of the t distribution with 29 degrees of freedom excluded by $t = 4.30$ is less than .005.

Test of Differences in Two Means, Independent Samples: $n \geq 30$

Marketers are frequently interested in learning of differences between groups created by exposure to marketing variables, such as the taste reactions of those tasting Bravo compared to those tasting Delight. Likewise, different responses to the same variable by groups with different characteristics are frequently of interest. The management group in our example was interested in differences in the consumption of carbonated beverages between males and females; it believed that males consumed more than females. Testing this "hypothesis" involves the use of the same logic and procedures used to test hypotheses about a single mean as described in the previous section. The only real difference in these procedures is that the *standard error of the difference between two means* is used rather than the standard error of the mean. Testing this hypothesis involves:

1. *The null hypothesis to be tested:* the null would be that mean consumption by males, M_m, is the same or less than mean consumption by females, M_f. Thus H_0: $M_m - M_f \leq 0$. From Table 17–2, we calculate the sample difference as $9.75 - 5.58 = 4.17$.

2. *The level of sampling error permitted:* judgmentally set at $\alpha = .10$ $(Z = 1.28)$

3. *The estimated standard error of the differences between two means:* calculate using

$$\hat{\sigma}_{\bar{x}_{m-f}} = \sqrt{\frac{\hat{\sigma}_m^2}{n_m} + \frac{\hat{\sigma}_f^2}{n_f}} \qquad (18-4)$$

where $\hat{\sigma}_m$ = estimated standard deviation of population m (males). This is calculated as before using equation $17-2$
$\hat{\sigma}_f$ = estimated standard deviation of population f (females) calculated as for males

$$n_m = \text{sample size for sample } m$$
$$n_f = \text{sample size for sample } f$$

$$\hat{\sigma}_{\bar{x}_{m-f}} = \sqrt{\frac{(10.78)^2}{60} + \frac{(12.02)^2}{40}} = 2.35$$

4. *The critical value is determined as*

$$\text{Critical value} = (M_m - M_f) + Z_\alpha \hat{\sigma}_{\bar{x}_{m-f}} \qquad (18\text{--}5)$$
$$= 0 + 1.28(2.35) = 3.01$$

5. *Since the sample difference, 4.17, is larger than the critical value (3.01), we can reject the null hypothesis that male consumption is equal to or less than female consumption.*

6. *The exact probability given our results can be calculated as*

$$Z = \frac{|(\bar{x}_m - \bar{x}_f) - (M_m - M_f)|}{\hat{\sigma}_{\bar{x}_{m-f}}} \qquad (18\text{--}6)$$

$$= \frac{4.17 - 0}{2.35} = 1.77$$

This value cuts off approximately 3½ per cent of the distribution. (See Appendix D.) Therefore, the exact probability of obtaining a sample difference of 4.17 or larger, given our sample sizes and the variances in our samples, if the male and female populations actually consume the same amount, is .035.

A nondirectional or two-tailed test can be conducted for a difference in two means using the same procedure that is appropriate for one mean.

Test of Differences between Two Means, Independent Samples: $n < 30$

If the size of one or both samples is below 30, a different method of calculating the standard error of the difference between two means must be used, and the appropriate t distribution must be used instead of the Z distribution. The appropriate t distribution is based on the degrees of freedom which is, $n_1 + n_2 - 2$. The formula for t is

$$t = \frac{(\bar{x}_1 - \bar{x}_2) - (M_1 - M_2)}{\sqrt{\dfrac{(n_1 - 1)s_1^2 + (n_2 - 1)s_2^2}{n_1 + n_2 - 2} \left(\dfrac{1}{n_1} + \dfrac{1}{n_2} \right)}} \qquad (18\text{--}7)$$

The denominator of 18–7 is the appropriate formula for the standard error of the difference between two means when the sample size is less than 30.

Other than these changes, the same six steps described in the previous section are followed. To test your understanding of this type of test, verify that the exact probability given the sample results and a null hypothesis of no difference in taste reaction between females tasting the Bravo brand and females tasting the Delight brand is .004. The standard deviation for the females tasting Bravo sample is 11.05 and for the females tasting Delight sample is 16.01. This is a two-tailed test, and once *df* exceeds 30, the Z distribution can be used as an approximation for the *t* distribution.

Test of Differences between Two Proportions, Independent Samples

Managers, and therefore researchers, are often interested in the difference between the proportion of two groups that engage in a certain activity or have a certain characteristic. In our example, management believed that the percentage of females who would report a zero level of carbonated beverage consumption would be larger than the percentage of males. Testing this hypothesis involves the use of the same logic and procedure used to test a difference between two means. The only difference is that the *standard error of the difference between two proportions* is used instead of the standard error of the difference between two means. The specifications required and the procedure for using them are:

1. *The null hypothesis to be tested:* the null would be that the proportion of females, P_f, reporting no consumption is equal to or less than the proportion of males, P_m. Thus, $H_0: P_f - P_m \leq 0$. From Table 17–2, we calculate the sample proportions and the difference as .50 − .317 = .183

2. *The level of sampling error permitted:* judgmentally set at $\alpha = .10$ (Z = 1.28)

3. *The estimated standard error of the differences between two proportions:* calculate using

$$\hat{\sigma}_{P_{f-m}} = \sqrt{\bar{p}(1 - \bar{p}) \left[\frac{1}{n_f} + \frac{1}{n_m} \right]} \qquad (18-8)$$

where $\bar{p} = \dfrac{n_f p_f + n_m p_m}{n_f + n_m}$

p_f = proportion in sample f (females) who are nonconsumers
p_m = proportion in sample m (males) who are nonconsumers
n_f = size of sample f
n_m = size of sample m

Therefore,

$$\bar{p} = \frac{40(.50) + 60(.317)}{40 + 60} = .39,$$

and

$$\hat{\sigma}_{p_{f-m}} = \sqrt{.39(.61)\left[\frac{1}{40} + \frac{1}{60}\right]} = .10$$

4. The null hypothesis is $H_0: P_f - P_m \leq 0$. *The critical value is then*

$$(P_f - P_m) + Z_\alpha \hat{\sigma}_{p_{f-m}}$$ $$(18-9)$$
$$0 + 1.28(.10) = .128$$

5. *Since the sample difference, .183, is larger than the critical value, we reject the null hypothesis and conclude that more females report no consumption than males.*

6. *The exact probability given our results can be determined as*

$$Z = \frac{|(p_f - p_m) - (P_f - P_m)|}{\hat{\sigma}_{p_{f-m}}} \qquad (18-10)$$

$$= \frac{.183 - 0}{.10} = 1.83$$

This value cuts off approximately 3 per cent of the distribution.

To confirm your understanding of this procedure, verify that the exact probability associated with the null hypothesis based on the belief that "the proportion of males who drink 12 or more glasses of carbonated beverages per week is greater than the proportion of females who drink 6 or more glasses per week" is approximately .38.

There are no separate large and small sample versions of hypothesis tests involving proportions. As long as the population proportion is midrange, say .3 to .7, small samples (10 or more) can be used in the tests described.

Test of Differences between Two Means, Related Samples

Samples from independent populations are the usual case in marketing research studies. However, there are occasions when it is desirable to have related samples — parent–child, husband–wife, salesperson–sales manager, gift department–accessories department, and the like. In related samples, the *selection of a sample element from one population limits the sample elements that can be selected from the second population.*

Since the statistical techniques we have discussed thus far are based on independent samples, they are not appropriate if the samples are related. Suppose we placed Bravo and Delight in six stores around campus and observed sales of these brands for a week as follows:

Store	Delight	Bravo
1	130	111
2	82	76
3	64	58
4	111	103
5	50	48
6	56	61
Total	493	457

This would be a situation involving related samples since the same stores are involved with both product versions. How can we test the hypothesis, using an alpha of .05, that Delight would outsell Bravo in all stores? The appropriate procedure is to use the t test for related samples, or t_r. The underlying logic is the same as for the previous tests we have described. However, a different procedure and different calculations are required.

Rather than focus on the differences in the means between the two groups, we need to analyze the differences between each individual pair of observations.

1. *The null hypothesis to be tested:* the difference in sales of Delight and Bravo in all stores, D, will be zero, or $H_0: D = 0$.

2. *We calculate a variable,* d_i, *which is the difference in sales between group 1 (Delight) and group 2 (Bravo) for the ith store:*

$$d_1 = 130 - 111 = 19$$
$$d_2 = 82 - 76 = 6$$
$$d_3 = 64 - 58 = 6$$
$$d_4 = 111 - 103 = 8$$
$$d_5 = 50 - 48 = 2$$
$$d_6 = 56 - 61 = -5$$

3. *The mean difference is*

$$\bar{d} = \frac{\sum_{i=1}^{n} d_i}{n} \qquad (18-11)$$
$$= 6.00$$

4. *The standard deviation of the differences is*

$$s_d = \sqrt{\sum_{i=1}^{n} \frac{(d_i - \bar{d})^2}{n-1}} \qquad (18-12)$$

$$= \sqrt{\frac{310}{5}} = 7.87$$

5. *The estimated standard error of the difference can then be calculated as*

$$\hat{\sigma}_{\bar{d}} = \frac{s_d}{\sqrt{n}} \qquad (18-13)$$

$$= \frac{7.87}{2.45} = 3.21$$

6. *The critical value is determined:* critical value $= D + t_\alpha \hat{\sigma}_{\bar{d}}$, where

$D =$ difference expected under the null hypothesis, or 0.

In our example, there are $n - 1 = 5$ degrees of freedom. Using the t table (Appendix E), the t value for $\alpha = 0.5$ is found to be 2.015. Therefore,

$$\text{critical value} = 0 + 2.015(3.21) = 6.47.$$

Since our sample value, 6.00, is less than our critical value of 6.47, we cannot reject the null hypothesis that Delight will sell no better than Bravo.

7. *An exact probability value for t can then be calculated in the same general manner described in the earlier sections on small sample means tests:*

$$t = \frac{|\bar{d} - D|}{\hat{\sigma}_{\bar{d}}} \qquad (18-14)$$

$$= \frac{6 - 0}{3.21} = 1.87$$

This value cuts off approximately 6.3 per cent of the curve.

Tests of Differences among Two or More Means, Independent Samples

Analysis of variance (ANOVA) is the most common approach to test for differences among three or more means. Actually, ANOVA is a set of techniques that can be used with two, three, or more means of the same variable, multiple variables, and even means of multiple variables that interact with each other. The Z and t tests described earlier are generally used when only two means are involved. However, the procedure we describe using three means will work for any number of means from two to n. We describe multivariate versions of ANOVA in the next chapter. Univariate ANOVA is often referred to as *one-way* ANOVA.

One-way ANOVA is commonly used in the analysis of experimental results. It is a method of determining the probability that the observed differences of the mean responses of groups receiving different experimental treatments are the result of sampling variation.

This procedure can help answer such questions as: "Is there a significant difference in sales per salesperson between our straight salary, straight commission, and combination salary/commission plans?"; "Does the color of our package — red, blue, green, or yellow — affect sales?"; and "Which, if any, of these five advertisements will produce the greatest attitude change?"

The bases of one-way ANOVA — both intuitive and mathematical — are explained in the following steps. We use a hypothetical example involving our new carbonated beverage. Suppose management is considering three different types of bottles: A — a tall, slender, clear bottle, B — a tall, slender, shaded bottle, and C — a short, shaded bottle. Since the costs of the bottles are not equal, management will use the least expensive version (C) unless there is a sales advantage associated with the other designs.

Three random samples of 25 stores each are selected and one version of the bottle is placed in each sample of stores. The same point-of-purchase display is used in all three stores. The sales results are shown in Table 18–2. Does the type of bottle affect sales?

(1.) Intuitive Logic.   In an experiment, the greater the effect of the treatment, the greater is the variation between group (treatment) means.

Table 18–2   Unit Sales Response to Varying Bottle Types

A			B		C	
125	142	143	125	146	137
149	160	116	171	91	160
189	145	170	162	148	123
107	131	201	148	130	168
136	162	141	185	138	139
153	155	168	98	145	141
156	165	126	137	169	138
196	188	138	149	168	196
151	153	140	139	140	97
139	162	146	140	114	138
148	142	87	132	124	183
154	134	150	141	96	135
133	$\bar{x} = 151$	147	$\bar{x} = 144$	136	$\bar{x} = 140$

Mathematical Measurement. The variation among group means is measured by the *mean squares* between groups (*MST*) calculation. *MST* is calculated as

$$MST = \frac{\text{sum of squares among groups}}{\text{degrees of freedom}} = \frac{\text{(SST)}}{df}$$

$$= \frac{\begin{array}{c}\text{sum of squared deviations of group sample}\\ \text{means } (\bar{x}_j) \text{ from overall sample mean } (\bar{x}_t),\\ \text{weighted by sample size } (n_j)\end{array}}{\text{number of groups } (G) - 1}$$

$$MST = \frac{\sum_{j=1}^{G} n_j(\bar{x}_j - \bar{x}_t)^2}{G - 1} \qquad (18\text{--}15)$$

Example: The overall sample mean is calculated from Table 18–2 as:

$$\bar{x}_t = \frac{25(151) + 25(144) + 25(140)}{75}$$

$$\bar{x}_t = 145$$

Then,

$$MST = \frac{25(151 - 145)^2 + 25(144 - 145)^2 + 25(140 - 145)^2}{3 - 1}$$

$$= 775$$

Notice that the greater the differences among the sample means (evidence of strong treatment effects), the larger *MST* will be.

(2.) Intuitive Logic. Although the variation among group sample means will change as a result of treatment effects (as just discussed), the variation *within* the group samples should not. The addition (or subtraction) of a fixed amount to each of a series of numbers does not change the variation of the numbers. Thus, the variance of the series [1, 3] (not from the carbonated beverage bottle example) is

$$\sigma^2 = \frac{(1 - 2)^2 + (3 - 2)^2}{2} = 1.0, \text{ which}$$

is the same as the variance of the series [1 + 4, 3 + 4], or

$$\sigma^2 = \frac{(5 - 6)^2 + (7 - 6)^2}{2} = 1.0$$

Therefore, a variable such as the bottle type could be presented in a different form to each of three sample groups. It could affect the *means* of each group, but it should not affect the *variance* of each group.

Illustration. The means for the sample groups are different, as shown in Table 18–2. Because the three groups of stores were randomly selected, one would expect that the variances of the three samples would have been the same (within sampling error) before the test was conducted. There is no reason to believe that they are different (again, beyond sampling error differences) for the period of the test. Therefore, we need an estimate of the variance within the samples.

Mathematical Measurement. The variation within the sample groups is measured as the *mean sum of squares within groups*. It is generally referred to as *mean square error* (*MSE*). It represents the natural and random variation in the data. It is calculated as

$$MSE = \frac{\text{sum of squares within groups}}{\text{degrees of freedom}} = \frac{SSE}{df}$$

$$= \frac{\begin{array}{l}\text{sum of the squared deviations of each}\\ \text{observation in the group sample } (x_{ij}) \text{ from}\\ \text{the mean of the observations for that group}\\ \text{sample } (\bar{x}_j), \text{ summed for all group samples}\end{array}}{\begin{array}{l}\text{sum of the sample sizes for all groups}\\ \text{minus the number of groups } (G)\end{array}}$$

$$MSE = \frac{\displaystyle\sum_{j=1}^{G} \sum_{i=1}^{n_j} (x_{ij} - \bar{x}_j)^2}{\displaystyle\sum_{j=1}^{k} n_j - G} \qquad (18\text{--}16)$$

The sum of the squared deviations for group A is obtained by taking each observation in the group A sample (125, 149, ... 134, as shown in Table 18–2), subtracting the group A mean from each ($x = 151$, also shown in Table 18–2) squaring the resulting difference for each observation, and summing the results, or

$$(125 - 151)^2 + (149 - 151)^2 + . . . + (134 - 151)^2 = 9,620$$

The same procedure is followed to obtain the sum of the squared deviations for group B (14,464) and for group C (15,490). The result of this procedure is

$$= \frac{(9,620) + (14,464) + (15,490)}{(25 + 25 + 25 - 3)} = 549.64$$

(3.) Intuitive Logic. Although the variation between sample means will increase as the effect of the treatment increases, variation within each of the samples should not change with treatment effects. The ratio of measurements of

576

$$\frac{\text{variation } \textit{between} \text{ sample means}}{\text{variation } \textit{within} \text{ samples}}$$

should, therefore, reflect the effect of the treatment, if any. The higher the ratio, the more probable it is that the treatment(s) actually had an effect.

Illustration. If we compute a ratio of measurements of the *between* variation to the *within* variation, we should be able to make an inference about the probability that the observed difference between the group sample means was the result of packaging and not of sampling variation.

Mathematical Measurement. A sampling distribution known as the *F* distribution allows us to determine the probability that an observed value of *F*, where

$$F = \frac{MST}{MSE} \qquad\qquad (18-17)$$

(with specified degrees of freedom in both the numerator and denominator) could have occurred by chance rather than as the result of the treatment effect.

The *F* distribution is a sampling distribution just like the *Z* and *t* distributions described earlier. Like the *t* distribution, the *F* distribution is really a set of distributions whose shape changes slightly depending upon the number and size of the samples involved. Therefore, using the *F* distribution requires that we calculate the degrees of freedom for the numerator and the denominator.

The numerator is *MST* and the degrees of freedom for it are the number of groups minus one $(G - 1)$. The denominator is *MSE* and the degrees of freedom for it are the total number of units in all the samples minus the number of samples (G) or $\sum_{j=1}^{G} n_j - G = 25 + 25 + 25 - 3 = 72$ for the problem at hand.

We can calculate *F* as

$$F = \frac{775}{549.64} = 1.41$$

Our null hypothesis is that there are no treatment effects, or

$$H_0: M_1 = M_2 = M_3 .$$

Using an alpha of .10, we find that the critical value for *F* with 2 and 72 degrees of freedom in Appendix F is approximately 2.38. Since 1.41 is less than the critical value, we cannot reject the null hypothesis of no differences between the groups. (Consulting a more detailed set of *F* distribution tables reveals that the exact probability is approximately .25.) Since management was concerned about the differential cost of the bottles, it might decide to use the least expensive version.

Table 18–3 ANOVA Output

Markstat ANOVA Regression Results

Data variable =			Sales				
Categorical variable =			Bt1Type				
Category	Val.	Mean	Source	DF	Sum of Squares	Mean Squared	F Ratio
Bt1A	1	151.00	Total	74	41124.00	555.73	
Bt1B	2	144.00	Between	2	1550.00	775.00	1.410
Bt1C	3	140.00	Within	72	39574.00	549.64	

Table 18–3 shows a common way of displaying the results of an ANOVA. Most computer programs display results in this manner. The usefulness of this display will be more apparent in the next chapter when we consider ANOVA with more than one variable.

Thus far, we have not described the formal assumptions involved in the ANOVA model. They are as follows:

1. *Treatments are assigned at random to test units.*
2. *Measurements are at least intervally scaled and are taken from a population that is normally distributed.*
3. *The variances in the test and control groups are equal.*
4. *The effects of treatments on response are additive.*

One of the assumptions of the ANOVA is that treatments are assigned at random to test units. This is often overlooked in practice by using pseudo-treatments such as occupation, stage of life cycle, or urban or rural residency, and analyzing to see what effect these factors have on the mean amounts of a particular product purchased. This use of nonrandomly assigned pseudotreatments greatly increases the possibility that other variables associated with them will affect responses, and these effects will be attributed to the pseudo-treatment.

Test of Differences Among Two or More Means, Related Samples

On occasion, it is desirable to test for differences among means from two or more related samples. Such occasions could include attitude scores for mother, father, and child; sales of three or more product versions of all which are sold in the same set of stores; or attitude scores for purchasing agents, operators, and managers from a set of manufacturers. ANOVA is not appropriate for such situations. Instead, a series of t_r tests can be conducted on all possible pairs of group means.

Hypothesis Tests Using Ordinal Data

Test of Rank Order in a Single Sample

At times it is desirable to determine if a set of rank orderings by a sample differs from a theoretical or hypothetical rank ordering. For example, the researcher in our example from Chapter 17 may wish to determine if the ranks assigned price importance in beverage purchases are random or if they indicate some shared preference.

The Kolmogorov-Smirnov test is appropriate for such situations. It is concerned with the degree of agreement between a set of observed ranks (sample values) and the values specified by the null hypothesis. The steps involved in the Kolmogorov-Smirnov test are

1. *Establish the cumulative frequency distribution that would be expected under the null hypothesis.* Our null is that there is no difference in the proportion assigning price to each rank, so 1/7 or .143 of the responses, would go to each rank if the null is correct (excluding sampling variations).

2. *Calculate the cumulative frequency distribution from the sample.* This is done using the data in Table 17 – 2.

Table 18 – 4   Worksheet for the Kolmogorov-Smirnov D

Price Importance	Observed Number	Observed Prop.	Observed Cum. Prop.	Null Prop.	Null Cum. Prop.	Absolute Difference Observed and Null Cum.
7 Extremely Important	25	.25	.25	.143	.143	.107
6 Very Important	15	.15	.40	.143	.286	.114
5 Somewhat Important	6	.06	.46	.143	.429	.030
4 Neither Important Nor Unimportant	14	.14	.60	.143	.572	.028
3 Somewhat Unimportant	5	.05	.65	.143	.715	.065
2 Very Unimportant	18	.18	.83	.143	.858	.028
1 Extremely Unimportant	17	.17	1.000	.143	1.000	.000

3. *Determine the Kolmogorov-Smirnov D—the largest deviation in absolute terms between the observed cumulative frequency proportions and the expected cumulative frequency proportions.* This is illustrated in Table 18–4.

The largest absolute difference is .114, which then serves as the Kolmogorov-Smirnov D value. Appendix G reveals that this value is not significant at an alpha of .10, but is at an alpha of .20. The exact probability is approximately .15.

Test of Differences in Rank Orders of Two Independent Samples

Does the rank assigned Bravo by females differ from the rank females assigned to Delight? As indicated in Table 18–1, the question can be answered by several techniques. However, the Mann-Whitney U test is generally the best approach. It is basically the ordinal data substitute for the *t* and *Z* tests for differences between the sample means described earlier. In fact, there are even large and small sample versions of this test. We illustrate the large-sample version that can be used if one sample is larger than 20 or if both samples are larger than 10.[2]

1. *The null hypothesis implied by our question at the beginning of this section is that the two distributions are equal.*
2. *The raw scores (rank assigned Bravo or Delight by each individual respondent) from the two groups are treated as one set and are placed in order of increasing size. Each raw score is then assigned to a rank. Ties are assigned the average rank of the group of raw scores they are in.* In Table 18–5 the ranks are

Raw Score	Number with Same Raw Score	Range of Ranks	Combined Average Rank
1	12	1–12	6.5
2	12	13–24	18.5
3	10	24–34	29.5
4	2	35–36	35.5
5	4	37–40	38.5

3. *The ranks for each treatment group are then summed.*
4. *A statistic called U is computed as*

Table 18-5 Combined Rank Calculation for the Mann-Whitney U Test

Raw Scores		Combined Ranks	
Bravo	*Delight*	*Bravo*	*Delight*
5	2	38.5	18.5
2	1	18.5	6.5
3	3	29.5	29.5
1	2	6.5	18.5
5	1	38.5	6.5
3	3	29.5	29.5
2	2	18.5	18.5
3	1	29.5	6.5
1	5	6.5	38.5
4	2	35.5	18.5
2	1	18.5	6.5
2	1	18.5	6.5
3	3	29.5	29.5
1	5	6.5	38.5
2	2	18.5	18.5
1	3	6.5	29.5
3	1	29.5	6.5
3	1	29.5	6.5
2	1	18.5	6.5
2	4	18.5	35.5
		$R_1 = 445$	$R_2 = 375$

$$U = n_1 n_2 + \frac{n_1(n_1 + 1)}{2} - R_1 \qquad (18-18)$$

or

$$U = n_1 n_2 + \frac{n_2(n_2 + 1)}{2} - R_2 \qquad (18-19)$$

where

n_1, n_2 = sample size in groups 1 and 2, respectively
R_1, R_2 = sum of the ranks assigned to groups 1 and 2, respectively

Thus,

$$U = (20)(20) + \frac{20(21)}{2} - 375$$

$$U = 235$$

5. *For small samples, the critical value for* U *with a specified alpha is ascertained with special tables.*[3] *For large-sample cases such as this one, a* Z *value is calculated and the standard* Z *table or normal distribution is used. The value for* Z *is calculated as*[4]

$$Z = \frac{U - \frac{n_1 n_2}{2}}{\sqrt{\frac{(n_1)(n_2)(n_1 + n_2 + 1)}{12}}} \qquad (18\text{--}20)$$

$$= \frac{235 - \frac{(20)(20)}{2}}{\sqrt{\frac{(20)(20)(20 + 20 + 1)}{12}}} = 0.95$$

Appendix D reveals that the probability of obtaining these results if the null hypothesis of no difference in the rankings assigned the two brands is correct is approximately .33. Therefore, the null hypothesis cannot be rejected.

Test of Differences in Rank Orders of Two Related Samples

Researchers occasionally need to evaluate differences in rank-order data between two related samples. Preference ratings between a set of brands, colors, or styles between husbands and wives or purchasing agents and users, and attitudes before and after an advertising campaign are relevant examples. The appropriate techniques for such situations include the *sign test* and the *Wilcoxon matched-pairs signed-ranks test* which is the ordinal version of the t_r test. We illustrate the large sample ($n > 25$) version of the Wilcoxon test.[5] Assume that 40 consumers taste our new beverage. *Each* consumer tastes it twice: once labeled as Bravo and once labeled as Delight. After tasting each version, the consumers rate its taste on a scale of 1 (terrible) to 10 (excellent). Management wants to know if the name of the beverage will affect the perceived taste. Therefore, a null hypothesis of no difference in the ratings given the two versions is established. The steps are as follows:

1. *Calculate the signed difference* (d_i) *between the two scores for each pair. Pairs with no difference are dropped from the analysis.*
2. *Ignoring the sign* ($+$ *or* $-$), *rank the* d's *from smallest to largest.* For ties, assign the average of the tied ranks.
3. *Assign each rank the sign of the* d *that it represents.*
4. *Determine whether the* $+$ *ranks or* $-$ *ranks have the smallest sum* (add all the $+$ ranks and all the $-$ ranks and select the smaller absolute value). *The smaller value is designated as* T.
5. *Determine* N *by counting the number of pairs that have a nonzero* d (have one value larger than the other).

Table 18–6 Worksheet for the Wilcoxon Matched-Pairs, Signed-Ranks Test

Respondent #	Delight Rating	Bravo Rating	d_i	Signed Rank of d_i	Rank with Less Frequent Sign
1	5	1	4	25	
2	7	7	0		
3	4	6	−2	−14	14
4	8	6	2	14	
5	6	6	0		
6	3	5	−2	−14	14
7	9	6	3	21	
8	10	10	0		
9	7	5	2	14	
10	6	7	−1	−5	5
11	5	5	0		
12	1	3	−2	−14	14
13	3	1	2	14	
14	9	6	3	21	
15	8	7	1	5	
16	7	8	−1	−5	5
17	6	6	0		
18	5	3	2	14	
19	8	5	3	21	
20	7	6	1	5	
21	4	4	0		
22	9	4	5	27.5	
23	2	5	−4	−25	25
24	6	6	0		
25	3	9	−6	−29.5	29.5
26	7	2	5	27.5	
27	4	1	3	21	
28	8	8	0		
29	9	3	6	29.5	
30	3	1	2	14	
31	5	8	−3	−21	21
32	6	7	−1	−5	5
33	7	5	2	14	
34	5	6	−1	−5	5
35	6	5	1	5	
36	8	4	4	25	
37	7	7	0		
38	3	4	−1	−5	5
39	1	2	−1	−5	5
40	3	3	0		
			$N = 30$		$T = 147.50$

These five steps are illustrated for our example in Table 18–6.

6.   *Calculate the Z value using the following formula:*

$$Z = \frac{T - \dfrac{N(N+1)}{4}}{\sqrt{\dfrac{N(N+1)(2N+1)}{24}}} \qquad\qquad (18\text{--}21)$$

$$= \frac{147.5 - \dfrac{(30)(30+1)}{4}}{\sqrt{\dfrac{(30)(30+1)(60+1)}{24}}} = -1.75$$

The probability associated with our results is less than .10 (see Appendix D). Therefore, management would probably conclude that the name Delight elicits more favorable taste ratings than the name Bravo.

Test of Differences in Rank Orders of Two or More Independent Samples

It is frequently desirable to analyze ordinal data provided by two or more independent samples. Common examples include ratings given two or more products, packages, or advertisements in which each version is rated by an independent sample. Similarly, having independent samples, such as lower-income, middle-income, and upper-income individuals, rate the same product or advertisement is quite common. The *Kruskal-Wallis one-way analysis of variance by ranks* is the appropriate test for such situations.

Part of the marketing strategy for the new beverage calls for a major effort to have the brand served in fast-food restaurants. As part of an attempt to determine the effect of brand name on obtaining restaurant distribution, 15 restaurant managers rated the taste of the beverage without a brand label on a 1 (terrible) to 10 (excellent) scale. This procedure was repeated using separate samples of restaurant managers with Bravo and Delight labels attached to the product. (The three samples were therefore independent.)

The steps involved in the Kruskal-Wallis one-way analysis of variance are:

1.   *Establish the null hypothesis that there is no difference in the average ratings assigned by the restaurant managers in the three samples.*

2.   *Rank order the scores from all of the groups together* (treat all the scores as one set).

3. *Determine the value of* R *for each group by summing the ranks of the scores for that group.* This is shown in Table 18–7 where $R_1 = 361.50$, $R_2 = 252.50$, and $R_3 = 421.00$.

4. *Calculate* H *as*

$$H = \frac{12}{N(N+1)} \sum_{j=1}^{k} \frac{R_j^2}{n_j} - 3(N+1) \qquad (18-22)$$

where k = number of samples
$\quad n_j$ = size of sample j
$\quad N$ = total number of observations in all samples
$\quad R_j$ = sum of ranks in the j_{th} sample

For our example

$$H = \frac{12}{45(45+1)} \left[\frac{(361.50)^2}{15} + \frac{(252.50)^2}{15} + \frac{(421.00)^2}{15} \right] - 3(45+1)$$

$$H = 5.64$$

5. *The probability associated with this value can be determined from the chi square table (Appendix H) with* $k - 1 (3 - 1 = 2)$ *degrees of freedom.* Since the probability is less than .10, one may conclude that brand name affects restaurant managers' perceptions of beverage taste.

Test of Differences in Rank Orders of Two or More Related Samples

If the ratings shown in Table 18–7 had been provided by *one* sample of 15 restaurant managers rather than three separate samples, the Kruskal-Wallis ANOVA would not be appropriate. Instead, the *Friedman two-way analysis of variance by ranks* should be used. The Friedman analysis is appropriate when there are two or more related samples and the data are ordinal. We illustrate this procedure using the data in Table 18–7 as though they had been generated by a single sample of 15 managers who rated each version of the product. The steps are as follows:

1. *Place the sample observations in a table such that the columns (k) represent treatments and the rows represent sample units (respondents).*

2. *Assign ranks to the scores in each row from 1 to* k, *with 1 representing the smallest score.*

3. *Sum the ranks for each column.*

585

Table 18–7 Calculations of Combined Taste Ranks for the Kruskal-Wallis ANOVA

Unlabled		Bravo		Delight	
Rating	Combined Rank	Rating	Combined Rank	Rating	Combined Rank
7	30.5	5	20	8	36.5
5	20	2	5.5	6	25
6	25	4	14.5	3	9.5
4	14.5	6	25	9	41.5
7	30.5	3	9.5	7	30.5
2	5.5	1	2	10	44.5
8	36.5	4	14.5	8	36.5
4	14.5	5	20	4	14.5
1	2	2	5.5	9	41.5
7	30.5	8	36.5	1	2
9	41.5	3	9.5	7	30.5
5	20	7	30.5	8	36.5
3	9.5	6	25	2	5.5
10	44.5	4	14.5	6	25.0
8	36.5	5	20	9	41.5
	$R_1 = 361.5$		$R_2 = 252.5$		$R_3 = 421.0$

Table 18–7 presents the data in the appropriate format for step 1. Table 18–8 illustrates steps two and three.

4. A value for χ_r^2 is calculated using the formula:

$$\chi_r^2 = \frac{12}{nk(k+1)} \sum_{j=1}^{k} (R_j)^2 - 3n(k+1) \qquad (18-23)$$

where n = sample size (number of matched subjects)
k = number of treatments (columns)

For our example

$$\chi_r^2 = \frac{12}{(15)(3)(4)} [(30.5)^2 + (25.0)^2 + (34.5)^2] - (3)(15)(4)$$

$$= 3.0$$

5. For all but very small sample sizes, the probability associated with χ_r^2 can be determined from a standard chi square table with $k - 1$ degrees of freedom.[6] From Appendix H with two degrees of freedom we see that we would obtain results of this nature about 22 per cent of the time

Table 18–8   Calculation of Ranks for the Friedman ANOVA

Respondent Number	Treatment		
	Unlabeled	Bravo	Delight
1	2	1	3
2	2	1	3
3	3	2	1
4	1	2	3
5	2.5	1	2.5
6	2	1	3
7	2.5	1	2.5
8	1.5	3	1.5
9	1	2	3
10	2	3	1
11	3	1	2
12	1	2	3
13	2	3	1
14	3	1	2
15	2	1	3
	$\Sigma R = 30.5$	25.0	34.5

given a true null hypothesis of no difference in scores among the various labels. Therefore, the evidence suggests that labeling affects taste perceptions.

Hypothesis Tests Using Nominal Data

Test of Distributions by Categories of a Single Sample

Often a researcher needs to determine if the number of subjects, objects, or responses that fall into some set of categories differs from chance (or some other hypothesized distribution). This could involve the partitioning of users into gender, geographic, or social-status categories. Conversely, it could involve the distribution of a particular sample, such as males, into heavy user, light user, or nonuser categories.

Suppose the advertising manager for our beverage wants to test three direct mail formats, each of which offers a $.75 discount coupon for a purchase of a six-pack of Delight at the campus bookstore. Five hundred of each version are mailed to students selected at random. The coupons were redeemed as follows:

587

Version A	135
Version B	130
Version C	155
Total	420

Is there a significant difference?

The chi square (χ^2) one-sample test is an appropriate way to answer this question. The χ^2 test requires the following steps:

1. *Determine the number that would be in each category if the null hypothesis were correct (E_i).* In our example, the null hypothesis would be that there is no difference in the response to each version. Therefore, we would expect an equal number of the total responses to fall in each category, or $E = 420/3 = 140$ per category. Check for small expected frequencies which can distort χ^2 results. No more than 20 per cent of the categories should have expected frequencies less than 5, and none should have an expected frequency less than 1.

2. *Calculate χ^2 as follows*

$$\chi^2 = \sum_{i=1}^{k} \frac{(0_i - E_i)^2}{E_i} \qquad (18\text{--}24)$$

where 0_i = observed number in i^{th} category
E_i = expected number in i^{th} category
k = number of categories

For our example

$$\chi^2 = \frac{(135 - 140)^2}{140} + \frac{(130 - 140)^2}{140} + \frac{(155 - 140)^2}{140}$$

$$= 2.5$$

3. *The probability associated with this value is determined from Appendix H with $k - 1$ degrees of freedom.* The probability is slightly less than .30.

Test of Distributions by Categories of Two Independent Samples

We often need to determine if two sample groups differ in the way they are distributed into a number of discrete categories. This would involve questions such as: "Are males and females equally divided into heavy, medium, and light user categories?" and "Are purchasers and nonpurchasers equally divided into blue-collar, white-collar, and managerial-professional occupation categories?'' An appropriate test for such questions is the chi square (χ^2) test for two independent samples.

We illustrate this technique using the data from Table 17–2 and the following question: "Is there a difference between males and females in terms of their reported frequency of carbonated beverage consumption?" Our null hypothesis is that there is no difference. For convenience, we collapse the eight response categories into three: 0, 1–3, and 4–7 days per week. The steps are:

1. *Place the observed (sample) frequencies into a* k × r *table (called a contingency table) using the* k *columns for the sample groups and the* r *rows for the conditions or treatments. Calculate the sum for all the rows and columns. Record those totals at the margins of the table (they are called marginal totals). Also calculate the total for the entire table (N).* For our example:

Frequency	Male	Female	Totals
0	19	20	39
1–3	18	12	30
4–7	23	8	31
Totals	60	40	100

2. *Determine the expected frequency for each cell in the contingency table by finding the product of the two marginal totals common to that cell and dividing that value by* N. *Thus:*

	Male	Female
0	$\dfrac{60 \times 39}{100} = 23.4$	$\dfrac{40 \times 39}{100} = 15.6$
1–3	$\dfrac{60 \times 30}{100} = 18.0$	$\dfrac{40 \times 30}{100} = 12.0$
4–7	$\dfrac{60 \times 31}{100} = 18.6$	$\dfrac{40 \times 31}{100} = 12.4$

The χ^2 value will be distorted if more than 20 per cent of the cells have an expected frequency of less than 5, or if any cell has an expected frequency of 0. It should not be used in these conditions. In this case all cells exceed 5 so we may continue.

3. *Calculate the value of χ^2 using*

$$\chi^2 = \sum_{i=1}^{r} \sum_{j=1}^{k} \frac{(O_{ij} - E_{ij})^2}{E_{ij}} \qquad (18\text{--}25)$$

where O_{ij} = observed number in the ith row of the jth column
E_{ij} = expected number in the ith row of the jth column

For our example

$$\chi^2 = \frac{(19 - 23.4)^2}{23.4} + \frac{(20 - 15.6)^2}{15.6} + \frac{(18 - 18)^2}{18}$$

$$+ \frac{(12 - 12)^2}{12} + \frac{(23 - 18.6)^2}{18.6} + \frac{(8 - 12.4)^2}{12.4}$$

$$\chi^2 = 4.67$$

4. *The probability associated with our results can be determined from Appendix G with $(r - 1)(k - 1) = 2$ degrees of freedom.* The chance of obtaining these results if the null hypothesis of no difference is correct is approximately .10. We therefore cannot reject the null.

Test of Distributions by Categories of Two Related Samples

At times we want to analyze category changes by individuals following some event. For example, a common form of testing advertising effectiveness is to (1) allow a sample of consumers to select a brand from a set of brands, (2) watch a pilot television show that contains a commercial for one of the brands, and (3) make a second choice from the same set of brands. The researcher is interested in the change in the number of consumers choosing the advertised brand after seeing the commercial. The *McNemar test* is appropriate for such situations.

Suppose an advertising test such as just described were conducted for the Delight brand of carbonated beverage. Prior to seeing the commercial, 80 respondents chose Delight and 420 chose one of the other brands. After seeing the commercial, 65 of those who originally chose Delight selected it again and 15 chose another brand. Of the 420 who originally selected another brand, 370 did so again on the second trial, whereas 50 selected Delight. Was the advertisement effective in inducing viewers to select Delight? The steps required to determine this are:

1. *Establish the null hypothesis that the advertising had no effect on inducing viewers to select Delight.*

2. *Place the observations in a 2 × 2 contingency table as in the following:*

		After Advertisement	
		Chose Other	Chose Delight
Before Advertisement	Chose Delight	15 (A)	65 (B)
	Chose Other	370 (C)	50 (D)

3. *Make certain that the sum of the expected values (E) in cells* **A** *and* **D** *under the null hypothesis of no difference is larger than 5 (if not, the binomial test must be used). The calculation is*

$$E = .5(A + D) \qquad (18\text{--}26)$$
$$= .5(15 + 50)$$
$$= 32.5$$

4. *Calculate a χ^2 value as follows:*

$$\chi^2 = \frac{(|A - D| - 1)^2}{A + D} \quad \text{with 1 degree of freedom} \qquad (18\text{--}27)$$
$$= \frac{(|15 - 50| - 1)^2}{15 + 50} = 17.78$$

5. *Determine the probability by consulting Appendix G. In this case, there is less than a .001 chance that results this extreme would have occurred by chance if the null is the actual situation. We can therefore reject the null and conclude that the advertising did influence viewers to select Delight.*

Test of Distributions by Categories of Two or More Independent Samples

Do white-collar, blue-collar, and managerial-professional groups differ in terms of being heavy, medium, light, and nonusers of this product? Do purchasing agents, operators, and supervisors differ in terms of having favorable, neutral, or unfavorable attitudes toward our brand? Such questions, which involve categorical (nominal) data and two or more independent samples, can be answered by using the chi square (χ^2) test for k independent samples. The procedure and formula for three or more samples is the same as for two samples. Therefore, we do not repeat the procedure here.

Test of Distributions by Categories of Two or More Related Samples

Do the husbands, wives, and oldest children from the same families differ in terms of being heavy, medium, or light television viewers? Do purchasing agents, operators, and supervisors from the same firms differ in terms of having favorable, neutral, or unfavorable attitudes toward our product? Would the same individual differ in categorizing our product as being "for men," "for women," or "for everyone" depending on which of four labels is used? Questions such as these can be answered using the *Cochran Q test*.

Suppose we allow 20 consumers to taste each of three "versions" of our beverage—unlabeled, Bravo, and Delight. After tasting each, they are allowed to choose either a six-pack of that version of the beverage or $2.00. The steps involved are:

Table 18–9   Worksheet for the Cochran Q Test

	Treatment[a]				
Respondent	Unlabeled	Bravo	Delight	L_i	L_i^2
1	0	0	0	0	0
2	0	0	1	1	1
3	1	0	1	2	4
4	1	1	1	3	9
5	0	0	0	0	0
6	1	0	0	1	1
7	0	1	1	2	4
8	1	0	1	2	4
9	0	0	0	0	0
10	1	1	0	2	4
11	0	0	0	0	0
12	1	0	0	1	1
13	0	1	1	2	4
14	0	0	0	0	0
15	0	1	1	2	4
16	1	0	1	2	4
17	0	0	0	0	0
18	0	0	1	1	1
19	0	0	0	0	0
20	1	1	1	3	9
	$G_1 = 8$	$G_2 = 6$	$G_3 = 10$	$\sum_{i=1}^{20} L_i = 24$	$\sum_{i=1}^{20} L_i^2 = 50$

[a] 1 = product selected, 0 = money selected

1. *Establish the null hypothesis that there is no effect of the label versions on choice of product versus money.*

2. *For dichotomous data, let 1 represent each "success" and 0 represent each "failure."*

3. *Arrange these scores in a* k *by* n *table where* k *columns represent treatments or conditions and* n *rows represent respondents.*

4. *Calculate the number of successes per treatment (*G_j*) and the number of successes per respondent (*L_i*). This is illustrated in* Table 18–9 *where choosing the beverage is considered a success.*

5. *The value for* Q *is calculated as*

$$Q = \frac{(k-1)\left[k \sum_{j=1}^{k} G_j^2 - \left(\sum_{j=1}^{k} G_j \right)^2 \right]}{K \sum_{i=1}^{n} L_i - \sum_{i=1}^{n} L_i^2} \qquad (18\text{--}28)$$

$$= \frac{(3-1)\{3[(8)^2 + (6)^2 + (10)^2] - (24)^2\}}{3(24) - 50}$$

$$= 2.18$$

6. *The probability associated with the* Q *value is determined from the chi square distribution (Appendix H) with* k − 1 *(*3 − 1 = 2*) degrees of freedom.* Results such as those obtained would occur by chance more than a third of the time if the treatments had no effect at all.

Review Questions

18.1. What are *statistical techniques?*

18.2. What is the purpose of a hypothesis test of differences between groups?

18.3. What is a *univariate hypothesis test?*

18.4. What are the five questions that lead to the selection of an appropriate univariate hypothesis test of differences?

18.5. What characterizes *independent* samples?

18.6. What conditions would lead to the use of _____?
   a. Z test of a mean
   b. *t* test of two means
   c. χ^2 two-sample test
   d. Kruskal-Wallis one-way ANOVA
   e. Wilcoxon matched-pairs signed-ranks test
   f. Kolmogorov-Smirnov one-sample test
   g. Mann-Whitney U test

  h. t_r test
  i. one-way ANOVA
  j. Friedman two-way ANOVA
  k. Cochran Q test
  l. McNemar test
  m. χ^2 one-sample test
  n. Z test of two proportions

18.7. What test(s) would be appropriate in the following situations?

	Data	Sample Size	Independent Samples?	# Samples
a.	interval	20	Yes	1
b.	nominal	35	Yes	2
c.	interval	100	Yes	2
d.	ordinal	40	No	2
e.	ratio	90	Yes	3
f.	ordinal	100	Yes	4
g.	nominal	36	No	2
h.	interval	120	No	4
i.	interval	80	Yes	1
j.	nominal	45	No	3
k.	ratio	60	Yes	2
l.	ordinal	50	Yes	2
m.	ordinal	30	No	3
n.	ordinal	21	Yes	1
o.	nominal	100	Yes	1
p.	nominal	80	Yes	6
q.	interval	90	No	2

Discussion Questions/Problems

18.8. Do you agree that the exact probability should always be reported in decisional research? Why?
      Use the data in Table 17–2 to perform the following tests. Use the following definitions: Group 1 = the population represented by males, treatment 1; Group 2 = the population represented by females, treatment 1; Group 3 = the population represented by males, treatment 2; Group 4 = the population represented by females, treatment 2; Group 5 = the population represented by all males; and Group 6 = the population group represented by all females. For hypothesis tests use an α of .05 and also report the exact probability.

18.9. Is the mean age of group 1 equal to the mean age of group 2?

18.10. Is the mean age of group 5 equal to the mean age of group 6?

18.11. Are the mean ages of groups 1, 2, 3, and 4 equal?

18.12. Is the mean taste reaction of group 5 greater than 45?

18.13. Is the mean taste reaction of group 4 greater than 55?

18.14. Is the proportion of group 1 having zero consumption equal to the proportion of group 2 having zero consumption?

18.15. Is the proportion of group 6 having a purchase probability of more than .5 greater than .30?

18.16. Assume the sample from group 2 was randomly selected and the sample from group 4 was matched to it in terms of age, classification and college major such that respondent 031 "matched" 081, 032 matched 082 and so forth. Is the mean taste reaction of group 2 equal to the mean taste reaction of group 4?

18.17. Do the ranks assigned price importance by group 5 indicate a preference?

18.18. Do the ranks assigned Bravo by group 1 equal the ranks assigned Delight by group 3?

18.19. Using the same assumptions as 18.16, do the ranks assigned Bravo by group 2 equal the ranks assigned Bravo by group 4?

18.20. Assume that the samples from groups 1, 2, 3, and 4 represent repeated measures on the same 20 individuals (use the first 20 from groups 1 and 3). Do the ratings assigned price importance differ across the four measurements?

18.21. Do the ratings assigned price importance differ between groups 1, 2, 3, and 4?

18.22. For groups 5 and 6 combined are there equal numbers of students in the age groups ≤ 19, $20-21$, ≤ 22?

18.23. Is there a difference between groups 5 and 6 in the number having a taste reaction ≤ 50, $51-60$, or > 60?

18.24. Assume that the choices from the sample from group 1 represent the same individuals in the same order as the sample from group 3. However, the choices shown for the sample from group 3 were made before seeing an ad for the product whereas the choices shown for the sample from group 1 were made after seeing the ad. Was the ad effective?

18.25. Is there a difference between groups 1, 2, 3, and 4 in the number having a taste reaction ≤ 50, $51-60$, > 60?

18.26. Assume that the samples from Groups 2, 3, and 4 represent the same individuals in the same order as the sample from group 1 (use the first 20 from groups 1 and 3). Assume that the choice column for group 1 was generated by an unlabeled version of the product whereas the choices in groups 2, 3, and 4 were generated by the same individuals tasting the product labeled Bravo, Delight, and Spring. Does brand name affect choice?

References

[1] Additional details on techniques available for ratio and interval data can be found in W. Mendenhall and J. E. Reinmuth, *Statistics for Management and Economics* (New York: Duxbury Press, 1986). The best source for details on techniques for ordinal and nominal data is S. Siegel, *Nonparametric Statistics* (New York: McGraw-Hill Book Co., Inc., 1956).

[2] Details on, and tables for, the small-sample versions are available in Siegel, op. cit., 116–127.

[3] Siegel, op. cit., 272–277.

[4] When there are a *very* large number of ties, a correction formula should be used. However, even with as many ties as were present in this example, the correction formula only changed Z from 1.05 to 1.09. See Siegel, ibid., 123–126.

[5] The small-sample version and appropriate tables are described in ibid., 77–79.

[6] For small samples see ibid., 166–172.

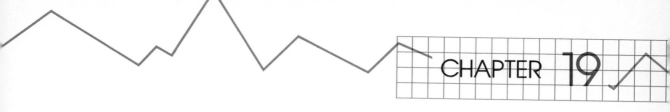

CHAPTER 19

Multivariate Hypothesis Tests

Safeway Stores, like other retailers, must decide which products and brands to advertise, which to place in special displays, and which to reduce in price. The problem is compounded by the fact that (1) each approach has different costs associated with it and (2) these effects may not be independent. That is, advertising a particular product or brand may increase sales 20 per cent. Likewise, featuring that product or brand in a point-of-purchase display may also increase sales by 20 per cent. What will happen to sales if the product or brand is both placed in a point-of-purchase display *and* advertised. Will sales increase 40 per cent? Less than 40 per cent? More?

In this chapter, we examine techniques for testing hypotheses about differences between groups when more than one variable may be causing these differences. This will enable us to answer questions such as the following: *"Do differing price levels, package sizes and point-of-purchase displays combine to have a unique influence on sales? Which has the strongest effect? Are their effects when used simultaneously different from the sum of their individual effects?"* When we examine the effects of two or more variables (say price and package, or brand name and gender, or all four) on a dependent variable, such as sales or preference, we must make one of two assumptions. We can assume that the effects of the independent variables are independent of each other and that no interactions (joint effects) occur. Or, we can assume that the effect of the independent variables taken together is different than the sum of their effects one at a time. This latter situation is known as *interaction.* You may recall from Chapter 7 that different experimental designs may be required if interaction is likely to occur. Different analytical techniques are also required when interaction may be present.

597

ANOVA Without Interaction

Recall also from Chapter 7 that randomized blocks designs (RBD) and Latin square designs are used when more than one variable may affect the results and there is no interaction expected. The basic ANOVA approach is the same for both designs. However, since the Latin square design involves an additional variable, some additional calculations are required. We illustrate both approaches.

Before reading the following discussion, you should review the material presented in Chapter 18 (pages 573–580) on univariate (one-way) ANOVA. The logic and basic procedures are the same for the multivariate approach. Therefore, a sound understanding of univariate ANOVA is essential for understanding the more advanced forms.

ANOVA for Randomized Blocks Designs *(RBD)*

Assume that the experimental design described in the main example in Chapter 17 (pages 525–527) was a simple RBD with gender as the blocking variable and brand name as the treatment variable. This would mean that we are assuming that gender and treatment do not interact. We would, in effect, be saying "I think gender will affect response to this product and I want to see if brand name will. I'm sure that gender won't affect the response to the brand name. Therefore, I will control for gender's effects on response to the product by blocking on it."

Let us accept this logic for a moment and test the null hypothesis that the brand name has no effect on the stated purchase probability. The results from Table 17–2 are summarized in Table 19–1 with two treatments and two blocks. Treatments generally form the column (c) and blocks form the rows (r).

How do we proceed? Recall from Chapter 18 that ANOVA utilizes an F ratio that has a measure of the variance associated with a treatment (MST) as the numerator and a measure of random, natural, or unexplained variances (MSE) as the denominator. Extending the one-way ANOVA to the RBD re-

Table 19–1 Mean Purchase Probability by Gender and Brand Name*

	Bravo (c = 1)	*Delight (c = 2)*	$\overline{X}$
Male (r = 1)	49.17	26.67	37.92
Female (r = 2)	49.25	62.50	55.88
$\overline{X}_j$	49.20	41.00	45.10

* Derived from Table 17–2.

quires computing a mean sum of squares for blocks as well as for treatments. In addition, the calculation of the mean sum of squares error is altered to reflect the effect of the blocks. The required formulas are as follows:

$$\text{Mean square treatment } (MST) = \frac{\text{Sum of squares treatments } (SST)}{df}$$

$$= \frac{\sum\limits_{j=1}^{c} n_j(\overline{X}_j - \overline{X}_T)^2}{c - 1} \qquad (19\text{-}1)$$

$$\text{Mean square blocking } (MSB) = \frac{\text{Sum of squares blocking } (SSB)}{df}$$

$$= \frac{\sum\limits_{i=1}^{r} n_i(\overline{X}_i - \overline{X}_T)^2}{r - 1} \qquad (19\text{-}2)$$

$$\text{Total mean square } (TMS) = \frac{\text{Total sum of squares } (TSS)}{df}$$

$$= \frac{\sum\limits_{i=1}^{r} \sum\limits_{j=1}^{c} \sum\limits_{k=1}^{n_{ij}} (X_{ijk} - \overline{X}_T)^2}{n_T - 1} \qquad (19\text{-}3)$$

$$\text{Mean square error } (MSE) = \frac{\text{Sum of squares error } (SSE)}{df}$$

$$= \frac{\sum\limits_{i=1}^{r} \sum\limits_{j=1}^{c} \sum\limits_{k=1}^{n_{ij}} (X_{ijk} - \overline{X}_i - \overline{X}_j + \overline{X}_T)^2}{n_T - r - c + 1} \qquad (19\text{-}4)$$

$$= \frac{TSS - SSB - SST}{n_T - r - c + 1}$$

where n_j = sample size of treatment group j
n_i = sample size of block group i
$\overline{X}_j$ = mean of treatment j
$\overline{X}_i$ = mean of block i
$\overline{X}_T$ = total or grand mean
n_{ij} = number of respondents (observations) receiving treatment i and blocking variable j
X_{ijk} = the kth observation in treatment i and block j
n_T = total number of observations

The ANOVA table takes the form shown in Table 19–2. The calculations for our example are:

Table 19-2 ANOVA Output Format for RBD

Source of Variation	Degrees of Freedom	Sum of Squares	Mean Square	F	P
Between Blocks	$r - 1$	SSB	$\dfrac{SSB}{r-1}$	$\dfrac{MSB}{MSE}$	F Table
Between Treatments	$c - 1$	SST	$\dfrac{SST}{c-1}$	$\dfrac{MST}{MSE}$	F Table
Error	$n_T - r - c + 1$	SSE	$\dfrac{SSE}{n_T - r - c + 1}$		
Total	$n_T - 1$	TSS	$\dfrac{TSS}{n_T - 1}$		

$$\bar{X}_T = \frac{30(49.17) + 30(26.67) + 20(49.25) + 20(62.50)}{100}$$

$$= 45.10$$

$$MST = \frac{50(49.20 - 45.10)^2 + 50(41.00 - 45.10)^2}{2 - 1}$$

$$= \frac{1,681.00}{1} = 1,681.00$$

$$MSB = \frac{60(37.92 - 45.10)^2 + 40(55.88 - 45.10)^2}{2 - 1}$$

$$= \frac{7,741.48}{1} = 7,741.48$$

$$TMS = \frac{(30 - 45.10)^2 + (100 - 45.10)^2 \cdots + (0 - 45.10)^2}{100 - 1}$$

$$= \frac{142,099.00}{99}$$

$$= 1,435.34$$

$$MSE = \frac{142,099.00 - 1,681.00 - 7,741.48}{100 - 2 - 2 + 1}$$

$$= 1367.80$$

These values are then used for calculating **F** ratios with the formulas

$$F_{\text{Blocks}} = \frac{MSB}{MSE}$$

Table 19-3 ANOVA Output for Purchase Probability in an RBD

Source of Variation	Degrees of Freedom	Sum of Squares	Mean Square	F	P
Gender	1	7,741.48	7,741.48	5.66	<.025
Name	1	1,681.00	1,681.00	1.23	>.250
Error	97	132,676.52	1,367.80		
Total	99	142,099.00			

$$F_{\text{Treatment}} = \frac{MST}{MSE}$$

The results are shown in Table 19-3. The data in the table indicate that the blocking variable, gender, is associated with a differential purchase probability. However, the observed differences between the treatment groups could have easily occurred by chance. Remember that we assumed that there was no interaction between our treatment and blocking variables. In the section on ANOVA with interaction, (pages 604-606) we reexamine these same data. We reach strikingly different conclusions, which indicates the importance of specifying properly both the experimental design and the ANOVA version.

ANOVA for Latin Square Designs

Latin square designs are an efficient way of blocking or controlling two variables that might affect our experimental results. Like the RBD, Latin square designs assume that there is no interaction among the variables.

The calculations are similar to those described for the RBD. However, it is necessary to calculate the effects of the second blocking variable. Table 19-4 illustrates a Latin square design in which the effects of three versions of a point-of-purchase display were tested. The Latin square design was used to control for store type (grocery, discount, and department) and store location (urban, suburban, and rural). The required formulas are

$$\text{Total means square } (TMS) = \frac{\text{Total sum of squares } (TSS)}{df}$$

$$= \frac{\sum\limits_{i=1}^{r} \sum\limits_{j=1}^{c} (X_{ij} - \bar{X}_T)^2}{rc - 1} \qquad (19\text{-}5)$$

$$\text{Mean square row block } (MSR) = \frac{\text{Sum of squares row block } (SSR)}{df}$$

$$= \frac{r \sum\limits_{i=1}^{r} (\bar{X}_i - \bar{X}_T)^2}{r - 1} \qquad (19\text{-}6)$$

Table 19–4 Latin Square Experiment Design and Results

	Design				Results (Sales)			
	Store Type					Store Type		
Store Location	Gr	Di	De	Store Location	Gr	Di	De	$\bar{X}$
U	C	A	B	U	51	59	67	59
S	A	B	C	S	32	66	49	49
R	B	C	A	R	37	52	37	42
				$\bar{X}$	40	59	51	50

where U = urban   Gr = grocery   A = point-of-purchase display A
S = suburban   Di = discount   B = point-of-purchase display B
R = rural   De = department   C = point-of-purchase display C

$$\text{Mean square column block } (MSC) = \frac{\text{Sum of squares column block } (SSC)}{df}$$

$$= \frac{c \sum_{j=1}^{c} (\bar{X}_j - \bar{X}_T)^2}{c - 1} \qquad (19\text{--}7)$$

$$\text{Mean square treatment } (MST) = \frac{\text{Sum of squares treatment } (SST)}{df}$$

$$= \frac{t \sum_{k=1}^{t} (\bar{X}_k - \bar{X}_T)^2}{t - 1} \qquad (19\text{--}8)$$

$$\text{Mean square error } (MSE) = \frac{\text{Sum of squares error}}{df}$$

$$= \frac{TTS - SSR - SSC - SST}{(r - 1)(c - 2)}$$

$$\text{F for column block} = \frac{MSC}{MSE}$$

$$\text{F for row block} = \frac{MSR}{MSE}$$

$$\text{F for treatment} = \frac{MST}{MSE}$$

where $c = r = t = $ number of columns, rows, and treatments respectively

$\overline{X}_T = $ grand mean (mean of all cells),

$\overline{X}_j = $ mean of column j,

$\overline{X}_i = $ means row i, and

$\overline{X}_k = $ mean of cells having treatment k.

The calculations for our example are

$$TMS = \frac{(51 - 50)^2 + (59 - 50)^2 + \cdots + (37 - 50)^2}{(3)(3) - 1}$$

$$= \frac{1294}{8} = 161.75$$

$$MSR = \frac{3[(59 - 50)^2 + (49 - 50)^2 + (42 - 50)^2]}{3 - 1}$$

$$= \frac{438}{2} = 219.00$$

$$MSC = \frac{3[(40 - 50)^2 + (59 - 50)^2 + (51 - 50)^2]}{3 - 1}$$

$$= \frac{546}{2} = 273.00$$

$$MST = \frac{3[(42.67 - 50)^2 + (56.67 - 50)^2 + (50.67 - 50)^2]}{3 - 1}$$

$$= \frac{296.00}{2} = 148.00$$

$$MSE = \frac{1294 - 438 - 546 - 296}{(3 - 1)(3 - 2)}$$

$$= \frac{14}{2} = 7.00$$

$$F_{columns} = \frac{219.00}{7.00} = 31.29$$

$$F_{rows} = \frac{273.00}{7.00} = 39.00$$

$$F_{treatment} = \frac{148.00}{7.00} = 21.14$$

The ANOVA table for this problem is Table 19–5. As the table indicates, store location, store type, and type of point-of-purchase display all appear to affect sales.

$$= \frac{125,008.14}{96} = 1,302.17$$

These results are summarized in Table 19–6, which indicates that brand name has an effect when considered in conjunction with gender. Reexamine Table 19–1. Males and females have a similar response to Bravo; however, males appear to dislike Delight whereas females like it. Thus, brand name interacts with gender to influence purchase probability. Compare these conclusions with the conclusions reached from examining Table 19–3 in which no test was made for interaction. Obviously, it is important to test for interaction if there is a reasonable possibility that it could occur.

Table 19–5   ANOVA Output for a Latin Square Design

Source of Variation	Degrees of Freedom	Sum of Squares	Mean Square	F	P
Location	2	438	219	31.29	<.05
Type	2	546	273	39.00	<.05
Point-of-Purchase	2	296	148	21.14	<.05
Error	2	14	7		
Total	8	1294			

Table 19–6   ANOVA Output for a Factorial Design

Source of Variation	Degrees of Freedom	Sum of Squares	Mean Square	F	P
Gender	1	7,741.48	7,741.48	5.92	<.025
Brand Name	1	1,681.00	1,681.00	1.29	>.250
Name ° Gender	1	7,668.38	7,668.38	5.86	<.025
Error	96	125,008.14	1,302.17		
Total	99	142,099.00			

Name ° Gender = interaction of name and gender

ANOVA Assumptions

Using ANOVA properly requires attention to the assumptions underlying the approach. In addition to requiring interval data, all of the versions of ANOVA discussed assume that

1. the sample in each cell is random and independent from samples in the other cells;
2. the dependent variable is normally distributed in each of the populations; and
3. the dependent variable's variance is the same in each population.

In addition to these three general assumptions, the randomized block and Latin square ANOVAs assume that the block and treatment effects are additive. That is, they assume that if a 10 per cent price reduction increases sales an average of 10 units a week and a point-of-purchase display increases sales an average of 15 units, using both simultaneously will increase sales by 25 units. The factorial approach allows a test of this assumption. As we saw in the last section, a failure to test for interaction when it exists can result in incorrect decisions.

Review Questions

19.1.   What is a *multivariate hypothesis test* of differences between groups?

19.2.   What is *interaction?*

19.3.   For what kinds of analytic problems is ANOVA used?

19.4.   What experimental design is required before ANOVA can be used to detect interaction?

Discussion Questions/Problems

19.5. Analyze the following data generated by an **RBD** design.

	Treatment		
Block	A	B	C
1	65	69	89
2	50	63	65
3	67	61	70
4	52	70	65
5	50	47	63
6	37	50	55
7	40	39	40
8	37	43	42
9	35	41	50

19.6. Repeat number 19.5 but treat blocks 1–3 as 9 measures within block **I**, blocks 4–6 as 9 measures within block **II**, and blocks 7–9 as 9 measures within block **III**.

19.7. Analyze the following data generated by a Latin square design.

	Design			Results		
	Store Type			Store Type		
Time Period	G	D	S	G	D	S
1	B	A	C	51	59	69
2	A	C	B	30	68	51
3	C	B	A	36	53	39

A, B, C, = different **POP** material
G = grocery, D = Department, S = Specialty

19.8. Analyze the experimental data in Table 17–2 as though they were obtained from a factorial design with taste reaction as the dependent variable and gender and brand name as treatments.

19.9. Analyze the experimental data in Table 17–2 as though they were obtained from a RBD with gender as the block, brand name as the treatment, and taste reaction as the dependent variable.

19.10. Data from a factorial experiment on the effectiveness of price reductions, point-of-purchase displays (POP) and newspaper advertising (Ad) are in the following table. The numbers in the table are average weekly units sold under each condition at the 60 stores involved in the study. What impact did each variable have on sales. Were interaction effects present? What would you recommend based on these results

Regular Price				Price − 10%				Price − 20%			
POP		No POP		POP		No POP		POP		No POP	
Ad	No Ad	Ad	No Ad	Ad	No Ad	Ad	No Ad	Ad	No Ad	Ad	No Ad
50	35	40	10	65	45	47	12	90	70	67	15
55	30	32	8	58	45	42	10	95	65	72	12
30	40	36	15	55	50	48	13	80	80	81	16
40	25	27	12	60	30	28	16	85	67	60	15
45	30	29	9	70	38	45	11	92	50	52	20

CHAPTER 20

Measures of Association

American Express, like other credit card firms, earns more return from card holders who use their card extensively than from those who are light users. They also have considerable data on each of their card holders from their credit application. This information includes such items as age, occupation, area of residence, income, and other financial data. Both mass media such as magazines and mailing lists from direct mail firms have similar data on their subscribers or lists.

One challenge facing American Express is to attract those customers most likely to make extensive use of their card. Target advertising is a means to accomplish this. Thus, American Express needs to be able to understand which demographic data are associated with heavy use of the American Express card. Multiple regression analysis, one of the techniques described in this chapter, can be used for this purpose.

Marketing managers are very often interested in the degree of association between variables. That is, they want to know if a high level of one variable tends to be associated with ("go with") a high or low level of another variable. Depending upon the purpose(s) for which the data were obtained, one may be interested in examining the degree of association of such variables as price, amount of advertising, perceived quality, life-cycle stage, social class, income, or education with variables such as purchaser-nonpurchaser of brand, attitudes toward brands, brand preference, sales, or market share.

In analyzing associative relationships, two types of variables are used: *predictor* (independent) variables and *criterion* (dependent) variables. Predictor variables are used to help predict or "explain" the level of criterion variables. Market share is an example of a criterion variable that such predictor variables as relative price, amount of advertising, and number of outlets are often used to explain.

Three important considerations in choosing a method of analyzing an associative relationship are (1) *the number of criterion variables,* (2) the number of *predictor variables,* and (3) *the scale(s) used for the measurements.*

Number of Criterion and Predictor Variables. The minimum number of criterion and predictor variables is one each, because at least two variables are necessary to have association. The techniques appropriate for analysis of two variable association are known as *bivariate techniques.* When more than two variables are involved in the analysis, the techniques employed are known as *multivariate techniques.* We cover bivariate techniques in this section of this chapter; multivariate techniques are covered in the next section.

The Scale(s) Used for the Measurement. As discussed earlier, measurements may be made using a *nominal, ordinal, interval,* or *ratio* scale. Association techniques that are appropriate for analyzing the degree of association between intervally scaled variables may be entirely inappropriate for use with variables measured in other scales. We describe techniques for use with interval, ordinal, and nominal data.

There are two components to measures of association. First, we want to know the *nature of the association.* That is, we want to be able to predict the level or magnitude of the criterion variable if we know the value of the predictor variable. If our advertising is $1.9 million, what will our sales be?

Second, we want to know the *strength of the association.* That is, we want to know how widely the actual value may vary from the predicted value. This concept is similar to the idea of a confidence interval discussed previously.

Misuse of Measures of Association. Each of the techniques we describe has assumptions that should be met before the technique is used. These are indicated in the appropriate sections. However, a common error in using measures of association is to assume that association represents causation. As we saw in Chapter 3 (page 49), this is not the case.

Even if we demonstrate statistically that two (or more) variables vary together in a manner that is unlikely to be due to sampling variation, two problems exist in concluding that changes in variable B cause changes in variable A. The first is *directionality.* Does an increase in a measure of overall attitude toward a brand increase brand usage? Or, does an increase in brand usage cause an increase in attitude? Or, might a third factor be causing both changes?

A second problem often occurs in practice. A number of measures, say 20, are taken of an attitude and one or more measures of purchasing are made. The analyst then runs 20 correlations and finds two that are statistically significant at an alpha of .10. However, by chance one would expect to find 2 out of 20 significant results with an alpha of .10. This practice accounts for some of the strange findings of correlations between such things as changes in the daily noon temperatures of some towns and changes in the Dow Jones average. Such findings are termed *spurious correlations.* Thus, one should be very careful in using any measure of association that was not *prespecified* in advance based on theory or practical intuition.

Measures of Association Between Two Variables

Bivariate Measures of Association Using Ratio/Interval Data

Most analyses of association are conducted by computer. However, before the analysis is conducted, the data should be plotted either by hand or by the computer. This plot generally is called a *scatter diagram.* It is important to examine the scatter diagram to determine if the association in the data, if any, is linear or curvilinear. If the data are nonlinear, standard techniques (linear regression analysis) may indicate no relationship when, in fact, there is one. If a nonlinear relationship is indicated, appropriate curve-fitting techniques should be used.

Figure 20–1 contains several scatter diagrams. Diagrams A and F suggest that there is no relationship between X and Y. Diagrams B and C indicate a strong positive and a strong negative relationship, respectively. Diagram D indicates a positive but weaker relationship. A nonlinear relationship between X and Y is indicated in Diagram E.

Let us assume that the taste reaction scores and the purchase probability scores in Table 17–2 are interval data. The first step in analyzing the relationship between the stated purchase probability and the taste reaction for the 20 females who tasted the Delight brand is to plot the data, as shown in Figure 20–2.

A visual examination of Figure 20–2 indicates that the purchase probability appears to increase as the taste reaction increases. How can we describe this relationship? The general equation for a straight line fitted to the variables X and Y is

$$Y = a + bX \qquad (20-1)$$

where Y is the criterion variable, X the predictor variable, a a constant that represents the intercept, and b the amount Y changes for each unit of change in X. Both a and b are unknown and must be calculated.

Approximations to the a and b values may be made by *graphic analysis.* A line can be fitted visually to a plot of the values of the two variables such as shown in Figure 20–2. The line is fitted in such a way as to attempt to make the

611

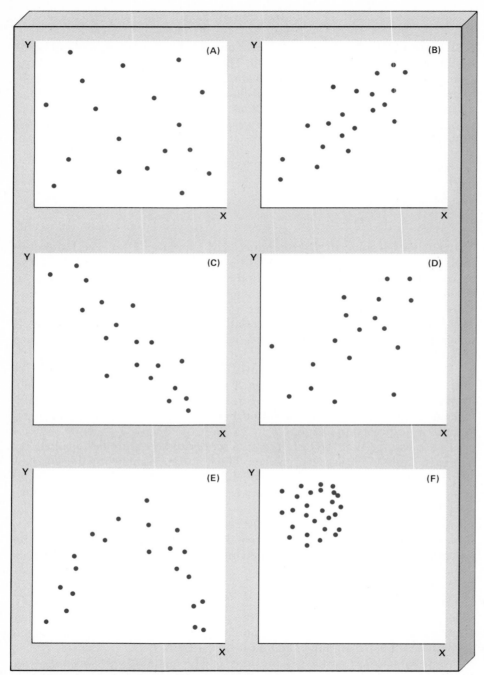

Figure 20–1   *Various Scatter Diagrams*

612

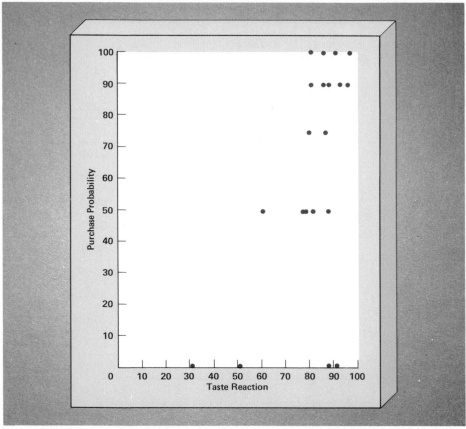

Figure 20–2 *Plot of Taste Reaction and Purchase Probability Values*

sum of all the distances of points above the line equal the sum of all those below the line. (The number of points above and below the line need not be equal, however.) The estimate of the a value is the intercept of the Y axis. The estimate of the b value may be determined by solving the equation, $\overline{Y} = a + b\overline{X}$, after substituting in the numerical values of $\overline{Y}$, a, and $\overline{X}$.

Bivariate least squares *regression analysis* is the mathematical technique for the fitting of a line to measurements of the two variables such that the algebraic sum of deviations of the measurements from the line are zero and the sum of the squares of the deviations are less than they would be for any other line. Table 20–1 shows the worksheet that is necessary to calculate a least squares regression analysis for our problem. Using the values from this worksheet, we calculate b as follows:

Table 20-1 Worksheet for Regression Analysis

Respondent No.	Purchase Probability Y	Taste Reaction X	Y^2	X^2	YX
81	100	85	10000	7225	8500
82	90	95	8100	9025	8550
83	0	90	0	8100	0
84	90	80	8100	6400	7200
85	50	77	2500	5929	3850
86	50	81	2500	6561	4050
87	75	79	5625	6241	5925
88	90	87	8100	7569	7830
89	0	50	0	2500	0
90	50	87	2500	7569	4350
91	100	90	10000	8100	9000
92	90	85	8100	7225	7650
93	50	60	2500	3600	3000
94	0	30	0	900	0
95	100	80	10000	6400	8000
96	50	78	2500	6084	3900
97	90	92	8100	8464	8280
98	75	86	5625	7396	6450
99	100	96	10000	9216	9600
100	0	87	0	7569	0
Total	1,250	1,595	104,250	132,073	106,135

$$b = \frac{\sum_{i=1}^{n} YX - n\overline{Y}\,\overline{X}}{\sum_{i=1}^{n} X^2 - n(\overline{X})^2} \qquad (20\text{–}2)$$

$$= \frac{106{,}135 - (20)(62.5)(79.75)}{132{,}073 - 20(79.75)^2}$$

$$= 1.32$$

The value for a can then be determined as

$$a = \overline{Y} - b\overline{X}$$
$$= 62.5 - 1.32(79.75) \qquad (20\text{–}3)$$
$$= -42.77$$

Thus, our data can be described by the line

$$\hat{Y} = -42.77 + 1.32X$$

This means that for every unit increase in taste reaction (X), the purchase probability tends to increase by about 1.3 units. Although this is the best mathematical description of our data, there is nothing in the formula itself that indicates how good (accurate) a description it is. Refer again to Figure 20–1. The data in scatter diagrams B and D would be represented by nearly identical lines. However, a visual inspection suggests that the line will describe the data in diagram B more accurately than it will the data in D. Stated another way, the observations (data points) in B will fall much closer to the line than will those in D.

The *coefficient of determination,* generally referred to as r^2, is the measure of the strength of association in a bivariate regression analysis. It can vary from 0 to 1, and represents the proportion of total variation in Y (criterion variable) that is accounted for, or explained, by variation in X (the predictor variable). Thus, an r^2 of 0 would indicate that none of the variation in Y is explained by the variation in X whereas one of 1.0 would indicate that it all is.

Scatter diagrams A and F in Figure 20–1 would have near 0 r^2 values. Diagram E would also have a near 0 r^2 if a linear rather than a curvilinear trend line were fitted. Diagram D would have an r^2 near .5, indicating that about half the variation in Y is accounted for by variation in X. Finally, diagrams B and C would have r^2 values near .9, indicating that most of the variation in Y is explained by variation in X.

What is the coefficient of determination for our example? Mathematically,

$$r^2 = 1 - \frac{\text{unexplained variance}}{\text{total variance}} = \frac{\text{explained variance}}{\text{total variance}}$$

$$r^2 = 1 - \frac{\sum\limits_{i=1}^{n} (Y_i - \hat{Y}_i)^2}{\sum\limits_{i=1}^{n} (Y_i - \bar{Y})^2} \qquad (20\text{--}4)$$

where $\hat{Y}_i$ = the predicted value of Y for the ith data point using the regression formula.

Thus,

$$r^2 = 1 - \frac{17,592}{26,125} = .33$$

About one-third the variation in stated purchase probability is accounted for or explained by changes in taste reactions.

Some degree of association will often occur between two variables because of random sampling variation. Therefore, it is generally desirable to test the null hypothesis that $r^2 = 0$. This can be tested as:

$$t = \frac{r\sqrt{n-2}}{\sqrt{1-r^2}} \quad \text{with } n-2 \text{ degrees of freedom.} \qquad (20\text{--}5)$$

For our example,

$$t = \frac{.57\sqrt{20-2}}{\sqrt{1-.33}} = 2.95$$

Examination of Appendix E reveals that an r^2 value this large would occur by chance less than 1 per cent of the time. A null hypothesis of no association between taste reaction and purchase probability would therefore have to be rejected if $\alpha \geq .01$.

Bivariate Measures of Association Using Ordinal Data

We often want to examine the degree of association between two ordinally scaled variables such as two attitudes or two rank orderings. Suppose we believe that our taste reaction and purchase probability scales produced only ordinal data. How should we analyze them? The *Spearman rank correlation coefficient*, r_s, is the most common approach. The steps involved in its calculation are:

1. *Establish the null hypothesis that there is no association between taste reaction and purchase probability.*

2. *Rank order all the observations of* **Y** *from 1 to* **N**. *Do the same for the sample observations of* **X**.

3. *Assign each subject two scores: the rank of his or her value on* **Y** *and the rank of his or her value on* **X**.

Table 20–2 Worksheet for Spearman Rank Correlation Coefficient

Respondent #	Y	X	di	di²
81	18.5	10.5	−8.0	64.00
82	14.0	19.0	5.0	25.00
83	2.5	16.5	14.0	196.00
84	14.0	7.5	−6.5	42.25
85	7.0	4.0	−3.0	9.00
86	7.0	9.0	2.0	4.00
87	10.5	6.0	−4.5	20.25
88	14.0	14.0	0	0
89	2.5	2.0	−0.5	0.25
90	7.0	14.0	7.0	49.00
91	18.5	16.5	−2.0	4.00
92	14.0	10.5	−3.5	12.25
93	7.0	3.0	−4.0	16.00
94	2.5	1.0	−1.5	2.25
95	18.5	7.5	−11.0	121.00
96	7.0	5.0	−2.0	4.00
97	14.0	18.0	4.0	16.00
98	10.5	12.0	1.5	2.25
99	18.5	20.0	1.5	2.25
100	2.5	14.0	11.5	132.25

$$\sum_{i=1}^{N} d_i^2 = 722.0$$

4. *Determine a value, d_i, for each individual by subtracting each person's Y score (rank) from his or her X score (rank). Square this result for each individual and sum for the entire group.* Table 20–2 illustrates these steps based on the raw scores from Table 20–1 (assuming that these are now ordinal rather than interval).

5. *Calculate r_s using the following formula:*[1]

$$r_2 = 1 - \frac{6 \sum\limits_{i=1}^{n} d_i^2}{n^3 - n} \qquad\qquad (20-6)$$

$$= 1 - \frac{6(722)}{(20)^3 - 20} = .46$$

6. *The probability associated with this value (the probability of obtaining a measure of association this strong or stronger given a true null hypothesis of no association) can be determined using a t value calculated as follows:*

$$t = r_s \sqrt{\frac{n-2}{1-r_s}} \qquad\qquad (20-7)$$

For our example

$$t = .46 \sqrt{\frac{20-2}{1-.46}}$$

$$= 2.66$$

with $n - 2$ degrees of freedom. As Appendix E indicates, an association this strong would be very unlikely to occur because of sampling error (less than 2 per cent) if the null of no difference were indeed true. We may therefore reject the null and conclude that there is in fact association between taste reaction and purchase probability.

Bivariate Measures of Association Using Nominal Data

Occasionally, we want to measure the degree of association between two sets of data, one or both of which are nominally scaled. We previously (pages 589–590) tested the null hypothesis that there was no difference in reported frequency of carbonated beverage consumption between males and females. Another question would be, "What is the degree of association between gender and reported frequency of carbonated beverage consumption?" The *contingency coefficient, C,* is the appropriate measure of association in such situations.

The procedure is simple.

1. *Establish the null hypothesis that there is no association between gender and reported frequency of carbonated beverage consumption.*
2. *Calculate χ^2 as previously described (pages 589–590).*
3. *Calculate C as*

$$C = \sqrt{\frac{\chi^2}{n + \chi^2}}$$

$$C = \sqrt{\frac{4.67}{100 + 4.67}} \qquad (20\text{--}8)$$

$$C = .21$$

4. *The probability associated with* **C** *is the same as for* χ^2 (approximately .16 in our example). We therefore conclude that we cannot reject the null of no association between gender and consumption frequency.

The contingency coefficient *C* is difficult to interpret. Although no association at all will produce a *C* of 0, the upper limit depends on the number of categories. However, values close to 0, such as the one obtained in our example, indicate a limited association.

Multivariate Measures of Association

In this section of this chapter, we cover multivariate measures of association. Like bivariate measures, the appropriate multivariate measure depends on the scale of measurement used (ratio/interval, ordinal, or nominal). In addition, the number of predictor and the number of criterion variables influence the choice of a statistical measure of association. A number of analytical situations require unique statistical measures. In the following sections, we provide descriptions of those techniques that are most useful in marketing research.

Recall that in Chapter 12 we covered a group of statistical techniques used for a unique measure of association — perceptual mapping. We do not repeat that discussion here, although additional applications of two of the techniques, factor analysis and discriminant analysis, are discussed.

Multiple Regression Analysis

Multiple regression analysis is used to examine the relationship between two or more intervally scaled predictor variables and one intervally scaled criterion variable. Ordinal data that are "near interval," such as semantic differential scale data, can generally be used also. In addition, we describe special techniques that allow some nominal predictor variables to be used.

Multiple regression is simply a logical and mathematical extension of bivariate regression, as described in the previous section. However, instead of fitting a straight line through a two-dimensional space, multiple regression fits a plane through a multidimensional space. The output and interpretation are exactly the same as for a bivariate analysis:

$$\hat{Y} = a + b_1 X_1 + b_2 X_2 + b_3 X_3 + \cdots + b_i X_i$$

where $\hat{Y}$ = estimated value of the criterion variable

a = constant derived from the analysis

b_i = coefficients associated with the predictor variables such that a change of one unit in X_i will cause a change of b_i units in $\hat{Y}$. The values for the coefficients are derived from the regression analysis.

X_i = predictor variables that influence the criterion variable

For example

$$\hat{Y} = 117 + .3X_1 + 6.8X_2$$

where $\hat{Y}$ = sales

X_1 = advertising expenditures

X_2 = number of outlets

would be interpreted as: "Sales tend to increase by .3 units for every unit increase in advertising and 6.8 units for every unit increase in the number of outlets."

An examination of two formulas derived by the General Electric Company will indicate the usefulness of multiple regression. The goal of the GE research project was to isolate the factors associated with a high price for a product relative to one's immediate competitors. A number of industries were examined and the following partial results were obtained for the consumer durables and capital equipment industries:

Consumer Durables: RP = 60.75 + 0.07RQ + 0.34RDC + 0.06ME + 1.15RS

Capital Equipment: RP = 71.88 + 0.09RQ + 0.27RDC + 0.02ME + 0.43RS

where RP = firm's price as a percentage of the average price of its leading competitors

RQ = relative product quality

RDC = relative direct cost

ME = marketing effort

RS = relative service

Relative price is influenced by the same variables in both industries (different variables were found for other industries). However, marketing effort (a measure of advertising, sales promotion, and sales force expenses) is more important (larger b) in the consumer durables industry, whereas product quality is more important in the capital equipment industry. Relative direct cost is important in both industries. Such analyses can provide significant marketing strategy implications.

Other marketing applications of multiple regression analysis include

1. *Forecasting* where either company variables such as relative price, relative advertising, and so forth; or external variables such as population growth, disposable income, and so forth; or both are used to forecast sales, demand, or market share.

2. *Outlet location decisions* where traffic counts, location of competitors, square footage available, and so on, are used to analyze the attractiveness of outlet locations for chain stores.

3. *Quota determination* involves using territory size, last period sales, competitor strength and related variables to determine sales quotas or objectives.

4. *Marketing mix analysis* by analyzing the relationship between elements in the marketing mix and market share or sales.

5. *Determining the relationship between the criterion variable and one predictor variable while the effects of other predictor variables are held constant:* An example is the estimate of the reliance on price as an indicator of quality of furniture while other factors, such as brand of product and stores in which it is available, are held constant.

6. *Estimating values for missing data (item nonresponse) in surveys.* For example, one can estimate income from occupation, age, and education data.

As these examples indicate, multiple regression can serve two primary purposes: (1) to *predict* the level of the criterion variable given certain levels of the predictor variables, or (2) to *gain insights* into the relationships between the predictor variables and the criterion variable.

The Strength of Multiple Regression Measures of Association

Recall from our discussion of bivariate regression that a coefficient of determination, generally called r square (r^2), can be calculated. This statistic can range from 0 to 1 in value and, in multiple regression, indicates the percentage of the variation in the criterion variable that is explained by the entire set of predictor variables. The r^2 for the capital equipment formula shown earlier is .32, which means that 32 per cent of the variation in relative price in this industry can be explained by the four variables in the equation.

In addition to measuring the strength of association reflected by the overall regression formula, it is necessary to assess the likelihood that each individual predictor variable's association with the criterion variable is the result of chance. The calculation is routinely performed by all packaged computer programs. The standard output is the probability of error if the null hypothesis of $b_i = 0$ is rejected. Each of the variables in the two GE equations had a probability of error of less than .10.

Multiple regression analysis is invariably conducted through the use of a computer. The computer program places all the predictor variables into the formula unless it is instructed to do otherwise. Therefore, it is customary to specify a cutoff point for inclusion into the final model. The cutoff point in the GE model was specified as .10. Thus, only those predictor variables with a probability of falsely rejecting the null hypothesis, $b_i = 0$, of less than .10 are included in the final model.

No single alpha level is appropriate for all such tests. As discussed in the section on hypothesis tests, it is generally worthwhile to examine the probability level associated with each variable that logically or theoretically "should" influence the criterion variable. The final regression formula should contain predictor variables that (1) are logically related to the criterion variable, and (2) have a probability level that is appropriate for the problem at hand.

Nominal Variables in Regression Analysis

Frequently it is desirable to include nominally scaled predictor variables, such as gender, marital status, or occupational category, in a multiple regression analysis. *Dummy variables* can be used for this purpose as long as there are relatively few such variables. For natural dichotomies, such as gender, one response is coded 0 and the other is coded 1. For polytomous data (multiple categories), such as occupation, each category serves as a variable. Thus, a three-category occupation scale could be coded as three variables:

$X_5 = 1$ (professional/managerial) or 0 (not professional/managerial)
$X_6 = 1$ (white collar) or 0 (not white collar)
$X_7 = 1$ (blue collar) or 0 (not blue collar)

The occupational scale just described could also be coded by using only X_5 and X_6. When these are both coded 0, the respondent must be blue collar. However, interpretation of the equation is easier if all categories are included.

The two GE regression formulas described earlier tested for the effect of patents, a dichotomous (yes/no) variable. For these two industries, patent protection was not associated (with a .10 α level for $b_i = 0$) with relative price. However, for consumer nondurables (whose formula is not shown), it had a b of $+2.05$. Thus, if a consumer nondurable product had patent protection, its relative price tended to be 2.05 per cent higher relative to competition.

Cautions in Using Multiple Regression

Multiple regression is a very useful technique. However, several cautions need to be observed when using it.

1. **Presence of Multicollinearity.** Multiple regression is based on the assumption that the predictor variables are independent (are *not* correlated). If they are, the b values are very unstable. However, the predictive ability of the equation is not affected. Therefore, multicollinearity is not a serious problem in forecasting applications but is very serious when the formula is used to gain an understanding of *how* the predictor variables influence the criterion variable.

It is always advisable to check for multicollinearity before or during a multiple regression analysis. This is done by requesting the computer to print a *correlation matrix*, which shows the correlation (r) of each variable in the analysis with every other variable in the analysis. The correlation matrix for the variables in the GE capital equipment relative price analysis is shown in Table 20–3.

An examination of the table indicates that relative quality and relative service are modestly correlated. When two predictor variables are correlated above .35, potential distortion of the b_i values should be checked (although serious problems are unlikely unless the r value is well above .50). A simple way to do this is to run the equation with both variables and with each variable separately. The b_i values should be similar in all three cases. If they are not similar, a multicollinearity problem exists.

Multicollinearity can be dealt with in three ways. First, it can be ignored. This is acceptable in forecasting applications but should be avoided in other situations. The second approach is to delete one of the correlated predictors. This is recommended when two variables are clearly measuring the same thing

Table 20–3 Correlation Matrix for Relative Price Regression Analysis

	RP	RQ	RDC	ME
RQ	.47			
RDC	.33	.09		
ME	.12	.11	−.03	
RS	.19	−.38	−.12	.19

(number of sales personnel and sales force salary expense) or when one variable has a clearer logical or theoretical link to the criterion variable. Finally, the correlated variables can be combined or otherwise transformed to produce unrelated variables. The marketing effort variable in the GE equation was constructed by combining measures of advertising effort, sales promotion effort, and sales force effort because the three variables were highly correlated with each other.

2. Interpretation of Coefficients.   Care must be taken in interpreting the coefficients of the predictor variables. Consider the following equation

$$\hat{Y} = 100 + .01 X_1 + .01 X_2$$

where $\hat{Y} =$ sales estimate,
$X_1 =$ advertising in thousands of dollars, and
$X_2 =$ salesforce expenditures in dollars.

At first glance it appears that a dollar spent on advertising and a dollar spent on the sales force would have an equal effect on sales. However, this is not true since different units of measurement (thousands of dollars and dollars) are used for the two variables. Thus, in our example, it would take a $1,000 increase in advertising to equal the effect of a $1 increase in sales force expenditures.

When it is desirable to compare the relative effects of predictor variables, they should be coded using the same measurement units. If this is not possible, most packaged computer programs will run a regression on standardized scores (each observation is converted to the number of standard deviations it is from its mean). Thus, a standardized predictor coefficient of 1.3 would be interpreted as "a one standard deviation change in this predictor will produce a 1.3 standard deviation change in the criterion variable." This allows a direct comparison of the effects of relative changes in variables measured in different units.

3. Causation.   It is very tempting to assume that levels of predictor variables *cause* the level of the criterion variable. However, all they indicate is *association* between the variables. Association is evidence of causation, but it is not proof of it. Assume that a group of firms base their advertising budgets on current sales. Thus, sales are causing advertising, and changes in sales cause changes in advertising. A regression analysis with sales as the criterion variable and advertising as one of the predictor variables would indicate a strong association. However, to conclude that advertising *causes* sales would not be justified in this case.

This example indicates the critical importance of developing a strong logical or theoretical relationship between the criterion and predictor variables before the analysis is conducted. Even with a strong theoretical base, the results can, at most, be treated only as *evidence* of causation.

Discriminant Analysis

Multiple regression allows us to use an intervally scaled criterion variable such as sales, market share, relative price, or attitude. Often the criterion variable that we are interested in is nominal, that is, purchaser – nonpurchaser, heavy user – light user – nonuser, foreign – domestic car purchaser, credit card – cash purchase, and so forth. Regression analysis is inappropriate in such situations. Instead, *discriminant analysis* should be used.

The objective of discriminant analysis is to classify persons or objects into two or more categories, using a set of intervally scaled predictor variables.[2] Examples of the use of discriminant analysis in marketing include classification of buyers versus nonbuyers of generic brand grocery products,[3] classification of credit applicants into 'good' versus 'bad' risks,[4] the "early" versus "late" timing of market research in new industrial product situations,[5] an analysis of supermarket buyer decisions,[6] a determination of the characteristics of users of *Crest* toothpaste following its endorsement by the American Dental Association,[7] the selection of store sites,[8] and an analysis of the factors that differentiate high-status gift purchases from low-status purchases.[9] As described in Chapter 12, discriminant analysis is also used to generate perceptual maps.

The mathematical logic of discriminant analysis is similar to regression analysis and is not developed here.[10]

When a discriminant analysis is run, the goal is to develop a model that will result in a large proportion of the cases being correctly classified. The discriminant equation can then be used to predict to which class a new case will belong, or, more importantly, to demonstrate which variables are most important in distinguishing between the classes. For example, a discriminant analysis of attitudes toward a department store found that the perceived price level of the store was the major discriminating factor between shoppers and nonshoppers. This alerted management to a need to increase its price-oriented advertising.

Discriminant analysis is generally conducted by a computer. Part of the output is a set of $n - 1$ formulas where n is the number of categories. Thus, a heavy user – light user – nonuser criterion variable set would produce two discriminant functions (formulas). For the two category case, some programs will produce two functions whereas others will produce only one. The programs will also indicate the statistical significance of the function(s). If a desired level of significance is not reached, the formulas are not used.

Suppose we run a discriminant analysis of a two-category case and obtain the following function:

$$Y = -.07X_1 + .03X_2 + .17X_3$$

where Y = user/nonuser cable TV
X_1 = years schooling completed
X_2 = family size
X_3 = years in residence

The following steps are required to use the formula:

1. The means of the predictor variables of the user group are used in the formula to produce a value for Y for users.
2. The means of the predictor variables of the nonuser group are used in the formula to produce a value for Y for nonusers.
3. The midpoint between these two Y values serves as the critical value.
4. The values of an individual case are used in the formula to produce a Y value. The individual is assigned (predicted to belong) to the group whose average value his or her value is nearest. The critical value is simply the dividing point between the two values.

Most computer programs supply the critical value(s). The same general logic applies in multicategory situations.

The accuracy of the discriminant analysis is tested by a *classification matrix* (also called a *confusion matrix*). This is a table that shows the number (and percentages) of correct and incorrect classifications based on the discriminators used. An example is a study of the determinants of car pooling versus solo driving.[11] The discriminators used were respondent attitudes toward car pooling. The classification matrix that resulted is shown in Figure 20–3.

The percentage of correct classifications is a measure of the accuracy of the discriminant functions. As shown in Figure 20–3, the car pooling attitude measurements used predicted correctly 70 per cent of those respondents who were car poolers and 77 per cent of those who were solo drivers.

The percentage of correct classifications is a measure of the accuracy of the functions. However, testing a model on the data used to develop it will produce a biased (upward) estimate of its accuracy. Therefore, it is desirable to keep a *holdout sample* when conducting a discriminant analysis. That is, as many cases as practical (up to 50 per cent) of the original sample are not used to develop the discriminant model. Instead, they are held out and used to develop the confusion matrix. This approach gives a more valid estimate of the accuracy of the discriminant function.

Discriminant analysis is a very useful analytical tool. However, the same cautions involved in using multiple regression apply to discriminant analysis.[12]

626

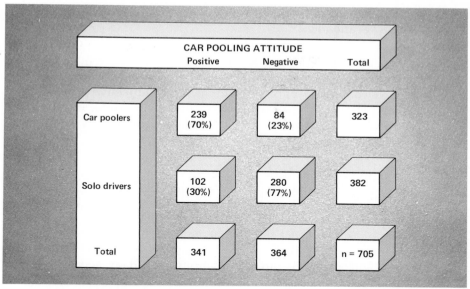

Figure 20–3   *Classification Matrix for Car-Pooling Study*

Factor Analysis

The objective of *factor analysis* is to summarize a large number of original variables into a small number of synthetic variables, called *factors*. Determining the factors that are inherent in a data array has a number of applications in marketing. These applications, and an example of each, are as follows:

1. **Development of perceptual maps.** As described in depth in Chapter 12, factor analysis is often used to determine the dimensions or broad criteria by which consumers evaluate brands or products and how each brand is seen on each dimension.

2. **Determining the underlying dimensions of the data.** A factor analysis of data on TV viewing indicates that there are seven different types of programs that are independent of the network offering them, as perceived by the viewers; (1) movies, (2) adult entertainment, (3) westerns, (4) family entertainment, (5) adventure plots, (6) unrealistic events, and (7) sin.[13]

3. **Identifying market segments and positioning products.** A factor analysis of data on desires sought on the last vacation taken by 1,750 respondents revealed six benefit segments for vacationers: those who vacation for the purpose of (1) visiting friends and relatives and not sightseeing, (2) visiting friends and relatives plus sightseeing, (3)

627

sightseeing, (4) outdoor vacationing, (5) resort vacationing, and (6) foreign vacationing.[14]

4. **Condensing and simplifying data.** In a study of consumer involvement across a number of product categories, 19 items were reduced to the 4 factors of (1) perceived product importance/perceived importance of negative consequences of a mispurchase, (2) subjective probability of a mispurchase, (3) the pleasure associated with owning and using the product, and (4) the value of the product as a cue to the type of person who owns it.[15] Each of these factors are independent (no multicollinearity).

5. **Testing hypotheses about the structure of a data set.** *Confirmatory factor analysis* can be used to test whether the variables in a data set come from a specified number of factors. Tests of significance are built in for the number of underlying factors present in the data. An example of an application of confirmatory factor analysis in marketing research is its use in determining whether or not there are four factors that account for aggregate audience exposure to a daily newspaper, and that those factors represent the public affairs, sports, business, and women's sections of the newspaper. (The findings of the study suggest that this is the case.)[16]

Unlike the techniques described previously, factor analysis does not use criterion and predictor variables. Instead, it attempts to determine the relationships among a set of variables. The mathematics of factor analysis are beyond the scope of this text.[17] However, the analysis is conducted on the correlation matrix that shows the correlation (r) between all pairs of variables in the original data set. Since correlation analysis requires interval (or near interval) data, so does factor analysis.

Factor analysis can best be explained by considering an example. A sample of 100 consumers rated a Safeway store on 24 seven-point semantic differential scales. While management would be interested in average score (or distribution of scores) on each of the 24 items, a number of other questions might also arise.

Do consumers think of Safeway in terms of all 24 of these items or do they use a smaller set?

If we want to conduct a large scale telephone survey, do we need to ask about all 24 items or can we use a smaller set?

We need to use these results in a discriminant analysis to understand what differentiates a Safeway shopper from a nonshopper. What do we do about multicollinearity?

Figure 20–4 presents the factor loadings associated with a factor analysis of the Safeway store data just described.

Three factors emerged from the analysis, which suggests that this group of consumers does not use 24 distinct attributes when evaluating this store. Instead, the consumers mentally group these attributes into three distinct characteristics or factors.

A *factor* is identified by those items that have a relatively high factor loading on that factor and a relatively low loading on the other factors. This means that they tend to vary (be associated) with other items that load high on that factor but not with items that load high on other factors. Factor I in Figure 20–4 is defined by the variables well-spaced merchandise, bright store, well-organized layout, pleasant store to shop in, attractive store, neat, spacious shopping, clean, and good displays. Thus, it could be labeled a *store atmosphere* factor. Factors II and III could be labeled *store personnel* and *value* factors, respectively.

Several useful implications are associated with Figure 20–4. First, it pro-

	Factors		
	I	II	III
1. Well-Spaced Merchandise	.68	.10	.21
2. Bright Store	.55	.14	.18
3. Ads Frequently Seen by You	.08	.14	.28
4. High-Quality Products	.25	.04	.55
5. Well-Organized Layout	.45	.14	.05
6. Low Prices	.03	.22	.17
7. Good Sales on Products	.10	.19	.59
8. Pleasant Store to Shop In	.54	.38	.22
9. Convenient Location	.04	.36	.45
10. Good Buys on Products	.14	.30	.78
11. Attractive Store	.71	.14	.11
12. Helpful Salespersons	.13	.65	.19
13. Good Service	.23	.79	.12
14. Friendly Personnel	.19	.85	.07
15. Easy-to-Return Purchases	.18	.49	.29
16. Big Selection of Products	.36	.35	.29
17. Reasonable Prices for Value	.05	.09	.62
18. Neat	.62	.20	.12
19. Spacious Shopping	.75	.04	.03
20. Clean	.58	.27	.15
21. Fast Check-Out	.42	.15	.37
22. Good Displays	.60	.16	.33
23. Easy-to-Find Items You Want	.14	.01	.22
24. Good Specials	.24	.13	.75
Eigen Value	12.35	4.60	1.95
Explained Variance	51.4%	19.2%	8.1%

Figure 20–4 *Factor Loadings from an Image Study of Safeway*

vides a better understanding of how consumers perceive or think about grocery stores. This can assist management in developing marketing strategies. Note, however, that the validity of this understanding depends in part on the completeness of the 24 items used to generate the factor structure. For example, had management omitted items 4, 7, 10, 17, and 24 from the semantic differential, the *value* dimension would have not been reflected in the results.

Second, it suggests that a much simpler measuring scale can be used in future attitude measures. Since the nine items that loaded high on Factor I appear to be measuring the same underlying characteristic, future scales could use three or four of these items rather than all nine.

Finally, factor scores can be created for each individual and used in further analyses. While the computation of factor scores is somewhat involved, most computer programs provide a factor score for each individual for each factor. In our example, each individual would have 3 factor scores rather than 24 item scores. Since factor scores are constructed in a manner that ensures independence, discriminant analysis could be run using each individual's three derived factor scores as the predictor variables.

Issues in Using Factor Analysis

A number of decisions and issues must be considered when a researcher uses factor analysis.

1. *Initial variable set.* As mentioned earlier, factor solutions are critically dependent on the initial data set that is analyzed. Failure to include variables associated with a key dimension will result in that dimension being omitted from the solution.

2. *Number of factors to use.* Principle components factor analysis is a widely used type of factor analysis. It produces up to one factor for each variable in descending order of the amount of variance explained by the factor. Thus, our earlier example could have resulted in 24 factors—hardly a simplification of the data. However, since factors are calculated such that the first factor explains the most variance in the data, the second factor the second most variance, and so forth, a variety of approaches exist to limit the final number of factors.

   Where practical, theory should be used to specify the number and nature of the factors. The results are then used to test or confirm the theory (confirmatory factor analysis).

   Unaided judgment is sometimes used. This generally involves the researcher stopping at the first factor that is difficult to interpret. Obviously, this approach is subject to potential biases.

   The most common approach is to use a rule of thumb referred to as the *eigenvalue-greater-than-one* rule. Eigenvalues are a measure of the variance explained such that

$$\begin{array}{l}\text{Per cent variation in} \\ \text{original variables} \\ \text{accounted for by the} \\ j\text{th factor}\end{array} = \frac{\text{Eigenvalue}_j}{\text{Number of variables}} \qquad (20-9)$$

All computer programs provide either the eigenvalue, the variance explained, or both.

Another rule of thumb requires that enough factors be retained to explain a "satisfactory" per cent of the total variance. Unfortunately, "satisfactory" is difficult to specify. A final, commonly used approach is to require that each additional factor explain a substantial or meaningful amount of the residual variance. Note that each guideline can result in a different number of factors.

The three factors included in our example in Figure 20–4 all have eigenvalues above 1.0 and together explain almost 79 per cent of the variance in the data.

3. *If and how to rotate.* Rotation involves moving the components or axes to improve the "cleanness" or fit of the solution. This will *not* change the total variance explained by the retained factors but may shift the relative percentage explained by each factor.

A number of rotation schemes exist. Choosing and using them wisely requires considerable expertise. Most computer programs will either automatically or on request provide what is called a *varimax rotation.* The loadings produced by this procedure are the best ones to use in the absence of a specific reason to use another approach.[18]

4. *Naming the factors.* We described this process earlier. However, it is a subjective process and you should always examine the variables that load highly on a factor rather than relying on a name provided by someone else. For example, we chose to call Factor III in Figure 20–4 *value.* Another researcher might call it *price* or *sale oriented.* Yet these terms have different connotations.

Cluster Analysis

The purpose of *cluster analysis* is to separate objects into groups such that the groups are relatively homogeneous. There is an important and obvious application in marketing for such a technique — its use for market segmentation. More than one-half of the published applications in marketing since the late 1960s have been for this purpose,[19] Other applications include its use for test market selection and to establish groupings of products within a product line.[20]

Several different algorithms are available for conducting cluster analyses. Depending upon the choice of method, the data used may be nominal, ordinal, interval, or ratio in nature.[21] There are likewise several different methods of testing the clustered results.[22]

Review Questions

20.1. What is a *criterion variable?*

20.2. What is meant by the *nature* of association?

20.3. What is meant by the *strength* of association?

20.4. What is a *scatter diagram?* Why is it useful?

20.5. What is *regression analysis?*

20.6. What is the *coefficient of determination?*

20.7. What does an r^2 of 1.0 mean? .5? 0?

20.8. What technique is used to measure bivariate association in ordinal data?

20.9. What technique is used to measure bivariate association in interval data?

20.10. What technique is used to measure bivariate association in nominal data?

20.11. What purposes does *multiple regression* serve? How is it used in marketing research?

20.12. How is the strength of multiple regression measures of association determined?

20.13. What is a *dummy variable?*

20.14. What is meant by *multicollinearity?* When is it a problem?

20.15. What problems can arise in interpreting the coefficients in a multiple regression equation?

20.16. Discuss the relationship of causation to multiple regression analysis.

20.17. What is *discriminant analysis?* How is it used in marketing?

20.18. What is *factor analysis?*

20.19. How is factor analysis used in marketing?

20.20. What are the major decisions involved in using factor analysis?

20.21. What is *confirmatory factor analysis?* Describe a marketing application.

20.22. What is *cluster analysis?* For what purposes is it used in marketing?

Discussion Questions/Problems

20.23. Provide a verbal description of the meaning of each of the following regression analysis outputs.
a. $\hat{Y} = 400 + 900X_1$
b. $\hat{Y} = 3,300,000 + .043X_2$

    c. $\hat{Y} = 432{,}000 - 12{,}615X_3$
    d. $\hat{Y} = 550{,}000 + .029X_4$
        where $\hat{Y}$ = predicted annual sales
            X_1 = number of outlets
            X_2 = annual advertising expenditure
            X_3 = number of competitors within one mile
            X_4 = average per capita income in the region

20.24. For each of the formulas in 20.23 prepare an explanation to management for the following r^2 values:
    a. $r^2 = .74$
    b. $r^2 = .62$
    c. $r^2 = .23$

20.25. What is the association between taste reaction and purchase probability for _____. (Assume interval data using the same group definitions given on page 594.)
    a. Group 2
    b. Group 3
    c. Group 4
    d. Group 5
    e. Group 6

20.26. Repeat 20.25 but assume ordinal data.

20.27. What is the association between gender and having a taste reaction of ≤ 50, $51-60$ or >60 (see Table $17-2$)?

20.28. Describe a management problem for which each of the following techniques might be useful. Describe the nature of the data required and how you would obtain it.
    a. multiple-regression analysis
    b. discriminant analysis
    c. factor analysis
    d. cluster analysis

20.29. Describe the managerial implications of the following multiple-regression formula when $r^2 = $ _____.
    a.   .78   b.   .48   c.   .23

$$Y = 908 + 4.96X_1 + 1.5X_2 - 11.2X_3$$

where Y = annual sales in thousands
          X_1 = hourly auto traffic during working hours
          X_2 = average household income in thousands within a 2.5-mile radius
          X_3 = number of competitors within a 15-minute drive

20.30. Given the following data, what would you estimate the annual sales to be for an outlet of 1,800 square feet, with a traffic flow of 3,000 people per hour, in a shopping center with 400,000 square feet, in a trade area with an average income of $20,000, with customers with an average income of $22,000, and with a competitor in the center? How much confidence would you have in your prediction?

Outlet	Annual Sales (000)	Foot Traffic Per Hour (00)	Center Square Footage	Average Income Shoppers (000)	Outlet Square Footage	Income Trade Area (000)	Competitor in Center
1	$1,300	42	300,000	$10.0	900	$ 8.2	No
2	1,750	20	275,000	17.1	1,500	15.2	Yes
3	950	32	250,000	10.5	1,000	8.4	Yes
4	2,000	48	290,000	20.8	1,800	18.9	No
5	1,350	15	260,000	12.4	1,200	10.2	No
6	1,600	26	280,000	15.7	900	13.6	Yes
7	2,150	31	350,000	23.2	2,000	21.5	Yes
8	1,100	37	200,000	12.1	1,000	10.8	No
9	3,250	22	440,000	26.3	2,200	23.9	Yes
10	2,600	27	360,000	24.8	1,800	22.7	No
11	1,900	29	310,000	20.5	1,600	18.8	No
12	1,500	35	360,000	13.8	1,450	11.2	Yes
13	1,800	31	320,000	16.2	1,700	14.1	No
14	1,650	43	220,000	15.4	1,500	13.8	Yes
15	1,200	36	210,000	13.1	1,200	10.0	No
16	1,760	21	420,000	14.6	1,400	12.5	Yes
17	1,880	18	310,000	15.9	1,200	12.5	No
18	1,950	27	260,000	20.5	1,900	18.9	No
19	2,050	33	290,000	21.3	1,900	19.1	Yes
20	1,720	45	230,000	14.3	1,700	12.8	Yes
21	1,340	19	220,000	12.6	1,300	11.1	Yes
22	1,460	23	290,000	14.2	1,400	13.0	No
23	1,820	28	310,000	17.4	1,700	15.3	No
24	1,990	26	300,000	21.1	1,900	19.2	Yes
25	2,060	30	360,000	22.1	1,800	20.3	No

20.31. Suppose that instead of having sales data on each outlet, the outlets were simply classified by management as "successful" or "unsuccessful." Given the following classification, would you predict the outlet described in 20.30 to be successful or unsuccessful? How much confidence would you have in your answer?

1. U	6. U	11. S	16. U	21. U
2. U	7. S	12. U	17. S	22. U
3. S	8. U	13. S	18. S	23. S
4. U	9. S	14. U	19. S	24. S
5. U	10. S	15. S	20. U	25. S

20.32. Prepare a *classification matrix* for the 25 stores described in 20.30 and 20.31.

References

[1] If there are large numbers of long (many ties for the same rank) ties, a correction formula should be used. See S. Siegel, *Nonparametric Statistics* (New York: McGraw-Hill Book Co., 1956), pp. 206–210.

[2] W. R. Dillon, M. Goldstein, and L. G. Schiffman, "Appropriateness of Linear Discriminant and Multinomial Classification Analysis in Marketing Research," *Journal of Marketing Research* (February 1978), 103–112.

[3] M. R. McEnally and J. M. Hawes, "The Market for Generic Brand Grocery Products: A Review and Extension," *Journal of Marketing* (Winter 1984), 75–83.

[4] J. R. Nevin and G. A. Churchill, Jr., "The Equal Credit Opportunity Act: An Evaluation," *Journal of Marketing* (Spring 1979), 95–104.

[5] R. A. More, "Timing of Market Research in New Industrial Product Situations," *Journal of Marketing* (Fall 1984), 84–94.

[6] D. B. Montgomery, "New Product Distribution: An Analysis of Supermarket Buyer Decisions," *Journal of Marketing Research* (August 1975), 255–264.

[7] A. Shuchman and P. C. Riesz, "Correlates of Persuasibility: The Crest Case," *Journal of Marketing Research* (February 1975), 7–11.

[8] S. Sands, "Store Site Selection by Discriminant Analysis," *Journal of the Market Research Society* (1981), 40–51.

[9] D. M. Andrus, E. Silver, and D. E. Johnson, "Status Brand Management and Gift Purchase," *Journal of Consumer Marketing* (Winter 1986), 5–13.

[10] See P. E. Green, D. S. Tull and G. Albaum, *Research for Marketing Decisions* (Englewood Cliffs, N.J.: Prentice Hall, 1988), 508–28.

[11] J. N. Sheth and G. L. Frazier, "A Model of Strategy Mix Choice for Planned Social Change," *Journal of Marketing* (Winter 1982), 15–26.

[12] See S. C. Richardson, "Assessing the Performance of a Discriminant Analysis," *Journal of the Market Research Society* (1982), 65–67; and M. R. Crask and W. D. Perreault, Jr., "Validation of Discriminant Analysis in Marketing Research," *Journal of Marketing Research* (February 1977), 60–68.

[13] V. R. Rao, "Taxonomy of Television Programs Based on Viewing Behavior," *Journal of Marketing Research* (August 1975), 355–358.

[14] S. Young, L. Ott, and B. Feigin, "Some Practical Considerations in Market Segmentation," *Journal of Marketing Research* (August 1978), 405–412.

[15] G. Laurent and J. N. Kapferer, "Measuring Consumer Involvement Profiles," *Journal of Marketing Research* (February 1985), 41–53.

[16] V. J. Jones and F. H. Siller, "Factor Analysis of Media Exposure Data Using Prior Knowledge of the Medium," *Journal of Marketing Research* (February 1978), 137–144.

[17] For a definitive discussion of the various types of factor analytic techniques and the assumptions of each see P. E. Green, *Analyzing Multivariate Data* (New

York: Holt, Rinehart, and Winston, Inc., 1978), 341–386, 403–411. See also D. W. Stewart, "The Application and Misapplication of Factor Analysis in Marketing Research," *Journal of Marketing Research* (February, 1981), 51–63.

[18] D. R. Lehmann, *Market Research and Analysis* (Homewood, Ill.: Irwin, 1989), 610.

[19] See the listing of "recent" applications of cluster analysis in marketing in G. Punj and G. W. Stewart, "Cluster Analysis in Marketing Research: Review and Suggestions for Application," *Journal of Marketing Research* (May 1983), 137. A more recent application for this purpose is R. K. Srivastava, M. I. Alpert, and A. D. Shocker, "A Customer-Oriented Approach for Determining Market Structures," *Journal of Marketing* (Spring 1984), 32–45.

[20] See Punj and Stewart, op. cit. for citations.

[21] Fourteen different clustering packages/programs are described in Punj and Stewart.

[22] Punj and Stewart provide a summary of empirical comparisons of performance of the various clustering algorithms (Table 4, pp. 141–143). Several testing methods are given in T. D. Klastorin, "Assessing Cluster Analysis Results," *Journal of Marketing Research* (February 1983), 92–98.

CHAPTER 21

Sales Forecasting

Management at Texas Instruments has monitored the personal computer market since the first PC was introduced in the 1970s. By the late 1970s, both private and public forecasts of the size of this market during the 1980s began to appear. These forecasts shared one common feature — they indicated that sales of PCs during the 1980s would be modest. Managers at most companies made market entry and production decisions on these forecasts.

Then, between 1980 and 1982, sales exploded from 300,000 units worldwide to 1.5 million. Hundreds of forecasts were made of future sales. Below are the average forecast figures (in $ billions) from reputable industry sources and actual sales from 1982 to 1986:

Year	Forecast	Actual	Actual as % of Forecast
82	NA	$1.95	NA
83	7.6	4.50	59%
84	11.6	5.61	48%
85	14.1	5.00	35%
86	16.5	6.00	36%

Actual sales averaged only 45 per cent of forecast sales and some forecasts were 700 per cent above actual sales. As a result of the forecasts, many new firms, including Texas Instruments and IBM, entered the market and existing firms made dramatic capacity additions. Unfortunately, since actual sales were

637

less than half the forecast sales, firms lost hundreds of millions of dollars, many went bankrupt, and others such as Texas Instruments and IBM had to withdraw from all or part of the market.[1]

Forecasting is a necessary part of every decision. A purposive choice among alternative actions in a problem situation requires that an outcome for each action be predicted. We can no more avoid forecasting than we can avoid making decisions.

Forecasting sales of both present and potential products, an integral part of most marketing decisions, is usually the responsibility of the marketing research department. A study sponsored by the American Marketing Association shows that 51 per cent of the marketing research departments in responding companies do short-term forecasting and 49 per cent do long-term forecasting.[2]

To be useful, a forecast must *provide a specified level of accuracy over a specified future time period.* Both the required level of accuracy and the time period are functions of the decision at hand. The accuracy of the forecast and the time period of the forecast are *not* independent. In general, short-run forecasts are more accurate than long-run forecasts.

One special aspect of accuracy involves *turning points.*[3] A turning point occurs when there is a relatively abrupt change in the direction or rate of growth of the forecast variable. Consider the standard product life-cycle chart shown in Figure 21 – 1. Many forecasting techniques will do a reasonably good job of predicting sales between $A-B$, $C-D$, $E-F$, and $G-H$.[4] However, the

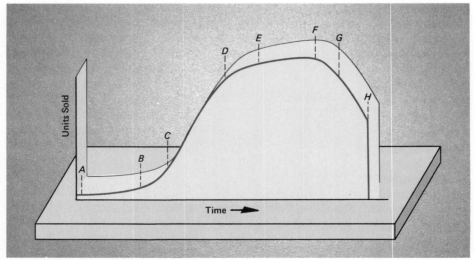

Figure 21 – 1   *The Product Life Cycle*

most critical marketing decisions generally involve predicting the turning points shown in the areas $B-C$, $D-E$, and $F-G$.

Aside from astrology and other forms of the occult, there are three major methods of forecasting: (1) *judgmental* methods, (2) *time series analysis and projection*, and (3) *causal methods*. Each of these general methods are described in this chapter as are the costs of incorrect forecasts and approaches to selecting a forecasting method.

Judgmental Methods of Forecasting

Some element of judgment is, of course, involved in all methods of forecasting. A method is classified as "judgmental," however, when the forecasting procedure used cannot be described well enough to allow more than one forecaster to use it and to arrive at substantially the same result. Three methods of making judgmental forecasts of sales are (1) *sales force composite,* (2) *expert consensus,* and (3) the *Delphi* method. A brief description of each method, its applications, the data and time required to use it, and an assessment of its accuracy and ability to identify turning points is provided in Table 21-1.

Sales Force Composite

One of the oldest methods of sales forecasting is to ask sales representatives to estimate their sales by product for the forecast period. The overall forecast is then arrived at by summing the individual forecasts.

This technique is widely used, especially by manufacturers of industrial products.[5] It has the virtues of being relatively accurate over the short term (the next one or two quarters); of being inexpensive to use; and, for industrial products forecasting, of providing a record on a customer-by-customer basis of the sales that the representative expects to make during the forecast period. These customer forecasts often are used for monitoring and evaluating performance during the forecast period, as well as for making the sales forecast itself.

There are problems in using this method, however. One of them is in motivating the sales force to do a conscientious job in forecasting customers' requirements, rather than to look on the entire procedure as being only more "paperwork" from the home office. Another problem is to adjust the estimates made for any consistent optimistic or pessimistic biases they may display. In addition to individual biases, at times the entire sales force may tend to over- or underpredict sales.[6] Undue optimism or pessimism is contagious; when it exists within a company, it is likely to be reflected in the estimates of a majority of the sales force, as well as others involved in forecasting company

Table 21-1   Judgmental Methods of Forecasting

	Sales Force Composite	*"Expert" Consensus*	*Delphi Method*
Description	Sales representatives are asked to make estimates of sales by product to each customer and potential customer for the forecast period. These are aggregated (after adjustment for any biases observed in past forecasts) to obtain an overall sales forecast by product.	A panel of "experts" (company executives, economists, and/or consultants) makes individual forecasts from which a consensus is reached through discussion. Social factors (dominance due to personality, rank, and the like) may play an important role in the weighting of individual forecasts in the consensus reached.	A panel of "experts" responds individually to questionnaires that ask for a forecast and a series of questions about the assumptions that underlie it. The responses are kept anonymous and provided to all forecasters. Successive questionnaires are sent out and responses exchanged until a working consensus is reached.
Accuracy			
Short term (0–6 months)	Good	Poor to good	Fair to very good
Medium term (6 months to 1 year)	Fair to good	Poor to good	Fair to very good
Long term (1 year or more)	Poor	Poor to fair	Fair to very good
Identification of turning points	Poor	Poor to fair	Fair to good
Typical applications	Next-quarter and annual sales forecast by product	Next-quarter, annual, and long-range sales forecasts of existing and new products; forecasts of margins	Annual and long range only; forecasts of existing and new products; forecasts of margins.
Data required	Data on past sales for the appropriate period for each customer of the sales representative are provided.	No data are provided other than (a) those requested by the individual forecasters as they prepare the initial forecast and (b) any additional data requested during the meeting(s) held to reach consensus.	A coordinator edits, consolidates, and distributes the responses to each round of questionnaires.
Time required	2–3 weeks	1–2 weeks	2–3 weeks

sales. In cases where the individual sales representative's estimates by customers are to be used for establishing sales quotas, there may be an understandable tendency for them to be deliberately conservative. An opposite bias may be introduced when a product is expected to be in short supply during the forecast period; the sales representatives may believe that their customers will get larger allocations if they forecast them as having greater requirements than they are actually expected to have.

Allowance for such biases must be made if they exist. This requires a continuing comparison of each representative's estimates with the actual sales made for each period and making appropriate adjustments.[7]

Although sales representatives are usually aware of, and sensitive to, any changes anticipated in purchase levels by their customers during the next few months, they are often unaware of broad economic movements or trends and their likely effects on the industries of the customers on which they call. For this reason, aggregating their individual forecasts produces overall forecasts of questionable accuracy beyond, say, the next two quarters. This technique is weak in identifying turning points, for the same reasons.

Expert Consensus

Expert consensus, often referred to as the *jury of expert opinion* method, is also widely used in forecasting.[8] An *expert* is anyone whom we judge has acquired special skill in or knowledge of a particular subject. Experts in sales forecasting include marketing researchers, executives of the company, consultants, trade association officials, trade journal editors, and, in some cases, officials in government agencies. The expertise of marketing researchers, company executives, and consultants can be used for forecasts of either company sales or industry sales, whereas that of the other categories of experts normally applies only to forecasts of industry sales.

Sales forecasts can be obtained from experts in one of three forms. In ascending order of the amount of information provided (and the difficulty of obtaining it), these are (1) *point* forecasts, (2) *interval* forecasts, and (3) *probability distribution* forecasts.

A *point forecast* of sales is a sales forecast of a specific amount. A forecast by an executive of the Winchester Bay Company, a builder of boats, might be that "sales will be $11,604,000 during the coming fiscal year." Point forecasts are the simplest forecasts to make because they give the least information. They are almost certain to be wrong but there is no indication of how much or with what probability. Although sales forecasts eventually must be stated as point estimates for production scheduling and inventory management purposes, information on the likely range and probability of errors is useful to help set the specific number. For this reason, it is desirable to obtain forecasts in either an interval or a probability distribution form.

An *interval sales* forecast is a forecast that sales will fall within a stated range with a given level of confidence. An example is the statement that "I am 80 per cent confident that Winchester Bay Company sales during the coming year will be between $11,000,000 and $12,200,000." An interval forecast is directly analogous to an interval estimate except that the probability attached to it is subjective in nature.

A *probability distribution* forecast is one in which probabilities are assigned to two or more possible sales intervals. An example is the following forecast for the Winchester Bay Company:

Sales of Winchester Bay Co.	Probability
$10,500,000 – $11,299,000	.25
$11,300,000 – $11,899,000	.50
$11,900,000 – $12,700,000	.25

Although the executive would no doubt concede that there is some chance of sales being less than $10,500,000 or more than $12,700,000, this likelihood is small enough to be ignored for planning purposes.

The intervals used represent low, medium, and high sales levels, also designated as *pessimistic, most probable,* and *optimistic* levels. Although the distribution can be broken down into as many intervals as desired, a distribution with three intervals is easier for executives to use than is one with four or more intervals.[9]

The procedures we have discussed thus far have been concerned with getting forecasts from a single executive. We now need to consider obtaining a joint forecast from several experts. One approach is to obtain individual forecasts from each "expert" and to combine them using some method of weighting. Four methods are possible:

1. Use equal weights (simple averaging) if degree of expertise is believed to be the same.

2. Use weights that are proportional to a subjective assessment of expertise.

3. Use weights that are proportional to a self-assessment of expertise.

4. Use weights that are proportional to the relative accuracy of past forecasts.[10]

The choice among these methods must rest with the judgment of the analyst in each specific situation. None are demonstrably superior for all situations.

An obvious alternative to combining differing forecasts into a joint forecast is to have the executives make a joint forecast initially. If this is done in a group meeting, however, level of rank and strength of personality become biasing factors in reaching a consensus. This is to be avoided if possible, because there is no evidence to suggest that ability to forecast is highly correlated with position held or ability to present one's views in a forceful manner.

The Delphi Method

A method of avoiding both the problems of weighting individual forecasts of experts and the biases introduced by rank and personality in the consensus method is provided by the *Delphi* method. The method consists of (1) *having the participants make separate forecasts* (point, interval, probability distribution, or some combination of the three), (2) *returning forecasts to the analyst, who combines them using one of the weighting systems described previously*, (3) *returning the combined forecast to the forecasters*, (4) *who make a new round of forecasts with this information*. This process is continued until it appears that further rounds will not result in an added degree of consensus.

The underlying premises on which the Delphi method is based are (1) *that successive estimates will tend to show less dispersion*, and (2) *that the median of the group response will tend to move toward the true answer*. Convergence of the group estimates is almost invariably observed. The critical issue is whether the movement is toward the true value.

The method has been applied in sales forecasting for short-, medium-, and long-range forecasts for existing products, for forecasting interest rates, and in forecasting demand for new products for introductory periods. American Hoist & Derrick used the Delphi technique for a five-year sales forecast, for example, and both Corning Glass and IBM have been reported as using it for forecasting demand for new products.[11]

The Delphi technique has also been used in technological forecasting, the outcomes of which are used in long-term sales forecasts. A comparison of final round forecasts with initial round individual forecasts for reported applications suggests that forecasting accuracy is improved by using the method.[12]

Forecasting by Time Series Analysis and Projection

A *time series* is a set of observations on a variable, such as sales, such that the observations are arranged in relation to time. Table 21-2 provides the time series for the consumption of malt beverages in the United States from 1980 through 1986. The sales data in this table are presented for both months and years. Quarterly, weekly, and occasionally daily sales figures are also subject to time series analysis.

Table 21–2 Shipments of Malt Beverages in the United States, by Months 1980–1986 (in barrels, 000 omitted)°

Month	1980	1981	1982	1983	1984	1985	1986
Jan	12,859	12,775	13,063	12,863	12,823	13,594	14,368
Feb.	12,517	12,346	12,956	12,894	13,162	12,900	13,057
Mar.	14,213	14,752	15,410	14,590	15,382	14,332	15,049
Apr.	14,658	15,911	16,225	16,058	15,302	16,528	16,468
May	16,246	17,374	16,722	16,967	17,062	17,889	17,603
June	16,944	17,424	17,625	17,736	17,700	16,731	17,509
July	17,474	17,962	16,869	17,625	18,218	17,711	17,857
Aug.	16,897	17,166	16,958	17,530	17,825	17,314	17,292
Sept.	15,127	15,477	15,357	15,850	14,761	14,511	15,270
Oct.	14,898	14,093	14,235	14,430	14,614	14,681	14,744
Nov.	13,073	13,607	13,809	13,462	13,259	13,073	13,738
Dec.	12,907	13,382	13,122	12,975	12,368	13,208	13,578
Total	177,813	182,269	182,351	182,980	182,476	182,472	186,533

° *Source:* United States Brewers Association, Inc., *Brewers Almanac,* 1988. Used with permission of the United States Brewers Association, Inc.

Forecasting using time series analysis is based on the assumption that *patterns observed in the changes in past periods' sales can be used to predict sales in future periods.*[13] A time series such as that shown in Table 21–2 is usually considered to be comprised of four separate types of movements or variations—*trend, cycle, seasonal,* and *random* variations.

Trend is the basic, long-term underlying pattern of growth, stability, or decline in the series. The plot of annual shipments of malt beverages for the period 1980 through 1986 shown in Figure 21–2 indicates that shipments increased slightly at the beginning and ending of the period but were otherwise stable. Thus, the overall trend was very slightly upward.

The level of sales of most companies shows considerably greater fluctuations over time than the annual data plotted in Figure 21–2. Sales rise and fall depending upon the general state of business, the level of demand for the products the company produces, the activities of competitors, and other factors. When a fluctuation is of more than a year's duration, it is said to be a *cyclical variation.* These variations usually do not occur on a regular basis and predicting their occurrence, or even isolating their past effects, is thus difficult.

Seasonal variations are regular, recurring fluctuations with a duration of one year or less. An examination of the monthly data in Figure 21–2 reveals that malt beverage shipments peak sharply during the summer months. Sales of children's shoes tend to increase markedly prior to the start of the school year and to have smaller peaks prior to Christmas and Easter. Periodic effects

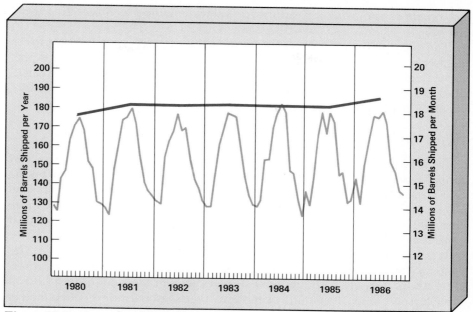

Figure 21-2   *Annual and Monthly Shipments of Malt Beverages in the United States, 1980–1986*

on retail sales are reflected in the sales for particular days of the week or week of the month; the custom of concentrating retail newspaper advertising in the Wednesday or Thursday editions and of holding end-of-the-month sales is based on these patterns.

The final group of forces affecting time series sales data is *random variation.* Random variation, sometimes called *residual variation* or *statistical noise,* is the effect of such unexplained (statistically) occurrences as unusual weather, strikes, and nonrecurring political events. It is that part of the time series data that cannot be explained as trend, cycle, or seasonal variation.

A number of forecasting methods are in use that consist of formal, explicit models for analyzing time series data and forecasting by projecting on the basis of an identified or assumed pattern. These methods vary in complexity from those that involve only some simple form of trend projection up through sophisticated, computerized models in which trend, cyclical, and seasonal variations are analyzed and projected.

Isolating Seasonal Fluctuations

Seasonal fluctuations are generally large enough to be taken into account in monthly and quarterly sales forecasts (the same general principles apply to daily and weekly forecasts). This is typically done by computing a *seasonal index number* and using it to adjust the values obtained by forecasting trend alone.

The many methods of computing seasonal indexes differ with respect to the number of past periods of data required, technical considerations with respect to the "centering" of the period for which the index number is to be calculated, whether trend and cyclical influences in the data are removed before the calculation is made, and other considerations.

Simple Average Method

In its simplest form, a seasonal index number for a period is the *value for that period divided by the average value for all periods for a year*. The resulting ratio is usually multiplied by 100, so that 100 represents an average value, an index number of less than 100 a lower than average value, and one of more than 100 a higher than average value. This approach is not appropriate if there is significant trend in the data.

It is unwise to use a simple average calculated on only one year's sales. The reason is that any month's sales may be unusually high or low due to weather, competitors' activities, the number of weekends in the month, or a host of other reasons. Thus, the monthly simple average seasonal indexes contained in Table 21-3 vary from year to year, sometimes significantly. When possible, an average of indexes from two or more years should be used.

In addition to random fluctuations from year to year, seasonal indexes for some product categories shift over time as the product becomes more or less appropriate as a gift, as new uses for the product evolve, as the product moves through its life cycle, and so forth. Thus, one should always examine the

Table 21-3   Simple Average Seasonal Indexes for Malt Beverage Shipments

Month	1980	1981	1982	1983	1984	1985	1986	$\bar{x}$
Jan.	86.8	84.1	86.0	84.4	84.3	89.4	92.4	86.8
Feb.	84.5	81.3	85.3	84.6	86.6	84.8	84.0	84.4
Mar.	95.9	97.1	101.4	95.7	101.2	94.3	96.8	97.5
Apr.	98.9	104.8	106.8	105.3	100.6	108.7	105.9	104.4
May	109.6	114.4	110.0	111.3	112.2	117.6	113.2	112.6
June	114.3	114.7	116.0	116.3	116.4	110.0	112.6	114.3
July	117.9	118.3	111.0	115.6	119.8	116.5	114.9	116.3
Aug.	114.0	113.0	111.6	115.0	117.2	113.9	111.2	113.7
Sept.	102.1	101.9	101.1	103.9	97.1	95.4	98.2	100.0
Oct.	100.5	92.8	93.7	94.6	96.1	96.5	94.9	95.6
Nov.	88.2	89.6	90.9	88.3	87.2	86.0	88.4	88.4
Dec.	87.1	88.1	86.4	85.1	81.3	86.9	87.3	86.0

underlying annual values if a multi-year average is used, to be certain that the average is not concealing a trend.

Centered Average Method

Another relatively simple method of calculating a seasonal index number is the *centered average* method. To illustrate its use, suppose that in early 1987 we had wanted to calculate a seasonal index number for malt beverage shipments for the month of June. Using the centered average method, we would have gone through the following steps:

1. *Decide how many years of data are to be included in the calculation.* Although an index number can be calculated using only one year's data, data for at least two years are necessary to determine seasonal variation with reasonable accuracy. If seasonal effects seem to fluctuate very much, a longer period may be required. We use two years in this example.

2. *Calculate a weighted average of monthly sales for the 13 months in which June 1986 is the middle month.* The use of 13 months of data allows the index to be "centered" on the month for which it is being calculated. In the example, the average is calculated using data for the months of December 1985 through December 1986. In order that December shipments are not overweighted in the average, a weight of "1" is assigned them, a weight of "2" is assigned the sales of the other 11 months, and the sum of the weighted shipment values is divided by 24.

In the example this weighted average is calculated as follows:

$$\frac{\begin{array}{c}(\text{Dec. 1985 shipments} \times 1)\\ + (\text{the sum of Jan. 1986 through Nov. 1986 shipments} \times 2)\\ + (\text{Dec. 1986 shipments} \times 1)\end{array}}{24}$$

$$= \frac{\begin{array}{c}(13{,}208 \times 1)\\ + ((14{,}368 + 13{,}057 + 15{,}049 + 16{,}468 + 17{,}603 + 17{,}509\\ + 17{,}857 + 17{,}292 + 15{,}270 + 14{,}744 + 13{,}738) \times 2) + (13{,}578 \times 1)\end{array}}{24}$$

$$= \frac{372{,}696}{24} = 15{,}529 \text{ thousand barrels.}$$

3. *Calculate an index number for June 1986 by dividing the weighted average monthly sales into the sales for June 1986 and multiply by 100.*

The resulting index number is

$$\frac{17{,}509}{15{,}529} \times 100 = 112.75$$

4. *Repeat steps 2 and 3 for the 13 months in which June 1985 is the middle month.*

The resulting index number is 110.28.

5. *Average the single year index numbers obtained in steps 3 and 4.* The average is

$$\frac{112.75 + 110.28}{2} = 111.52$$

This is the unadjusted seasonal index for June.[14]

6. *Add the unadjusted monthly index numbers for each month of the year and divide by 12. If the average obtained is not equal to 100.0, divide each unadjusted monthly index number by the average and multiply by 100 to obtain an adjusted monthly index number.* Analogous procedures are used for calculating seasonal index numbers for quarters, weeks, or days when using the centered average approach.

The average seasonal index for each month using this method for the data on malt beverage shipments from 1980 through 1986 is shown in Table 21 – 4.

Census X-11 Method

An advanced form of the centered average approach to calculating seasonal indexes is the Census X-11 technique. A computer program eliminates the trend and cycle component from the data utilizing complex centered averages. In addition, irregular or random fluctuations are removed by averaging

Table 21 – 4 Seasonal Indexes for Malt Beverage Shipments[*]

Month	Seasonal Index Computed by			
	Centered Average	Census X-11		Simple Average
Jan.	85.8[a]	85.2[b]	85.2[c]	86.8[a]
Feb.	84.3	85.2	85.3	84.4
Mar.	97.6	97.2	97.1	97.5
Apr.	105.2	107.4	107.5	104.4
May	113.0	112.7	112.9	112.6
June	114.1	114.6	114.5	114.3
July	116.2	117.0	117.1	116.3
Aug.	113.6	114.3	114.4	113.7
Sept.	102.3	97.5	97.3	100.0
Oct.	95.1	95.5	95.6	95.6
Nov.	87.7	87.1	87.0	88.4
Dec.	85.1	86.0	86.0	86.0

[*] Based on data from 1980 through 1986
[a] Average for 1980 through 1986
[b] Calculated for 1986
[c] Forecast for 1987

seasonal indexes over the time period covered by the data with controls for periods containing extreme fluctuations. Finally, the program provides a forecast of seasonal indexes for one year in advance. Such a forecast of seasonal indexes is provided for 1987 malt beverage shipments in Table 21-4. Note that the forecasts for 1987 differ only slightly from the calculated values for 1986, indicating a stable seasonal pattern.

As Table 21-4 indicates, all three methods produce similar results. However, this is due in part to the stable nature of this data set. It is generally worthwhile to try several techniques and then utilize the one which best fits the data.

Time Series Forecasting Models

In this section, we examine six formal approaches to making extrapolative forecasts from time series data. These approaches are (1) *naïve model forecasts.* (2) *moving average,* (3) *exponential smoothing,* (4) *statistical trend analysis,* (5) *the Box-Jenkins model,* and (6) *the X-11 model.* Summary comments on each of these methods are given in Table 21-5.

Naïve Model Forecasts

Naïve model forecasts are characterized by reliance on the last period's sales as a forecast of the next period's sales. The simplest possible model is "next period's sales will be the same as the present period's sales." This model provides accurate sales forecasts only to the extent that the trend in sales is "flat," rather than increasing or decreasing, and when random and cyclical effects are believed to be negligible. One can, and should, adjust for seasonal effects when they are known to be present.

As an example, suppose that at the beginning of December 1986 we had wanted to forecast shipments of malt beverages for that month using this simple naïve model. The forecast would have been made as follows:

1. *Determine the deseasonalized value for November 1986 shipments.*

$$Y_{Nov.\ desea.} = (Y_{Nov.}/\text{seasonal index for Nov.})100$$
$$= (13{,}738/87.1°)100 = 15{,}773 \text{ thou. bbls.}$$

2. *Seasonalize this value using the December seasonal index to obtain the forecast for December.*

$$\hat{Y}_{Dec.} = (Y_{NOV.\ desea.} \times \text{seasonal index for Dec.})/100$$
$$= (15{,}773 \times 86.0°)/100 = 13{,}565 \text{ thou. bbls.}$$

° index numbers determined by using the Census X-11 method.

Table 21-5 Forecasting by Use of Time Series Anaylsis and Projection

	"Naïve" Model	*Moving Average*	*Exponential Smoothing*	*Statistical Trend Analysis*	*Box-Jenkins*	*Census X-11*
Description	Forecasts are made using a deliberately naive model such as "next period sales will be the same as this period sales," or "next period sales will be the same as this period sales adjusted for the change from last period sales."	The forecast consists of an average of the sales for the last X periods, where X is chosen so that the effects of seasonal factors on sales are eliminated.	Similar to a moving average, except that the more recent period sales have a greater weight.	Uses regression analysis to determine the underlying pattern of growth, stability, or decline in the data.	A technique for selecting the optimal model in terms of "fit" to the time series.	Techniques for breaking a time series into seasonal cyclical, trend, and random components.
Accuracy Short term (0–6 months)	Poor to very good	Poor to very good	Fair to very good	Fair to very good	Fair to excellent	Fair to excellent

Medium term (6 mos–1 year)	Poor	Poor	Poor to good	Poor to good	Fair to good	Fair to good
Long term (1 year or more)	Very poor	Very poor	Very poor	Poor to fair	Poor to good	Poor to good
Prediction of turning points	Never forecasts turning points; incorporates them after they occur	Never forecasts turning points; incorporates them after they occur	Never forecasts turning points; incorporates them faster than moving average after they occur	Never forecasts turning points; late in incorporating them after they occur	Fair	Fair
Typical applications	A standard for judging accuracy of other techniques; short-term sales forecasts	Inventory control for standard items; short-term sales forecasts	Inventory control for standard items; short-term sales forecasts	Inventory control for standard items; short-term sales forecasts	Inventory control, forecasts of fund flows; short-term sales forecasts	Forecasting sales
Data required	Data for the preceding periods	A minimum of 8 quarters, or 25 months, if seasonals are present, otherwise less data	Same as for a moving average	Same as for a moving average	A minimum of 45 observations	12 quarters, or 36 months of data
Time required	1 day	1 day	1 day	1 day	1–2 days	1 day

Table 21-6 Forecasts of Annual Malt Beverage Shipments Using the Forecasting Model $Y_{t+1} = Y_t + (Y_t - Y_{t-1})$, 1982-1986 (000s of barrels)

	Actual Shipments	Forecast Shipments	Error (in %)
1980	177,813	—	—
1981	182,268	—	—
1982	182,351	186,723	02.4
1983	182,980	182,434	00.2
1984	182,476	183,609	00.6
1985	182,472	181,972	00.3
1986	186,533	182,468	02.2

As shown in Table 21 – 2, the actual value for shipments for December 1986 was 13,578 thousand barrels, and so the forecast would have been a remarkably accurate one.

A similar but somewhat more sophisticated model is, "next period's sales will be equal to last period's sales adjusted for the change from the sales for the period before that." One approach to the adjustment is to add or subtract the difference between the last two periods' sales to present sales, or $Y_{t+1} = Y_t + (Y_t - Y_{t-1})$. As long as the trend in sales consists of a relatively fixed amount of increase or decrease each period, and any cyclical and seasonal effects are negligible, this model will work well.

The forecasts that would have resulted from using this method of forecasting for malt beverage consumption for the years 1982 – 1986 are shown in Table 21 – 6. As is indicated by the low error percentages, this method would have provided very accurate annual forecasts for those five years.

However, as shown in Table 21 – 7, this approach would not have produced a very good forecast for the first six months of 1986. The reason for this is the relatively high shipments in January 1986. If one month deviates sharply from the normal pattern, its effects on forecast accuracy will be reflected in the deviate month *and* in the next two months' forecasts when this model is used.

Moving Average Forecasts

A moving average is an average of the values for the last X periods that is updated—"moved"—each period. As the value for the new period becomes available, it is added and the value for the $X + 1$ period back is dropped. For example, if the moving average is for 8 quarters, the value for the most recent quarter is added when it becomes available and the value for the 9th quarter back is dropped.

Moving averages are most commonly used for forecasting sales for short

Table 21–7 Forecasts of Monthly Malt Beverage Shipments for January–June, 1986*

Month	Actual Shipments (000 bbls.)	Adjusted Last Period Estimate[a]	Error (in %)	24-Month Moving Average[b]	Error (in %)	Exponential Smoothing,[c] α = 0.1	Error (in %)	Linear Regression[b]	Error (in %)	Box-Jenkins	Error (in %)
Jan.	14,368	13,811	−03.9	13,199	−08.1	13,159	−08.4	13,364	−07.0	14,170	−01.4
Feb.	13,057	14,989	14.8	12,889	−01.3	12,913	−01.1	13,001	−00.4	13,694	04.9
Mar.	15,049	14,017	−06.9	14,848	−01.3	14,933	−00.8	15,025	−00.2	14,953	−00.6
Apr.	16,468	16,088	−02.3	15,923	−03.3	16,002	−02.8	16,095	−02.3	16,196	−01.7
May	17,603	18,120	06.2	17,229	01.0	17,309	−01.7	17,366	01.8	17,165	00.6
June	17,509	17,704	01.1	17,514	00.0	17,600	00.5	17,636	00.7	16,341	−06.7
Average (absolute) per cent error			05.9		02.5		02.6		02.1		02.7

* The linear regression and Box-Jenkins forecasts are for 6 months in advance. The others are for 1 month.

[a] Using the naive model $\hat{Y}_{t+1} = Y_t + (Y_t - Y_{t-1})$ with deseasonalized data and then seasonally adjusting the forecast using the simple average method.

[b] Seasonally adjusted using index numbers arrived at by the simple average method.

[c] Calculated based on data deseasonalized by the simple average method and then seasonally adjusted in the same manner.

periods: a week, a month, or a quarter is the usual time period involved. A moving average is typically computed for 8 quarters, 24 months, or 104 weeks. In situations with little or no seasonal variations, moving averages can be used as computed as a forecast for the next period's sales. As such, the model involved is "sales for the next period will be equal to the average sales for the last X periods."

The usual situation is that the seasonal effects on sales are large enough so that the forecast should be adjusted by the appropriate seasonal index. The moving average value for shipments of malt beverages in the United States for the period December 1984 through November 1986 is 15,325 thousand barrels. The seasonally adjusted forecast of shipments for December 1986 is

$$\hat{Y}_{Dec.} = (15{,}325 \times 86.0)/100 = 13{,}180 \text{ thousand barrels.}$$

This forecast is fairly close to the actual shipment (13,578 thousand barrels) because there is limited trend in the data. Forecasts made using a two-year moving average will tend to be low, or high, by an amount equal to slightly more than one-half of any increases, or decreases, as a result of (linear) trend over the two years. For forecasts made using moving averages of a longer duration, the average error resulting from the effects of trend will be proportionately greater.

This is a forecast for only one month in advance. Longer-term forecasts tend to lose accuracy rapidly. In addition, the moving average never forecasts turning points; it only incorporates changes in sales in the average after they occur. The length of the lag before turning points are incorporated depends on the length of the data period; a moving average of quarterly data will have a longer lag than one of monthly data, for example.

The primary use of moving average forecasts (as for exponentially smoothed forecasts, the next method discussed) is in inventory control systems for standard items. A company producing and selling many items must develop systematic methods of forecasting inventory requirements, as the cost of non-systematic individual forecasts would be prohibitive. The Crane Company, for example, manufactures and sells thousands of valves, fittings, meters, pumps, and other items. To attempt to forecast sales of each product by any of the judgmental methods discussed earlier would be very cumbersome and costly. Computer programs are available for inventory control systems that provide both perpetual inventory data and an updated moving average (or exponentially smoothed) forecast at the desired intervals.

Exponential Smoothing

Exponential smoothing is a technique for obtaining a *weighted moving average* such that the more recent the observation, the heavier is the weight assigned. The logic of such a weighting pattern in sales forecasting is that the more recent periods' sales are more likely to be better predictors of next period's sales than are those for earlier periods.

In its simplest form, the exponential smoothing forecasting equation is

$$\hat{Y}_{t+1} = \alpha Y_t + (1 - \alpha)\overline{Y}_t$$

where $\hat{Y}_{t+1}$ = forecast sales for next period
α = the weight for the present period actual sales
Y_t = present period sales, and
$\overline{Y}_t$ = present period smoothed sales

The initial level of smoothed sales $(\overline{Y}_t)$ can be an average of sales for the last few periods. After the first exponentially smoothed forecast is made, the present period smoothed sales are then used for $\overline{Y}_t$. If the data show seasonal variation, they should be deseasonalized before being smoothed.

An important step in making an exponentially smoothed forecast is the selection of the α value. The usual method of selecting an α value is to try several different levels of α to "forecast" known values of recent periods in the time series. The α level that gives the best "forecast" of these values is then used for forecasting future period values. Since the computations are normally made by computer, the larger number of calculations required by this procedure is usually not a problem.

For the malt beverage shipment data, an α of .1 provided the most accurate forecasts for 1985. Therefore, this value was used for the 1986 forecasts shown in Table 21–7.

Because of the heavier weighting of the recent observations, the accuracy of exponentially smoothed forecasts is generally somewhat better than that for moving average forecasts. The forecasts obtained by exponential smoothing for malt beverage shipments for the period January through June of 1986, however, have a slightly lower average accuracy than those arrived at by the seasonally adjusted moving average method. As shown in Table 21–7, the average per cent of error for the exponentially smoothed ($\alpha = .1$) forecasts is 2.6 per cent and that for the 24-month moving average forecasts is 2.5 per cent. This equivalence is the result of the absence of an increasing or decreasing trend in the data for this time period.

The exponential smoothing model discussed here (and used for these forecasts) is the simplest of a series of forecasting methods using this general technique. *Double exponential smoothing, adaptive smoothing,*[15] and *Winter's extended exponential smoothing*[16] are examples of more complex smoothing models.

Statistical Trend Analysis

Statistical trend analysis involves a determination of the underlying trend or pattern of growth, stability, or decline in the series. A *regression analysis* is run using time as one variable and the variable to be forecast (sales in this case) as the other. For a simple linear regression (other regression models can be used) the equation obtained from the analysis is

$$\hat{Y}_{t+1} = a + b(t + 1)$$

where $\hat{Y}_{t+1}$ = a forecast of next period sales,
$\quad\quad a$ = a constant,
$\quad\quad b$ = the slope of the trend line (the amount of change per period), and
$\quad t + 1$ = the number of periods plus 1 of data in the time series used for deriving the value of the slope.

If the number of months used to develop the regression formula is a multiple of 12, it is not necessary to deseasonalize the data before developing the regression model. However, this is generally wise as a visual inspection of the plot of the deseasonalized data will indicate if a linear or curvilinear regression model should be used. If the data set is composed of other than several complete years' data (i.e., not a multiple of 12), it is essential to deseasonalize the data before developing the regression model. Otherwise, the seasonal variations in the partial year will distort the final formula.

The value forecast by the regression equation should be adjusted by the relevant seasonal index number to produce the final forecast. Table 21–7 contains seasonal adjusted forecasts of January through June 1986 using the monthly data from 1980 through 1985 to derive the regression formula. As can be seen, the linear regression model shown below also does a good job of forecasting the next six months of shipments.

$$\hat{Y} = 14,927 + 6.445t$$

Time Series Models That Deal with Cycles as Well as Trends and Seasonal Fluctuations

At the beginning of this chapter, we pointed out that the most critical marketing decisions generally involve forecasting turning points. An abrupt change in the rate of change or direction of sales of a product or company often signals the need for significant change in the level of price or advertising, the kind and extent of distribution, production and inventory levels, and/or the products offered.

The time series forecasting models discussed thus far are not capable of forecasting turning points. They can do a good, even excellent, job of forecasting sales when only a trend and/or a seasonal pattern is present in the data. When, however, cyclical changes are present—when turning points occur periodically—large errors can occur.

The X-11 method was referred to earlier as a means of obtaining seasonal indexes. This is a by-product (albeit an important one) of its use to decompose the time series into its components of trend, cycle, seasonal, and random elements. Once these elements are identified, extrapolations of them can be made and used as forecasts.[17]

The *Box-Jenkins method* involves a different approach to forecasting than any of the methods discussed thus far. Using it, the forecaster first identifies a tentative model of the nature of the past data and enters it, and the data, in the computer. The Box-Jenkins program then estimates the parameters of the model and conducts a diagnostic check to determine if the model is an adequate description of the data. If it is, the model is used to make the forecast; if it is not, the computer prints out diagnostic information that assists the forecaster in revising the model. This iterative process continues until a satisfactory model is obtained and the forecast is made.[18] Box-Jenkins was used to make forecasts for malt beverage shipments for each of the months from January through June of 1986. As shown in Table 21–7, its forecasts were similar to those of the other methods used.

A limitation on the use of the Box-Jenkins model is that it requires a minimum of 45 observations in the time series.

Selecting One or More Times Series Forecasting Models

The researcher using time series analysis as a sales forecasting technique must keep in mind that this approach is based on the assumption that *patterns observed in the past will continue in the future*. This often is not true for industry sales and frequently does not hold for individual firm sales. Thus, any time series forecast should be carefully evaluated in light of management's knowledge of changing future events. For example, a firm planning a major price decrease should not naïvely rely on forecasts based on sales at the old price. Formal, as well as informal, techniques are available for incorporating anticipated atypical events into time series forecasts.

Patterns in time series change over time. For that reason, *it is important that the forecaster examine a plot of the data before selecting a time series forecasting model* and *before deciding how far back to use the observations for making the forecast*.

A comparative evaluation of time series forecasting models, both against each other and against other types of models, is given in a later section of the chapter. An interesting finding that is reported there is that *combining* the forecasts from two or more time series models generally gives a better forecast than that from any individual model.

Causal Methods of Forecasting

A *causal* method of sales forecasting involves the development and use of a forecasting model in which changes in the level of sales are the result of changes in one or more variables other than time.

Causal methods of forecasting require the identification of causal (predictor) variables, measuring or estimating the change in them, and establishing the functional relationship between them and sales. A local utility supplying water to an Arizona community, for example, may have found that water usage is a function of the number of residential meters, income, the rate charges, and

Table 21–8 Causal Methods of Forecasting

	Regression Model	Econometric Model	Surveys of Buyer Intentions	Barometric Forecasting
Description	An equation relating sales to predictor variables (e.g., disposable income, relative price, level of promotion) is derived using multiple regression analysis	A system of interrelated regression equations used to forecast sales (or profits)	Surveys that measure buyer intentions for selected durable goods and industrial products	A time series whose movements precede those of the series to be predicted
Accuracy				
Short term (0–6 months)	Fair to very good	Fair to very good	Poor to good	Poor to good
Medium term (6 months–1 year)	Fair to very good	Fair to very good	Poor to good	Poor to good
Long term (1 year or more)	Poor to fair	Poor to good	Poor to fair	Poor to good
Identification of turning points	Fair to good	Poor to good	Poor to good	Tend to identify most turning points but also falsely signal turns
Typical applications	Forecasts of brand and product line sales	Forecasts of industry sales and economic changes	Forecasts of product line sales	Forecasts of changes in the economy
Data required	Sales and values of predictor variables by region over time. Need 20 or more observations	Similar to data required for regression model	Several periods of data are required to determine relationship of intentions to company sales	The indicators most widely used are published by U.S. government agencies
Time required	1 day once variables are identified and data available	1–2 months initially, 2–4 weeks thereafter	2–6 weeks	1 day

Source: Adapted from J. C. Chambers, S. K. Mullick, and D. D. Smith, "How to Choose the Right Forecasting Technique," *Harvard Business Review* (July–August 1971), 45–74.

the amount of rainfall. By forecasting any changes in the level of these variables, and knowing the functional relationship between them and residential usage of water, a forecast can be made.

The illustration just given involves a *causal regression model* in the forecast. Of the many other kinds of causal methods of forecasting, the most commonly used, in addition to regression models, include *leading indicators, survey of buyer intentions,* and *econometric models.* These methods are each discussed, and a brief description of them and their salient characteristics is given in Table 21–8.

Barometric Forecasting—Leading Indicators

A baby food manufacturer has found that the number of births in each state for the past three years, lagged by six months, is a good leading indicator of nonmilk baby food sales. The marketing research department of a manufacturer of industrial packaging materials has found that changes in the Federal Reserve Board *Index of Industrial Production* tend to lead changes in company sales by about three months. A plumbing specialty products manufacturer has determined that orders for its products typically come in about five months after the contract award, and so the monthly *F. W. Dodge Construction Statistics* based on contract awards provide a sound basis for forecasting plumbing product sales five months later.[19]

These are examples for which one would intuitively expect lead-lag relationships to exist between the indicator and company sales. The company that has products with such dependent relationships on variables whose changes precede changes in the firms's sales can make profitable use of leading indicators as a forecasting technique.

Most companies are not in this fortunate position, however. As a consequence, leading indicators have been used more widely in forecasting changes in overall business conditions than for directly forecasting sales for individual companies. The level of sales of most companies is at least partially dependent on general business conditions. In those cases, some forecast of the overall level of economic activity is necessary before a company sales forecast can be made.

The Department of Commerce collects and publishes data each month on forty different time series that tend to lead the overall economy. Among these leading indicators are series on the *average workweek in manufacturing, new business formation, new orders in durable goods industries, contracts and orders in plant and equipment, new building permits, industrial materials prices,* and *stock prices of 500 common stocks.*[20]

The use of individual leading indicators presents two interpretive problems to the forecaster. The first arises from *mixed* signals. The direction of movement signaled (that is, an indication that the economy is rising or falling) by each of a group of indicators is rarely the same for all indicators. In such a case it is difficult to know which direction to accept as the correct one. The second problem is one of *false* signals. Most leading indicators have a reasonably good record of predicting turning points that actually occur. The problem is that they also predict turning points that do *not* occur. (As the economist Paul Samuelson noted a few years ago, leading indicators "have forecast nine of the last five recessions.")

A *diffusion index* is one means of dealing with the mixed signals problem. The index number for a given group of indicators during a specified time period is the percentage of the indicators that have risen (shown an increase in economic activity) during the period. An index number of 100 indicates that all the series have risen, whereas one of 0 indicates that they have all fallen. Series that are unchanged are counted as one-half having risen and one-half having fallen.

The use of a diffusion index may help solve the false signal problem as well, depending on the series used and the skill of the analyst. A succession of low index numbers over a number of months in an expansionary period should precede a down-turn. A high index number in a recessionary period generally signals an upturn. Interpretation of the movements of the index is something similar to that for movements of a barometer; data on other variables and forecasting skills are required to predict accurately the nature of the coming (economic) weather.

Surveys of Buyer Intentions

One might reasonably conclude that a good way of forecasting sales is to ask customers to forecast their purchases. After all, customers know more about their prospective purchases than anyone else.

This reasoning has led many companies and a number of agencies to conduct periodic surveys of buyer intentions. A major steel company conducts a survey each quarter among companies in each of thirteen steel-using industries to determine their expected purchases during the next quarter and the next twelve months. Several surveys of planned business plant and equipment expenditures are conducted in the United States, including those taken by the Bureau of Economic Analysis, McGraw-Hill Publishing Company, The Conference Board, and *Fortune* magazine.[21]

These are all surveys of industrial products. Many private surveys of consumer durables are conducted as are a number that are publicly available. The General Electric Company has used a panel to obtain purchase intention information on appliances on a continuing basis. Published surveys are conducted regularly by the Survey Research Center, the University of Michigan, and others.[22]

Rather than to ask the respondent for either a "will buy" or "will not buy" answer, the usual procedure is to ask how *probable* it is that the item will be purchased during the indicated period. Either a 5-point or 11-point scale of the type used in product concept evaluations (examples are given on pp. 331–332) are commonly employed for this purpose.

The forecasting record of these surveys has been an uneven one. Although no data on private surveys are available, it appears safe to conclude that the forecasts of industrial products provided by such surveys have been substantially better than those of consumer products. The Bureau of Economic Analysis survey of new plant and equipment expenditures for 1981, for example, had an error of 3.4 per cent for manufacturing companies and 0.2 per cent for nonmanufacturing companies, both small errors.[23] However, the Bureau of the Census discontinued the Consumer Buying Expectations Survey in the early 1970s because a "large number of data users and subject analysts representing universities, private firms, nonprofit research organizations, and other government agencies" invited to review the results of the operation of the survey concluded the data it provided were "only marginally useful." [24]

One consulting firm uses a rule-of-thumb that only one third of those consumers who check the top two boxes on a five-point intent to purchase scale (*definitely will try* or *probably will try*) actually try the product being tested.

At the present stage of development, forecasts of consumer goods are best made by means other than the collection and use of buying intentions data. However, the forecasting of industrial goods using intentions data is a reasonable approach for at least some industries.

Causal Regression Models

A regression model is perhaps the most widely used causal model for forecasting sales. A causal regression model is an equation relating sales to predictor variables such as disposable income, price relative to competitive products, level of advertising, and others. The equation is derived using multiple regression analysis (see Chapter 20).

The steps involved in developing a regression model for forecasting are the following:

1. *Select the predictor variables that are believed to be the major determinants of sales.* These variables are selected on the basis of judgment. In order to be useful they should be variables that can either be measured (the number of color television sets now in use as a predictor of next period color television set sales, for example) or can be forecast more easily than can sales (price of own product relative to that of competitive products, for example).

2. *Collect time series and/or cross-sectional data for each predictor variable.* In general, 20 or more observations for each predictor variable are necessary for acceptable results.

661

Exhibit 21–1 *Forecasts Made Using Causal Regression Models*

American Can Company: Beer Can Sales

The American Can Company forecasts the demand for beer cans with a regression equation of the form

$$Y_{t+1} = a + b_1\hat{I}_{t+1} + b_2D_t + b_3A_t$$

where Y_{t+1} = forecast sales for the coming year

a = a constant derived from the regression analysis

$\hat{I}_{t+1}$ = estimated disposable income for the coming year

D_t = number of drinking establishments in the current year

A_t = age distribution of the current year

b_1, b_2, b_3 = the coefficients or weights derived from the regression analysis.[25]

Ski Area Sales in Northern New England and New York State

A study of the usage of 26 ski areas in northern New England and New York State indicates that the equation

$$Y_{i+1} = -1681 + .3095X_1 + 781.6X_2 - .0030X_1X_3 - 83.79X_2^2$$

where Y_{t+1} = forecast sales for the coming year

X_1 = average total advertising budget

X_2 = the average of the sum of driving time from Boston, Hartford, New York, and Albany

X_3 = average per cent of advertising budget spent on radio, television, and magazine advertising

provides a highly accurate forecast of use of each ski area.[26]

California Bakery: Sales of Hamburger Buns

Sales of hamburger buns for a California bakery were predicted accurately by the equation

$$Y_{t+1} = 1,028.7 + .0007T^3 + 172.4D$$

where Y_{t+1} = forecast sales of hamburger buns in packages

T = average weekly high temperature (degrees)

D = dummy variable: 1 if the first of the month falls on Monday, Thursday, or Friday; 0 otherwise.[27]

3. *Decide whether the relationship between each predictor variable and sales is likely to be linear or curvilinear.* Many demand functions are more nearly logarithmic than linear. When this is believed to be the case, the data should be converted to a logarithmic form.

4. *Run the regression analysis to obtain the coefficients and determine goodness of fit.*

5. *Repeat steps (1) through (4) until a satisfactory model is obtained.* A "satisfactory" model is one that forecasts historical sales data with an acceptable degree of accuracy.

Regression models are used for forecasts of both consumer and industrial products. Exhibit 21–1 provides several illustrations.

Econometric Models

The amount of water resistance a new design for a sailboat hull will have can be determined by two methods. The first is to build a scale model of the hull, provide instruments as needed, and test it in a boat tank. This method employs a model that is a physical analog of the hull. The second method is to simulate the hull with a series of mathematical equations and calculate the water resistance it will have. This method uses a model that is a mathematical analog of the hull. If the two methods are competently carried out, they will produce comparable results, and excellent predictions of the actual resistance of the hull when the boat is built.

Physical analogs of economic processes are rarely built. However, a conspicuous part of the economic literature in recent years has been devoted to the development and description of mathematical analogs, called *econometric models.*

An econometric model consists of a set of interrelated equations that jointly define the variable to be forecast and those of its predictor variables whose levels are determined within the economic unit being modeled. For example, a simplified econometric model for forecasting sales for a company might consist of the following six equations:

1. sales $= f$ (gross national product, price, marketing expenditures)
2. price $= f$ (marketing expenditures, production cost, prices of competitive products)
3. marketing expenditures $= f$ (advertising, personal selling, and distribution expenditures)
4. advertising expenditures $= f$ (sales, price, profitability, and levels of competitive advertising)
5. production costs $= f$ (production levels, inventory level)

6. profitability $= f$ (sales, production costs,
           marketing expenditures, administrative costs).[28]

Given the specification of the model, it is necessary to (1) determine the functional form of the equations, (2) determine the values of their parameters, and (3) solve the equations simultaneously in order to produce a forecast. Considerable statistical expertise is required for the first two of these steps; econometric forecasting is not a task for those who are uninitiated in the more complex methods of curve fitting and statistical estimation.

There is no evidence of the relative accuracy of econometric forecasting versus that of other methods at the individual firm level. There is substantial evidence, however, that the use of econometric models for sales forecasting has increased dramatically over the last few years. Many forecasting services are now available that provide econometric forecasts of sales for their clients, and many large companies, including Hunt-Wesson, Alcoa, and Corning Glass have econometric sales forecasting models of their own.

Error Costs and the Value of Forecasts

Errors in forecasts result in costs that are either *outlay* or *opportunity* in nature. In general, a forecast that is too high results in outlay costs and one that is too low results in opportunity costs.

Forecasts that are too high result in prospective new products being introduced when they should not be, and in excess inventories for existing products. The extra costs incurred as a result of sales being less than they were forecast to be are actual dollar and cents outlays that appear in the appropriate cost accounts in the income statement.

The new-product failures that occur as a result of overly optimistic forecasting are the most visible and dramatic evidences of forecast error. The Gourmet Foods line of General Foods, Hunt's Flavored Ketchups, and the IBM PC Jr. are examples of costly product misfires.

The costs of carrying excess inventory for a successful product as a result of a forecast that was too high are just as real, if not as apparent, as those incurred from product failures. For example, the overly optimistic forecasts of the PC market described at the beginning of this chapter cost PC manufacturers an estimated $2.5 billion in inventory losses in the mid 1980s.[29]

The costs incurred from lost opportunities as a result of overly conservative forecasts do not appear in the cost section of the income statement. The fact that current accounting practice does not permit these "costs" to be entered in a set of accounts does not make them any less real, however. A missed opportunity for a profitable new product, or the sales lost on existing products because of inventory outages, result in lower revenues and profits than would have been the case with more accurate forecasting.

Lost opportunities for new products are sometimes as dramatic, although seldom as well publicized, as product failures. Sperry-Rand developed and marketed the first commercial electronic computer, the *Univac I,* in the early 1950s. A point forecast of the potential market in the United States for computers of that size and capability (larger in size but smaller in capability and slower than today's minicomputers) was a total of 20! This forecast was made before IBM had placed its first computer on the market and undoubtedly contributed to Sperry-Rand's loss of position in the field. In an interesting twist of fate, IBM later turned down the rights to Xerox technology for the same reason.

Misforecasting markets can be as costly as misforecasting new product sales. Montgomery Ward did not expand the number of its retail stores at the end of World War II because its then chairman forecast that a recession would occur similar to the one following World War I. Sears, Roebuck, on the other hand, began a major program of expansion then. The recession did not occur. Forty years later, Montgomery Ward still has not overcome the lead attained by Sears, Roebuck as a result of the divergent postwar forecasts of the two companies.

The costs of forecasting errors are usually asymmetrical. That is, the cost of errors of high forecasts will usually not be the same as the cost of errors of low forecasts. This suggests that one will ordinarily want to make the forecast such that *the risk of incurring the higher cost error is less than that for the lower cost error.*

The Choice of Forecasting Model(s)

More than a dozen different forecasting methods have been presented in this chapter, and variations of most of them exist that have not been discussed. Because such a variety of methods exists, the question may legitimately be raised, "How does one go about selecting a forecasting method?"

In selecting a method in a specific forecasting situation, one should first compare the requirements of the forecast with the capabilities of the method. In general, forecast requirements consist of (1) *accuracy* specification, (2) *data* requirement, and (3) *time* availability. If accuracy to within ±5 per cent is required, methods that are judged to yield forecasts of no better than ±5 per cent accuracy (singly or in combination) need no longer be considered (unless, of course, no other method is expected to give better accuracy than that). If the *data* required by the method are not available (as, for example, time series data in forecasting sales of new products), then some other method must be found.

A similar situation exists with respect to *time;* if a method cannot reasonably be expected to produce a forecast within the time available, it logically cannot be considered further for use.

The application of these screening criteria will usually eliminate a sizeable number of potential forecasting methods. The choice among those remaining methods is essentially a cost/benefit type of decision when greater accuracy is weighted against added costs.

A review by Mahmoud of the findings of some 25 studies comparing the accuracy of different forecasting methods indicates that quantitative methods tend to outperform those based on judgment. In the same review, however, 8 studies showing that judgmental methods forecasts tend to outperform quantitative method forecasts, and another 5 studies indicating that there were no differences in the accuracies of judgmental and quantitative forecasts, were cited. The reviewer concludes that "On the whole, past research suggests that quantitative methods outperform qualitative (judgmental) methods." [30]

There is also some consensus on which quantitative methods are best. One empirical study (known as the *Makridakis competition,* or *M-competition*) of time series forecasting methods found that exponential smoothing (after seasonally adjusting the data) produced more accurate forecasts, on the average, for 111 times series than did 13 other time series techniques.[31] Box-Jenkins was one of the 13 techniques that were outperformed. In the comparison of accuracies of 5 time series methods of forecasting malt beverage shipments for January–June 1986 (Table 21–7), linear regression was first, the 24-month moving average was second and single exponential smoothing was third. The conclusions concerning exponential smoothing from a follow-up M-competition with 1,001 time series were more qualified, however. Single exponential smoothing with deseasonalized data still was found to be the best of 24 forecasting methods for monthly data for forecasts of one or two months ahead, and performed relatively well for forecasts up to six months ahead. It did not do well for longer periods, however, and especially so when there was a substantial trend in the data, since it does not take trend into account. It also did not do well for annual data.[32] Recent reviews have concluded that no one method is clearly superior to other methods.[33]

Rather than to use only a single forecasting method, however, there is a substantial amount of evidence that combining the results of two or more methods of forecasting into a single forecast usually outperforms any one of the constitutive forecasts. In the same review of forecasting accuracies referred to earlier, 21 studies of combined versus individual method forecasting accuracies are cited, and the combined forecast comes out the winner in 18 of them (in the other 3 studies the results of the combined forecasts were "acceptable.") [34] The theoretical basis for combining sales forecasts is that different methods provide different information on the potential market.

As Table 21–9 demonstrates, combining the forecasts of different

Table 21–9 Combined Forecasts of Monthly Malt Beverage Shipments for January–June, 1986

Month	Actual Shipments (000 bbls.)	Comb. A°	Error (in %)	Comb. B°°	Error (in %)	Comb. C°°°	Error (in %)	Comb. D°°°°	Error (in %)
Jan.	14,368	13,767	−04.2	13,262	−07.7	13,664	−04.9	13,541	−05.8
Feb.	13,057	13,348	02.2	12,957	−00.8	13,304	01.9	13,497	03.4
Mar.	15,049	14,989	−00.4	14,979	−00.5	14,943	−00.7	14,755	−02.0
Apr.	16,468	16,146	−02.0	16,049	−02.5	16,097	−02.2	16,061	−02.5
May	17,603	17,266	−01.9	17,338	−01.5	17,237	−02.0	17,438	−00.9
June	17,509	16,989	−03.0	17,618	00.6	16,971	−03.1	17,359	−00.9
Average (Absolute) Per Cent Error			02.3		02.3		02.5		02.6

° Simple average of linear regression and Box-Jenkins forecasts.
°° Simple average of exponential smoothing and linear regression forecasts.
°°° Simple average of exponential smoothing and Box-Jenkins forecasts.
°°°° Simple average of forecasts of the five methods shown in Table.

methods does not always improve accuracy. Four different combinations (using simple averages) of forecasts of beer shipments in each of the first six months of 1986 are given in the table. None of the combinations provides forecasts as accurate as the linear regression forecasts (see Table 21–7). In order to improve accuracy, the constituent forecasts used in the combination need to have compensating errors. In general, this did not occur in the beer shipment forecasts.

There are a number of ways of combining forecasts. They include *simple averaging, historical weighting* (each forecast is weighted by the ratio of its mean squared error to the total of the mean squared error for all forecasts), *subjective weightings,* and other, more technical methods.[35]

Evaluation of Forecasts

Forecasts should initially be made using as many methods as practical, including at least one naïve model. Not only should multiple methods be used, but multiple combinations of these should be used as well. After each forecast period, the forecast of each method and combination should be compared to actual sales. Further, reasons for discrepancies should be noted. For example, the seasonal effects may be overforecast due to mild weather, or the growth trend may have slowed. Over time, the firm will learn which approach is most accurate under which environmental conditions. Then the firm can continue to use a smaller subset of techniques that work well across the environmental conditions the firm faces.

Review Questions

21.1. What are the three major methods of *forecasting?*

21.2. What are three methods of making *judgmental forecasts?*

21.3. What problems arise in using *sales force composite* forecasts?

21.4. What is (i) a *point* forecast, (ii) an *interval* forecast, (iii) a *probability distribution* forecast?

21.5. What are the methods that can be used to obtain a joint forecast from several persons ("experts")?

21.6. What problems arise in forming a consensus of expert opinion?

21.7. What is the *Delphi* method?

21.8. What is the underlying assumption in forecasting by *time series analysis and projection?*

21.9. What are the components of a statistical time series?

21.10. What is a *seasonal index number?*

21.11. What are the methods that can be used to obtain *seasonal index numbers?*

21.12. What are the steps involved in the *centered average* method of calculating index numbers?

21.13. What are the steps involved in calculating index numbers using the *simple average* method?

21.14. Describe two *naïve models* for forecasting.

21.15. Describe the *moving average method* of forecasting.

21.16. The formula for the single stage *exponential smoothing* forecasting model is

$$\hat{Y}_{t+1} = \alpha Y_t + (1 - \alpha)\overline{Y}_t$$

Explain what each term on the right-hand side of this equation means and how the value for it is derived.

21.17. The formula for a *linear regression model* for forecasting is

$$\hat{Y}_{t+1} = \alpha + b(t + 1).$$

Explain what each term on the right-hand side of the equation means and how the value for it is derived.

21.18. Describe how, in general, the *Box-Jenkins* model for forecasting works.

21.19. What are *causal models* for forecasting?

21.20. What is required to make a forecast using a causal model?

21.21. What are four methods of making causal forecasts?

21.22. What is *barometric* forecasting?

21.23. What is a *diffusion index?*

21.24. Has the record of forecasting using *surveys of buying intentions* been a good, poor, or an uneven one? Explain.

21.25. What is a *causal regression* model?

21.26. What is an *econometric* model?

21.27. What are the considerations that should be used in selecting a forecasting model?

21.28. According to available evidence, which, on the average, produces the more accurate forecasts, judgmental methods or quantitative models?

21.29. What are the findings of empirical studies of the accuracies of time series analysis and projection models?

21.30. What are the findings of empirical studies concerning the gain or loss in accuracy from combining individual forecasts?

21.31. How should an evaluation of sales forecasts be made for a company?

Discussion Questions/Problems

21.32. Most of us probably find it hard to accept the empirical evidence that quantitative models, in general, outperform human judgment as forecasting methods. What do you perceive as being the characteristics of human judgment that cause it to provide inferior forecasts?

21.33. Few companies seem to make systematic periodic evaluations of their forecasts and forecasting methods. Why do you believe this is the case?

21.34. Very few persons seem to want to be the chief forecaster for a company. Yet, there are some reasons why this is often a good position for a person in marketing research. What do you see as the likely (a) advantages (b) disadvantages of such a position?

21.35. Between 1967, when Super Bowl I was played, and 1985, when Super Bowl X was played, the winning team was an accurate predictor of whether or not the stock market would go up that year in 17 of the 19 years. If a team from the "old" National Football League (the league before the merger with the American Football League) or a team from the National Football Conference in the "new" National Football League won, the stock market would go up in that year. If the NFL team lost, the market would go down in that year.

Suppose that both the probability of an NFL team (old or new) winning the Super Bowl and of the stock market going up is .5. The chance of 17 of 19 correct predictions occurring is then .0004.

Since there are only 4 chances in 10,000 that this would occur by chance, shouldn't the winner of the Super Bowl be treated seriously as a predictor of the direction of stock market prices for the coming year? Why or why not?

21.36. Explain why sales forecasts made by using a moving average of 104 weeks of sales data could be expected to be low or high by an average of 53.5 times the slope of the linear regression equation for the 104 weeks of data.

21.37. Calculate a sales forecast based on problem 20.30 (pages 633–634).

21.38. Complete Table 21–7 for the second half of 1986. What do you conclude concerning the merits of each technique relative to this data set?

21.39. The world record times for the mile run for the 124 years from 1864 through 1988 are as follows:

1864 — Charles Law, Britain, 4:56

1865 — Richard Webster, Britain, 4:36.5

1874 — Walter Slade, Britain, 4:26

1875 — Walter Slade, Britain, 4:24.5

1880 — Walter George, Britain, 4:23.2

1884 — Walter George, Britain, 4:18.4

1884 — Fred Bacon, Scotland, 4:18.2

1895 — Thomas Conneff, U.S., 4:15.6

1911 — John Paul Jones, U.S., 4:15.4

1913 — John Paul Jones, U.S., 4:14.6

1915 — Norman Taber, U.S., 4:12.6

1923 — Paavo Nurmi, Finland, 4:10.4

1931 — Jules Ladoumegue, France, 4:09.2

1933 — Jack Lovelock, New Zealand 4:07.6

1934 — Glenn Cunningham, U.S., 4:06.8

1937 — Sydney Wooderson, Britain, 4:06.4

1942 — Gunder Haegg, Sweden, 4:06.2

1942 — Arne Andersson, Sweden, 4:06.2

1942 — Gunder Haegg, Sweden, 4:04.6

1943 — Arne Andersson, Sweden, 4:02.6

1944 — Arne Andersson, Sweden, 4:01.6

1945 — Gunder Haegg, Sweden, 4:01.4

1954 — Roger Bannister, Britain, 3:59.4

1954 — John Landy, Australia, 3:58

1957 — Derek Ibbotson, Britain, 3:57.2

1958 — Herb Elliot, Australia, 3:54.5

1962 — Peter Snell, New Zealand, 3:54.4

1964 — Peter Snell, New Zealand, 3:54.1

1965 — Michel Jazy, France, 3:53.6

1966 — Jim Ryun, U.S., 3:51.3

1967 — Jim Ryun, U.S., 3:51.1

1975 — Filbert Bayi, Tanzania, 3:51

1975 — John Walker, New Zealand, 3:49.4

1979 — Sebastian Coe, Britain, 3:48.95

1980 — Steve Ovett, Britain, 3:48.8

1981 — Sebastian Coe, Britain, 3:48.53

1981 — Steve Ovett, Britain, 3:48.40

1981 — Sebastian Coe, Britain, 3:47.33

1985 — Said Audito, Morocco, 3:46.92

1985 — Steve Cram, Britain, 3:46.31

Using linear regression make a forecast of

a. what the world record time for the mile will be on December 30, 1999.

b. when the world record for the mile will be at or below 3:30.

c. Do you have any reservations about the accuracy of either of these forecasts? If so, what are they?

21.40. The costs of a 30-second commercial on the Super Bowl telecast for each of the 16 years from 1973 through 1989 are given below.

a. What is your point estimate (based on judgment) of the cost of a 30-second commercial for the 1989 Super Bowl? the 1992 Super Bowl?

b. What is your subjective interval estimate of the cost of the commercial in 1990 such that there is a 50 per cent probability that it will include the actual cost? the 1992 Super Bowl?

c. Based on extrapolation of the linear trend for the portion of the data that you choose, what is the estimate of the cost of a 30-second commercial for the 1990 Super Bowl? (Show your calculations) the 1991 Super Bowl? 1992? 1993?

d. If the answers in (a) and (c) differ, indicate which you believe to be the better forecast and explain why.

Super Bowl VII — 1973	$103,500	Super Bowl XVI — 1982	$345,000
Super Bowl VIII — 1974	107,000	Super Bowl XVII — 1983	400,000
Super Bowl IX — 1975	110,000	Super Bowl XVIII — 1984	450,000
Super Bowl X — 1976	125,000	Super Bowl XIX — 1985	500,000
Super Bowl XI — 1977	162,000	Super Bowl XX — 1986	550,000
Super Bowl XII — 1978	185,000	Super Bowl XXI — 1987	600,000
Super Bowl XIII — 1979	222,000	Super Bowl XXII — 1988	650,000
Super Bowl XIV — 1980	275,000	Super Bowl XXIII — 1989	675,000
Super Bowl XV — 1981	324,300		

21.41. Assume the following data represent factory shipments to retailers of compact disk players by one manufacturer.

a. Develop a set of seasonal indexes. Justify the method you use.

b. Forecast deseasonalized trend sales for 1989 using the following:

i. the naïve model $Y_{t+1} = Y_t$

ii. the naïve model $Y_{t+1} = Y_t + (Y_t - Y_{t-1})$

iii. the naïve model $Y_{t+1} = Y_{t-11} + (Y_{t-11} - Y_{t-13})$

iv. a 24-month moving average

v. exponential smoothing with $\alpha = 0.1$

vi. exponential smoothing with $\alpha = 0.2$

vii. exponential smoothing with an optimal α

viii. a linear statistical trend analysis

ix. a nonlinear statistical trend analysis

c. The actual sales for 1989 were 77,650; 87,100; 113,700; 86,500; 92,150; 125,050; 96,200; 106,500; 174,650; 144,050; 160,950; and 258,700. Which method was most accurate? Why?

    d. Given the nature of this product, would you have any concerns using the forecasting method selected in (c) for 1991? 1992? 1993? What would these concerns be and how would you deal with them?

	1983	1984	1985	1986	1987	1988
Jan.	2,750	4,600	8,050	16,000	22,300	43,250
Feb.	2,950	6,550	11,000	17,250	24,600	49,400
March	5,500	8,450	12,450	20,500	28,250	53,300
April	5,400	4,200	6,200	15,900	23,100	45,650
May	6,100	5,350	9,000	17,400	20,950	54,420
June	6,200	6,750	10,400	22,000	28,050	69,700
July	4,150	4,800	10,600	17,350	28,200	64,900
Aug.	4,500	7,250	11,250	19,850	27,800	49,800
Sept.	11,300	10,550	18,700	32,000	48,600	91,200
Oct.	11,500	12,200	19,300	28,550	40,150	79,750
Nov.	10,000	11,400	19,550	29,300	46,450	86,800
Dec.	10,550	12,550	25,600	37,700	66,300	120,350

Projects

20.42. Obtain the data from a local company necessary to make a sales forecast. Prepare forecasts using what you believe to be appropriate individual methods and combinations of the forecasts from them. Discuss the forecasts with the company management.

20.43. Consult the most recent issues of *Brewers Almanac* and update Tables 21–2, 21–7, and 21.9. What do you conclude concerning the merits of each technique relative to this data set?

References

[1] D. R. Wheeler and C. J. Shelley, "Toward More Realistic Forecasts for High-Technology Products," *Journal of Business and Industrial Marketing* (Summer 1987), 55–63.

[2] D. W. Twedt, *1983 Survey of Marketing Research* (Chicago: American Marketing Association, 1983), 41. See also D. J. Dalrymple, "Sales Forecasting Practices Results from a United States Survey," *International Journal of Forecasting* (#3, 1987), 379–91.

[3] J. L. King, "Predicting the Turning Points of Business and Economic Time Series," *Journal of Business* (April 1987), 201–38.

4. See E. Mahmoud, G. Rice, and N. Malhotra, "Emerging Issues in Sales Forecasting and Decision Support Systems," *Journal of the Academy of Marketing Science,* (Fall 1988), 47–61; and S. K. Mullick et al., "Life-Cycle Forecasting" in S. Makridakis and S. C. Wheelwright, *The Handbook of Forecasting* (New York: John Wiley, 1987).

5. Dalrymple, op. cit.; and D. Weinstein, "Forecasting for Industrial Products," in Makridakis and Wheelwright, op. cit.

6. A. D. Cox and J. D. Summers, "Heuristics and Biases in the Intuitive Projection of Retail Sales," *Journal of Marketing Research* (August 1987), 290–97.

7. See M. M. Moriarity, "Design Features of Forecasting Systems Involving Management Judgments," *Journal of Marketing Research* (November 1985), 353–364, for a discussion of how to detect, measure, and reduce bias in forecasts. See also A. J. Adams, "Procedures for Revising Management Judgments Forecasts," *Journal of the Academy of Marketing Science* (Fall 1986), 52–57.

8. Dalrymple, op. cit.

9. An examination of probabilistic forecasts is given in J. F. Yates and S. P. Curley, "Conditional Distribution Analyses of Probabilistic Forecasts," *Journal of Forecasting"* (1985), 61–73.

10. See S. Makridakis and R. L. Winkler, "Averages of Forecasts: Some Empirical Results," *Management Science,* (1983A), 987–996.

11. S. Basu and R. G. Schroeder, "Incorporating Judgments in Sales Forecasts: Applications of the Delphi Method at American Hoist and Derrick," *Interfaces* (May 1977), 18–23; and D. L. Hurwood, E. S. Grossman, and E. L. Bailey, *Sales Forecasting* (New York: The Conference Board, 1978), 13, 15. Other examples of use are given in R. D. Hisrich and M. P. Peters, *Marketing a New Product* (The Benjamin/Cummings Publishing Company, Inc., 1978), 206–207; K. Brockhoff, "Forecasting Quality and Information," *Journal of Forecasting,* (1984), 417–428; and F. J. Parente, J. K. Anderson, P. Myers, and T. O'Brien, "An Examination of Factors Contributing to Delphi Accuracy," *Journal of Forecasting,* (1984), 173–182.

12. See, for example, R. Best, "An Experiment in Delphi Estimation in Marketing Decision Making," *Journal of Marketing Research* (November, 1974), 448–452; Brockhoff, op. cit.; Parente, et al, op. cit.; and G. M. Estes and D. Kuespert, "Delphi in Industrial Forecasting," *Chemical and Engineering News,* August 23, 1976, 40–47; S. Basu and R. G. Schroeder, op. cit.; and Hurwood et al., op. cit.

13. M. D. Geurts, "The Impact of Misrepresentative Data Patterns on Sales Forecasting Accuracy," *Journal of the Academy of Marketing Science* (Fall 1988), 88–94.

14. The centered moving average index number for June given in Table 21–4 differs from the one just calculated. The reasons are that (i) more than two years of data were used in calculating the index number in Table 21–4 and (ii) the one just calculated is unadjusted.

15. Makridakis and Wheelwright, op. cit.

[16] For details see J. T. Mentzer, "Forecasting with Adaptive Extended Exponential Smoothing," *Journal of the Academy of Marketing Science* (Fall 1988), 62–70.

[17] See S. C. Wheelwright and S. Makridakis, *Forecasting Methods for Management*, 3d ed. (New York: John Wiley & Sons, Inc., 1980).

[18] G. E. P. Box and G. M. Jenkins, *Time Series Analysis, Forecasting and Control* (San Francisco: Holden-Day, Inc., 1970). See also Wheelwright and Makridakis, op. cit. (1980), 171–196, for a description of the method.

[19] R. R. Rosenberg, "Forecasting Derived Product Demand in Commercial Construction," *Industrial Marketing Management* (1982), 39–46.

[20] These series are published by the Social and Economics Statistics Administration, in *Business Conditions Digest* (U.S. Department of Commerce).

[21] Results from the Bureau of Economic Analysis are published in the *Survey of Current Business*. The McGraw-Hill survey results are published in *Business Week*. The Conference Board survey results are published in the *Survey of Current Business* and the Board's own publications. *Fortune* publishes its own survey results.

[22] The results of the Survey Research Center survey are published in the Center's own publications. A private survey done by the Albert Sindlinger Co. is published in the *Business Record*, a publication of The Conference Board.

[23] J. T. Woodward, "Plant and Equipment Expenditures: First and Second Quarters and Second Half of 1982," *Survey of Current Business* (March 1982), 26. See also R. Rippe, M. Wilkinson, and D. Morrison, "Industrial Market Forecasting with Anticipations Data," *Management Science* (February 1976), 639–650; and D. G. Morrison, "Purchase Intentions and Purchase Behavior," *Journal of Marketing* (Spring 1979), 65–74, for favorable assessments of anticipations data accuracy.

[24] "Consumer Buying Indicators," *Current Population Reports*, Series P-65, no. 46, (U.S. Department of Commerce, April 1973), 5. See also J. McNeil, "Federal Programs to Measure Consumer Purchase Expectations, 1946–73: A Post-Mortem," and F. G. Adams and F. T. Juster, "Commentaries on McNeil," *Journal of Consumer Research* (December 1974), 1–15.

[25] G. E. S. Parker and E. C. Segura, "How to Get a Better Forecast," *Harvard Business Review* (March–April 1971), p. 101.

[26] The r^2 for the equation for a two-year period was .89. H. E. Echelberger and E. L. Shofer, Jr., "Snow + (X) = Use of Ski Slopes," *Journal of Marketing Research* (August 1970), 388–392.

[27] G. Albaum, R. Best, and D. I. Hawkins, "The Marketing of Hamburger Buns: An Improved Model for Prediction," *Journal of the Academy of Marketing Science* (Summer 1975), 223–231. See also R. D. Carlson, "The Marketing of Hamburger Buns," *Journal of the Academy of Marketing Science* (Spring 1974), 309–315.

[28] Adapted from a similar conceptual model presented in Wheelwright and Makridakis, op. cit., 205.

[29] J. Sculley, *Odyssey* (New York: Harper & Row, 1987), 270.

[30] E. Mahmoud, "Accuracy in Forecasting: A Survey," *Journal of Forecasting* (1984), 141.

[31] S. Makridakis and M. Hibon, "Accuracy of Forecasting: An Empirical Investigation," *Journal of the Royal Statistical Society* Series A (February, 1979), 97–145.

[32] S. Makridakis et al, "The Accuracy of Extrapolation (Time series) Methods: Results of a Forecasting Competition," *Journal of Forecasting* (1982), 111–153.

[33] S. Makridakis, "The Future of Forecasting," in Makridakis and Wheelwright, op. cit.; and Mahmoud, Rice, & Malhotra, op. cit.

[34] Mahmoud, op. cit., 150–152.

[35] For methods of weighting see R. L. Winkler and S. Makridakis "The Combination of Forecasts," *Journal of the Royal Statistical Society* Series A, 1984; B. E. Flores and E. M. White, "A Framework for the Combination of Forecasts," *Journal of the Academy of Marketing Science* (Fall 1988), 95–103; and R. J. Thomas, "Forecasting New Product Market Potential," *Journal of Product Innovation Management* (#4, 1987), 109–19.

CASE IV–1 WEYERHAEUSER VIII: SAMPLE DESIGN, SIZE, AND SELECTION

Review Cases I–2 and II–3. Weyerhaeuser was very interested in its image compared to that of Georgia-Pacific. The company's aim was to learn how sponsoring "This Old House" would influence its image over time. Therefore, Weyerhaeuser decided to conduct a benchmark study of DIYers' images of the two firms, prior to the beginning of the company's sponsorship of the program. Repeated annually, the study would track changes in consumers' perceptions of the firms.

Initially a national sample was considered, perhaps using an interval panel such as NFO's for a sample frame. The primary reason this option was not chosen was that most lumber companies are not well-known outside their areas of major operations but are very well-known within those areas. A national probability sample would generate respondents from throughout the United States. Determining which respondents were located in areas where a given lumber producer was particularly well-known would be difficult. Furthermore, subsequent surveys would have to match the geographic distribution of the initial survey, or another source of variance would be introduced.

A second reason for not using a national sample is the uneven availability of "This Old House." Since not all towns receive the series, calling into areas where it is not available would add to the cost of the survey.

Based on this logic, Boston, Chicago, Miami, and Phoenix were selected. All four are above-average DIY areas that also have above-average viewing patterns for "This Old House." Thus, they represent important markets and areas where contacting sufficient numbers of viewers would be practical. However, consultations with the interviewing firm resulted in the dropping of Miami as a site, due to the high cost of having to provide bilingual interviewers.

A sample size of 600 completed interviews, 200 per city, was chosen. Available funding was considered but was not a significant constraining factor. The basic logic was that within city comparisons between viewers and nonviewers broken down by at least one additional variable would be desirable. Thus, cell sizes would quickly become too small unless the obtained sample per city were at least 200. The following table indicates how this logic would work, given a 60/40 viewer/nonviewer split.

Since the primary emphasis was on the effect of sponsorship, a quota sample was used. Viewership of at least once a month was the quota variable and it was set at 60 per cent. All respondents were screened for DIY activity over the past 10 months. Those spending less than $200 on materials for home

| | Phoenix (200) | |
	(Viewer = 120)	(Nonviewer = 80)
Heavy DIYer (top 1/3 in expenditures)	40	27
Moderate DIYer (middle 1/3 in expenditures)	40	26
Light DIYer (bottom 1/3 in expenditures)	40	27

improvement were excluded from the survey (see questions 1 through 4 in the questionnaire in Case III – 1 for the screening and quota procedure).

1. Evaluate the sampling procedure used and suggest improvements as appropriate.
2. Develop an alternative sampling plan.

CASE IV – 2 WEYERHAEUSER IX: DATA ANALYSIS

The response rate for the survey was 83 per cent. That is, 17 per cent refused to answer even the screening questions. The impact of the screening questions is shown below.

| | % of Respondents Screened | | | |
	Total (8346)	Boston (2646)	Chicago (3265)	Phoenix (2435)
Household did no DIY projects in 1987	87.2%	87.5%	86.6%	87.8%
1987 DIY Household but spent less than $200	4.3	3.9	5.1	3.6
1987 DIY, $200+ Household, but overquota program nonviewer	1.3	1.1	2.2	0.4
Completed interview	7.2	7.6	6.1	8.3
	100.0%	100.0%	100.0%	100.0%

1. How would you deal with the nonresponse issue (note that there were only a few weeks available to conduct and analyze the survey)?
2. How would the fact that this is a quota sample affect your analysis?
3. Analyze the data to provide information that will help Weyerhaeuser's management deal with the issues raised in Case I–2. (The data from a random selection of 498 of the original 600 respondents are available in the data disk that accompanies the teachers' manual and in the **MARKSTAT** disc.

CASE IV – 3 BURGOYNE INFORMATION SERVICE'S SAMPLING PLAN FOR A MINI-MARKET CONTROLLED STORE TEST*

Burgoyne's sampling plan for selecting outlets for a mini-market controlled store test is described in the following paragraphs.

Audit Panel

The audit panel chosen for the test design can be either "trend" or "projectable." In the trend design, Burgoyne would audit a "representative" number of stores from the major factions in the market. Representation is typically determined by share of market. In the projectable design, Burgoyne would statistically determine the audit sample size needed to yield results at a prescribed confidence level with a set percentage of maximum safe error.

Test Market

To demonstrate the execution of the Mini-Market technique, we selected Omaha, Nebraska as an average Mini-Market city for testing. Our coverage area will include the following counties:

A. Douglas County (Nebraska)
B. Sarpy County (Nebraska)
C. Pottawattamie County (Iowa)

NOTE: Three basic alternatives exist in defining your geographical location for a Mini-Market:

* Used with permission from Burgoyne Information Services.

    A.   Metropolitan Area

    B.   SMSA

    C.   AOI (Area of Dominant Influence)

Sample Size

In order to project the sales data for the entire Omaha MSA, a projectable audit panel of forty-one (41) stores (29 Chain and 12 High Volume Independents) is necessary. This audit panel would yield results at the 90% confidence level with a maximum safe error of 10%.[*]

Furthermore, given a distribution target level for the test product at 70% of the universal all commodity volume (ACV), it will be necessary to obtain penetration in at least 66 stores within the coverage area.

Therefore, the remaining 25 stores (66 – 41) would comprise the "distribution only" panel.

Graphically, the 66 store test sample looks like this:

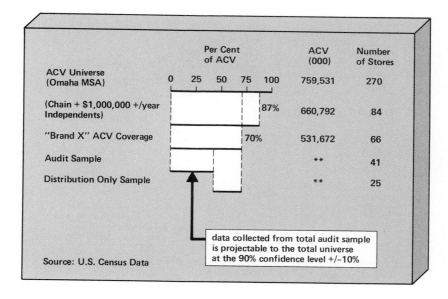

	Per Cent of ACV	ACV (000)	Number of Stores
ACV Universe (Omaha MSA)	0 25 50 75 100	759,531	270
(Chain + $1,000,000 +/year Independents)	87%	660,792	84
"Brand X" ACV Coverage	70%	531,672	66
Audit Sample		**	41
Distribution Only Sample		**	25

data collected from total audit sample is projectable to the total universe at the 90% confidence level +/–10%

Source: U.S. Census Data

[*] A "representative" trend audit panel would require approximately 20 audit stores. The results however would be nonprojectable.

[**] It is impossible to determine the per cent of ACV or the total ACV for the audit sample and/or the distribution only sample without actually knowing which particular outlets would comprise the panels. Once the panel was selected, ACV estimates for each individual store would be calculated.

Another approach is available. Distribute the test product in audit panel stores which account for the clients anticipated level of distribution once a rollout is enacted. Have the rest of the audit panel represent those outlets which will not buy the product. Let's assume the client expects to achieve a distribution level of 80 per cent. The total audit panel remains projectable to the entire universe. Graphically:

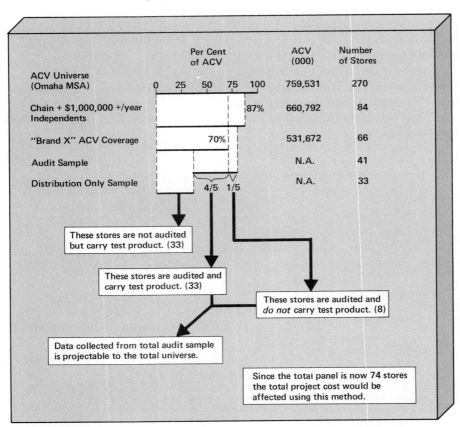

Store Panel

The store panel in Omaha would be comprised of chain and high-volume independents (ACV $1,000,000 + /year) grocery outlets within the three (3)-county MSA or universe.

Based on past experience we would anticipate cooperation on this project from the following accounts:

Name	# of Stores	% of Market ACV
Bakers	9	21.5
Hy-Vee	9	11.3
Albertsons	5	9.6
Food 4 Less	5	4.7
Randalls	1	4.6

plus voluntary/cooperative and independent outlets.

1. Evaluate this sampling plan.

IV-4 CLASSIC COKE, NEW COKE, PEPSI-COLA TASTE TEST

Can people really distinguish between new Coke and Classic Coke? Is there a clear preference in taste between new Coke and Pepsi-Cola? Is it mostly younger people who prefer the sweeter colas? Given a choice of a free can of cola, will people tend to take the brand that they have just chosen in a taste test?

To get at the answer to these and other questions, a taste test of Classic Coke, new Coke, and Pepsi-Cola was carried out. It was conducted at two of the entrances to a shopping mall using a quota sample of 78 persons. The samples of the three colas to be tasted were labeled "K," "L," and "M." The test was 'double blind' in nature in that neither the persons administering nor the persons taking it knew which cola was labeled with which letter.

Each subject was asked to make paired taste comparisons of the cola combinations K/L, K/M, and L/M. The combinations were administered in random order, as were the individual colas in each combination. The subject was asked to rinse out his or her mouth with water after each sample was tasted. After completing the third taste comparison, the subject was interviewed using the following questionnaire.

1. Compare the design of this taste test with that used by Coca-Cola USA (described on pp. 42–43). Which design do you think was better? Why?

2. Analyze the results of the test. What do you consider to be the findings that would be relevant to Coca-Cola USA management? To Pepsi-Cola management? Give the supporting analysis for each of these findings.

3. If Coca-Cola and/or Pepsi-Cola management were to take actions based solely on these findings, what should they do? Why?

Cola Questionnaire   Resp. No. _____

Please respond to the following questions as accurately as possible. Thank you for your cooperation and willingness to assist in our research project.

1. For each combination of soft drinks listed below, please indicate which one you prefer.
    a. Brand K or Brand L? _____
    b. Brand L or Brand M? _____
    c. Brand K or Brand M? _____

2. If a free can of cola were offered to you, which would you select?
    a. New Coke _____
    b. Classic Coke _____
    c. Pepsi _____
    d. Other _____
    e. None _____

3. Gender
    a. female _____
    b. male _____

4. What is the occupation of the head of your household? _____

5. What is the latest grade of school you have completed?
    a. grade school   _____
    b. high school, no diploma   _____
    c. graduated high school   _____
    d. some college, no degree   _____
    e. junior college certificate _____
    f. 4-year college degree   _____
    g. some graduate school   _____
    h. masters/doctoral degree   _____

6. What is your best estimate of the amount of cola you personally drink in one week?
    a. none   _____   e. 13–18 cans   _____
    b. 1–3 cans   _____   f. 19–24 cans   _____
    c. 4–6 cans   _____   g. 25–36 cans   _____
    d. 7–12 cans   _____   h. more than 36 cans _____

7. What is your household's yearly family income?
    a. under $10,000   _____
    b. $10,000 – $14,999   _____
    c. $15,000 – $24,999   _____
    d. $25,000 – $34,999   _____
    e. $35,000 – $49,999   _____
    f. $50,000 and above   _____

8. Age
    a. 14 – 19 _____   e. 45 – 54 _____
    b. 20 – 24 _____   f. 55 – 64 _____
    c. 25 – 34 _____   g. 65 and over _____
    d. 35 – 44 _____

9. Race
    a. white/caucasian _____   d. Hispanic _____
    b. black _____   e. Oriental _____
    c. Indian _____   f. Other, please specify _____

Cola Taste Test Data

Subject	Pepsi-Cola or Classic Coke	Classic Coke or New Coke	New Coke or Pepsi-Cola	Choice of Free Can	Gender	Head's Occupation	Education Level	Amount Cola/wk.	Income	Age	Race	Best Liked Cola	Least Liked Cola
1	1	3	1	1	1	3	5	2	4	3	1	1	2
2	1	3	1	2	1	5	1	1	2	6	1	1	2
3	2	2	3	4	1	2	4	2	3	6	1	2	1
4	2	3	3	2	2	4	4	4	2	3	1	3	1
5	2	2	1	2	1	4	3	2	1	4	2	2	3
6	1	3	3	2	2	2	2	4	3	7	1	3	2
7	1	3	1	3	2	2	1	1	3	6	1	1	2
8	1	3	1	1	2	3	4	2	5	1	1	1	2
9	1	3	3	1	2	2	4	2	4	1	1	3	2
10	1	3	1	2	2	2	6	3	3	3	1	1	2
11	2	2	3	1	1	2	3	1	3	7	1	2	1
12	2	3	3	1	2	4	3	6	2	3	1	3	1
13	1	3	1	1	1	3	4	1	1	3	1	1	2

683

Cola Taste Test Data (Continued)

Subject	Pepsi-Cola or Classic Coke	Classic Coke or New Coke	New Coke or Pepsi-Cola	Choice of Free Can	Gender	Head's Occupation	Education Level	Amount Cola/wk.	Income	Age	Race	Best Liked Cola	Least Liked Cola
14	2	3	3	1	2	3	4	4	5	2	1	3	1
15	1	3	1	2	2	3	4	4	9	2	5	1	2
16	2	3	3	4	1	4	6	4	4	5	1	3	1
17	1	3	1	1	1	2	5	4	5	4	1	1	2
18	1	2	1	1	1	2	3	3	1	7	1	1	3
19	1	2	1	1	1	3	4	3	6	4	1	1	3
20	1	3	3	1	1	3	4	3	6	2	1	3	2
21	1	3	1	2	2	3	4	2	3	6	1	1	2
22	2	2	3	2	2	2	3	2	2	2	1	2	1
23	2	2	3	2	1	2	3	2	3	5	1	2	1
24	2	2	1	1	2	3	4	2	3	3	1	2	3
25	1	3	1	1	1	2	4	4	3	2	1	1	2
26	2	2	3	2	2	1	4	3	2	2	1	2	1
27	2	2	3	4	1	2	5	2	4	4	1	2	1
28	1	3	1	1	1	2	4	3	4	2	1	1	2
29	1	3	1	3	2	3	5	2	5	3	1	1	2
30	2	2	1	2	2	3	5	3	5	3	1	2	3
31	1	3	3	1	2	1	3	6	1	1	1	3	2
32	1	3	1	1	1	3	1	2	9	1	6	1	2
33	1	3	1	1	2	2	2	1	3	7	1	1	2
34	2	2	3	1	1	5	1	1	1	7	1	2	1
35	1	3	1	1	2	2	3	3	6	2	1	1	2
36	1	3	1	1	2	2	3	1	6	2	1	1	2
37	1	3	1	2	1	4	4	1	2	7	1	1	2
38	2	2	1	1	2	1	4	3	1	2	1	2	3
39	1	3	1	2	2	2	2	2	4	1	1	1	2
40	1	3	3	1	1	6	3	2	2	1	1	3	2
41	1	3	3	1	2	2	6	3	5	4	1	3	2
42	1	3	1	1	2	1	4	1	1	2	5	1	2
43	1	2	1	2	2	4	5	3	6	4	1	1	3
44	1	3	1	1	2	3	6	2	6	5	1	1	2
45	1	3	1	2	1	3	4	2	3	5	1	1	2
46	1	3	1	2	2	3	6	2	4	6	1	1	2

Cola Taste Test Data (Continued)

Subject	Pepsi-Cola or Classic Coke	Classic Coke or New Coke	New Coke or Pepsi-Cola	Choice of Free Can	Gender	Head's Occupation	Education Level	Amount Cola/wk.	Income	Age	Race	Best Liked Cola	Least Liked Cola
47	1	2	1	2	1	3	4	1	3	7	1	1	3
48	2	2	3	4	2	3	8	2	5	4	1	2	1
49	1	3	3	2	1	2	4	2	2	6	1	3	2
50	2	2	3	1	1	2	3	2	2	6	1	2	1
51	1	3	1	1	1	3	8	6	5	5	1	1	2
52	2	3	3	1	2	2	2	3	2	4	1	3	1
53	1	3	1	1	1	2	3	3	3	5	1	1	2
54	1	3	3	3	2	2	4	2	3	3	1	3	2
55	1	2	1	2	1	2	5	1	3	7	1	1	3
56	2	3	3	2	1	3	2	5	9	1	1	3	1
57	1	2	1	1	1	3	4	8	6	2	1	1	3
58	1	3	3	2	1	3	4	2	5	1	1	3	2
59	1	3	3	2	1	3	4	2	4	1	1	3	2
60	1	3	1	1	1	1	4	1	1	2	1	1	2
61	1	3	1	4	1	1	7	3	2	2	1	1	2
62	1	3	3	2	2	3	4	2	5	2	1	3	2
63	1	3	3	2	2	1	4	2	4	2	1	3	2
64	1	3	1	1	2	1	4	3	1	2	1	1	2
65	1	2	1	2	2	1	7	1	1	2	1	1	3
66	2	3	3	2	1	1	5	2	1	2	1	3	1
67	1	3	1	4	1	2	4	2	3	1	1	1	2
68	1	2	1	2	1	3	4	2	6	2	2	1	3
69	2	2	3	2	2	3	4	4	6	1	1	2	1
70	2	3	3	1	1	3	4	4	6	1	5	3	1
71	1	3	3	1	1	2	4	2	2	1	1	3	2
72	2	3	3	1	2	3	4	2	3	1	1	3	1
73	2	3	3	3	2	3	4	3	6	2	1	3	1
74	1	3	1	1	1	3	4	4	6	1	1	1	2
75	2	2	1	1	2	6	4	2	5	2	1	2	3
76	2	2	3	2	2	3	4	5	6	1	1	2	1
77	1	3	3	2	2	3	4	3	6	1	1	3	2
78	1	3	3	4	2	2	4	2	2	2	1	3	2

Value Labels:

Cola Brands	1 Pepsi-Cola, 2 Classic Coke, 3 New Coke, 4 Other
Gender	1 Female, 2 Male
Occupation	1 Student, 2 Blue Collar, 3 White Collar, 4 Service Worker, 5 Housewife, 6 Farmworker
Education	1 Grade School, 2 High School — No Diploma, 3 High School Diploma, 4 Some College, 5 Junior College Graduate, 6 4-Year College Graduate, 7 Some Graduate School, 8 Masters or Doctoral Degree
Amount of Cola (Cans or Equiv) per Week	1, None; 2, 1–3; 3, 4–6; 4, 7–12; 5, 13–18; 6, 19–24; 7, 25–36; 8, More Than 36
Income	1, Under $10,000; 2, $10,000–14,999; 3, $15,000–24,999; 4, $25,000–34,999; 5, $35,000–49,999; 6, $50,000 and Over; 9, Refused
Age	1, 14–19; 2, 20–24; 3, 25–34; 4, 35–44; 5, 45–54; 6, 55–64; 7, 65 and Older
Race	1 White, 2 Black, 3 Indian, 4 Hispanic, 5 Oriental, 6 Other
Best Liked Cola/Least Liked Cola	Derived from paired comparisons

CASE IV–5 NATIONAL PIANO AND ORGAN SURVEY PROPOSAL*

Recently the National Piano and Organ Co. solicited proposals for a market study from three research agencies. The proposal submitted by one of the agencies, Product Acceptance and Research (**PAR**), follows.

Purpose: The purpose of this study is two-fold:

    A. To determine the share of market by brand of pianos and organs on a national basis.

    B. To gather data on attitudes, thoughts, and opinions of piano and organ owners concerning American-made versus foreign-made products.

Tentative Starting Date: June 1

° Used with permission from Product Acceptance & Research, Evansville, Indiana.

Length of Study:	From questionnaire approval by the client to the final report would require about seven (7) weeks.
Criteria for Respondent Selection:	On a systematic random sample basis from telephone books in our test cities, respondents would be screened for piano/organ ownership. Respondents would be in the 21–65 age group.
Type of Interviewing:	We would plan to use central location telephone interview technique, to ensure quality of interviews.
Sample:	In our conversations, it appears that the thrust of your marketing effort is aimed at major markets. Hence, we would plan to draw our sample using twenty-five (25) of the largest metro markets in the United States (see attached map). This sample would have interviewing in 18 states and the District of Columbia.
	Using a sample of 25 piano owners and 25 organ owners in each city, our sample would be 625 each for share of market data. The American vs. foreign-made question would have a sample of 1,250. On a city by city basis, our sample error would be relatively high (estimated at 13 per cent), but on a national level, the sampling error would be in the magnitude of 3 per cent.
Research Design and Procedure:	PAR would design two (2) questionnaires. The first, envisioned to be one page, would be the screener. From it, we would determine the number of piano homes and organ homes in our sample cities. Additionally, we would ask brands of pianos and organs known and the brand they would purchase if circumstances were such that they were to make such a purchase.
	When piano and organ owners were found, a second questionnaire would be executed. Research areas to be covered would include:

A. Unaided piano and organ brand awareness, then aided.
B. Brand of instrument owned.
C. Age of instrument.
D. Why they purchased the brand they own.
E. What motivated them to make the purchase.
F. Product satisfaction.

                                        G. If they were to buy today, what brand would they purchase.

                                        H. What brand(s) of auto(s) do they own.

                                         I. What brand(s) of TV(s) do they own.

                                        J. How do they feel about American- vs. foreign-made products.

                                        K. Demographic data

Additional areas, or areas of special interest, could be added by the client, if desired.

It is estimated that a 12-minute questionnaire will be required to obtain the desired data.

Tabulation and Reporting: The screeners and main questionnaires would be tabulated, analyzed, and reported. From the screener questionnaires, data would be developed on piano and organ ownership, brand awareness, and preferred brand if a purchase were to be made. The report for the main questionnaire would address each of our objectives plus "profile" owners of each brand of pianos and organs.

Responsibilities and Procedures: PAR would be responsible for the following:

A. Drawing of the sample.

B. Questionnaire design with client approval.

C. Pilot testing of the questionnaire.

D. Interviewing, interviewer instruction, quality control, and verification.

E. Coding and verifying.

F. Tabulation.

G. Analysis.

H. Final report.

1. Evaluate the adequacy of this proposal as a research proposal.
2. Evaluate the sampling plan.
3. Evaluate the overall research design.

CASE IV–6 VERNON STEEL SUPPLY

Vernon Steel Supply sells iron and steel reinforcing rods. These products are used to provide structural strength to concrete. Thus, they are used almost any time large quantities of concrete are used.

Management has been concerned with the firm's ability to forecast demand. Forecast errors had averaged almost 10 per cent during 1987 and 1988 and the error in the first quarter of 1989 had been almost 13 per cent.

Sales forecasts were made for two quarters ahead, with a new forecast made each quarter. The forecasting was done by the president and the marketing manager, using what they referred to as their "wet finger in the wind" method. Once each quarter, they met in the president's office with data on orders, construction contract awards for the market area, salesman call reports, and other information. After reviewing these data, they each wrote their forecasts for the next two quarters on a piece of paper. Differences were discussed and a final sales forecast (usually a compromise that was close to the average of their individual forecasts) was made for each quarter.

As a result of its inability to forecast accurately, the company had been forced to keep large inventories on hand to avoid losing sales when demand was unexpectedly high. The president decided that some means had to be found to make better forecasts so the company could reduce inventories and operating costs.

A consultant was called in to work on the problem. She found that a trade association provided data on reinforcing rod sales each month in each of the counties of Vernon's market area. She ran an analysis of past sales data for the industry and for Vernon and found that Vernon's market share had remained close to 9.2 per cent for some time. In discussions with the president and marketing manager, they stated that it was reasonable to expect that the company's share would continue to be at about this same level unless some major change took place in the industry.

The consultant planned to run simple linear regression analyses with the contract awards lagged by four through eight months to see which gave the best "fit." She then planned to use the regression equation for the lag period with the best fit to forecast industry reinforcing rod sales for each month for the number of months that the equation permitted. This, of course, would also require relevant seasonal adjustments.

1. What logic supports "lagging" the construction awards?
2. Prepare monthly sales forecasts as far into the future as possible using the optimal lag period.

Monthly Construction Activity (X) and Rod Consumption (Y)

Year	Month	X Seasonally Adjusted, 1980 Dollars (000)	Y Rod Consumption in Meters° (000)	Year	Month	X Seasonally Adjusted, 1980 Dollars (000)	Y Rod Consumption in Meters° (000)
				1987	Jan.	108,300	74.3
					Feb.	110,000	79.2
					Mar.	108,300	82.3
					Apr.	111,200	83.2
					May	109,300	91.2
1985	Jan.	93,300	67.8		June	106,900	94.6
	Feb.	93,300	71.8		July	107,500	99.4
	Mar.	91,700	78.4		Aug.	105,400	99.7
	Apr.	94,100	75.9		Sept.	106,200	94.5
	May	91,600	79.6		Oct.	103,600	85.4
	June	87,100	83.9		Nov.	107,000	80.8
	July	84,700	84.0		Dec.	106,500	73.2
	Aug.	84,800	82.1	1988	Jan.	105,800	73.1
	Sept.	89,200	78.7		Feb.	102,200	76.9
	Oct.	92,000	71.3		Mar.	102,800	81.5
	Nov.	90,000	64.6		Apr.	98,300	86.4
	Dec.	90,400	58.4		May	99,500	86.1
1986	Jan.	88,400	59.1		June	99,800	93.5
	Feb.	93,200	67.2		July	101,700	89.4
	Mar.	91,000	72.9		Aug.	106,200	97.9
	Apr.	88,900	73.1		Sept.	106,500	79.1
	May	94,000	73.1		Oct.	108,100	74.6
	June	103,700	79.2		Nov.	110,500	78.0
	July	109,200	85.9		Dec.	113,400	68.9
	Aug.	109,000	85.1	1989	Jan.	115,000	73.8
	Sept.	103,600	74.6		Feb.	105,800	80.9
	Oct.	105,000	72.9		Mar.	102,600	83.3
	Nov.	103,800	81.1				
	Dec.	108,100	73.5				

° Unadjusted.

Marketing Research Reports and Ethical Issues

The results of the marketing research project have to be reported effectively if they are to receive the proper attention from management. Marketing research reports are the subject of Chapter 22.

Ethical concerns exist in all activities, and research is no exception. The ethical issues that arise in marketing research, and the practice of corporate espionage, are the topics of Chapter 23.

Marketing Research Reports

"One of the most popular studies of the past at Coca-Cola nearly went astray. Two days after a three-hour presentation by the researchers who supervised and conducted the study, I was told by a senior top manager, 'We have scheduled a meeting in three weeks for you to tell us what they said. The only thing we're sure of is that there's some important findings in that study.'

I basically reduced the presentation by leaving out technical details and using the same key charts with minor brands eliminated, and after a four-hour presentation and discussion, everyone was happy with the study." [1]

The results of a research project may be reported in written or oral format, or both. The importance of *effective* reporting cannot be overemphasized. Regardless of the quality of the research process and the accuracy and usefulness of the resulting data, the findings will not be utilized if they are not communicated effectively to the appropriate decision makers.

Furthermore, many executives cannot easily ascertain the quality of a research design, questionnaire, or experiment. They can, however, easily recognize the quality level of a report. Therefore, *the quality of the report is often used as a major indicator of the quality of the research itself.*

Preparing the Written Research Report

Good research reports begin with *clear* thinking on the part of a researcher.[2] The researcher should *analyze the reader's needs* carefully and prepare a detailed outline *prior* to writing the first draft. The first draft should be considered just that — a *first* draft. Few of us write well enough to produce a polished draft the first time. The writer should plan on at least one major rewrite.

Focus on the Audience

The only reason for writing a research report is to communicate something to someone. The *someone* is the most important aspect of the communications process. The entire research project is performed to generate information that will aid one or more decision makers. The research report must convey that information to those decision makers.

Several facts must be kept in mind. First, managers are extremely busy. Second, they are much less interested in the technical and logical aspects of a research problem than the researcher is. Third, they are seldom well versed in research techniques and terminology. Fourth, if there is more than one reader, and there usually is, they are likely to differ in terms of interests, training, and reasons for reading the report. Finally, managers, like everyone else, prefer interesting reports over dull ones. With these facts in mind, a number of general guides to writing are offered here.

Focus on the Objective of the Study

The research was initiated to help make a decision. The report should be built around the decision and how the resultant information is relevant to the decision. This is what the manager is interested in. Researchers are often more interested in the research problem and the methodology used to solve it. Unfortunately, many research reports reflect the interest of the researcher rather than the manager. This can result in unread (and perhaps unreadable) reports, an "ivory tower" image, and a resulting erosion of the effectiveness of the research department.

Minimize the Reporting of the Technical Aspects of the Project

Researchers have an unfortunate, if natural, tendency to attempt to convince management of their expertise and thoroughness in the research report. This leads to detailed discussions of the sampling plan, explorations of why it is superior to alternative sampling plans, and so on. Yet, few executives are interested in this level of detail. However, the research department should keep such a detailed report *internally* to serve as a guide for future studies, and to answer any question that might arise concerning the methodology of the study. Technical details that might be of use to some, but not all readers, should be placed in an appendix.

Use Terminology That Matches the Vocabulary of the Readers

"Few managers can balance a research report, a cup of coffee, and a dictionary at the same time." [3] Terms such as *skewed distribution, correlation coefficient,* or even *significance level* are not necessarily familiar to all marketing managers. In many research reports, it is often necessary to utilize the concepts that underlie these terms. Three strategies are available for dealing with this problem. The term can be used, followed by a brief description or explanation; the explanation can be provided first followed by the term; or the technical terms can be omitted altogether. Which approach, or combination of approaches, is best depends upon the nature of the audience and the message.

Avoid errors in grammar and spelling

One incorrect sentence or misspelled word can undermine the credibility of the entire research project, and it can seriously harm your career. Use a dictionary and grammar guide any time that you are in doubt. [4]

Which of the following words are spelled incorrectly?

acknowledgement	beneficial	correspondant	maintenance
accross	commitee	descrepency	necessary
astericks	congradulate	inclose	ocurrence

Which of the following sentences are incorrect?

- The firm applied for it's license after the deadline.
- The reports laid there unused for a week.
- I lead a fund drive last year.
- Your prospective on the matter differs from mine.
- I like writing, to read, and cross-country ski trips.

All of the words and sentences listed are incorrect. Since mistakes are hard to detect, two proofreaders should be used for any important document. Word processors with spelling checks can also be used to minimize such errors.

Develop an Interesting Writing Style

Research reports should be interesting to read. There is no inherent reason for a research report to be dull, tedious, or boring. Consider the following statement written by a well-known research executive:

> The use of analytical techniques of the behavioral sciences will gradually revolutionize the communication arts by predicating their prac-

tice upon a body of demonstrably general principles which will be readily available to creative people for increasing their knowledge of consumer response to advertising communications.[5]

Can you imagine reading a report composed of such statements? Unfortunately, most researchers have not been trained in effective writing. Self-instruction is, therefore, often necessary.

We should strive for simplicity and conciseness. Simplicity does not mean that the audience is talked down to, nor does conciseness mean that the report necessarily be short. However, unnecessary complexity in sentence structure and long-windedness in reporting should be avoided. Consider the following two sentences:

As Table 6 indicates, our survey found that 86.3 per cent of those surveyed said that they would be extremely likely or very likely to purchase Whifle if it were available at their supermarket.

versus

As Table 6 indicates, consumers are enthusiastic about Whifle.

It is important to "break up" the text of the report. Page after page of type looks dull, and probably is dull. Headings and subheadings with ample white space are essential. Fortunately, word processors make proper layout easy to achieve. Use bullets (the round, black symbols shown below) and indentation to highlight key points:

- Key points must stand out
- Break up the text of the report
- Focus on the audience

Use Visual Aids Whenever Practical

Exhibit 22–1 illustrates three different ways of presenting numerical data. As a general rule, a sentence in the text of a report should contain no more than

---

Exhibit 22–1 *Three Ways of Presenting Sales Data*

Sentence

Monthly sales by department were appliances, $453,268 (35.1%); hardware, $362,197 (28.0%); drugs and cosmetics, $198,415 (15.4%); household supplies, $169,327 (13.1%); sporting goods, $69,462 (5.4%); and toys, $38,917 (3.0%). Total sales were $1,291,586.

Table

Monthly Sales by Department

Department	Sales	Total (in %)
Appliances	$ 453,268	35.1
Hardware	362,197	28.0
Drugs and cosmetics	198,415	15.4
Household supplies	169,327	13.1
Sporting goods	69,462	5.4
Toys	38,917	3.0
Total	$1,291,586	100.0

Pie Chart

Monthly Sales by Department

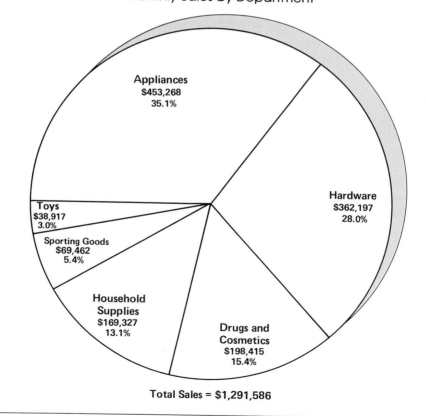

Appliances
$453,268
35.1%

Hardware
$362,197
28.0%

Toys
$38,917
3.0%

Sporting Goods
$69,462
5.4%

Household
Supplies
$169,327
13.1%

Drugs and
Cosmetics
$198,415
15.4%

Total Sales = $1,291,586

two or three numerical values. Sentences containing more numbers than this are difficult to read and understand. The table in the exhibit is much easier to read than the sentence. However, the pie chart contains the same information and provides a quick, strong impression of the relative sales by each department.

Exhibit 22–2 illustrates three different ways to describe changes in the number of individuals in various age groups between 1980 and 1990. Again, the advantage of graphics is apparent. Descriptions of several of the more common graphic techniques follow.

A *pie chart* is a circle divided into sections, such that each section represents the percentage of the total area of the circle associated with one variable. For example, in Exhibit 22–1, 35.1 per cent of the firm's monthly sales were appliances. Therefore, 35.1 per cent of the area of the circle was assigned to appliances. Since there are 360 degrees to a circle, 3.6 degrees comprise 1 per cent of the circle. The section of the circle representing appliance sales has a central angle of $3.6 \times 35.1 = 126.4$ degrees.

Another useful visual aid is the *bar chart,* which may be either vertical or horizontal. Because the same principles apply in either case, we limit our discussions to the vertical bar chart. A vertical bar chart is constructed by placing rectangles or bars over each value or interval of the variable of interest. The height of the bar represents the level of the variable on the vertical axis. Vertical bar charts are often used to represent changes in a variable over time. Figure 22–1 illustrates two bar charts. Another type of bar chart is shown in Exhibit 22–2.

The data shown in the bar chart in Figure 22–1B could also be shown in the form of a *line chart,* such as Figure 22–2. The bar chart is somewhat less complex in appearance and may be more suited to those unaccustomed to dealing with figures. Line charts are generally superior under the following conditions: (1) *when the data involve a long time period,* (2) *when several series are compared on the same chart,* (3) *when the emphasis is on the movement rather than the actual amount,* (4) *when trends rather than a frequency distri-*

Exhibit 22–2 *Three Ways of Presenting Population Change Data*

Sentence

Between 1980 and 1990, the population of the various age groups in the United States changed as follows: (1) under 5, +3.2 million; (2) 5–13, +0.6 million; (3) 14–17, −3.4 million; (4) 18–24, −5.0 million; (5) 24–34, +4.3 million; (6) 35–44, +10.2 million; (7) 45–54, +2.2 million; (8) 55–64, −0.8 million; and (9) 65 and over, +4.3 million.

Table

Age Group	Numerical Changes, 1980–1990 (In Millions)
Under 5	+3.2
5–13	+0.6
14–17	−3.4
18–24	−5.0
25–34	+4.3
35–44	+10.2
45–54	+2.2
55–64	−0.8
65+	+4.3

Bar Chart

Numerical Changes in Population by Age Group: 1980–1990 (in Millions)

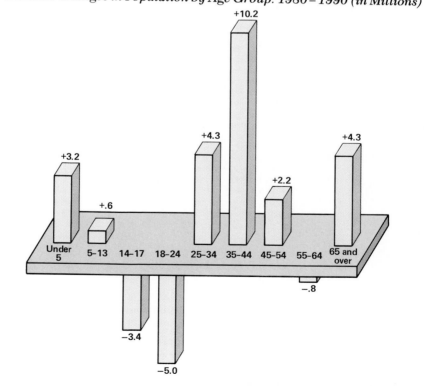

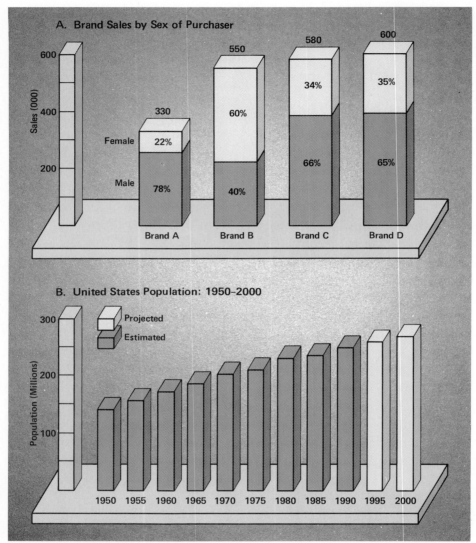

Figure 22–1 *Bar Charts*

bution are presented, (5) *when a multiple-amount scale is used,* and (6) *when estimates, forecasts, interpolations, or extrapolations are to be shown.*

A *histogram* is a vertical bar chart in which the height of the bars represents the relative or cumulative frequency of occurrence of the variable of interest. For example, assume that 730 respondents rate the service provided by a restaurant on a six-point semantic differential scale bounded by *poor* on the

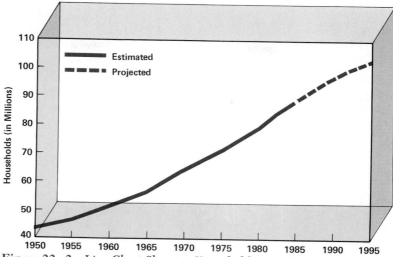

Figure 22-2 *Line Chart Showing Household Growth, 1950-1995*

left and *excellent* on the right. The number of respondents marking each response from left to right is 154, 79, 50, 112, 198, and 146. Stated in percentages, the responses from left to right would be 21.2, 10.8, 6.8, 15.3, 25.9, and 20.0. Figure 22-3 demonstrates the advantages of presenting this type of data in the form of a histogram.

The histogram makes clear at a glance the bimodal nature of the response (that is, the fact that responses are clustered in two groups). A textual presen-

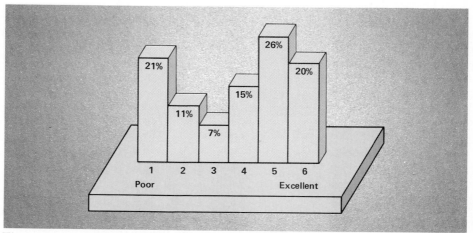

Figure 22-3 *Relative Frequency Histogram of the Poor Service—Excellent Service Semantic Differential Item*

701

Exhibit 22–3 *Effective and Ineffective Tables*

Table 1. United Auto Rental Inc. Performance 1976–1986

Performance Indicator	1976	1981	1986
Days Rental			
All vehicles	3,692	5,402	5,802
Compact	312	1,248	2,621
Standard	2,891	3,469	2,359
Luxury	489	685	822
Mileage			
All vehicles	155,066	246,347	293,981
Compact	20,592	82,368	172,973
Standard	121,422	145,706	99,080
Luxury	13,052	18,273	21,928
Revenue			
All vehicles	$151,963	$223,040	$241,222
Compact	$12,973	$51,892	$108,973
Standard	$117,193	$140,632	$95,630
Luxury	$21,797	$30,516	$36,619

Table 2. United Auto Rental Inc. Performance 1976–1986

Performance Indicator	1976	1981	1986
Days Rental			
Compact	300	1,200	2,600
Standard	2,900	3,500	2,400
Luxury	500	700	800
ALL VEHICLES	3,700	5,400	5,800
Mileage			
Compact	21,000	82,000	173,000
Standard	121,000	146,000	99,000
Luxury	13,000	18,000	22,000
ALL VEHICLES	155,000	246,000	294,000
Revenue			
Compact	$ 13,000	$ 52,000	$109,000
Standard	117,000	141,000	96,000
Luxury	22,000	31,000	37,000
ALL VEHICLES	$152,000	$224,000	$242,000

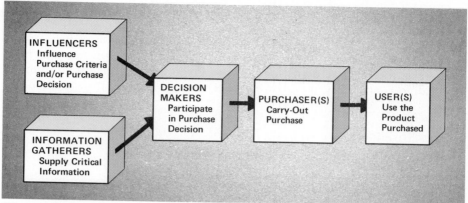

Figure 22 – 4   *Use of a Flow Diagram to Introduce a Set of Topics*

tation of the raw data and/or a comment on the fact that the responses were bimodal would not have the same impact on many readers as the histogram.

It is often necessary to present numerical data that cannot be converted to graphic format. When this is the case or when the data underlying the graph need to be presented in numerical form as a supplement to the graph, tables should be used. Exhibit 22 – 3 shows both an effective and ineffective presentation of the same data.

Flow diagrams are a visual presentation of a sequential process or logic. They are very effective for introducing topics and summarizing results. Figure 22 – 4 was used to introduce the key areas covered in a study to determine which individuals in various industries are involved in the purchase and use of microcomputers.

Most data analysis software programs will prepare standard graphic displays. Likewise, most word processing and spread sheet software can produce pie charts, bar charts, and so forth. Specialized graphics software can develop elaborate, multicolor charts, graphs, headings, and diagrams. Coupled with high-quality printers, such software is making effective visuals a standard part of research reports. However, there are readers who prefer text and tables. If the preferences of the key individual commissioning the study is known, the report should conform to his or her preferences.

Rounding of Numbers

All too often one reads statements in research reports such as "the average age of the buyer of standard sized Chevrolets has climbed from 38.72 years in 1980 to 51.65 years in 1990." Such statements are usually the product of a computer analysis having been made in which all calculated numbers are routinely rounded to two places following the decimal point. The analyst then simply copies the data as they are given on the printout and that is the way they appear in the report.

The reporting of data to a number of decimal places that is either unwarranted or unnecessary is a practice to be avoided. There is a spurious accuracy implied by the last two digits for the ages given in the preceding example. There almost certainly were errors in the reporting of ages by buyers when the

---

Exhibit 22–4   *Hints for Constructing an Interesting Research Report*

- Use present tense and active voice. Results and observations expressed in *now* terms sound better. Don't say: *"The respondents liked the taste of Whiffey."* Say, *"People like the taste of Whiffey."* Managers use research to make decisions now. If the research results are not valid in the present tense, there is no use presenting them to management.

    The active voice should be used when possible. Why said, *"It is believed that . . . ;"* when you mean, *"We believe that . . ."*

- Use information headlines. A headline that says "Convenience is the product's major advantage" is more meaningful and interesting to a manager than a heading such as "Results of Product Benefit Analysis."

- Let tables and charts do the work. The purpose of a table or a chart is to simplify. Use your words to point out significant items in the table — something that is not readily clear. Or use your words to offer interpretive comments. Use verbatims from sample respondents to support a point. Don't repeat in words what the chart or table already communicates.

- Use the double-sided presentation whenever possible. This format will reduce the verbiage in your report. It simply presents the table on the left side of the open report. Your informative headline and interpretive comments are on the right-hand page.

- Make liberal use of verbatims. Great nuggets of marketing wisdom have come from people's comments. Use verbatims if you have them. They make tables, charts, and text much more interesting. Remember, marketing managers are ultimately interested in the customer's thoughts, not yours.

Source: Adapted from H. L. Gordon, "Eight Ways to Dress a Research Report," *Advertising Age,* October 20, 1980, S-37.

data were collected that would have made the calculated mean age questionable to an accuracy of more than one year. To imply that the data are accurate to one-hundredth of a year is thus both inaccurate and misleading.

Reporting data to several significant digits is often unnecessary, even when accurate. It is important for Chevrolet officials to know that the average age of the buyers of their standard-sized cars is increasing. It is probably sufficient, however, for this information to be reported as "the average age of the buyers of standard-sized Chevrolets (*Impala* and *Caprice*) has climbed from under 40 to over 50 in the last 10 years."

Writing an interesting research report is not easy. Exhibit 22–4 provides eight "hints" from an experienced marketing researcher.

The Organization of the Report

No one format is best for all occasions. The nature of the audience and the topic of the report combine to determine the most desirable format. However, a general format is suggested in Table 22–1 that can be altered to meet the requirements of most situations.

Title Page. The title page should identify the topic, for whom the report is prepared, the date of the report and the researcher(s). If the report is for limited distribution, this fact should also be noted on the title page. The title of the report should indicate the nature of the research project as precisely and as succinctly as possible.

Executive Summary. The executive summary is the most important part of the research report. It must clearly and concisely present the heart of the report. The objectives, findings, and conclusions, and recommendations must be presented forcefully and briefly.

Many executives will read only this part of the report. In fact, the executive summary may be all that is provided to some managers. Others will use the

Table 22–1 Generalized Format for a Research Report

I. Title page
II. Executive summary
III. Table of contents
IV. Introduction
V. Methodology
VI. Findings
VII. Limitations
VIII. Conclusions and recommendations
IX. Appendixes

executive summary to determine if, and what, they should read in the main report.

Table of Contents. Unless the report is exceptionally brief, it should contain a table of contents, including the page numbers of major sections and subdivisions within the sections, and a list of all appendixes. If numerous tables or charts are used, they should also be listed on a separate page immediately following the table of contents.

Introduction. The introduction should provide (1) *background material*, (2) *a clear statement of the research objectives*, and (3) an *overview of the organization of the report*. The first section of the introduction should contain a description of the management problem and the factors that influence it. The researcher cannot assume that everyone who will read the report is familiar with the underlying problem.

The next section of the introduction should be a concise statement of the objectives, which will involve the management problem and its translation into a research problem. The objectives arise out of the background data, but are so critical that they should be stated explicitly. The introduction should conclude with a brief overview of the organization of the report.

Findings. The major portion of the report should be devoted to the findings, which should be organized around the objectives of the study. This section generally has a title such as Marketing Implications. The findings should not consist of an endless series of statistical tables. Instead they should describe, in meaningful terms, what the research found. Summary tables and visual aids (charts, graphs, and the like) should be used to clarify the discussion. Relevant action recommendations based on the objectives and findings are also included. Detailed findings are presented in appendixes.

Methodology. This section *summarizes* the methodology used to meet the objectives of the research project. Technical details should be minimized. Where necessary, such details should be placed in appendixes. The researcher must remember that, although he or she is deeply interested in research design, managers are not. This should *not* be the major section of the report.

Limitations. The researcher should not overlook or hide any problems in the research. Furthermore, care should be taken to point out limitations that are apparent to skilled researchers but that a manager might overlook. For example, the danger in generalizing to the national market from local studies or the potential problems of nonresponse error are often overlooked by executives. The limitations section should, without unduly degrading the overall quality of the work, indicate the nature of any potential limitations.

Appendixes. Items that will appeal to only a few readers or that may be needed only for occasional references should be confined to an appendix. Details of the sampling plan, detailed statistical tables, interview verification procedures, copies of questionnaires and interview instructions, and similar items generally belong in an appendix.

An Example. Many of the points we have been discussing are illustrated in Exhibit 22–5. This table of contents was taken from a report conducted for a margarine producer. The purpose of the study was to "gain an understanding of consumer behavior within the margarine market" in order to "create more effective marketing strategies" for the firm's two margarine brands. The impetus for the study was a decline in brand share for both brands. The study involved a series of focus groups followed by a major survey.

Notice that the headings are *action-oriented*—"How the Study Was Done" not "Methodology." This is much more likely to attract the manager's interest. Although the titles are different, the table of contents parallels the

Exhibit 22–5 ***Table of Contents from a Research Report***

Table of Contents

	Page No.
Major Findings and Recommendations	1
Why This Study Was Done	5
How the Study Was Done	8
Qualitative Phase	
I. What Do Women Say About Margarine?	11
II. What Do They Use It For?	14
III. How Do They Feel About Different Brands?	16
IV. Hypotheses Generated	20
Quantitative Phase	
I. What Does the Market Look Like?	22
II. How Do Premier and Delight Fit into the Margarine Market?	32
III. A Closer Look at Premier	36
IV. A Closer Look at Delight	48
V. What About Butter?	62
VI. Some Special Issues	70
Marketing Implications	76
Detailed Tables	82
Questionnaire Material	104

one we have recommended except that there is not a separate section on limitations. Some of the more important limitations were covered in the "methodology" section. This table of contents serves as an effective invitation to read the report as well as a guide to its contents. The report itself encouraged readership through its quality typing, ample white space, effective graphics, and limited verbiage.

Transmittal Letter.   A research report is not simply dropped on a manager's desk. Instead, it is delivered with a transmittal letter (or memo if it is an internal research department). The transmittal letter (1) identifies the research report, (2) restates the authorization for the study, and (3) indicates who is receiving copies of the report. It may also focus the manager's attention on key aspects of the report. Finally, it is the appropriate place to initiate follow-up research — "I'll call you after you've had a chance to read this to discuss some follow-up suggestions."

Preparing Oral Presentations

Most research proposals and projects involve one or more oral reports. Major projects frequently require a series of interim reports that are generally oral. Oral reports are also commonly made at the proposal and the conclusion of projects. These oral reports may follow or precede the preparation and distribution of a written report. Upper-level managers will often base decisions on the oral report. Therefore, we cannot overemphasize how critical this task is. As one successful researcher states: "After working 6 months or more on a project, the researcher may get 30 to 60 minutes of top management's time. The oral report had better be effective!"

The first step in ensuring that the oral report is effective is the same as for a written report — an analysis of the audience. The next step is the development of a detailed report outline or, preferably, a written *script* for the report. Once the oral presentation is prepared, it should be rehearsed. Even highly trained actors and speakers typically rehearse material prior to making a formal presentation. Researchers, generally with limited training in oral presentations, should plan on several "dry runs" before making a presentation to management. If practical, these dry runs should be recorded on VCR equipment and carefully analyzed.

The use of visual aids is essential for oral presentations. The oral presentation of a list of several numbers or percentages simply will not register on many listeners. Even the visual presentation of the numbers in a table will often not have the necessary impact. Most people have to "study" a table to understand it. Therefore, oral presentations should make extensive use of the various charting techniques referred to earlier as well as any other appropriate visual aids. In fact, most research presentations are built around a complete set of visual aids.

Exhibits 22–6 and 22–7 show two visual aids used in a presentation by Booz-Allen & Hamilton, Inc. Exhibit 22–6 is a chart used to structure and highlight the overview, whereas Exhibit 22–7 serves to present numerical data.

A number of kinds of equipment are available to assist in the presentation of visual materials. A *chalkboard* allows the researcher to write out and manipulate numbers. It is particularly useful when technical questions concerning the findings are anticipated. A *magnetic board* and a *felt board* offer some of the same advantages but are not as flexible. They do, however, allow the rapid presentation of previously prepared materials.

A *flip chart* is a large pad of blank paper mounted on an easel. Visual aids are drawn on the pages in advance, and the speaker flips to the appropriate chart while progressing through the talk. The use of colored felt-tip pens can

---

Exhibit 22–6 *Text Visual Aids Used by Booz-Allen & Hamilton, Inc.*

PROJECT OVERVIEW . . .

STUDY RESULTS SUGGEST . . .

- Managers have set higher new product targets for the next five years
- A complex external environment will challenge new product managers during the 1980s
- From an internal perspective, a short-term orientation by management is the major obstacle to successful new product development today
- Over the last decade, several refinements have been made to the new product process
  —New products frequently fulfill defined strategic roles
  —Many companies establish formal criteria to measure new product performance
  —Greater prescreening and planning have improved the effectiveness of new product expenditures
  —New product requirements drive the choice of new product organization

Exhibit 22–7 *Graphic Visual Aid Used by Booz-Allen & Hamilton, Inc.*

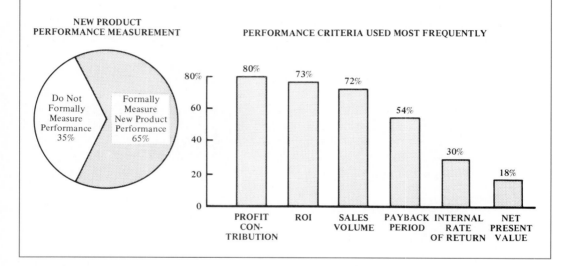

CURRENT PRACTICES AND TRENDS . . .

TODAY, ONE THIRD OF THE COMPANIES SURVEYED DO NOT FORMALLY MEASURE NEW PRODUCT PERFORMANCE

NEW PRODUCT PERFORMANCE MEASUREMENT

Do Not Formally Measure Performance 35%

Formally Measure New Product Performance 65%

PERFORMANCE CRITERIA USED MOST FREQUENTLY

80% PROFIT CONTRIBUTION
73% ROI
72% SALES VOLUME
54% PAYBACK PERIOD
30% INTERNAL RATE OF RETURN
18% NET PRESENT VALUE

increase the impact of the flip chart. Blank pages can be left at appropriate intervals and the speaker can create new exhibits as the need arises.

Overhead projectors are widely used to show previously prepared images against a screen or wall. The materials presented in this manner can range from simple charts to complex overlays. An overlay is produced by the successive additions of new images to the screen without removing the previous images. In addition, the speaker can write on the transparency (the acetate sheet on which the image is carried) and the writing will appear on the screen.

Overhead transparency masters can be prepared from the printouts generated by the graphics software described earlier. In addition, colored transparencies can be produced by color plotters that work in conjunction with personal computers or independently. There are also companies that specialize in preparing color transparencies. A variety of kits and accessories are available to assist in the manual preparation of transparencies.[6]

Table 22 – 2 Influence of Overhead Projectors (OHP) on Group Decisions

OHP used to promote "Go" position	Go	67%
	No Go	33%
OHP used to promote "No Go" position	Go	33%
	No Go	67%
No projector used to promote either position	Go	50%
	No Go	50%

Source: The Wharton Applied Research Center, the Wharton School, The University of Pennsylvania (1981).

The potential impact of overhead projectors was reflected in a study involving 36 group meetings in which two speakers presented pro and con positions concerning the introduction of a new product. The use of overhead projectors was systematically varied between the speakers. The results shown in Table 22 – 2 indicate the positive effect of this visual aid.

Slides of anything that can be photographed can be projected onto a screen. Although these slides are not as flexible as those used on overhead projectors (that is, they cannot be written on while in use), remote-control, magazine-loaded projectors allow a smooth, evenly paced presentation using this technique. The ability to make color slides directly from computer monitors is a significant advantage of this approach.

Videotape equipment (VCR) coupled with large-screen projectors is gaining use in research presentations. It is particularly useful for presenting parts of focus group interviews, showing how product tests were conducted, and presenting other material that does not lend itself to a static presentation.

Finally, *projectors* similar to VCR projectors can be attached to personal computers to project the monitor image onto a wall or screen. This is particularly useful when mathematical or accounting models or formulas have been developed. Executives can then ask "what if" questions that can be answered immediately.

For example, a research project might forecast a market share of 40 per cent for a new product. Part of the report might contain a five-year cash flow and income statement projection. If this is contained in a personal computer, an executive can ask: "What if our market share is actually 35 per cent (or 55 per cent)?" and the researcher merely needs to enter this one number. The computer will quickly produce new five-year cash flow and income statements that can be projected onto the screen.

Reading Research Reports

Substantially more people read research reports than write them. Managers need to develop skill in reading research reports (and listening to research presentations) in order to evaluate the usefulness of the research results. The Advertising Research Foundation has developed a set of guidelines that managers can follow to evaluate research reports.[7] A brief summary follows.

Origin — What Is Behind the Research. The report should contain a clear statement of why the research was conducted, who sponsored it, and who conducted it. Key questions:

- Does the report identify the organizations (divisions, departments) that requested the research?
- Does it contain a statement of purpose that clearly states what the research was to accomplish?
- Are the organizations that defined and conducted the research identified?

Design — The Concept and the Plan. The research approach, the sample, and the analysis should be described clearly and they should be appropriate for the purpose of the study. Key questions:

- Is there a complete, nontechnical description of the research design?
- Is the design consistent with the purpose for which the research was conducted?
- Does any aspect of the design, including the measuring instrument(s), induce any bias (particularly bias in favor of the sponsor)?
- Does the design control for patterns of sequence or timing or other external factors that might prejudice the results?
- Are the respondents capable of answering the questions raised?
- Is there a precise statement of the populations the research is to represent?
- Does the sampling frame fairly represent the population?
- Does the report specify the type of sample used and describe the method of sample selection?
- Does the report describe how the data are analyzed?
- Are copies of the questionnaire, field and sampling instructions, and other materials available in the appendix or on file?

Execution — Collecting and Handling the Information. Data should be carefully collected by competent people using forms and methods appropriate for the task. Key questions:

- Does the report describe the data-collection procedures including "quality control" procedures?
- Does the report specify the proportion of the selected sample from which information was collected?
- Were those who collected the data treated in a manner that would minimize any bias they might introduce?

Stability — Sample Size and Reliability. The sample size should be reported and it should be large enough to yield stable results. Key questions:

- Is the sample large enough to provide stable findings?
- Are sampling error limits shown (if applicable)?
- Is the calculation of sampling error, or the lack of such a calculation, explained?
- Does the treatment of sampling error make clear that it does not include nonsampling error?
- For the major findings, are the reported error tolerances based on direct analysis of the variability of the collected data?

Applicability — Generalizing the Findings. The research report should clearly indicate the boundaries which limit the findings. Key questions:

- Does the report specify when the data were collected?
- Does the report state clearly whether its results apply beyond the direct source of the data?
- Is it clear which groups, if any, are underrepresented in the data?
- If the research has limited applications, is there a statement describing who or what it represents and the times and conditions under which it applied?

Meaning — Interpretations and Conclusions. All assumptions and judgments involved in reaching any findings, conclusions or recommendations should be clearly specified. Key questions:

- Are the measurements described in simple and direct language?
- Does the use of the measurements make sense?

- Are the actual findings clearly differentiated from any interpretation of the findings?
- Has rigorous objectivity and candid reporting been used in interpreting research findings as evidence of causation or as predictive of future behavior?

Candor — Open Reporting and Disclosure.   The research report should be an honest, complete description of the research process and outcome. Key questions:

- Is there a full and forthright disclosure of how the research was done?
- Have all the potentially relevant findings been presented?

As a user of a research project, you need to know what the results of the study are and how accurate they are likely to be. The Advertising Research Foundation guidelines can assist you in this evaluation.

Review Questions

22.1.   What is meant by "focus on the audience" when writing a research report?

22.2.   How do the objectives of the study relate to the writing of the research report?

22.3.   What is a *horizontal bar chart?*

22.4.   What is a *vertical bar chart?*

22.5.   What is a *line chart?*

22.6.   When is a *line chart* preferred over a *bar chart?*

22.7.   What is a *pie chart?*

22.8.   What is a *histogram?*

22.9.   What is a *flow diagram?*

22.10.   How should numbers be rounded for use in research reports?

22.11.   How should a report be organized?

22.12.   What should go on the title page?

22.13.   What should go in the introduction section?

22.14.   What should go in the methodology section?

22.15.   What should go in the limitations section?

22.16.   What should go in the conclusions section?

22.17.   What should go in the transmittal letter?

22.18. How should one prepare for an oral presentation?

22.19. What visual aids are available for oral presentations?

22.20. How does one read or evaluate a research report?

22.21. Why is it critical to avoid spelling and grammar errors in research reports?

Discussion Questions/Problems

22.22. Develop one or more visual aids to present the following data, showing the relationship between store sales and profits and the computer software department's sales and profits. Do you prefer a graphic presentation or the table? Which do you think the typical executive prefers? Why?

	Sales		Profits	
Year	Store	Software	Store	Software
1981	$7,500,000	$ 785,000	$ 695,000	$ 98,900
1982	7,700,000	863,000	760,000	99,700
1983	8,056,000	927,000	846,000	102,400
1984	7,624,000	908,000	796,000	103,200
1985	8,681,000	1,101,000	852,000	127,600
1986	9,022,000	1,197,000	892,000	138,500
1987	9,383,000	1,305,000	933,000	152,600
1988	9,766,000	1,536,000	967,000	158,200
1989	9,913,000	1,756,000	1,023,000	162,300
1990	9,991,000	1,987,000	1,096,000	165,100

22.23. Using the data in problem 22.22, develop a visual aid to emphasize:
a. the growth of store sales
b. the growth of software sales
c. the growth of store profits
d. the growth of software profits
e. the impact of software profits on store profits for 1990
f. the impact of software sales on store sales for 1990
g. the change in profits as a per cent of sales over time

22.24. As a new marketing researcher for a medium-sized department store, you have been asked to prepare a report showing what happens to sales revenue after it is received. The report will be presented in the local newspaper in an in-depth examination of the store. Investigation reveals the following figures. Prepare a visual aid for use in the newspaper article.

Net sales (revenue)	$7,000,000
Cost of goods sold	3,500,000
Sales force compensation	1,300,000
Administrative salaries	350,000
Overhead (rent, insurance, etc.)	450,000
Inventory shrinkage (spoilage, theft, etc.)	100,000
Advertising	125,000
Taxes (local, state, and federal)	875,000
Aftertax profit	300,000

22.25. Average daily sales for a grocery store were found to be Monday, $120,000; Tuesday, $100,000; Wednesday, $145,000; Thursday, $150,000; Friday, $140,000; Saturday, $275,000. Prepare a visual aid to show this information.

22.26. A survey produced the following data on television viewing during weekday evenings. Prepare one or more visual aids for presentation of these data.

	Absolute Frequency	Relative Frequency	Cumulative Frequency
Less than 0.1 hrs	12	06.8	06.8
0.1 – 1.0 hrs	33	18.8	25.6
1.1 – 2.0 hrs	26	14.8	40.4
2.1 – 3.0 hrs	50	28.4	68.8
3.1 – 4.0 hrs	55	31.2	100.0
	176	100.0	

22.27. Prepare a visual aid for presentation of the following annual sales data (in thousands).

1967	$2,220	1973	$2,515	1979	$2,600	1985	$3,400
1968	2,460	1974	2,970	1980	2,510	1986	3,800
1969	2,800	1975	2,770	1981	2,580	1987	4,200
1970	2,815	1976	2,950	1982	2,800	1988	4,375
1971	2,920	1977	3,125	1983	3,080	1989	4,850
1972	2,850	1978	3,230	1984	3,175	1990	5,100

22.28. Using the following data, develop a visual aid to emphasize the growth of sales and profits and a second visual aid to emphasize the change in profits as a per cent of sales.

Year	Sales (000)	Profits (000)	Year	Sales (000)	Profits (000)
1985	$16,200	$2,000	1988	$21,000	$3,900
1986	17,400	2,800	1989	24,100	4,800
1987	19,200	3,200	1990	26,000	6,300

22.29. The following paragraph was part of a research report presented to a group of small retailers. The preceding paragraphs had described a semantic differential as "a seven-point scale with bipolar adjectives on either end of a continuum."

"Each person interviewed was asked to rate each store along this seven-point scale. From their individual positioning on the continuum we compiled an overall mean score with a standard deviation of means on each set of descriptive adjectives. These mean scores and their standard deviations were then used to form a profile. The profile presented in graphic form gives a quantitative expression of the total group mean responses. From the profile, we are able to analyze and pinpoint specific factors relating to each store that are viewed favorably or unfavorably."

Rewrite the paragraph so that it is stated in the way you think is appropriate for the readers (small retailers).

22.30. Two samples of consumers were asked to evaluate two versions of a new product. Attitude measurements were made for one sample for version **A** and for the other sample for version **B**.

Write a paragraph describing the fact that the mean attitude score for version **A** of the new product was 83 compared to a mean score of 74 for version **B** of the product. Assume that a **Z** test indicates that the probability of a Type I error is .01. Also assume that the audience for the report does not have a background in statistics.

22.31. Develop a visual aid to introduce and summarize the following discussion: "We will first work with management to clarify the problem. Then we will simultaneously develop our sampling plan and develop and pretest the questionnaire. Then we will conduct the survey, analyze the results, and prepare the final report."

22.32. Prepare a visual aid to summarize the following conclusions from a series of focus group interviewers: "The decision to insulate an existing home is determined primarily by the household's perception of the economic savings generated by the insulation and their perception of their financial liquidity. Secondary influencing factors are the length of time the family plans to live in the home and their environmental sensitivity."

717

Projects

22.33. In 1983 a report was published on the findings of a survey of American firms with regard to their use of marketing research. (Dik W. Twedt, *1983 Survey of Marketing Research*, American Marketing Association: HF, 5415.2, A12, 1983). Similar studies were published by the American Marketing Association in 1947, 1959, 1963, 1968, 1973, and 1978. Evaluate the 1983 report as a report of the findings (not on the basis of its substantive content).

22.34. Examine several issues of the *Journal of Marketing Research* or the *Journal of Marketing*. Find two cases in which data could have been presented more effectively. Prepare a more effective presentation and show both versions to the class.

22.35. Using the data in Table 17–2, write a research report.

22.36. Repeat 22.35 but instead of a report prepare and give an oral presentation.

22.37. Examine the annual reports from several companies. Identify exceptionally good and exceptionally weak presentations of data.

22.38. Read several articles in the *Journal of Marketing Research.* Find five sentences that are unnecessarily complex or are otherwise unclear. Prepare more effective sentences and show both versions to the class.

References

[1] R. G. Stout, "Intangibles Add to Results," *Advertising Age*, October 20, 1980, S–39.

[2] This section is based on A. S. C. Ehrenberg, "Rudiments of Numeracy," in J. Sheth, *Research in Marketing*, 2 (New York: JAI Press Inc., 1979) 191–216; and B. D. Sorrels, *Business Communication Fundamentals* (New York: Merrill Publishing, 1984).

[3] S. H. Britt, "The Writing of Readable Research Reports," *Journal of Marketing Research* (May 1971), 265.

[4] For example, see Sorrels, op. cit.

[5] Britt, op. cit.

[6] For example, see *3M Meeting Graphics Catalog* (St. Paul, Minn.: 3M Corporation, undated).

[7] Public Affairs Council, *Guidelines for the Public Use of Market and Opinion Research* (New York: Advertising Research Foundation, 1981).

CHAPTER 23

Ethical Issues in
Marketing Research

The commercial featured a well-known fashion model saying: "In shampoo tests with over 900 women like me, *Body on Tap* got higher ratings than *Prell* for body. Higher than *Flex* for conditioning. Higher than *Sassoon* for strong, healthy-looking hair."

The supporting research had several groups of approximately 200 women each test just one shampoo. They rated it on a six-step scale, from "outstanding" to "poor," for 27 separate attributes, such as body and conditioning. Nine hundred women did not make product-to-product comparisons between *Body on Tap* and *Sassoon*, or between *Body on Tap* and any of the other brands mentioned. In fact, no woman in the tests tried more than one shampoo.

The basis for the claim that the women preferred *Body on Tap* to *Sassoon* for "strong, healthy looking hair" was to combine the data for the "outstanding" and "excellent" ratings and discard the lower four ratings on the scale. The figures then were 36 per cent for *Body on Tap* and 24 per cent (of a separate group of women) for *Sassoon*. When the "very good" and "good" ratings were combined with the "outstanding" and "excellent" ratings, however, there was no difference between the two products in the category of "strong, healthy looking hair."

The research was conducted for Bristol-Myers by Marketing Information Systems, Inc. (MISI), using a technique known as blind monadic testing. The president of MISI testified that this method typically is employed when what is wanted is an absolute response to a product "without reference to another specific product." Although he testified that blind monadic testing was used in connection with comparative advertising, that was not the purpose for which

719

Bristol-Myers retained MISI. Rather, they wished to determine consumer reaction to the introduction of *Body on Tap*.

Sassoon also found some other things wrong with the tests and the way they were represented in the Bristol-Myers advertisements. The fashion model said 900 women "like me" tried the shampoos. Actually, one-third of the women were aged 13 to 18. This was significant because *Body on Tap* appealed dispro-portionately to teenagers, and the advertising executive who created the cam-paign for Bristol-Myers testified that its purpose was to attract a large portion of the *adult* women's shampoo market.

Sassoon commissioned its own research to support its legal position. ASI Market Research, Inc. showed the *Body on Tap* commercial, along with other material, to a group of 635 women and then asked them several questions individually.

Some 95 per cent of those who responded said each of the 900 women referred to in the commercial had tried two or more brands. And 62 per cent said that the tests showed [that] *Body on Tap* was competitively superior.[1]

Is it ethical to use research data as Bristol-Myers did in this example? Earlier, both observational and projective techniques were described as means of gathering data that respondents are unable or *unwilling* to provide in response to direct questioning. Should opinions be elicited that the respon-dent does not want to give? Many questions such as these — *ethical questions* — are involved in the marketing research process.[2] Exhibit 23–1 presents several specific research practices that some individuals might view as being less than completely ethical.

It is essential that we, as marketing research students, practitioners, and professors, develop an awareness of and concern for the ethical issues of our profession. The process of studying and practicing a profession can apparently alter an individual's perceptions of the rights and prerogatives of that profes-sion.[3] For example, evidence suggests that the pursuit of a business education leads to more tolerant attitudes toward "questionable" business practices than those held by students with other majors.[4]

Thus, a person engaging in marketing research may unknowingly use tech-niques and practices that the general public considers unethical. Therefore, we should examine our field for activities that may be questionable in the view of the general public. Such an examination should lead to research practices in line with the general ethical expectations of society. This approach is not only "good" in some absolute sense, but it is also self-serving. Most of us would prefer to maintain high standards of conduct voluntarily rather than have standards set and enforced by governmental action.[5] For example, the Privacy Act of 1974 requires that respondents in a federal government survey be explicitly informed, both verbally and in writing, of (1) whether the survey is voluntary or mandatory, (2) the purpose of the survey, (3) how the information

Exhibit 23-1 *Specific Research Practices with Ethical Implications*

1. Research has consistently found that including a small amount of money in a mail survey will greatly increase the response rate. Promises of money for returning the questionnaire are much less effective. One explanation is that respondents experience guilt if they do not complete a questionnaire for which they have already been "paid," but find it not worth their while to complete a questionnaire for the amount of money usually promised. Based on this, a research firm puts 25¢ in all its mail surveys.

2. A research firm specializes in telephone surveys. It recently began using voice pitch analysis in an attempt to determine if respondents were distorting their answers to sensitive questions.

3. A mall intercept facility recently installed hidden eye-tracking equipment. Now, when respondents are asked to view advertisements or packages, they are not told that their eye movements are being recorded.

4. The research director of a large corporation is convinced that using the company's name in surveys with consumers produces (1) lowered response rates and (2) distorted answers. Therefore, the firm routinely conducts surveys using the title Public Opinion Institute.

5. A company dramatically cuts the price of its products in a city where a competitor is test marketing a new product.

6. An insurance company uses a variety of projective techniques to assist in preparing advertisements for life insurance. Potential respondents are told that the purpose of the tests is to isolate factors that influence creativity.

7. A survey finds that 80 per cent of the doctors responding do not recommend any particular brand of margarine to their patients who are concerned about cholesterol. Five per cent recommend Brand A, four per cent recommend Brand B, and no other brand is recommended by over 2 per cent of the doctors. The company runs an advertisement that states: "More doctors recommend Brand A margarine for cholesterol control than any other brand."

is to be used, and (4) the consequences to the individual of not participating in the survey.

Few commercial researchers would welcome this level of control. However, every year numerous state legislatures consider bills regulating various

Table 23 – 1 Public Perceptions of Survey Research

	1978	1980	1982	1984	1986
Positive Image Attributes	%	%	%	%	%
The research industry serves a useful purpose	85	85	84	81	85
Polls and research surveys are used to help manufacturers produce better products	81	80	80	82	83
Answering questions in polls or surveys is an interesting experience	70	64	66	60	67
Answering questions in polls or research surveys is in my own best interest	72	70	68	60	70
Survey research firms maintain the confidentiality of answers	—	60	61	54	62
Negative Image Attributes					
Some questions asked in polls or research surveys are too personal	42	47	49	51	45
The information obtained in polls or research surveys helps manufacturers sell consumers products they don't want or need	38	45	43	44	43
The term "poll" or "research survey" is used to disguise a sales pitch	43	38	38	39	40
Polls or research surveys are an invasion of privacy	31	25	26	28	24
Answering questions in polls or research surveys is a waste of time	17	18	21	22	19
The true purpose of some surveys is not disclosed	—	68	65	61	68
Last Interview Evaluation					
Pleasant experience	84	76	83	79	78
Too long	14	21	19	23	21
Overly personal questions	17	17	13	14	14
Questions confusing	—	14	13	16	15
Unpleasant experience	6	9	6	12	9

n = approximately 500 each year
Source: B. J. Kyzr-Sheeley, "Results of Walker's 1986 Industry Image Study," *The Marketing Researcher,* Vol. 16, No. 3.
Used with permission from Walker Research Inc.

aspects of the research process. For example, California, Florida, Michigan, New Jersey, Ohio, and Wyoming recently considered laws that would permit persons to have an asterisk beside their names in phone books indicating they do not want unsolicited calls. Survey researchers would be bound by this as would the various telemarketing organizations.[6]

A final benefit from a highly ethical approach to the marketing research process is improved public acceptance. Public acceptance is absolutely essential for the survival of marketing research. This is true for the general public, which provides most of the data, and for managers who base decisions on the data.

Survey research is the type of research most likely to involve the general public directly. Table 23–1 indicates that it enjoys a reasonable degree of acceptance among the general population. However, it should be noted that almost half the households contacted for this "survey on surveys" refused to participate. It is very likely that those who refuse to participate in a survey have substantially more negative attitudes toward research than those who participate.[7]

The Nature of Ethical Issues in Marketing Research

Unfortunately, we do not have a list of ethical and unethical marketing practices that covers all the situations the marketing researcher may face. Several issues are controversial within the profession.[8] Some widely accepted social values, such as the individual's right to privacy, support one position; whereas equally accepted values, such as the individual's right to seek knowledge, may support an opposing position. Where does one turn for guidance in ethical conduct when engaged in marketing research? Models for ethics in the general field of marketing have been proposed by a number of authors.[9] Each of those models provides useful insights and a general guide for action. However, none is specific enough to provide an unambiguous guide to behavior in specific marketing research situations.

The American Marketing Association provides a Marketing Research Code of Ethics, which is reproduced in Exhibit 23–2. The International Chamber of Commerce and the European Society for Opinion and Marketing Research have developed the ICC/ESOMAR International Code of Marketing and Social Research Practice, which is much more detailed and situation specific.[10]

Recent research indicates that the presence of an explicit, company specific code of ethics has a substantial impact on the behavior of those engaged in the research process.[11] Therefore, organizations should formulate, communicate, and enforce explicit statements of ethical expectations in marketing research.

Five distinct entities are affected by the research process: (1) the general public (2) the respondents in the specific study, (3) the client, (4) the researcher, and (5) the research profession. Specific ethical issues relating to each of these groups are discussed next.

Exhibit 23-2 *Marketing Research Code of Ethics**

The American Marketing Association, in furtherance of its central objective of the advancement of science in marketing and in recognition of its obligation to the public, has established these principles of ethical practice of marketing research for the guidance of its members. In an increasingly complex society, marketing management is more and more dependent upon marketing information intelligently and systematically obtained. The consumer is the source of much of this information. Seeking the cooperation of the consumer in the development of information, marketing management must acknowledge its obligation to protect the public from misrepresentation and exploitation under the guise of research.

Similarly, the research practitioner has an obligation to the discipline and to those who provide support for it — an obligation to adhere to basic and commonly accepted standards of scientific investigation as they apply to the domain of marketing research.

For Research Users, Practitioners, and Interviewers

1. No individual or organization will undertake any activity which is directly or indirectly represented to be marketing research, but which has as its real purpose the attempted sales of merchandise or services to some or all of the respondents interviewed in the course of the research.

2. If respondents have been led to believe, directly or indirectly, that they are participating in a marketing research survey and that their anonymity will be protected, their names shall not be made known to any one outside the research organization or research department, or used for other than research purposes.

For Research Practitioners

1. There will be no intentional or deliberate misrepresentation of research methods or results. An adequate description of methods employed will be made available upon request to the sponsor of the research. Evidence that fieldwork has been completed according to specifications will, upon request, be made available to buyers of the research.

2. The identity of the survey sponsor and/or the ultimate client for whom a survey is being done will be held in confidence at all times, unless this identity is to be revealed as part of the research design. Research information shall be held in confidence by the research organization or department and not used for personal gain or made available to any outside party unless the client specifically authorizes such release.

3. A research organization shall not undertake marketing studies for competitive clients when such studies would jeopardize the confidential nature of client-agency relationships.

For Users of Marketing Research

1. A user of research shall not knowingly disseminate conclusions from a given research project or service that are inconsistent with or not warranted by the data.

2. To the extent that there is involved in a research project a unique design involving techniques, approaches, or concepts not commonly available to research practitioners, the prospective user of research shall not solicit such a design from one practitioner and deliver it to another for execution without the approval of the design originator.

For Field Interviewers

1. Research assignments and materials received, as well as information obtained from respondents, shall be held in confidence by the interviewer and revealed to no one except the research organization conducting the marketing study.

2. No information gained through a marketing research activity shall be used, directly or indirectly, for the personal gain or advantage of the interviewer.

3. Interviews shall be conducted in strict accordance with specifications and instructions received.

4. An interviewer shall not carry out two or more interviewing assignments simultaneously, unless authorized by all contractors or employers concerned.

Members of the American Marketing Association will be expected to conduct themselves in accordance with the provisions of this code in all of their marketing research activities.

° Reprinted with permission from the American Marketing Association.

Ethical Issues Involving Protection of the Public

A true profession focuses first on the needs of the public or innocent third parties. A falsified research report used to justify funding for the client by a bank would be unethical (and illegal), despite the fact that it might be economically advantageous to *both* the researcher and the client. Three major areas of concern arise in this context: *incomplete reporting, misleading reporting,* and *nonobjective research.* The Advertising Research Foundation's *Guidelines for the Public Use of Market Research* described in Chapter 22 focuses on these issues.[12] Additional discussion is provided here.

Incomplete Reporting

A client or researcher withholding information that could be harmful to the public is analogous to a seller of a product not disclosing potentially damaging information about a product in a sales presentation to the buyer. Both attempt to mislead potential buyers by leaving them uninformed about undesirable features or characteristics of the product.

More common than the temptation to omit negative information is the temptation to avoid reporting situational details that are necessary to interpret the obtained results properly. For example, a common use of test market data is to persuade the trade (wholesalers and retailers) to stock and promote the new item. Therefore, some firms choose to conduct test markets in areas where their distribution or reputation is particularly strong.[13] Failure to report this fact could cause the trade to misinterpret the market response to the item.

Misleading Reporting

Misleading reporting involves presenting the research results in such a manner that the intended audience will draw a conclusion that is not justified by the results. This sometimes occurs when research results are used in advertising campaigns.

For example, an ad claimed that following comparison tests, "an amazing 60 per cent" of a sample of consumers said that Triumph cigarettes tasted as good or better than Merit. This was indeed indicated by the results. However, since many respondents said the brands tasted the same (as good as), the results also indicated that *64 per cent said that Merit tasted as good or better than Triumph!*[14] The public presentation of the results as done for Merit cigarettes would most likely mislead a substantial portion of the general public. The *Body on Tap* story at the beginning of this chapter provides a more detailed example of misleading reporting of research results.

Nonobjective Research

The researcher, the client, or both would often benefit if certain research findings were obtained. There is no doubt that the "intentional or deliberate misrepresentation of research methods or results," specified in the American Marketing Association code, is unethical. However, research techniques can be selected that will maximize the likelihood of obtaining a given finding.

Conducting test markets in areas where the firm has an unusually strong distribution system or reputation is one example of nonobjective research. The question phrasing used by Burger King to support a comparative advertisement (see page 285) is another example. Calculating and reporting means rather than medians when a few extreme values distort the mean is a third form of nonobjective research.

It is the researcher's obligation to warn management in advance of any nonobjective aspects contained in a proposed research project. The researcher should also clearly indicate in the final report the existence and probable effects of any research biases. Managers should use the resultant data in a manner consistent with the probable biases.

Ethical Issues Involving Protection of Respondents

Three ethical issues confront researchers in their relationships with respondents; namely, the use of the guise of conducting a survey to sell products, the invasion of the privacy of the respondent, and abuse of the respondents.

Use of "Marketing Research" Guise to Sell Products

The use of the statement, "I am conducting a survey," as a guise for sales presentations or to obtain information for sales leads is a major concern of legitimate researchers. Both telephone and personal "interviews" have been used as an opportunity for sales solicitation. Some mail "surveys" have served to generate sales leads or mailing lists.

Forty per cent of those interviewed in a recent national survey reported exposure to a sales pitch disguised as a survey.[15] Table 23–1 indicates widespread belief that this is a common practice. This level of abuse has occurred despite the fact that the practice is illegal as well as unethical.

A related ploy is to use a "survey" as a guise to solicit funds. Unfortunately, this technique appears to have been used by such respectable organizations as the Democratic Congressional Campaign Committee (DCCC) and the League of Women Voters.

For example, the DCCC sent a mailing with PRESIDENTIAL SURVEY ENCLOSED, 1984 DEMOCRATIC PRESIDENTIAL SURVEY, in large dark type on the envelope. The heading on the cover letter, OFFICIAL 1984

DEMOCRATIC PRESIDENTIAL SURVEY, was printed in large, bright blue letters. The same heading appeared on the "questionnaire" in bright red letters. However, the "questionnaire" contained only two questions and a "contribution" form. The majority of the four-page cover letter and the one-page "questionnaire" focused on encouraging a monetary contribution.

The authors of this text believe that this use of "survey research" is unethical. In our view, any communication described to a respondent as a survey or interview should have the collection of data as its *sole* purpose.

Invasion of Privacy of Respondents

The *right to privacy* refers to the public's general feeling or perception of its ability to restrict the amount of personal data it will make available to outsiders. The three important elements involved in this "right" are the *concept of privacy* itself, the concept of *informed consent* by which an individual can waive the right to privacy, and the concept that *anonymity and confidentiality* can help protect those whose privacy has, to some extent, been invaded.

The *right to privacy is the right of individuals to decide for themselves how much they will share with others* their thoughts, feelings, and the facts of their personal lives. What is private varies between individuals and within individuals from day to day and setting to setting. The essence of the concept is the right of *each individual to decide in each particular setting or compartment of his or her life how much to reveal.* As Table 23–1 shows, the public is concerned about the intrusion of marketing research into their privacy.[16]

Because the essence of the right of privacy is the individual's ability to *choose* what will be revealed, the marketing researcher must not abrogate the respondent's ability to choose. This requires the researcher to obtain the *informed consent* of the potential respondents.

Informed means providing potential respondents with sufficient information for them to determine whether participation is worthwhile and desirable, *from their point of view.* This would, in general, involve a description of the types of questions to be asked or the task required, the subject areas covered, the time and physical effort involved, and the ultimate use to which the resultant data will be put.

Few requests for cooperation for marketing research studies convey all of this information.[17] However, several studies on the effect of providing full information, including statements stressing the respondent's right *not* to participate, have found these procedures to have no or minimal effects on the overall response rate, item response rate, or the nature of the obtained responses.[18] In addition, these procedures do not appear to affect the respondents' evaluations of the interview itself.[19]

Some marketing studies and techniques may be less able to withstand full disclosure. Disguised techniques are based on the premise that more accurate or meaningful answers can be obtained if the respondent is not aware of the purpose of the questions. Revealing the sponsor's name can, in some circumstances, affect responses.

As Table 23–1 indicates, most respondents believe that the "true purpose of some surveys is not disclosed." However, this does not seem to deter their willingness to participate in surveys or to lower their overall belief in the value of marketing research.

To the extent that full informed consent cannot be obtained, *anonymity* and *confidentiality* are important. *Anonymity* means that the identity of the subject is never known to anyone. *Confidentiality* means that the respondent's identity is known to only a limited number of investigators but is otherwise protected from dissemination.

Unfortunately, there is increasing concern about the ability or willingness of research firms to maintain the confidentiality of their data. This increased concern probably arises from a combination of publicity about: (1) the use of research to generate sales leads, (2) the theft and/or transferral of computerized data, and (3) the practice of magazines and other organizations selling their mailing lists.

Abuse of Respondents

Respondents can be abused in a variety of ways. Frequent interviewing of the same respondents is a form of abuse. For example, middle-class, younger (under 35) females are particularly likely to be interviewed frequently.[20]

Overly long interviews are an abuse of the respondents. Table 23–1 indicates that many respondents view their last interview as lasting too long. This is particularly serious when respondents are uninformed or are misled concerning the length of the interview.

Asking personal questions that are not absolutely required to solve the problem at hand should be avoided. For example, if the managerial problem requires a comparison of households with incomes over $50,000 with those under $50,000, respondents should not be asked their exact household income. Instead, they can be asked to indicate if their household income is above or below $50,000.

Confusing questions, poorly trained interviewers, hard-to-read questionnaires, and other factors that place an unnecessary burden on respondents should be avoided.[21] When respondents agree to give the researcher their time and energy, it is the researcher's responsibility to minimize the effort required of them.

Ethical Issues Involving the Protection of the Client

Every professional has the obligation to protect the client in matters relating to their professional relationship. The marketing researcher is no exception. The matters in which the client may expect protection when authorizing a marketing research project include protection against (1) *abuse of position arising from specialized knowledge*, (2) *unnecessary research*, (3) *an unqualified researcher*, (4) *disclosure of identity*, (5) *treating data as nonconfidential and/or nonpropriety*, and (6) *misleading presentation of data*.

Protection Against Abuse of Position

The marketing manager is generally at a substantial disadvantage in discussing a research project. Most researchers have specialized knowledge and experience that the marketing manager cannot match. Therefore, the manager is frequently forced to accept the researcher's suggestions at face value, just as we often accept the advice of medical doctors or lawyers. Like other professionals, the marketing researcher often has the opportunity to take advantage of specialized knowledge to the detriment of the client. Recommending expensive primary data collection when less expensive secondary data would provide adequate information is an example of abuse of position.

Protection Against Unnecessary Research

Researchers are sometimes requested to engage in a specific research project that is unrelated to the underlying problem, has been done before, or is economically unjustified. The researcher can often benefit from such an activity. This gain will frequently exceed whatever goodwill might be generated by refusing to conduct unwarranted research. Should the researcher accept such assignments?

A sales representative may not feel obligated to be certain that the customer really needs the product (although a careful application of the marketing concept requires it). Yet, a doctor or lawyer is ethically prohibited from prescribing unwarranted medicine or legal action. A marketing researcher has a professional obligation to indicate to the client that, in his or her judgment, the research expenditure is not warranted. If, after this judgment has been *clearly* stated, the client still desires the research, the researcher should feel free to conduct the study. The reason for this is that the researcher can never know for certain the risk preferences and strategies that are guiding the client's behavior.

Protection Against Unqualified Researchers

Another area of concern involves the request for research that is beyond the capabilities or technical expertise of the individual researcher or research organization. The cost, both psychological and economic, from saying, "I cannot do this as well as some other individual" can be quite high. However, accepting a project beyond the researcher's capacities typically results in time delays, higher costs, and decreased accuracy.

Again, professional ethics should compel the researcher to indicate to the potential client the fact that the research requires the application of techniques that are outside his or her area of expertise.

Protection of Anonymity of Client

The client will have authorized a marketing research project either to help identify or to help solve marketing problems. In either case, it may well be to the advantage of competitors to know that the study is being done. The researcher is therefore obligated ethically to preserve the anonymity of the client. The fact that a particular firm is sponsoring a study should not be revealed to *any* outside party unless the client so agrees. This includes respondents and other existing and potential clients.

Protection of Confidential and Proprietary Information

The data generated for a particular client and the conclusions and interpretations from those data are the exclusive property of the client. It is obvious that a researcher should not turn over a client's study to one of the client's competitors. However, what if the researcher gathers basic demographic material on a geographic area for one client and the same information is required for a study by a noncompeting client? The American Marketing Association code is not clear on this point, but it seems to suggest that such data cannot be used twice without the explicit consent of the original client. Reuse of the data, assuming that permission is granted, should result in the two clients sharing the cost of this aspect of the research rather than the research organization charging twice.

One researcher expresses the pressures and problems generated by this issue clearly:

> I get involved in a number of proprietary studies. The problem that often arises is that some studies end up covering similar subject matter as previous studies. Our code of ethics states that you cannot use data from one project in a related project for a competitor. However, since I often know some information about an area, I end up compromising my original client. Even though upper management formally states that it should not be done, they also expect it to be done to cut down on expenses. This conflict of interest situation is difficult to deal with. At least in my firm, I don't see a resolution to the issue. It is not a one time situation, but rather a process that perpetuates itself. To make individuals redo portions of studies which have recently been done is ludicrous, and to forgo potential new business is almost impossible from a financial perspective.[22]

Protection Against Misleading Presentations of Data

Reports that are represented orally or are written in such a way as to give deliberately the impression of greater accuracy than the data warrant are obviously not in the best interest of the client. Such an impression can be left by reports by a number of means. These include the use of *overly technical jargon, failure to round numbers properly, unnecessary use of complex analytic procedures,* and *incomplete reporting.*

Overly Technical Jargon. All specialties tend to develop a unique terminology. By and large, this is useful as it allows those familiar with the field to communicate in a more concise and precise way. However, technical jargon and extensive mathematical notation can also convey a false aura of complexity and precision. The research report's primary function is to convey *to the client* the results of the research. It is not the proper place to demonstrate the complexity of sampling formulas or the range of terms that are unique to the research process.

Failure to Round Numbers Properly. An impression of greater precision than the data warrant can also be created through the failure to round numbers properly. For example, a statement that the average annual expenditure by some group for furniture is $261.17 implies more precision than is generally warranted. If the researcher believes that the data are accurate to the nearest $10, the average should be rounded to $260. If the data were developed from a sample, the use of a confidence interval might be appropriate, as well.

Unnecessary Use of Complex Analytic Procedures. The transformation of the data into logarithms when they could just as well be analyzed in arithmetic form, and the normalizing of data when they would be better left in nonnormalized states are examples of needlessly complex analytic procedures. When unnecessary, the use of such procedures is confusing at best and misleading at worst.

Incomplete Reporting. Incomplete reporting renders an objective appraisal of the research report impossible. It can create false impressions of the accuracy of the research or even of the meaning of the resultant data. Both the initial client and any concerned third party have a right to expect a report that will allow them to make a reasonable assessment of the accuracy of the data.

An example should make this point clear. Assume that a sample is drawn from a population of 10,000 firms and the final report shows an obtained sample size of 750. On the surface, this may appear to be a reasonable sample size. However, unless other descriptive data are given, there is no way to estimate the potential impact of nonresponse error. An evaluation of the probable effects of this source of error requires a knowledge of the response

Exhibit 23-3 *Information to Be Included in the Research Firm's Report**

Every research project differs from all others. So will every research report. All reports should nonetheless contain specific reference to the following items:

1. The objectives of the study (including statement of hypotheses)
2. The name of the organization for which the study is made and the name of the organization that conducted it
3. Dates the survey was in the field and date of submission of final report
4. A copy of the full interview questionnaire, including all cards and visual aids, used in the interview; alternatively, exact question wording, sequence of questions, etc.
5. Description of the universe(s) studied
6. Description of the number and types of people studied:
   a. Number of people (or other units)
   b. Means of their selection
   c. If sample, method of sample selection
   d. Adequacy of sample representation and size
   e. Percentage of original sample contacted (number and type of callbacks)
   f. Range of tolerance (sample error)
   g. Number of cases for category breakouts
   h. Weighting and estimating procedures used

Where trend data are being reported and the methodology or question wording has been changed, these changes should be so noted.

On request — clients and other parties with legitimate interests may request and should expect to receive from the research firm the following:

a. Statistical and/or field methods of interview verification (and percentage of interviews verified)
b. Available data on validation of interview techniques
c. Explanation of scoring or index numbers devices

* *Source:* Paper developed by The Market Research Council's Ethics Committee. Reprinted with permission from Leo Bogart, ed., *Current Controversies in Marketing Research* (Rand McNally College Publishing Company, 1969), 156. Copyright © 1969 by Markham Publishing Company, Chicago, Reprinted by permission of Rand McNally College Publishing Company.

rate. The 750 respondents could represent a response rate as low as 10 or 20 per cent or as high as 100 per cent. One's confidence in the resulting data would vary considerably between these two extremes.

One guide to what should be presented in a research report, from an ethical standpoint, is presented in Exhibit 23–3.

Ethical Issues Involving Protection of the Research Firm

Several issues can arise in the research firm-client relationship in which the research organization needs protection. These include protection against *improper solicitation of proposals, disclosure of proprietary information on techniques,* and *misrepresentation of findings.*

Protection Against Improper Solicitation of Proposals

Research proposals should be requested *only* as an aid in deciding whether to conduct the research and/or which research firm to use. Similarly, proposals should be evaluated solely on their merit unless the other criteria (size and/or special capabilities of the research firm) are made known in advance. Proposals from one research firm should not be given to a second firm or an in-house research department for implementation.

Protection Against Disclosure of Proprietary Information or Techniques

Research firms often develop special techniques for dealing with certain types of problems. Examples are models predicting the success of new products, models for allocation of advertising expenditures among media, and simulation techniques for predicting effects of changes in the marketing mix variables. Research firms properly regard these techniques as being proprietary. The client should not make these techniques known to other research firms or appropriate them for its own use without the explicit consent of the developer.

Protection Against Misrepresentation of Findings

Suppose the *Honest and Ethical Research Firm* is commissioned to do a study of analgesics by the manufacturer of *Brand A* aspirin. In its report of the findings the statement is made that "Brand A aspirin was reported to be the aspirin most preferred by two of three respondents using only aspirin as an analgesic for headaches." In its advertising on television to consumers, however, the firm makes the statement, "According to a study conducted by the *Honest and Ethical Research Firm*, two of three consumers preferred *Brand A* aspirin to all other products for treatment of headaches."

This is a clear distortion of the findings. It not only misleads the viewer, but is potentially damaging to the research firm as well. Other manufacturers of analgesics will recognize that this is not a true statement and may conclude that the research firm is guilty either of a careless piece of research or of dishonesty in reporting the results.

Ethical Issues Involving Protection of the Research Profession

There is debate as to whether marketing research is a profession or not.[23] It is the belief of your authors that the long-run viability of marketing research hinges on its being recognized as a profession.[24] All of the issues we have described thus far affect the professional status of marketing research. In addition, two other concerns emerge.

Use of Accepted Research Procedures

Whereas there are multiple ways to generate data relevant to most marketing problems, marketing researchers should follow sound research procedures or *clearly* indicate any departures. A profession attempts to "do it right" and treats "doing it right" as an end in itself.

Marketing research professionals recognize that research that produces wrong managerial decisions harms the entire practice of marketing research. If marketing research is to become a true profession, quotations such as the one that follows must become nonexistent:

> The most difficult moral problem is how to handle a situation in which our company has made a mistake in study design (or in study execution) which results in obtaining results that are unreliable or invalid. We try to bury the mistake and concentrate on the valid parts of the study in those cases.[25]

Would you like your doctor to have this attitude?

Inappropriate Use of Marketing Research Techniques

Marketing research firms and others often use marketing research techniques in areas that at least some of the public feel should not be studied in this manner.

Most major political campaigns make extensive use of marketing research.[26] There is concern about our national leaders using marketing research to develop positions that reflect what the public wants rather than trying to persuade the public to support what it needs. In addition, the early and frequent release of opinion poll results influences the ability of candidates to raise funds and otherwise gain support.

Exhibit 23–4 describes another controversial use of marketing research technology. Although there are no easy answers to the ethical questions raised by applying marketing research methodologies in courtroom situations, these questions have serious implications for both legal practice and marketing research.[27]

Exhibit 23–4 *The Ethics of Using Marketing Research Technology to Select Juries and Develop Appeals to Juries*

- A teenage girl is left a quadriplegic after an automobile accident. The defendant in a law suit for damages was the teenage driver of the car in which the girl was riding. The fact that the driver was heavily insured could not be admitted into evidence. The girl's lawyer was afraid the jury would be reluctant to impose a large judgment against the teenager.

The girl's lawyer hired a marketing research firm to conduct a community survey to determine the demographic characteristics of people most likely to hold a teenager liable for large damages. This information was used by the attorney to guide his jury selection.

- A simulated jury is a group of individuals with similar characteristics — such as age, gender, and political affiliation — as the members of the actual jury. The simulated jury either sits in the audience of the courtroom and reports its reactions to the actual proceedings or listens to lawyers present arguments that they plan to use in the trial and responds to both the content and the style of the presentation.

A simulated jury was used by IBM in a $300 million antitrust unit. Six individuals with backgrounds similar to the actual jury were paid to attend the trial each day (they did not know which side employed them). They weighed the evidence and reported their impressions each evening. IBM developed much of its strategy around this information. It won the case.

MCI Communications used simulated juries in an antitrust suit against AT&T. It used several mock juries that allowed its attorneys to try out various arguments *before* presenting them in front of the real jury. It won the largest award in history.

Source: L. B. Andrews, "Mind Control in the Courtroom," *Psychology Today* (March 1982).

Corporate Espionage

In the section of Chapter 14 that dealt with observation techniques, it was suggested that observation techniques were widely used to monitor shifts in competitor's prices, advertising, products, and the like. No ethical issue is involved in observing the *public* behavior of competitors.[28] Corporate espionage is not concerned with this type of observation, however. Rather, it refers to observations of activities or products that the competitor is taking reasonable care to conceal from public view. Activities of this nature pose both ethical and legal questions.

Espionage techniques include such activities as electronic eavesdropping, bribing competitors' employees, planting "spies" in a competitor's organization, sifting through garbage, eavesdropping at bars frequented by competitor's employees, and hiring away competitor's employees to learn of their future plans or secret processes.

The threat, real or imagined, of espionage by competitors has led many firms to engage in elaborate security systems. These systems may be internal or external. It is a sad comment that the industrial counterespionage business is apparently flourishing, although it is not clear that espionage is actually a widespread practice.

Techniques of corporate espionage have not been described in any detail in this text. We do not consider such activities to be a legitimate part of the business world, much less an acceptable part of the marketing research function. Many of these practices are illegal and all are unethical. They are referred to in this section of the text only to prevent the student from naïvely thinking that they do not exist.

Review Questions

23.1. What does the Privacy Act of 1974 require with respect to federal government surveys?

23.2. Describe the Marketing Research Code of Ethics developed by the American Marketing Association.

23.3. Describe the ethical issues involving the *protection of the public.*

23.4. Describe the ethical issues involving the *protection of the client.*

23.5. Describe the ethical issues involving the *protection of the research firm.*

23.6. Describe the ethical issues involving the *protection of the respondents.*

23.7. What is *informed consent?*

23.8. What is the difference between *anonymity* and *confidentiality?*

23.9. Describe the ethical issues involving the *protection of the marketing research profession.*

23.10. What is meant by *corporate espionage?* How does it differ from standard observation techniques?

Discussion Questions/Problems

23.11. Discuss the ethical issues involved in the situations described in Exhibit 23–1.

23.12. Discuss the ethical implications of Exhibit 23–4.

23.13. Evaluate the code of ethics presented in Exhibit 23–2.

23.14. Evaluate the reporting requirements suggested in Exhibit 23–3.

23.15. Discuss the ethical implications of the following situations:°

    a. A project director recently came in to request permission to use ultraviolet ink in precoding questionnaires on a mail survey. He pointed out that the cover letter referred to an anonymous survey, but he said he needed respondent identification to permit adequate cross tabulations of the data. The M. R. director gave his approval.

    b. One product of the X company is brassieres, and the firm has recently been having difficulty making some decisions on a new line. Information was critically needed concerning the manner in which women put on their brassieres. So the M. R. director designed a study in which two local stores cooperated in putting one-way mirrors in their foundations dressing rooms. Observers behind these mirrors successfully gathered the necessary information.

    c. In a study intended to probe rather deeply into the buying motivations of a group of wholesale customers by use of a semistructured personal interview form, the M. R. director authorized the use of the department's special attaché case equipped with hidden tape recorders.

    d. Some of X company's customers are busy executives, hard to reach by normal interviewing methods. Accordingly, the market research department recently conducted a study in which interviewers called "long distance" from nearby cities. They were successful in getting through to busy executives in almost every instance.

    e. In another study, this one concerning magazine reading habits, the M. R. director decided to contact a sample of consumers under the name of Media Research Institute. This fictitious company name successfully camouflaged the identity of the sponsor of the study.

° C. M. Crawford, "Attitudes of Marketing Executives Toward Ethics in Marketing Research," *Journal of Marketing* (April 1970, 46–52. Used with permission of the American Marketing Association. See also I. P. Akaah and E. A. Riordan, "Judgments of Marketing Professionals About Ethical Issues in Marketing Research" *Journal of Marketing Research* (February 1989), 112–120.

      f. In the trial run of a major presentation to the board of directors, the marketing vice-president deliberately distorted some recent research findings. After some thought, the M. R. director decided to ignore the matter since the marketing head obviously knew what he was doing.

23.16. Is it ethical to utilize projective techniques to determine an individual's attitudes about a product without disclosing the reason? Justify your answer.

23.17. Should the response rate always be reported when reporting the results of survey research? Why?

23.18. A manufacturer of small appliances issues a guarantee with each appliance that covers more variables and a longer time period than any of its competitors. This guarantee is featured in the firm's advertising and on the product packages. However, for the guarantee to be effective, the consumer must first complete a questionnaire designed by the marketing research department. Is this an ethical approach to data collection?

23.19. "Individuals acquire telephones so that they can talk with whomever they wish and so that those wishing to talk with them can do so easily. If they do not wish to be called by people other than those they select, they can obtain an unlisted phone number. Therefore, marketing research techniques such as random digit dialing, which results in contacts with persons with unlisted numbers, are a direct invasion of a person's privacy. These techniques should be illegal. They are clearly unethical." Comment.

23.20. "Observational studies in which the subjects are not first informed that their behavior is being observed are unethical." Comment.

23.21. Clients sometimes request and even insist that a specific question be included in a questionnaire. How should the researcher react to this if it is felt that the question will produce biased data?

23.22. Develop a marketing research code of ethics. How, if at all, would this code be enforced?

23.23. Discuss the ethical implications of the following situations:°
      a. Researcher poses as graduate student working on a thesis in order to gain information that competitors might not otherwise give.
      b. Researcher calls the vice-president while he is at lunch, hoping to find the secretary who may have some information but is less likely to be suspicious about researcher's motives.
      c. Researcher calls competitor's suppliers and distributors, pretending to do a study of the entire industry. Researcher poses as a representative of a private research firm and works at home during the project so that the company's identity is protected.

° Adopted from B. Whalen, "Business Ethics Are Taking a Beating," *Marketing News*, May 25, 1984, 1+.

    d. The competitor's representative is coming to a local college to recruit employees. Researcher poses as a student job-seeker to learn recruiting practices and other general information about competitor.

    e. The researcher is asked to verify rumors that the competitor is planning to open a new plant in a small southern town. The researcher poses as an agent from a manufacturer looking for a site similar to the one that the competitor supposedly would need. Researcher uses this cover to become friendly with local representatives of the Chamber of Commerce, newspapers, realtors, etc.

    f. Researcher corners a competitor's employee at a national conference and offers to buy drinks at the hotel bar. Several drinks later, the researcher asks the hard questions.

    g. Researcher hires an individual who works for the competitor to serve as an informant to researcher's company.

23.24. Discuss the ethics of the following situations:

    Pretests show that the average time to complete a particular telephone interview is 20 minutes. They also show a sharp drop in the response rate if respondents are told in advance that the interview will last 20 minutes. Telling them it will take 15 minutes does *not* reduce the response rate. The researcher:

    a. does not provide any information in advance on the length of the interview

    b. tells the respondents it "will take only a few minutes"

    c. tells the respondents it "will take about 15 minutes"

Projects

23.25. Develop a 10-point 'ethical-unethical' and a 10-point 'common-uncommon' scale for each of the situations in problem 23–15. Have 25 marketing majors and 25 nonbusiness majors evaluate each situation. Analyze the results and prepare a report.

23.26. Repeat 23.25 using the situations in problem 23.23.

23.27. Repeat 23.25 using the situations in Exhibit 23–1.

23.28. Repeat 23.25 using a nonstudent group for the 25 nonbusiness majors.

23.29. Repeat 23.26 using a nonstudent group for the 25 nonbusiness majors.

23.30. Repeat 23.27 using a nonstudent group for the 25 nonbusiness majors.

23.31. Interview a marketing researcher. Report on his or her perceptions of the major ethical problems in the field.

23.32. Read (a) "Mind Control in the Courtroom," *Psychology Today* (March 1982), 66–73; and (b) "Marketing Research and Corporate Ligation," *Journal of Business Ethics*, 3 (1984), 185–194. Prepare a report presenting your evaluation of the ethics of this use of marketing research.

References

[1] S. A. Diamond, "Market Research Latest Target in Ad Claims," *Advertising Age,* January 25, 1982, 52. Used with permission.

[2] S. D. Hunt, L. B. Chonko, and J. B. Wilcox, "Ethical Problems of Marketing Researchers," *Journal of Marketing Research* (August 1984), 309–324.

[3] See W. French and M. Ebner, "A Practical Look at Research Ethics," *Journal of Data Collection* (Fall 1986), 49–53; and O. C. Ferrell and S. J. Skinner, "Ethical Behavior and Bureaucratic Structure in Marketing Research Organizations," *Journal of Marketing Research* (February 1988) 103–109.

[4] D. I. Hawkins and A. B. Cocanougher, "Student Evaluations of the Ethics of Marketing Practices: The Role of Marketing Education," *Journal of Marketing* (April 1972), 61–64. See also F. K. Shuptrine, "Evaluating the Ethics of Marketing Practices," in N. Beckwith et al. *1979 Educators' Conference Proceedings* (Chicago: American Marketing Association, 1979), 124–127.

[5] C. J. Frey and T. C. Kinnear, "Legal Constraints and Marketing Research," *Journal of Marketing Research* (August 1979), 295–302; and R. Schweizer, "Present and Future Data Flow Legislation," *European Research* (January 1986), 29–34.

[6] "Self-Regulated Research," *Marketing News,* January 2, 1987, 1.

[7] See also S. W. McDaniel, P. Verille, and C. S. Madden, "The Threats to Marketing Research," *Journal of Marketing Research* (February 1985), 74–80; and J. Goyder, "Surveys on Surveys," *Public Opinion Quarterly* (Spring 1986), 27–41.

[8] J. G. Smith, "Should We Measure Involuntary Responses?" *Journal of Advertising Research* (October 1979), 35–39; A. M. Tybout and G. Zaltman, "Ethics in Marketing Research: Their Practical Relevance," *Journal of Marketing Research* (November 1974), 357–368; R. L. Day, "A Comment on 'Ethics in Marketing Research," *Journal of Marketing Research* (May 1975), 232–233; and A. M. Tybout and G. Zaltman, "A Reply to Comments on 'Ethics in Marketing Research: Their Practical Relevance," *Journal of Marketing Research* (May 1975), 234–237.

[9] See P. E. Murphy and G. R. Laczniak, "Marketing Ethics," *Review of Marketing 1984,* edited by B. M. Enis and K. J. Roering (Chicago: American Marketing Association, 1981), 251–266; G. R. Laczniak, "Framework for Analyzing Marketing Ethics," *Journal of Macromarketing* (Spring 1983), 7–18; G. R. Laczniak and P. E. Murphy, *Marketing Ethics* (Lexington, Mass.: Lexington Books, 1985); and O. C. Ferrell and L. G. Gresham, "A Contingency Framework for Understanding Ethical Decision Making in Marketing," *Journal of Marketing Research* (Summer 1985), 87–96.

[10] C. H. Winquist and C. C. J. de Koning, "ICC/ESOMAR International Code of Marketing and Social Research Practice," in R. Worcester and J. Downham, *Consumer Market Research Handbook* (New York: North-Holland, 1986), 813–826.

[11] Ferrell and Skinner, op. cit.

[12] Advertising Research Foundation, *Guidelines for the Public Use of Market and Opinion Research* (New York: Advertising Research Foundation, 1981). See also D. H. Furse and D. W. Stewart, "Standards for Advertising Copytesting," *Journal of Advertising* (4, 1982), 30–38.

[13] C. L. Hodock, "Intellectual Dishonesty," *Marketing News,* January 20, 1984, 1.

[14] S. A. Diamond, "Market Research Latest Target in Ad Claims," *Advertising Age,* January 25, 1982, 52.

[15] B. J. Kyzr-Sheeley, "Results of Walker's 1986 Industry Image Study," *The Marketing Researcher* (Indianapolis; Walker Research, Inc., 1986), 3.

[16] E. D. Godfield, "Two Studies Probe Public's Feelings on Being Surveyed," *Marketing News* (March 25, 1977), 6; and E. Singer, "Public Reactions to Some Ethical Issues of Social Research," *Journal of Consumer Research* (June 1984), 501–509.

[17] J. Sobal, "The Content of Survey Introductions and the Provision of Informed Consent," *Public Opinion Quarterly* (Winter 1984), 788–793.

[18] E. Singer, "Informed Consent: Consequences for Response Rate and Response Quality in Social Surveys," *American Sociological Review* (April 1978), 144–162; D. I. Hawkins, "The Impact of Sponsor Identification and Direct Disclosure of Respondents' Rights on the Quantity and Quality of Mail Survey Data," *Journal of Business* (October 1979), 577–590; and E. Singer and M. R. Frankel, "Informed Consent Procedures in Telephone Interviews," *American Sociological Review* (June 1982), 416–427.

[19] E. Singer, "The Effects of Informed Consent Procedures on Respondents' Reactions to Surveys," *Journal of Consumer Research* (June 1978), 49–57.

[20] Kyzr-Sheeley, op. cit., 4; and S. Schleifer, "Survey Participation," *Marketing News,* February 15, 1985, 1.

[21] See L. M. Sharp and J. Frankel, "Respondent Burden," *Public Opinion Quarterly* (Spring 1983), 36–53.

[22] Hunt, Chonko, and Wilcox, op. cit., 314.

[23] K. C. Schneider, "Marketing Research 'Industry' Isn't Moving Toward Professionalism," *Marketing Educator* (Winter 1984), 1.

[24] For a discussion of professionalism, see T. E. Schaefer, "Professionalism," *Journal of Business Ethics,* 3 (1984), 269–277.

[25] Hunt, Chonko, and Wilcox, op. cit.

[26] See J. J. Honomichl, "President Reagan's Marketing Plan" and "The Big Four of Political Research" in J. J. Honomichl, *Marketing Research People* (Lincolnwood, Ill.: Crain Books, 1984), 67–84 and 85–94.

[27] S. M. Smith, "Marketing Research and Corporate Litigation," *Journal of Business Ethics,* 3 (1984),185–194; and C. Schleier, "Lawyers, Court Help in Jury Selection," *Advertising Age,* November 14, 1985, 30–32.

[28] See L. M. Fuld, *Competitor Intelligence* (New York: John Wiley & Sons, 1985).

CASE V–1 WEYERHAEUSER X: RESEARCH REPORT

Use the information in the previous Weyerhaeuser cases to prepare (a) a written report and (b) a 20-minute oral report to Weyerhaeuser's top management committee. The report should deal with the issues raised in Case I–2.

1. Base your report on an actual analysis of the real data from Case IV–2.
2. Base your report on what such an analysis might logically produce.

CASE V–2 MARKETING RESEARCH AND COMPARATIVE ADVERTISING

Variety Brands has had several brands of both canned and dry dog food on the market for over 30 years. However, its market share lagged far behind such competitors as Gaines Foods, Ralston Purina, and Carnation. It recently developed and introduced a special food for puppies.

Variety's scientists assured management that the new product was nutritionally superior to any product on the market. However, sales were disappointing. Management asked the marketing research department to demonstrate the superiority of the product.

Kevin Perez was placed in charge of the project. He decided to elicit opinions from veterinarians. Past experience had convinced Kevin that Variety would lose in a direct comparison with its leading competitors because of their strong overall reputations. He felt that this would occur even if the Variety product were superior.

With this concern in mind, Kevin conducted a large-scale survey of vets engaged in small animal practice. A virtually perfect sampling frame was obtained since all vets are licensed. Prenotification, initial questionnaire with $1.00 enclosed, reminder postcard, second questionnaire with $1.00 enclosed, and a final postcard produced a response rate of 76 per cent.

The questionnaire asked the vets to compare blind product descriptions (formulas and nutritional content *without* brand names) of Variety and the three leading puppy foods.

Based on the results of the survey, an advertising campaign was launched with the key claim—"Variety puppy food was preferred by responding vets more than two to one over other leading brands of puppy food."

1. Evaluate the methodology used.

2. Comment on Kevin's ethics in using a blind product description comparison.

3. Comment on the ethics of using the survey results as described in the case. Would your response change if the claim had been for "Variety's puppy food formula" rather than "Variety puppy food"?

CASE V – 3 HYDRA PRODUCTS

Hydra Products manufactures and markets a number of products, including a low-cholesterol cooking oil. The firm's brand, H-P Oil, is the leading selling oil. As part of a major evaluation of the marketing mix used for H-P Oil, the firm hired a nationally known marketing research firm to assess physicians' knowledge, attitudes, and behavior with respect to this product category.

The researchers interviewed 2,000 physicians in a nationwide survey. One of their most significant conclusions was that "Most physicians lack sufficient knowledge of the relationship between heart disease and diet to provide meaningful recommendations on diet to their patients." In addition, the following specific findings were of particular interest to Hydra Products' management.

1. Of the 2,000 doctors surveyed, 1,400 recommended the use of a low-cholesterol cooking oil to patients who need to lower their cholesterol levels. Of those 1,400, 600 doctors recommended a specific brand. However, a doctor's recommendation often appeared to be based on factors other than a depth of knowledge of the health-related attributes of the various brands. The distribution of those doctors recommending a specific brand was as follows:

Brand	%
H-P Oil	34
A	15
B	14
C	12
D	8
All others	17

2. Of the 2,000 doctors surveyed, 1,200 were unaware of the brand of oil used in their own homes. The distribution of brands among those who were aware of the brand used was as follows:

Brand	%
H-P Oil	14
A	12
B	10
C	6
D	6
All others	52

Based on these findings, Hydra Products developed a new advertising campaign that featured the following claims:

- Of those doctors interviewed in a national survey, more than twice as many recommend H-P Oil than any other brand to their patients.
- Of those doctors interviewed in a national survey, more reported using H-P Oil in their own home than any other brand.

1. Was Hydra Products' use of the research data ethical? Why?

2. Assume that the Federal Trade Commission believed that the advertisements were misleading. Devise a research project that would provide information on whether the advertisements were, in fact, misleading.

745

Expected Value Analysis

In this appendix we develop, and apply, the formal mathematical analysis that underlies the expected value approach. We include a discussion of risk preferences and how they can be included in the calculation of expected value of information.

A Decision about Test Marketing a New Product

A few years ago, a product manager and the marketing research manager of the General Mills Company disagreed about the need for having a potential new product test marketed. The research manager wanted to run a market test before deciding whether to introduce the new product, and the product manager thought that this would be a waste of time and money. Their disagreement was so strong and the discussion became so heated that the research manager accused the product manager of misleading management. The product manager in turn accused the research manager of not recognizing a sound new product idea when he saw one.

After their tempers had cooled somewhat, they agreed to write down the estimates that were the basis for their respective conclusions. The estimates were as follows:[1]

[1] These estimates are contrived, although the situation described is an actual one.

Break-Even Sales for New Product	Research Manager 500,000 Units	Product Manager 500,000 Units
Forecasts of sales and profits	"Good chance" (odds of about 7 out of 10, or 70%) that sales for the 3-year planning period would be between 500,000 and 800,000 units, with 650,000 units as the most likely level. With sales of 650,000 units, profits are estimated to be $2,650,000. "Fair chance" (about 30%) that sales for the 3 years will be between 300,000 and 500,000 units, with most likely level (if so) of 400,000 units. With sales of 400,000 units, losses are estimated to be $2,120,000.	"Very good chance" (odds of about 8 out of 10, or 80%) that sales would be between 500,000 and 1,100,000 units during the 3-year planning period, with 800,000 units as the most likely level. With sales of 800,000 units, profits are estimated to be $4,250,000. "Not very likely but some chance" (about 20%) that sales will be between 400,000 and 500,000 units, with most likely level (if so) of 450,000 units. With sales of 450,000 units, losses are estimated at $1,100,000.
Cost of test marketing the product in four cities for one year	$350,000	$350,000
Accuracy of market test	"Very good." About 85% chance of the test correctly indicating whether the break-even sales volume would be reached.	"Very good." About 85% chance of the test correctly indicating whether the break-even sales volume would be reached.
Conclusion	Run market test before deciding whether to introduce the product.	Introduce the product without running a market test.

As may be seen, the differences that had caused the dispute were concerned with both the *chance* and the *amount* of profits. The research manager was not as optimistic as the product manager, either with respect to the chance that the product would be profitable or, if it were, the amount of profit that would result. They had no disagreement about the break-even point in terms of sales, however, or the accuracy or estimated cost of the market test.

Both managers used the *intuitive approach* to making their initial decisions about whether or not the market test should be conducted. We are now going to apply *expected value* analysis to their estimates to see if their earlier decisions are consistent with the results we get from it.

Initially we will calculate the expected value of the market test information on the assumption that both managers were *risk neutral* (neither risk assuming nor risk averse.) Later we examine the implications of that assumption.

The Expected Value Approach to Determining the Value of Information

The Conditional Payoff Table

Before explaining the expected value model, let us summarize the data from the example using a *conditional payoff table*. Although not required, it is generally wise to start any expected value analysis by constructing such a table. This serves as a convenient visual display and helps ensure that no data are overlooked.

A conditional payoff table provides data on the payoffs for each alternative being considered for each state of the market. The personal probabilities associated with each market state are also shown.

In the General Mills problem, a conditional payoff table is required for both the research manager and the brand manager since both their payoff and

Table A – 1 Conditional Payoff Table for the Research Manager

	State of Market 1 (S₁) (Favorable Market)		State of Market 2 (S₂) (Unfavorable Market)	
	Probability— P(S₁)	Payoff	Probability— P(S₂)	Payoff
A₁ Introduce	.70	$2,650,000	.30	<$2,120,000>°
A₂ Do not introduce	.70	0	.30	0

° <denotes loss>.

Table A–2 Conditional Payoff Table for the Product Manager

	State of Market 1 (S₁) (Favorable Market)		State of Market 2 (S₂) (Unfavorable Market)	
	Probability — $P(S_1)$	Payoff	Probability — $P(S_2)$	Payoff
A_1 Introduce	.80	$4,250,000	.20	<$1,100,000>°
A_2 Do not introduce	.80	0	.20	0

° <denotes loss>.

probability estimates differed. The required data were given in the initial description of the problem and are reproduced in Tables A–1 and A–2.

Expected Value of Perfect Information (EVPI)

Imagine for the moment that the market test could provide *perfect information*. That is, if the market test were run, the indication provided by it as to which market state was the true state would be *certain* to be correct. Practically speaking, this level of accuracy of information is never obtained. The concept is useful, however, because assuming perfect accuracy allows us to calculate the *maximum* value of a given research project. That is, we would never pay more for a research project that provided potentially inaccurate information than we would for one that we knew would give us perfectly accurate information.

How do we calculate the expected value of information? The *expected value of perfect information* (EVPI) *is the expected value of the decision with perfect information* (EVDPI) *minus the expected value of the decision with no additional information* (EVD), or

$$EVPI = EVDPI - EVD$$

Let us go through the calculation of EVPI for the product manager first. The first step is to calculate the expected value of the decision (EVD). This involves (1) *computing for each alternative the sum of the payoffs for each market state weighted by the probability for that state* and (2) *selecting the alternative with the highest sum.* Since the payoffs are weighted (multiplied) by their associated probabilities, *expected values* (EV) are obtained. In the case of the product manager, the expected values for the two alternatives are obtained as follows:

EV (Introduce) $= (.80)(\$4,250,000)$
$+ (.20)(<\$1,100,000>) = \$3,180,000$

EV (Do not introduce) $= (.80)0(.20)0 \qquad\qquad = 0$

Since the decision to introduce has the higher expected value,

$$EVD = \$3,180,000.$$

If the product manager were a risk neutral decision maker — that is, if he made decisions only on the basis of the possible monetary outcomes, each weighted by the probability of its occurring — and if the only choices were to introduce or not to introduce the product — he would have introduced the product. The expected value of this decision would have been expected value of the "introduce" alternative, or $EVD = \$3,180,000$.

The second step is to calculate the expected value of the decision with perfect information. Computationally, this involves (1) *for each market state, selecting the highest payoff from among those for the various alternatives,* (2) *multiplying each payoff selected by the probability of the market state occurring,* and (3) *summing the resulting weighted payoffs.*

The reason that we use only the highest payoff for each market state is apparent once we think about it. If we were to obtain perfect information and learn that a particular market state was the true state, *we would obviously choose the alternative with the highest payoff for that state.*

It is also clear why we must multiply each of the selected payoffs by the probability of occurrence of the associated market state. Before the perfect information is obtained, we do not know which state will be the actual one. We have made assessments of the *probability* of each state occurring, however, and so we can weight the payoff selected for each state by the probability that it will be the true state. This gives an expected payoff for each alternative under conditions of perfect information.

The payoff for the product manager that is the highest for market state 1 is $4,250,000, and is for the "Introduce" alternative. The payoff that is the highest for market state 2 is $0, and is for the "Do Not Introduce" alternative.

The EVDPI for the product manager is then determined as follows:

EV (Introduce)	= .80 ($4,250,000)	= $3,400,000
EV (Do not introduce) =	.20(0) =	0
EVDPI	=	$3,400,000

The expected value of perfect information (EVPI) is the difference in the expected value of the decision with perfect information and with no additional information, or

$$EVPI = EVDPI - EVD$$
$$= \$3,400,000 - \$3,180,000$$
$$= \$220,000$$

Note that the EVPI for the product manager is *less* that the $350,000 it was estimated that the market test would cost. Thus, given the estimates of payoffs and probability assessment by the product manager, and assuming that he is a risk neutral decision maker, he was *correct* to argue that the market test should not be run. The expected value of even *perfect* information would not have

750

been worth the cost of the test. (It is possible, however, that some other, lower-cost project might have been worth conducting, given the product manager's estimates and probability assessments.)

What about the EVPI for the research manager? It will be different than that for the product manager because of different estimates of payoffs and personal probabilities assigned to the occurrence of the favorable and unfavorable market states. It can be calculated (from the data given in Table A – 1) as $636,000. (You should verify this by making your own calculation.) Because this is greater than the estimated cost of the market test ($350,000), conducting the market test *might* have been worthwhile for the research manager. If the market test would, in fact, have provided perfect information, conducting it *would* have been worthwhile for the research manager. Since the market test was judged to be only 85 per cent accurate, however, the information it would provide would have been worth *less* than $636,000.

The expected value of imperfect information (EVII) for the research manager therefore has to be calculated before we can tell whether he was correct in arguing that a market test should be run that would cost $350,000 and would be 85 per cent accurate, assuming that he was a risk-neutral decision maker.

Expected Value of Imperfect Information

Perfect information never really occurs in marketing research. Practically speaking, the researcher must deal with information that has some probability of being incorrect. In a research project involving a sample, for example, we know that the possibility of sampling error is always present. As we saw in Chapter 3, there are many potential nonsampling errors as well. Therefore, as a practical matter we are dealing with the *expected value of imperfect information* (EVII) in making the decision of whether to conduct a research project.

How does one calculate EVII? *The expected value of imperfect information is simply the *expected value of perfect information* (EVPI) minus the *expected cost of errors* (ECE) caused by *the inaccuracy,* or

$$EVII = EVPI - ECE$$

Two kinds of errors are possible in the market test information. If T_1 is the designation for the market test indicating that market state S_1 is the true state and, similarly, T_2 is the indication for market state S_2, then we can get a T_1 indication from a market in which S_2 is the actual situation, or a T_2 indication given a market in which S_1 is the true state.

The error of T_1 given S_2 is known as a *Type I* error.[2] It is a conditional error since the indication T_1 is in error only under the condition that S_2 is the true

---

[2] The Type I error is the result of falsely rejecting the null hypothesis. In this case, the null hypothesis would be that the break-even point could not be reached—that is, that S_2 is the true market state.

state of the market. The conditional probability of this error occurring is shown symbolically as

$$P(T_1|S_2),$$

where the vertical line means "conditional on."

The probability of a Type I error is traditionally denoted as α. Therefore, in this context $\alpha = P(T_1|S_2)$.

A *Type II* error is the other kind of error possible, the one of the market test giving a T_2 indication when S_1 is the true state. It is denoted by β. We may, therefore, write $\beta = P(T_2|S_1)$.

The expected cost of an error is the conditional probability of the error times the prior probability of the state times the payoff of the state. The expected cost of the two types of errors is

$$\text{expected cost of Type I error} = P(T_1|S_2) \cdot P(S_2) \cdot |V_2|$$
$$= \alpha P(S_2)|V_2|$$

where $|V_2|$ is the absolute value of the payoff for state 2, and

$$\text{expected cost of Type II error} = P(T_2|S_1) \cdot P(S_1) \cdot V_1$$
$$= \beta P(S_1)V_1$$

where V_1 is the value of the payoff for state 1.

We now can determine the expected error costs for the marketing research manager's formulation of the General Mills problem. Recall that the research manager's assessment (and that of the product manager, as well) of the predictive accuracy of the proposed market test was 85 per cent. That is, there was only a 15 per cent chance of the market test giving an incorrect indication of the sales volume in the three year planning period, or

$$P(T_1|S_2) = \alpha = .15$$
$$P(T_2|S_1) = \beta = .15$$

Using this information and that in Table A–1, we can then calculate

$$\text{expected cost of Type I error} = \alpha P(S_1)|V_2|$$
$$= .15 \times .30|\$2,120,000|$$
$$= \$95,400$$

and

$$\text{expected cost of Type II error} = \beta P(S_1) \cdot V_1$$
$$= .15 \times .70|\$2,650,000|$$
$$= \$278,250$$

We have determined the expected value of perfect information and the expected costs of the errors for the research manager. The expected value of imperfect information (EVII) for him is then

$$\text{EVII} = \text{EVPI} - \text{ECE}$$
$$= P(S_2)|V_2| - \alpha P(S_2)|V_2| - \beta P(S_1)V_1$$
$$= \$636,000 - \$95,400 - \$278,250 = \$262,350$$

Recall that the estimated cost of the market test was $350,000. If the research manager was a risk-neutral decision maker, it must be concluded that the test was *not* worth its estimated cost. In that case, the research manager was wrong to argue that the test should be conducted. The research manager may not have been neutral in his risk preference, however. If that were so he may have been correct in arguing that the market test should be run. We explore that possibility in a later section of the appendix.

Table of Values for Venture Analysis Problems

Although the calculations required for determining the EVII are not overly complex, they can become tedious. For *venture analysis* problems, however, a table has been developed that eliminates the need for making such calculations. Table A – 3 contains the tabular values necessary for determining EVII for this class of problems.

A *venture analysis* problem is the general type of problem of which the General Mills case is an example. In such problems, two actions are considered: a *go* action (introduce the product, in the General Mills case) and a *no go* action (do not introduce the product). Two market states are also considered, one a *favorable state* and the other an *unfavorable state*.

We can use Table A – 3 to determine EVII for a venture analysis problem by following the steps to be outlined subsequently. The EVII for the research manager for the market test in the General Mills case will be determined to illustrate the procedure.

1. *Estimate the gain to the company over the planning period resulting from the change if it is made and is successful (conditional gain).* *Example:* The gain estimated by the research manager for the planning period is $2,650,000 if the new product is introduced and is successful.

2. *Estimate the loss to the company over the planning period resulting from the change if it is made and is unsuccessful (conditional loss).* *Example:* The estimated loss by the research manager is $2,120,000 if the new product is introduced unsuccessfully.

3. *Calculate the ratio of conditional gain to conditional loss for the change.* (Divide the estimate in step 1 by the estimate in step 2.)

4. *Assess the chance of the proposed change being successful if made.* *Example:* The assessment by the research manager of the chance of the new product being a success if introduced is 70 per cent.

753

Table A – 3 Expected Value of Imperfect Information for Venture Analysis Problems[°]

Chance that the research project being considered will indicate correctly whether the change being considered should be made[†]	Chance of the change being a success is estimated to be														
	50% (even odds)					60% (6 out of 10 odds)					67% (2 out of 3 odds)				
	Ratio of estimated gain if change is successful to loss if it is unsuccessful														
	1.0	2.0	3.0	4.0	5.0	1.0	2.0	3.0	4.0	5.0	1.0	2.0	3.0	4.0	5.0
%	EVII = the maximum percentage of the potential loss that should be spent on research =														
55	5.0														
60	10.0														
65	15.0		zero			5.0									
70	20.0	5.0				10.0		zero			3.3				
75	25.0	12.5				15.0					8.3	zero			
80	30.0	20.0	10.0			20.0	8.0				13.3				
85	35.0	27.5	20.0	12.5	5.0	25.0	16.0	7.0			18.3	8.3			
90	40.0	35.0	30.0	25.0	20.0	30.0	24.0	18.0	12.0	6.0	23.3	16.7	10.0	3.3	
95	45.0	42.5	40.0	37.5	35.0	35.0	32.0	29.0	26.0	23.0	28.3	25.0	21.7	18.3	15.0
99	49.0	48.5	48.0	47.5	47.0	39.0	38.4	37.8	37.2	36.6	32.3	31.7	31.0	30.3	29.7

Chance that the research project being considered will indicate correctly whether the change being considered should be made	Chance of the change being a success is estimated to be														
	70% (7 out of 10 odds)					75% (3 out of 4 odds)					80% (8 out of 10 odds)				
	Ratio of estimated gain if change is successful to loss if it is unsuccessful														
	1.0	2.0	3.0	4.0	5.0	1.0	2.0	3.0	4.0	5.0	1.0	2.0	3.0	4.0	5.0
%	EVII = the maximum percentage of the potential loss that should be spent on research =														
55															
60															
65															
70															
75	5.0		zero												
80	10.0					5.0		zero							
85	15.0	4.5				10.0					5.0	zero			
90	20.0	13.0	6.0			15.0	7.5				10.0	2.0			
95	25.0	21.5	18.0	14.5	11.0	20.0	16.3	12.5	8.7	5.0	15.0	11.0	7.0	3.0	
99	29.0	28.3	27.6	26.9	26.2	24.0	23.3	22.5	21.8	21.0	19.0	18.2	17.4	16.6	15.8

[°] Research to evaluate change being contemplated (new product, new advertising campaign, change in sales program, different price, change in distribution channel, adjustment of production process, etc.). Before using the table, read the definition of a venture analysis problem given on p. 753.

[†] The values in this table were found from using a formula whose underlying logic is

$$\begin{array}{l} \text{the expected value of} \\ \text{the information from} \\ \text{the research} \end{array} = \begin{array}{l} \text{the expected value of} \\ \text{perfect information} \end{array} - \begin{array}{l} \text{the expected out-of-pocket} \\ \text{cost of undertaking the} \\ \text{venture when it should not} \\ \text{be undertaken} \end{array} - \begin{array}{l} \text{the expected opportunity} \\ \text{cost of not undertaking} \\ \text{the venture when it should} \\ \text{be undertaken} \end{array}$$

5. *For the research project being considered, assess the chance of it pre-dicting correctly whether the change would be successful if made. Example:* There is an estimated 85 per cent chance of correct predic-tion by the market test.

6. *For the research project being considered, look up in the table the maximum percentage of the conditional loss that should be spent on research.* (The estimates made in steps 3, 4, and 5 are used in looking up the percentage in the table. Interpolate when required.)

7. *For the research project being considered, multiply the conditional loss (estimate from step 2) by this percentage (obtained in step 6) and divide by 100 to obtain the maximum amount that should be spent for it. Example:*

$$\frac{12.375 \times \$2,120,000}{100} = \$262,350$$

8. *Estimate the cost of each research project.* (Include estimates of the out-of-pocket cost of doing the research and opportunity costs re-sulting from disclosure and/or delay.) *Example:* The estimate was $350,000.

9. *For the research project being considered, subtract the estimated cost (step 8) from the maximum amount that should be spent (step 7). Example:*

$$\$262,350 - \$350,000 = <\$87,650>$$

10. *Repeat this process for other potential research projects for the same problem. Select the research project with the highest positive differ-ence. If none has a positive difference, do not do research. Example:* The market test should not be conducted.

It will be observed that the EVII determined from the table was the same as that calculated earlier.

Determining EVII for Problems Other Than Venture Analysis Problems

What about determining EVII for problems in which more than two actions are being considered, more than two market states are of interest, or both of these situations exist? Can it be done and, if so, how is it done?

The answer to these questions is that there is a *general solution* for prob-lems that are formulated with as many actions as desired and for as many states

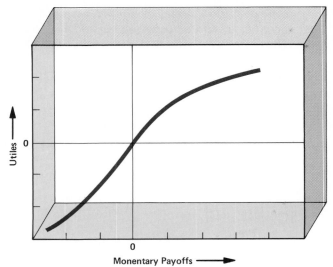

Figure A – 1 *Utility Function for a Decision Maker with a Low Level of Risk Aversion*

Source: R. O. Swaim, "Utility Theory — Insights into Risk Taking," *Harvard Business Review* (November – December, 1966), 132.

as may be of interest. The computations become more lengthy and somewhat more complex, but the underlying concepts remain the same.[3]

The Assumption Concerning Risk Preferences

As stated before we began the calculations of the **EVII** for the research manager and the product manager, they were to be made on the assumption that both managers were *risk neutral.* If one or both of them were *risk averse* or *risk assuming,* however, the assumption that they are risk neutral may lead to misleading results. *A person who is risk averse will value information from a research project more highly than one who is risk neutral, and a person who is risk assuming will value information less highly than one who is risk neutral.*

The available evidence suggests that most executives — not all, but most — are risk averse. This is true of marketing executives as well as for those in other fields. One of the present authors has measured the risk preferences of some three hundred marketing executives, for example, and found that all but a few of them were risk averse. (You may measure your own risk preferences by doing the exercise in question A – 18 at the end of this appendix.)

[3] See P. E. Green, D. S. Tull, and G. Albaum, *Research for Marketing Decisions* (Englewood Cliffs: Prentice Hall, 1988), 57 – 93.

Whenever there is reason to believe that an executive involved in the do — do not do research decision is risk averse, or risk assuming, a measure of his or her *utility function* should be made and used in the calculations of expected value. A *utility function* is a representation of the amount of utility, measured in *utiles* and either positive or negative, a person has for given amounts of monetary gains and losses. An example of such a measurement is given in Figure A–1. The expected value of the information in this case is known as the *certainty monetary equivalent of imperfect information* (CMEII).

The calculations to determine CMEII are similar to those for EMVII except that monetary values initially have to be converted into utiles and converted back at a later stage of the calculations.[4]

Review Questions

A.1. What is EVPI?

A.2. What is EVDPI?

A.3. What is EVD?

A.4. What is EVII?

A.5. What is ECE?

A.6. What is the equation that relates EVPI, EVDPI, and EVD? State what it means in words.

A.7. What is the equation that relates EVII, EVPI, and ECE? State what it means in words.

A.8. What is a *utility function?*

A.9. What is CMEII?

Discussion Questions/Problems

A.10. How do you make a decision about how much to study before an exam? Is this an analogous decision to deciding whether or not to do a research project? Why or why not?

A.11. Juries in criminal cases are instructed to find the defendant guilty only if they believe he or she is guilty "beyond a reasonable doubt."
  a. What probability do you assign to this phrase?
  b. There are two possible errors that a jury can make. It can find a guilty person innocent or an innocent person guilty. What effect does the previous instruction have on the relative size of these errors?
  c. Sometimes the phrase "clear and abiding conviction" is used instead of "beyond a reasonable doubt." Do the two phrases mean the same thing to you in numerical probabilities?

[4] See ibid.

A.12. Shoppers continually make decisions about whether to get more information before they buy. How should the decision be made on whether to go to one more store before buying

    a. pants in the $40 price range?

    b. a suit in the $300 price range?

A.13. Timberlane, a West Coast lumber firm, is considering introducing a new charcoal lighter. This new material, tentatively named *Starter Chips,* is simply chips of pitch pine. Pitch pine is a tree containing a high level of pine resin. The chips light at the touch of a match and burn for about 20 minutes. The product manager involved is considering a controlled store test (placing the product in a limited number of stores and monitoring both purchases and user attitudes). Assume that a national introduction would produce profits of $3,600,000 over the planning period if successful and a loss of $1,800,000 if unsuccessful. Timberlane executives feel that there is a 60 per cent chance the product will be successful.

    a. If the controlled store test would produce perfectly accurate information, what is the *maximum* they would be willing to pay if they were risk neutral decision makers?

    b. As (a) but assuming 95 per cent accuracy?

    c. As (a) but assuming 85 per cent accuracy?

    d. As (a) but assuming 75 per cent accuracy?

    e. As (a) but assuming 65 per cent accuracy?

A.14. How would your answers to problem A.13 change if the Timberlane executives' initial estimate was that the product had:

    a. a 70 per cent chance of success?

    b. an 80 per cent chance of success?

A.15. Green Giant recently developed a line of *Boil'n Bag* frozen entrées. Assume that prior to introduction, Green Giant's management felt the product had an 80 per cent chance of success. If successful the new line would generate $12 million profits over the planning period. If unsuccessful, it would generate the same amount of losses.

    a. Using an expected value approach, how much would Green Giant be willing to pay for a perfectly accurate test market?

    b. a .99 accurate test market?

    c. a .95 accurate test market?

    d. a .90 accurate test market?

    e. an .85 accurate test market?

    f. an .80 accurate test market?

A.16. Repeat problem A.15 except change management's prior expectations from 80 per cent to 70 per cent.

A.17. Repeat problem A.15 except change the potential loss from $12 million to $10 million.

A.18. Say you have a cash balance of $1,000 above your living costs for the rest of this term. This $1,000 is money you have earned and for which you are not accountable to anyone else. Further suppose that you are faced with the situations described here.

a. You are forced either to accept a gamble with an equal chance of winning $50 or losing $250 or else making an immediate payment to avoid the gamble.

    i. Would you accept the gamble? Yes ____ No ____

> If your answer is yes, make a dot at the intersection of the zero payment and the #1 lines in the diagram below.
> Then go to question (b).
> If your answer is no, answer part (ii) of this question.

    ii. What is the maximum amount you would pay to avoid the gamble? $ ____

> Enter this amount in the diagram below by making a dot at the appropriate point on line #1.

b. You are forced either to pay an immediate sum to obtain a gamble with an equal chance of winning $400 and losing $200 or else to turn it down at no cost.

    i. Would you turn it down at no cost? Yes ____ No ____

> If your answer is yes, make a dot at the intersection of the zero payment and the #2 lines in the diagram below. Then go to question (c).
> If your answer is no, answer part (ii) of this question.

    ii. What is the maximum amount you would pay for the gamble? $ ____

> Enter this amount in the diagram below by making a dot at the appropriate point on line #2.

c. You are forced either to accept a gamble with an equal chance of winning $100 or losing $200, or else making an immediate payment to avoid the gamble.

    i. Would you accept the gamble? Yes ____ No ____

> If your answer is yes, make a dot at the intersection of the zero payment and the #3 lines in the diagram below. Then go to question (d).
> If your answer is no, answer part (ii) of this question.

    ii. What is the maximum amount you would pay to avoid the gamble? $ ____

> Enter this amount in the diagram below by making a dot at the appropriate point on line #3.

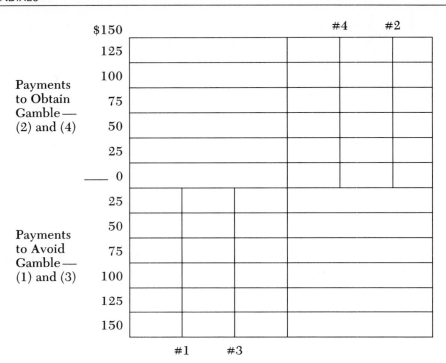

d. You are forced either to pay an immediate sum to obtain a gamble with an equal chance of winning $200 and losing $100, or else to turn it down at no cost.

    i. Would you turn it down at no cost? Yes ＿＿ No ＿＿

> If your answer is yes, make a dot at the intersection of the zero payment and the #4 lines in the diagram below.
> If your answer is no, answer part (ii) of this question.

    ii. What is the maximum amount you would pay for the gamble? $ ＿＿

> Enter this amount in the diagram below by making a dot at the appropriate point on line #4.

1. Enter your answers to questions (a) through (d) as previously instructed.
2. Connect the resulting four points with a smoothed-in line.
3. If the line is *straight* you are *risk neutral*;
   if the line is *concave downward* [⌒] You are risk averse;
   if the line is *concave upward* [⌣] you are *risk seeking*.

Projects

A.20. Decide what numerical probability you assign to each of the following phrases. Record these probabilities. Without indicating your answers, ask ten other people to tell you the numerical probabilities they associate with each phrase.

    a. It is unlikely that . . .
    b. It is doubtful that . . .
    c. It may be that . . .
    d. It is improbable that . . .
    e. There is a good chance that . . .
    f. There is a possibility that . . .
    g. It is very likely that . . .
    h. It is probable that . . .
    i. It is very unlikely that . . .
    j. It is highly doubtful that . . .
    k. There is not a good chance that . . .
    l. It is very doubtful that . . .
    m. It is very improbable that . . .
    n. There is a good possibility that . . .
    o. It is uncertain that . . .
    p. It is likely that . . .
    q. It is highly probable that . . .

What conclusion do you draw about the precision with which your assessments of probabilities are communicated by these phrases?

A.21. Ask ten people whether

    a. they would prefer to have the weatherman report that there is "a 60 per cent chance of rain," "a better than average chance of rain," or "a good chance of rain."

    b. they would prefer to have the anchor person on a program covering results on election night report that "according to our projections, candidate X has a 90 per cent chance of being elected," or "according to our projections, candidate X has a very good chance of being elected."

What tentative conclusions do you draw about the relative communication content of quantitative versus verbal descriptors of probabilities?

A.22. Ask five people if they consider themselves to be risk seeking, risk neutral, or risk averse. Then have them complete A–18. Did they accurately categorize themselves?

Sample Size Determination: Two Additional Methods

The discussion of the size of probability samples in Chapter 16 was confined to the determination of the size of simple random samples. In this appendix, we extend the discussion of traditional models of sample-size determination to include two other types of probability samples — single-stage stratified random samples (proportional and nonproportional) and single-stage cluster samples.

Sample Size for Single-Stage Stratified Random Samples

A *stratified random sample* is one in which the population is first divided into strata, and a probability sample is then taken from each stratum. The strata are ideally selected in such a way as to provide the maximum variance *between* them and minimum variance *within* them. In practice, this ideal can rarely be met, as stratification is limited to those characteristics of the population that can be identified: age, sex, income, education, and the like. These demographics often do not correlate highly with the measure of the attitude, actual behavior, or planned behavior being studied. However, to the extent that they do, stratification provides a gain in sample efficiency over a srs.

In this section we assume that the sample from each stratum is selected as a srs. This is an unrealistic assumption for most stratified samples taken from human populations because of the lack of adequate sample frames. However, the simplification is warranted here, as one of our purposes is to illustrate the application of srs principles to other kinds of probability samples.

There are two kinds of single-stage stratified samples, *proportional* and *nonproportional*. It is useful to discuss them separately.

762

Sample Size for Proportional Single-Stage Stratified Random Samples

Suppose that the invoices that we examined in Chapter 16 are for sales to companies in two industries. Further suppose that 750 of these invoices were to companies in industry 1 and 500 were to companies in industry 2. Finally, suppose that there is reason to believe that the variances of the two strata are different; the standard deviation for industry 1 is estimated to be $20.00 ($\hat{\sigma}_1 = \$20.00$) and for industry 2 is $30.00 ($\hat{\sigma}_2 = \$30.00$). Given the same allowable error ($\bar{x} - M = \$8.00$) and the same confidence coefficient (90 per cent, $Z = 1.64$) as used before, what size single-stage stratified random sample should be taken?

In order to answer this question, it is first necessary to specify whether the sample is to be a *proportional* or a *nonproportional* stratified random sample. A proportional sample is one in which the proportion of the sample assigned to each stratum is the same as it is in the population. That is, if we let

n_1 = the sample size for industry 1,
n_2 = the sample size for industry 2,
N_1 = the population size of industry 1, and
N_2 = the population size of industry 2,

then a proportional sample is one in which

$$\frac{n_1}{n} = \frac{N_1}{N} = \frac{750}{1250} = .60, \text{ and}$$

$$\frac{n_2}{n} = \frac{N_2}{N} = \frac{500}{1250} = .40$$

A *nonproportional* sample is one in which the strata proportions in the sample and the population are not equal. (We discuss nonproportional samples shortly.)

The formula for the sample size of an srs in an estimation of the mean problem was given in equation 16–6 (in Chapter 16) as

$$n = \frac{Z^2 \sigma^2}{e^2} \qquad (16-6)$$

The formula for the sample size of a stratified sample is of the same general form, the only difference being that the formula for the variance of a stratified sample is substituted. For a proportional stratified sample, the estimated variance about the mean is

$$\hat{\sigma}_{st}^2 = \sum_{h=1}^{k} W_h \frac{\hat{\sigma}_h^2}{n} \qquad (B-1)$$

763

where

$$W_h = \text{weight of stratum } h = \frac{N_h}{N}$$

$\hat{\sigma}_h^2 = \text{estimated variance of stratum } h$
$k = \text{total number of strata}$

Substituting this variance formula for the one in equation $16-6$ gives the comparable formula for sample size for a proportional stratified sample, namely

$$n = \frac{Z^2}{e^2} \sum_{h=1}^{k} W_h \hat{\sigma}_h^2 \qquad (B-2)$$

We can now answer the question concerning sample size in the example. Substituting the appropriate values in equation $B-2$ we get

$$n = \frac{1.64^2(.60 \times \$20.00^2 + .40 \times \$30.00^2)}{(\$8.00)^2}$$

$$= \frac{2.69(.60 \times 400 + .40 \times 900)}{64}$$

$$= 26 \text{ (rounded to the next larger number)}$$

The sample sizes for each stratum are determined as

$n_1 = W_1 n = .60 \times 26 = 16$ (rounded to nearest number), and
$n_2 = W_2 n = .40 \times 26 = 10$

Recall the sample size calculated for a simple random sample with the same specifications was 35. This reduction illustrates the principle that *stratification permits a smaller sample size with the same error specification* or *a smaller error specification with the same sample size.* This assumes that the stratification is done with stratifying characteristics that are related to the variance, and that variances differ among strata.

The formula for the sample size for a single-stage stratified proportional random sample for estimation of proportions is derived similarly to that for the mean. It is

$$n = \frac{Z^2}{e^2} \sum_{h=1}^{k} W_h P_h (1.0 - P_h) \qquad (B-3)$$

where

$P_h = \text{proportion of stratum } h \text{ having the characteristic of interest, and}$

$$W_h = \frac{N_h}{N}$$

Sample Size for Nonproportional Single-Stage Stratified Random Samples

In the ideal situation, one would almost always choose to take a nonproportional rather than a proportional stratified sample. The reason for this can be seen by examining an extreme case. Suppose industry 1 has a zero standard deviation (all of the invoices are for the same amount). All of the standard deviation would then necessarily be in industry 2. We would then want a sample size of only 1 in industry 1 ($n_1 = 1$) and the rest of the sample in industry 2. This would clearly be a nonproportional sample.

This suggests that stratum sample size should be proportional to stratum standard deviation. This inference is correct but not complete; optimum stratum sample size is proportional to both the proportion of the population contained in the stratum and the stratum standard deviation. The formula for the optimum allocation of a sample of size n to stratum h is

$$n_h = n \frac{N_h \hat{\sigma}_h}{\sum\limits_{h=1}^{k} N_h \hat{\sigma}_h} \qquad (B-4)$$

Thus, it would only be in those cases in which the strata have equal variances that we would want a proportional sample, at least insofar as sampling theory is concerned.

The formula for the sample size of a single-stage nonproportional stratified sample for an estimation problem concerned with a mean is

$$n = \frac{Z^2}{e^2} \left(\sum\limits_{h=1}^{k} W_h \hat{\sigma}_h \right)^2 \qquad (B-5)$$

If our previous statements concerning the optimum allocation of a sample among strata are correct, it should also follow that a nonproportional stratified sample should require a smaller sample for the same error specification so long as strata variances are unequal. We may test this inference by working through our example again.

Substituting values and solving for overall sample size gives

$$n = \frac{Z^2}{e^2} \left(\sum\limits_{h=1}^{k} W_h \hat{\sigma}_h \right)^2$$

$$= \frac{1.64^2}{\$8.00^2} (.60 \times \$20.00 + .40 \times \$30.00)^2$$

$$= 25 \text{ (rounded to next larger number}$$

This compares with a sample size of 26 ($n = 26$) for the proportional sample. The difference is small insofar as the example is concerned, but the point is illustrated.

The nonproportional sample is allocated among strata (using equation B–4) as

$$n_1 = \frac{25(750 \times \$20.00)}{(750 \times \$20.00) + (500 \times \$30.00)}$$
$$= 13$$

and

$$n_2 = 12$$

The corresponding formula for the sample size for a nonproportional sample involving estimation of a proportion is

$$n = \frac{Z^2}{e^2} \left(\sum_{h=1}^{k} W_h \sqrt{P_h(1.0 - P_h)} \right)^2 \qquad (B-6)$$

The sample size for each stratum is found by the formula

$$n_h = \frac{W_h \sqrt{P_h(1.0 - P_h)}}{\sum\limits_{h=1}^{k} W_h \sqrt{P_h(1.0 - P_h)}} \qquad (B-7)$$

Sample Size for Single Stage Cluster Sample

A single-stage *cluster sample* is a simple random sample in which each sampling unit is a collection, or cluster, of elements. When the sampling units are geographic subdivisions, such as counties, townships, or blocks, the sample resulting from taking a simple random sample of each of them is known as an *area sample*.

Cluster sampling (area sampling) is common in the sampling of human population when *personal interviews* are to be used, for two reasons. First, a good cluster sampling frame usually exists (blocks or census tracts in a city, for example) whereas a good element sampling frame usually does not (a good listing of households, for example). Second, the cost of personal interviewing increases as a function of the distance between sampling units. If one conducts interviews within a series of geographic clusters, the per-interview cost is less, and often substantially so, than it would be if the interviews were dispersed geographically as in the case with a simple random sample of elements.

The per-interview cost by telephone and the mailing cost per questionnaire are not more for a simple random than for a cluster sample. The element sampling frame problem is also much less severe for both telephone and mail surveys than for personal interviews. For these reasons cluster sampling is rarely used for telephone and mail surveys.

Although the average cost per personal interview for a cluster sample is lower than for a srs, total sampling costs are not necessarily reduced proportionately. A larger sample size usually has to be taken because of the intracluster similarities of sampling elements. Persons who live on the same block, for example, tend to have similar incomes, attitudes, and shopping patterns. Interviewing two people on the same block is therefore likely to provide less information about characteristics of the population as a whole than would interviewing two persons selected at random from the population.

As in the case for a srs, the formulas for determining sample size for estimating means and for estimating proportions using a cluster sample are different. We first discuss the determination of the sample size for the estimation of a mean.

Sample Size for Single-Stage Cluster Sample for Estimating a Population Mean

Suppose that the invoice values discussed in Chapter 16 are for sales to 250 different companies. Assume further that there are five invoices for each company. If we let the companies each form a cluster, the number of clusters is $N = 250$, and the number of elements per cluster is $l = 5$. Suppose finally that the variance between clusters is estimated to be $10,000 ($\hat{\sigma}_{ct}^2 = \$10,000$). Using the same allowable error ($e = \bar{x} - M = \pm \$8.00$) and confidence coefficient ($z = 1.64$) as used in Chapter 16 in calculating the size of the srs, how large a cluster sample should be taken to estimate the population mean?

The formula for the number of clusters to include in the sample is

$$n = \frac{N\hat{\sigma}_{ct}^2}{\dfrac{Ne^2l^2 + \hat{\sigma}_{ct}^2}{Z^2}} \qquad (B\text{--}8)$$

where

n = number of clusters in the sample,
N = number of clusters in the population,
$\hat{\sigma}_{ct}^2$ = estimated variance between cluster totals,
$e = \bar{x} - M$ = allowable error,
Z = the confidence coefficient, and
l = the average number of elements per cluster.

For the example the number of clusters that should be included in the sample is

$$n = \frac{250(\$10,000)}{\dfrac{250(\$8.00^2)5^2}{1.64^2} + \$10,000}$$

$= 15.8$ or, rounding up,
$= 16$ clusters

The size of the sample in terms of elements is then $16 \times 5 = 80$ invoices. This compares with the sample size for the srs of 35 invoices.

Although the calculation of the number of clusters to include in a single-stage cluster sample is straightforward, how, you may ask, does one estimate the variance between clusters?

The variance between cluster totals is the sum over all clusters of the squared variation of each actual cluster total from the average cluster total divided by the number of clusters, or

$$\sigma_{ct}^2 = \frac{\sum_{i=1}^{N} (Y_i - M\bar{l})^2}{N} \qquad (B-9)$$

where

$Y_i =$ the total for the ith cluster
$M =$ the population mean
$\bar{l} =$ the average number of elements per cluster, and
$N =$ the number of clusters in the population

The variation between cluster totals is much greater than that between element values, and so the variance between clusters is many times that of the variance for a simple random sample.

This does not mean that it is necessarily more difficult to estimate variance between clusters. The same procedures for estimating population variance (described on page 501) are available for estimating the variance between clusters.

If a pilot sample is used to obtain a sample variance to estimate the population variance between cluster means, the appropriate formula to use is

$$s_c^2 = \sum_{i=1}^{n} \frac{(y_i - \bar{x}\bar{l})^2}{n-1} \qquad (B-10)$$

where

$n =$ number of clusters in the sample
$y_i =$ the total of the ith cluster in the sample,
$\bar{x} =$ the sample mean of the element values, and
$\bar{l} =$ the average number of elements per cluster

Sample Size for a Single-Stage Cluster Sample for Estimating a Population Proportion

The formula for determining the sample size for a cluster sample for estimating a proportion is similar to that for estimating a mean. It is

$$n = \frac{N\sigma_{cp}^2}{\frac{Ne^2\bar{l}}{Z^2} + \sigma_{cp}^2} \qquad (B-11)$$

where

n = the number of clusters to be included in the sample,
N = the number of clusters in the population,
σ_{cp}^2 = the estimated variance between cluster proportions,
$\bar{l}$ = the average number of elements per cluster,
e = the allowable error, and
Z = the confidence coefficient

Let a_i be the number of elements in cluster i and $\bar{a}$ be the average number of elements in each cluster that possess a characteristic of interest. The variance between cluster proportions is then the sum over all clusters of the squared variation of each a_i from $\bar{a}$ divided by the total number of clusters, or

$$\sigma_{cp}^2 = \sum_{i=1}^{N} \frac{(a_i - \bar{a})^2}{N}. \qquad (B-12)$$

It can be estimated by a pilot sample variance between cluster proportions using the formula

$$s_{cp}^2 = \sum_{i=1}^{n} \frac{(a_i - \bar{a})^2}{n-1} \qquad (B-13)$$

where $\bar{a}$, in this case, is the average for the sample clusters.

An example illustrates the application of these formulas. Suppose that we want to estimate the proportion of the invoice values in the table discussed in Chapter 16 that are $20.00 or less. Suppose further that 250 companies have 5 invoices each and that we want to take a simple random sample of companies and use all 5 invoices of each company. N is then 250 and $\bar{l}$ is 5. Further assume that we want to have a confidence level of 95.4 per cent ($Z = 2.0$) that the sample proportion will not vary from the population proportion by more than .08 ($e = p - P = .08$, or 8 percentage points.) Finally, suppose we have taken a pilot sample of five companies and recorded the following values for their sales invoices:

C_1	C_2	C_3	C_4	C_5
$18	$42	$13	$93	$33
32	86	27	54	39
15	65	38	12	63
64	74	29	26	27
49	59	15	77	40

769

How many companies should we include on our sample?

The first step in determining the sample size is to calculate the sample variance between clusters, s_{cp}^2. From the data given in the example the values for a_i are

$$a_1 = 2, a_2 = 0, a_3 = 2, a_4 = 1, \text{ and } a_5 = 0.$$

The value for $\bar{a}$ is then

$$\bar{a} = \frac{\sum\limits_{i=1}^{n} a_i}{n} = \frac{5}{5} = 1$$

The sample variance between cluster proportions is then calculated as

$$s_{cp}^2 = \frac{(2-1)^2 + (0-1)^2 + (2-1)^2 + (1-1)^2 + (0-1)^2}{5-1}$$

$$= \frac{4}{4} = 1.0$$

Using this value as the estimator of σ_{cp}^2, we can calculate the number of clusters to include in the sample using equation $(B-11)$ as

$$n = \frac{250(1.0)^2}{\dfrac{250(.08)^2 5^2}{2^2} + 1.0}$$

$$= 22.7 = 23 \text{ companies}$$

Conjoint Analysis Calculations

Table 12–1, reproduced on page 772 as Table C–1, contains an orthogonal array based on the situation presented in Chapter 12 (pages 360–370). Conjoint analyses can be based on linear programming techniques (**LINMAP**) or analysis of variance techniques (**MONANOVA**). However, dummy variable linear regression using effects coding is most common.

Regression is most appropriately run on rating scores rather than rank-order scores. If run on ranks, the ranks should first be inverted such that higher numbers represent increasing levels of preference or purchase likelihood. Effects coding requires that each attribute be treated as a *dummy variable*. For each attribute, one level will be omitted from the regression formula. This level can be selected arbitrarily. Thus, the regression model for our problem could be

$$\text{Rating} = \text{Constant} + B1(\text{Moist}) + B2(\text{Canned}) + B3(\text{Mamacat}) + B4(\text{Plus}) \\ + B5(\$.55) + B6(\$.65) + B7(\text{Endorsement}) + B8(\text{Guarantee})$$

This formula omits the dry version, the Formula 9 name, the $.75 price level, and the "no" option for both endorsement and guarantee.

The variables in the formula are coded either + 1 (that level of the attribute is present), 0 (that level of the attribute is not present but a level of that attribute represented in the formula is present), or − 1 (that attribute is represented by the level that is not in the formula). Thus, form in our formula would be coded as follows:

Table C – 1   Attribute Combinations for Evaluation of a Cat Food

No.	Form	Name	Price	Endorsement	Guarantee	Respondent's Evaluation Ranking	Respondent's Evaluation Rating
1	Canned	MamaCat	$.75	No	Yes	12	50
2	Canned	Formula 9	.55	Yes	No	7	78
3	Canned	Plus	.65	No	No	9	66
4	Dry	MamaCat	.75	Yes	No	18	15
5	Dry	Formula 9	.55	No	Yes	8	72
6	Dry	Plus	.65	No	No	15	32
7	Moist	MamaCat	.55	No	No	4	90
8	Moist	Formula 9	.65	Yes	No	6	80
9	Moist	Plus	.75	No	Yes	5	84
10	Canned	MamaCat	.65	No	No	10	52
11	Canned	Formula 9	.75	No	No	16	28
12	Canned	Plus	.55	Yes	Yes	1°	95
13	Dry	MamaCat	.55	No	No	13	42
14	Dry	Formula 9	.65	No	Yes	11	50
15	Dry	Plus	.75	Yes	No	17	20
16	Moist	MamaCat	.65	Yes	Yes	2	92
17	Moist	Formula 9	.75	No	No	14	38
18	Moist	Plus	.55	No	No	3	90

° Most preferred.

Actual Form	Coding Moist	Coding Canned
moist	1	0
canned	0	1
dry	−1	−1

The eight options in Table C – 1 would be coded:

| | Form | | Name | | Price | | | |
No.	Moist (X1)	Canned (X2)	MamaCat (X3)	Plus (X4)	$.55 (X5)	$.65 (X6)	Endorsement (X7)	Guarantee (X8)
1	0	1	1	0	−1	−1	−1	1
2	0	1	−1	−1	1	0	1	−1
3	0	1	0	1	0	1	−1	−1
4	−1	−1	1	0	−1	−1	1	−1
5	−1	−1	−1	−1	1	0	−1	1
6	−1	−1	0	1	0	1	−1	−1
7	1	0	1	0	1	0	−1	−1
8	1	0	−1	−1	0	1	1	−1
9	1	0	0	1	−1	−1	−1	1
10	0	1	1	0	0	1	−1	−1
11	0	1	−1	−1	−1	−1	−1	−1
12	0	1	0	1	1	0	1	1
13	−1	−1	1	0	1	0	−1	−1
14	−1	−1	−1	−1	0	1	−1	1
15	−1	−1	0	1	−1	−1	1	−1
16	1	0	1	0	0	1	1	1
17	1	0	−1	−1	−1	−1	−1	−1
18	1	0	0	1	1	0	−1	−1

Effects coding allows a straightforward interpretation of the coefficients generated in the regression program. Each individual's rating score or inverse ranking is then treated as the dependent variable and the coded values associated with the item receiving each rating are considered independent variable values. An ordinary least-squares regression analysis is run with, in our example, 18 observations for each individual.

Using the ratings and inverse rankings in Table C–1, we would obtain coefficients for each variable as follows:

$$\text{Rating} = 64.13 + 19.33(\text{Moist}) + 1.83(\text{Canned}) - 2.83(\text{MamaCat})$$
$$+ 4.83(\text{Plus}) + 18.17(\$.55) + 2.33(\$.65) + 2.75(\text{Endorsement})$$
$$+ 10.63(\text{Guarantee})$$

$$\text{Ranking} = 8.5 + 3.83(\text{Moist}) + .33(\text{Canned}) - .33(\text{MamaCat})$$
$$+ 1.17(\text{Plus}) + 3.50(\$.55) + .67(\$.65) + .75(\text{Endorsement})$$
$$+ 2.25(\text{Guarantee})$$

The coefficients of the variables in the equation indicate the contribution that level of that attribute made toward the rating (or ranking) given the item. This represents the utility or value that the level of that attribute provides the respondent. These are termed *part-worths*.

Note that the magnitude of the part-worths differs between the two formulas. This is to be expected, as the first formula predicts ratings ranging from 15 to 95, whereas the second predicts ranks that are much smaller (1 to 18). However, the relative differences between the part-worths within each formula are similar. Thus, using either ratings or rankings would lead to similar conclusions.

Effects coding is done in such a manner that the sum of the effects (part-worths) of each attribute must equal zero. Thus, the part-worth of the omitted level of each attribute is simply that value which will make the sum of all the part-worths associated with a variable equal to zero. Thus, the part-worths for the respondent in our example using the ranking data are:

		Original	*Rescaled*
		Part-worths	*Part-worths*
I.	*Form*		
	Dry	−4.17	0.00
	Moist	3.83	1.00
	Canned	.33	.56
II.	*Name*		
	MamaCat	−.33	.48
	Formula 9	−.84	.42
	Plus	1.17	.67
III.	*Price*		
	$.55	3.50	.96
	.65	.67	.61
	.75	−4.17	.00
IV.	*Endorsement*		
	Yes	.75	.62
	No	−.75	.43
V.	*Guarantee*		
	Yes	2.25	.80
	No	−2.25	.24

The relative importance of each attribute can be estimated by the difference between the part-worths (utility) of the most valued and least valued levels of that attribute relative to the differences associated with the other attributes. Thus, if an individual's choice is strongly influenced by a movement from dry to moist food (a large difference in part-worths), this attribute is more important than one for which changing levels does not affect his or her choice (a small difference in part-worths). This is calculated as:

$$RIA_i = \frac{A_i \text{ (largest part-worth — smallest part-worth)}}{\sum_{i=1}^{n} A_i \text{ (largest part-worth — smallest part-worth)}}$$

where

$$RIA_i = \text{relative importance of attribute } i$$
$$A_i = \text{attribute } i$$

For our example, the relative importance values are:

	Highest Utility	−	Lowest Utility	=	Difference	÷	Sum	=	Relative Importance
Form	3.83	−	(−4.16)	=	7.99	÷	23.67	=	.34
Name	1.17	−	(− .84)	=	2.01	÷	23.67	=	.08
Price	3.50	−	(−4.17)	=	7.67	÷	23.67	=	.32
Endorsement	.75	−	(− .75)	=	1.50	÷	23.67	=	.06
Guarantee	2.25	−	(−2.25)	=	4.50	÷	23.67	=	.19
Sum					23.67				

As described in Chapter 12, relative importance values should be used with care because they are heavily dependent on the levels associated with each attribute. Thus, an unrealistically high or low price would dramatically increase the importance score for the price attribute relative to the others. Within the ranges used in this example, this respondent assigns highest importance to form and price, moderate importance to a guarantee, and limited importance to the name and an endorsement.

With effects coding it is not necessary to rescale the original part-worth values, as they can be directly compared. However, many analysts prefer to rescale by setting the highest obtained part-worth across all attributes equal to 1.0, the lowest equal to zero, and the others placed on this 0–1 scale by linear interpolation or by using the following formulas:

$$(1) \quad U_i = \frac{X_i + |L|}{H + |L|}$$

$$(2) \quad U_i = \frac{X_i - L}{H - L}$$

where

$U_i = $ rescaled part-worth for attribute level i
$X_i = $ original part-worth for attribute level i
$L = $ lowest original part-worth
$H = $ highest original part-worth

Formula 1 is used when the lowest original part-worth is less than zero. Formula 2 is used when it is greater than zero.

Part-worths are typically shown graphically as in Figure 12–1, part of which is reproduced below:

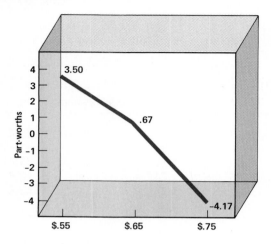

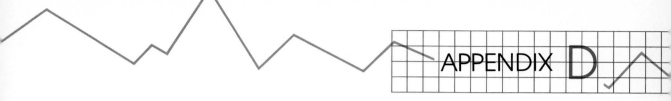
Area Under the Normal Curve

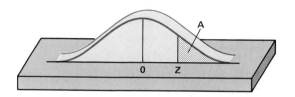

Z	A	Z	A	Z	A	Z	A
0.00	.5000	.036	.3594	0.72	.2358	1.06	.1446
0.02	.4920	.038	.3520	0.74	.2296	1.08	.1401
0.04	.4840	0.40	.3446	0.76	.2236	1.10	.1357
0.06	.4761	0.42	.3372	0.78	.2177	1.12	.1314
0.08	.4681	0.44	.3300	0.80	.2119	1.14	.1271
0.10	.4602	0.46	.3228			1.16	.1230
0.12	.4522	0.48	.3156	0.82	.2061	1.18	.1190
0.14	.4443	0.50	.3085	0.84	.2005	1.20	.1151
0.16	.4364	0.52	.3015	0.86	.1949	1.22	.1112
0.18	.4286	0.54	.2946	0.88	.1894	1.24	.1075
0.20	.4207	0.56	.2877	.090	.1841	1.26	.1038
0.22	.4129	0.58	.2810	0.92	.1788	1.28	.1003
0.24	.4052	0.60	.2743	0.94	.1736	1.30	.0968
0.26	.3974	0.62	.2676	0.96	.1685	1.32	.0934
0.28	.3897	0.64	.2611	0.98	.1635	1.34	.0901
0.30	.3821	0.66	.2546	1.00	.1587	1.36	.0885
0.32	.3745	0.68	.2483	1.02	.1539	1.38	.0838
0.34	.3669	0.70	.2420	1.04	.1492	1.40	.0808

Z	A	Z	A	Z	A	Z	A
1.42	.0778	1.86	.0314	2.34	.0096	2.80	.0026
1.44	.0749	1.88	.0301	2.36	.0091	2.82	.0024
1.46	.0721	1.90	.0287	2.38	.0087	2.84	.0023
1.48	.0694	1.92	.0274	2.40	.0082	2.86	.0021
1.50	.0668	1.94	.0262	2.42	.0078	2.88	.0020
1.52	.0643	1.96	.0250			2.90	.0019
1.54	.0618	1.98	.0239	2.44	.0073	2.92	.0018
1.56	.0594	2.00	.0228	2.46	.0070	2.94	.0016
1.58	.0571	2.02	.0217	2.48	.0066	2.96	.0015
		2.04	.0207	2.50	.0062	2.98	.0014
1.60	.0548	2.06	.0197	2.52	.0059	3.00	.0014
		2.08	.0188	2.54	.0055	3.05	.0011
1.62	.0526	2.10	.0179	2.56	.0052	3.10	.0010
1.64	.0505	2.12	.0170	2.58	.0049	3.15	.0008
1.66	.0485	2.14	.0162	2.60	.0047	3.20	.0007
1.68	.0465	2.16	.0154	2.62	.0044	3.25	.0006
1.70	.0446	2.18	.0146	2.64	.0042	3.30	.0005
1.72	.0427	2.20	.0139	2.66	.0039	3.35	.0004
1.74	.0409	2.22	.0132	2.68	.0037	3.40	.0003
1.76	.0392	2.24	.0125	2.70	.0035	3.45	.0003
1.78	.0375	2.26	.0119	2.72	.0033	3.50	.0002
1.80	.0359	2.28	.0113	2.74	.0031		
1.82	.0344	2.30	.0107	2.76	.0029	3.55	.0002
1.84	.0329	2.32	.0102	2.78	.0027	3.60	.0002

Percentiles of the *t* Distribution (One- and Two-Tailed Tests)*

df	.30 (.15)	.20 (.10)	.10 (.05)	.050 (.025)	.02 (.01)	.01 (.005)
1	1.963	3.078	6.314	12.706	31.821	63.657
2	1.386	1.886	2.920	4.303	6.965	9.925
3	1.250	1.638	2.353	3.182	4.541	5.841
4	1.190	1.533	2.132	2.776	3.747	4.604
5	1.156	1.476	2.015	2.571	3.365	4.032
6	1.134	1.440	1.943	2.447	3.143	3.707
7	1.119	1.415	1.895	2.365	2.998	3.499
8	1.108	1.397	1.860	2.306	2.896	3.355
9	1.100	1.383	1.833	2.262	2.821	3.250
10	1.093	1.372	1.812	2.228	2.764	3.169
11	1.088	1.363	1.796	2.201	2.718	3.106
12	1.083	1.356	1.782	2.179	2.681	3.055
13	1.079	1.350	1.771	2.160	2.650	3.012
14	1.076	1.345	1.761	2.145	2.624	2.977
15	1.074	1.341	1.753	2.131	2.602	2.947
16	1.071	1.337	1.746	2.120	2.583	2.921
17	1.069	1.333	1.740	2.110	2.567	2.898
18	1.067	1.330	1.734	2.101	2.552	2.878
19	1.066	1.328	1.729	2.093	2.539	2.861
20	1.064	1.325	1.725	2.086	2.528	2.845
21	1.063	1.323	1.721	2.080	2.518	2.831

df	.30 (.15)	.20 (.10)	.10 (.05)	.050 (.025)	.02 (.01)	.01 (.005)
22	1.061	1.321	1.717	2.074	2.508	2.819
23	1.060	1.319	1.714	2.069	2.500	2.807
24	1.059	1.318	1.711	2.064	2.492	2.797
25	1.058	1.316	1.708	2.060	2.485	2.787
26	1.058	1.315	1.706	2.056	2.479	2.779
27	1.057	1.314	1.703	2.052	2.473	2.771
28	1.056	1.313	1.701	2.048	2.467	2.763
29	1.055	1.311	1.699	2.045	2.462	2.756
30	1.055	1.310	1.697	2.042	2.457	2.750

° The P in parentheses is for one-tailed test.

Source: R. A. Fisher, *Statistical Methods for Research Workers,* 14th ed. (Copyright © 1972 by Hafner Press, a Division of Macmillan Publishing Company, Inc.).

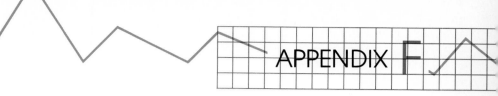
Percentiles of the *F*-Distribution for α Values of .01, .05, and .10

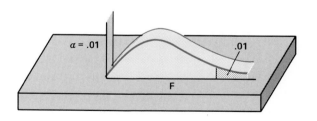

$v_2/v_1°$	1	2	3	4	5	6	8	12	15	20	30	60	∞
1	4052	4999.5	5403	5625	5764	5859	5982	6106	6157	6209	6261	6313	6366
2	98.50	99.00	99.17	99.25	99.30	99.33	99.37	99.42	99.43	99.45	99.47	99.48	99.50
3	34.12	30.82	29.46	28.71	28.24	27.91	27.49	27.05	26.87	26.69	26.50	26.32	26.13
4	21.20	18.00	16.69	15.98	15.52	15.21	14.80	14.37	14.20	14.02	13.84	13.65	13.46
5	16.27	13.26	12.06	11.39	10.97	10.67	10.29	9.89	9.72	9.55	9.38	9.20	9.02
6	13.75	10.92	9.78	9.15	8.75	8.47	8.10	7.72	7.56	7.40	7.23	7.06	6.88
7	12.25	9.55	8.45	7.85	7.46	7.19	6.84	6.47	6.31	6.16	5.99	5.82	5.65
8	11.26	8.65	7.59	7.01	6.63	6.37	6.03	5.67	5.52	5.36	5.20	5.03	4.86
9	10.56	8.02	6.99	6.42	6.06	5.80	5.47	5.11	4.96	4.81	4.65	4.48	4.31
10	10.04	7.56	6.55	5.99	5.64	5.39	5.06	4.71	4.56	4.41	4.25	4.08	3.91
11	9.65	7.21	6.22	5.67	5.32	5.07	4.74	4.40	4.25	4.10	3.94	3.78	3.60
12	9.33	6.93	5.95	5.41	5.06	4.82	4.50	4.16	4.01	3.86	3.70	3.54	3.36
13	9.07	6.70	5.74	5.21	4.86	4.62	4.30	3.96	3.82	3.66	3.51	3.34	3.17
14	8.86	6.51	5.56	5.04	4.69	4.46	4.14	3.80	3.66	3.51	3.35	3.18	3.00
15	8.68	6.36	5.42	4.89	4.56	4.32	4.00	3.67	3.52	3.37	3.21	3.05	2.87

v_2													
16	8.53	6.23	5.29	4.77	4.44	4.20	3.89	3.55	3.41	3.26	3.10	2.93	2.75
17	8.40	6.11	5.18	4.67	4.34	4.10	3.79	3.46	3.31	3.16	3.00	2.83	2.65
18	8.29	6.01	5.09	4.58	4.25	4.01	3.71	3.37	3.23	3.08	2.92	2.75	2.57
19	8.18	5.93	5.01	4.50	4.17	3.94	3.63	3.30	3.15	3.00	2.84	2.67	2.49
20	8.10	5.85	4.94	4.43	4.10	3.87	3.56	3.23	3.09	2.94	2.78	2.61	2.42
21	8.02	5.78	4.87	4.37	4.04	3.81	3.51	3.17	3.03	2.88	2.72	2.55	2.36
22	7.95	5.72	4.82	4.31	3.99	3.76	3.45	3.12	2.98	2.83	2.67	2.50	2.31
23	7.88	5.66	4.76	4.26	3.94	3.71	3.41	3.07	2.93	2.78	2.62	2.45	2.26
24	7.82	5.61	4.72	4.22	3.90	3.67	3.36	3.03	2.89	2.74	2.58	2.40	2.21
25	7.77	5.57	4.68	4.18	3.85	3.63	3.32	2.99	2.85	2.70	2.54	2.36	2.17
26	7.72	5.53	4.64	4.14	3.82	3.59	3.29	2.96	2.81	2.66	2.50	2.33	2.13
27	7.68	5.49	4.60	4.11	3.78	3.56	3.26	2.93	2.78	2.63	2.47	2.29	2.10
28	7.64	5.45	4.57	4.07	3.75	3.53	3.22	2.90	2.75	2.60	2.44	2.26	2.06
29	7.60	5.42	4.54	4.04	3.73	3.50	3.20	2.87	2.73	2.57	2.41	2.23	2.03
30	7.56	5.39	4.51	4.02	3.70	3.47	3.17	2.84	2.70	2.55	2.39	2.21	2.01
40	7.31	5.18	4.31	3.83	3.51	3.29	2.99	2.66	2.52	2.37	2.20	2.02	1.80
60	7.08	4.98	4.13	3.65	3.34	3.12	2.82	2.50	2.35	2.20	2.03	1.84	1.60
120	6.85	4.79	3.95	3.48	3.17	2.96	2.66	2.34	2.19	2.03	1.86	1.66	1.38
∞	6.63	4.61	3.78	3.32	3.02	2.80	2.51	2.18	2.04	1.88	1.70	1.47	1.00

• v_1 = degrees of freedom in numerator; v_2 = degrees of freedom for denominator.

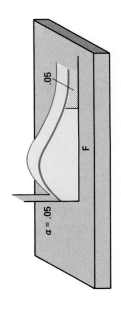

$\alpha = .05$

v_2/v_1	1	2	3	4	5	6	8	12	15	20	30	60	∞
1	161.4	199.5	215.7	224.6	230.2	234.0	238.9	243.9	245.9	248.0	250.1	252.2	254.3
2	18.51	19.00	19.16	19.25	19.30	19.33	19.37	19.41	19.43	19.45	19.46	19.48	19.50
3	10.13	9.55	9.28	9.12	9.01	8.94	8.85	8.74	8.70	8.66	8.62	8.57	8.53
4	7.71	6.94	6.59	6.39	6.26	6.16	6.04	5.91	5.86	5.80	5.75	5.69	5.63
5	6.61	5.79	5.41	5.19	5.05	4.95	4.82	4.68	4.62	4.56	4.50	4.43	4.36
6	5.99	5.14	4.76	4.53	4.39	4.28	4.15	4.00	3.94	3.87	3.81	3.74	3.67
7	5.59	4.74	4.35	4.12	3.97	3.87	3.73	3.57	3.51	3.44	3.38	3.30	3.23
8	5.32	4.46	4.07	3.84	3.69	3.58	3.44	3.28	3.22	3.15	3.08	3.01	2.93
9	5.12	4.26	3.86	3.63	3.48	3.37	3.23	3.07	3.01	2.94	2.86	2.79	2.71
10	4.96	4.10	3.71	3.48	3.33	3.22	3.07	2.91	2.85	2.77	2.70	2.62	2.54
11	4.84	3.98	3.59	3.36	3.20	3.09	2.95	2.79	2.72	2.65	2.57	2.49	2.40
12	4.75	3.89	3.49	3.26	3.11	3.00	2.85	2.69	2.62	2.54	2.47	2.38	2.30
13	4.67	3.81	3.41	3.18	3.03	2.92	2.77	2.60	2.53	2.46	2.38	2.30	2.21
14	4.60	3.74	3.34	3.11	2.96	2.85	2.70	2.53	2.46	2.39	2.31	2.22	2.13
15	4.54	3.68	3.29	3.06	2.90	2.79	2.64	2.48	2.40	2.33	2.25	2.16	2.07

v_2												
16	4.49	3.63	3.24	3.01	2.85	2.74	2.59	2.42	2.35	2.28	2.19	2.11
17	4.45	3.59	3.20	2.96	2.81	2.70	2.55	2.38	2.31	2.23	2.15	2.06
18	4.41	3.55	3.16	2.93	2.77	2.66	2.51	2.34	2.27	2.19	2.11	2.02
19	4.38	3.52	3.13	2.90	2.74	2.63	2.48	2.31	2.23	2.16	2.07	1.98
20	4.35	3.49	3.10	2.87	2.71	2.60	2.45	2.28	2.20	2.12	2.04	1.95
21	4.32	3.47	3.07	2.84	2.68	2.57	2.42	2.25	2.18	2.10	2.01	1.92
22	4.30	3.44	3.05	2.82	2.66	2.55	2.40	2.23	2.15	2.07	1.98	1.89
23	4.28	3.42	3.03	2.80	2.64	2.53	2.37	2.20	2.13	2.05	1.96	1.86
24	4.26	3.40	3.01	2.78	2.62	2.51	2.36	2.18	2.11	2.03	1.94	1.84
25	4.24	3.39	2.99	2.76	2.60	2.49	2.34	2.16	2.09	2.01	1.92	1.82
26	4.23	3.37	2.98	2.74	2.59	2.47	2.32	2.15	2.07	1.99	1.90	1.80
27	4.21	3.35	2.96	2.73	2.57	2.46	2.31	2.13	2.06	1.97	1.88	1.79
28	4.20	3.34	2.95	2.71	2.56	2.45	2.29	2.12	2.04	1.96	1.87	1.77
29	4.18	3.33	2.93	2.70	2.55	2.43	2.28	2.10	2.03	1.94	1.85	1.75
30	4.17	3.32	2.92	2.69	2.53	2.42	2.27	2.09	2.01	1.93	1.84	1.74
40	4.08	3.23	2.84	2.61	2.45	2.34	2.18	2.00	1.92	1.84	1.74	1.64
60	4.00	3.15	2.76	2.53	2.37	2.25	2.10	1.92	1.84	1.75	1.65	1.53
120	3.92	3.07	2.68	2.45	2.29	2.17	2.02	1.83	1.75	1.66	1.55	1.43
∞	3.84	3.00	2.60	2.37	2.21	2.10	1.94	1.75	1.67	1.57	1.46	1.32

(last column, v_2:) 16: 2.01, 17: 1.96, 18: 1.92, 19: 1.88, 20: 1.84, 21: 1.81, 22: 1.78, 23: 1.76, 24: 1.73, 25: 1.71, 26: 1.69, 27: 1.67, 28: 1.65, 29: 1.64, 30: 1.62, 40: 1.51, 60: 1.39, 120: 1.25, ∞: 1.00

$^\circ$ v_1 = degrees of freedom in numerator; v_2 = degrees of freedom for denominator.

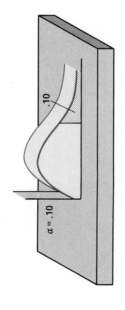

$\alpha = .10$

v_2/v_1°	1	2	3	4	5	6	8	12	15	20	30	60	∞
1	39.86	49.50	53.59	55.83	57.24	58.20	59.44	60.71	61.22	61.74	62.26	62.79	63.33
2	8.53	9.00	9.16	9.24	9.29	9.33	9.37	9.41	9.42	9.44	9.46	9.47	9.49
3	5.54	5.46	5.38	5.34	5.31	5.29	5.25	5.22	5.20	5.18	5.17	5.15	5.13
4	4.54	4.32	4.19	4.11	4.05	4.01	3.95	3.90	3.87	3.84	3.82	3.79	3.76
5	4.06	3.78	3.62	3.52	3.45	3.40	3.34	3.27	3.24	3.21	3.17	3.14	3.10
6	3.78	3.46	3.29	3.18	3.11	3.05	2.98	2.90	2.87	2.84	2.80	2.76	2.72
7	3.59	3.26	3.07	2.96	2.88	2.83	2.75	2.67	2.63	2.59	2.56	2.51	2.47
8	3.46	3.11	2.92	2.81	2.73	2.67	2.59	2.50	2.46	2.42	2.38	2.34	2.29
9	3.36	3.01	2.81	2.69	2.61	2.55	2.47	2.38	2.34	2.30	2.25	2.21	2.16
10	3.29	2.92	2.73	2.61	2.52	2.46	2.38	2.28	2.24	2.20	2.16	2.11	2.06
11	3.23	2.86	2.66	2.54	2.45	2.39	2.30	2.21	2.17	2.12	2.08	2.03	1.97
12	3.18	2.81	2.61	2.48	2.39	2.33	2.24	2.15	2.10	2.06	2.01	1.96	1.90
13	3.14	2.76	2.56	2.43	2.35	2.28	2.20	2.10	2.05	2.01	1.96	1.90	1.85
14	3.10	2.73	2.52	2.39	2.31	2.24	2.15	2.05	2.01	1.96	1.91	1.86	1.80
15	3.07	2.70	2.49	2.36	2.27	2.21	2.12	2.02	1.97	1.92	1.87	1.82	1.76

v_2													
16	3.05	2.67	2.46	2.33	2.24	2.18	2.09	1.99	1.94	1.89	1.84	1.78	1.72
17	3.03	2.64	2.44	2.31	2.22	2.15	2.06	1.96	1.91	1.86	1.81	1.75	1.69
18	3.01	2.62	2.42	2.29	2.20	2.13	2.04	1.93	1.89	1.84	1.78	1.72	1.66
19	2.99	2.61	2.40	2.27	2.18	2.11	2.02	1.91	1.86	1.81	1.76	1.70	1.63
20	2.97	2.59	2.38	2.25	2.16	2.09	2.00	1.89	1.84	1.79	1.74	1.68	1.61
21	2.96	2.57	2.36	2.23	2.14	2.08	1.98	1.87	1.83	1.78	1.72	1.66	1.59
22	2.95	2.56	2.35	2.22	2.13	2.06	1.97	1.86	1.81	1.76	1.70	1.64	1.57
23	2.94	2.55	2.34	2.21	2.11	2.05	1.95	1.84	1.80	1.74	1.69	1.62	1.55
24	2.93	2.54	2.33	2.19	2.10	2.04	1.94	1.83	1.78	1.73	1.67	1.61	1.53
25	2.92	2.53	2.32	2.18	2.09	2.02	1.93	1.82	1.77	1.72	1.66	1.59	1.52
26	2.91	2.52	2.31	2.17	2.08	2.01	1.92	1.81	1.76	1.71	1.65	1.58	1.50
27	2.90	2.51	2.30	2.17	2.07	2.00	1.91	1.80	1.75	1.70	1.64	1.57	1.49
28	2.89	2.50	2.29	2.16	2.06	2.00	1.90	1.79	1.74	1.69	1.63	1.56	1.48
29	2.89	2.50	2.28	2.15	2.06	1.99	1.89	1.78	1.73	1.68	1.62	1.55	1.47
30	2.88	2.49	2.28	2.14	2.05	1.98	1.88	1.77	1.72	1.67	1.61	1.54	1.46
40	2.84	2.44	2.23	2.09	2.00	1.93	1.83	1.71	1.66	1.61	1.54	1.47	1.38
60	2.79	2.39	2.18	2.04	1.95	1.87	1.77	1.66	1.60	1.54	1.48	1.40	1.29
120	2.75	2.35	2.13	1.99	1.90	1.82	1.72	1.60	1.55	1.48	1.41	1.32	1.19
∞	2.71	2.30	2.08	1.94	1.85	1.77	1.67	1.55	1.49	1.42	1.34	1.24	1.00

^{a} v_1 = degrees of freedom in numerator; v_2 = degrees of freedom for denominator.

Source: M. Abramewitz and I. A. Stegan, *Handbook of Mathematical Functions — AMS 55,* National Bureau of Standards and Applied Mathematics, Series (Washington, D.C.: U.S. Government Printing Office, 1964).

787

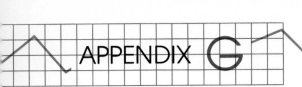
Table of Critical Values of D in the Kolmogorov-Smirnov One-Sample Test

	Level of Significance for $D = maximum$ $\|F_o(X) - S_N(X)\|$			
Sample Size (N)	.20	.10	.05	.01
1	.900	.950	.975	.995
2	.684	.776	.842	.929
3	.565	.642	.708	.828
4	.494	.564	.624	.733
5	.446	.510	.565	.669
6	.410	.470	.521	.618
7	.381	.438	.486	.577
8	.358	.411	.457	.543
9	.339	.388	.432	.514
10	.322	.368	.410	.490
11	.307	.352	.391	.468
12	.295	.338	.375	.450
13	.284	.325	.361	.433
14	.274	.314	.349	.418
15	.266	.304	.338	.404
16	.258	.295	.328	.392
17	.250	.286	.318	.381
18	.244	.278	.309	.371

Sample Size (N)	Level of Significance for $\mathbf{D} = maximum$ $\|F_0(X) - S_N(X)\|$			
	.20	*.10*	*.05*	*.01*
19	.237	.272	.301	.363
20	.231	.264	.294	.356
25	.21	.24	.27	.32
30	.19	.22	.24	.29
35	.18	.21	.23	.27
Over 35	$\dfrac{1.07}{\sqrt{N}}$	$\dfrac{1.22}{\sqrt{N}}$	$\dfrac{1.36}{\sqrt{N}}$	$\dfrac{1.63}{\sqrt{N}}$

Table of Values of Chi Square

How to use the table and interpret the probability found:

1. Find the *degrees of freedom* (df) of the contingency table for the problem by multiplying the number of rows minus one $(r - 1)$ times the number of columns minus one $(k - 1)$:

$$df = (r - 1)(k - 1)$$

2. Look up the probability for the number of degrees of freedom and the calculated value of χ^2, approximating if necessary. This will be the *probability that the differences between the observed and the expected values occurred because of sampling variation.*

Probability of χ^2 Occurring Because of Sampling Variation

df	.99	.98	.95	.90	.80	.70	.50	.30	.20	.10	.05	.02	.01	.001
1	.00016	.00063	.0039	.016	.064	.15	.46	1.07	1.64	2.71	3.84	5.41	6.64	10.83
2	.02	.04	.10	.21	.45	.71	1.39	2.41	3.22	4.60	5.99	7.82	9.21	13.82
3	.12	.18	.35	.58	1.00	1.42	2.37	3.66	4.64	6.25	7.82	9.84	11.34	16.27
4	.30	.43	.71	1.06	1.65	2.20	3.36	4.88	5.99	7.78	9.49	11.67	13.28	18.46
5	.55	.75	1.14	1.61	2.34	3.00	4.35	6.06	7.29	9.24	11.07	13.39	15.09	20.52
6	.87	1.13	1.64	2.20	3.07	3.83	5.35	7.23	8.56	10.64	12.59	15.03	16.81	22.46
7	1.24	1.56	2.17	2.83	3.82	4.67	6.35	8.38	9.80	12.02	14.07	16.62	18.48	24.32
8	1.65	2.03	2.73	3.49	4.59	5.53	7.34	9.52	11.03	13.36	15.51	18.17	20.09	26.12
9	2.09	2.53	3.32	4.17	5.38	6.39	8.34	10.66	12.24	14.68	16.92	19.68	21.67	27.88
10	2.56	3.06	3.94	4.86	6.18	7.27	9.34	11.78	13.44	15.99	18.31	21.16	23.21	29.59
11	3.05	3.61	4.58	5.53	6.99	8.15	10.34	12.90	14.63	17.28	19.68	22.62	24.72	31.26
12	3.57	4.18	5.23	6.30	7.81	9.03	11.34	14.01	15.81	18.55	21.03	24.05	26.22	32.91
13	4.11	4.76	5.89	7.04	8.63	9.93	12.34	15.12	16.98	19.81	22.36	25.47	27.69	34.53
14	4.66	5.37	6.57	7.79	9.47	10.82	13.34	16.22	18.15	21.06	23.68	26.87	29.14	36.12
15	5.23	5.98	7.26	8.55	10.31	11.72	14.34	17.32	19.31	22.31	25.00	28.26	30.58	37.70
16	5.81	6.61	7.96	9.31	11.15	12.62	15.34	18.42	20.46	23.54	26.30	29.63	32.00	39.29
17	6.41	7.26	8.67	10.08	12.00	13.53	16.34	19.51	21.62	24.77	27.59	31.00	33.41	40.75
18	7.02	7.91	9.39	10.86	12.86	14.44	17.34	20.60	22.76	25.99	28.87	32.35	34.80	42.31
19	7.63	8.57	10.12	11.65	13.72	15.35	18.34	21.69	23.90	27.20	30.14	33.69	36.19	43.82
20	8.26	9.24	10.85	12.44	14.58	16.27	19.34	22.78	25.04	28.41	31.41	35.02	37.57	45.32
21	8.90	9.92	11.59	13.24	15.44	17.18	20.34	23.86	26.17	29.62	32.67	36.34	38.93	46.80
22	9.54	10.60	12.34	14.04	16.31	18.10	21.34	24.94	27.30	30.81	33.92	37.66	40.29	48.27
23	10.20	11.29	13.09	14.85	17.19	19.02	22.34	26.02	28.43	32.01	35.17	38.97	41.64	49.73
24	10.86	11.99	13.85	15.66	18.06	19.94	23.34	27.10	29.55	33.20	36.42	40.27	42.98	51.18
25	11.52	12.70	14.61	16.47	18.94	20.87	24.34	28.17	30.68	34.38	37.65	41.57	44.31	52.62
26	12.20	13.41	15.38	17.29	19.82	21.79	25.34	29.25	31.80	35.56	38.88	42.86	45.64	54.05
27	12.88	14.12	16.15	18.11	20.70	22.72	26.34	30.32	32.91	36.74	40.11	44.14	46.96	55.48
28	13.56	14.85	16.93	18.94	21.59	23.65	27.34	31.39	34.03	37.92	41.34	45.42	48.28	56.89
29	14.26	15.57	17.71	19.77	22.48	24.48	28.34	32.46	35.14	39.09	42.56	46.69	49.59	58.30
30	14.95	16.31	18.49	20.00	23.36	25.51	29.34	33.53	36.25	40.26	43.77	47.96	50.89	59.70

Source: R. A. Fisher, Statistical Methods for Research Workers, 14th ed. (Copyright © 1972 by Hafner Press, a Division of Macmillan Publishing Company, Inc.)

Table of Random Numbers

69	47	26	60	28	33	65	51	63	91	41	07	85	54	48	47	89	89	28	16	53	63	25	95	88
36	14	60	08	90	71	30	34	43	18	96	70	86	34	51	06	51	11	14	03	33	67	85	71	90
62	16	07	76	94	09	32	30	74	76	86	78	75	52	70	37	57	13	08	29	32	23	91	70	56
75	46	96	99	49	03	54	14	38	20	58	77	01	14	85	16	66	99	28	95	46	57	76	48	08
32	53	72	54	45	60	27	95	50	61	94	74	24	19	78	12	00	75	85	97	32	75	62	45	62
66	09	42	47	16	57	33	42	44	67	41	75	32	43	09	79	78	39	01	27	21	30	48	49	20
12	56	30	19	62	47	50	43	45	05	13	13	79	58	36	73	10	71	17	77	56	92	66	44	72
93	63	44	66	76	44	76	82	75	38	09	46	79	96	66	80	57	46	23	99	32	05	27	34	43
99	96	86	08	57	19	62	73	25	37	61	76	95	17	07	61	40	57	34	44	54	85	84	40	08
92	95	55	56	71	43	44	26	00	73	43	15	01	66	82	74	35	10	28	92	17	90	92	95	63
88	77	70	08	13	16	60	87	60	67	80	97	39	58	27	90	59	22	75	49	43	63	83	03	90
71	43	59	44	65	08	48	18	95	88	73	16	98	95	53	70	49	86	71	25	87	37	88	73	79
81	71	50	68	32	00	95	95	39	17	83	77	07	95	65	90	61	10	52	48	74	48	32	49	54
85	35	17	54	65	57	99	07	07	65	21	93	79	91	42	77	75	10	96	19	13	78	19	34	56
97	98	88	17	00	58	81	12	61	35	25	42	21	18	68	84	37	73	30	88	85	19	59	16	47
40	50	04	89	66	51	21	91	82	71	15	80	17	88	38	27	49	65	30	34	49	28	22	14	67
22	73	51	48	82	14	87	85	46	89	19	46	67	54	20	61	33	11	68	14	55	25	25	25	92
21	29	99	31	69	64	45	42	00	84	18	46	43	44	30	16	40	07	95	26	63	24	69	37	48
18	09	80	67	79	82	33	35	05	92	31	34	64	39	62	35	51	99	31	87	41	61	85	97	94
26	72	96	60	46	44	75	28	54	62	38	92	97	05	53	34	53	64	56	43	93	64	05	68	42
66	28	80	86	71	43	11	46	59	63	17	27	36	56	92	37	11	11	86	57	44	98	34	87	82
62	99	58	99	85	78	25	10	31	75	63	00	87	08	78	22	12	12	52	85	49	86	18	07	70
55	60	57	69	48	19	41	83	50	67	59	12	99	19	02	00	28	19	08	11	96	28	36	61	43
76	62	89	95	48	58	09	12	03	61	59	06	54	85	46	84	63	96	51	96	65	12	98	54	11
94	66	26	20	23	40	59	39	40	32	15	16	54	81	79	63	12	78	47	16	58	70	58	97	02
50	73	51	48	98	54	66	93	14	37	81	30	87	07	65	99	95	12	72	94	81	51	49	09	37
94	11	04	04	22	92	49	83	08	57	01	85	53	53	23	75	41	14	29	11	66	15	93	94	90
97	87	81	59	36	66	29	96	73	78	67	53	01	98	78	74	15	70	42	62	68	10	52	98	34
46	50	73	23	03	04	37	49	13	66	97	24	11	63	83	18	23	87	99	66	21	91	79	12	63
43	85	00	91	54	39	67	34	53	17	21	10	43	16	80	81	09	79	08	82	51	07	40	95	83
18	20	00	87	87	11	61	72	26	45	62	83	74	27	48	29	35	71	96	66	24	78	91	94	06
68	94	94	68	84	27	04	78	14	17	14	84	79	82	01	96	90	62	31	73	19	12	96	97	05
04	19	46	04	41	94	03	09	64	84	26	45	84	77	37	82	23	36	75	78	06	25	19	44	15
18	58	79	01	03	59	56	25	50	68	29	21	93	72	00	20	31	12	49	91	03	44	85	01	90

Glossary

Accuracy The degree to which research data are free from both systematic and variable errors.

Add-a-Digit Dialing A sampling technique for telephone surveys that requires a researcher to select a sample from an existing directory and add one to each number thus selected.

After-Only Experimental Design Involves manipulating the independent variable and following this with a postmeasurement.

Aggregate-of-Sales-Representatives Forecast A judgmental method of forecasting sales; it involves asking sales representatives to estimate their sales by product for the forecast period. The overall forecast is then arrived at by summing the individual forecasts.

Aided Recall Provides the respondents with all or some of the aspects of an original event to help them remember it.

Allowable Error The amount of sampling error in the estimate (of the parameter) that is acceptable to the researcher.

Alternative-Form Reliability A method for determining reliability by giving two "equivalent" questionnaires to the same group of people and comparing the results on a question-by-question basis.

ANOVA (Analysis of Variance) Is used to test for differences among two or more means to determine if the observed differences of the mean responses of groups receiving different experimental treatments are the result of sampling variation.

Area Sample A type of cluster sample in which geographic subdivisions (countries, towns, blocks, etc.) serve as the sampling units.

Attitude Scale Sets of rating scales constructed to measure one or more dimensions of an individual's attitude toward some object. Attitude scales are constructed using Likert, Semantic Differential, and Stapel scales.

Banners Are a way of displaying several cross tabulations in one table.

Bar Chart A chart in which the length of the bar represents the amount of the item associated with the bar.

Bayesian Statistical Model A statistical procedure for incorporating subjective probabilities and data costs into sample size calculations and statistical decision making.

Before-After Experimental Design Involves measuring the dependent variable before (premeasurement) and after (postmeasurement) the introduction or manipulation of the independent variable. The result of interest is the difference between the pre- and postmeasurement.

Bivariate Analysis of Association An analysis of the relationship between two variables, a predictor (independent) variable and a criterion (dependent) variable, for the purpose of using the predictor variable to help predict or "explain" the level of criterion variable.

Box-Jenkins Forecasting Method A computer assisted iterative forecasting process that involves identifying a tentative model, testing it to see if it adequately describes the data, and, if need be, revising the model and retesting it until a satisfactory model is obtained and a forecast is made.

Blind Use Test A test in which consumers are asked to use several alternative products and then evaluate the relative desirability of the products without knowing the brand names.

Brain Wave Analysis A technique that provides measurements of a physiological response to a stimulus and that differentiates between rational responses and emotional responses by measuring changes in brain wave patterns.

Branching Questions Questions that require respondents to answer differing subsequent questions depending on their response to the original question.

Cartoon Technique A projective technique requiring the subject to "fill in" the thought or comments of people depicted in a cartoon situation.

Causal Research Attempts to specify the cause-and-effect relationship between two or more variables in the problem model.

Census A measurement of each element in the group or population of interest.

Centered Moving Average A method used to calculate seasonal index numbers in which a moving average of the data for one year plus one period is used to calculate the average value for the period in the center of the data. Example: use a weighted average of the sales data for December through December (13 months) to find the average sales for the center month (June); use January through January to find July, etc.

Chi-Square Test A statistical test for analyzing significance in analysis of frequencies.

Cluster Analysis **A** set of techniques for separating objects into mutually exclusive groups such that the groups are relatively homogeneous.

Cluster Sampling **A** probability sampling method in which the sampling units are selected in groups.

Codebook **A** set of instructions used to inform data coders how to code the responses to each question on a questionnaire and to indicate the format to use to input the data into the computer.

Coding The process of establishing categories for responses to questions, such as Male = 1 and Female = 2, and then assigning each response to a category.

Coefficient Alpha **A** measure of the degree of internal comparison reliability possessed by a measurement instrument. It can range from 0 to 1. A value below .6 if viewed as being relatively low and a value above .9 is relatively high.

Coefficient of Determination (r^2) The proportion of total variation in the criterion variable that is accounted for by variation in the predictor variable(s). It measures the strength of association in a regression analysis and ranges from 0 (none of the variation is explained) to 1.0 (all of the variation is explained).

Comparative Concept Tests Tests conducted by presenting several ideas or concepts to the subject and asking him/her to evaluate each concept in terms of purchase intentions or preferences relative to the other concept(s).

Comparative Rating Scale Requires the respondent to evaluate one item in light of or in comparison to a specified other item.

Completely Randomized Experimental Design An after-only with control or a before-after with control design involving more than one level or version of the independent variable.

Computer Interview In a computer interview, the computer presents the questions to the respondents on a TV-type screen and the respondents answer via a console.

Computerized Data Base **A** collection of information or data that are available to users by means of a computer terminal. Many commercial computerized bases, such as mailing lists, industry analyses, and governmental indexes, are available for lease or outright purchase.

Concept Test The consumers are exposed to a verbal and/or pictorial representation of the product, rather than a physical prototype, and their reactions to it are obtained.

Conceptual Definition Defines a concept in terms of other concepts and is similar to definitions found in a dictionary. It represents the concept's major characteristics. This allows one to distinguish Concept **A** from Concept **B**, a *similar* but *different* concept, for example, Brand Loyalty vs. Repeat Purchasing Behavior.

Concurrent Validity **A** measure of how accurate a description of an object, state, or event is now, as opposed to how accurate it will be in the future, (predictive validity). One measure of concurrent validity is how comparable the results of Instrument A and Instrument B are when both are used to measure the same characteristics in the same object at the same point in time.

Conditional Payoff Table A matrix in which each cell contains an estimate of the financial outcome if the action (indicated on one axis) and environmental event (indicated on the other axis) both occurred.

Conditional Probability The probability of event B occurring, given that event A has occurred.

Confidence Interval The range of values within which a population value is likely to fall. It is created when making an interval estimate. The degree of confidence (confidence coefficient) is usually specified by the researcher.

Conjoint Analysis A set of techniques used to derive the relative importance respondents assign to each attribute when selecting from among several brands. It also allows an estimate of the best combination of attributes.

Consistent Preference Discrimination Test Conducted by having the subject repeat a paired comparison test several times. The CPDT measures both preference and the ability of the subject to discriminate between two or more stimuli (brands, product formulations).

Constant Sum Scale Requires the respondent to divide a constant sum, generally 10 or 100, among two or more objects or attributes in order to reflect the respondent's relative preference for each object, the importance of the attribute, or the degree to which an object contains each attribute.

Construct Validity Understanding the factors that underlie the obtained measurement. It involves knowing how well and why a given measure works by having a sound theory of the nature of the concept being measured and how it relates to other concepts.

Content Validity Exists when a panel of "experts" considers the measuring instrument appropriate for obtaining the information desired.

Contingency Coefficient A measure of the degree of association between two sets of data, one or both of which are nominally scaled.

Control Group The group of subjects not exposed to the experimental treatment.

Controlled-Store Test A market test utilizing a limited number of outlets in several areas. A research firm typically pays the selected outlets to let it place its product in their stores, and handles all the warehousing, distribution, pricing, and shelving.

Convenience Sample A sample chosen solely because it is a convenient sample for the researcher to interview or study. Friends, employees, and college students are examples of commonly used convenience samples.

Convergent Validity When two different measures of the same concept produce similar results. For example a positive score on an attitude scale for brand A and frequent use of brand

A would be evidence of convergent validity.

Correlation A number between -1 and $+1$ that reflects the nature (direct or inverse) and the degree of the association between two or more variables.

Counterbiasing Statements Used to begin a question in a way which makes a potentially embarrassing response seem ordinary. They are used to reduce distortion in responses by making it easier for respondents to admit potentially embarrassing behavior.

Criterion Variable The dependent variable in an associative relationship among variables. (See Predictor Variable.) Example: A criterion variable such as Market Share is often explained by such predictor variables as relative price or amount of advertising.

Cross Sectional Study A study, usually a survey, measuring a sample of respondents at a single point in time.

Cross Tabulation A table constructed to show how a given value on one variable (for example, Male or Female) is associated with one or more other variables (such as Education Level and/or Income).

Cumulative Distribution A table or graph that indicates the percentage (or number) of cases having a value less than or equal to the table or graph value.

Data Reduction The activities involved in developing a basic data array as complete and error-free as possible and calculating the appropri-ate summarizing statistics (mean, median, etc.).

Day-After Recall (DAR) A widely used method of copy testing television advertisements based on telephone interviews of TV viewers in sample cities where a TV advertisement is being tested. Viewers are contacted the day after the ad is broadcast and asked to describe the advertisement using an aided recall method.

Decision Support System An interactive system of data and decision rules or models designed to assist managers make specific decisions.

Delphi Method A judgmental method of forecasting that avoids the problem of weighting individual expert forecasts while eliminating rank and personality bias. Experts are asked their judgments, the researcher summarizes the expert's opinions and returns the summary to each expert who is asked to make another forecast now that he/she has received a summary of other experts' thoughts. The process is repeated until either a consensus is reached or as much convergence as seems likely has been attained.

Dependent Variable A variable whose value Depends on the level or magnitude of the independent variable. Sales of automobiles (dependent variable) may Depend on the level of interest rates (independent variable). (See Criterion Variable.)

Depth Interview An interviewing procedure in which the interviewer does not have a prespecified list of questions. The interviewer is free to create questions and probe responses that appear relevant. Respondents are free to respond to questions in any way they think appropriate. Types of depth interviews include individual, mini group, and focus group.

Descriptive Research A type of research that focuses on providing an accurate description of the variables in the problem model. Examples include market-potential studies, attitude surveys, media research, and price studies.

Diary Panel A group of households each of which records purchases of selected products for a specified time period using a predetermined diary format. Consumer diary panels are available commercially (for example, the National Purchase Diary Panel, Inc.).

Dichotomous Question An extreme form of the multiple-choice question in which only one of two responses is allowed; usually framed as yes-no, agree-disagree, or did-did not.

Discriminant Analysis A statistical technique for classifying persons or objects into two or more categories, using a set of intervally scaled predictor variables.

Discriminant Validity A form of validity in which there is a *low* correlation between the measure of interest (for example, number of magazines read) that are supposedly not measuring the same variable or concept.

Double-Barreled Question A question in which two or more questions are asked as one. Example: "Do you think Coke has the right level of carbonation and sweetness?"

Double-Triangle Discrimination Test (See Triangle Taste Test)

Dummy Variable An artificially scaled variable created by a researcher when a nominally scaled predictor variable is to be included in a regression equation. Dummy variables are scaled 1 (indicating the presence of a characteristic) or 0 (indicating its absence). For example, $1 = $ Male, $0 = $ Not Male (i.e., female).

Editing The process of ensuring that the data requested are present, readable, and accurate. Editing involves determining how to treat ambiguous or illegible responses, what to do with inconsistent responses, and whether or not to use a set of responses or delete them from analysis.

Electronic Test Market Similar to minimarket tests except the research firm has (1) the ability to collect on-going scanner based sales data from the major food and drug outlets, (2) a UPC scanner-based household panel that also has its television viewing monitored electronically, and (3) the capability of sending differing commercials to varying households in the panel.

Executive Summary A brief summary of the results of the research project commissioned by the client. It stresses the major findings, conclusions, and recommendations of the research team.

Expected Value The estimated value of a decision calculated by multiplying the payoff of each possible outcome by the probability of the outcome occurring, and adding the products generated.

Expected Value of Perfect Information The difference between the expected value of a decision outcome with certain knowledge and the expected value of the decision with current knowledge.

Experimentation A controlled situation in which the experimenter systematically changes the values of one or more variables [the independent variable(s)] to measure the impact of these changes on one or more other variables [the dependent variable(s)].

Exploratory Research A type of research concerned with discovering the general nature of a problem and the factors that relate to it. The design is flexible and may proceed without a fixed plan. It is generally based on secondary data and convenience samples.

Exponential Smoothing A forecasting technique in which the forecast for the next period is a weighted average of sales over the past X time periods. The more recent periods are weighted more heavily than the earlier periods.

Ex Post Facto Study A study in which the researcher starts with some currently existing condition, then attempts to discover the events (variables) which caused it. This is not an experimental design because variables are not manipulated and subjects are not assigned to treatment/control groups.

Expressive Projective Techniques Require the consumer to assume the role or behavior of an object or another person. They are used to uncover information (about an individual's attitudes and values) not available through direct questioning or observation.

External Validity The ability of the results from an experiment to predict the results in the actual situation.

Eye Tracking A procedure in which the subject's eye movements are tracked to determine the extent to which each element in a stimulus object (such as a package design) is noted, including the speed, sequence, and time spent noting each element.

Face Validity A form of content validity that exists when "nonexperts" such as respondents or executives judge the measuring instrument as appropriate for the task at hand.

Factor Analysis A type of analysis used to determine the underlying dimensions of a set of data, to determine relationships among variables, and to condense and simplify a data set.

Factor Loading The correlation between a specific attribute or variable and a factor identified in a factor analysis.

Factorial Design A statistical experimental design used to measure the effect of two or more independent variables on a dependent variable, especially when they may interact with each other.

Field Experiment An experiment conducted in a "real-world" environment such that the respondents are unlikely to be aware that an experiment is under way.

Field Work The portion of the research process during which data are actually collected from respondents or subjects. Examples include telephone interviews, mall intercepts, and taste tests.

Focus Group Interview A form of depth interview generally involving 8–12 people chosen because they are from a market segment of interest. The group is interviewed for 1–3 hours by a moderator who guides discussion about a product, a concept, or an advertisement.

Forced Choice Scale A rating scale that does not allow for a "no opinion" or "undecided" response. The scale "forces" the respondent to make a choice, to express his or her attitude.

Free Word Association A projective technique that requires the respondent to give the first word or though that comes to mind after the researcher presents a word or phrase.

Frequency Distribution A table that provides a summary of the number of times various responses were given by the respondents.

Full Profile Conjoint The more realistic version of conjoint analysis in which subjects evaluate complete product descriptions developed from an orthogonal array.

Graeco-Latin Square Experimental Design An experimental design that allows the researcher to control statistically for three noninteracting extraneous variables in addition to the independent variable.

Graphic Rating Scale A scale that measures a subject's attitude concerning an object by requiring the subject to make a mark on a line in which the end points are identified by adjectives such as "excellent" and "very poor."

Histogram A vertical bar chart in which the height of the bars represents the relative or cumulative frequency of occurrence of the variable of interest.

History Error An experimental error that occurs when changes in extraneous variables (those outside the control of the researcher) affect the outcome of the experiment. Examples include weather, competitors' actions, general economic events.

Hypothesis An "educated guess" about the outcome of an empirical test designed to answer a research question.

Implied Alternative A question asked in a way which leaves unstated other alternatives. Example: "Should the state legislature use the budget surplus to give state employees a raise?" The implied alternative is other uses for the monies, such as " . . . or should the money be used to lower the tax rate."

Implied Assumption A question asked in a way that the answer given depends on the assumptions made about relevant factors outside the question itself. Example: many students might respond positively to the question "Are you in favor of reducing class periods from 50 minutes to 30 minutes?" unless they considered the implied assumption that the number of class periods would be increased so that total time spent in class during a semester would remain constant.

Imputation Estimates Involve assigning attributes to the nonrespondents (of a survey) based on the characteristics of the respondents in order to adjust for nonresponse.

Independent Samples Two or more samples are said to be independent if the selection of sample elements to be included in one sample does not affect the sample elements to be included in the other sample(s).

Independent Variable The variable that is manipulated by the experimenter to see if and how it affects the value of the dependent variable.

Instrumentation Error An experimental error that occurs when the measurement instrument changes over time. For example, an experimenter may become more skilled at recording subjects responses to a new ad as an experiment progresses.

Interaction Error An experimental error that occurs when subjects react differently to the independent variable because of a previous measurement. Example: if you were asked to participate in an opinion survey concerning Ford automobiles, your reactions to subsequent Ford commercials would be different from those who did not participate in the opinion survey. If you participate in another survey to measure the effectiveness of the advertisement, interaction error may occur.

Internal Comparison Reliability Exists when the scores on several questions, all of which were designed to measure a characteristic such as a person's Brand Loyalty proneness, are all highly correlated with each other.

Internal Validity The degree of replicability of an experiment or assurance that experimental results are due to the variables manipulated in the experiment in that specific environment.

Interval Estimate A statistical estimate of a range of values with a known probability of including a parameter (such as a population mean).

Interval Panel A sample of respondents who have agreed to complete a number of questionnaires during their tenure as panel members.

Interval Scale Numbers used to rank items such that numerically equal distances on the scale represent equal distances in the property being measured. The location of the zero point and the unit of measurement are determined by the researcher; consequently, ratios calculated on data from interval scales are not meaningful.

Interviewer Effect The effect the interviewer has on the responses received from sample members. Results can be affected by the interviewer's age, sex, appearance, mannerisms, race, opinions, social class and voice.

Itemized Rating Scale A rating scale that has a limited number of categories ordered in terms of their scale positions, e.g., very satisfied—satisfied—dissatisfied—very dissatisfied.

Item Nonresponse Occurs when a respondent to a survey fails to answer one or more questions on an otherwise complete questionnaire.

Judgment Sampling The sampling process that uses "expert" judgment to select a representative sample. For example, several U.S. cities may be "judged" to be "typical" of the rest of the country and are used to represent all cities in the United States.

Laboratory Experiment An experiment conducted in an artificial environment with the subjects frequently aware that they are involved in an experiment.

Latin Square Design A statistical experimental design in which two noninteracting extraneous variables in addition to the independent variable may be controlled. For example, what is the effect on sales (the dependent variable) of three different alternative package designs in three different types of retail stores under three different economic conditions?

Leading Question A question that suggests what the answer should be, or that reflects the researcher's point of view. Example: "Do you agree, as most people do, that TV advertising serves no useful purpose?"

Likert Scale A rating scale that requires the subject to indicate his/her degree of Agreement or Disagreement with a statement.

Line Chart A two-dimensional chart in which the X axis represents one variable (often time) and the Y axis another. Both variables are generally continuous.

Longitudinal Study A study in which the same respondents are measured repeatedly over time.

Mail Interview Delivering the data collection instrument to the respondent using the postal service.

Mall Intercept Survey A survey conducted in a shopping mall that involves approaching shoppers and asking them to take part in the survey being conducted.

Marketing Information System (MIS) A system designed to generate, store, and disseminate relevant information to the appropriate marketing decision makers.

Marketing Research A formalized means of obtaining information to be used to make marketing decisions.

Maturation Error An experimental error that occurs because biological or psychological processes change during the time of the experiment. Examples include hunger, boredom, fatigue.

Mean A measure of central tendency; obtained by adding all observations and dividing the sum by the number of observations.

Measurement The assignment of numbers to characteristics of objects, persons, states, or events, according to rules.

Measurement Timing Error Occurs when the pre- or postmeasurement is made at an inappropriate time to indicate the effect of the experimental treatment.

Median   A measure of central tendency; the value below which 50 per cent of the observations lie.

Mode   A measure of central tendency; the value that occurs most frequently.

Monadic Tests   A product concept or use test in which subjects are asked to evaluate the product or concept and then rate it on an intention-to-buy, preference, or attitudinal scale without examining other products.

Mortality Error   An experimental error that occurs when multiple groups are used and some groups lose subjects who are fundamentally different from those subjects lost by other groups. This error does not necessarily occur simply because a group loses some members.

Moving Average Forecast   A forecasting model where the value for the next period will be equal to the average value for the last x periods, where x is some multiple of the number of periods in a year.

Multicollinearity   A potential problem in multiple regression analysis when two or more of the predictor variables are correlated with each other.

Multidimensional Scaling   A variety of techniques for representing objects as points in multidimensional space (where the dimensions are the attributes that respondents use to differentiate the objects) such that the Euclidian distance between the objects will reflect the original rank order of similarities between the pairs of objects as perceived by the respondents.

Multiple-Choice Question   A question that requires the respondent to choose among a set of predetermined alternative responses.

Naïve Forecasting Model   A time series forecasting model that relies heavily on the value of the variable in the most recent period to forecast a value for the variable in the next period in a time series.

Nominal Scales   Comprised of numbers used to categorize objects or events without ordering the categories.

Nomological Validity   A form of validity in which a measure correlates positively in the theoretically predicted way with measures of different but related constructs. For example, the tendency to purchase prestige brands should show a high correlation with a person's need for status and materialism and a negative correlation with price sensitivity.

Noncomparative Rating Scales   A rating scale in which respondents are not given a standard to use when asked to assign a rating to some object. There is no referent given, such as "compared to your favorite brand," when noncomparative rating scales are used.

Nonparametric Statistics   Statistics and statistical tests designed for nominal and ordinal data.

Nonprobability Sample   One in which chance selection procedures are not used to draw the sample.

803

Nonresponse Error Variation between the selected sample and the sample that actually participates in the study; caused by a failure to contact all members of a sample, and/or the failure of some contacted members of the sample to respond to all or specific parts of the measurement instrument.

Nonsampling Error All the errors that can arise in research other than those associated with the sampling process.

Null Hypothesis (H_O) One that, if accepted, will result in no opinion being formed and/or action being taken that is different from any currently held or being used.

Observation Systematically planned and recorded observation that serves a specifically formulated research purpose, is related to more general propositions, and is subjected to checks and controls on its total accuracy.

One-on-One Interviews In-depth interviews involving a one-to-one relationship between the interviewer and the respondent.

One-Tailed Test A statistical hypothesis test in which the alternative hypothesis specifies the direction of anticipated difference between two values. Examples include 'sales greater than 100 units per week,' 'consumption is less than 10 units per month,' or 'males consume more than females.' Values in only one tail of the normal distribution are used in the test of the null hypothesis. (See two-tailed test.)

One-Way Frequency Distribution A frequency distribution for a single variable. It is a list of the number of times each response occurred.

On-Line Data Base A computerized data base to which the user has direct access, typically by telephone connection. An example is the **PREDICAST** System.

Open-Ended Question A question that leaves the respondent free to offer any response that he or she thinks appropriate. Open-ended questions may vary in degree of openness.

Operational Definition A description of the activities the researcher must complete in order to assign a value to the concept to be measured. It translates the concept (e.g., Brand Loyalty) into one or more measurable events (e.g., purchase frequency).

Order Bias Bias that results from the order in which alternatives in a multiple-choice question, or the order in which questions in a questionnaire are presented.

Ordinal Scale A rating scale in which numbers, letters, or other symbols are used to assign ranks to items. An ordinal scale requires the respondent to indicate if one item has more or less of a characteristic than another item. The magnitude of the differences between the items is not estimated.

Paired Comparison A method of ranking objects by presenting all possible pairs of the objects, one pair at a time, to subjects who identify which of the two objects possesses more of the characteristic of interest. Example: three brands of soda may be ranked by presenting the three pairs: A-B; A-C; and B-C to subjects, who state their preference for one brand in each pair.

Panel Refers to a group of individuals who have agreed to provide information to a researcher over a period of time.

Parameter The numerical characteristics of a model or a population. Examples include the a and b terms in a regression equation for a population, the mean and standard deviation of a population.

Part-worth A measure of utility or value that respondents assign specific levels of attributes in a conjoint analysis.

Perceptual Map A graphic representation of the perceived relationships among elements in a set, where the elements could be brands, services, or product categories. Commonly used to describe the output of a multidimensional scaling (MDS) analysis.

Personal Interviews Face-to-face situations in which the interviewer asks the respondent questions about the survey's topic of interest.

PERT (Program Evaluation Review Technique) Identifies and displays the activities and associated time requirements needed to complete a research project.

Physiological Measures Direct observations of physical responses (controllable or uncontrollable) to a stimulus.

Picture-Response Technique A projective technique requiring the subject to use his or her imagination to describe what is happening in a series of vaguely structured pictures. (A construction type projective technique.)

Pie-Chart A circle divided into sections, such that each section represents the percentage of the total area of a circle associated with one variable.

PIMS Database A computerized data base maintained by the Strategic Planning Institute, containing data on over 200 marketing, financial, and operating performance variables collected from almost 2,000 business units.

Plus-One Dialing A sampling technique for telephone surveys that requires the researcher to select a sample from an existing directory and add one to each number thus selected.

Point Estimate A statistical estimate of a parameter (such as a population mean) involving only a single value. Example: if a single sample mean is used as the estimate of the population mean, the sample mean is a point estimate.

Politz-Simmons Method A method of adjusting survey results for nonresponse. It assumes that the responses of "not-at-home" (nonrespondents) would have been similar to the actual responses of respondents who characterize themselves as "seldom at home."

Population   The group the researcher wants to generalize to or learn about.

Population Specification Error   Variation between the population required to provide the needed information and the population selected by the researcher.

Position Bias   The tendency on the part of respondents to favor responses occupying certain positions in lists of responses. Examples include middle positions in lists of numbers, first or last item in a list of long alternatives.

Precoding   Establishing categories for responses to open-ended questions *before* a questionnaire is presented to a respondent. The researcher must know all possible responses or use a category labeled "other," to be able to precode a questionnaire.

Predictive Validity   The extent to which the future level of some variable can be predicted by a current measurement of the same or a different variable. Examples include using a person's current score on the GMAT exam to predict his or her future success in a graduate program; using a person's current attitude about a product to predict his or her future purchase of the product.

Predictor Variable   The independent variable in an associative relationship among variables. (See Criterion Variable.) A predictor variable, such as a SAT or GMAT score, is often used to "predict" how well a person will do in pursuing a college degree.

Premeasurement Error   An experimental error that occurs when subjects are measured two or more times, and the first measurement influences the responses to the second measurement. Example: students often score higher on the SAT or ACT exam the *second* time they take it because of their experience taking it the first time.

Pretest   A pretest is a field test of the data collection instrument. It is designed to discover those questions that will cause the respondent problems, which questions are unclear and need to be reworded, and which questions need to be added, dropped or repositioned.

Primary Data   Original data collected specifically for the problem at hand.

Probability Sample   One in which the sampling units are selected by chance and for which there is a known chance of each unit being selected.

Product Audit   A survey of sales of a specified product in all types of retail outlets during a given time period. Product audits are commercially available. An example is the National Total Market Index from Audits and Surveys, Inc.

Profile Analysis   Used to depict attribute by attribute differences in how two or more groups of subjects view a specified object, such as a grocery store. It can also be used to show how Store A is different from Store B on several dimensions such as cleanliness, honesty, dependability, etc.

Projective Technique   The technique of inferring a subject's attitudes or values based on his or her description of vague objects requiring interpretation. Common types used in market research include cartoons, picture-response, third-person, and sentence-completion.

Proportion   The number of the elements of the population that have a particular characteristic divided by the total number of elements in the population (a per cent).

Psychogalvanometer   A device that measures a person's reactions to various stimuli by measuring changes in the rate of perspiration. It identifies only the presence or absence of an emotional response, not the nature of the response.

Purposive Sample   A nonprobability sample selected with some specific objective(s) in mind. For example, selecting geographically dispersed people who possess a valid driver's license and a good driving record to test drive a new front-wheel drive car.

Quota Sample   A nonrandom sample selected such that the demographic characteristics of interest are represented in the sample in the same proportion as they are in the population. If 20 per cent of the population of interest is Irish, 25 – 40 years old, and Catholic, then 20 per cent of the quota sample used should be Irish, 25 – 40 years old, and Catholic.

Random-Digit Dialing   A technique for obtaining a representative sample in a telephone interview; requires that at least some of the digits of each sample phone number be generated randomly.

Random Error   A variable error (see reliability).

Randomized Block Design   An experimental design in which experimental and control groups are created in a way that assures that the effects of a single extraneous variable are more or less equal among all groups. For example, if gender is an important variable, the proportion of males and females would be the same across all groups in this design.

Randomized Response Technique   An approach to overcoming nonresponse or biases in the responses to potentially embarrassing questions by asking a respondent to answer at random one of two dichotomous questions — the first meaningless, the second potentially embarrassing — without telling the researcher which question is being answered. Based on the total responses, the researcher can estimate the response to the embarrassing question.

Rank-Order Scale   A scale that requires the subject to rank a set of stimuli, such as soft drinks, according to some criterion, such as degree of sweetness, without estimating the size of the differences between the stimuli.

Rating Scales   A variety of scales usually used to measure attitudes towards an object, the degree to which an object contains a particular attribute, one's feelings (like or dislike) toward some attribute, or the importance attached to an attribute. Rating scales require the rater to place an attribute of the object being rated at some point along a numerically valued continuum or in one of a numerically ordered series of categories.

Ratio Scale A rating scale in which items are ranked so that numerically equal scale distances represent equal distances in the property being measured. These scales have a natural and known zero point, such as returns to a mail survey or unit sales for Brand X.

Reactive Error Occurs when the artificiality of the experimental situation or the behavior of the experimenter causes effects that emphasize, dampen, or alter any effects caused by the treatment variable.

Refusal Rate (R) The percentage of subjects who would not participate when asked to take part in a research study:

$$R = \frac{\text{number who did not respond}}{\text{number contacted}}$$

Regression Analysis A mathematical technique for fitting a line to measurements of two variables such that the algebraic sum of the deviations of the measurements from the line is zero and that the sum of the squares of the deviations is less than it would be for any other line. It indicates how one variable's value changes as the second variable's value changes.

Reliability The extent of variable error in a measurement. Reliability exists when repeated measures of the same stable characteristic (e.g., education level) in the same objects or persons (e.g., consumer panel members) show limited variation.

Research Design Involves defining the research problem, determining how to collect the data and from whom, establishing the ways the data will be analyzed, estimating costs and the preparation of the research proposal.

Research Proposal A document that describes the objectives and purpose(s) of the research, the questions to be answered, the methodologies to be employed, the expected outcome and benefits to be derived from the proposed research, and the cost and time required.

Response Latency The time delay before a respondent answers a question. It is used as an indicator of the respondent's certainty or confidence in his/her answer. It is also used as an indicator of a respondent's "guessing" responses to factual questions and for strength of preference when used with paired comparisons.

Sample Those individuals chosen from the population of interest as the subjects in an experiment or to be the respondents to a survey.

Sampling Distribution of the Mean The frequency distribution created by the means of all possible samples of a specified size taken from a specified population. The sampling distribution of the mean is a normal distribution regardless of the sample size if the population is normally distributed. It is also normally distributed if samples of at least 30 are used regardless of the distribution of the population.

Sampling Distribution of the Proportion The frequency distribution similar in concept to the sampling distribution of the mean, but using sample proportions instead of sample means. (See Sampling Distribution of the Mean.)

Sampling Error Variation between a representative sample and the sample obtained by using a probability sampling method; caused by chance variations in the elements selected for a sample.

Sampling Frame The physical means of representing the elements of the population from which a sample will be drawn. Examples include telephone books, class rosters, the listing of New York Stock Exchange members.

Scanner Data A scanner is a machine that reads the universal product code (UPC) on a package. Scanner data may include package price, size, brand, weight, or other predetermined data that are recorded and summarized for later analysis.

Scanner Panel A group of consumers with identification numbers who use the numbers to identify their purchases of selected products. The retail checker records the consumer's ID number, then reads the scanner code on the product(s) purchased, both data items along with the store ID number and the date are automatically recorded in computer memory and/or magnetic tape.

Scorer Reliability The extent of agreement among judges (scorers) working independently to categorize a series of objects. Example: two judges view 100 TV commercials. Each judge independently categorizes each commercial as humorous,

musical, or straight sell. The higher the degree of agreement between judges, the greater the degree of reliability of the categorization.

Seasonal Index Number A number used to adjust monthly or quarterly data or forecasts for seasonal fluctuations. A seasonal index number is the ratio of the value of a variable for a period to the average value of the variable for all periods within the time interval used. Often used in time series analysis.

Secondary Data Data potentially useful in solving a current problem but that were collected for a different purpose. Examples include government data bases (e.g., the *Census of Population*) used to forecast population shifts, industry trade data used to evaluate new product acceptance, corporate annual reports used to determine market shares.

Selection Error Occurs when a nonrepresentative sample is obtained by nonprobability sampling methods.

Semantic Differential Scale An attitude scaling device, it requires the respondent to rate the attitude object on a number of itemized rating scales bounded on each end by one of the two bipolar adjectives.

Sensitivity Analysis A procedure used to identify the range of values a variable may have without affecting the decision outcome.

Sentence-Completion Technique A projective technique requiring the subject to complete a sentence using the first phrase which comes to mind. The subject is not required to associate himself or herself with the response, and so is more likely to give a more revealing response. (A completion-type projection technique.)

Simple Random Sample   A probability sample in which single units are drawn from an unstratified population by a single stage procedure. Each unit has a known and equal chance of being included in the sample.

Simulated Before-After Experimental Design   Controls for premeasurement and interaction errors by using separate groups for the pre- and postmeasurements. The measure of interest is the difference between postmeasurement and premeasurement.

Simulated Test Market   Involves mathematical estimates of market share based on consumers' initial reactions to the new product; consumers are exposed to the product in a laboratory setting.

Solomon Four-Group Design   A basic experimental design consisting of four groups (two treatment; two control) and six measurements (two premeasurements; four postmeasurements). It is a before-after with control experiment run simultaneously with an after-only with control experiment. It controls all sources of experimental error subject to control by design.

Split-Ballot Technique   Involves the use of two or more versions of a questionnaire to measure the same thing. This technique is used to reduce the effect of position bias when using multiple choice questions.

Split-Half Reliability   A measure of reliability in which the results from half the items on a multi-item measure are compared with the results for the remaining items. If there is substantial variation between the groups, the reliability of the instrument is in doubt.

Spurious Correlation   A correlation that "happens" to exist between two data sets without any underlying cause. A random correlation.

Standard Deviation   A measure of dispersion; indicates how "spread out" the data are; the square root of the variance.

Standard Error of the Mean   The standard deviation of a sampling distribution of the mean. It is equal to the population standard deviation divided by the square root of the sample size.

Standard Market Test   The product is sold through regular marketing channels to a predetermined sample (typically 2 or 3) of marketing areas using one or more marketing strategies. Selection of the sample of test areas is a critical issue.

Standard Metropolitan Statistical Area (SMSA)   An integrated social and economic unit such as a city, or a city and its surrounding suburbs, with a population nucleus of 50,000 or more inhabitants.

Stapel Scale   A unipolar (only one characteristic used) ten-interval rating scale with values which range from $+5$ to -5. Subjects are asked to choose a response category which reflects the amount of the characteristic possessed by the object.

Statistic   A characteristic or measure of a sample (in contrast to a parameter, which is a characteristic of a population).

Statistical Estimation Involves the estimation of a population value we do not know from a sample value we do know.

Store Audit Detailed sales reports by product category and brand for a sample of specified retailers (typically food and drug stores) during a given period of time. Store audits are commercially available. An example is the Nielsen Retail Index.

Stratified Sampling Involves treating each relevant stratum in the population of interest as a separate subpopulation for sampling purposes. For example, the total population might be divided into three age groups, under 25, 25–45, 45 and older. If stratified sampling were used, a separate sample would be drawn from each group and combined to yield a stratified sample.

Stress A measure of how well a given multidimensional scaling solution "fits" the original data.

Structured Interview The extent to which an interviewer is restricted to following the question instructions, wording, and sequence in a questionnaire. Each subject is asked the same set of questions in the same predetermined order.

Surrogate Information Error Variation between the information required to solve the problem and information sought by the researcher.

Surrogate Situation Error An experimental error which occurs when the test situation differs from the real

situation in some fundamental way. For example, in a test of alternative advertising copy actual competitor messages were used. When the product was introduced to the real market, the competitors changed their messages.

Survey of Buying Intentions A causal method of sales forecasting in which customers are asked to forecast their purchases. The survey is designed to measure the likelihood that an individual or organization will purchase a given product in the future.

Syndicated Research Services A number of firms that regularly collect data of relevance to marketers, which they sell on a subscription basis.

Tachistoscope A slide projector with adjustable projection speeds and levels of illumination. These devices are widely used in copy testing. A tachistoscope is used to test ads to determine at which speeds elements such as the product, brand, and headline are recognized.

Telephone Interview Using the telephone to ask the subjects of a survey to respond to a set of questions developed to collect information.

Telescoping A tendency to remember events as occurring more recently than they actually did.

Test Marketing "Trying out" alterations of the marketing mix in a limited geographic area (such as one or more test cities).

Test-Retest Reliability Repeating the measurement using the same instrument under as nearly equivalent conditions as possible to compare the similarity of responses. The greater the similarity, the greater the presumed reliability of the instrument.

Theater Test A technique for testing television commercial effectiveness; involves showing the commercial to a theater audience and obtaining pre- and post-exposure attitudes and/or preferences. The measure of interest is the difference between postmeasurement and premeasurement.

Third-Person Technique A construction projective technique allowing the subjects to project their attitudes onto some vague third person (an "average consumer," "a typical shopper," "your friends").

Time Series Analysis A method of forecasting based on a time series — i.e., data arranged in relation to time, such as annual sales data. Analysis of time series isolates four separate effects — trend, cycle, seasonal and random variations — then uses these effects to forecast future values of the variable (such as sales).

Treatment Group The portion of the sample that is exposed to the changes made in the independent variable in an experiment. For example, in a taste test trying to measure consumer acceptance of a new flavor, those people testing the new flavor are part of the treatment group; those tasting the original flavor are part of the control group.

Triangle Taste Test A technique for determining the percentage of respondents who can differentiate one version of a food product from another. It is used for developing and altering food products.

Two-Tailed Test A statistical hypothesis test in which the alternative includes all values (both higher and lower) of the parameter except the null hypothesis value.

Type I Error An error caused by accepting the alternate hypothesis when the null hypothesis is true.

Type II Error An error caused by accepting the null hypothesis when the alternate hypothesis is true.

Unaided Recall Involves asking respondents a question and *NOT* giving them any clues as to what answers might be appropriate responses. For example, "What commercials did you see on TV last night?"

Uninformed Respondent A respondent who has never known the answer to a question (not a respondent who has forgotten or who is unwilling to communicate the answer). These respondents are a source of error when they pretend to know and report the response to such questions.

Universal Product Code (UPC) A product identification code on most packaged goods; it contains information on product category, package size, brand, flavor, and so on. The UPC is read by optical scanners at the check out counter.

Validity The amount of systemic error in a measurement.

Voice Pitch Analysis A little-used technique that examines changes in the relative vibration frequency of the voice to measure emotional response to stimuli. Such analysis can be used to determine which verbal responses reflect an emotional commitment and which are merely low-involvement responses.

Word Association **A** set of techniques that require the subjects to respond to a word with the first thing(s) that come to mind.

X-11 Technique **A** time series based forecasting model that provides information on seasonals, trends, and cycles and measures of how closely they fit the data. It also provides a measure of growth rate that can be used or forecasting turning points.

Index

Company Index

Name Index

Subject Index

information value estimating, 49–53
management problem/opportunity clarification, 46
measurement technique selection, 55
model development, 47–48
research proposal preparation, 57–58
sample selection, 55–56
situation analysis, 46–47
time estimation, 56–57
Research process, 43
Research proposal, 57–58
Response latency, 341–342, 343
Risk taking, 51–52

Sales forecasting, 637–639
causal methods, 657–659
barometric, 659–660
buyer intention surveys, 660–661
econometric models, 663–664
regression models, 661–663
error costs, 664–665
judgmental methods, 639–643
model choices, 665–667
time series analysis and projection, 643–
645
isolating seasonal fluctuations, 645–649
models, 649–657
Sampling, 459, 461–462, 464–465
census versus, 462–464
control, 152–154
distribution, 494–495
of the mean, 495–500
of the proportion, 500
error, 60, 499
hypothesis testing, 514–516
relative allowable, 504
frame specification, 466–467, 469, 470
method selection, 471–472
equal unit probability versus unequal unit
probability, 478–479
probability versus nonprobability, 472–
477
single-stage versus multistage, 479
single-unit versus cluster, 477
stratified versus unstratified, 477–478
plan specification, 479–481
population definition, 465–466, 467–468
primary considerations, 55
selection, 481
situations, 481–487
size determination, 479, 491–492

estimation problems involving means,
500–505, 506
estimation problems involving proportions, 505, 507–508
hypothesis testing, 513–516
incidence, 517–518
methods, 492–494
nonproportional single-stage stratified
random samples, 765–766
nonresponse, 517–518
non-SRS random samples, 512
proportional single-stage stratified random samples, 763–764
single-stage cluster sample, 766–770
single-stage stratified random samples,
762
SRS samples for multinomial problems,
508–512
unit specification, 469, 471
SAMSCAN, 118
Scanner data, 118–119
See also Panels; Survey research
SCANTRACK, 118
Scatter diagram, 611, 612
Seasonal variation, 644–645
Secondary data
advantages, 78
applications, 100–102
external sources, 84–89
associations, 93
computerized databases, 89–93
directories, 98–99
experts, 99–100
government agencies, 94–98
published, 99
syndicated services, 98
internal sources
accounting records, 81–82
internal experts, 83–84
miscellaneous reports, 82–83
sales force reports, 82
problems, 78
accuracy, 80–81
availability, 79
relevance, 79–80
sufficiency, 81
Securities and Exchange Commission (SEC),
97
Selective Dissemination of Information (SDI),
93
Semantic differential scale, 346–348
Sensitivity analysis, 33

835

HF
5415.5
T91
1990

Tull, Donald S.
Marketing research :
    measurement & method

DUE DATE

	201-6503		Printed in USA